Handbook of
Clinical Behavior
Therapy with the
Elderly Client

APPLIED CLINICAL PSYCHOLOGY

Series Editors:
Alan S. Bellack, *Medical College of Pennsylvania at EPPI, Philadelphia, Pennsylvania,*
and Michel Hersen, *University of Pittsburgh, Pittsburgh, Pennsylvania*

Current Volumes in this Series

ACTIVITY MEASUREMENT IN PSYCHOLOGY AND MEDICINE
  Warren W. Tryon

BEHAVIORAL CONSULTATION AND THERAPY
  John R. Bergan and Thomas R. Kratochwill

BEHAVIORAL CONSULTATION IN APPLIED SETTINGS
An Individual Guide
  Thomas R. Kratochwill and John R. Bergan

THE CHALLENGE OF COGNITIVE THERAPY
Applications to Nontraditional Populations
  Edited by T. Michael Vallis, Janice L. Howes, and Philip C. Miller

CLINICAL PSYCHOLOGY
Historical and Research Foundations
  Edited by C. Eugene Walker

ETHNIC VALIDITY, ECOLOGY, AND PSYCHOTHERAPY
A Psychosocial Competence Model
  Forrest B. Tyler, Deborah Ridley Brome, and Janice E. Williams

HANDBOOK OF BEHAVIOR MODIFICATION WITH THE MENTALLY RETARDED
Second Edition
  Edited by Johnny L. Matson

HANDBOOK OF CLINICAL BEHAVIOR THERAPY WITH THE ELDERLY CLIENT
  Edited by Patricia A. Wisocki

PSYCHOLOGY
A Behavioral Overview
  Alan Poling, Henry Schlinger, Stephen Starin, and Elbert Blakely

USING RATIONAL-EMOTIVE THERAPY EFFECTIVELY
A Practitioner's Guide
  Michael E. Bernard

A Continuation Order Plan is available for this series. A continuation order will bring delivery of each new volume immediately upon publication. Volumes are billed only upon actual shipment. For further information please contact the publisher.

Handbook of Clinical Behavior Therapy with the Elderly Client

Edited by

Patricia A. Wisocki

University of Massachusetts
Amherst, Massachusetts

Plenum Press • New York and London

Library of Congress Cataloging-in-Publication Data

Handbook of clinical behavior therapy with the elderly client / edited
  by Patricia A. Wisocki.
        p.   cm. -- (Applied clinical psychology)
    Includes bibliographical references and index.
    ISBN 0-306-43756-2
    1. Behavior therapy for the aged.   I. Wisocki, Patricia A.
  II. Series.
    [DNLM: 1. Behavior Therapy--in old age.   WT 150 H233]
  RC489.B4H376 1991
  618.97'689'142--dc20
  DNLM/DLC
  for Library of Congress   91-1962
                                                              CIP

ISBN 0-306-43756-2

© 1991 Plenum Press, New York
A Division of Plenum Publishing Corporation
233 Spring Street, New York, N.Y. 10013

Printed in the United States of America

To my parents, Anne and Peter Wisocki, role models for graceful and successful aging, and to my husband, John L. Tierney

Contributors

THOMAS F. BERGQUIST, Department of Psychology, University of Alabama at Birmingham, Birmingham, Alabama 35294

RICHARD R. BOOTZIN, Department of Psychology, University of Arizona, Tucson, Arizona 85721

KATHRYN LARSEN BURGIO, University of Pittsburgh School of Medicine, Pittsburgh, Pennsylvania 15213·

LOUIS D. BURGIO, University of Pittsburgh School of Medicine, Pittsburgh, Pennsylvania 15213

LAURA L. CARSTENSEN, Department of Psychology, Stanford University, Stanford, California 94131

BRAD CRENSHAW, Department of Psychology, University of Massachusetts, Amherst, Massachusetts 01003

PATRICIA C. DICKERSON, Behavioral Medicine Unit, Division of General and Preventive Medicine, University of Alabama at Birmingham, Birmingham, Alabama 35294

JEFFREY J. DOLCE, Behavioral Medicine Unit, Division of General and Preventive Medicine, University of Alabama at Birmingham, Birmingham, Alabama 35294

LINDA WARREN DUKE, Department of Psychology, University of Alabama at Birmingham, Birmingham, Alabama 35294

MARY-LOUISE ENGELS, Behavior Therapy Unit, Douglas Hospital Center, Verdun, Quebec, Canada H4H 1R3

MINDY ENGLE-FRIEDMAN, Baruch College, City University of New York, New York, New York 10010

JANE E. FISHER, Department of Psychology, Northern Illinois University, DeKalb, Illinois 60115

CHARLES J. FOGELMAN, The Baltimore Psychologists, Baltimore, Maryland 21420

WILLIAM E. HALEY, Department of Psychology, University of Alabama at Birmingham, Birmingham, Alabama 35294

BENJAMIN L. HANDEN, Children's Hospital of Pittsburgh, Pittsburgh, Pennsylvania 15213-3417

PATRICIA HANRAHAN, University of Chicago, Chicago, Illinois 60637

ARTHUR MACNEILL HORTON, JR., Department of Psychiatry, University of Maryland Medical School, Baltimore, Maryland 21218

ROBERT C. INTRIERI, Pennsylvania State University, State College, Pennsylvania 16802

JEFFREY A. KELLY, Department of Psychiatry and Human Behavior, University of Mississippi Medical Center, Jackson, Mississippi 39216

KIM E. KENDALL, 416 17th Avenue East, Seattle, Washington 98102

NANCY KEUTHEN, Psychosomatic Medicine Unit, Massachusetts General Hospital, Boston, Massachusetts 02114

NATHAN L. LINSK, Department of Medical Social Work, College of Associated Health Professions, University of Illinois at Chicago, Chicago, Illinois 60680

CLAIRE MORSE, Department of Psychology, Guilford College, Greenboro, North Carolina 27410

WILLIAM O'DONOHUE, Department of Psychology, Northern Illinois University, DeKalb, Illinois 60115

DANI B. PERS, Amherst Medical Associates, Amherst, Massachusetts 01002

ELSIE M. PINKSTON, School of Social Service Administration, University of Chicago, Chicago, Illinois 60637

JOSEPH E. STRUCKUS, Department of Psychology, Gaylord Hospital, Wallingford, Connecticut 06492

LINDA TERI, Department of Psychiatry and Behavioral Sciences, University of Washington Medical School, Seattle, Washington 98195

PATRICIA A. WISOCKI, Department of Psychology, University of Massachusetts, Amherst, Massachusetts 01003

JUDY M. ZARIT, Child, Adult, and Family Psychological Center, State College, Pennsylvania 16801

STEVEN H. ZARIT, Department of Individual and Family Studies, Pennsylvania State University, University Park, Pennsylvania 16803

Preface

Although we speak of "the elderly" as if there were one body of people with common characteristics, older adults are more heterogeneous than any other population. People over the age of 65 are also the fastest-growing segment of the population in the United States, currently numbering 25 million. The majority of older adults reside in their communities; a small fraction of them are cared for in institutions. Most may expect to experience some kind of physical impairment. Approximately a quarter of the population may expect to suffer a mental health impairment.

While traditional therapies have not been especially effective for older adults, behavior therapy has shown exceptional promise as a treatment modality. This book presents a comprehensive explication of the relatively new field of behavioral gerontology. It was written for the clinician interested in the interaction of medical, environmental, and psychological variables and their effects on treatment of elderly clients and for the researcher who will be looking to extend knowledge about interventions with this population. It will be useful for the graduate student in clinical psychology, as well as the experienced clinician, who will want to include the elderly in his or her therapeutic population.

This book was designed in four parts. The first part contains an overview of the field of behavioral gerontology, including its distinguishing characteristics and a review of the behavioral intervention research, categorized by problem area. In the second part authors discuss the influence of medication, nutrition, residential placement, social support, and cognitive impairment on treatment, all factors essential to the design of an intervention program. In the third part chapters are presented about treatment applications for individuals presenting with a variety of problems, including anxiety, social skills deficits, dating–marital–sexual dilemmas, depression, memory impairment, insomnia, institutionalization, health, and pain problems. In the fourth part authors address ways of intervening in the health care system: staff training, family care, health service providers, and community services.

The authors of these chapters are experts in their fields. Most are clinicians who have had direct experience with aging clients. Most are researchers who have carved out the areas of study they have written about. They have brought together a compendium of work valuable for practitioner and researcher alike. I am grateful for their efforts and acknowledge their significant contributions to the field of behavior gerontology.

I am also grateful to the secretarial staff in the psychology department at the University of Massachusetts, especially Melanie Bellenoit, who was tireless in preparing much of this work and didn't object as strenuously as she could about doing multiple rewrites. My husband, John Tierney, deserves a special note of thanks because for three years he allowed me to spread my notes, manuscripts, references, diskettes, and soda cans into his section of our study without complaining.

Patricia A. Wisocki

Amherst, Massachusetts

Contents

I
The Behavioral Approach
to Aging

Behavioral Gerontology

PATRICIA A. WISOCKI

CHARACTERISTICS OF BEHAVIORAL GERONTOLOGY

Behavioral gerontology is probably best defined as the application of behavioral principles and procedures to the problems of the elderly and the issues of aging. As such, it is a specialty area in behavior therapy and shares the identifiable characteristics of the parent field, as defined by Kazdin (1975): (1) a focus on current determinants of behavior rather than historical antecedents; (2) an emphasis on overt behavior change as the proper subject matter by which effective treatment is judged; (3) the specification of treatment procedures in objective terms; (4) a reliance upon basic research in psychology as a source of hypotheses about treatment and specific therapeutic techniques; (5) specificity in defining, treating, and measuring target populations. While the roots of behavior therapy are planted in the early learning theories, its contemporary branches have extended into a variety of conceptual models and sophisticated methodologies, including applied behavioral analysis, neo-behaviorism, social learning theory, and cognitive behavior therapy (cf. Eysenck & Martin, 1987; Hersen, Kazdin, & Bellack, 1983; Wilson & Franks, 1982).

There are at least two significant implications of using a behavioral approach to gerontology. First, as O'Donohue, Fisher, and Krasner (1986) point out, such an approach means that the variable of chronological age is not causal, but correlational and descriptive. Behavior is not considered differently within each developmental stage. The same principles of learning apply to those who are old and not old. Thus, behaviorists reject a developmental model of aging. Second, the method of analysis is functional. That is, behaviorists study the effects of antecedent and consequent environmental events—the conditions necessary for behavioral change—on the behavior of aging men and women. They do not ignore the influence of biological variables on environmental events—certain abilities undeniably decline with age and certain factors associated with age influence a person's response to events—but they recognize that biology interacts with environment in the production of behavior: biological conditions influence behavior and behavioral

PATRICIA A. WISOCKI • Department of Psychology, University of Massachusetts, Amherst, Massachusetts 01003.

changes influence biological conditions (Burgio & Burgio, 1986). Thus, the behaviors exhibited by old people are modifiable, even if there are biological factors contributing to them.

The range of possible antecedents to the behaviors of the old include physical decline, disease, social conditions, environmental factors, self-attitudes and statements, nutritional practices, medication effects, and so forth. The responses elicited by these antecedent stimuli are often those which characterize a person as elderly, such as cautiousness, decreased mobility, withdrawal from social contact, negative self-statements, and so forth. Consequences of "behaving old" may be further physical decline, poor personal attitudes, loss of social connections, poor health, and so forth. These consequences may then become stimuli for other behaviors. Behaviorists maintain that an intervention made at either the antecedent or consequence level will affect the behavior of the old.

Behavioral gerontology is a recent addition to the fields of both behavior therapy and gerontology. It has maintained a slow but steady rate of growth since the mid-sixties, when a handful of psychologists suggested the application of a behavioral model to the problems of the aged (e.g., Cautela, 1966; Cohen, 1967; Hoyer, 1973, 1974; Lindsley, 1964). The behavioral model was touted for its cost-effectiveness; its focus on the present, immediate problem; its applicability to populations often ignored by other treatment systems, like the chronically or organically impaired elderly; its ability to accommodate the interindividual variability found among the elderly with the use of functional analyses and single case design research strategies; and its commonsense approach to training caregivers dealing with the elderly in institutions (Wisocki, 1984).

Despite the enthusiasm of some behaviorists, little behavioral research using the elderly as subjects was actually done until 1973 (Wisocki & Mosher, 1982), and even since then, the number of research studies per year has been small. Less than a shelf-full of books has been published describing behavioral gerontological research and clinical practice (e.g., Carstensen & Edelstein, 1987; Hussian, 1981; Hussian & Davis, 1985; Lewinsohn & Teri, 1983; Pinkston & Linsk, 1985; Teri & Lewinsohn, 1984). Special-interest groups in behavioral gerontology have been formed in the two primary professional organizations for behaviorists (The Association for Advancement of Behavior Therapy and The Association for Behavioral Analysis), but the membership of each group is small.

It is possible that the lack of interest in gerontology among behaviorists reflects the lack of interest by professionals in other fields who maintain that the elderly suffer irreversible biological decline and cannot benefit from intervention attempts, or that it is not cost-effective to expend our energies on an aging population when the needs of youth are so great. It is also possible that the lack of focus on elderly as a population is explicable, to some extent, by the belief of many behaviorists that such variables as age, gender, and diagnostic condition are not limiting factors in the application of behavioral technology. Many believe that research findings with younger populations can simply be applied to older populations and that it is not necessary to replicate work with each behavioral strategy or procedure with the elderly. Indeed, the evidence confirms this argument, although modifications are required of some procedures in order to accommodate particular age-related factors. Carstensen (1988) has offered additional practical reasons: that working with elderly requires lower expectations about the amount of gain possible in treatment; and that few publication outlets exist for behavioral gerontological research, citing what appears to be an antiaging bias in behavioral and clinical journals and an antibehavioral bias in gerontological journals. Finally, Mosher-Ashley (1986–1987) has pointed out serious design problems in much of the early behavioral research.

Whatever the reasons, it is clear that the field of behavioral gerontology is a small one. In 1982, Wisocki and Mosher undertook a comprehensive review of all behavioral gerontological articles published in established journals between 1963 and 1980. They presented data on the types of problems explicated in the articles, the distribution of articles by journal type, and the specific distribution by age of all research subjects used in studies reported in the behavioral journals. They found that only 11 articles were published, on average, each year between 1973 and 1980; that most of the behavioral gerontological work was published in gerontological journals (40% as opposed to 17% in behavioral journals); that subjects over age 65 were represented in only 0.6% of all the articles published in behavioral journals; that most of the work was done with institutionalized elderly; and that, therefore, most of the behaviors targeted for study were relevant to that group of subjects, such as social interaction, participation in events, management issues, self-care, declining cognitive abilities, and related behavioral excesses or deficits. Psychotherapy concerns, health and disease problems, and life satisfaction issues were addressed in only a few studies.

In 1985, Louis Burgio extended the review by four years and found no differences in the average rate of publication. He did find that behavioral journals had increased their rate of publication of gerontological research, although it was still less than one article per year per journal, and that medical/nursing journals had decreased their rates of publication of that type of research. The other types of journals contained roughly the same numbers of articles as they had previously. Burgio (1985) also found that the types of problem areas addressed by this research changed somewhat. There was a substantial decrease in the application of behavioral procedures to the problems of self-care, participation, and social interaction, and a substantial increase in articles dealing with psychotherapy and behavioral medicine for the elderly. Programs in environmental management were presented at the same rate; programs dealing with the modification of cognitive abilities increased slightly. According to these two reviews, between 1964 and 1984 a total of 151 articles describing behavioral research in gerontology was published in established journals.

Several reviews of behavioral gerontology were written during this time period. In 1977, Baltes and Barton made a "case for the operant model" in gerontology by cogently arguing that it demonstrates the plasticity of old age and that environmental conditions may be arranged so as to maximize the functioning of the old. Most of the behavioral gerontological research that occurred around that time was directed at environmental management (antecedent stimulus control) with institutionalized elderly who experienced severe response deficits, to some extent attributable to the fact that they had grown old within the institution, not that they had entered it when or because they became old. There were several reviews that examined the behavioral work of that period (e.g., Baltes & Barton, 1979; Got-testam, 1980; Hussian, 1984; Patterson & Jackson, 1980; Reidel, 1981; Richards & Thorpe, 1978; Williamson & Ascione, 1983) and concluded that, although there were severe design flaws, the use of such a model showed clear promise for gerontologists.

In later reviews (Burgio & Burgio, 1986; Carstensen, 1988; Mosher-Ashley, 1986–1987; Wisocki, 1984) suggestions were made to extend behavioral gerontological work beyond the operant model and beyond institutionalized elderly populations.

This chapter is organized into topical categories of clinical interventions that roughly correspond to the historical development of behavioral gerontology. The field began with a focus on elderly in confined-care environments. Behaviorists had already established a reputation for dealing effectively with "forgotten" or "neglected" populations, and it was logical for them to transfer their attention and skills from chronic wards to geriatric units (which sometimes were the same thing anyway). The usual problems targeted for intervention with these populations included self-care (feeding, ambulation, continence, hygiene); social interaction and participation in activities; and idiosyncratic problems, like disruptive behavior, stereotypy, repetitive verbalizations, and self-injury. The first half of this review deals with those problem areas. The second half focuses on more recent innovations in behavioral gerontological research: problems associated with cognitive decline; treatment of problems related to health and disease; and psychotherapy issues.

Included in this review are those research studies that described the use of behavioral procedures and principles in the treatment of problems experienced by clients who were at least 60 years old. When subjects in experiments were of mixed ages, I included only those in which the majority were at least 60 years old and/or analyzed results by age. I have included some case studies when there has been no research in a particular area. I have excluded studies described in papers presented at conventions unless the results added significantly to the conclusions in a particular area of intervention. I have also excluded work on assessment scales, staff training, observational studies, and descriptions of clinical work from book chapters or popular articles.

REVIEW OF THE LITERATURE

Self-Care Programs

Self-care behaviors include eating, ambulating, and maintaining personal hygiene. They are behaviors which were once in a person's behavior repertoire, but were lost in old age, more often due to lack of reinforcement than to the aging process or disease. In a series of studies, Margaret Baltes and her colleagues have demonstrated the powerful influence of others' responses in creating dependency in older people (Baltes, Burgess, & Stewart, 1978; Baltes, Honn, Barton, Orzech, &

Lago, 1983; Barton, Baltes, & Orzech, 1980; Lester & Baltes, 1978). From her work, Baltes (1988) has also concluded that the elderly in such situations often learn to use dependent behavior functionally in order to obtain social contact. Thus, in attempting to establish independence in the population by teaching self-maintenance skills, the behavior therapist must take care to establish a more appropriate method of interaction. Unless an alternate form of social reinforcement can be arranged, it is probably neither useful nor ethical to target self-care behaviors for change.

The therapist also has a responsibility to assess the extent to which an elderly client is capable of meeting the demands of a program. For exam-ple, a client's arthritis may make self-feeding difficult. In such a case the goal of self-feeding is most realistically achieved by supplementing a reinforcement program with environmental modifications, such as specially designed utensils, plates with rubberized bottoms to reduce slippage from the table, and so forth. Mosher-Ashley (1986–1987) has pointed out that many of the studies designed to assess the influence of staff behavior on fostering dependency in elderly institutionalized patients did not consider physical disabilities as a differentiating factor in treatment and that, therefore, conclusions from those studies are limited.

Let us turn now to the specific behavioral research conducted in each of the self-care skill areas.

Self-Feeding

Of the four studies investigating methods of teaching the elderly to feed themselves, all used contingent positive reinforcement (food and praise) as the primary intervention. The first three used a reversal design and demonstrated that eating behavior was functionally dependent on reinforcement. Geiger and Johnson (1974) used reinforcement alone and reported various levels of improvement in their six subjects who were required to complete the consumption of a meal at one sitting. To their design, Baltes and Zerbe (1976) added verbal prompting and a timeout procedure for refusal to eat, which produced a dramatic improvement in the eating behavior of one subject who had not eaten on her own in 5 months. For a second subject, they first padded the eating utensils to make them easier to hold, and praised the subject when she fed herself. Risley and Edwards (1978) included manual prompting with their reinforcement program and demonstrated a positive effect on their sample of nursing home residents. None of these studies sampled behavior during a follow-up period, nor did they describe a maintenance program that continued after the experimental program.

In the fourth study in this category (Lewin, Lundervold, Saslow, & Thompson, 1989), the investigators worked with two patients who were unable to eat independently and a third patient whose visual impairments inhibited the amount of food she ate. All patients were cognitively and medically impaired and their ages were in the nineties. After measuring the percentages of independent eating and food intake, the investigators prompted the first two patients to eat on their own and praised them whenever they complied. One patient improved significantly. The third patient was given preferred food and the physical environment was made more accommodating. She increased food intake by 33%.

Independent Mobility

There were four studies that examined the effects of reinforcement on ambulation, or independence from a wheelchair, or on self-wheeling. Using a reversal design, MacDonald and Butler (1974) successfully demonstrated the positive effect of prompting and contingent staff praise on the walking behavior of two nursing home residents. They did not conduct a generalization program or collect follow-up data. Sachs (1975) described work with two nursing home residents who were given tokens contingently upon amount of time or distance walked, using an AB design. The behavior increased, but important details about the methods of observation and coding were not explicated, and there was no follow-up component to the program. Using an AB design, Sperbeck and Whitbourne (1981) studied the effect of verbal praise given by nursing home staff on the walking and self-wheeling of four elderly residents. Only one client demonstrated any improvement in distance walked. The investigators made no attempt to assess the differential value of the reinforcers for each of the clients, so the effect of praise was not established. No follow-up data were presented. Burgio, Burgio, Engel, and Tice (1986) designed a more complex study that included a generalization assessment. Using a multiple-baseline across-settings-and-subjects design, staff prompted eight nursing home residents to walk independently and reinforced them with praise. Six of the subjects increased the distances they were able to walk to the dining room for a meal where additional praise was given. In an experimental condition in which praise in the dining room was withheld, the subjects also increased the distance walked, thereby demonstrating a generalization effect. They did not increase their walking in other areas of the nursing home, however. Walking to the dining room was maintained afterward at a 4-month follow-up. The other two subjects were unable to progress beyond the baseline level.

Carstensen and Fisher (Chapter 15, this volume) have pointed out that the mobility of elderly clients may be influenced by physical limitations, such as cerebrovascular accidents, the architectural design of a residence, and the absence of staff attention for walking independently. They also suggest that wheelchairs are often associated with privilege and cite the example of wheelchair-bound patients allowed into meals or events before ambulatory patients, thereby possibly reinforcing that form of dependency.

Personal Hygiene

This category includes programs designed for reestablishing behaviors of independent oral hygiene, bathing, and toileting. Sachs (1975) developed a token program to improve the oral hygiene of three nursing home residents. Two of the subjects successfully learned the complete program, which consisted of picking up their toothbrushes from the nursing station, brushing their teeth, and returning the toothbrushes to the station. There was only partial success with the third subject. As case studies in which important details about experimental procedures have been omitted, however, these results are mainly suggestive.

Rinke, Williams, Lloyd, and Smith-Scott (1978) tested the effectiveness of prompting and reinforcement on the self-bathing skills of elderly nursing home residents in a multiple-baseline design across bathing behaviors. Although they reported that each technique, and a combination of both techniques, was useful in increasing independence, they did not control for sequence effects. Mishara (1978) designed a token economy program for elderly hospitalized demented patients. Patients earned tokens for completing their own self-care skills and engaging in social activities. After 6 months, results indicated that the patients in the program required significantly less care from nursing staff and that significantly fewer of them (6%) showed declines in their self-care abilities when compared with the patients who had not been in a token program (39%), suggesting that the treatment may have slowed the disability from dementia. Mishara was careful to point out that some patients in the groups showed no change whatsoever.

McEvoy and Patterson (1986) added skills-training modules to their token economy program for 30 demented patients. Each module covered a different self-care skill area, such as bathing, hygiene, hair care, doing laundry, managing money, selecting meals, and so forth. Each skill was reduced to its component parts and demonstrated by the trainer, who then prompted the patients to practice and reinforced their attempts with praise and tokens. Prompts occurred in gradually decreasing specificity. After 3 months, the investigators noticed a difference in improvement rates for the group of demented patients, when compared with a control group of nondemented psychiatric patients. The investigators found that the demented patients were able to relearn basic hygiene skills, which they had had previously in their behavioral repertoires, as well as the control group, but not the skills which were more complex and cognitively demanding. The patients also learned most effectively when engaged in physical practice and when many sensory systems were involved in the feedback process. Individual differences were also noted. The demented patients learned basic skills within an average of 7.4 to 15.4 weeks, while the nondemented patients required 4.4 weeks for the same skills. Of the participants in the study, 80% were discharged to boarding houses or private residences. The investigators said that they were unable to collect follow-up data in those circumstances.

In comparison with the amount of work on the aforementioned behaviors, the work on incontinence is quite extensive and includes both community-dwelling elderly and those who live in institutions. Of the four types of incontinence identified by Burgio and Burgio (Chapter 14, this volume), only one (overflow incontinence, in which the bladder does not empty fully) requires surgery for correction. The other three types have been effectively modified with behavioral procedures. These types include: functional incontinence, which occurs in people who have normal physiological responses, but have cognitive or mobility impairments that prevent them from using the toilet consistently; urge incontinence, in which a person is unable to inhibit bladder contractions; and stress incontinence, in which overflow is not effectively inhibited during periods of pressure caused by lifting, laughing, sneezing, and so forth.

Functional incontinence is most common to nursing home residents and is affected by staff attention, environmental factors, memory deficits, or psychological problems such as fear, confusion, or depression. Behavioral treatment efforts for functional incontinence have included the use of voiding schedules or habit training (Burgio, Engel, McCormick, Hawkins, & Scheve, 1988; Sogbein & Awad, 1982; Spangler, Risley, & Bilyew, 1984); contingency management (Grosicki, 1968; Pollock & Liberman, 1974); and a combination of the two procedures (Chanfreau-Rona, Bellwood, & Wylie, 1984; Pinkston, Howe, & Blackman, 1986–1987; Sanavio, 1981; Schnelle, Traughber, Morgan, Embry, Binion, & Colemen, 1983).

When voiding schedules are used, fluid intake is controlled and the patients are checked for wetness or dryness at frequent regular intervals (usually 1 or 2 hours). With this strategy the majority of patients significantly decreased episodes of incontinence in all studies, but they did not learn to control their bladders. The effectiveness of the procedures depends on the consistency of the caregiver.

Burgio *et al.* (1988) tried to determine if the voiding schedule could be increased from the usual 2-hour period to 3 or 4 hours. They studied four functionally incontinent and cognitively impaired elderly in a nursing home using an AB design. After a 2-week assessment of the frequency of incontinent episodes and independent toilet use, the investigators placed three of the patients on a 2-hour prompt schedule and the fourth on a 3-hour schedule. If the patient was dry during the time period, he or she was verbally praised; if he or she had been incontinent, verbal corrective feedback was given. All occurrences of self-initiated toileting were praised. If there was little or no improvement, voiding schedules were reduced; when there was improvement, the schedules were doubled. Treatment required between 43 and 127 days and varied according to the response of the individual patient. All patients had fewer incontinent experiences. The average percent of dry pants increased from 30% to 62% during treatment. It was possible to thin the prompting schedule to 3 hours for two patients and 4 hours for one patient. One patient did not go beyond the 2-hour schedule, perhaps due to a decline in health. Burgio *et al.* also found that patients became dependent on the staff-initiated prompts to signal their use of the toilet, instead of their own internal cues. After treatment, two patients returned to baseline levels, while two patients maintained improvement.

In the two studies in which contingency management procedures were assessed alone, rewards for dryness (tokens, social attention, tangible items) and punishment for incontinent episodes (clean up urine and stay in wet pants, loss of tokens) did not effectively improve clients' voiding behavior. In fact, in the Grosicki study, the control group subjects improved their continence levels more than the experimental group subjects. Within the experimental group, subjects improved more when they were given social reinforcement for continence and not at all when tokens were used. In the Pollock and Liberman study, the patients, who had severe cerebral dysfunctions and memory impairment that affected their ability to locate the bathroom, increased incontinent episodes after treatment. There were also design problems with this study that make it difficult to evaluate objectively.

When contingency management procedures were combined with voiding schedules, there was more success. Sanavio (1981) taught two subjects a toileting sequence that included fluid loading every hour, dry pants inspection every 20 minutes, reinforcement for voiding on the toilet and for dry pants or punishment for incontinence (cleaning themselves and repeatedly practicing toileting behaviors). Sanavio demonstrated the effectiveness of the procedure with a reversal design and maintenance supported by follow-up data. A carefully controlled study by Schnelle *et al.* (1983) was done with 11 geriatric subjects who were given social approval when their clothes were dry or when they asked for toileting help and mild disapproval when they were incontinent. Clothes were checked every hour and subjects were reminded to void if necessary. The number of incontinent episodes was reduced by half, and correct toileting increased by 45%.

Chanfreau-Rona *et al.* (1984) combined stimulus control procedures (a large picture of a person toileting appropriately and cut-out footsteps leading to the bathroom) with a 2-hour voiding schedule and verbal reinforcement for dryness for three geriatric wards of a hospital. In two of the wards, patients increased incontinent episodes, while on the third ward, there was only a slight decrease. The investigators attributed the failures to staff behavior more than to the procedures.

Pinkston and her colleagues (1986–1987) had more success with their program of stimulus cues and reinforcement for three wheelchair-bound elderly women in a nursing home. In a multiple-baseline design across residents, every hour the patients were asked if they wanted to use the toilet and were taken to the bathroom every 2 hours. Whenever they used the toilet appropriately they were given praise and cookies. After the intervention program there was a decrease in incontinence and an increase in appropriate toileting.

For urge and stress incontinence, effective behavioral interventions have included the use of voiding schedules (Clay, 1978); bladder retraining, in which the client learns to void under different stimulus cues than those produced by the physical urge and thereby learns to increase bladder capacity (Frewen, 1978, 1979, 1982), and biofeedback (Burgio, Whitehead, & Engel, 1985; Engel, Nikcomanesh, & Schuster, 1974; Smith, Smith, Rose, & Newman, 1989; Whitehead, Burgio, & Engel, 1985; Willington, 1978), in which clients learn to control bladder and sphincter responses through operant conditioning.

In Clay's study, 31 patients learned to manage their voiding schedules, with the diligence of their caretakers. He reported that 63% of the males and 73% of the females were successfully managed. In a series of studies by Frewen with females of different ages, cure rates from 82% to 97% were reported.

Biofeedback is a promising treatment for incontinent elderly. In 1974, Engel *et al.* demonstrated that five of six elderly subjects were able to learn the procedure and become continent after several training sessions. Subjects were taught to distinguish between their typical sphincter responses and normal responses. They were praised whenever they produced normal graphs and were told whenever their graphs were poor. Four subjects maintained continence after the study was terminated. Two remained continent for at least 5 years. The lack of control measures restrict the conclusions of this study, however. Willington (1978) also studied the effects of biofeedback information on a group of elderly outpatients and reported that 62% were cured of urge incontinence and 34% showed improvement after one to three training sessions. Working with 17 elderly patients, Whitehead *et al.* (1985) reported a 78% reduction in incontinence episodes with a combination of biofeedback and self-directed toileting schedules. In a second study, Burgio, Whitehead, and Engel (1985) designed a more elaborate program in which biofeedback was combined with pelvic exercises, self-monitoring, self-directed toileting schedules, and relaxation techniques. Subjects were 39 elderly people who lived in their own homes. After an average of 3.5 training sessions, subjects reduced the frequency of incontinent episodes by an average of 87%.

Smith *et al.* (1989) extended this work with 54 community-dwelling elderly who had a 12-year median duration of urge and stress incontinence. After filling out daily bladder records for 2 weeks, subjects were taught pelvic exercises and given biofeedback and verbal feedback about their behavior. Relaxation techniques, habit training, diet modification, and bowel regimens were discussed with them as well. They were instructed to do the pelvic exercises 50 times each day. They returned for follow-up visits every 2 weeks until improvement was shown, and they were seen for 1-, 3-, 6-, and 12-month evaluations. Assessment measures at those times included a review of the bladder records and direct demonstration of control via the clinical perineometer. This program proved quite successful. At all follow-up evaluations, subjects reported a significant decrease in the mean number of urinary accidents. Between baseline and the end of the formal treatment sessions, subjects improved by a mean percentage of 78%. For the most part, this improvement was accomplished within three training visits. The study, which took 2 years to complete, effectively demonstrated the value of biofeedback training for establishing continence in this group of subjects. As the authors point out, however, there were no attempts to randomize subjects or compare the biofeedback program with appropriate control groups. There was also no verification of whether or not the participants actually practiced at home and recorded data properly. The fact that 25% of the subjects dropped out of the program suggests the need for further exploration of motivation factors in this type of program.

Conclusions about Self-Care Research

These studies on self-care represent an important phase of behavioral gerontology. The behaviors targeted by the researchers are ones which have been regarded as distinctive hallmarks of aging and as unmodifiable. The investigators working in this area explored the value of contingent reinforcement for older people with severe losses and found it useful.

Conclusions about the actual value of the interventions are limited, however, because the research designs were generally flawed and incomplete. Subjects were usually few in number, randomly assigned, and were studied in a within-subject design. Studies were generally conducted within a short time period, there were few follow-up assessments, and rarely were generalization programs built into the treatment programs. There were few controls for experimenter bias and novelty effects. Staff, the primary implementors of the treatments, were seldom involved in the designs of the studies; they were often not assessed for their knowledge of the treatment procedures or their ability to carry out the programs; and they were infrequently trained in the procedures. The subjects themselves, mainly institutionalized elderly, were never consulted about elements of the treatment that may have enhanced the intervention effects. For example, idiosyncratic selection of reinforcers did not occur, although there is evidence that staff and patients often disagree about what stimuli are reinforcing to patients (Wisocki, 1982). Some behavioral gerontologists (Page, Caron, & Yates, 1973; Richards & Thorpe, 1978) have been troubled by the idea that the use of behavioral procedures in institutions may enforce traditional institutional values or may only address the concerns of staff and family members, rather than ameliorate the problems of the elderly themselves. A few of the later studies, however, were better designed and executed and seem to show more concern for these sensitive issues.

Social Interaction and Participation Programs

The behavioral research into increasing social interactions, social activities, and the social skills of elderly occupies a substantial part of the overall contribution of behavior therapy to gerontology. I have divided this research into four types of intervention. In the first type, environmental changes, like the inclusion of food and beverages into the patient's schedule or furniture arrangement, were employed as independent variables. In the second type, recreational activities or objects were provided to a sample of elderly who were either prompted or reinforced to use them. The goal of this research was to increase participation in social activities. In the third type, investigators aimed their interventions at increasing verbal interaction. In the fourth type, subjects were in social skills or assertiveness programs. I will discuss each of these in turn.

Environmental Changes

The most striking aspect of this body of research is that the intervention was small and inexpensively achieved, but the effect on behavior was significant. Blackman, Howe, and Pinkston (1976) designed a study in which juice and coffee were available on 3 alternating days a week, inter-spersed with 2 days when no beverages were available. Their data show clear differences in the number of residents in attendance and the amount of interaction among the residents during the days when juice and coffee were available. Carroll (1978) instituted a social hour at which residents of a state hospital could request their own beverages and found an increase in residents' participation in recreational, occupational, and musical activities. Quattrochi-Tubin and Jason (1980) provided coffee to nursing home residents during a morning exercise program, using an ABAB design. They found increases in program participation and increased social enjoyment. Two groups of investigators (Peterson, Knapp, Rosen, & Pither, 1977; Sommer & Ross, 1958) observed that interactions increased when chairs were arranged around small tables rather than along the walls. Risley and Edwards (1978) found that social activity during mealtime increased when institutional-style food service was re-placed with family-style serving. Family-style service also improved residents' memories of the previous day's meal. Melin and Gotestam (1981) reported an increase in interaction among patients and improvement in the use of tableware when staff served meals and snacks at small tables instead of placing them on serving trays.

This research was conducted with the small percentage of elderly who are "captive" populations in institutions, where environmental stimulation is often low. It is, therefore, not surprising to find that a small change in residential setting or a demonstration of personal interest produced a noticeable show of activity. In none of these studies, unfortunately, were measures taken of the maintenance of the targeted behaviors over time. Neither was there control for the novelty of the manipulation. Such design problems are often encountered when one is doing research in the natural setting, where the experimenter cannot control all the relevant factors in a program. For example, Carroll (1978) reported that his follow-up program was hampered by the lack of support from the staff and hospital administration. The inclusion of large groups of clients in the treatment programs is a noteworthy feature of this research, in marked contrast to the single-subject designs used in the bulk of behavioral-gerontological research.

Carstensen and Erikson (1986) have cautioned that a simple increase in rates of interaction is insufficient as a measure of success. It is also necessary to examine the quality of the social interaction. To arrive at this conclusion they executed a well-controlled and elaborate study, using a group reversal design, to investigate the effect of juice and cookies on the interaction behavior of 30 nursing home residents. Data were taken on eye contact, body movements, sounds, lip movements, physical contacts, gestures, and facial expressions. The actual verbalizations made by subjects were repeated into a tape recorder. Results indicated that attendance rates and number of interactions increased during the treatment conditions and decreased during the withdrawal condition. When the content of the vocal behavior was analyzed, however, Carstensen and Erikson found that the increase was due to more frequent episodes of ineffective communication. During the treatment conditions, ineffective communications substantially increased over baseline, while the verbalizations of facts, opinions, and questions decreased.

Participation

Several studies were designed to increase the involvement of elderly in a number of scheduled activities. For example, Bingo playing was encouraged among 43 institutionalized elderly by awarding badges that could later be used for obtaining refreshments (Quilitch, 1974). When this condition was in force (using a reversal design), the number of players increased from 3 to 15. The provision of puzzles, simple dexterity toys and games, with prompts for their use (Jenkins, Felce, Lunt, & Powell, 1977), or an opportunity to garden indoors (Powell, Felce, Jenkins, & Lunt, 1979) increased the activity level of nursing home residents. No baseline data are reported in these last two studies, making it impossible to judge the significance of the interaction. Furthermore, the availability of activities is confounded with intermittent and ongoing praise and attention, so that the separate effects are unknown. Finally, the studies were flawed by the lack of controls for novelty effects and the absence of a measure for maintenance and generalization.

As Morse and Wisocki have pointed out elsewhere in this text (Chapter 4), the results of these studies buttress the general agreement that inactivity is not a necessary condition of the institutionalized elderly, and they demonstrate that the strategy of providing and reinforcing participation may work effectively in institutional settings. Their positive results also underscore the impoverished nature of the geriatric wards in the 1970s. Such studies, however, do not provide the systematic data needed to understand how best to utilize limited resources to obtain maximum participation.

In a series of studies, McClannahan and Risley systematically investigated the effects of alterations in the environment on activity rates. In one study (1973), they opened a store in the activity area of a nursing home and observed the amount of interaction outside the store during times when it was open and closed. The program was conducted over a 9-month period, but "shopping" was possible for only 36 days (1 hour per day). Interactions were dependent on the store's availability and increased somewhat over time. In a second study (1975a) they found that the placement of small objects in the trays of residents' gerry chairs increased their activities and conversation.

McClannahan and Risley (1975b) also conducted two experiments designed to increase activity among a population of 100 elderly nursing home residents. In the first experiment they investigated the influence of randomly distributed prizes on attendance at various activities—bingo games, art programs, and reading programs—using a reversal design over a 20-week period. In the second experiment they followed the same design, but used servings of snack foods during the activity. In both conditions the numbers of residents attending the activity sessions significantly increased from baseline conditions, although the actual numbers of participants were small.

McClannahan and Risley (1974) investigated the effects of prompts on activity levels of nursing home residents. In a counterbalanced design, they compared types of announcements made to residents during nine intervals over a 3-week period. The announcements were made via signs, the loudspeaker system, table placards, and all three concurrently. There was also a control group in which no announcement was made. In comparing monetary rewards for attendance and no monetary rewards, they found no difference between the types of announcements, but some announcement was significantly better than no announcement. The use of all three types of announcements was slightly better than the use of any one individual type. They also found that residents' presence in a lounge area increased substantially when they were paid 25 cents to answer questions while sitting there. They noticed increases in both lounge attendance and mutual assistance among the residents. When the money was withdrawn, participation was reduced nearly to zero.

Newkirk, Feldman, Bickett, Gipson, and Lutzker (1976) provided supporting evidence for the effect of prompts on activity. Employing a group design, they found that attendance at activities was increased when a room was centrally located and when the residents were called by name to the activity, rather than simply announcing the activity over a loudspeaker.

McClannahan and Risley demonstrated functional relationships between prompting and participation, but they did not address the benefits of the intervention. They examined only one residential setting and a limited range of behaviors over a relatively short time period. This work is important, however, because it forces us to consider environmental elements that facilitate or hinder participation by residents. McClannahan and Risley indicated that 3 of the 10 residents in the 1975b study failed to utilize any of the materials. One of these was hostile to the intervention, and all three patients had impaired vision. It is necessary to know more about the match between residents' particular specifications and the environmental factors that would facilitate interactions. These points were made by the investigators themselves.

Verbal Interactions

The findings from the Carstensen and Erikson (1986) study cause us to consider carefully the work that specifically targeted verbal interactions. In the studies described below, the investigators made no attempt to examine the quality of the verbal behavior. The question under consideration was whether or not rates of verbal behavior could be increased by the application of contingent reinforcement. Mueller and Atlas (1972) tested two methods of increasing verbal behavior among five institutionalized elderly: the use of primary reinforcers and the use of prompts and tokens. Only the second treatment provoked a change in the clients' verbal exchange in group discussions. The use of prompts was not separated from the use of tokens, however, making it impossible to differentiate the relative merits of each treatment factor. The experimental design was a simple one; no effort was made to vary or withdraw the experimental conditions. There were no follow-up or maintenance data. With a reversal design, Hoyer, Kafer, Simpson, and Hoyer (1974) contingently reinforced the verbalizations of two elderly mentally ill clients while two other clients looked on. The reinforcers were pennies, candy, or cigarettes. They found that both word production and verbal interaction increased for all clients, including those who only observed the exchange. Their conclusions are limited by the lack of data on generalization or follow-up. MacDonald (1978) used contingent verbal reinforcement on the verbalizations of three elderly nursing home residents to get them to talk to each other. When the reinforcement was withdrawn, however, the verbal exchanges diminished. In an attempt to extend MacDonald's study and obtain maintenance and generalization of behavior, O'Quinn, O'Dell, and Burnett (1982) employed a multiple baseline design with two pairs of two nursing home residents. The clients were instructed to ask questions of each other at the evening meal. If no verbal activity occurred, the experimenter modeled the desired behavior and reinforced verbalizations whenever they were made. The presence of the experimenter was faded after 10 days. Two months later the number of interactions was measured in three follow-up visits. While rates of verbalizations increased for all clients, interaction was apparently dependent on the presence of the facilitating experimenter.

Social Skills Training

This is an area that has been extensively investigated by behaviorists for every population but the elderly, despite Welford's (1980) prediction that social skills would be a primary focus in applied gerontology during the 1980s. There are a few studies, however, in which elderly clients were taught the essentials of social interaction. All but one study were conducted with institutionalized elderly as subjects.

Goldstein and Baer (1976) approached the problem of interaction from the standpoint of written correspondence. When residents of a nursing home complained that they received few letters, Goldstein and Baer identified letter-writing strategies that would most likely generate responses. Three residents were selected by staff for participation in a multiple-baseline design study. These residents were taught to ask questions in their letters and to include stamped, self-addressed envelopes. The strategy successfully increased the amount of correspondence each person received, and the residents increased their social arena beyond the confines of the nursing home.

Praderas and MacDonald (1986) tried to teach four elderly nursing home residents to use the telephone by means of instructions, modeling, role-playing, feedback, and reinforcement in a multiple-baseline design across behaviors. All of the subjects improved to some extent, but only two subjects clearly acquired the targeted skills. There was no increase in the use of the telephone and no generalization to the natural environment.

Berger and Rose (1977) asked nursing home residents to identify difficult social situations, 34 of which were later rated and defined by staff. Twenty five residents were randomly assigned to one of three conditions: interpersonal skills training, a discussion control, and assessment-only control. Those in the skills-training group were taught to respond appropriately to half of the situations originally identified, while the rest were used as an indication of generalization. The investigators took behavioral measures of performance and the residents rated themselves on interpersonal competence. The residents who received the training were significantly more effective in responding to social events than the residents in the control conditions in both the targeted and non-targeted situations. After a 2-month follow-up, only the responses to the targeted events were maintained, but the training did not generalize to non-targeted situations. No difference in self-ratings were found between the groups.

In a well-controlled study, Lopez, Hoyer, Goldstein, Gershaw, and Sprafkin (1980) taught conversational skills to 56 elderly institutionalized patients with the use of modeling, role-playing, and contingent social reinforcement. All subjects acquired the targeted skills, and the skill transferred to structured interactions with staff, but not to unstructured situations. In a second study with a similar design, Lopez (1980) taught 70 elderly residents who were about to reenter the community how to express appreciation. The findings from this study paralleled those of the first one: skills did not transfer outside the experimental situation. In this study, skills transfer was enhanced by medium overlearning, but high overlearning decreased both the acquisition of skills and their transfer.

Engels and Poser (1987) described a program in which community-dwelling elderly clients established their own goals and learned social skills through role-playing, modeling, cognitive training, and homework assignments. After 10 weeks of training and at follow-up, clients indicated positive gains in the targeted areas. The details of this work are reported by Engels in Chapter 8 of this volume.

Assertiveness training, an established behavioral treatment package heavily reliant on role-playing procedures, has had mixed results with elderly adults. Corby (1975) found that elderly nursing home residents significantly improved in assertion after training, but two other investigators found no significant effects. Rose (1977) found some increase in assertion for elderly study participants, but the increase was less than that shown by groups of younger subjects. Edinberg, Karoly, and Gleser (1977) found no differences between older adults who participated in assertiveness training, discussion groups, or no treatment.

Franzke (1987) compared the effects of a 6-week assertiveness training program with a no-treatment control group. There were 42 community-dwelling elderly subjects in each group, with some control for socioeconomic status. Those subjects trained in assertion scored significantly better on self-report measures of self-concept and assertiveness. Subjects were not tested outside the training sessions, there were no controls for expectancy effects, and there were no follow-up measures.

Assertive behavior is affected greatly by situational contexts and must be taught and practiced in those contexts for generalization to occur. None of these studies met that requirement. The question of whether or not assertiveness training is appropriate for elderly clients is still an open one.

Treatment Outcome Studies

Two sets of investigators conducted comparison studies of the differential effects of treatment programs. In 1973, Mishara and Kastenbaum designed a token economy program for male residents of a geriatric facility and compared its effects with those of a noncontingent "enriched" control ward. Residents in the experimental group earned tokens for self-care activities, helping on the ward after mealtimes, and talking with others. Residents were able to exchange their tokens for wine, if they wished. In the control ward, wine was given noncontingently. After 21 months, results were assessed. Both groups used fewer medications, but the subjects in the control group showed a greater decline in medication usage. There was more socialization in both groups, but the control group showed a greater increase. The investigators judged the token economy program more effective for the active residents. The staff preferred it because it maintained more self-care activities in residents (Mishara, 1978).

In 1982, MacDonald, Davidowitz, Gimbel, and Foley also found that some patients benefitted more from some treatments than others did. They examined the effects of three treatment programs on the activity level of patients in a geriatric ward. In the first treatment sequence, the physical environment of the dayroom was rearranged to encourage interaction, and various recreational items were available for use. In the second treatment sequence, staff were trained in general reinforcement principles and gave attention contingently whenever they observed patients being active. In the third treatment sequence, after training in prompting techniques, staff prompted activity from inactive patients, while continuing to deliver contingent attention to patients who were active. For both the second and third interventions, a multiple-baseline design across subjects was used to assess the effects. For further analysis, patients were divided into high and low-activity levels during baseline. After 103 days of treatment, there were three follow-up probes at 21, 41, and 61 days. The authors found that each of the three treatments effectively increased activity levels and that there were differential effects for high- and low-active patients. High-active patients became more active when exposed to the first two treatments, while the third treatment (prompting) had little impact on their activity levels. Patients with initially low activity levels responded only to the prompt condition. At follow-up, activity levels were not maintained, most likely because the interventions were not continued by staff, despite training in the procedures.

Conclusions about Social Interaction and Participation Research

The ability to relate socially to others is important in the maintenance of good mental and physical health for people of all ages. As people age, they often lose friends and relatives from long-established social networks, and they must then take special care of those relationships that remain or they must cultivate new ones. Sometimes long-held interaction patterns are ineffective in establishing new friendships, and the elderly person is required to learn new behaviors.

It would seem, then, that this area of research has great potential for benefiting the elderly population. As this review indicates, however, little has been done with those elderly who are not residents of nursing homes or mental hospitals. With impaired elderly, researchers have learned that social and verbal behaviors occurring initially at a low rate are amenable to change when contingent reinforcement is used consistently. Subjects were able to acquire the desired behavior, but the behavior was not self-sustaining, and rates of performance did not generalize to conditions outside the experimental situation.

Various explanations have been proposed to explain this lack of maintenance and generalization. Carstensen (1988) has pointed out that elderly residents of nursing homes may not want more interaction with peers. There is evidence that the elderly in institutions do not find other elderly men or women reinforcing (Wisocki, 1982). Another reason may be due to the staff's behavior. Romaniuk, Wilcox, and Romaniuk (1982) reported that elderly in a day-treatment facility were frequently devalued by patronizing comments made by the staff. It is also possible that the problem of social inactivity is more complex than researchers have believed. Carstensen and Fremouw (1988) have proposed that depression, anxiety, and mental status are correlates of social isolation and must be included as targets in treatment programs. Also, in this body of research, experimenters on the whole did not incorporate maintenance plans into their program designs. Most often, they simply waited to see if the behavior would continue after the treatment was withdrawn. The interventions were generally short term, although the target behavior was complex and the subjects often seriously impaired. The researchers most frequently used a within-subject ABAB reversal design in these studies, with only one treatment phase.

The studies were generally well-designed, however, and often demonstrated innovative strategies for developing more social behaviors for institutionalized elderly. On the whole, they indicated that the treatment procedures exerted functional control over the behavior of those elderly often considered unable to change their condition.

Idiosyncratic Behavior Problems

Behavior therapists are often asked to consult to geriatric wards about patients' behaviors that are either dangerous or troublesome to themselves or others. For example, Zimmer, Watson, and Treat (1984) found that nurses in 42 nursing homes indicated that 64% of their 3,456 patients presented significant behavior problems and that 23% of these had "serious problems." Burgio, Tice, and Engel (1985) provided more specific details about these problems. In surveying an urban nursing home about the number and kinds of problems presented by their 160 patients, they found that the most common problems were with mobility, incontinence, dressing, confusion/disorientation, low activity level, language, depression, and feeding. The next most frequent problems were tantrums, verbal abuse, noncompliance, aggression, bedtime difficulties, disruptive behavior, stereotypic behavior, wandering, fecal smearing, self-injurious behavior, vomiting, and inappropriate sexual behavior. Low-frequency problems (those occurring less than 5% of the time) included stealing, destruction of property, spitting, high activity level, and pica. Ryan, Tainsh, Kolodny, Landrum, and Fisher (1988) identified 30% of residents in two long-term care facilities as "noisemakers." Noisy residents were those who displayed a "chronic pattern of perseverative verbal behavior . . . in a pattern (which) may be continuous or intermittent, goal directed or without apparent purpose. It may vary in loudness, content, and impact" (p. 370).

Many of these problems are positively correlated with organic impairment, a fact that does not preclude treatment, but that does complicate treatment because staff are often unwilling to acknowledge that environmental events may have a bearing on the occurrence of such problems.

Although there are several anecdotal reports about various methods of treatment for elderly who display these behavior problems, most of the research studies have been conducted with younger subjects. In this section we shall look at the existing behavioral research in this category.

Aggression

Using an ABCDA multiple-baseline experimental design across behaviors, Rosberger and MacLean (1983) demonstrated the value of contingent attention to positive behaviors and contingent extinction of a variety of disruptive behaviors exhibited by an elderly female nursing home patient who had suffered a cerebrovascular accident. These behaviors included throwing and banging dishes, pushing objects at others, fecal smearing, kicking and tripping others, and self-exposure. Within 3 weeks all behaviors but fecal smearing were reduced to zero and were maintained at least 5 months when a follow-up assessment was done. The authors pointed out, however, that this study had serious design problems that interfered with the integrity of the program.

Vaccaro (1988) examined the effect of a DRO schedule on the aggressive behavior of six elderly men in a state hospital. Using a well-controlled ABAB design, Vaccaro established a 3-week baseline by meeting with the clients for 1 hour twice a week to discuss weekly events and to remind clients of what constituted aggressive and nonaggressive behaviors. During the first experimental condition, if the clients exhibited no aggressive behavior, they were rewarded with food or juice every 10 minutes; every aggressive action was consequated with a verbal reprimand and a 10-minute time-out period. This condition lasted for 6 weeks. A second 3-week baseline period was followed by a second 6-week experimental condition. During the last 2 weeks of this phase, reinforcers were delivered every 20 minutes instead of every 10 minutes. Clients were informed about this change in advance. Finally, Vaccaro implemented a 16-week phase-out program in which clients were rewarded for a day of nonaggressive behavior by being able to select two out of three tangible reinforcers. After 4 consecutive days of nonaggressive behavior, clients were rewarded with two recreational trips each week, planned around their interests. Presumably, this pattern continued as a regular ward routine after the study was over. Follow-up data after phase-out were not taken.

Physical and verbal aggressive acts were measured both in the context of the group sessions with the experimenter and on the ward. In both settings Vaccaro successfully demonstrated that the DRO schedule had functional control over the aggressive behavior of all six clients and that the effect continued during the phase-out period. This phase-out period, in which clients learned to extend the time between reinforcers, is an especially notable feature of this study.

Stereotypy

Hussian (1982a) studied two elderly institutionalized patients who displayed a variety of stereotypic behaviors. Hussian targeted only the behavior of clothing manipulation. With a multiple-baseline design, he taught patients to associate a large, red, cardboard circle with positive reinforcement, which was presented when no stereotypic behavior occurred. He reported a significant reduction in clothing manipulation after training, but no generalization to the other stereotypic behaviors that were not treated, thereby demonstrating a functional relationship between the intervention and the behavior.

Repetitive or Disruptive Vocalizations

In this same study of stimulus control, Hussian (1982a) included a third patient who had a high rate of repetitive verbalizations. Using the same methodology, he found that he was able to reduce the frequency of this patient's behavior by nearly half. In another study, Hussian (1982b) compared the effects of extinction and the use of positive self-statements on the repetitive verbalizations about death made by one nursing home patient. While there was a reduction in the behavior, the experimental design was inadequate to draw conclusions about treatment effects.

Several years earlier, Baltes and Lascomb (1975) published a study in which they differentially consequated the screaming behavior of one elderly patient with a time-out intervention and appropriate behaviors with social and tangible rewards. They demonstrated the functional relationship between the intervention and the behavior by means of an ABA design, but they did not measure maintenance.

Patterson and Teigen (1973) executed a nicely controlled study with a female patient who had a 26-year history of giving bizarre information about her personal life. Their target behaviors were factual information and reality-oriented conversation. The experimenters devised five different types of questions and varied their presentation across three conditions. In the first condition the patient received tokens whenever her verbalizations were correct; in the second condition the patient was not reinforced for accuracy; in the third condition the tokens were given contingently again. The patient was discharged home and the program continued. The data from the home environment indicated a clear relationship between the contingently given tokens and accuracy. When the tokens were given on a random basis, accuracy declined. At a 2-month follow-up the behavior was maintained, demonstrating the efficacy of the procedure.

Haley (1983) developed a comprehensive program for an elderly woman who often cried out for assistance from her family whenever she was left alone. After taking a baseline of the number of minutes she was able to be alone without shouting, Haley taught the patient a relaxation procedure to use when she began to feel anxious. He also used a kitchen timer, with gradually increasing intervals and a message board to remind the patient of the location of all family members. When the patient was able to tolerate a new level of time without calling out, she was rewarded with food or wine. Eventually the family was able to leave her alone for nearly an hour. In this case report, the author has described a successful and practical intervention for a difficult problem, which enabled the patient to remain at home. He has also focused on a stimulus condition of the patient (anxiety), as well as the problem behavior (calling out). These clinical considerations, however, limit the conclusions we might draw about the differential effects of the treatment methods.

Green, Linsk, and Pinkston (1986) taught the use of contingent reinforcement and extinction to the spouses of two mentally impaired elderly who lived at home. The wives identified the goals for treatment, took baseline data on targeted verbal behavior (accusatory verbalizations, appropriate verbal responses, and spontaneous verbalizations), and learned to evaluate their progress. Maintenance procedures were taught as well. The investigators employed an ABAB design for one client and an AB design for the other to evaluate the effect of the interventions. For the first client, the frequency of incidents did not change, but the duration of the incidents decreased dramatically. For the second client, there was an increase in the number of spontaneous verbalizations, but it was not substantial, due apparently to the incorrect application of reinforcement by the spouse. At a 6-month follow up, the behavioral improvements were maintained. As the authors point out, an important feature of this study was that the wives learned better coping skills and institutional placement was averted.

Wandering and Disorientation

Hussian and Davis (1985) have characterized wandering behavior as ambulation that is not under the control of the typical environmental cues, although it is
under some degree of stimulus control. Hussian (1982b) used a stimulus control
method to modify the wandering behavior of three demented patients. He paired
the presentation of two different-colored stimuli with the delivery of positive and
negative consequences (food and a loud noise) respectively. Once the associations
were established, each stimulus was placed in areas where ambulation was permitted (the orange stimulus) and discouraged (the blue stimulus). The cues were
eventually faded. The wandering behavior was effectively reduced and success was
maintained for 2 months. Hussian found, however, that even after four booster
sessions during the course of a year, the cues were required for control. This study
is particularly noteworthy because it was conducted after a careful analysis of the
behavior and included a long-term follow-up of the effects of the intervention.

Earlier, Cuvo (1976) worked with an elderly retarded woman who had trouble
returning to her ward after an activity. Using a reversal design in which a candy bar
was either given or withheld whenever the patient returned with a set time period,
Cuvo demonstrated functional control over the dawdling behavior.

Hanley (1981) tried a different strategy. He first assessed the ability of five
demented patients to locate eight different places on their hospital ward. Any place
the patients were unable to locate became the target for their training program. The investigator showed the area to the patients, described it verbally, and coached the patient
to repeat the name of the place. Four patients demonstrated improvement in place finding after a 2-week follow-up, but after 5 months these gains were not maintained.

McEvoy and Patterson (1986) used a chaining procedure with demented patients on their ward. They determined the patients' abilities to find specific locations
and then taught them the route to the places they were unable to find in a back-
wards chaining sequence. Successful completion of each part of the chain was
reinforced with tokens and praise and another part was added to the trip. Within 1
month of training, the patients were successful 80% of the time in completing the
entire route and the behavior was maintained at a 1-month follow-up.

Hussian and Brown (1987) used a very simple manipulation to reduce exiting
from hospital wards. They placed eight strips of masking tape on the floor in a two-
dimensional grid pattern in front of exit doors and observed a 68% reduction in
attempts to open the doors among seven of eight patients with Alzheimer's disease.
The one person who did not respond to this treatment seldom looked down at the
floor, and the investigators speculated that he probably never noticed the tape.
Hussian and Brown suggest that the grid pattern was the effective variable in
maintaining confinement of these patients, but there was no mention of controls for
other environmental events. They did not take follow-up or maintenance data.
Chafetz and West (1987) incorporated a similar intervention into their ward for
demented patients and, in conducting a longitudinal evaluation of the ward, found
that while the grid pattern was effective in reducing the number of exit attempts,
after the tape was removed, attempts to exit continued to decrease. They felt that
other changes in the general environment accounted for the behavioral success.

Self-Injury

Mishara, Robertson, and Kastenbaum (1973) tried to stop the self-injurious behavior of an elderly man by giving him a variety of tasks to perform. While the strategy worked during the time he was occupied in some activity, it did not reduce his self-abuse at other times. This case study, like others, cannot be evaluated empirically.

Mishara and Kastenbaum (1973) conducted a more elaborate study on self-injurious behavior in which they compared the effects of two different hospital milieux on the self-injurious behavior of three wards of elderly patients. On one ward a token economy was instituted. In two other wards they increased the number of available activities, gave clients more opportunities to select reinforcers for themselves, and tried to alert staff to the contingencies which affected clients. The clients in the two control conditions decreased self-injurious behavior significantly more than the clients in the token economy condition. Clients on the token economy ward, however, required less help from staff for self-care, and they demonstrated more appropriate social behaviors. This study is difficult to evaluate, however, because neither baseline nor follow-up measures were taken.

Conclusions about Research on Idiosyncratic Behavior Problems

Despite the number and variety of idiosyncratic problems occurring frequently with the elderly in institutional settings, the research work with those problems is scanty. Fewer than 20 studies have been published. Excluding three studies conducted with entire wards of patients, very few patients have been included in these research programs.

The quality of the work is variable. Some of the studies lack crucial design elements, especially in the areas of generalization and maintenance of the experimental effects. Many of them, however, have incorporated clever, innovative, and practical strategies into the treatment plans for clients. While this research, like research cited previously, demonstrated the benefits of the contingent application of reinforcement and extinction, it tested a greater variety of behavioral procedures than work in other areas, and the interventions were more complex. This research was also distinguished by the fact that investigators attended to individual details of the clients and the conditions contributing to the presenting problems, tailoring many of the programs to individual needs.

Memory Training and Language Programs

Decrements in a variety of cognitive abilities are typically associated with the aging process. Older adults can expect to experience losses in short-term memory, information acquisition and retrieval, and response speed, but the declines are generally small and vary greatly between individuals.

Researchers have used behavioral principles and procedures in their investigations of ways to remediate age-related declines in cognitive abilities, with test-taking strategies as the target behaviors. Contingent reinforcement (in the form of money or verbal feedback) was used effectively to increase response speed (Hoyer, Hoyer, Treat, & Baltes, 1978; Hoyer, Labouvie, & Baltes, 1973), to increase the number of correct responses and decrease particular kinds of errors (Perone & Baron, 1983; Schultz & Hoyer, 1976), and to decrease cautiousness and increase risk-taking in testing situations (Birkhill & Schaie, 1975). In two studies in which praise was the reinforcer given for correct test responses, however, the elderly did not improve their performance levels (Hutchison, 1974; Kausler & Lair, 1968).

Modeling strategies have also been used effectively for improving the test-taking performance of elderly subjects. Crovitz (1966) trained elderly subjects to verbalize the principles involved in concept formation, with a resulting performance improvement. In several studies, Denny and her colleagues (Denny, 1974; Denny & Denny, 1974; Denny, Jones, & Krigel, 1979) used models to teach elderly subjects to ask effective problem-solving questions. Meichenbaum's (1974) self-instruction training, basically a modeling procedure, was not only used to teach elderly subjects to attend to relevant stimulus cues and to cope with anxiety in the test-taking situation, but produced superior performances on the categories subtest of the Halstead battery. Labouvie-Vief and Gonda (1976) used Meichenbaum's procedure and discovered that self-instruction training raised performance scores on both the training and transfer task in reasoning, which were then maintained for 2 weeks.

Some investigators used a combination of procedures to enhance the test-taking performance of elderly participants. For example, Sanders, Sterns, Smith, and Sanders (1975) taught subjects to solve a concept identification task by means of a programmed learning sequence based on shaping and a token reinforcement system. Beres and Baron (1981) based their training program on instruction, practice, and feedback and found improvements on tests of fluid intelligence. Hill, Sheikh, and Yesavage (1988) found that active pretraining in a variety of methods, such as imagery, affective judgment, and relaxation, helped elderly learn mnemonic methods.

Other investigators tried to reduce the anxiety experienced by nondemented elderly in test-taking situations with either a relaxation procedure (Yesavage, 1984; Yesavage, Rose, & Speigel, 1982) or stress inoculation training (Hayslip, 1989). Yesavage and colleagues found that highly anxious subjects benefitted from relaxation training. Their decreases in anxiety were positively correlated with improved performance in test-taking after memory training. Subjects who were not anxious, however, showed learning decrements after relaxation, perhaps an indication that anxiety had a functional value in their learning. Hayslip compared induction training and stress inoculation training with a no-contact control on measures of fluid ability. He found that both experimental groups demonstrated greater immediate posttest gains on the Letter Sets task than the control group. At a 1-month follow-up, the stress inoculation training group and the control group experienced slight performance declines on that test. For a Letter Series task both experimental groups showed improvement 1 week after posttest, but after a 1-month follow-up, only the stress inoculation group demonstrated gains. According to Hayslip these data suggested alternative ways to facilitate intellectual competence in older adults.

Some cognitive losses, dementia and aphasia, for example, occur as a result of organic disorders. Even in such cases, the accompanying troubling deficits are amenable to intervention. The behavioral literature on these disorders, presented below, is extremely small. I have divided it into work on memory deficits and language programs.

Coping with Memory Deficits

Using fluids as reinforcers, Ankus and Quarrington (1972) successfully conditioned elderly patients with severe memory loss to respond to specific requirements for lever pulling. Zarit, Zarit, and Reever (1982) were moderately successful in teaching demented patients to use imagery-based techniques to learn lists and pairs of words. At posttest, however, the patients were unable to recall their words. Hill, Evandovich, Sheikh, and Yesavage (1987) had more success in using an imagery technique to teach a demented patient to connect names and faces. They measured the interval over which the patient could recall names and found that it increased from 2 to 6 minutes. At a 1-month follow-up, the interval of 6 minutes was maintained.

Hanley and Lusty (1984) worked with an 84-year-old institutionalized demented patient who had trouble remembering personal information and her daily schedule. The investigators gave her a diary with the relevant information, and she was prompted to look at it when her memory failed her. She learned to consult her diary after 4 weeks of training, but she was not taught to initiate the behavior on her own and, consequently, was dependent on staff for prompts.

Bourgeois (1988) tried a similar strategy with three moderately demented patients who lived at home with their husbands and who often forgot specific information about family matters. Bourgeois and the patients' husbands constructed "communication wallets," which contained sentences and pictures representing the information needed for communication. The patients were then prompted to use the wallet when topics included in it were discussed. Bourgeois assessed the number of correct statements made by the patients and found an increase when the wallets were in use. After the prompts were discontinued, the habit of using the wallets was maintained.

Scogin, Storandt, and Lott (1985) gave a group of elderly a graduated, self-paced program for improving memory skills to teach themselves at home and compared their results to those of a wait-list control group. The experimental subjects improved on 6 of 11 measures of memory, but they did not decrease their complaints about memory loss or their scores on a depression inventory. Treatment effects were maintained after 1 month, according to a follow-up measure. There was no indication that the training generalized into the natural environment, however.

Language Programs

Many of the current language rehabilitation programs involve behavioral elements, such as shaping, fading, reinforcement, and modeling. Elderly patients are not generally considered good candidates for rehabilitation programs because their prospects for recovery are poor and because retraining is an intensive process, made more difficult by the physical limitations elderly often experience.

Behaviorists have made forays into this area, but the work has not been extensive. Wisocki and Mosher carried out two studies in which elderly aphasic patients were taught sign language as an alternative to verbal communication. In the first study (Wisocki & Mosher, 1980) they treated an elderly male aphasic patient in a VA hospital. They used shaping procedures for the client and involved a peer in the program for generalization purposes. The patient not only learned 14 signs that enabled him to communicate with others for the first time in years, but he also significantly increased the mean frequency of social interactions with other patients. Both targets were maintained at a 4-month follow-up. The experimental design of this study did not include a phase that would have conclusively demonstrated the value of including the peer in the intervention program. This study took place over 66 weeks and used a great deal of person power to teach a small number of signs, calling into question its cost-effectiveness. Its main value was in demonstrating that a severely impaired elderly client could acquire a workable communication system.

In the second study, reported by Wisocki (1986), Wisocki and Mosher taught sign language to six nursing home residents whose language was impaired due to cerebral vascular accidents. After a baseline period, residents were taught 70 signs in 10 weeks by means of manual shaping and modeling. The program continued for an additional 20 weeks while staff were incorporated into the program and patients were encouraged to use sign in the normal course of their daily routines. The investigators found that individual patients learned at different rates. Some acquired only 15% of the signs, while others learned 100% of them. At a 5-week follow-up, retention levels were between 15% and 65% for different patients. Generalization occurred for all patients. Staff involvement made little difference in the use of sign. No longer-term follow-up was taken, and there was no maintenance program built into the study.

Conclusions about Research on Memory and Language Programs

The basic research presented initially in this section effectively demonstrates the plasticity of intellectual behaviors in the elderly (see a review by Baltes, Dittman-Kohli, & Kliegl (1986) for further elucidation). The applied work, however, is still preliminary. There is evidence that severely impaired elderly are able to recover some functioning, but strict testing of methods for enhancing recovery has yet to be done.

Health Programs

Health is a major concern for elderly citizens. An elderly person can expect to suffer from at least one chronic health problem and make frequent use of health care services during the course of his or her old age. Since most health problems are related to lifestyle and environmental factors, the development of positive strategies for remediating the effects of disease is important.

For this review I have described studies in which elderly people served as subjects for behavioral interventions for disease conditions and health-related problems, including arthritis, heart disease, dermatitis, cancer, choreal movements, pain, headache, eating disorders, alcoholism, compliance, increasing exercise levels, and increasing nutritious eating practices.

Arthritis

In two case studies, investigators worked with older arthritic patients. Czirr and Gallagher (1983) treated a man who suffered from severe rheumatoid arthritis and moderate depression. They taught the patient relaxation and imagery techniques and encouraged him to become actively involved in pleasant events. After 7 weeks of treatment, the patient reported a decrease in pain by 50% and a significant reduction in the depression. At a 3-month follow-up, the patient continued to report success in treatment. Using biofeedback procedures, Boczkowski (1984) taught an 80-year-old osteoarthritic woman to avoid contracting the muscles surrounding her joints so as to maintain a proper blood flow which, in turn, reduced the experience of pain. The patient reported a decrease in pain, stiffness, and medication after treatment. The conclusions of these studies are limited by the lack of controls typical of case reports.

Lorig, Laurin, and Holman (1984) prepared a self-management course in relaxation, problem solving, exercise, and instruction for middle-aged and elderly arthritis sufferers. After the program the participants demonstrated more knowledge about arthritis and reported a lessening of pain and fewer visits to a physician. A few years later, Lorig and Holman (1989) studied 589 arthritis sufferers who had taken the 6-week self-management course. They randomly assigned subjects to a group that received a bimonthly newsletter about arthritis, a group that attended an additional 6-week course in reinforcement, or a group that received no reinforcement. After 20 months all participants were queried about their pain experiences, feelings of depression, and visits to their physicians. There were no differences between the groups: all participants decreased pain by 20%, depression by 13%, and visits to physicians by 35%. The authors were confident that these trends would continue over time. They concluded that the additional feedback in newsletters about the course did not alter the effects of the self-care intervention.

Using the same educational program of Lorig et al. (1984), Keefe and his colleagues (1990) compared it with the effects of a cognitive-behavioral pain-coping skills-training program and a standard care control condition for 94 patients with osteoarthritic knee pain. The mean age of the group was 64 years. After random assignment to groups, patients in the behavioral treatment group were taught the following strategies: relaxation, imagery, distraction, task management, ways to schedule pleasant activities, and cognitive restructuring. Patients in the arthritis education group were simply given lectures about osteoarthritis and various treatment methods for it. Patients in the control condition continued regular treatment. After 10 weeks, patients reported on the coping strategies they used, their health status, and their use of medications. They engaged in a set of standard activities used to allow observers to record pain behavior. All these measures were taken at pre-intervention as well.

Results indicated that the patients in the cognitive-behavioral training group had significantly lower levels of pain and psychological disability after treatment than patients in the other two groups. The investigators also found that improvement was related to patients' perceptions of the effectiveness of their coping strategies. They found no improvement in physical disability or pain behavior in any group, a condition they related to the age of the subjects in this study.

Lindroth, Bauman, Barnes, and McCredie (1989) taught a program of pain and stress management and exercise to 100 arthritis sufferers in Australia and compared the results of the program with 100 outpatients in a control group. Self-report data on symptoms and treatment were collected before and immediately after treatment, and 3 and 12 months after the program was terminated. The participants in the treatment program showed significantly fewer problems attributable to arthritis, increased knowledge about arthritis, and changes in some health behaviors.

Heart Disease

Benson, Alexander, and Feldman (1975) included five elderly patients in their sample of eleven people with ischemic heart disease. After 4 weeks of relaxation training, three of the five elderly patients were able to decrease the number of premature ventricular contractions. The lack of a control group and the absence of follow-up data make it difficult to draw firm conclusions about this finding.

Dermatitis

Manuso (1977) used biofeedback-assisted handwarming training for a 60-year-old woman who suffered from chronic eczematous dermatitis of the hands. After a baseline period, the patient was trained in relaxation procedures, taught how to notice when her hand temperature was low and to use mental imagery to raise the temperature. The program went on for 13 weeks and the dermatitis disappeared. Six months after the program was over, the patient was still able to increase her hand temperature and was still symptom free.

Choreal Movements

Choreal movements occur in conjunction with Sydenham's Chorea and are often side effects of certain drugs, inducing tardive dyskinesia. Longin, Kohn, and Macurik (1974) trained a 63-year-old male suffering from Sydenham's Chorea to make incompatible responses on a lever-pull, button-press apparatus. During training the patient was able to demonstrate a decrease in spasmodic movements that generalized to other situations and was maintained 20 weeks later at follow-up.

Two sets of investigators successfully reduced the orafacial movements of tardive dyskinesia in elderly patients. Taylor, Zlutnick, and Hoehle (1979) did so through the use of overcorrection and feedback, while Jackson and Schonfeld (1982) trained their patient to gain control by practicing in a mirror and then used visual and aural feedback via a television monitor and a small microphone to prompt continued control.

Pain

In a controversial case report, Levendusky and Pankrantz (1975) described the treatment of a 65-year-old man who experienced intense abdominal pain and was dependent on pain medication. They diluted the pain medication with saline (without the patient's knowledge or consent) and gradually withdrew it. Simultaneously they taught the patient relaxation, imagery, and cognitive relabeling for the pain behaviors. According to self-report measures, the patient improved significantly and was still doing well at a 6-month follow-up.

Pearson (1987) described an interesting application of imagery procedures in a case study of an 84-year-old woman who experienced severe pain in her foot and ankle. Relying on the patient's devout Catholicism, the nurse asked the patient to visualize the characteristics of the pain and what the inflamed area would be like without the pain. She was told to picture the Holy Spirit entering the body and the painful area to make the pain "escape." Such instruction was apparently effective in this case.

In a nicely controlled study, Puder (1988) examined the value of stress inoculation training for 69 patients experiencing chronic pain. The subjects ranged in age from 27 to 80, with a mean age of 53 years. Twenty two of the subjects were over age 60. Subjects were divided into two groups: immediate and delayed treatment. After a week of baseline in which subjects recorded and rated their daily pain experiences, indicated the amount of pain-induced interference in their daily activities, reported on their abilities to cope with pain, and their use of medication and other treatments, the participants were instructed in the procedures. Their progress was reviewed during each session, and problems were discussed. Therapy was conducted once a week for 10 weeks in a group format. The self-report measures continued throughout treatment and a 1-month follow-up. At 6 months the participants collected the same data for 1 week. Results indicated that the treatment was effective in managing the pain experience, but that it only slightly affected perceived intensity of pain.

The author also analyzed the effect of age on treatment outcome. He found that age was not a factor in the treatment success and recommended the inclusion of older adults in programs for chronic pain as an alternative to drug therapy, which may be risky for elderly people. The author points out that reliance on self-report data and the lack of an alternative treatment group are limitations of the study.

Achterberg, Kenner, and Lawlis (1988) included several elderly subjects in their study of 149 severely burn-injured patients. They compared three treatment groups (relaxation alone; relaxation and imagery; relaxation, imagery and thermal biofeedback) with a no-treatment control group, using daily measures of discomfort, anxiety, mood, blood pressure, heart rate, respiration, medication usage, EMG, and thermal responses. They found that all three experimental groups benefitted from treatment, but subjects in the group with the biofeedback component showed the most success. However, the authors cautioned that the benefits of biofeedback in this case did not justify the costs required and instead recommend the relaxation and imagery treatment.

Cancer

As a conditioned response to chemotherapy treatments for cancer, patients often experience anticipatory nausea and vomiting. An elderly female patient, seen by Hamburger (1982), continued to feel the side effects long after chemotherapy whenever she felt anxious or angry. She learned to use relaxation procedures to cope with the emotional stimuli and reported satisfaction with the technique, even after a year had passed. Green and Seime (1987) were more sophisticated in their study of an elderly woman patient who experienced nausea in conjunction with her chemotherapy. In a single-case reversal design, they successfully used a taste-masking solution to reduce the effect of the chemotherapy and were able to maintain the benefits after withdrawing the solution.

Headache

In two case studies, investigators reported success with relaxation procedures (Linoff & West, 1982) and biofeedback (King & Arena, 1984) for elderly patients suffering with headache pain. In the first study, an 89-year-old male resident of a nursing home received 19 sessions of taped relaxation instructions, accompanied by soothing background music. At the end of treatment he reported a significant reduction in pain and other somatic problems. Staff reported that he had requested pain medication only once in 3 weeks, a change they regarded as significant. There were no follow-up measures. In the second study, a 69-year-old man with cluster headaches was trained in biofeedback and self-monitoring. His wife was taught to avoid reinforcing the headache behavior. Intensity of headache pain decreased by 44% after treatment, and the couple attributed improvement in their relationship to the treatment. There were no follow-up measures.

Arena, Hightower, and Chong (1988) evaluated the effects of an 8-week relaxation treatment on the tension headaches of 10 elderly subjects. At a 3-month posttreatment assessment they found a significant decrease (50%) in overall headache activity in seven subjects, a significant increase in the number of headache-free days, and significantly less peak headache activity and use of medication. These results challenge previous findings from retrospective studies that indicated a negative linear relationship between age and outcome success (i.e., Blanchard, Andrasik, Evans, & Hillhouse, 1985, who studied five elderly subjects; Diamond & Montrose, 1983, who included data from one elderly subject; Holroyd & Penzien, 1986, who conducted a meta-analysis of the tension headache literature). However, there are limitations of the study, as the authors themselves point out. There is no control group; the sample size is small; the sample is limited to healthy, white, nonurban residents; only relaxation methods were used in the study.

Eating Disorders

It is likely that eating disorders generally go unreported among elderly patients because they are usually seen and treated as symptoms of a physical disorder

(Stelnicki & Thompson, 1989). Yet there have been reports in the literature of behavioral treatment programs for elderly who experience anorexia nervosa, bulimia, and pica. All of the behavioral interventions for these problems have been described in a single-subject case study format and, therefore, their conclusions must be considered tentative.

Of the three studies of anorexia (Launer, 1978; Price, Giannini, & Colella, 1985; Ronch, 1985), behavioral treatment programs resulted in successful weight gain, but the programs were incomplete and the likelihood of continued maintenance after release from the hospital was considered poor. Follow-up information was lacking in all cases. Barry and Salamon (1987) described the unsuccessful cognitive-behavioral assessment and treatment of a 78-year-old institutionalized bulimic male patient. Nash, Broome, and Stone (1987) successfully treated an elderly male patient with pica by using contingent brief physical restraint. Follow-up data taken several months later indicated a 98% reduction in pica behavior and a total lack of pica-related physical complications.

Alcoholism

There are four reports on the use of behavioral treatment strategies with elderly alcoholics. In the first study, Horton and Howe (1982) describe the contingent use of response cost whenever the breathalyzer reading of an elderly demented nursing home resident exceeded a specific point. As long as the contingency was in effect, the patient refrained from drinking.

The other three reports are based on work with larger numbers of subjects and involve more complex programs. Wiens, Menustik, Miller, and Schmitz (1982–1983) founded their program on aversive conditioning principles. The investigators reported that the older subjects experienced success rates comparable to those of younger subjects 1 year after completion of the intervention. Dupree, Broskowski, and Schonfeld (1984) centered their program around five training modules in which the following goals were emphasized: the functional assessment of drinking behaviors; the establishment of self-management skills for high-risk situations; the acquisition of information about alcohol and alcohol abuse; ways of generating problem-solving skills; and ways of expanding social support networks. The treatment program went on for more than a year and experienced a high dropout rate. Of those 17 subjects who remained in the study, 82% were successful abstainers a year after the program was completed. Carstensen, Rychatavik, and Prue (1985) evaluated a 28-day inpatient program for 16 elderly alcoholics at a VA Medical Center. Patients received medical care, individual counseling, education about alcoholism, training in self-management and problem solving, and marital therapy or vocational rehabilitation if needed. Carstensen *et al.* found that 50% of the sample maintained abstinence for 2 years and that another 12% had significantly decreased their usage of alcohol.

Horton and Fogelman expand on the treatment literature for elderly alcohol and drug abusers later in this text (Chapter 13).

Compliance

There are three studies which investigated ways to teach elderly to adhere to medical regimens or follow treatment recommendations. Dapcich-Miura and Hovell (1979) worked with an 82-year-old heart patient who successfully improved his compliance with a complex medical regimen by means of a token reinforcement program. The patient was reinforced with poker chips if he engaged in three specific types of "healthy behavior" every day: taking his pills, drinking orange juice, and taking walks. The poker chips could be exchanged for the privilege of deciding what to eat for dinner or what restaurant to visit. The authors demonstrated that the patient increased his target behaviors as a function of the token program. When the tokens were withdrawn, the behaviors rapidly returned to baseline levels. Wandless and Davies (1977) demonstrated that tear-off calendars or tablet identification cards were more useful for elderly patients in avoiding errors in medication compliance than standard instructions. Patients who used the calendars made fewer errors than patients who used cards, and those with either a card or a calendar made significantly fewer errors than those given only standard instructions. Waggoner and LeLieuvre (1981) used visual feedback displays to enhance compliance with exercise regimens for elderly with rheumatoid arthritis.

Increasing Exercise Levels

Using a simple AB design, Libb and Clements (1969) reinforced four demented elderly patients with tokens (marbles that could be exchanged for tangible items) for 5 minutes of riding on a stationary bike. After 14 sessions, three patients met the exercise goals established for them. Those patients with the lowest baseline levels showed the greatest effect. There was no attempt to measure maintenance. Without a reversal phase in the design, however, it is difficult to ascertain the relationship between the behavior and the intervention.

Perkins, Rapp, Carlson, and Wallace (1986) used a multiple-baseline design across subjects to increase the rate of exercise by eight male residents of a nursing home who ranged in age from 46 to 78 years, with a mean of 66 years. The program included a 6-week baseline phase; an intervention consisting of goal setting, posting of performance feedback, and contingent reinforcement; and a maintenance phase of goal setting and posting without contingent reinforcement. Goals were set each week at 10% above the previous week's average daily distance achieved on a stationary bike. A participant was required to meet his goal four out of five days before establishing a new target. Reinforcement was given in the form of a gold star placed next to the participant's name, praise, colored buttons, a tee shirt, and publication of the participant's name in a newsletter. After four to six goals were met, the reinforcers were eliminated. Goals were posted for an additional 6 weeks. The intervention consistently increased the exercise levels of all subjects until the contingent reinforcement was withdrawn. At that point one of the eight subjects stopped bike riding altogether, and a second subject returned to his baseline level. The exercise behavior of the other six subjects remained fairly stable. No follow-up data are reported.

In a study by Matteson (1989), 36 elderly subjects participated in a 3-month program of supervised and unsupervised stretching exercises, walking, and other exercise activities. The first group of subjects received positive reinforcement from the facilitator each week; the second group received positive reinforcement each month; and the third group received no reinforcement. All groups significantly increased their exercise levels by approximately 1 hour per week, but the second group had significantly lower levels of exercise than the other groups.

Increasing Nutritious Eating Practices

Bunck and Iwata (1978) tackled a more general problem. They investigated two ways of improving participation in community meal programs by using a multiple-baseline design across three groups of elderly citizens in 292 households. In the first experiment they compared the effectiveness of providing public service radio announcements about the availability of meal programs and free transportation, a home visit in which the citizen was personally invited to attend, a follow-up phone call, and a mailing announcing a list of rewards for participation. Giving rewards for participation was the most effective method for increasing attendance at meal programs (it was also the least expensive method). The home visit was also an effective strategy. Overall, however, they managed to increase participation only by 25 people. In the second experiment Bunck and Iwata used the 25 participants from the first experiment and evaluated the differential effects of allowing the elderly citizens to select their own rewards versus experimenter-selected rewards (i.e., movies and bingo provided after the meal). Both strategies improved attendance, but the self-selected reward program was more cost-effective.

Conclusions about Health Behavior Research

Of the research reported in this section, more than two-thirds was conducted in a single-case design format without benefit of the controls described as appropriate for such research (see Hersen & Barlow, 1976). Many of the remaining studies lacked controls for expectancy effects, objective measures of treatment effects, reliability measures, adequate sampling, and follow-up data. In the area of physical health, like mental health, clients are influenced by a variety of placebo factors. Spontaneous remission of some types of diseases is not uncommon. It is, therefore, necessary that experimental work in the health field be as carefully controlled as other areas of scientific investigation.

The range of problems addressed in these studies was impressive, however, and the findings from them offer promise for the alleviation of a variety of health problems experienced by older adults, in both community and institutional settings. Behavioral interventions seem as effective for elder subjects as they are for younger ones, although more comparative studies are necessary to determine the fact of that conjecture. As Keuthen and Wisocki point out in Chapter 16 (this volume), the potential for substantive contributions by behavior therapists in the field of behavioral medicine is vast.

Psychotherapy

Psychotherapy with the elderly, no matter the mode of intervention, is a poorly researched area. A small number of case studies exists to show the potential benefits of behavior therapy for the psychological problems experienced by elderly clients, but there is very little systematic research available to guide therapeutic activities.

As in the review of health programs, I have divided the relevant studies on intervention by problem area: anxiety, anger, depression, bereavement, paranoia, obsessive-compulsive behavior, self-esteem, insomnia, and mixed problems. I have mentioned case study evidence to illustrate the range of possible directions for therapy, but the benefits of those studies are limited.

Anxiety and Stress

There are several case studies in which the authors reported successful implementation of stress management procedures. Friedman (1966) employed desensitization and anesthesia-assisted relaxation to treat a 66-year-old man with a severe fear of dogs. Wander (1972) used 23 sessions of systematic desensitization and thought stopping to reduce the phobic behavior of a 60-year-old man. Garrison (1978) helped a 65-year-old man cope with a fear of leaving home by teaching him relaxation techniques. Garfinkel (1979) decreased anxiety and agitation in an elderly patient through relaxation and systematic desensitization. Thyer (1981) used *in vivo* desensitization to eliminate the dog phobia of a 70-year-old woman. In all cases the patients improved as a result of treatment and demonstrated gains at follow-up, but there was no demonstration of a functional relationship between intervention and outcome.

In two studies, DeBerry (1981–1982, 1982) compared the use of progressive muscle relaxation therapy with a placebo control for anxious elderly women. Treatment occurred over a 5-month period. Subjects who received the relaxation training were significantly less anxious at posttreatment and at follow-up than were the subjects in the control group. Anxiety was measured only by self-report, however.

Downs, Rosenthal, and Lichstein (1988) conducted two studies comparing participant modeling and filmed peer modeling to decrease anxiety about whirlpool bathing among fearful elderly patients in a nursing home. In the first study, 24 patients were assessed for avoidance behaviors in the bathing routine, matched on assessment scores, and assigned to one of the treatment groups or the control group. Treatment occurred twice a week for 2 weeks. In groups of four, patients in the participant modeling group observed the therapist and several volunteer patients sequence the procedure, with and without assistance from the therapist. The same series of events occurred for patients in the filmed modeling condition, except that they observed two peers engage in the behaviors and were encouraged to imagine themselves in the film and anticipate possible problems. Patients in the control group received only pre- and post treatment assessment.

The participant modeling group showed greater behavioral improvements than the filmed modeling group. Both modeling conditions produced better results than the control group. There were no significant differences between groups in patients' subjective evaluations of distress or ratings by aides. Gains were maintained at lower levels after 4 weeks. No additional follow-up data were taken.

In the second study by these investigators, 48 patients with similar avoidance problems were included. Assessment, matching, and treatment procedures were the same as in the first study, except that the patients were seen individually rather than in groups. Findings were the same.

In Chapter 5 (this volume), Handen outlines a number of problems with the treatment of anxious elderly.

Anger

Wisner and Green (1986) treated a 73-year-old demented man who had frequent outbursts of anger. After a 2-week baseline period in which angry episodes were charted, the patient participated in a 6-week program in cognitive-behavioral strategies for controlling anger. At a 3-month follow-up, the authors concluded that the treatment was effective in helping the patient control his anger.

Depression

In the first case report of the behavioral treatment of depression, Falloon (1975) described the combined use of *in vivo* desensitization, social skills training, anti-anxiety medication, and contingency management by staff to eliminate various fears of two depressed elderly women. According to measures taken by staff, the patients experienced less depression and anxiety.

Hussian and Lawrence (1981) and Hussian (1983) adopted Lewinsohn's model of treatment for a group of institutionalized elderly and reported success with a program of social reinforcement for increased levels of activity and instruction in problem-solving techniques.

Goddard and Carstensen (1986) also used Lewinsohn's conceptualization of depression to treat an 86-year-old female nursing home resident. A functional analysis of the problem (which the client participated in) identified that the reduced availability of reinforcers was a primary factor in the depression. Treatment consisted of increasing access to self-initiated reinforcing events, extinction by staff for the patient's crying spells, social reinforcement for positive behaviors, and individual therapy sessions. Behavior change was determined by scores on a mood rating scale and the Geriatric Depression Scale. After 10 days of intervention and 28 days of maintenance, the patient was markedly improved. At a 6-week follow-up the gains were maintained.

Two sets of investigators examined the effects of a treatment strategy on the number of complaints emitted by depressed elderly institutionalized patients.

Williams and Dorow (1983) used music and verbal feedback in various degrees to reinforce and punish noncomplaining and complaining behavior, respectively. In the first condition their patient, a 79-year-old man, was given sympathy whenever he complained and praise for not complaining. In the second condition, he was reprimanded for complaining, his favorite music was discontinued, and he was praised for not complaining. In the third condition, his music was interrupted whenever he complained, but there was no other feedback. In the final condition, no music was presented. The investigators found that complaints decreased and noncomplaining behavior increased when music was used contingently.

Using an ABAB design, Williamson (1984) treated an elderly female patient in individual sessions, where she was encouraged to talk about nonsomatic things by making such talk contingent on time to discuss somatic complaints. For example, at first only 1 minute of appropriate talk was required for 4 minutes of "somatic talk." Over time, the ratio changed in favor of the appropriate conversation. The amount of somatic talk decreased by 20% by the end of therapy, and a functional relationship between the intervention and the rate of somatic complaints was demonstrated.

Thompson, Davies, Gallagher, and Krantz (1986) have reviewed Beck's ideas about depression, the critical therapeutic ingredients, the stages of therapy, and the empirical research in light of their relevance for elderly adults. They also present four case studies exemplifying the range of clinical problems to which one might adapt Beck's therapy model for the elderly.

Several investigators have compared group behavior therapy for elderly depressed clients with other forms of psychotherapy. The results have been interesting. On the whole, there have been no differences between therapies when measures were taken immediately after the termination of treatment. Subjects improved in all treatment conditions. For example, Steurer *et al.* (1984) found that both cognitive-behavioral and psychodynamic therapies were equally effective. Gallagher (1981) and Gallagher and Thompson (1982, 1983) reported that behavior therapy was as effective as supportive psychotherapy, cognitive therapy, and insight-oriented therapy. However, when the results were examined more closely, patients in the behavior therapy condition showed more gains. Observers who were recording social interaction data in the Gallagher (1981) study reported significant increases for the patients in the behavior therapy condition. These patients also indicated more satisfaction than those in the supportive therapy group when posttreatment interviews were done. Subjects in the study by Gallagher and Thompson (1982) who were in the control condition showed a significantly greater rate of relapse at a 1-year follow-up (56%) than patients in either behavior therapy or cognitive therapy (11%). In Chapter 10 (this volume) Teri presents the details of therapy with depressed clients.

Bereavement

Flannery (1974) described the treatment of an elderly bereaved man who was suffering with agitated depression and a variety of somatic complaints. Flannery made therapy with himself contingent upon the patient agreeing, in a written contract, to seek medical services, dispose of all inappropriate medications, and attend activities at the senior center. During therapy Flannery reinforced positive self-statements and prompted and shaped the discussion of grief-related topics. The treatment was regarded as successful, but many important details of it were not spǫcified.

For more information about the use of behavioral methods for dealing with the grief experiences of older adults the reader is referred to Wisocki and Averill (1987).

Paranoia

The only evidence pertinent to the treatment of paranoia in elderly clients is currently derived from case reports. All treatment strategies in these reports are highly dependent on the behavior of others in the client's environment and involve careful use of reinforcement for positive behaviors and extinction for the paranoid statements. Brink (1980) significantly reduced the paranoid statements of an 81-year-old female by instructing the patient's daughter to engage in positive discussions with her mother every day and to briefly confront and then ignore paranoid complaints. Observing that institutional staff intermittently reinforced the paranoid delusions of a 68-year-old woman on the ward, Carstensen and Fremouw (1981) instructed the staff members to terminate all verbal interactions that contained paranoid statements and to engage in conversation with her at least once a day when she was not expressing paranoid statements. The patient was also instructed to keep a diary of positive events, and she was seen in individual therapy, where she was encouraged to discuss her feelings of dependency, mistrust, and isolation. After 14 weeks of this type of treatment, the patient stopped speaking in delusional language and was on good terms with the staff. Haley (1983) used eight sessions of cognitive-behavior therapy, which included role playing, assertive training, relaxation, and self-disclosing statements to reduce the paranoid behavior of a 71-year-old nursing home patient. He also suggested that staff relabel the patient's behavior as "healthy assertiveness." Incidents of conflicts decreased by half after treatment. In the treatment of a 78-year-old paranoid demented male patient, Proulx and Campbell (1986) achieved significant decreases in confused and paranoid behavior by having an observer chart the relationships of antecedents and consequences to the behavior.

Obsessive-Compulsive Behavior

Four case studies have been reported in which patients with obsessive-compulsive disorders have been treated by behavioral methods. Two involved handwashing compulsions (O'Brien, 1978; Rowan, Holborn, Walker, & Siddiqui, 1984) and two involved compulsive checking (Junginger & Ditto, 1984; Melamed & Siegel, 1975).

In the first set of reports, O'Brien instructed his client, a 70-year-old woman who also had a fear of contracting smallpox, to read and write whenever she felt like washing her hands, behaviors incompatible with handwashing. The client and her husband were also trained in assertion and in the use of contingent reinforcement and extinction. Therapy continued for 16 sessions. O'Brien reported that the client was free of all symptoms at the termination of therapy and that she had maintained this success at a 2-year follow-up visit. Rowan *et al.* treated a 67-year-old woman who had problems similar to those of O'Brien's client. They used response prevention and *in vivo* exposure to contaminated items through a modeling sequence. The treatment was considered a success when the patient demonstrated that she could make prolonged contact with 44 previously contaminated items. The client maintained gains at an 18-month follow-up.

For those clients who experienced checking obsessions, Melamed and Siegel used self-directed *in vivo* procedures, while Juninger and Ditto designed a more elaborate program of response prevention—having the client exaggerate the description of her fears, role-playing experiences of inflicting injury to nurses, and medication. Both forms of intervention were highly effective.

Self-Esteem

Bellucci and Hoyer (1975) compared the behavior of young and old women given noncontingent positive feedback when they performed simple tasks, reinforced themselves (by taking available rewards), and made self-evaluations, in an attempt to determine age differences in susceptibility to extrinsic rewards. They found that, with this strategy, elderly women learned to significantly increase their self-reinforcing behavior.

Insomnia

Puder, Lacks, Bertelson, and Storandt (1983) tested the effect of stimulus control instructions on the sleep onset insomnia of 16 elderly clients, using a between-subjects multiple-baseline design. Clients were trained to develop regular sleep schedules and to use the bed only for sleeping. After 4 weeks of intervention, there were significant improvements in sleep behavior, which were maintained at a 6-week follow-up. In a second study by these same investigators (Davies, Lacks, Storandt, & Bertelson, 1986), testing the effects of countercontrol therapy with sleep maintenance problems, older insomniacs were as amenable to treatment as younger ones.

Kolko (1984) developed a treatment program consisting of biofeedback-enhanced relaxation training for a 61-year-old woman who experienced excessive daytime sleepiness. The patient was instructed to pay particular attention to her abdominal and sphincter muscles during the relaxation training to reduce the probability that she would be awakened during the night to urinate. After treatment, she reduced the number of daytime sleep episodes almost to zero, and she maintained those rates at 6- and 12-month follow-ups.

Hoelscher and Edinger (1988) evaluated a behavioral treatment package for use with four elderly subjects experiencing sleep-maintenance insomnia. The treatment package consisted of reducing wake time spent in bed, education about sleep patterns, and stimulus control techniques. Using a multiple-baseline design and four hour-long sessions of training, Hoelscher and Edinger reported that three of their four subjects significantly reduced the amount of wake time after sleep onset and that these gains were maintained at a 3-month follow-up.

Piercy and Lohr (1989) treated a 73-year-old female patient who complained of intermittent insomnia. After a 4-week baseline in which the patient recorded the number of times she awoke during the night, she was given relaxation training for 6 weeks. For the following 2 weeks she was expected to control her own behavior without the help of the therapist. The patient showed consistent reductions in EMG activity as the program progressed, which the investigators regarded as indication of successful treatment.

In Chapter 12 of this text, Engle-Friedman and Bootzin apply their work in insomnia to the problems of the elderly.

Sexual Problems

There are three references to the use of behavioral methods for the treatment of sexual problems experienced by elderly clients. In the first study, Rowland and Haynes (1978) described a 6-week sexual enhancement program for 10 married couples in a group format. In the program, participants were given information about sexuality among older adults, discussed various relevant topics, learned communication and pleasuring strategies, and were given homework assignments to enhance their learning. According to the subjects, the program was successful in increasing sexual satisfaction, some sexual behaviors, and positive attitudes toward marriage and life in general. No follow-up measures were taken.

In the second study, Kaas and Rousseau (1983) treated an elderly impotent divorced male by group therapy and individual behavioral counseling. The client was educated in the effects of various conditions on sexual attitudes and performance and self-pleasuring activities. After 1 month, the client reported satisfaction with the treatment and was able to achieve erections during masturbation.

In the third study, Whitlatch and Zarit (1988) present a case report on successful behavior therapy for a sexually dysfunctional elderly married couple.

In Chapter 9 (this volume), Fisher and O'Donohue discuss behavioral approaches to various aspects of dating, marriage, and sexuality proposed by elderly clients.

Mixed Problems

Tauber (1982) treated a 64-year-old woman who had a variety of physical and psychological problems, including high blood pressure, neck pain, bruxism, alcoholism, insomnia, depression, and obsessive thoughts. While the patient was enrolled in group therapy, Tauber treated her with biofeedback-assisted relaxation and autogenic training. After seven sessions, the patient reported improvement in sleep, bruxism, and blood pressure. At a 2-month follow-up the patient reported maintenance of the effects. It is impossible to say which, if any, of the methods used were effective in eliminating the patient's problems.

In the following three studies, the authors employed group designs to assess the benefits of treatment, with varying degrees of control. Ingersoll and Silverman (1978) compared two approaches to therapy with the elderly: behavior therapy, where a group of patients were taught relaxation techniques, modeling, reinforcement and role playing; and an insight-oriented therapy, where a group of patients participated in sessions involving the life-review process, keeping journals, and devising genograms. Both groups improved on measures of self-esteem and anxiety reduction, but only patients in the "insight condition" showed significantly greater improvement on the measure of somatic behavior only. These conclusions are difficult to evaluate because the study lacked a control group and the investigators did not take measures of generalization and maintenance.

Weldon and Yesavage (1982) taught relaxation and self-hypnosis to 25 demented elderly and compared the effects of that intervention to a matched control group who participated in a discussion of current events. The groups met 3 times a week for 3 months. At the end of the treatment period, subjects given the relaxation and hypnosis training showed significant improvements in self-help, communication, and social skills, as well as significant reductions in psychiatric problems. There were no follow-up measures taken.

Finally, Sallis, Lichstein, Clarkson, Stalgaitis, and Campbell (1983) worked with 24 community-dwelling elderly who were assessed as both anxious and depressed. They designed their treatment groups around common elements of skill learning, group discussion, and homework. Subjects were assigned to either an anxiety treatment condition, in which they were taught relaxation and visualization, a depression treatment condition, in which the focus was on increasing participation in pleasant events and learning the rational disputation method, or a placebo condition, in which subjects learned techniques of self-disclosure and reflection of feelings. Treatment was conducted for 10 sessions.

Subjects in all conditions improved equally on systolic and diastolic blood pressure and on self-rated depression. Only subjects in the placebo condition showed any improvements on trait anxiety. There were no differences between the groups on heart rate measures or participation in pleasant activities. The authors cite, however, problems with compliance among the subjects and the lack of a waitlist control group, which further limits the reliability of these conclusions.

Conclusions about Behavioral Psychotherapy Research

The bulk of this literature is constructed of individual therapy reports which, while often ingenious in method and far-ranging in scope, do not meet the requirements of solid scientific research criteria. The majority of the case studies have not been designed in an appropriate single-case framework (Hersen & Barlow, 1976) and therefore do not show a functional relationship between the intervention and the outcome. Often designs, when they do exist, are confounded by the use of medication and other factors, making it impossible to conclude with any confidence that the procedure was responsible for the successful outcome attributed to it. Self-report measures most often served as the determinant of treatment success; actual tests of objective behavioral performance were rarely used.

In group studies of treatment outcome, many of the designs were flawed in one way or another; follow-up measures were rare, there were few tests or training for generalization from the therapeutic environment to the natural environment, and most experimenters relied on self-report measures of success. If observers were used in studies, reliability measures were seldom reported. There have been no studies that adequately assessed the effects of various components in therapy. As in every area of intervention research cited in this chapter, more and better research is necessary with and for elderly clients.

Summary and General Conclusions

Behavioral gerontologists have produced a small mass of data on the value of a behavioral approach to the treatment of elderly clients suffering a wide variety of problems. Behavioral programs for self-care, social interaction and participation, disruptive behavior, memory and language problems, health, and psychological problems have been described in this review. Many of these programs have been innovative, imaginative, and well executed. Most were first attempts to conduct research in a difficult area with an often forgotten or ignored population. The investigators were enthusiastic and eager to demonstrate the applicability of a behavioral intervention to problems long regarded as unchangeable. This research has demonstrated the possibility of positive change in old age and has contributed to the development of a more hopeful attitude about elderly people and aging in general.

The bulk of the research, however, has serious design flaws that inhibit our ability to assert that a functional relationship does indeed exist between the intervention and the behavior change. In most cases generalization and maintenance programs were lacking, making it impossible to conclude that the results were relevant beyond the immediate parameters of the study itself. A good deal of the research was conducted with a single subject or only a few subjects. And, although a technology exists for designing a well-controlled single-case experiment (e.g., Hersen & Barlow, 1976), only a few of these studies conformed to the rules of the design. These complaints are particularly pertinent for the research of the early days of behavioral gerontology. As the field has developed, the research has improved significantly.

Much of the research focused on the remediation of deficits, instead of on the prevention of future losses. It was done primarily with institutionalized elderly and demonstrated that small, inexpensive interventions could produce impressive changes. It is time to devote more attention to the problems of the community-dwelling older adults, with particular emphasis on the areas of physical and mental health. Investigators need to examine the value of more behavioral procedures than the contingent application of reinforcement, extinction, and punishment. Cognitive methods, the reciprocal inhibition techniques, and social learning procedures should be incorporated into intervention programs and examined for the benefit of the elderly. We need to do studies that compare various treatments and which partial out the elements of treatment responsible for behavior change.

The field of behavioral gerontology has passed through its own youth and is reaching maturity. The next decade presents us with an exciting challenge.

REFERENCES

Achterberg, J., Kenner, C., & Lawlis, G. (1988). Severe burn injury: A comparison of relaxation, imagery, and biofeedback for pain management. *Journal of Mental Imagery, 12*, 71–87.

Ankus, M., & Quarrington, S. (1972). Operant behavior in the memory-disordered. *Journal of Gerontology, 27*, 500–501.

Arena, J., Hightower, N., & Chong, G. (1988). Relaxation therapy for tension headache in the elderly: A prospective study. *Psychology & Aging, 3*, 96–98.

Baltes, M. (1988). The etiology and maintenance of dependency in the elderly: Three phases of operant research. *Behavior Therapy, 19*, 301–320.

Baltes, M., & Barton, E. (1977). New approaches toward aging: A case for the operant model. *Educational Gerontology: An International Quarterly, 2*, 383–405.

Baltes, M., & Barton, E. (1979). Behavioral analysis of aging: A review of the operant model and research. *International Journal of Behavioral Development, 2*, 297–320.

Baltes, M., & Lascomb, S. (1975). Creating a healthy institutional environment for the elderly via behavior management: The nurse as a change agent. *International Journal of Nursing Studies, 12*, 5–12.

Baltes, M., & Zerbe, M. (1976). Independence training in nursing home residents. *The Gerontologist, 16*, 419–432.

Baltes, M., Burgess, R., & Stewart, R. (1978). Independence and dependence in self-care behaviors in nursing home residents: An operant-observational study. *International Journal of Behavioral Development, 3*, 489–500.

Baltes, M., Honn, S., Barton, E., Orzech, M., & Lago, D. (1983). On the social ecology of dependence and independence in elderly nursing home residents: A replication and extension. *Journal of Gerontology, 38*, 556–564.

Baltes, P., Dittman-Kohli, F., & Kliegl, R. (1986). Reserve capacity of the elderly in age-sensitive tests of fluid intelligence: Replication and extension. *Psychology & Aging, 2*, 172–177.

Barry, B., & Salamon, M. (1987). Psychologically based idiosyncratic bulimia in a 78-year-old institutionalized male. *Clinical Gerontologist, 6*, 71–73.

Barton, E., Baltes, M., & Orzech, M. (1980). Etiology of dependence in older nursing home residents during morning care: The role of staff behaviors. *Journal of Personality & Social Psychology, 38*, 423–431.

Bellucci, G., & Hoyer, W. (1975). Feedback effects on the performance and self-reinforcing behavior of elderly and young adult women. *Journal of Gerontology, 30*, 456–460.

Benson, H., Alexander, J., & Feldman, C. (1975). Decreased premature ventricular contractions through use of the relaxation response in patients with stable ischemic heart disease. *Lancet, 2*, 380–382.

Beres, C., & Baron, A. (1981). Improved digit symbol substitution by older women as a result of extended practice. *Journal of Gerontology, 36*, 591–597.

Berger, R., & Rose, S. (1977). Interpersonal skill training with institutionalized elderly patients. *Journal of Gerontology, 32*, 346–353.

Birkhill, W., & Schaie, K. (1975). The effect of differential reinforcement of cautiousness in intellectual performance among the elderly. *Journal of Gerontology, 5*, 578–583.

Blackman, D., Howe, M., & Pinkston, E. (1976). Increasing participation in social interaction of the institutionalized elderly. *The Gerontologist, 16*, 69–76.

Blanchard, E., Andrasik, F., Evans, D., & Hillhouse, J. (1985). Biofeedback and relaxation treatments for headache in the elderly: A caution and a challenge. *Biofeedback & Self-Regulation, 10*, 69–73.

Boczkowski, J. (1984). Biofeedback training for the treatment of chronic pain in an elderly arthritic female. *Clinical Gerontology, 2*, 39–46.

Bourgeois, M. (1988). *Training caregivers to facilitate the generalization and maintenance of communicative behaviors in patients with Alzheimer's disease.* Paper presented at the Association for Behavior Analysis, Philadelphia, PA.

Brink, T. (1980). Geriatric paranoia: Case report illustrating behavioral management. *Journal of the American Geriatric Society, 28*, 519–522.

Bunck, T., & Iwata, B. (1978). Increasing senior citizen participation in a community-based nutritious meal program. *Journal of Applied Behavior Analysis, 11*, 75–86.

Burgio, K., Whitehead, W., & Engel, B. (1985). Urinary incontinence in the elderly: Bladder-sphincter biofeedback and toileting skills training. *Annals of Internal Medicine, 103,* 507–515.

Burgio, L. (1985). *Behavior analysis and intervention in geriatric long-term care.* Paper presented at the Florida Association for Behavior Analysis, Tampa, FL.

Burgio, L., & Burgio, K. (1986). Behavioral gerontology: Application of behavioral methods to the problems of older adults. *Journal of Applied Behavior Analysis, 19,* 321–328.

Burgio, L., Tice, L., & Engel, B. (1985). *Behavioral gerontology: Where are the data?* Paper presented at the Association for Behavior Analysis, Columbus, OH.

Burgio, L., Burgio, K., Engel, B., & Tice, L. (1986). Increasing distance and independence of ambulation in elderly nursing home residents. *Journal of Applied Behavior Analysis, 19,* 357–366.

Burgio, L., Engel, B., McCormick, K., Hawkins, A., & Scheve, A. (1988). Behavioral treatment for urinary incontinence in elderly inpatients: Initial attempts to modify prompting and toileting procedures. *Behavior Therapy, 19,* 345–357.

Carroll, P. (1978). The social hour for geropsychiatric patients. *Journal of the American Geriatrics Society, 26,* 32–35.

Carstensen, L., & Edelstein, B. (Eds.). (1987). *Handbook of clinical gerontology.* New York: Pergamon Press.

Carstensen, L., & Erickson, R. (1986). Enhancing the social environments of elderly nursing home residents: Are high rates of interaction enough? *Journal of Applied Behavioral Analysis, 19,* 349–355.

Carstensen, L., & Fremouw, W. (1981). The demonstration of a behavioral intervention for late life paranoia. *The Gerontologist, 21,* 329–333.

Carstensen, L., & Fremouw, W. (1988). The influence of anxiety and mental status on social isolation among the elderly in nursing homes. *Behavioral Residential Treatment, 3,* 63–80.

Carstensen, L., Rychtarik, R., & Prue, D. (1985). Behavioral treatment of the geriatric alcohol abuser: A long-term follow-up study. *Addictive Behaviors, 10,* 307–311.

Cautela, J. R. (1966). Behavior therapy and geriatrics. *Journal of Genetic Psychology, 1-8,* 9–17.

Chafetz, P., & West, H. (1987). *Longitudinal control evaluation of a special care unit for dementia patients: Initial findings.* Paper presented at the Gerontological Society of America convention, Washington, DC.

Chanfreau-Rona, D., Bellwood, S., & Wylie, B. (1984). Assessment of a behavioral programme to treat incontinent patients in psychogeriatric wards. *British Journal of Clinical Psychology, 23,* 273–279.

Clay, E. (1978). Incontinence of urine: A regimen for retraining. *Nursing Mirror, 146,* 23–24.

Cohen, D. (1967). Research problems and concepts in the study of aging: Assessment and behavior modification. *The Gerontologist, 7,* 13–19.

Corby, C. (1975). Assertion training with aged populations. *Counseling Psychologist, 5,* 69–74.

Crovitz, E. (1966). Reversing a learning deficit in the aged. *Journal of Gerontology, 21,* 236–238.

Cuvo, A. (1976). Decreasing repetitive behavior in an institutionalized mentally retarded resident. *Mental Retardation, 15,* 22–25.

Czirr, R., & Gallagher, D. (1983). Case report: Behavioral treatment of depression and somatic complaints in rheumatoid arthritis. *Clinical Gerontologist, 2,* 63–66.

Dapcich-Miura, E., & Hovell, M. (1979). Contingency management of adherence to a complex medical regimen in an elderly heart patient. *Behavior Therapy, 10,* 193–201.

Davies, R., Lacks, P., Storandt, M., & Bertelson, A. (1986). Countercontrol treatment of sleep maintenance insomnia in relation to age. *Psychology & Aging, 1,* 233–238.

DeBerry, S. (1981–1982). An evaluation of progressive muscle relaxation on stress-related symptoms in a geriatric population. *International Journal of Aging & Human Development, 14,* 255–269.

DeBerry, S. (1982). The effects of meditation-relaxation on anxiety and depression in a geriatric population. *Psychotherapy, Theory, Research, & Practice, 19,* 512–521.

Denny, N. (1974). Classification abilities in the elderly. *Journal of Gerontology, 20,* 309–314.

Denny, N., & Denny, D. (1974). Modeling effects on the questioning strategies of the elderly. *Developmental Psychology, 10,* 458–460.

Denny, N., Jones, F., & Krigel, S. (1979). Modifying the questioning strategies of young children and elderly adults with strategy-modeling techniques. *Human Development, 22,* 23–36.

Diamond, S., & Montrose, D. (1983). The value of biofeedback in the treatment of chronic headache: A four-year retrospective study. *Headache, 16,* 70–71.

Downs, A., Rosenthal, T., & Lichstein, K. (1988). Modeling therapies reduce avoidance of bath-time by institutionalized elderly. *Behavior Therapy, 19,* 359–368.

Dupree, L., Broskowski, H., & Schonfeld, L. (1984). The Gerontology Alcohol Project: A behavioral treatment program for elderly alcohol abusers. *The Gerontologist, 24*, 510–516.

Edinberg, M., Karoly, P., & Gleser, G. (1977). Assessing assertion in the elderly: An application of the behavioral-analytic mode of competence. *Journal of Clinical Psychology, 33*, 869–874.

Engel, B., Nikcomanesh, P., & Schuster, M. (1974). Operant conditioning of rectosphincteric responses in the treatment of fecal incontinence. *New England Journal of Medicine, 290*, 646–649.

Engels, M. L., & Poser, E. (1987). Social skills training with older women. *Clinical Gerontologist, 6*, 70–73.

Eysenck, H., & Martin, I. (Eds.). (1987). *Theoretical foundations of behavior therapy*. New York: Plenum.

Falloon, L. (1975). The therapy of depression: A behavioral approach. *Psychotherapy & Psychosomatics, 25*, 69–75.

Flannery, R. (1974). Behavior modification of geriatric grief: A transactional perspective. *International Journal of Aging & Human Development, 5*, 192–203.

Franzke, A. (1987). The effects of assertiveness training on older adults. *Gerontologist, 27*, 13–16.

Frewen, W. (1978). An objective assessment of the unstable bladder of psychosomatic origin. *British Journal of Urology, 50*, 246–249.

Frewen, W. (1979). Role of bladder training in the treatment of the unstable bladder in the female. *Urologic Clinics of North America, 6*, 273–277.

Frewen, W. (1982). A reassessment of bladder training in detrusor dysfunction in the female. *British Journal of Urology, 54*, 372–373.

Friedman, D. (1966). Treatment of a case of dog phobia in a deaf mute by behavior therapy. *Behavior Research & Therapy, 4*, 141.

Gallagher, D. (1981). Behavioral group therapy with elderly depressives: An experimental study. In D. Upper & S. Ross (Eds.), *Behavioral group therapy* (Vol. 3, pp. 91–122). Champaign, IL: Research Press.

Gallagher, D., & Thompson, L. (1982). Treatment of major depressive disorder in older adult outpatients with brief psychotherapies. *Psychotherapy, Theory, Research, & Practice, 19*, 482–490.

Gallagher, D., & Thompson, L. (1983). Effectiveness of psychotherapy for both endogenous and non-endogenous depression in older adult outpatients. *Journal of Gerontology, 38*, 707–712.

Garfinkel, R. (1979). Brief behavior therapy with an elderly patient: A case study. *Journal of Geriatric Psychiatry, 12*, 101–109.

Garrison, J. (1978). Stress management for the elderly: A psychoeducational approach. *Journal of the American Geriatrics Society, 26*, 397–403.

Geiger, O., & Johnson, L. (1974). Positive education for elderly persons. *The Gerontologist, 14*, 432–436.

Goddard, P., & Carstensen, L. (1986). Behavioral treatment of chronic depression in an elderly nursing home resident. *Clinical Gerontologist, 4*, 13–20.

Goldstein, R., & Baer, D. (1976). A procedure to increase the personal mail and number of correspondents for nursing home residents. *Behavior Therapy, 7*, 348–354.

Gotestam, K. G. (1980). Behavioral and dynamic psychotherapy for the elderly. In J. Birren & R. Sloan (Eds.), *Handbook of mental health and aging* (pp. 775–805). Englewood Cliffs, NJ: Prentice-Hall.

Green, R., Linsk, N., & Pinkston, E. (1986). Modification of verbal behavior of the mentally impaired elderly by their spouses. *Journal of Applied Behavior Analysis, 19*, 329–336.

Greene, P., & Seime, R. (1987). Stimulus control of an anticipatory nausea in cancer chemotherapy. *Journal of Behavior Therapy & Experimental Psychiatry, 18*, 61–64.

Grosicki, J. (1968). Effect of operant conditioning on modification of incontinence in psychiatric geriatric patients. *Nursing Research, 17*, 304–311.

Haley, W. (1983). A family-behavioral approach to the treatment of cognitively impaired elderly. *Gerontologist, 23*, 18–20.

Hamburger, L. (1982). Reduction of generalized aversive responding in a post treatment cancer patient: Relaxation as an active coping skill. *Journal of Behavior Therapy & Experimental Psychiatry, 13*, 229–233.

Hanley, I. (1981). The use of signposts and active training to modify ward disorientation in elderly patients. *Journal of Behavior Therapy & Experimental Psychiatry, 12*, 241–247.

Hanley, I., & Lusty, K. (1984). Memory aids in reality orientation: A single case study. *Behavior Research & Therapy, 22*, 709–712.

Hayslip, P. (1989). Alternative mechanisms for improvements in fluid ability performance among older adults. *Psychology & Aging, 4,* 122–124.

Hersen, M., & Barlow, D. (1976). *Single case experimental designs: Strategies for studying behavior change.* New York: Pergamon Press.

Hersen, M., Kazdin, A., & Bellack, A. (Eds.). (1983). *The clinical psychology handbook.* New York: Plenum.

Hill, R., Evandovich, K., Sheikh, J., & Yesavage, J. (1987). Imagery mnemonic training in a patient with primary degenerative dementia. *Psychology & Aging, 2,* 204–205.

Hill, R., Sheikh, J., & Yesavage, J. (1988). Pretraining enhances mnemonic training in elderly adults. *Experimental Aging Research, 14,* 207–211.

Hoelscher, T., & Edinger, J. (1988). Treatment of sleep-maintenance insomnia in older adults: Sleep period reduction, sleep education, and modified stimulus control. *Psychology & Aging, 3,* 258–263.

Holroyd, K., & Penzien, D. (1986). Client variables and the behavioral treatment of recurrent tension headache: A meta-analytic review. *Journal of Behavioral Medicine, 9,* 515–536.

Horton, A. M., & Howe, N. (1982). Behavior therapy with an aged alcoholic: A case study. *International Journal of Behavioral Geriatrics, 1,* 17–18.

Hoyer, F., Hoyer, W., Treat, N., & Baltes, P. (1978). Training response speed in young and elderly women. *International Journal of Aging & Human Development, 9,* 247–253.

Hoyer, W. (1973). Application of operant techniques to the modification of elderly behavior. *The Gerontologist, 13,* 18–22.

Hoyer, W. (1974). Aging as intraindividual change. *Developmental Psychology, 10,* 821–826.

Hoyer, W., Labouvie, G., & Baltes, P. (1973). Modification of response speed and intellectual performance in the elderly. *Human Development, 16,* 233–242.

Hoyer, W., Kafer, R., Simpson, S., & Hoyer, F. (1974). A reinstatement of verbal behavior in elderly patients using operant procedures. *The Gerontologist, 14,* 149–152.

Hussian, R. (1981). *Geriatric psychology: A behavioral perspective.* New York: Van Nostrand Reinhold.

Hussian, R. (1982a). Stimulus control in the modification of problematic behavior in elderly institutionalized patients. *International Journal of Behavioral Geriatrics, 1,* 33–46.

Hussian, R. (1982b). The combination of operant and cognitive therapy with geriatric patients. *International Journal of Behavioral Geriatrics, 1,* 57–61.

Hussian, R. (1983). A combination of operant and cognitive therapy with geriatric patients. *International Journal of Behavioral Geriatrics, 1,* 57–61.

Hussian, R. (1984). Behavioral geriatrics. In M. Hersen, R. Eisler, & P. Miller (Eds.), *Progress in behavior modification* (Vol. 6, pp. 159–183). New York: Academic Press.

Hussian, R., & Brown, D. (1987). Use of two-dimensional grid patterns to limit hazardous ambulation in demented patients. *Journal of Gerontology, 42,* 558–560.

Hussian, R., & Davis, R. (1985). *Responsive care.* Champaign, IL: Research Press.

Hussian, R., & Lawrence, P. (1981). Social reinforcement of activity and problem-solving training in the treatment of depressed institutionalized elderly patients. *Cognitive Therapy & Research, 1,* 57–69.

Hutchison, S. (1974). An investigation of learning under two types of social reinforcers in young and elderly adults. *International Journal of Aging & Human Development, 5,* 181–186.

Ingersoll, B., & Silverman, A. (1978). Comparative group psychotherapy for the aged. *Gerontologist, 18,* 201–206.

Jackson, G., & Schonfeld, L. (1982). Comparisons of visual feedback, instruction prompts, and discreet prompting in the treatment of orafacial tardive dyskinesia. *International Journal of Behavioral Geriatrics, 1,* 35–46.

Jenkins, J., Felce, D., Lunt, B., & Powell, L. (1977). Increasing engagement in activity of residents in old people's homes by providing recreational materials. *Behavior Research & Therapy, 15,* 429–434.

Junginger, J., & Ditto, B. (1984). Multitreatment of obsessive compulsive checking in a geriatric patient. *Behavior Modification, 8,* 379–390.

Kaas, M., & Rousseau, G. (1983). Geriatric sexual conformity: Assessment and intervention. *Clinical Gerontologist, 2,* 31–34.

Kausler, D., & Lair, C. (1968). Informative feedback conditions and verbal-discrimination learning in elderly subjects. *Psychonomic Science, 10,* 193–194.

Kazdin, A. (1974). *Behavior modification in applied settings.* Belmont, CA: Wadsworth.

Keefe, F., Caldwell, D., Williams, D., Gil, K., Mitchell, D., Robertson, C., Martinez, S., Nunley, J., Beckham, J., Crisson, J., & Helms, M. (1990). Pain coping skills training in the management of osteoarthritic knee pain: A comparative study. *Behavior Therapy, 21,* 49–62.

King, A., & Arena, J. (1984). Behavioral treatment of chronic cluster headache in a geriatric patient. *Biofeedback & Self Regulation, 9,* 201–208.

Kolko, D. (1984). Behavioral treatment of excessive daytime sleepiness in an elderly woman with multiple medical problems. *Journal of Behavior Therapy & Experimental Psychiatry, 15,* 341–345.

Konarski, E., Johnson, M., & Whitman, T. (1980). A systematic investigation of resident participation in a nursing home activities program. *Journal of Behavior Therapy & Experimental Psychiatry, 11,* 249–257.

Labouvie-Vief, G., & Gonda, J. (1976). Cognitive strategy training and intellectual performance in the elderly. *Journal of Gerontology, 31,* 327–332.

Launer, M. (1978). Anorexia nervosa in late life. *British Journal of Medical Psychology, 51,* 375–377.

Lester, P., & Baltes, M. (1978). Functional interdependence of the social environment and the behavior of the institutionalized aged. *Journal of Gerontology, 37,* 443–449.

Levendusky, P., & Pankrantz, L. (1975). Self-control techniques as alternatives to pain medication. *Journal of Abnormal Psychology, 84,* 165–168.

Lewin, L., Lundervold, D., Saslow, M., & Thompson, S. (1989). Reducing eating dependency in nursing home patients: The effects of prompting, reinforcement, food preference, and environmental design. *Journal of Clinical & Experimental Gerontology, 11,* 47–63.

Lewinsohn, P., & Teri, L. (Eds.). (1983). *Clinical geropsychology.* New York: Pergamon Press.

Libb, J., & Clements, C. (1969). Token reinforcement in an exercise program for hospitalized geriatric patients. *Perceptual & Motor Skills, 28,* 975–978.

Lindroth, Y., Bauman, A., Barnes, C., & McCredie, M. (1989). A controlled evaluation of arthritis education. *Advances, 6,* 17–19.

Lindsley, O. (1964). Geriatric behavioral prosthetics. In R. Kastenbaum (Ed.), *New thoughts on old age* (pp. 41–61). New York: Springer.

Linoff, M., & West, C. (1982). Relaxation training systematically combined with music: Treatment of tension headaches in a geriatric patient. *International Journal of Behavioral Geriatrics, 1,* 11–16.

Longin, H., Kohn, J., & Macurik, K. (1974). The modification of choreal movements. *Journal of Behavior Therapy & Experimental Psychiatry, 5,* 263–265.

Lopez, M. (1980). Social skills training with institutionalized elderly: Effect of pre-counseling structuring and overlearning on skill acquisitions and transfer. *Journal of Counseling Psychology, 27,* 286–293.

Lopez, M., Hoyer, W., Goldstein, A., Gershaw, N., & Sprafkin, R. (1980). Effects of overlearning and incentive on the acquisition and transfer of interpersonal skills with institutionalized elderly. *Journal of Gerontology, 35,* 403–408.

Lorig, K., & Holman, H. (1989). Long term outcomes of an arthritis self-management study: Effects of reinforcement efforts. *Social Science & Medicine, 29,* 221–224.

Lorig, K., Laurin, J., & Holman, H. (1984). Arthritis self-management: A study of the effectiveness of patient education for the elderly. *The Gerontologist, 24,* 455–457.

MacDonald, M. (1978). Environmental programming for the socially isolated aging. *The Gerontologist, 18,* 350–354.

MacDonald, M., & Butler, A. (1974). Reversal of helplessness: Producing walking behavior in nursing home wheelchair residents using behavior modification procedures. *Journal of Gerontology, 29,* 97–101.

MacDonald, M., Davidowitz, J., Gimbel, B., & Foley, L. (1982). Physical and social environmental reprogramming as treatment for psychogeriatric patients. *International Journal of Behavioral Geriatrics, 1,* 15–32.

Manuso, S. (1977). The use of biofeedback-assisted handwarming training in the treatment of chronic eczematous dermatitis of the hands: A case study. *Journal of Behavior Therapy & Experimental Psychiatry, 8,* 445–446.

Matteson, M. (1989). Effects of a cognitive-behavioral approach and positive reinforcement on exercise for older adults. *Educational Gerontology, 15,* 497–513.

McClannahan, L., & Risley, T. (1973). A store for nursing home residents. *Nursing Homes, 22,* 10–29.

McClannahan, L., & Risley, T. (1974). Design of living environments for nursing home residents: Recruiting attendance at activities. *The Gerontologist, 14,* 236–240.

McClannahan, L., & Risley, T. (1975a). Activities and materials for severely disabled geriatric patients. *Nursing Homes, 24,* 10–13.

McClannahan, L., & Risley, T. (1975b). Design of living environments for nursing home residents: Increasing participation in recreation activities. *Journal of Applied Behavior Analysis, 8,* 261–268.

McEvoy, C., & Patterson, R. (1986). Behavioral treatment of deficit skills in dementia patients. *The Gerontologist, 26,* 475–478.

Meichenbaum, D. (1974). Self-instructional strategy training: A cognitive prosthesis for the aged. *Human Development, 17,* 273–280.

Melamed, B., & Siegel, L. (1975). Self-directed *in vivo* treatment of an obsessive-compulsive checking ritual. *Journal of Behavior Therapy & Experimental Psychiatry, 6,* 31–35.

Melin, L., & Gotestam, K. G. (1981). The effects of rearranging ward routines on communication and eating behavior of psychogeriatric patients. *Journal of Applied Behavior Analysis, 14,* 47–52.

Mishara, B. (1978). Geriatric patients in token economy and milieu treatments: A multivariate analysis. *Journal of Consulting & Clinical Psychology, 46,* 1340–1348.

Mishara, B., & Kastenbaum, R. (1973). Self-injurious behavior and environmental change in the institutionalized elderly. *International Journal of Aging & Human Development, 4,* 133–145.

Mishara, B., Robertson, B., & Kastenbaum, R. (1973). Self-injurious behavior in the elderly. *The Gerontologist, 13,* 311–314.

Mosher-Ashley, P. (1986–1987). Procedural and methodological parameters in behavioral-gerontological research: A review. *International Journal of Aging & Human Development, 24,* 189–229.

Mueller, D., & Atlas, L. (1972). Resocialization of regressed elderly residents: A behavioral management approach. *Journal of Gerontology, 27,* 390–392.

Nash, D., Broome, J., & Stone, S. (1987). Behavior modification of pica in a geriatric patient. *Journal of the American Geriatric Society, 35,* 79–80.

Newkirk, J., Feldman, S., Bickett, A., Gipson, M., & Lutzker, J. (1976). Increasing extended care facility residents' attendance at recreational activities with convenient locations and personal invitations. *Journal of Applied Behavior Analysis, 9,* 207.

O'Brien, J. (1978). The behavioral treatment of a thirty-year smallpox obsession and handwashing compulsion. *Journal of Behavior Therapy & Experimental Psychiatry, 9,* 365–368.

O'Donohue, W., Fisher, J., & Krasner, L. (1986). Behavior therapy and the elderly: A conceptual and ethical analysis. *International Journal of Aging & Human Development, 23,* 1–15.

O'Quinn, J., O'Dell, S., & Burnett, R. (1982). Effects of brief behavioral intervention on verbal interactions of socially inactive nursing home residents. *International Journal of Behavioral Geriatrics, 1,* 3–9.

Page, S., Caron, P., & Yates, E. (1973). Behavior modification methods and institutional psychology. *Professional Psychology, 6,* 175–181.

Patterson, R., & Jackson, G. (1980). Behavioral approaches to gerontology. In L. Michelson, M. Hersen, & S. Turner (Eds.), *Future perspectives in behavior therapy* (pp. 293–313). New York: Plenum.

Patterson, R., & Teigen, J. (1973). Conditioning and post-hospital generalization of non-delusional responses in a chronic psychotic patient. *Journal of Applied Behavior Analysis, 6,* 65–70.

Pearson, B. (1987). Pain control: An experiment with imagery. *Geriatric Nursing, 8,* 28–30.

Perkins, K., Rapp, S., Carlson, C., & Wallace, C. (1986). A behavioral intervention to increase exercise among nursing home residents. *The Gerontologist, 26,* 479–481.

Perone, M., & Baron, A. (1983). Reduced age differences in omission errors after prolonged exposure to response pacing contingencies. *Developmental Psychology, 19,* 915–923.

Peterson, R., Knapp, T., Rosen, J., & Pither, B. (1977). The effects of furniture arrangement on the behavior of geriatric patients. *Behavior Therapy, 8,* 464–467.

Piercy, J., & Lohr, J. (1989). Progressive relaxation in the treatment of an elderly insomniac. *Clinical Gerontologist, 8,* 3–11.

Pinkston, E., & Linsk, N. (1985). *Care of the elderly: A family approach.* New York: Pergamon Press.

Pinkston, E., Howe, M., & Blackman, D. (1986–1987). Medical social work management of urinary incontinence in the elderly: A behavioral approach. *Journal of Social Service Research, 10,* 179–194.

Pollock, D., & Liberman, R. (1974). Behavior therapy for incontinence in demented patients. *The Gerontologist, 24,* 576–583.

Powell, L., Felce, D., Jenkins, J., & Lunt, B. (1979). Increasing engagement in a home for the elderly by providing an indoor gardening activity. *Behaviour Research & Therapy, 17,* 127–135.

Praderas, K., & MacDonald, M. (1986). Telephone conversational skills training with socially isolated impaired nursing home residents. *Journal of Applied Behavior Analysis, 19,* 337–348.

Price, W., Giannini, A., & Colella, J. (1985). Anorexia nervosa in the elderly. *Journal of the American Geriatric Society, 33,* 213–215.

Proulx, G., & Campbell, K. (1986). The management of apparent "paranoid" behaviour in a patient with multi-infarct dementia. *Clinical Gerontologist, 6,* 121–128.

Puder, R. (1988). Age analysis of cognitive-behavioral group therapy for chronic pain outpatients. *Psychology & Aging, 3,* 204–207.

Puder, R., Lacks, P., Bertelson, A., & Storandt, M. (1983). Short-term stimulus control treatment of insomnia in older adults. *Behavior Therapy, 14,* 424–429.

Quattrochi-Tubin, S., & Jason, L. (1980). Enhancing social interactions and activity among the elderly through stimulus control. *Journal of Applied Behavior Analysis, 13,* 159–164.

Quilitch, H. (1974). Purposeful activity increase in a geriatric ward through programmed recreation. *Journal of the American Geriatrics Society, 22,* 226–229.

Reidel, R. (1981). Behavior therapies. In C. Eisdorfer (Ed.) *Annual review of gerontology & geriatrics* (pp. 160–195). New York: Springer.

Richards, W., & Thorpe, G. (1978). Behavioral approaches to the problems of later life. In M. Storandt, I. Siegler, & M. Elias (Eds.). *The clinical psychology of aging* (pp. 253–267). New York: Plenum.

Rinke, C., Williams, J., Lloyd, K., & Smith-Scott, W. (1978). The effects of prompting and reinforcement on self-bathing by elderly residents of a nursing home. *Behavior Therapy, 9,* 873–881.

Risley, T., & Edwards, A. (1978). *Behavioral technology for nursing home care: Toward a system of nursing home organization and management.* Paper presented at the Nova University Conference on Aging, Port St. Lucie, FL.

Romaniuk, M., Wilcox, F., & Romaniuk, J. (1982). Modification of patronizing verbalizations in a geriatric day treatment program. *International Journal of Behavioral Geriatrics, 1,* 13–24.

Ronch, J. (1985). Suspected anorexia nervosa in a 75-year-old institutionalized male: Issues in diagnosis and intervention. *Clinical Gerontologist, 4,* 31–38.

Rosberger, Z., & MacLean, J. (1983). Behavioral assessment and treatment or "organic" behavior in an institutionalized geriatric patient. *International Journal of Behavioral Geriatrics, 1,* 33–46.

Rose, S. (1977). Assertiveness training in groups: Research in clinical settings. *Scandinavian Journal of Behavior Therapy, 6,* 61–86.

Rowan, V., Holborn, S., Walker, J., & Siddiqui, A. (1984). A rapid multi-component treatment for an obsessive-compulsive disorder. *Journal of Behavior Therapy & Experimental Psychiatry, 15,* 347–352.

Rowland, K., & Haynes, S. (1978). A sexual enhancement program for elderly couples. *Journal of Sex & Marital Theory, 4,* 91–113.

Ryan, D., Tainsh, S., Kolodny, V., Landrum, B., & Fisher, R. (1988). Noise-making among the elderly in long-term care. *The Gerontologist, 28,* 369–371.

Sachs, D. (1975). Behavioral techniques in a residential nursing home facility. *Journal of Behavior Therapy & Experimental Psychiatry, 6,* 123–127.

Sallis, J., Lichstein, K., Clarkson, A., Stalgaitis, S., & Campbell, M. (1983). Anxiety and depression management for the elderly. *International Journal of Behavioral Geriatrics, 1,* 3–12.

Sanavio, E. (1981). Toilet retraining psychogeriatric residents. *Behavior Modification, 5,* 417–427.

Sanders, J. C., Sterns, H., Smith, M., & Sanders, R. (1975). Modification of concept identification performance in older adults. *Developmental Psychology, 11,* 824–829.

Schnelle, J., Traughber, B., Morgan, D., Embry, J., Binion, A., & Coleman, A. (1983). Management of geriatric incontinence in nursing homes. *Journal of Applied Behavior Analysis, 16,* 235–241.

Schultz, N., & Hoyer, W. (1976). Feedback effects on spatial egocentrism in old age. *Journal of Gerontology, 30,* 72–75.

Scogin, F., Storandt, M., & Lott, L. (1985). Memory-skills training, memory complaints and depression in older adults. *Journal of Gerontology, 40,* 562–568.

Smith, J., Smith, D., Rose, M., & Newman, D. (1989). Managing urinary incontinence in community-residing elderly persons. *The Gerontologist, 29,* 229–233.

Sogbein, S., & Awad, S. (1982). Behavioral treatment of urinary incontinence in geriatric patients. *Canadian Medical Association Journal, 127*, 863–864.

Sommer, R., & Ross, H. (1958). Social interaction on a geriatric ward. *International Journal of Social Psychiatry, 4*, 128–133.

Spangler, P., Risley, T., & Bilyew, D. (1984). The management of dehydration and incontinence in nonambulatory geriatric patients. *Journal of Applied Behavior Analysis, 17*, 397–401.

Sperbeck, D., & Whitbourne, S. (1981). Dependency in the institutionalized setting: A behavioral training program for geriatric staff. *The Gerontologist, 21*, 268–275.

Stelnicki, G., & Thompson, J. (1989). Eating disorders in the elderly. *Behavior Therapist, 12*, 7–9.

Steurer, J., Mintz, J., Hammen, C., Hill, M., Jarvik, L., McCarley, T., Motoike, P., & Rosen, R. (1984). Cognitive-behavioral and psychodynamic group psychotherapy in treatment of geriatric depression. *Journal of Consulting & Clinical Psychology, 52*, 180–189.

Tauber, L. (1982). Biofeedback as an adjunct in treating elders. *Clinical Gerontologist, 11*, 72–73.

Taylor, C., Zlutnick, S., & Hoehle, W. (1979). The effects of behavioral procedures on tardive dyskinesia. *Behavior Therapy, 10*, 37–45.

Teri, L., & Lewinsohn, P. (1984). *Clinical geropsychology: New directions in assessment and treatment.* New York: Pergamon Press.

Thompson, L., Davies, R., Gallagher, D., & Krantz, S. (1986). Cognitive therapy with older adults. *Clinical Gerontologist, 5*, 245–279.

Thyer, B. (1981). Prolonged *in vivo* exposure therapy with a 70-year-old woman. *Journal of Behavior Therapy & Experimental Psychiatry, 12*, 69–71.

Vaccaro, F. (1988). Application of operant procedures in a group of institutionalized aggressive geriatric patients. *Psychology & Aging, 3*, 22–28.

Waggoner, C., & LeLieuvre, R. (1981). A method to increase compliance to exercise regimens in rheumatoid arthritis patients. *Journal of Behavioral Medicine, 4*, 191–201.

Wander, T. (1972). Existential depression treated by desensitization of phobias: Strategy and transcript. *Journal of Behavior Therapy & Experimental Psychiatry, 3*, 111–116.

Wandless, I., & Davies, J. (1977). Can drug compliance in the elderly be improved? *British Journal of Medicine, 1*, 359–361.

Weldon, S., & Yesavage, J. (1982). Behavioral improvement with relaxation training in senile dementia. *Clinical Gerontologist, 1*, 43–49.

Welford, A. (1980). Epilogue: Where do we go from here? In L. Poon (Ed.), *Aging in the 1980s: Psychological issues* (pp. 615–621). Washington DC: American Psychological Association.

Whitehead, W., Burgio, K., & Engel, B. (1985). Biofeedback treatment of fecal incontinence in geriatric patients. *Journal of the American Geriatrics Society, 33*, 320–324.

Whitlatch, C., & Zarit, S. (1988). Sexual dysfunction in aged married couple: A case study of a behavioral intervention. *Clinical Gerontologist, 8*, 43–62.

Wiens, A., Menustik, C., Miller, S., & Schmitz, R. (1982–1983). Medical-behavioral treatment of the older alcoholic patient. *American Journal of Drug & Alcohol Abuse, 9*, 461–475.

Williams, G., & Dorow, L. (1983). Changes in complaints of a chronically depressed psychiatric patient as a function of an interrupted music/verbal feedback package. *Journal of Music Therapy, 20*, 143–155.

Williamson, P. (1984). An intervention for hypochondriacal complaints. *Clinical Gerontology, 3*, 64–68.

Williamson, P., & Ascione, F. (1983). Behavioral treatment of the elderly: Implications for theory and therapy. *Behavior Modification, 7*, 583–610.

Willington, F. (1978). Urinary incontinence and urgency. *Practitioner, 220*, 739–747.

Wilson, G. T., & Franks, C. (Eds.). (1982). *Contemporary behavior therapy: Conceptual & empirical formulations.* New York: Guilford Press.

Wisner, E., & Green, M. (1986). Treatment of a demented patient's anger with cognitive-behavioral strategies. *Psychological Reports, 59*, 447–450.

Wisocki, P. A. (1982). Actual and predicted responses of institutionalized elderly to the Psychiatric Reinforcement Survey Schedule. *International Journal of Behavioral Geriatrics, 1*, 47–55.

Wisocki, P. A. (1984). Behavioral approaches to gerontology. In M. Hersen, R. Eisler, & P. Miller (Eds.), *Progress in behavior modification* (Vol. 6, pp. 121–157). New York: Academic Press.

Wisocki, P. A. (1986). *A behavioral program for teaching sign language to elderly aphasic patients.* Paper presented at the University of Chicago School of Social Work, Charlotte Towle Symposium on Behavioral Research on Aging, Chicago.

Wisocki, P. A., & Averill, J. (1987). The challenge of bereavement. In L. Carstensen & B. Edelstein (Eds.), *Handbook of clinical gerontology* (pp. 312–321). New York: Pergamon Press.

Wisocki, P. A., & Mosher, P. (1980). Peer-facilitated sign language training for a geriatric stroke victim with chronic brain syndrome. *Journal of Geriatric Psychiatry, 13,* 89–102.

Wisocki, P. A., & Mosher, P. (1982). The elderly: An understudied population in behavioral research. *International Journal of Behavioral Geriatrics, 1,* 5–14.

Yesavage, J. (1984). Relaxation and memory training in 39 elderly patients. *American Journal of Psychiatry, 141,* 778–781.

Yesavage, J., Rose, T., & Spiegel, D. (1982). Relaxation training and memory improvement in normals. *Experimental Aging Research, 8,* 195–198.

Zarit, S., Zarit, J., & Reever, K. (1982). Memory training for severe memory loss: Effects on senile dementia patients and their families. *Gerontologist, 22,* 373–377.

Zimmer, J., Watson, N., & Treat, A. (1984). Behavioral problems among patients in skilled nursing facilities. *American Journal of Public Health, 74,* 1118–1121.

Factors Affecting Treatment of the Elderly

Medication and the Aging Organism
A Guide for the Non-Prescribing Clinician

Nancy Keuthen

The elderly as an age group are major consumers of prescription medications. The total number of drugs prescribed for the elderly is disproportionately high, relative to their representation in the population. Individuals 65 years of age and older spend one-quarter of the total national expenditure for medication (Vestal, 1984), though they comprise under 12% of the population (Bureau of the Census, 1985). Nearly two-thirds of this group receive medications regularly (Guttmann, 1978). Physicians often simultaneously prescribe from three to twelve medications per day for elderly patients (Lamy, 1980) and more than thirteen prescriptions per year (Lamy & Vestal, 1976). Less than 5% of all individuals 65 years of age or older abstain from all drug use (Guttmann, 1978). The elderly also use over-the-counter preparations, but it is unclear from existing statistics whether or not they use them more than other age groups.

Pharmacological treatment can be more complicated in the elderly than in younger cohorts, making safe and effective treatment more difficult. Many factors contribute to this situation, including increased use of drugs, decreased functioning of organs involved in drug metabolism and elimination, drug-drug, drug-disease, and drug-food interactions, poor medication compliance, use of over-the-counter preparations, and problems with assessment and diagnosis. In light of the fact that the etiology of undesired drug reactions may involve the confluence of

Nancy Keuthen • Psychosomatic Medicine Unit, Massachusetts General Hospital, Boston, Massachusetts 02114.   This chapter was written for the purpose of alerting non-prescribing clinicians to the issues and pitfalls accompanying pharmacological treatment of the elderly. It is in no way intended to be used as a set of guidelines for actual prescribing practices with this population.

multiple factors, treatment interventions may accordingly require multipronged approaches.

DRUG SIDE EFFECTS

In this chapter I have reviewed the nature and incidence of drug side effects and toxic reactions in the elderly as well as the multiple variables that may contribute to their occurrence. I have also highlighted two arenas in which the practicing behavioral clinician may enhance the pharmacological treatment of the elderly client.

Accompanying their high use of prescription drugs and their use of over-the-counter medications is a greater risk for adverse reactions even in normal doses (Cooper, 1975). The elderly are also more likely to experience side effects with a broader range of drugs (Morrant, 1975; Shader, 1972). In an investigation of 521 consecutive admissions to an acute geriatric unit in England, Leach and Roy (1986) documented adverse drug reactions in 18.8% of medicated patients. Hurwitz (1969) reports the prevalence of adverse drug reactions by age group as follows: 20–29 years of age—3%, 40–49 years of age—7.5%, and 70–79 years of age—21.3%. Thus, side effects are more prevalent in the elderly than in middle-aged individuals by a factor of three, and more prevalent in the elderly than in young adults by a factor of seven. Not only is the potential for side effects greater in this age group, but their occurrence may have more serious ramifications, as the elderly may be less able to recover from them due to the presence of multiple life stresses (Schuckit & Moore, 1979). Adverse drug reactions contributed to more than 10% of approximately 2,000 consecutive hospital admissions to geriatric departments in Great Britain (Williamson & Chopin, 1980). In some cases, adverse reactions to some drugs, including anticoagulants, antibiotics, and cardiovascular drugs, have been noted to contribute toward fatalities (Lamy, 1980).

Both psychiatric and nonpsychiatric medications may have toxic effects that mimic the symptomatology seen in psychiatric and medical disorders. Among these are psychosis, agitation, motor restlessness, lethargy, depression, mania, affective lability, confusion, and disorientation. In such circumstances, symptom alleviation may occur simply upon the adjustment or withdrawal of the responsible agent. Table 1 presents a summary of psychiatric, physical, and cognitive problems that may occur in the elderly when they ingest frequently prescribed drugs.

When side effects or toxic outcomes from these drugs are misattributed to other physical or psychiatric disorders, iatrogenic problems may result from inappropriate treatment interventions. To exemplify these points, I will next discuss some of the more problematic responses in the elderly to common psychoactive agents, as well as potential pitfalls resulting from the misattribution of these effects.

Both psychotropic and cardiovascular medications are responsible for the most serious drug reactions in the elderly. Despite repeated evidence attesting to the harmful potential of psychotropic drugs for older individuals (Boston Collaborative Drug Surveillance Program, 1973; Davies, 1971; Greenblatt, Allen, & Shader, 1977; Paulson, 1968), statistics reveal their frequent use. Some of the more hazardous side

Table 1

Commonly Prescribed Drugs and Possible Side Effects in the Elderly

Medication	Typically prescribed for	Behavioral signs as side effects
Anti-Parkinson	Symptoms of Parkinson's disease and pseudo-Parkinson's	Psychotic behavior
Digitalis	Hypertension	Hallucinations, confusion, nightmares, disorientation
Dilantin (toxicity)	Seizure disorders	Lethargy, confusion
Diuretics	Edema	Sexual disturbances, confusion
Antihypertensive	High blood pressure	Lethargy, depression, sexual disturbances, headache, psychotic behavior
Antiarrhythmics	Irregularities in heart rate	Psychotic behavior, rashes
Gastrointestinal	Acidity, upset, gas	Confusion
Steroids	Arthritis	Mania, hallucinations, delusions, emotional variability
Major tranquilizers		
Phenothiazines		
Aliphatics		
Chlorpromazine	Combativeness, extreme agitation, hallucinations, delusions, hostility	Drowsiness, withdrawal, rigidity, akinesia,[a] tremor, obesity
Promazine		
Piperazines	Combativeness, extreme agitation, hallucinations, delusions, hostility	Motor restlessness (akathesia), insominia, muscle spasms, (dystonias), tongue, lip, and jaw movements (tardive dyskinesia)[b]
Fluphenazine		
Trifluoperazine		
Piperidines		
Thioridazine		Sexual dysfunction, rashes
Butyrophenones	As above and mania, paranoid ideation	Extrapyramidal (rigidity, tremors)
Haloperidol		
Thioxanthenes	As above and severe depression	Extrapyramidal
Thiothixene		
Antidepressants		
Tricyclics (Desipramine, amitriptyline, nortriptyline, doxepin)	Motor retardation, hypochondriasis, poor appetite, insomnia, and self-neglect symptomatic of depression	Agitation, psychotic behavior, urinary retention, paresthesia
MAO-inhibitors	Same as above	Same as above and hypertensive crisis
Minor tranquilizers		
Benzodiazepines	Anxiety, multiple somatic complaints, convulsions, insomnia, agitation	Visual hallucinations, confusion, disorientation. Psychotic behavior may follow withdrawal
Chlordiazepoxide		
Diazepam		
Oxazepam		
Diphenylmethane		
Hydroxyzine		
Lithium carbonate	Racing thoughts, mania, manic-depression	Anorexia, psychotic behavior

Note. From R. Hussian (1981). *Geriatric psychology: A behavioral perspective.* Princeton, NJ: Van Nostrand Reinhold.
[a]Mimics depression.
[b]Mimics Huntington's chorea.

effects caused by neuroleptic medications include extrapyramidal and anti-cholinergic symptoms as well as excessive sedation. The potency of neuroleptics is positively correlated with extrapyramidal symptoms and negatively correlated with the frequency and severity of sedation, orthostatic hypotension, and anti-cholinergic symptoms. The elderly are especially sensitive to extrapyramidal symptoms such as akinesia, akathisia, parkinsonism, and tardive dyskinesia. Approximately one-half of all patients between 60 and 80 years of age treated with neuroleptics have developed extrapyramidal symptoms (Hamilton, 1966). Incorrect diagnoses of akathisia and akinesia as agitation and depression, respectively, may result in unwarranted pharmacological interventions and additional side effects. Undesired sedative effects in the aged organism can exacerbate confusion and disorientation in the demented or worsen nocturnal insomnia as a result of daytime sleep. If neuroleptics are used to treat the increased agitation that often accompanies confusion and disorientation, the clinical situation will be exacerbated. Orthostatic hypotension may result in falls and subsequent fractures or broken bones. Anticholinergic side effects may include dry mouth, urinary retention, constipation, blurred vision, and an exacerbation of glaucoma. Dry mouth may result in denture misfit and thus interfere with food intake. Constipation may be an especially salient problem for the older individual with limited mobility and poor dietary intake, and may lead to noncompliance with instructions to take medication.

Tricyclic antidepressant medications, like neuroleptics, can cause orthostatic hypotension and anticholinergic symptoms, as well as cardiac toxicity. Another anticholinergic toxic effect, CNS anticholinergic toxic syndrome, is characterized by confusion, disorientation, memory loss, tactile hallucinations, and, occasionally, visual hallucinations and assaultiveness. In the event that this syndrome is misdiagnosed as psychosis or dementia, subsequent treatment with neuroleptics might only worsen the anticholinergic effects of the initial tricyclic drug. Lastly, MOAI medications, in general, are relatively contraindicated for use with this population because there is an elevated potential for toxicity.

Side effects to lithium, which are common among the elderly, can mimic the overt manifestations of other physical and psychiatric disorders. For example, a lithium-related tremor might be misdiagnosed as a side effect of other medications; nausea and vomiting from lithium toxicity might be assigned other medical etiologies; confusion caused by low lithium levels can be misdiagnosed as dementia-related confusion. Lithium toxicity occurs more rapidly in the elderly than in younger individuals.

Antianxiety medications, commonly prescribed and often abused, may cause apathy, prolonged sedation, impaired motor coordination, disorientation, and confusion. Lethargy and apathy may be misdiagnosed as depression; disorientation and confusion may be misinterpreted as symptoms of an organic brain disorder. Limited mobility due to lethargy can create further problems. Reductions in alertness, when coupled with hypotension, can often result in falls. Failure to recognize the involvement of medication in these symptom pictures can result in further unwarranted therapeutic efforts or inappropriate placement, clouding the clinical picture and often creating iatrogenic problems.

VARIABLES CONTRIBUTING TO DRUG REACTIONS

To more fully understand the complexities of pharmacological treatment of the elderly, we will now review some other variables that affect drug reactions. These variables include altered pharmacokinetics, greater intraindividual variability in this age cohort, increased incidence of illness and disability, the common practice of polypharmacy, limited compliance with medication instructions and self-medication, the prescribing practices of physicians for this group, and problems with assessment of the elderly.

Altered Pharmacokinetics

Age-related physiological changes in the elderly often result in altered patterns of drug responsivity. Drug absorption, distribution, metabolism, excretion, and receptor sensitivity may all be affected to varying extents. The elderly experience decreases in gastrointestinal absorptive surface and in blood flow through the gastrointestinal tract; altered gastrointestinal motility and sphincter activity; decreases in lean body mass and increases in body fat relative to total body weight; reduction in total body fluids, serum albumin, liver and renal blood flow, liver mass and enzyme activity; and alterations in the number and affinity of receptors. Thompson, Moran, and Nies (1983) summarized the resultant changes in the pharmacokinetic effects of psychotropic drugs in the elderly by saying that there are increases in plasma concentration of water-soluble drugs; decreases in plasma concentration and slower elimination of fat-soluble drugs; higher percentages of unbound, metabolically active drugs; decreased effectiveness of the body's ability to metabolize foreign substances; decreases in renal excretion; and prolonged half-lives of drugs that are excreted unchanged. For a more in-depth review of the changes in drug responsivity in the aging organism, see articles by Goldberg and Roberts (1983) and Ouslander (1981).

The clinical utility of findings from pharmacologic studies in the elderly are somewhat limited. The majority of the research is cross-sectional rather than longitudinal in design, so that empirical findings are more applicable to the group of surviving elderly and may be discrepant with changes deriving from the aging process itself. Population samples utilized in research protocols often are healthy, ambulatory individuals, a group that does not adequately represent the elderly population as a whole. Generally, concurrent effects from other environmental and subject characteristics have not been evaluated, thus confounding the interpretation of age-related alterations in pharmacokinetic and pharmacodynamic findings.

Unfortunately, due to our limited knowledge about the effects of aging on the pharmacokinetic properties of drugs, physicians often prescribe reflexively (Ouslander, 1981) and extrapolate dosages from those recommended for the "average" young adult to the elderly. In general, most age-related changes intensify the effects of the drugs. Elderly individuals usually require dosages of one-half to one-third those recommended for young adults. Failure to recognize these age-related physiological changes may lead to toxic drug levels, dangerous side effects, and increased susceptibility to drug interactions.

Intraindividual Variability

The variability among individuals in any sample is expected to increase with age. Alterations in physiological processes also occur as a function of the number and severity of disease processes in each individual case (Salzman & Shader, 1974). In view of the large differences noted between elderly individuals, normative data are much less likely to represent adequately the individual case for the elderly than that for younger adults. The specification of guidelines for prescribing medication is more difficult to achieve. Not unexpectedly, elderly samples experience greater variability in drug response and an increased incidence of paradoxical effects.

Increased Incidence of Illness and Disability

As a group, the elderly are more likely to have a greater number and severity of chronic medical illnesses and to exhibit high frequencies of many psychiatric problems as well. The more common chronic medical illnesses include arthritis, diabetes, high blood pressure, and heart disease. The most frequently prescribed medications to treat the elderly are cardiovascular drugs, psychotropic drugs, analgesics, and laxatives (Lamy, 1980; Williamson & Chopin, 1980). Among psychotropic medications, the elderly receive a disproportionately high number of prescriptions for tranquilizers and antidepressants, while the number of stimulant drugs ordered for this age group is disproportionately low. Phillipson (1976) reports that approximately 86% of elderly Americans have one or more chronic physical conditions and more than 50% of the elderly have two or more medical conditions. These physical conditions themselves may have psychiatric presentations (such as paranoid delusions secondary to uncontrolled diabetes mellitus or depressive symptomatology secondary to hypoglycemia), and the illnesses may interact with prescribed medications, altering drug responsivity.

Polypharmacy

In light of these high rates of illness and disability, it is not surprising that the practice of polypharmacy becomes increasingly more commonplace as a patient's age increases. Statistics on the incidence of polypharmacy are startling. A survey of elderly in Finland averaging over 70 years of age showed that one-third had taken four or more drugs during one week, with one-half using psychotropic drugs and 20% using more than one psychotropic medication (Hemminki & Heikkila, 1975). In a study of medication practices in one long-term care facility, Kalchthaler, Coccaro, and Lichtiger (1977) reported that the average number of drugs prescribed per patient was 3.33 and the average number of pills taken daily was 6.34. Prien (1975) found that one out of every six elderly VA hospital patients with a psychiatric disorder was treated with two or more psychoactive medications simultaneously. Guttmann (1978) reports that the elderly are inclined to take psychotropic drugs in combination with other medical prescriptions.

When polypharmacy occurs, the multiple drugs can interact antagonistically, cancelling out the effects of each other (e.g., oral antacids can inhibit absorption of digoxin, and tricyclics can decrease the effects of propranolol). Or they can interact synergistically, one potentiating the pharmacological effect of the other (e.g., alcohol increases the effects of barbiturates). In a review of the medication regimens in two nursing homes for the elderly, Brown, Boosinger, Henderson, Rife, Rustia, Taylor, and Young (1977) reported a potential for significant drug interactions in 53% of selected profiles. The picture becomes even more complicated when the roles of diet, physical health, and the use of over-the-counter preparations are considered. Just as chronic medical illnesses may alter drug responsivity, drug regimens will impact upon disease processes. Diet may also play a major role. The ramifications of nutrition are discussed in depth by Kendall, Wisocki, and Pers in Chapter 3 of this book.

Medication Compliance and Self-Medication

There is wide variability in the reported rates of noncompliance with medication among the elderly. In a summary of existing studies, Hussar (1978) cited that one-third to one-half of all patients were noncompliant. Gibson and O'Hare (1968) and Schwartz, Wang, Feitz, and Goss (1962) reported that more than half of elderly patients fail to take their drugs as prescribed. Some researchers maintain that the possibility for abuse of prescribed drugs increases with age for both sexes (Abrahams, Armstrong, & Whitlock, 1970; George, 1972; Swanson, Weddige, & Morse, 1973). For the most part, though, investigators (e.g., German, Klein, McPhee, & South, 1982; Weintraub, Au, & Lasagna, 1973) have failed to document increased noncompliance with increasing age. In fact, Hamblin, Wells, and Ellis (1979) reported the highest "compliance ratio" in patients over 70 years of age. Research exploring reasons for noncompliance in this age group as well as interventions to enhance compliance are sorely needed.

A host of reasons have been put forth to account for poor compliance, some of which are applicable to all age groups and others which are more salient for the elderly. In a study of 114 chronically ill medical patients with an average age of 70.2 years, Brand and Smith (1974) found a relationship between poor compliance with physician's recommendations (including medications and appointments) and the educational level, financial status, and severity of disease. The rate of noncompliance was significantly different between four marital status groups. Noncompliance was the highest for the widowed, followed by the single and divorced, and finally by married individuals. These authors also found that noncompliance was correlated with problems in community health and social agencies, limited understanding of instructions, a poor attitude toward treatment, and the cost of medications. Hemminki and Heikkila (1975) reported that 53% of the elderly take fewer drugs than prescribed, citing no further need for the medications, no benefit from them, excessive cost or negative side effects. It is always important to consider carefully the role of reported side effects in cases of undercompliance. In some cases, failure to ingest prescribed drugs may be beneficial to the individual (e.g., when the accompanying drug reactions are harmful and/or lethal). Hemminki and Heikkila also reported that the likelihood of misuse increases when the elderly have many drugs to take and when the medication regimen is complex. One expects that the probability of noncompliance is greater when the consequences of discontinuing treatment are delayed. The negative correlation between duration of treatment and compliance is particularly salient for the elderly, many of whom are on long-term prophylactic medication regimens for a variety of chronic illnesses.

Poor compliance with medications can involve underuse or overuse and may be intentional or inadvertent. In general, underuse comprises the majority of instances of drug noncompliance in the elderly (Raffoul, Cooper, & Love, 1981). With elderly populations, one needs to examine a wide range of variables, including physical, psychological, socioeconomic, and cultural ones, when attempting to account for limited compliance. Simple considerations such as physical access to a pharmacy must not be overlooked. Cultural sanctions against drug treatment, especially for psychiatric problems, may be meaningful for this age group. Cost factors are also critical, as the elderly American, on the average, spends over $100 on prescription medications annually (National Center for Health Statistics, 1977) and often has a limited income. Sensory and cognitive impairments may also account for poor compliance. Problems with hearing, reading, comprehending, and executing instructions may result from auditory or visual deficits, memory problems, or confusional states. Some medications whose side effects include a diminution of cognitive faculties may further exacerbate these problems. Medication misuse attributable to these sources may cause minor side effects or be lethal.

Unintentional drug overuse can be particularly problematic in view of the narrower margin between therapeutic and toxic drug levels in the elderly as well as a decreased tolerance for side effects. Overuse of prescription medications is also of concern in light of the high suicide rates among the elderly. We need to be especially cautious in prescribing drugs for depressed elderly. In the past, the prescription drugs for which the highest frequencies of abuse were reported for individuals over 50 years of age were barbiturates and benzodiazepine tranquilizers (Pascarelli, 1974). As few prescriptions are now written for barbiturates, the frequency of abuse is likely to be the highest with benzodiazepines.

Self-medication by the elderly is widely recognized as a problem (Lenhart, 1976). It may be a problem because elderly have limited accessibility to clinics, live on low incomes, and/or may be afraid to identify the nature and extent of an illness. Sharing prescriptions with friends (Gibson & O'Hare, 1968) and hoarding outdated medications are common. The practice of doctor-shopping may result in excessive drug-prescribing, fragmented care, and polypharmacy. Individual caregivers will be unaware of the potential for side effects from drug interactions. Frequent use of over-the-counter preparations, at times in combination with alcohol, can also be troublesome (Capel & Stewart, 1971). Contrary to patterns of use with prescribed psychoactive drugs, only 9% of men and 7% of women in the 60–74 age group reported using an over-the-counter psychoactive drug within the past year in a study by Parry, Balter, Mellinger, Cisin, and Manheimber (1973). As this study was conducted nearly two decades ago, its significance for current patterns of over-the-counter drug use is unclear.

Many health problems can be temporarily alleviated by over-the-counter drugs. Some of the most widely used preparations are aspirin and aspirin compounds and laxatives (Schuckit & Moore, 1979). Aspirin and antacids in particular often cause adverse reactions for the elderly. Gillies and Skyring (1972) found that 15% of women and 8% of men in one survey reported that they ingested aspirin daily. Chronic aspirin use may result in gastrointestinal disturbances, ulcers, gastric bleeding, asthmatic attacks, skin reactions, and, when consumed in high doses, confusion, excitement, delirium, or hallucinations. When abused, analgesic compounds can cause renal disease, anemia, peptic ulcers, and gastrointestinal bleeding. Even the short-term use of these substances may cause cerebral impairment (Johnson, 1972); longer-term use may result in depression, confusion, skin rashes, and varying neurological abnormalities. Laxatives are used on a weekly basis by approximately one-third of individuals over age 60. These preparations can cause cardiac and respiratory failure in certain cases (Lenhart, 1976), as well as dehydration, abdominal pain, thirst, muscular weakness, cramps, and electrolyte imbalances.

Abuse of cough preparations, sleep-inducing agents, antihistamines, and even vitamins can have serious side effects for this age group. Cough mixtures can produce blood pressure changes and psychiatric symptomatology. Antihistamines can cause agitation, excitement, or difficulties with concentration. Vitamins can have varying side effects depending upon the specific vitamin used. For instance, hypervitaminosis A can cause headache, bone pain and alopecia; megadoses of vitamin C can cause gastrointestinal disturbances; high doses of nicotinic acid may cause impairment of liver function. A therapist must assess usage patterns of over-the-counter agents. The elderly client and his or her family often deny or downplay the amount of drug usage, creating a serious problem for caregivers who must consider the possibility of hazardous side effects from the use of the over-the-counter drugs alone or in combination with prescription medications, alcohol, and/ or street drugs.

Little attention has been focused on the abuse of alcohol and narcotics by the elderly. In a large sample study conducted by Stephens, Haney, and Underwood (1982), 59.6% of their sample denied use of alcoholic beverages in the past month, and only 1.9% reported any lifetime use of illicit substances. In a similar vein, other studies have reported small percentages of the elderly using even moderate amounts of alcohol (e.g., Maultsby & Fortier, 1981). The consensus is that alcohol abuse is a significant problem in the elderly although it is underreported by both patients and their caregivers. While elderly narcotic abusers are not visible to the public, they are estimated to exist in increasing numbers (O'Donnell, 1969). Schuckit (1977) reports that older alcoholics are less likely to receive antabuse treatment in light of increased incidence of medical problems in this age cohort. Elderly abusers do not find the available treatment options of methadone maintenance programs or total abstinence appealing. Placement of such cases in long-term facilities can be difficult. New treatment programs for the elderly abuser are clearly warranted. In Chapter 13 (this volume), Horton and Fogelman further discuss the problem of elderly alcohol and drug abusers.

Medication Prescribing Practices for the Elderly

Medical care for the elderly is often fragmented. Frequently the elderly have multiple caregivers, who prescribe numerous different medications and communicate minimally among themselves. The elderly see many caregivers because they often have a number of disabilities that require a variety of specialists, and because they shop around for physicians. Most elderly do not discuss their prescriptions with different physicians and most do not ask questions about the prescriptions they are given (Doyle & Hamm, 1976). For these reasons caregivers should always ascertain the nature and extent of involvement of other professionals, as well as the kind of alternative medications that may have been prescribed.

The prescribing physician can be a source of drug misuse as much as the elderly consumer. Inappropriate medication practices can result from inaccurate assessment and diagnosis, improper medication for a specific diagnosis, failure to evaluate potential drug interactions, and overmedication. American physicians tend to add medications rather than subtract or substitute, particularly when the regimen is complex.

Accurate assessment and diagnosis is an especially important area, and it is difficult to achieve with this population: many caregivers are involved with the patient; one cannot depend on the patient's report; and the patient and family often deny that medication abuse occurs. (These factors will be discussed more fully in the next section.) A study by Stephens, Haney, and Underwood (1982) reported that physicians inquired about use of other medications in only 42.9% of their subjects who took at least four medications concurrently. Another confounding problem is the lack of direct contact with the patient. Doyle and Hamm (1976) reported that only 13% of an elderly sample actually saw their doctors to receive prescriptions, while 30.3% simply telephoned the practitioner, and 30.5% had their pharmacist contact the physician. A similar situation exists for elderly in nursing homes. In a 1971 DHEW investigation of 75 nursing homes, cited in the report on pharmaceutical use in nursing homes of the Subcommittee on Long Term Care of the U.S. Senate Special Committee on Aging (1975), investigators found that two-thirds of the patients had not received physical examinations upon admission and 40% of the patients had not been seen by a physician for over 3 months.

Physician error may also account for improper medications prescribed for a specific diagnosis or incomplete pharmacological treatment. Careless and automatic prescribing practices may have serious consequences. In American nursing homes, residents have received from four to seven drugs per day, many of which were inappropriate or ineffective (Subcommittee on Long Term Care, 1975). In one study, 46 of 58 elderly patients on diuretics were not simultaneously treated with potassium, leaving many of them lethargic, constipated, and dehydrated (Gibson & O'Hare, 1968). Beardsley, Heaton, Kabat, and Martilla (1975) reported that 37% and 35% of p.r.n. orders for tranquilizers and hypnotics, respectively, were not justified by reports in patient charts, reflecting inadequate record keeping or inappropriate prescribing practices.

There is evidence to suggest that overmedication of the elderly may occur in various settings. Ingman, Lawson, Pierpadi, and Blake (1975) studied patients in a nursing home and reported that "more neuroactive substances were prescribed for patients with superior mentation and minimal physical disability" (p. 309). In addition, while some psychoactive medications may be utilized to treat primarily nonpsychiatric disorders, the rationale for such prescribing practices is questionable and requires further exploration. In a survey of psychoactive drug use in 12 VA hospitals, Prien (1975) reported use of psychoactive drugs in one out of every six patients without a diagnosed mental disorder. For example, psychoactive drugs may be utilized to treat psychological distress accompanying physical illness when psychotherapy may be just as effective. One may also conjecture that pharmacological interventions are more readily utilized than alternative treatment options with the treatment of older populations, due to the oft-cited distaste for working with the elderly, the belief that the elderly are less amenable to psychotherapy, and the reality that alternative interventions may not be cost-effective in light of limited life expectancies.

Assessment of the Elderly Client

Physical and psychological problems in the elderly are often difficult to assess and correctly identify. As a result, many chronic conditions, often even potentially treatable ones, go undetected (Brocklehurst, Carty, Leeming, & Robinson, 1978; Williams, Hill, Fairbank, & Knox, 1973).

Numerous physical, socioeconomic, cultural, and psychological factors may be involved in symptom presentation by the older individual. The elderly often have multiple somatic concerns that may be presented in a diffuse fashion. A number of presenting complaints, such as confusion and urinary incontinence, may be symptomatic of a variety of illnesses, making specific disorders difficult to recognize. Physical concerns often accompany a picture of depression, and aches and pains may simply be depressive correlates. Since physical illness is often considered more culturally acceptable to the elderly, emotional distress may initially be manifested as somatic concerns. As stated earlier, both physical and psychological symptoms can result from drug side effects, interactions among several drugs, drug-food or drug-disease interactions, medical disorders, or psychological illnesses. As the number of chronic disabilities and prescribed medications rises rapidly, the overall clinical picture becomes increasingly more complex. Limited access to care providers as well as small, fixed incomes may prevent the individual from seeking help when early signs of an illness appear. The stigma placed on mental health problems by many elderly may deter them from seeking needed assistance or presenting themselves to medical professionals.

The elderly individual may be a poor and/or unreliable historian due to depression, denial of illness, lack of education, and altered cognitive states. Family members or friends may themselves be unaware of the individual's medication abuse or failing memory due to limited contact with them. In other cases, significant others are cognizant of these problems, but share in the patient's denial. Failure to report the complete clinical picture may result in misdiagnosis and subsequent inappropriate treatment interventions.

Caregivers assessing elderly patients need to ask simple, specific, direct questions to evaluate the broad clinical picture. Corroboration of information from a significant other is always useful. Narrow assessment may result in the misattribution of symptoms. For example, depression in the elderly is often readily related by professionals to the presence of multiple life stressors and frequent losses even when the clinical picture may also result from an untreated medical condition or a drug side effect. In light of this, it is crucial to rule out organic bases for presenting symptoms before acceptance of environmental causality. The careless attribution of symptoms, such as memory problems or depression, to the aging process itself, may result in a failure to treat what may be a readily reversible problem. Lastly, assessment is an ongoing process. The caregiver may need to revise initial clinical formulations when symptom relief does not occur within an expected time period after the initiation of a treatment intervention.

When assessing the etiology of a physical or psychiatric disturbance, caregivers need to know how to evaluate the role of medications in the current clinical picture, particularly in cases of acute behavioral alteration. As stated earlier, symptoms attributable to drug side effects may appear indistinguishable from those accompanying a functional psychiatric disorder. Consequently, when working with elderly clients who are on medications, the following considerations are recommended for clinicians:

1. Know all prescribed medications, their dosages, why they were prescribed, when drug treatment began, and current blood levels, if possible. Look for correlations between drug trials and parameters of the symptom picture.
2. Determine the necessary length of the therapeutic drug trial, possible side effects to drug use and drug withdrawal, as well as the length of time the drug remains in the body after discontinuation.
3. Evaluate for potential interactive drug effects (antagonistic or synergistic) when polypharmacy is involved. Encourage treatment with the fewest number of drugs possible.
4. Evaluate the presence of multiple symptoms known to co-occur in symptom complexes when questioning the presence of drug side effects.
5. Assess compliance with medications as prescribed. Seek data from significant others regarding medication compliance when there is a question of abuse or undermedication.
6. Assess the nature and frequency of over-the-counter medications used, as well as abuse of alcohol and street drugs.

7. Evaluate the possible roles of visual and auditory impairments, impoverished intellectual abilities, memory dysfunction, or confusional states in the patient's comprehension of instructions and compliance with medication regimens.
8. Investigate the presence of chronic physical disabilities and acute medical illnesses that may affect drug action as well as be altered by prescribed medications.
9. Assess nutritional status and the potential for drug-food interactions.
10. Evaluate access to the pharmacy, cost considerations, and the patient's beliefs and values in medication compliance.
11. Consider the possibility of an idiosyncratic drug reaction when alternative explanations are inadequate.

A PROPOSED INTERFACE BETWEEN PHARMACOLOGICAL AND BEHAVIORAL INTERVENTIONS

So far I have addressed many issues pertinent to the assessment of the elderly medicated client. I have stressed that physical conditions may mimic psychiatric disorders in their symptom presentation, that psychiatric difficulties may first present as physical problems, and that the direct, side, and interactive effects of medications may be difficult to distinguish in presentation from those of functional psychiatric disorders. At this juncture, I would like to present two areas in which behavioral treatment strategies may make a large contribution: medication compliance and the treatment of unavoidable medication side effects.

Compliance

As reviewed earlier, several characteristics of the elderly and their therapeutic regimens suggest that compliance might be problematic for this age cohort. Most studies demonstrate a negative effect on drug compliance of longer drug treatment, more frequent dosages, and a greater number of medications. This appears to bode poorly for the elderly, who are known to have a greater number and severity of chronic medical illnesses. It is not clear, however, from available data that elderly are less compliant than other age groups; in fact, most studies suggest that compliance in this age group is at least as good as in younger samples. But in any event, interventions to enhance compliance are required and may differ from those found to be effective with younger cohorts.

It is important to remember that the problem of compliance can have many facets. The patient may use drugs excessively or less than required to be of value. The individual may utilize alcohol or street drugs in conjunction with prescribed medications, or alone to self-medicate. Over-the-counter preparations may be mixed with prescribed medications or taken in lieu of them. The elderly individual may discontinue medications before the recommended time. These scenarios may be attributable to a lack of education regarding prescribed medications, their routes of action and potential side effects, or to entrenched negative ideas about the mental health profession that keeps the older person from consulting a professional when necessary. Educational programs designed to increase the level of understanding of medications and their uses, as well as to counter the negative image of the mental health system are sorely needed. Behaviorists could also make a significant contribution in the design and evaluation of much-needed treatment programs for the elderly abuser of prescription, over-the-counter, or street drugs.

Little research to date has systematically investigated the efficacy of interventions to enhance compliance in this age cohort. One study by Wandless and Davies (1977) successfully utilized tear-off calendars and tablet identification cards to reduce errors in medication compliance. Individuals with the calendars made fewer errors than those with cards, and those with either cards or a calendar made significantly fewer errors than those given only standard instructions. MacDonald, MacDonald, and Phoenix (1977) showed improvement in drug compliance and drug regimen comprehension with 15 minutes of pharmacist counseling prior to the discharge of geriatric patients. Other studies, though, have failed to document increased compliance as a consequence of educational interventions. A case study by Dapcich-Miura and Hovell (1979) showed the beneficial effects of token reinforcement for increasing compliance with a medication regimen, exercise, and fluid intake.

Future investigations need to address the extent to which techniques utilized in the classical compliance literature (Sackett & Haynes, 1976) may be tailored for the elderly to enhance their compliance. Among these behavioral strategies are reminders, contracting, tailoring the medication regimen, graduated medication implementation, self-monitoring, reinforcement, and family/peer support. The compliance literature has demonstrated that education in drug regimen improves medication compliance, while education about disease does not. It is unclear, as stated earlier, that this trend occurs to the same extent in the elderly as it does in other age groups. The effects of social isolation are particularly relevant for the elderly, yet few investigators have examined the impact of this factor on drug compliance. The optimal frequency and nature of supervisory contact needs to be identified as well as age-relevant reinforcement/feedback mechanisms to enhance drug compliance.

Tailoring of Medication Side Effects

The growing field of behavioral medicine has introduced interventions based on behavioral principles designed to prevent, treat, and/or assist patients in coping with symptoms typically considered the domain of physicians. In cases where the benefits of medication clearly outweigh the side effects experienced, the individual is left to cope with uncomfortable and, at times, socially embarrassing symptoms. As stated earlier, the elderly are at higher risk in general for such side effects.

Accordingly, the development of interventions to minimize adverse side effects would benefit this age group in particular and, in turn, be likely to enhance medication compliance.

One such example is the current research investigating treatment interventions for tardive dyskinesia. This movement disorder, which consists of stereotyped, repetitive movements of the lips, tongue, mouth, and jaw, and choreiform movements of the trunk and extremities, is traditionally attributed to the use of neuroleptic medications. The elderly, women in particular, are at increased risk for development of this disorder (Kane & Smith, 1982).

A number of researchers have conducted small sample investigations and case studies exploring the effectiveness of a variety of behavioral procedures in the reduction of dyskinetic symptomatology. Interventions purported to reduce anxiety and increase awareness of symptoms have been used with some success. Albanese and Gaarder (1977) treated two patients with biofeedback and reported symptom disappearance in one case and symptom improvement in the other. Farrar (1976) also reported on the successful use of EMG biofeedback to treat tremors and dystonias. Frederiksen and Rosenbaum (1979) compared binary feedback, simultaneous visual feedback, and self-monitoring in reducing the involuntary movements. The binary feedback and self-monitoring were effective with two patients, and one person given simultaneous visual feedback showed some symptom improvement. In another investigation, Taylor, Zlutnick, and Hoele (1979) exhibited the beneficial use of overcorrection and positive-negative feedback in reducing dyskinetic movements. The initial success of these researchers attests to the fact that nonmedical interventions can be effective in the treatment of disorders that initially were attributed to a medical etiology. In a similar fashion, researchers need to explore the potential efficacy of behavioral interventions in the treatment of other medication-related side effects.

SUMMARY

Behavioral clinicians treating elderly clients need to recognize the fact that similar symptom pictures may result from the use of prescribed or over-the-counter medications, physical problems, or psychiatric disorders. Awareness of the potential effects of medications on the aging organism and the necessity of a broad initial assessment will help ensure selection of the most appropriate treatment intervention. In addition, the efforts of behavioral researchers are needed to investigate strategies to enhance medication compliance in this age cohort as well as to minimize adverse side effects of these medications.

ACKNOWLEDGMENT

I would like to extend my heartfelt thanks to Paul Zusky, M.D., for his thoughtful review of the final draft of this chapter.

REFERENCES

Abrahams, M. J., Armstrong, J., & Whitlock, F. A. (1970). Drug dependence in Brisbane. *Medical Journal of Australia, 2*, 397–404.

Albanese, H., & Gaarder, K. (1977). Biofeedback treatment of tardive dyskinesia: Two case reports. *American Journal of Psychiatry, 134*, 1149–1150.

Beardsley, R., Heaton, A., Kabat, H., & Martilla, J. (1975). *Patterns of drug use in nursing home patients.* Minneapolis: University of Minnesota College of Pharmacy.

Boston Collaborative Drug Surveillance Program. (1973). Clinical depression of the central nervous system due to diazepam and chlordiazepoxide in relation to cigarette smoking and age. *New England Journal of Medicine, 288*, 277–280.

Brand, F. N., & Smith, R. T. (1974). Medical care and compliance among the elderly after hospitalization. *International Journal of Aging and Human Development, 5*, 331–346.

Brocklehurst, J. C., Carty, M. H., Leeming, J. T., & Robinson, J. M. (1978). Medical screening of old people accepted for residential care. *Lancet, 1*, 141–142.

Brown, M. M., Boosinger, J. K., Henderson, M., Rife, S. S., Rustia, J. K., Taylor, O., & Young, W. W. (1977). Drug-drug interactions among residents in homes for the elderly—a pilot study. *Nursing Research, 26*, 47–52.

Bureau of the Census. (1985). *Statistical abstract of the United States: 1986* (106th ed.). Washington, DC: U.S. Government Printing Office.

Capel, W. C., & Stewart, G. T. (1971). The management of drug abuse in aging populations: New Orleans findings. *Journal of Drug Issues, 1*, 114–120.

Cooper, J. W., Jr. (1975). Implications of drug reactions—recognition, incidences, and prevention. *Rhode Island Medical Journal, 58*, 274–280.

Dapcich-Miura, E., & Hovell, M. F. (1979). Contingency management of adherence to a complex medical regimen in an elderly heart patient. *Behavioral Therapy, 10*, 193–201.

Davies, R. K. (1971). Confusional episodes and antidepressant medication. *American Journal of Psychiatry, 128*, 95–99.

Doyle, J. P., & Hamm, B. M. (1976). *Medication use and misuse study among older persons.* Jacksonville, FL: The Cathedral Foundation of Jacksonville.

Farrar, W. B. (1976). Using electromyographic biofeedback in treating oraficial dyskinesia. *Journal of Prosthetic Dentistry, 35*, 384–387.

Frederiksen, L. W., & Rosenbaum, M. S. (1979). The behavioral control of tardive dyskinesia: Evaluation of three types of feedback. *Journal of Behavior Therapy and Experimental Psychiatry, 10*, 229–302.

George, A. (1972). Survey of drug use in a Sydney suburb. *Medical Journal of Australia, 2*, 233–237.

German, P. S., Klein, L. E., McPhee, S. J., & South, C. R. (1982). Knowledge of and compliance with drug regimens in the elderly. *Journal of the American Geriatrics Society, 30*, 568–571.

Gibson, S. S. J. M., & O'Hare, M. M. (1968). Prescription of drugs for old people at home. *Gerontologica Clinica, 10*, 271–280.

Gillies, M. A., & Skyring, A. P. (1972). The pattern and prevalence of aspirin ingestion as determined by interview of 2921 inhabitants of Sydney. *Medical Journal of Australia, 1*, 974–979.

Goldberg, P. B., & Roberts, J. (1983). Pharmacologic basis for developing rational drug regimens for elderly patients. *The Medical Clinics of North America, 67*, 315–331.

Greenblatt, D. J., Allen, M. D., & Shader, R. I. (1977). Toxicity of high dose flurazepam in the elderly. *Clinical Pharmacological Therapeutics, 21*, 355–361.

Guttmann, D. (1978). A study of drug-taking behavior of older Americans. In C. R. Beber & P. P. Lamy (Eds.), *Medication management and education of the elderly* (pp. 201–230). Amsterdam: Excerpta Medica.

Hamblin, D., Wells, F. O., & Ellis, S. (1979). A study of the compliance to prescribed treatment of patients under antihypertensive treatment. *Journal of Clinical and Hospital Pharmacy, 4*, 41–49.

Hamilton, L. D. (1966). Aged brain and the phenothiazines. *Geriatrics, 21*, 131–138.

Hemminki, E., & Heikkila, J. (1975). Elderly people's compliance with prescriptions and quality of medication. *Scandinavian Journal of Social Medicine, 3*, 87–92.

Hurwitz, M. (1969). Predisposing factors in adverse reactions to drugs. *British Medical Journal, 1*, 536–539.

Hussar, D. A. (1978). Patient noncompliance. *Journal of American Pharmacological Association, 15*, 183–190.

Hussian, R. (1981). *Geriatric psychology: A behavioral perspective*. New York: Van Nostrand Reinhold.

Ingman, S. R., Lawson, I. R., Pierpadi, P. G., & Blake, P. (1975). A survey of the prescribing and administration of drugs in a long-term care institution for the elderly. *Journal of American Geriatrics Society, 23*, 309–316.

Johnson, D. A. W. (1972). The psychiatric side effects of drugs. *Practitioner, 209*, 320–326.

Kalchthaler, T., Coccaro, E., & Lichtiger, S. (1977). Incidence of polypharmacy in a long-term care facility. *Journal of American Geriatrics Society, 25*, 308–313.

Kane, J. M., & Smith, J. M. (1982). Tardive dyskinesia. Prevalence and risk factors, 1959 to 1979. *Archives of General Psychiatry, 39*, 473–481.

Lamy, P. P. (1980). *Prescribing for the elderly*. Littleton, MA: PSG Publishing.

Lamy, P. P., & Vestal, R. E. (1976). Drug prescribing for the elderly. *Hospital Practice, 11*, 111–118.

Leach, S., & Roy, S. S. (1986). Adverse drug reactions: An investigation on an acute geriatric ward. *Age and Aging, 15*, 241–246.

Lenhart, D. G. (1976). The use of medications in the elderly population. *Nursing Clinics of North America, 11*, 135–143.

MacDonald, E. T., MacDonald, J. B., & Phoenix, M. (1977). Improving drug compliance after hospital discharge. *British Medical Journal, 2*, 618–621.

Maultsby, M. C., Jr., & Fortier, R. H. (1981). *Patterns of drug use by normal elderly people*. Lexington, KY: University of Kentucky Medical Center, Rational Behavior Therapy Center.

Morrant, J. C. A. (1975). Medicines and mental illness in old age. *Canadian Psychiatric Association Journal, 20*, 309–312.

National Center for Health Statistics. (1977). *Health interview survey: United States 1975*. Rockville, MD: Health Resources Administration.

O'Donnell, J. A. (1969). *Narcotic addicts in Kentucky*. Washington, DC: Public Health Service Publication.

Ouslander, J. G. (1981). Drug therapy in the elderly. *Annals of Internal Medicine, 95*, 711–722.

Parry, H. J., Blater, M. B., Mellinger, G. D., Cisin, I. H., & Manheimer, D. I. (1973). National patterns of psychotherapeutic drug use. *Archives of General Psychiatry, 28*, 769–783.

Pascarelli, E. F. (1974). Drug dependence: An age-old problem compounded by old age. *Geriatrics, 29*, 109–115.

Paulson, G. W. (1968). "Permanent" or complex dyskinesias in the aged. *Geriatrics, 9*, 105–110.

Phillipson, R. (1976). *Drugs and the aged: Policy issues and the utilization of research findings*. Paper presented at the American Association for the Advancement of Science, Boston, MA.

Prien, R. F. (1975). A survey of psychoactive drug use in the aged at Veterans Administration hospitals. In S. Gershon & S. Raskin (Eds.), *Aging* (pp. 143–154). New York: Raven Press.

Raffoul, P. R., Cooper, J. K., & Love, D. W. (1981). Drug misuse in older people. *The Gerontologist, 21*, 146–150.

Sackett, D. L., & Haynes, R. B. (Eds.). (1976). *Compliance with therapeutic regimens*. Baltimore, MD: Johns Hopkins Press.

Salzman, C., & Shader, R. I. (1974). Psychopharmacology in the aged. *Journal of Geriatric Psychiatry, 7*, 165–184.

Schuckit, M. A. (1977). Geriatric alcoholism and drug abuse. *Gerontologist, 17*, 168–174.

Schuckit, M. A., & Moore, M. A. (1979). Drug problems in the elderly. In O. Kaplan (Ed.), *Psychopathology of aging* (pp. 229–241). New York: Academic Press.

Schwartz, D., Wang, M., Feitz, L., & Goss, M. E. W. (1962). Medication errors made by elderly chronically ill patients. *American Journal of Public Health, 52*, 2018–2029.

Shader, R. I. (1972). *Psychiatric complications of medical drugs*. New York: Raven Press.

Stephens, R. C., Haney, C. A., & Underwood, S. (1982). *Drug taking among the elderly*. Washington, DC: U.S. Government Printing Office.

Subcommittee on Long Term Care of the U.S. Senate Special Committee on Aging. (1975). *Drugs in nursing homes: Misuse, high cost and kickbacks*. Washington, DC: U.S. Government Printing Office.

Swanson, D. W., Weddige, R. L., & Morse, R. M. (1973). Abuse of prescription drugs. *Mayo Clinic Proceedings, 48*, 359–367.

Taylor, C. B., Zlutnick, S. I., & Hoele, W. (1979). The effects of behavioral procedures on tardive dyskinesia. *Behavior Therapy, 10*, 37–45.

Thompson, T. L., Moran, M. G., & Nies, A. S. (1983). Psychotropic drug use in the elderly. *New England Journal of Medicine, 308,* 134–138.

Vestal, R. E. (Ed.). (1984). *Drug treatment in the elderly.* Boston, MA: ADIS Health Services Press.

Wandless, I., & Davies, J. W. (1977). Can drug compliance in the elderly be improved? *British Medical Journal, 1,* 359–361.

Weintraub, M., Au, W. Y.-W., & Lasagna, L. (1973). Compliance as a determinant of serum digoxin concentration. *Journal of the American Medical Association, 244,* 481–485.

Williams, T. F., Hill, J. G., Fairbank, M. E., & Knox, K. G. (1973). Appropriate placement of the chronically ill aged—a successful approach by evaluation. *Journal of the American Medical Association, 226,* 1332–1335.

Williamson, J., & Chopin, J. M. (1980). Adverse reactions to prescribed drugs in the elderly: A multicenter investigation. *Age and Aging, 9,* 73–80.

Nutritional Factors in Aging

KIM E. KENDALL, PATRICIA A. WISOCKI,
AND DANI B. PERS

An overwhelming number of elderly men and women are habitually undernour-ished. Estimates indicate that one-third to one-half of the health problems of the elderly are a direct or indirect consequence of nutritional deficiencies (Gershell, 1981). People over the age of 60 consume far less than what is believed necessary to meet nutrient standards for their age, sex, and weight. More than 15 years ago, the Ten-State Nutritional Survey (DHEW, 1972) found that, as a group, elderly citizens had insufficient caloric, iron, and vitamin A dietary intake. Since then, other nutritional surveys have confirmed these findings (Bowman & Rosenberg, 1982; Harrill & Cervone, 1977; National Center for Health Statistics, 1974; Pao & Hill, 1974) and estimated that 50% of the elderly population fall below adequate standards for vitamin C, vitamin A, and calcium intake. Many more do not take sufficient amounts of vitamin D. The percentage is even greater among elderly Blacks, Spanish-Americans, and poor.

Even those elderly in institutions, where adequate care is presumed, show poor nutritional status. According to a study by Baker, Frank, Thind, Jaslow, and Louria (1979), more than 30% of the institutionalized elderly in their sample showed low levels of vitamin B_6, folate, and nicotinate.

Nutrition is important to health, fitness, and a positive lifestyle. It has a profound effect on aging at every stage of the life cycle (Young, 1983). Improper eating habits over the long term have been associated with a variety of diseases and disorders, including diabetes, cancer of the colon, osteoporosis, arteriosclerosis, and periodontal disease.

The maintenance of adequate nutrition can be a complex and sometimes difficult process because there are a variety of interacting factors that determine one's nutritional status. In this chapter the authors discuss several of those factors, including physiological changes in the aging organism, disease conditions, medi-cations and drug intake, economic and social conditions, and physical limitations. They consider ways nutritional imbalances impact on two psychological problems

KIM E. KENDALL • 416 17th Avenue East, Seattle, Washington 98102.   PATRICIA A. WISOCKI • Depart-ment of Psychology, University of Massachusetts, Amherst, Massachusetts 01003.   DANI B. PERS • Amherst Medical Associates, Amherst, Massachusetts 01002.

common to the elderly (depression and mental deterioration), and describe the potential benefits of dietary modifications. They present guidelines for establishing good nutritional practices for an elderly individual including methods of assessment and interventions within a behavioral context. Finally, they present the results of recent research studies dealing with ways to change dietary practices.

INFLUENCES ON NUTRITIONAL STATUS

Physiological Changes

Normal aging is accompanied by decreased metabolism and diminished requirements for supporting active cell growth (Busse, 1980; Calloway & Zanni, 1980; Mayer, 1974). By age 70 the basal metabolic rate has dropped 16%. Active lean body mass is slowly replaced by fat, even in a person who is not overweight (Calloway & Zanni, 1980; Mayer, 1974). These physiological changes require an elderly person to maintain normal weight or even be slightly underweight, since there is an increase in body fat in proportion to body protein (Worthington-Roberts & Hazzard, 1982). Gastrointestinal secretions decrease with age, and there is a delay in emptying the esophagus, which may be annoying or frightening to an older person. Such changes, therefore, require that the elderly take care to consume a diet high in nutrients, while reducing the caloric content of their foods.

Effects of Disease

Infection, disease, injury, and the prospects of undergoing surgery raise the nutrient requirements of the elderly. Blood loss from tumors, ulcers, aspirin abuse, and diverticular disease often results in iron deficiency. Gastrointestinal diseases interfere with absorption and the utilization of nutrients so that even when intake is adequate, nutritional status may be depleted.

Deficiencies in calcium, chromium, and zinc, a common condition for many elderly, may contribute to osteoporosis and impaired glucose tolerance. Osteoporosis, a gradual loss of calcium from the bones, leads to porous and brittle bones and is especially common among elderly women. The increase in bone fractures seen in women above the age of 55 seems almost a normal by-product of aging, but may instead reflect a widespread and long-term inadequate dietary intake of calcium, coupled with inadequate levels of exercise.

Effects of Medication

Many of the drugs commonly prescribed to the elderly, the chief users of drugs in the United States, may induce vitamin or mineral deficiencies (Roe, 1980). Deficiencies of the B vitamins are produced by more drugs and with greater frequency than deficiencies of vitamin C or fat-soluble vitamins. Antituberculosis drugs can lead to a combined deficiency of folate, B_6, and niacin by affecting the absorption or utilization of these vitamins. Anticonvulsants can produce deficiencies in vitamin D and folate. Diuretics reduce serum levels of calcium, magnesium, and zinc.

Psychotropic drugs are especially problematic. For example, sedatives may reduce one's interest in food. Benzodiazepines may cause gastrointestinal symptoms and loss of appetite. Phenothiazines may lead to constipation, increased appetite, and weight gain. Perhaps the most dangerous psychotropic drug for the elderly is lithium, a salt which alters liver and thyroid function. Lithium is especially threatening for an elderly person who has a restricted salt intake, is dehydrated, and/or is on diuretics and has difficulty excreting excess salts (Sloan, 1982).

Nonprescription drugs have as many serious side effects. Chronic use of aspirin can lead to anemia secondary to gastrointestinal bleeding, which is a particular problem for the elderly who are already likely to be deficient in iron and who may be taking other drugs that compromise iron status, such as steroids or antiinflammatory agents (Michocki, 1982). Antacids, frequently used by the elderly as self-medication for indigestion or heartburn, often contain aluminum hydroxide, which when taken chronically can lead to phosphate depletion, osteomalacia, constipation, and intestinal blockage (Michocki, 1982).

Laxatives, the most frequently ordered drugs in geriatric facilities and used by at least 50% of all elderly, present a particularly serious problem. Elderly are predisposed to constipation due to poor dietary habits, which result from a decrease in saliva secretion, poor dentition, impaired sense of taste and smell, loss of appetite, insufficient intake of liquids, and inadequate exercise. Constipation can also be a side effect of antidepressants, antihistamines, opiates, and iron products. Or, as Michocki (1982) points out, it may be a symptom of a disease process. Laxatives may lead to phosphate depletion and electrolyte imbalance (Michocki, 1982; Roe, 1980). Whenever possible, laxatives should be avoided. Instead, dietary fiber in the form of high fiber vegetables, bulk and bran, and liquids should be added to the diet. Exercise is also helpful in reducing the problem of constipation, and it affects other physiological factors, such as reaction time, the capacity for physical labor, and general health.

Mineral oil, frequently used as a laxative, can lead to the loss of carotene and vitamins A, D, and K, which dissolve in the oil and are secreted. The oil also creates a barrier to the absorption of these same nutrients. Colchicine, used as an antiinflammatory agent in gout, can lead to the malabsorption of fat and depletion of carotene, sodium, potassium, vitamin B_{12} and lactose through interference with mitosis and damage of enzymes. Metformin and phenformin used as hypoglycemic agents in diabetes compete with vitamin B_{12} for absorption. Para-aminosalicylic acid used as an antituberculosis agent acts as a block to the mucosal uptake of vitamin B_{12}. Similarly, salicylazosulfapyridine blocks the mucosal uptake of folate when used for ulcerative colitis and regional enteritis as an antiinflammatory agent. Prednisone and other glucocorticoids block calcium transport and hence lead to the depletion of calcium when used in the treatment of autoimmune and collagen diseases. The anticonvulsants, phenobarbitol, diphenylhydantoin, and primidone accelerate the catabolism of vitamin D and other active metabolites, leading to the depletion of calcium absorption (Roe, 1980).

It is not true that alcohol consumption always leads to malnutrition. On the average, alcoholics may not differ from nonalcoholics in nutritional status (Roe, 1980). It is true, however, that excess alcohol consumption can lead to severe nutritional deficiencies. Even without depleting nutritional resources, alcohol can effect changes in bone marrow and red blood cells, and it has direct toxic effects on the pancreas and liver. Alcohol often leads to malabsorption of vitamins, resulting in decreases in thiamine, folic acid, riboflavin, niacin, ascorbic acids, B_6, B_{12}, and vitamin A (Roe, 1980). Alcohol also increases the excretion of magnesium, zinc, calcium, and potassium and may result in protein depletion.

With increasing age, drugs tend to remain in the body longer and have a more prolonged biological activity, so that clinical and toxic effects may be more common and pronounced in older people (Braithwaite, 1982; Dorsey, 1979; Gulevich, 1977; Roe, 1980). The ratio of fat to protein tissue is increased, and hence lipid-soluble medications, including many psychoactive drugs, tend to accumulate in the fatty tissues. The ability of the liver to metabolize drugs also decreases with age. These factors lead to a lowered threshold for the toxic side effects of many drugs. Drugs can deteriorate nutritional status by usually indirect means, and they involve changes that affect the absorption or metabolism of nutrients. In such cases, even when dietary intake appears sufficient, one's nutritional status may be inadequate.

Effects of Economic, Social, and Physical Limitations

It is not possible to neglect the role that economic concerns, social factors, and physical limitations play in the diet of elderly citizens. More than one-fourth of all elderly Americans are below the poverty index. Many lack transportation, physical mobility, and the capacity to shop. They may lack cooking facilities and utensils, along with companionship and a comfortable place to eat. Of those over 65, 31% live alone (Patten, 1982) and are likely to skip meals (Slesinger, McDivitt, & O'Donnell, 1980). Physical and financial limitations affect a person's ability to prepare meals, while social isolation decreases appetite and the motivation to eat nutritious meals.

Oral disease, lack of teeth, or poor-fitting dentures can also reduce a person's ability and willingness to eat. By the age of 65, 50% of Americans have lost many or most of their teeth. This percentage increases by the age of 75. Elderly may avoid hard or sticky food in preference for soft, more highly refined and less nutritious foods (Busse, 1980; Rivlin, 1981). Wisocki (1982) has found that this is especially true of elderly in institutions. Her sample of male geriatric residents of a VA hospital preferred ice cream, soft drinks, cookies, chips, and doughnuts, to other more healthful foods. Gradual decreases in the senses of taste and smell (Kamath, 1982; Spitzer, 1982) may also tend to reduce the appetite of elderly people (Mayer, 1974; Patten, 1982; Rivlin, 1981; Young, 1978). Decreased vision and hearing further isolate some elderly, making them more reluctant to eat in public places or at large social gatherings, because they are not able to enjoy conversation.

Growing old in America does not, in itself, assure high prestige and preferential treatment. It may be that the American culture allows the elderly to be at a greater nutritional risk than other age groups, unlike some nonindustrialized societies where older males (and sometimes females) have priority for high protein foods and are in this way assured of receiving adequate levels of protein and carbohydrates (Patten, 1982).

THE EFFECT OF NUTRITIONAL DEFICIENCIES ON PSYCHOLOGICAL STATUS

There is no doubt that an inadequate diet produces indications of psychological problems, particularly depression and mental deterioration. Roe (1980) has reported that a deficiency in vitamin B_6 has been associated with depression. Garetz (1976) has estimated that 8–15% of noninstitutionalized elderly are depressed and that up to 50% of people in geriatric facilities show significant clinical depression. Although we do not know what percentage of these people are depressed due to nutritional shortages, we cannot ignore the possibility that it may be a substantial number. Marginal or preclinical vitamin deficiencies may lead to nonspecific depression-like symptoms, such as malaise, irritability, sleepiness, loss of appetite and weight, apathy, and fatigue. Depression can, in turn, further compromise nutritional status by leading to overeating or undereating.

Mental deterioration is associated with vitamin B_{12} deficiency. Anemia induced by vitamin B_{12} loss has been associated with a higher incidence of psychiatric symptoms than anemia resulting from other causes (Baker *et al.*, 1979). A deficiency of niacin may lead to the development of severe psychological symptoms, including dementia, confused talking, disorientation of time and place, hallucinations, delusions, rigidity, depression, uncontrollable gasping and sucking (Gershell, 1981). Deficits in thiamine have been associated with muscle weakness, mental confusion, irritability, hallucinations, and disorientation. Deficits in iron, folate, and B_{12} may produce these behaviors: weakness, difficulty in concentration, confusion, apathy, depression, personality changes, paranoia, failure to initiate action, lack of appetite, shortness of breath. Deficiencies in vitamin B_1 and B_6 and nicotine acid have also been implicated in many similar behaviors. Given the range of problems linked to nutritional deficiencies, it is easy to assume that a good many elderly have been mistakenly diagnosed and treated for depression, organic brain syndrome, or paranoia without examination of their nutritional status.

To summarize, there are many factors that make the elderly especially prone to malnutrition and the effects of chronic subclinical malnutrition, including the fact that these symptoms are often interpreted as part of the normal aging process. Many interrelated factors, such as the effects of disease, drugs, surgery, poverty, social isolation, physical disabilities, perceptual changes, and educational level, all contribute in varying degrees to a given elderly person's nutritional status, and in turn, to his or her physical and mental health. The extensive degree of subclinical vitamin deficiency seen in the elderly may impact on physical and mental dysfunction more than has been previously recognized. The management of these interrelated factors presents a great challenge to medical and mental health professionals as well as to the elderly themselves. The benefits are worthwhile, however, as we shall see in the next section.

THE POTENTIAL BENEFITS OF DIETARY MODIFICATIONS

It is possible that the increased vitamin needs of elderly are a result of an age-related reduction in vitamin binding and an increased inability to store vitamins (Baker *et al.*, 1979). For instance, increasing dietary levels of niacin, folate, vitamin C, and vitamins B_6 and B_{12} lowers the likelihood of detecting inadequate levels of these nutrients in the elderly, and these vitamins quickly become deficient when supplementation is withdrawn (Baker *et al.*, 1979). It may therefore be useful to supplement diets with the water-soluble vitamins B, C, folate, and niacin, elements that are frequently at low levels for the elderly to begin with. Adequate vitamin intake often relieves fatigue, weakness, loss of appetite, irritability, and anxiety. Improvements in mental and physical condition have been seen in patients receiving vitamin B complex and vitamin C supplements (Bowman & Rosenberg, 1982; Gershell, 1981). Supplements of vitamin B_{12} and folate have reduced the percentage of those deficits in both institutional and noninstitutional elderly (Baker *et al.*, 1979). Calcium supplements may be indicated in cases where the diet cannot or does not include adequate amounts of dairy products and fresh, green leafy vegetables. Iron supplementation is useful in decreasing anemic signs (Worthington-Roberts & Hazzard, 1982).

It should be kept in mind, however, that dietary supplements alone do not guarantee adequate nutritional intake. Poor absorption and increased requirements for nutrients may compromise nutritional status even when supplements are added to the diet. It is especially important to avoid supplementation with high levels of fat-soluble vitamins (vitamins A, E, D, K) because they may produce toxicity. Though less common, neurotoxic effects of Vitamin B_6 supplements are also known to occur. Frequently those with poor diets may be taking supplements that do not replace the nutrients they are missing. Ironically, those elderly who take supplements are less likely to have had deficient diets to begin with and may not need the supplement once their diets have been improved.

MODIFICATION OF NUTRITIONAL HABITS

Because there are many and varied causes of poor nutritional status and because nutritional deficiencies may show themselves as psychological problems or physical decline, the behavioral clinician has many points of intervention in attempting to modify nutritional habits.

Poor nutritional habits will probably not be a presenting problem when an elderly client enters therapy, although in some cases they may be what alarms a family enough to make the referral. For example, a client may come into therapy complaining of fatigue or listlessness; a client may seek treatment for a drug or alcohol dependency; a client may complain of depression or loss of memory. In all cases, it is important to assess nutritional status along with the assessment of other variables and to establish treatment goals that will address dietary habits to some extent at least.

In this section we will describe ways a clinician may assess the nutritional status of elderly clients, establish treatment goals, and execute intervention strategies for improving the nutritional status of elderly clients.

Assessment Procedures

Thorough assessment of nutritional status includes some procedures generally unavailable to the gerontological psychologist, such as biochemical analysis and anthropomorphic measurements (Redfern, 1982)—methods used typically to determine malnutrition. A clinician who wants to make use of these procedures will be required to refer the client to a medical facility.

Dietary intake is normally assessed simply by asking a person to recall everything he or she has eaten within the last 24 hours or by using a food frequency checklist (Food & Nutrition Board, N.R.C., 1981). These measures, relying on memory, are prone to inaccuracies and are limited in value since they only sample one day's intake. A more accurate assessment can be obtained by means of a food diary of everything one puts into the mouth including medication and vitamins (Roe, 1980). The food diary, kept for 7 days, is then used to estimate intake or specific nutrients which may be of concern. Detailed food composition tables are available from which these estimations can be made (Adams, 1975). Self-imposed or therapeutic diets should also be examined with reference to which foods are allowed and whether the diet is strictly followed.

If an elderly person lives alone, he or she may be subsisting on processed soft foods, such as buns, pastry, cereals, baby foods, and pet foods, all of which are low in nutrients. Besides inquiring about what food is regularly consumed during the week, one should check the refrigerator and cupboards for available foods (Mayer, 1974). In order to obtain a complete picture, it is also important to ask questions about the availability of utensils, cooking equipment and eating facilities, one's housing arrangements, financial status, and access to transportation. Figure 1 presents a Nutritional Assessment Form developed by Wisocki and Kendall (1986), which includes a comprehensive set of questions dealing with medical, dietary, and physical factors that may affect nutritional status.

A weight chart is also useful in assessing nutritional status. A consistent weight loss of 2 to 4 pounds a week can indicate illness, depression, apathy, or a malignancy (Gershell, 1981). Thus, it would seem appropriate for patients to be weighed on a regular basis.

Routine questioning about self-medication with over-the-counter (OTC) drugs and about prescribed medications is essential to a complete history (Michocki, 1982;

Roe, 1980). One useful way to elicit a history is by listing specific symptoms for which someone might take an OTC drug (e.g., Do you take medications for constipation, indigestion, headache, nervousness, insomnia, pain, or colds? What do you take? How much? How frequently?). Inadequate nutritional status may certainly be indicated when a person on medication has symptoms that cannot be explained by primary disease or in relation to drug toxicity or hypersensitivity (Roe, 1980). It may be necessary to contact a client's present and past physicians in order to find out the length of time a drug has been used.

Levels of folic acid and vitamins B_{12}, B_6, and D are frequently lowered by drug intake. It is especially important to consider these nutrients when examining a dietary history. If a complete drug history is available, one may be more specific about which nutrients should be examined. For example, people who are taking anticonvulsant medication might experience depletion in folate and vitamin D, especially if they are avoiding fruits, vegetables, liver, and milk. Recommendations would be made to increase these foods in order to avoid serious problems. Elderly who have a high alcohol intake might expect depletions in folate, thiamin, magnesium, and zinc. If they also have a low intake of fruits, vegetables, liver, and animal protein and a high intake of refined cereals, they could expect trouble.

Treatment Goals and Intervention Strategies

Nutritional goals should be designed for each person, based on general guidelines and the specific factors involved in a given medical, drug, and dietary history. In general, one should encourage dietary patterns that reduce the incidence of disease, poor psychological conditions, and eating patterns associated with an existing disease. As Posner (1982) points out in making national policy recommendations for the nutrition education of elderly Americans, eating patterns should be designed to maintain ideal weight and follow healthful dietary guidelines by reducing total fat and saturated fat intake; increasing complex carbohydrates; increasing fiber intake; and increasing intake of vitamin B_{12}, folic acid, iron, calcium, and vitamin D. Exercise is also recommended because it is thought to prevent mineral loss in the elderly and decreases the risks of being overweight, hypertensive, and/or in possession of elevated cholesterol levels (Kohrs, 1982; Liebman, 1981; Mayer, 1974). A modest program of exercise—3 days a week for 30 minutes a day— over a 3-year period has also been shown to be effective in preventing bone loss and increasing bone mineral content for women between the ages of 69 and 95 when compared to a nonexercise control group (Smith & Reddan, 1976). Similar findings were reported by Aloia, Cohn, Ostuni, Cane, and Ellis (1976). Other researchers (Smith, Reddan, & Smith, 1981) have duplicated these findings by showing that aged women on an exercise program had bone mineral content similar to women on supplemental vitamin D, while untreated controls experienced a decrease in bone mineral content during the same period. Others (Aloia, Rasulo, Deftos, Kaswain, & Yen, 1985) found an additional effect of exercise: it induces hypercalcemia and the calciotrophic hormones, substances thought to mediate skeletal remodeling through

Nutritional Assessment Form for Elderly Clients

Name: _____   Date: _____
Address: _____   Birthdate: _____
                                                    Phone No.: _____

MEDICAL STATUS

Name of primary physician: _____
Address: _____
Phone: _____
Date of last medical exam: _____

Please list other physicians or specialists:

Name   Specialty   Problem he/she follows

List hospitalizations you've had from most recent:

Date   Problem/purpose   Procedures/surgery   Duration of stay

List regular forms of exercise:

Type   # of times per day/week/mo   Duration
Sitting
Walking
Running
Bicycling
Specific program
   (e.g., Jazzercise, aerobics)
Miscellaneous

Do you exercise with or without a partner? with/without

PHARMACOLOGICAL STATUS

Please list below any prescribed drugs you are taking:

| | | Frequency per | | | Prescribing |
Name	Purpose	day/week	Dosage	Length of time	physician
1.					
2.					
3.					
4.					
5.					

Please list any medications or preparations that you purchase over-the-counter and use for the following symptoms. (Please list all products used.)

	Product	Dosage	How often per week	How effective is it? very/some/not at all
Constipation:				
Indigestion:				
Headache:				
Nervousness:				
Pain:				
Colds:				
Other (specify):				

NUTRITIONAL STATUS

1. How many meals do you regularly eat per day? _____

2. List usual content of each meal (include vitamins and liquids such as, water, alcohol, coffee, tea, juice, soda, as well as foods):

Breakfast	Snack	Lunch	Snack	Dinner	Snack

3. Do you eat fresh/frozen/canned vegetables?
   _____ None
   Whole grains? _____ yes   _____ no
   Vegetables with fiber (celery, broccoli, carrots)? _____ yes   _____ no
   Milk? _____ yes   _____ no
   Liver/meat/poultry? _____ yes   _____ no
   Fruits? _____ yes   _____ no

4. List any vitamins you take regularly:

Vitamin	How often per week?	Dosage	Brand name	Weekly total

5. What dietary limitations have been recommended by your physician(s)?
   Please list:

6. How many days per week are you able to adhere to these recommendations?
   Comment on each recommendation:

7. Describe a "healthy" diet below (List content of 3 meals):

Breakfast	Lunch	Dinner	Snacks

8. Where do you eat?
   Is it comfortable? Yes/No Comment:
   Do you have companionship (include pets): Yes/No
   If yes, please list:

9. Who prepares your meals?

   How frequently?
   Where?
   What utensils are available (dishes, tableware, stove, refrigerator, etc.)?

10. Does someone shop for you?   Yes/No
    Who?
    How frequently?
    Who makes out the shopping list?

11. How much do you spend on food per week? _____

    Are you ever unable to buy foods you would like?   Yes/No
    Please list those foods you are unable to buy:

12. Do fruit juices upset your stomach?   Yes/No

    Do you drink fruit juice?   Yes/No
    How often?

13. Do you wear dentures?   Yes/No

    Do you have difficulty eating?   Yes/No
    Comment:

14. Have you noticed any decrease in your sense of smell?   Yes/No

    Has there been any decrease in your sense of taste?   Yes/No

15. Have you experienced any change in appetite over the last 6 months?
    Yes/No   If yes, was it an increase or decrease?

16. Have you lost/gained weight in the last 6 months?   Yes/No
    If so, how much weight?

17. Have you experienced a decrease in your energy level over the last six months?
    _____ Yes   _____ No
    In what way?

18. Have you experienced a decrease in your memory or ability to concentrate over the
    last 6 months?   Yes/No
    Comment:

FIGURE 1.   Nutritional Assessment Form for Elderly Clients. (Wisocki & Kendall, 1986)

their availability. A program of education about the value and requirements of good nutrition is a fourth area of intervention. Let us examine each of these points more carefully and consider ways behavioral interventions may help to meet these goals.

Maintain Ideal Weight

In achieving an ideal weight, an elderly person may need to gain or lose weight or if he or she is already at ideal weight, to stay there. Behaviorally managed weight control programs aim to alter a person's caloric intake while increasing caloric expenditure through physical exercise. The core elements in a program for changing caloric intake, as described by Wilson (1984), are these four: self-monitoring one's eating patterns and setting achievable goals for oneself; restructuring the environmental cues for eating (e.g., eating only in one place, doing nothing else while eating, etc.); changing the topography of eating patterns (e.g., making the eating setting more attractive, the food more palatable, eating more slowly, using smaller places, etc.); reinforcement of behavior change.

Clients may also be taught the use of coping skills for those interpersonal situations and emotional conditions, such as loneliness, frustration, or boredom, that may trigger inappropriate eating and the use of cognitive instructional strategies to endorse the efficacy of the therapeutic techniques.

Follow Healthful Dietary Guidelines

Reduce Fat Intake. This goal is especially important if one is at risk for heart attack, a likely possibility if one already has a high blood cholesterol level. High blood cholesterol levels are commonly attributed to diets high in saturated fats. To reduce fat intake, a diet of lean meats, fish, poultry, and dry legumes is recommended, along with a reduction in butter, cream, hydrogenated margarine and shortening and a moderate use of eggs and organ meats.

In trying to meet this goal one must be careful to avoid inadvertently restricting certain foods that provide valuable nutrients to elderly. Red meats are particularly important since they provide iron, protein, and zinc, elements often deficient in the elderly (Gersovitz, Motil, & Munro, 1982; Munro & Young, 1978). While iron requirements of the body are lowest in old age due to the lifelong accumulation of iron stores (Lynch, Finch, & Monsen, 1982), it is still important to maintain significant intake levels. In fact, there is evidence that iron supplementation in the elderly may reduce the incidence of stroke, but there is no evidence that cholesterol levels are related to stroke incidence in elderly men and women (Kohrs, 1982; Worthington-Roberts & Hazzard, 1982).

Zinc is found in crab, oysters, liver, beef, poultry, veal, milk, cheese, and eggs, foods which may be considered expensive or unappetizing by the elderly. Specific diseases prevalent among many elderly, such as hepatitis, alcoholic liver cirrhosis, intestinal malabsorption, and chronic renal failure, are associated with zinc deficiency (Young, 1983). Zinc is also seen as critical for the synthesis of nucleic acid, protein, and biological membrane metabolism, all functions involved in the healing of wounds (Hallbrook & Lanner, 1972) and in immune function (Gross & New-burne, 1980).

Increase Complex Carbohydrates. Since fats and carbohydrates supply a good part of the body's energy, when fats are decreased, carbohydrates should be increased. Complex carbohydrates are better than fats in general because they contain fewer than half the calories of fats and many essential nutrients besides. Examples of foods containing complex carbohydrates are legumes, nuts, fruits, vegetables, and whole grain breads and cereals.

Increase Fiber Intake. Fiber should be included in a diet because it relieves constipation and thus reliance on laxatives. It is also helpful in preventing diverticular disease and other gastrointestinal disorders. High fiber intake is not advisable, but the substitution of whole grain bread in place of white bread, or the addition of three tablespoons of bran to cereal once a day and the inclusion of high fiber vegetables is an easy way to increase fiber (Kohrs, 1982).

Increase Intake of Vitamins B_{12} and D, Folic Acid, Iron, and Calcium. Two of these nutrients, vitamin D and calcium, have been implicated in bone loss among elderly citizens (Heaney, Gallagher, & Johnston, 1982; Parfitt, Gallagher, & Heaney, 1982). Heaney, Gallagher, and Johnston (1982) have recommended that for males over the age of 60 and females over the age of 50, calcium levels be increased to 1,000 mg per day or more, an amount well beyond the current Recommended Dietary Allowances. Milk and cheese are good sources of calcium. Vitamin D is found naturally in fatty fish, eggs, and chicken liver; it is a supplement in milk and some other processed foods. Sunlight is a good source as well.

Consider Salt and Alcohol Intake. Although most current dietary recommendations include lowering salt intake for the reduction of high blood pressure, this is less of a problem for the elderly than it is for the middle-aged. Since taste acuity lessens with age, a low-salt diet may not be palatable for the elderly and may lead to reduced food intake. Therefore, it may not be prudent to restrict the salt intake of an underweight elderly person who has only a slight elevation in blood pressure (Kohrs, 1982).

Because alcohol adds large amounts of calories and few nutrients to the diet, lowered levels of alcohol intake are recommended. Alcohol should probably not be eliminated altogether from the diets of those who use it with meals since it improves social contact and enhances psychological functioning and appetite (Mishara & Kastenbaum, 1974). Alcohol can also improve the quality of sleep in the elderly (Busse, 1980).

Compliance Programs

Once the nutritional targets have been established, behavior therapists can design programs to enhance compliance to any specific food regimen. Together with a client and his or her family, the therapist might construct a multifaceted program, the basics of which are described as follows.

In the beginning it is important to take baseline data of what food is eaten for at least 4 weeks. The therapist can then get an idea of what the client's preferences are and what habits he or she has in eating. It would be helpful to enlist a family member to spot-check on a random basis certain meals and snacks a person eats at various times of the day, since self-reported dietary habits are often inaccurate (Lansky & Brownell, 1982; Rush & Kristal, 1982).

Next the client and therapist should spend time identifying various nutritious foods and problem foods and discussing the value of good nutritional practices. There should also be discussion about ways to adapt familiar recipes, ways to shop for healthy foods, and which restaurants feature nutritious menus. It helps at this point to compare prices of healthy foods with less nutritious foods by going over grocery lists. Many clients are unaware of the extra expense in impulse items and snack foods. Showing a decrease in grocery bills can be an effective reinforcer for changing eating habits. There is also a time when the therapist might introduce the use of cognitive restructuring for thoughts about certain foods or food groups that a person may not be familiar with and for thoughts about the value of healthy eating. Covert reinforcement is also helpful in encouraging people to select certain foods. When that procedure is used, a client imagines himself or herself making the correct choices in the market, preparing meals the correct way, enjoying the food, and telling himself or herself that he or she is now "eating smart."

Many changes often occur spontaneously at this point in time. When they happen, the client should be reinforced enthusiastically by both the therapist and any involved family members. Concrete gains should be identified whenever possible. For example, the client may get checked for blood pressure or cholesterol levels. Physical stamina, sleeping, or appearance might be slightly improved. The money saved from improved shopping habits might be spent on some special item.

Generally, however, the greatest changes are made later, when the client and therapist contract for the inclusion and exclusion of certain targeted foods for a specific period of time. Food categories, like fruits or vegetables, or specific items, like salt or sugar, can be targeted. Or the client can agree to make small changes in each food group. Whatever changes are made must be reinforced. The client can be taught to reinforce himself or herself for making appropriate food choices or for sticking to the contract. At this time, too, client and therapist should discuss the importance of self-monitoring and self-praise, because a therapeutic goal is the instillation of a lifelong habit of evaluating one's own progress and reliance on oneself for reward, rather than others.

We do not want to negate the value of family members as reinforcers. Often nothing is as effective for an older person as interest from the family, visits from family members, special outings, company at meals, and so forth. But it generally happens that interest from the family lags after a time despite good intentions, and it becomes increasingly difficult to reinforce someone for doing "what they should be doing anyway" or what they have been doing for a long time. Self-reinforcement helps to insure that the client's behavior continues independent of the vicissitudes of others.

It is likely that this program will continue for a year. After the first 3 or 4 months, the client need not attend weekly sessions with the therapist, but can reduce the number of visits to once every 3 or 4 weeks. When gains have been clearly established, the therapist's attention shifts to maintenance by providing reinforcement and feedback and by designing strategies to help overcome any specific difficulties that arise as a person progresses through the program.

Increase Exercise

One cannot make recommendations about nutrition without considering the value of exercise. Older people often do not feel that exercise is necessary or they exaggerate the risks involved in vigorous exercise. In fact, the need for exercise does not decrease with age. Some diseases (e.g., hypokinetic disease) may actually be caused or accelerated by inactivity and sedentary lifestyle (Wiswell, 1980). The benefits of exercise in physiological and psychological functioning are established (see review by DeVries, 1977). Investigators have found improved cerebrovascular circulation, neuroendocrine sensitivity and function, and motionality as a result of exercise. Cognitive and behavioral characteristics have improved (Spirduso, 1975), and there have been reductions in anxiety (Driscoll, 1976) and depression (Morgan & Pollock, 1970) with physical exercise. Dodson and Mullens (1969) have demonstrated that exercise programs for geriatric residents have resulted in significant decreases on the MMPI hypochondrial and psychothenic scales, while Powell (1974) has shown that increases on the Wechsler Memory Scale are an effect of exercise.

Most likely the clinical behavior therapist will need to include an exercise regimen in his or her overall therapeutic plan for an elderly client. An exercise program may be devised utilizing a pattern of gradually increasing demands, like the Royal Canadian Air Force Exercises. It is important to provide regular monitoring and positive feedback as the person follows an exercise program. In her clinical practice, Wisocki has found it helpful to establish assessment criteria by which the elderly client may determine progress and reinforce himself or herself for gain. These criteria should be reasonable and achievable without too much work. For example, after several weeks of exercise one criterion might be walking up a flight of stairs with fewer signs of exertion than previously experienced, or demonstrating increased flexibility in bending down to tie shoes. Another measure of progress may involve the number of blocks or miles walked, as measured by a pedometer. In any case, a tangible, realistic measure is important in maintaining a pattern of exercise.

Education

Probably the most significant inroads to the improvement of nutritional status among elderly individuals are made by educating people to the facts. Instruction is especially important in the areas of nutritional requirements, specific diets, ways to prepare food, the need for exercise, the changes one may expect in aging, with particular attention to sensory changes (e.g., in taste buds, olfaction, dentition) and digestive system changes, and the potential harm from medication and alcohol.

Instructions should be clear. The important points should be emphasized repeatedly. Various sensory modalities should be engaged when the instructions are given. Whenever possible, charts or other record-keeping systems should be used to enhance compliance, to aid failing memories, and as a tangible means of monitoring participation in any established program. It is necessary that clients participate in the educational process. Perhaps a system of programmed learning might be implemented to insure that the clients have grasped the major points of nutritional health.

Health care providers may also need to include instruction in budgeting, details about the federal and local systems of aid, the availability of special programs for the elderly—particularly Meals-On-Wheels and transportation aids—restaurant discounts to senior citizens, etc. Occasionally a psychologist encounters an older person who expresses reluctance to take advantage of these programs, believing that they are only for the infirm or poor. These beliefs must be considered in the intervention process.

It may also be necessary to explain the importance of properly fitted dentures, which will help make the food one eats more palatable and allow for greater variety of foods. Increasing the variety of one's diet may be the single most important change that can be made in an elderly person's eating habits. The improvement of one's visual acuity may also aid in making food appear more appetizing. For that reason alone it is important to encourage the elderly to maintain or update their eyeglass prescriptions.

Institutionalized elderly especially may be unaware of their personal limitations. They may express unrealistic complaints about what they would be eating if they were at home. They may reject food that looks unlike what they used to eat. The elderly person's anger over lack of food choice may reflect a more general anger and sense of frustration about loss of control over his or her environment that aging frequently elicits. Interventions are preferable that increase an elderly person's sense of control over his or her diet, increase choice, and increase variety. It is possible to influence the food choices of the elderly by introducing new foods gradually into their diets, by arranging their meals in an attractive way, and by explaining something about the value of food for health, taste, and convenience (Holdsworth & Davies, 1982).

Studies have shown that it can take up to 1 year of therapy to reverse nutritional deficiencies in the elderly (Howels, 1975). Perhaps it is that length of time which has discouraged many investigators from actively developing behavioral programs to modify the dietary habits of elderly citizens. Or it may be that the eating habits of the elderly are stronger, due to this longer eating history. Food preferences and food aversions can be very powerful and long lasting. If food choices are also dictated by cultural factors, they may be even more difficult to change. Some empirical work has been done, however, and the details of those studies are examined in the next section.

RESEARCH STUDIES

In 1973, Bechill and Wolgamot estimated that fewer than 1% of the eligible population participated in federal government programs that provided meals for the elderly. This statistic prompted Bunck and Iwata (1978) to investigate ways of improving participation in community meal programs. Using a multiple-baseline design across three groups composed from 202 households, these investigators conducted two experiments. In the first experiment, they compared the effectiveness of providing public service radio announcements about the availability of meal programs and free transportation, a home visit in which the citizen was personally invited to attend, a follow-up telephone call, and a mailing announcing a list of 58 "rewards" for participation. These rewards included activities, products, games, and services. When the data were analyzed, Bunck and Iwata found that home visits and rewards for participation were more effective in increasing attendance at meal programs than radio announcements or telephone contacts. The use of rewards was the most effective and least expensive of all methods. Overall, however, the number of participants for the meal program only increased by 25.

In the second experiment, Bunck and Iwata evaluated the effects of low-cost incentives in improving attendance, using the 25 participants from the first experiment. They provided movies and bingo games on one day following the meal, and on two other days, after the meal, participants could select rewards from a list. Both strategies improved attendance, but the reward program was more cost-effective.

Using employees of the National Institute of Health as subjects, Zifferblatt, Wilbur, and Pinsky (1980) monitored what foods were chosen in the cafeteria lunch line for 15 months. Next they introduced a nutrition education program on cards distributed along with food purchases. Each card described the nutritional value of a food available in the cafeteria. Sets of matching cards could be exchanged for small prizes at various times during the 8-week program. The investigators found significant changes in dietary habits after the program. Employees reduced caloric intake. They purchased fewer desserts and bread products, and they increased intake of skim milk. They did not, however, change their food preferences. One suspects that a more direct intervention, such as rewarding people for trying new foods, would be more likely to produce such changes than an educational program alone.

Stanford University, however, demonstrated that education about nutrition can be effective. Investigators at Stanford (Stern, Farquhar, Maccoby, & Russell, 1976) initiated an ambitious study involving three communities in Northern California. They targeted the dietary habits of two communities, while the third community served as a control. For 2 years the "treatment group" communities were exposed to a multimedia campaign of television, newspaper articles, billboards, radio announcements, and posters through which investigators attempted to educate and persuade people to change their nutritional practices. In addition to the media exposure, a random sample of residents at risk for heart disease were given a 9-week course in nutrition. Prior to these interventions all residents were evaluated for diet, knowledge of dietary risk factors, and plasma cholesterol. At 1 and 2 years of follow-up, the residents of the treatment communities reported significantly lower intakes of cholesterol and saturated fats and lower systolic blood pressure than the residents in the control community. They also were more knowledgeable about dietary risk factors. Those people who took the 9-week course improved significantly more than the other residents in the treatment communities in lowered consumption of cholesterol and saturated fats, but after 2 years these differences were eliminated due primarily to continued improvement in the general community group.

The study illustrates not only that dietary habits can be changed on a large scale, but that media presentations are as effective as the more intensive intervention programs for small groups. Cerqueria *et al.* (1979) reported similar findings from a study in Mexico.

A more simple strategy was devised by Mayer *et al.* (1986) and tested in a family-owned cafeteria. At various places in the cafeteria they displayed three posters listing the benefits of a low-fat diet and showing which low-fat entree dishes were available to customers. They also placed fliers with the same information on each dining table. Customers were 140 regular visitors to the cafeteria, including approximately 40 elderly men and women. Prior to the placement of the posters, the investigators collected baseline observational data on the entree and dessert selections made by all customers. The posters and fliers served as the only interventions. They were displayed after baseline and then removed while a second baseline was taken, and finally reinstated. Each phase occurred for 6 days.

Data analysis indicated significant changes in the proportion of low-fat entrees chosen by customers during the times the posters were shown. There were no increases in the number of desserts during the interventions, indicating that additional calories were not consumed in other food products.

These results compared favorably with results obtained in similar studies investigating the effects of providing information about nutrition at the point where consumers make a selection about the foods they buy (Davis-Chervin, Rogers, & Clark, 1985; Dubbert, Johnson, Schlundt, & Montague, 1984).

A great deal more work on changing nutritional practices has been done with children (e.g., Brownell & Kaye, 1982; Coates, Jeffrey, & Slinkard, 1981; Epstein, Masek, & Marshall, 1978; Herbert-Jackson & Risley, 1977; Madsen, Madsen, & Thompson, 1974; Stark, Collins, Osnes, & Stokes, 1986). They have all achieved good results with different procedures.

All the studies described indicate that good nutritional habits can be developed, even though the behavior is complex and maintained by a multiplicity of factors. Thus, it seems that the effort is worth the gain.

SUMMARY

In sum, the elderly present a unique set of nutritional needs and problems. The physical, emotional, and social changes that ordinarily accompany aging, all exert an influence upon nutrition. Physiological changes, such as decreased metabolic rate, may lower the caloric needs of the elderly, thereby contributing to the difficulty of obtaining adequate nutrition without gaining excess weight. Injuries and diseases increase the nutrient requirements of the elderly, while, ironically, medications often decrease the body's crucial supplies of vitamins and minerals. Laxatives, used by a majority of the elderly, pose a threat, as they may lead to phosphate depletion and electrolyte imbalance. Social factors, particularly poverty and isolation, exert a negative influence upon adequate nutritional intake in the elderly.

The psychological and physical effects of malnutrition may be misinterpreted as part of the normal aging process. Some of the mental deterioration and depression seen in the elderly may be due to deficiencies in vitamins or minerals. The importance of accurate assessment of nutritional status is essential even when a client presents with physical or psychological problems. The Nutritional Assessment Form (Figure 1) aids in the assessment of medical, dietary, and physical factors which may affect nutritional status.

Inadequate nutrition in the elderly may be improved through vitamin and mineral supplements. However, care should be taken to avoid the toxicity associated with the storage of fat-soluble vitamins such as A, E, D, and K, and also with the water-soluble vitamin B_6. Luckily, there are several avenues open to clinicians whose goal it is to improve the nutritional status of their elderly patients. Education in proper nutrition and good shopping habits is essential.

Nutritional goals should be individualized to meet the specific needs of each client. In general, eating patterns should be designed to aid in the maintenance of ideal body weight and overall health. The elderly will benefit from reducing their intake of saturated fat and increasing their intake of complex carbohydrates and fiber, as well as increasing their intake of a diverse selection of many foods rich in naturally found vitamins and minerals. Salt and alcohol intake should be reduced, and exercise strongly encouraged.

Nutritional habits may be difficult to change, but clinicians can develop incentives for their clients for improved shopping, food preparation, and eating habits. Current research indicates that behavioral programs that emphasize reward systems tend to be the most effective in altering nutritional habits. Even though nutritional behavior is complex and affected by numerous factors, research strongly suggests that good nutritional habits can be developed and enhanced via educational and behavioral programs that are individually tailored and systematically applied.

References

Adams, C. F. (1975). *Nutritive value of American foods in common units.* (Agriculture Handbook No. 456.) Washington, DC: Agriculture Research Service, U.S. Department of Agriculture.

Aloia, J. F., Cohn, S. H., Ostuni, J. A., Cane, R., & Ellis, K. (1976). Prevention of involutional bone loss by exercise. *Annals of International Medicine, 89,* 356–358.

Aloia, J. R., Rasulo, P., Deftos, L. J., Kaswain, A., & Yen, J. K. (1985). Exercise-induced hypercalcemia and the calciotropic hormones. *Journal of Laboratory and Clinical Medicine, 106,* 229–232.

Baker, H., Frank, O., Thind, I. S., Jaslow, S. P., & Louria, D. B. (1979). Vitamin profiles in elderly persons living at home or in nursing homes versus profiles in healthy young subjects. *Journal of American Geriatrics Society, 27,* 444–450.

Bechill, W. D., & Wolgamot, I. (1973). *Nutrition for the elderly,* DHEW Publication No. SRS 73-20236. Washington, DC: U.S. Government Printing Office.

Bowman, B. B., & Rosenberg, I. H. (1982). Assessment of the nutritional status of the elderly. *American Journal of Clinical Nutrition, 35,* 1142–1152.

Braithwaite, R. (1982). The pharmokinetics of psychotropic drugs in the elderly. In D. Wheatley (Ed.), *Psychopharmacology of old age* (pp. 46–54). New York: Oxford University Press.

Brownell, K., & Kaye, F. (1982). A school-based behavior modification, nutrition education and physical activity program for obese children. *American Journal of Clinical Nutrition, 35*, 277–283.

Bunck, T., & Iwata, B. (1978). Increasing senior citizen participation in a community-based nutritious meal program. *Journal of Applied Behavioral Analysis, 11*, 75–86.

Busse, E. W. (1980). Eating in late life: Physiologic and psychologic factors. *New York State Journal of Medicine, 80*, 1496–1497.

Calloway, D. H., & Zanni, E. (1980). Energy requirements and energy expenditure of elderly men. *The American Journal of Clinical Nutrition, 33*, 2088–2092.

Cerquera, M., Casanueva, E., Ferrer, A., Fontanot, G., Chavez, A., & Flores, R. (1979). A comparison of mass media techniques and a direct method for nutrition education in rural Mexico. *Journal of Nutrition Education, 11*, 133–137.

Coates, T., Jeffrey, R., & Slinkard, L. (1981). Heart healthy eating and exercise: Introducing and maintaining changes in health behaviors. *American Journal of Public Health, 71*, 15–23.

Davis-Chervin, D., Rogers, T., & Clark, M. (1985). Influencing food selection with point-of-choice nutrition information. *Journal of Nutrition Education, 17*, 18–22.

Department of Health, Education, and Welfare. (1972). *Ten-state nutrition survey, 1968–70 V. Dietary* (Publication Number HSM 71-8133). Atlanta: USDHEW, Center for Disease Control.

DeVries, H. (1975). Physiology of exercise and aging. In D. J. Woodruff & J. Birren (Eds.), *Aging: Scientific perspectives and social issues* (pp. 257–276). Englewood Cliffs: Prentice-Hall.

Dodson, L. C., & Mullens, W. R. (1969). Some effects of jogging on psychiatric hospital patients. *American Corrective Therapy Journal, 23*, 130–134.

Dorsey, F. G. (1979). Overview of aging and risk of susceptibility to pharmacologic iatrogenic problems in the elderly. In A. J. Levenson (Ed.), *Neuropsychiatric side-effects of drugs in the elderly* (pp. 1–3). New York: Raven Press.

Driscoll, R. (1976). Anxiety reducing using physical exertion and positive images. *The Psychological Record, 26*, 87–94.

Dubbert, P., Johnson, W., Schlundt, D., & Montague, N. (1984). The influence of caloric information on cafeteria food choices. *Journal of Applied Behavior Analysis, 17*, 85–92.

Epstein, L., Masek, B., & Marshall, W. (1978). A nutritionally based school program for control of eating in obese children. *Behavior Therapy, 9*, 766–778.

Food & Nutrition Board, National Research Council. (1981). *Assessing changing food consumption patterns.* Washington, DC: National Academy Press.

Garetz, F. K. (1976). Breaking the dangerous cycle of depression and faulty nutrition. *Geriatrics, 31*, 73–75.

Gershell, W. J. (1981). Psychiatric manifestations of nutritional deficiencies in the elderly. In A. J. Levenson & R. C. Hall (Eds.), *Neuropsychiatric manifestations of physical disease in the elderly* (pp. 119–132). New York: Raven Press.

Gersovitz, M., Motil, K., & Munro, H. (1982). Human protein requirements: Assessment of the adequacy of the current Recommended Dietary Allowance for dietary protein in elderly men and women. *American Journal of Clinical Nutrition, 35*, 6–14.

Gross, R. L., & Newburne, P. (1980). Role of nutrition in immunologic function. *Physiological Review, 60*, 188–302.

Gulevich, G. (1977). Psychopharmacological treatment of the aged. In J. D. Barchas, P. A. Berger, R. D. Ciaranello, & G. R. Elliott (Eds.), *Psychopharmacology: From theory to practice* (pp. 123–148). New York: Oxford University Press.

Hallbrook, T., & Lanner, E. (1972). Serum zinc and healing of venous leg ulcer. *Lancet, 2*, 780–782.

Harrill, I., & Cervone, N. (1977). Vitamin status of older women. *American Journal of Clinical Nutrition, 30*, 431–440.

Heaney, R., Gallagher, J., & Johnston, C. (1982). Calcium nutrition and home health in elderly. *American Journal of Clinical Nutrition, 36*, 986–1013.

Herbert-Jackson, E., & Risley, T. (1977). Behavioral nutrition: Consumption of foods of the future by toddlers. *Journal of Applied Behavior Analysis, 10*, 407–413.

Holdsworth, M. D., & Davies, L. (1982). Nutrition education for the elderly. *Human Nutrition: Applied Nutrition, 36A*, 22–27.

Howels, J. G. (1975). *Modern perspectives in the psychiatry of old age.* New York: Bruner/Mazel.

Kamath, S. K. (1982). Taste acuity and aging. *The American Journal of Clinical Nutrition, 36*, 766–775.

Kohrs, M. B. (1982). Introduction: Symposium on nutrition and aging. *The American Journal of Clinical Nutrition, 36*, 733–822.

Lansky, D., & Brownell, K. (1982). Estimates of food quantity and calories: Errors in self-report among obese patients. *American Journal of Clinical Nutrition, 35*, 727–732.

Liebman, B. (1981). A look at the benefits of exercise. *Nutrition Action, 8*, 9–11.

Lynch, S. R., Finch, C., & Monsen, E. (1982). Iron states of elderly Americans. *American Journal of Clinical Nutrition, 36*, 1032–1045.

Madsen, C. H., Madsen, C. K., & Thompson, F. (1974). Increasing rural Head Start children's consumption of middle-class meals. *Journal of Applied Behavioral Analysis, 7*, 257–262.

Mayer, J. (1974, May). Aging and nutrition. *Geriatrics*, pp. 57–59.

Mayer, J., Heins, J., Vogel, J., Morrison, D., Lankester, L., & Jacobs, A. (1986). Promoting low-fat entree choices in a public cafeteria. *Journal of Applied Behavioral Analysis, 4*, 397–402.

Michocki, R. J. (1982). What to tell patients about over-the-counter drugs. *Geriatrics, 37*, 113–124.

Mishara, B., & Kastenbaum, R. (1974). Wine in the treatment of long-term geriatric patients in mental institutions. *Journal of the American Geriatrics Society, 22*, 88–94.

Morgan, W., & Pollock, M. (1970). Physical activity and cardiovascular health: Psychological aspects. *Ergopsychology Laboratory Report, 26*, 1–15.

Munro, H. N., & Young, V. R. (1978). Protein metabolism. *Postgraduate Medicine, 63*, 143–149.

National Center for Health Statistics (NCHS) (1974). *Preliminary findings of the First Health and Nutrition Examination Survey (HANES), United States (1971–1972) Dietary intake and biochemical findings.* (HRA Pub. No. 74-1219-1). Washington, DC.

Pao, E. M., & Hill, M. M. (1974). Diets of elderly, nutrition labeling and nutrition education. *Journal of Nutritional Education, 6*, 96–99.

Parfitt, A., Gallagher, J., & Heaney, R. (1982). Vitamin D and bone health in the elderly. *American Journal of Clinical Nutrition, 36*, 1014–1031.

Patten, S. E. (1982). Nutrition and the elderly: A cultural perspective. *Geriatrics, 37*, 141–144.

Posner, B. M. (1982). Nutrition education for older Americans: National policy recommendations. *Journal of the American Dietetic Association, 80*, 455–458.

Powell, R. R. (1974). Psychological effects of exercise therapy upon institutionalized geriatric mental patients. *Journal of Gerontology, 29*, 157–161.

Redfern, D. E. (1982). *Assessing the nutritional status of the elderly—State of the art.* Report of the Third Ross Roundtable on Medical Issues. (Document No. 0556). Columbus, OH: Ross Laboratories.

Rivlin, R. S. (1981). Nutrition and aging: Some unanswered questions. *The American Journal of Medicine, 71*, 337–339.

Roe, D. A. (1980). *Drug-induced nutritional deficiencies.* Westport, CT: AVI Publishing.

Rush, D., & Kristal, A. (1982). Methodologic studies during pregnancy: The reliability of the 24-hour dietary recall. *American Journal of Clinical Nutrition, 35*, 1259–1268.

Slesinger, D. P., McDivitt, M., & O'Donnell, F. M. (1980). Food patterns in an urban population: Age and sociodemographic correlates. *Journal of Gerontology, 35*, 432–441.

Sloan, R. W. (1982). How to minimize side-effects of psychoactive drugs. *Geriatrics, 37*, 51–64.

Smith, E. L., & Reddan, W. (1976). Physical activity: A modality for bone accretion in the aged. *American Journal of Roentgenology, 126*, 1297.

Smith, E. L., Reddan, W., & Smith, P. E. (1981). Physical activity and calcium modalities for bone mineral increase in aged women. *Medical Science Sports Exercise, 13*, 60–64.

Spirduso, W. (1975). Reaction and movement time as a function of age and physical activity level. *Journal of Gerontology, 30*, 435–440.

Spitzer, M. (1982). *Taste acuity in institutionalized elderly.* Paper presented at the 35th Annual Scientific Meeting of the Gerontological Society of America, Boston, MA.

Stark, L., Collins, F., Osnes, P., & Stokes, T. (1986). Using reinforcement and cueing to increase healthy snack food choices in preschoolers. *Journal of Applied Behavioral Analysis, 19*, 367–379.

Stern, M., Farquhar, J., Maccoby, N., & Russell, S. (1976). Results of a two-year health education campaign on dietary behavior: The Stanford Three Community Study. *Circulation, 54*, 826–832.

Wilson, G. T. (1984). Weight control treatments. In J. Matarazzo, S. Weiss, J. Herd, N. Miller, & S. Weiss (Eds.), *Behavioral health* (pp. 657–670). New York: John Wiley & Sons.

Wisocki, P. A. (1982). Actual and predicted responses of institutionalized elderly to the Psychiatric Reinforcement Survey Schedule. *International Journal of Behavioral Geriatrics, 1,* 4–55.

Wisocki, P. A., & Kendall, K. (1986). *Nutritional Assessment Form for Elderly Clients.* Unpublished, University of Massachusetts, Amherst.

Wiswell, R. M. (1980). Relaxation, exercise, and aging. In J. Birren & R. B. Sloane (Eds.), *Handbook of mental health and aging* (pp. 943–958). Englewood Cliffs: Prentice-Hall.

Worthington-Roberts, B. S., & Hazzard, W. R. (1982). Nutrition and aging. In C. Eisdorfer (Ed.), *Annual review of gerontology and geriatrics,* (Vol. 3, pp. 297–329). NY: Springer Publishing.

Young, C. M. (1978). Nutritional counseling for better health. In G. D. M. Burdman & R. M. Brewer (Eds.), *Health aspects of aging* (pp. 118–124). Portland, OR: Continuing Education Books.

Young, E. A. (1982). Nutrition, aging and the aged. *Medical Clinics of North America, 67,* 295–313.

Zifferblatt, S., Wilbur, C., & Pinsky, J. (1980). Changing cafeteria eating habits. *Journal of the American Dietetic Association, 76,* 15–20.

Residential Factors in Behavioral Programming for Elderly

CLAIRE MORSE AND PATRICIA A. WISOCKI

INTRODUCTION

For most of us home means shelter and food, comfort and security, opportunities for socialization and intimacy, a place for beloved possessions, and one's own personal private space in the world. For the elderly home may also mean independence and family stability.

In this chapter we will be discussing housing for the elderly. We will first present some statistics that describe where home is for most elderly. Next we will briefly address the problems experienced by elderly in urban and rural residential settings and present various alternative housing options that have been developed in recent years for them. These options include public housing, foster care homes, home sharing, hotels and rooming homes, retirement communities, and community housing. Special attention is paid to architectural design and service features important to the elderly in public housing. We will also consider the living conditions of elderly in institutions and describe some of the environmental factors that contribute to behavioral and cognitive decline of the residents. We will review the environmental-behavioral research conducted with institutionalized elderly men and women that has direct relevance to promoting behavior change through a modification of environmental factors. Finally, we will offer some comments regarding the clinical relevance of this information.

Statistical Description

Most older people (about 70%) live in homes they own (Lawton, 1979). About 5% of the population live in institutions, either nursing homes or mental institu-

CLAIRE MORSE • Department of Psychology, Guilford College, Greensboro, North Carolina 27410. PATRICIA A. WISOCKI • Department of Psychology, University of Massachusetts, Amherst, Massachusetts 01003.

tions. Approximately 9% live in special housing for the elderly (Lawton, 1980). Although the majority of the elderly live with other people, women are more likely to live alone than men, who most often live with a spouse (Newman, Zais, & Struyk, 1984). About 12% live with a child or other family member (Newman, Morgan, Marans, & Pastalan, 1976).

As one ages further these figures change. The percentage of people over 85 who live in nursing homes, mental hospitals, or total care institutions is about 20% (Vincente, Wiley, & Carrington, 1979). The population over 85 is growing and will continue to do so for some time. Thus, while institutionalization is far from the normative experience of elders, the possibility has increased that the oldest group of the population will experience institutional living. McConnell (1984) has estimated that 40% or 50% of the elderly will at some time live in an institution.

Urban Settings

A large percentage of elderly live in urban areas. Rowles (1984) has estimated that 62% of the elderly fit this classification. More than half of these people live in the central areas of a city (Kennedy & DeJong, 1977), and another 15% live in apartments or hotels (Howell, 1980b). Most older urban dwellers have "aged in place," having lived in their current dwellings for a long time (often 18 years or more) (Myers, 1982; Newman et al., 1984). These elderly face deterioration of their property and may be unable to maintain it due to financial pressures from rising costs and their own relatively fixed incomes (Golant, 1984). Their houses may be too large and difficult to manage. Widows constitute a large group of aging community dwellers who are likely to be living in older housing in need of repair and maintenance (Arling, 1976). When "gentrification" affects a city, older people are likely to be displaced by increasing rents, taxes, and housing conversions, making the area too costly for them to live there (Myers, 1982).

If they remain in their neighborhoods there may be other problems. Older people generally have established patterns of shopping and daily activities in the neighborhood (Myers, 1982). Many older people do not drive cars (Ast, 1977; Lawton, 1972) but rely on walking, public transportation, or family and friends to transport them (Brody & Lang, 1982). Often unable to journey far from their residences, they are denied access to certain goods and services that are available in the larger community and are forced to satisfy their needs in a relatively circumscribed neighborhood (Walsh, Krauss, & Regnier, 1981). Cantor (in Myers, 1982) estimates that the neighborhood for urban elderly consists of about 10 city blocks. If urban renewal or revitalization causes local shops to close or move, as is frequently the case, older people may find their access reduced still further or eliminated altogether (Myers, 1982; Regnier, 1974; Teski, 1981). For those who are physically disabled the problem is even more severe.

Patterns of socialization also recur within the area delimited by the neighborhood. Families often live close by and render many services to their elderly relations (Bultena, 1969; Troll, Miller, & Atchley, 1979). Although widows retain contact with offspring, particularly with daughters, their morale is more dependent on friends and neighbors with whom they visit and exchange assistance (Arling, 1976).

Urban elderly often express a well-founded fear of crime (Harris, 1975). They are disproportionately the victims of certain crimes, including robbery, burglary, and larceny (Cunningham, 1976; Lawton, 1980). Their concentration in central areas of the city puts them in close proximity with the young, often unemployed males likely to be suspects in crimes committed against the elderly (Cunningham, 1976).

Rural Settings

About 38% of the elderly live in small towns or rural areas (Rowles, 1984). These elderly fare worst of all in terms of housing. They tend to live in old houses that are often in poor repair and lacking adequate plumbing and heat (Atchley & Miller, 1979); they have lower incomes than urban elders (Lee & Lassey, 1980); and they tend to be far away from the services and goods available to city dwellers (Coward, 1979; Taietz & Milton, 1979) and more distant from family (Powers, Keith, & Goudy, 1979). Those elderly rural dwellers who have stopped driving may have difficulty obtaining even minimal services (Golant, 1972) and opportunities for socialization, often leaving them isolated and lonely (Kivett, 1979).

The rural elderly do not feel less satisfied overall with their lives, however. Although they may evidence higher than average scores on some specific indicators, such as negation, hopelessness, and despair (Lee & Lassey, 1980), rural elderly report general satisfaction with housing. In a study of 771 rural dwellers in 17 counties, 96% of the population recognized the need for specific repairs in their housing, but felt that it fully met their needs (Montgomery, Stubbs, & Day, 1980).

The satisfactions resulting from owning their own homes in settings in which they have lived for years appear to compensate for the objectively poor conditions (Rowles, 1980, 1984). Rural or small town dwellers know most of their neighbors, and the neighbors are often willing to provide them with community services (Philblad, 1975). This stable, supportive environment may make possible a gradual transition from full-time work to eventual death, as has been documented among the people of rural Appalachia (Lozier & Althouse, 1975). In an extensive analysis of small-town dwellers in Kansas, Windley & Scheidt (1982) found that happiness and physical and mental health were highest among those people most involved in the community, and that satisfaction with one's dwelling was an important contributor to physical and mental health.

Few elderly in urban or rural settings want to move from their homes, and few do, hoping to remain independent for as long as they can. Those who wish to relocate within a community, however, may experience health and morale benefits (Carp, 1966; Lawton, 1979; Lawton & Cohen, 1974; Sherwood, Greer, Morris & Mor, 1979). In the next section of this chapter, we will examine current trends in housing alternatives available for elderly who wish to change their residences, and we will comment on the relative merits and flaws in each.

Housing Alternatives

There are various kinds of housing that provide some supportive care without the confines of a typical nursing home or mental institution. Some alternatives have been derived from the specific resources and needs of a community. Listed below, with brief descriptions, are several possibilities.

Foster Care Homes

Foster care homes generally house from one to four residents in a single household (Eckert & Murray, 1984). Because they are small they can provide a family-like atmosphere and highly individualized attention, although there is no guarantee that such will be the case. Possible benefits from this living arrangement include integration into the life of the community, lower cost, and greater privacy and freedom of activity than are available in nursing homes. While the possibility for such care is great in terms of quality of care and numbers served, the actual number of available homes is difficult to determine, in part because definitions vary from state to state (Eckert & Murray, 1984). The total cannot be very large: only about 10% of not currently married men and 5% of not now married women live with a person unrelated to them. The opportunity to expand the numbers of foster care homes may be blocked by reluctance among families of the elderly who feel an obligation to provide care. Potential foster care providers may also experience reluctance because they mistakenly fear that their responsibility may continue until the death of the old person (Dunkle, 1983).

Community Housing

Community housing has been viewed as an intermediate step between independent living and institutional residence. The Philadelphia Geriatric Center (PGC) is a good example of a model program. The PGC has converted several single-family residences into separate apartments with a common living room, for use by many older people. This housing appeals especially to the ill and lonely elderly who live alone and may fear crime in their current neighborhoods (Brody, 1978). Although the supportive services offered by the PGC are largely those common to apartment buildings, such as maintenance and janitorial service in the common areas, residents are able to take advantage of programs offered by the PGC, and can purchase some food and housekeeping services. When Brody (1978) compared groups of people who had moved into the PGC with those who had not, she found that although residents had some complaints about the particulars of the housing, they were generally satisfied with their move. They were more satisfied than the group of applicants who had not moved. Because it modified existing buildings, the creation of community housing was relatively simple and inexpensive. Such miniprojects could be part of housing authorities' responsibilities (Eckert & Murray, 1984) if local zoning ordinances permit them.

Home Sharing

Home sharing is a good alternative for elderly willing to give up some privacy. With this arrangement, an existing home is offered (generally under the auspices of a social agency or group) to another person who rents an apartment or room with kitchen privileges. There are numerous variants of this arrangement. In one example, a younger person may occupy a room in exchange for services such as housekeeping or meal preparation and monitoring the health status of the older resident. Or a person may provide health care services to the home owner. In another example, several elderly may live together (in mutual comfort) in a single home. In addition to providing housing and "employment" to renters, this arrangement has financial, social, and security benefits for older people willing to cooperate and share with each other. It can successfully allow people to lead relatively independent lives while gaining support from others. A national effort to assist in developing home-sharing projects has been initiated under the auspices of the Grey Panthers, but this type of housing has not yet appealed to a significant number of elderly (Eckert & Murray, 1984; Strieb, 1978).

Hotels and Rooming Houses

An estimated 397,000 people reside in hotels and rooming houses of variable quality and not subject to governmental regulations. For the most part these residents are male, older than 75, living in poverty, alone, and either never married or are divorced. The choice of this type of dwelling was apparently made by some before they became elderly; for others it was the only low-cost option available once they were older. These residents are rather suspicious of social services, fear that social service agents will force them to move into an institution, and value self-sufficiency highly (Lally, Black, Thornock, & Hawkins, 1979). While some residents may have a reduced social interaction network, they do not complain about being lonely. Some have interactions with many other people, including other hotel residents and employees and neighborhood residents (Cohen & Sokolovsky, 1980). Indeed, Lally *et al.* (1979) have pointed out that hotel staff often provide valuable assistance to their clientele.

Retirement Communities

Retirement communities, in general, are specifically planned in self-contained settings, often in the Sunbelt, where the climate is mild. They are relatively costly and available primarily to middle- and upper-class elders. They are often totally or partly age segregated and may have restrictions about visits from young children. Size varies from 100 to more than 5,000 residents (Marans, Hunt, & Vakalo, 1984). They offer their residents many recreational and cultural opportunities within the community. Many also offer a kind of governance structure that may be used to influence local government to provide services the community desires.

Marans *et al.* (1984) describe five types of retirement communities based on size, resident characteristics, levels of services, and sponsorship. These types have been designated as retirement new town, retirement village, retirement subdivision, retirement residence, and continuing care retirement center. Those who live in such communities (fewer than one million people) report satisfaction with them (Sherman, 1975); they view positively the activities and services offered and enjoy the congeniality of living with other retired people (Burby & Weiss, 1967). As the residents age and begin to need more services than these communities sometimes offer, difficulties may arise that force either the resident to relocate or the community to change its policy (Lawton, Greenbaum, & Liebowitz, 1980). Either option could be traumatic.

Public Housing

Elderly individuals currently occupy over one-third of the units in public housing, which is low-rent housing provided to low-income tenants. Public housing varies in the extent to which services are offered to residents. Some settings offer a complete range of services, including skilled nursing care, intermediate care, and independent apartment dwellings, while other projects offer apartments only.

There has been some debate over the amount of services that should be provided to clientele. Concern for maintaining the elderly person's independence is at the core of the debate. Investigators who studied the effect of providing different meal services found that dependency was not increased when elderly were offered meals (Gutman, 1978; Lawton, 1976). These investigators found other interesting data, however. Gutman noted more benefits (i.e., higher morale, more socialization in and outside the residence) after elderly moved to a facility that offered self-contained suites. Lawton found that residents of congregate housing who were given a minimum of one daily meal showed improved morale, lessened loner status, and greater housing satisfaction. They also showed some minimal losses in external orientation. On the other hand, residents of the traditional public housing projects who were not given a meal, nor any type of formal programming, participated more often in activities, interacted more with other people, and had more personal interests, including keeping abreast of the news. Lawton (1976) also noted that the behavioral changes (outer adaptations) and the emotional changes (inner aspects) were in opposite directions in the two settings, which may indicate a trade-off for residents of either type of public housing.

In all types of housing it is important to consider the overall design features and the availability of services. Both elements significantly affect the elderly residents' feelings of well-being and satisfaction. In the next section we will present the research pertinent to these two aspects.

ARCHITECTURAL DESIGN FEATURES

A number of investigators have examined the differential effects of living in a high-rise apartment and a garden-style apartment complex. Some studies have found that social contact among high-rise occupants is greater than among occupants of garden or court apartments, primarily because residents have a larger pool of people with whom to interact. High-rise buildings frequently have public or common areas in which residents can meet and socialize casually. These areas are most effectively located within 30 feet of paths for traffic flow, such as at building entrances or near the elevators or mailboxes (Howell, 1980a). Perhaps as a consequence of the richer opportunities available within the facility, residents may not go outside their dwellings as frequently as do low-rise residents (Devlin, 1980; Nahemov, Lawton, & Howell, 1972).

Residents frequently enjoy watching the comings and goings of others (Howell, 1980a), and any activity outside the building tends to increase perceived and actual security among residents (Devlin, 1980; Rowles, 1981). Some residents will not welcome surveillance of their activity, however, and will want to come and go unwatched (Lawton, 1979). A balance might be struck by partially screening the public area from visual observation or by creating a variety of entrances.

Seating arrangements are also important considerations. Ideally, seats should be designed for older arthritic people who may have difficulty arising from deep, soft seats, particularly those without armrests (Howell, 1980a). Social groupings are influenced by the kinds of chairs provided. If chairs are too large or too heavy to be moved easily, residents may avoid them (Howell, 1980a).

The common areas used by residents, such as lounges, entryways, and stairways, should be well lighted and visually interesting. These are the places to present information to residents about the location and scheduling of activities, for instance. Residents use lounges that are centrally located more than those located at the ends of corridors (Howell, 1980a). When possible, they like to look out of doors, and they welcome the placement of windows at a height to allow viewing from a seated position. Residents want each floor in a building identified in a distinctive way so as to minimize the possibility of confusion. They prefer short hallways; they like cross-ventilation in their apartments and trash disposals on each floor (Zube, 1974).

Well-designed public housing for the elderly attends to these considerations and others. Safety features that are mandated by building codes must be provided along with such things as barrier-free access for wheelchairs, call buttons or phones (or more sophisticated technology), sinks and appliances installed at the proper height, windows, adequate storage space, individual control of heating, and safety controls on appliances. The units should also be designed for privacy, decorum, and individual preference (Aranyl & Goldman, 1980; Gelwichs & Newcomer, 1974;

Rose, 1978). Costs are not necessarily increased when such features are included in a building (Lawton, 1979; Lipman & Slater, 1977). For additional information the interested reader is referred to *Nursing Homes and Hostels with Care Services for the Elderly* (1979), a manual that includes useful guidelines and comments for planning a housing facility with attention to architectural, general, operational, and recreational features.

Individual apartments should offer the resident maximum opportunity for individuality, flexibility, and continuity with his or her previous life patterns (Howell, 1980a). It should be possible for a resident to provide some or all of the furniture if he or she wishes it. At all times a resident should be encouraged to add some individualized decorations, such as pictures, wall-hangings, lamps, plants, and so forth. To the extent possible, available space should be divided in accord with the resident's wishes. Moveable walls are a desirable feature in this regard. Frustrations or hazards in these realms can influence the affective and behavioral state of the client. The practitioner needs to keep such features in mind as reasons for treatment "failures" or attitudinal dissatisfaction.

Service Features

In studies probing the services desired by public housing residents, medical services top most lists (Carp, 1976; Lawton, 1975). A study by Sherwood, Greer, Morris, & Mor (1981) showed that even though off-hours nursing services were not extensively used in a public housing facility, a proposal to eliminate them was adamantly resisted. Residents felt reassured that assistance was available if needed.

Other services important to residents for maintaining their independence include: transportation to medical service providers, assistance with chores and housekeeping, meal preparation, cleaning, shopping, personal assistance (e.g., in bathing, clipping toenails, or doing laundry), day or night care, care of some prostheses, and daily monitoring to assure that the resident remains well. Social, recreational, educational, and cultural programming are desirable as well.

Some or all of these services may be offered by the housing project itself; others may be available through local government agencies. Some may be purchased from local vendors, and some may be provided by volunteers, families, friends, neighbors, or through such institutions as churches, schools, or medical centers.

While it may be vital for the elderly to receive such services from others, it is also important that they provide an exchange of goods and services among themselves (Dowd, 1975). The process of helping others may contribute to one's own sense of self-esteem and independence and may be helpful in facilitating a resident's adjustment to life in a public residence. This is an area in which behaviorists may apply their skills by developing programs that foster cooperation among residents, encourage friendships and family relations outside the residence, and support the participation of residents in the larger community. If such programs are located in neighborhoods close to resources (e.g., near the center of the city) so that residents can walk to shopping areas, attend recreational events, visit the library, or attend religious functions, greater participation is assured.

Safety and security are also of prime concern (Lawton, Nahemov, Yaffe, & Feldman, 1976). Residents often express fear of going out, particularly at night. Buildings should have well-lighted entryways, without bushes and other obstructions that might hide potential attackers. Ideally, the traffic flow is safely distant from the route residents must take to and from their residences. Some surveillance should be provided, either by residents using the buddy system, by a hired security guard, or by local police.

Access to public transportation is also an important consideration. Public transportation is underutilized when schedules are inconvenient, stops do not have shelter, routes are limited, costs are high, and the resident has difficult getting on or off the vehicle. In some areas special services for handicapped or wheelchair users are available, but older people (and younger people) are often unaware of them, despite the efforts of agencies and service providers to inform the public of their existence (Hayslip, Ritter, Poltman, & McDonnell, 1980).

For reasons of sociability, security, and reduced generational conflicts, older citizens seem to prefer living in a neighborhood which is 50% occupied by older people. According to the results of a study by Weinicke (1973), when this proportion existed, people who were concerned about the age distribution had more contact with friends and saw their children less often than those who expressed less interest in the age distribution of a neighborhood. Of course, not all elderly people want to live in such a setting. For some residents the age distribution is less important than maintaining familiarity in their environment and making their surroundings meaningful (Kalish & Knudtson, 1976).

INSTITUTIONAL SETTINGS

We will now turn our attention to those elderly who, for one reason or another, will need to move from their neighborhoods and take up residence in an institutional setting.

Those elderly residing in mental institutions and nursing homes comprise a small proportion of the elderly population. Yet for behavioral researchers, they have been the most frequently studied group of elderly (Wisocki & Mosher, 1982). Their problems are probably the most severe of all elderly; their disabilities are greater; their resources are more depleted.

The elderly in mental hospitals are usually poor, have little or no family contact, are in advanced old age (over 80 years), and suffer from impaired mental and physical functioning and multiple chronic disabilities (Gottesman, 1971). In 1980, 5.9% of admissions to state and county mental hospitals were 65 or over, while 28.9% of the patients in the same institutions are over 65 (NIMH, 1983), a fact which suggests that the majority of elderly mental hospital residents grew old within the institution.

Nursing homes are presently used by the terminally ill who require intensive nursing care, patients recuperating from an illness, those infirm elderly who lack sufficient social resources to manage themselves in the community, and former residents of state mental hospitals who were transferred to make room for younger patients. Nursing homes are currently holding a larger number of chronic patients in need of long-term custodial care than they have had in the past, due somewhat to the existence of social service programs that allow elderly to remain longer in their own homes.

Institutionalized residents are often physically inactive and socially apathetic. There is evidence that institutional milieux create dependence and decrease the functional level of their residents (Baltes, 1982; Barton, Baltes, & Orzeck, 1980; Bayne, 1971). Staff behavior is important in shaping this change. Staff often attend to and reinforce dependent behaviors of the residents and ignore independently executed behaviors. For instance, they are reluctant to wait while a resident dresses or shaves. Instead of prompting and rewarding the appropriate behavior, or re-teaching it when necessary, they simply do it for the resident (Baum, 1977; Lester & Baltes, 1978; Mikulic, 1971). Thus, as demonstrated by Avorn and Langer (1982), some residents may lose the basic skills of feeding, dressing, grooming, toileting, and locomotion, even when they are physically capable of accomplishing those tasks. Other residents may even demonstrate what DiGiovanni (1978) calls "pseu-doretardation," a condition in which the behaviors of a resident seem to indicate mental incapabilities, but are actually the result of inadequate or inappropriate stimulation and lack of attention and social/cognitive interactions. In Chapter 19 (this volume) Lou Burgio expands on the ways staff may be trained to promote positive and independent behaviors among residents.

Depression is often seen among elderly institutionalized people (Power & McCaron, 1975). Blazer (1982) asserts that long-term care facilities, characterized by routine and structured to discourage identity, connection to others, and personal effectiveness, may bring about depression. Depression can also be engendered by a loss of self-esteem accompanied by loss of friends, and/or loss of physical or intellectual capabilities, and loss of control over one's life (Simpson, Woods, & Britton, 1981). All of these may be associated with moving to a nursing home and/or growing old.

While there has been a good deal of controversy regarding the findings, some studies do indicate that relocation to a nursing home can be a traumatic event, leading to an earlier death than would be predicted for some residents (Jasnau, 1967; Kastler, Gray, & Carruth, 1968; Schooler, 1976). Other studies, however, have not documented increased mortality or have shown beneficial effects from reloca-tion (see Coffman, 1981). The effects of relocation appear dependent on the choice or control that the potential mover has, both in the current and the new residence, the similarity of the new to the old residence, and the physical features of the new environment, such as space, prosthetic aids, orientational aids and safety features in comparison with the client's current housing (Kasl & Rosenfield, 1980; Moos & Lemke, 1984; Schultz & Brenner, 1977).

Coffman (1981) has used the multidimensional concept of social support in interpreting the contradictory relocation-effect literature. Any relocation means disruption and reestablishment and the disintegration of existing support systems that must be re-created in the new location. Older people vary in the skill and success they have in reestablishing themselves, and in the amount of assistance they require. The ill, the hopeless and despairing, and the disoriented are obviously at greater risk, although some of these people are just those for whom the move is required. In Chapter 7 (this volume) Ben Handen discusses the value of social support for the elderly in greater detail.

These data remind us that it is crucial to give careful attention to the process of moving. The older person must be informed, prepared, and assured that the move is a good one. His or her anxieties should be recognized and addressed (Coffman, 1981; Lieberman, 1974). Behavior therapists are well equipped to deal with this aspect of an elderly person's life. If relocation is clearly required, programs may be designed to desensitize a person to various aspects of institutional living and to reduce fears of relocating. The incorporation of architectural designs and service features outlined in this chapter into residential placements should also result in a reduction of stress on a resident.

Nursing homes and mental institutions have been faulted for failure to provide privacy and an atmosphere of dignity for the adults who live there (Wack & Rodin, 1978). Residents are called by their first names by people they do not know; they may be treated as children; they may be left unattended for long periods of time (Gottesman & Bourestom, 1974; Moss & Halamandaris, 1977).

For older people living in close proximity, privacy is an important issue. Lawton, Liebowitz, & Charon (1970) found that after a ward was remodeled to provide more privacy to elderly residents, there was an increase in personal hygiene and mobility. In asking institutional residents about their preferences, Lawton and Bader (1970) found single rooms preferable to double rooms, particularly if the resident was elderly and in good health. Those who expressed preference for double rooms, however, showed gains in security and companionship (Lawton & Bader, 1970). This was especially true for those who were more ill than others.

For one group of relatively ill people, the opportunity to share a room and to have visual access to the activities of the institution provided some pleasure and social interaction. The watching was resented by other residents, however, who preferred to maintain more privacy in their activities (Lawton, 1980). In any case, certain basic privacy and control requirements should be respected, particularly for bathing, toileting, dressing, and conversing. Residents enjoyed privacy before moving into the nursing home and are likely to want it afterward (Lipman & Slater, 1977; Moss, 1981).

Mental institutions that house a number of geriatric patients also evidence inadequate reward structures and activity options for patients. Self-injurious behavior occurs frequently (Mishara, Robertson, & Kastenbaum, 1973) and seems dependent upon the lack of environmental "enrichment" achieved by recreation and social stimulation and the opportunity to make individual decisions (Mishara & Kastenbaum, 1972).

Institutions vary considerably in their flexibility and tolerance of individual behavioral preferences, and in providing opportunities for resident participation in decision making about individual behavior, institutional policies, and evaluation of environmental design (Carp, 1976; Moos & Lemke, 1984). These dimensions have important consequences for individual satisfaction and the maximization of individual functioning. Residents seem to be happier, more autonomous, and feel a greater sense of responsibility and individual control in those institutions that allow them to schedule their own activities. Residents who were permitted to bathe or shower according to their own preferences rather than as scheduled by someone else, to choose clothing, arrange their own mealtimes as much as possible, to go to bed and awaken according to their own wishes, and to make other decisions about their daily lives were better off than those for whom decisions were made (Schultz & Brenner, 1977). The research supporting the importance of control for maintaining one's highest level of functioning seems to suggest that institutions should be structured to provide meaningful opportunity for individual decisions whenever possible (Lipman & Slater, 1977). Langer and Rodin, in a series of reports (Langer & Rodin, 1976; Langer, Rodin, Beck, Weinman, & Spitzer, 1979; Rodin & Langer, 1977), have documented the beneficial effects of stressing personal responsibility and choice on health and morale of institutionalized elders. These investigators found that even such relatively minor choices as deciding whether to accept and care for a plant or choosing to attend a movie significantly benefited resident morale, alertness, and attitude (Rodin & Langer, 1977). Banziger and Roush (1983) found increases in self-reported control over life events, greater life satisfaction, and improved mortality rate in a group of nursing home residents given responsibility for feeding birds. Similar changes were not found in the control group who did not feed the birds. Further evidence comes from work by Reid and Ziegler (1980) and Ziegler and Reid (1983) who found that desired control was positively associated with several measures of physical and psychological well-being.

In a related study, Schultz and Hanusa (1978) observed short-term, but not long-term, benefits of providing institutional residents the opportunity to schedule visits from college students who were taking courses that included conversations with elderly. They speculate that the absence of long-term benefits in their study may have resulted from the residents' lack of control in the larger sense. The students were coming for a finite period over which the residents in fact did not have control, while the responsibility for the items in the Langer and Rodin studies was truly in the hands of the residents. Moos (1981) remarks that control and participation may be relative. For example, former soldiers residing in a highly scheduled VA center may benefit from scheduling because it is consistent with the regimentation of their prior service lives. Former housewives, on the other hand, may find the tightly scheduled and inflexible life of some institutions in conflict with the autonomy and decision making they formerly exercised over such things as mealtimes and activities (see Weisz, 1983, for further comment).

Moos and Lemke have recently developed and tested a set of instruments for assessing the qualities and characteristics of supportive, specialized institutional environments (Moos & Lemke, 1980; 1984; Lemke & Moos, 1981). These instruments measure physical and architectural features, policy and program dimensions, factors describing the group of residents as a whole (termed "suprapersonal environment"), and the quality of the social climate—its organization, cohesiveness, conflict, and the degree of influence a resident has. These tools allow more refined description of environments than has been previously attempted and might be used in evaluating the suitability of a residence for a particular client contemplating a move.

One broad finding from studies with these instruments is that facilities offering more services serve those with greater resources in both the physical and recreational realms. The more active residents had more health and assistance services provided for them than the less active residents. Residents who were more active in initiating programs and events were treated as more autonomous and had more social activities scheduled for them. On the other hand, staff and resources were not concentrated in the facilities where the residents' functional abilities were lowest and presumably more needed (Lemke & Moos, 1981).

BEHAVIORAL-ENVIRONMENTAL RESEARCH

For the elderly living in institutions, research evidence indicates that the modification of environmental design factors has profound effects on the behavior of residents. In the next section we will examine the results of studies that manipulated four types of independent variables: the arrangement of furniture, architectural design, recreational activities and objects, and beverages and food. By far, the greatest body of behavioral-environmental research has been conducted among institutional populations where the functional relationships between environmental factors and behavior are more easily examined and demonstrated. This restricted focus, however, does limit the conclusions that may be drawn from this work.

Furniture Arrangement

A number of studies have demonstrated that resident behavior changed when furniture was rearranged in their environment. For example, interactions increased when chairs were arranged around small tables rather than along the walls (Peterson, Knapp, Rosen, & Pitcher, 1977; Sommer & Ross, 1958). Cheek, Maxwell, and Weisman (1971) reported that the installation of a carpet in a psychogeriatric ward was followed by improved patient attire and behavior. Social activity during mealtimes has been increased by replacing institutional-style with family-style food service (Risley & Edwards, 1978). In that study, family-style service also improved residents' memories of the previous day's meal. Melin and Gotestam (1981) found an increase in interaction among patients and improvement in the use of tableware when meals and snacks were served at small tables instead of placing them on serving trays. The fact that these behaviors were changed by such minor alterations in the environment underscores the need to be more aware of the effects of the physical setting in determining the behavior of residents. From a research standpoint, however, conclusions are limited by the fact that no measures were taken of the maintenance of the behaviors targeted and by the lack of follow-up data.

There remain many uninvestigated facets of the behavioral-environmental intervention potential. There have been no systematic investigations of the parameters of any environmental changes in influencing residents' conduct. We do not know, for instance, how much benefit can be expected in a facility in which chairs are optimally arranged. Indeed, we do not know whether chairs around many small tables is the optimal arrangement or simply better than many chairs around a single table or chairs along the walls. The studies cited report results from a single facility. We do not know how these results apply to other settings or other resident groups. For example, the study by Cheek, Maxwell, and Weisman (1971) demonstrated benefits in only one of the two wards studied, suggesting that other undefined factors played a role in the changed behavior. We do not know how long the beneficial effects persist, nor for what groups they are appropriate or inappropriate. We do not know what aspects of the general modifications are critical and which incidental. We have little idea of the costs of the programs, or what would happen to the elderly clients if we failed to initiate changes. Interpretation of the results of specific studies is often equivocal. In the Sommer and Ross (1958) study, for example, a physical therapist introduced knitting and crocheting to residents of the ward at approximately the same time the furniture was rearranged. Magazines were also provided and nurses were asked to encourage patients to read them. These activities alone could have been responsible for increased socialization, or they could have had an interactive effect. The need for more elaborate research in this area is obvious.

Architectural Changes

The importance of matching the program and physical facilities of a housing placement to the needs of residents emerges from a study by Cornbleth (1977). Cornbleth evaluated the differential effects of a unit that had access to a large, outdoor, enclosed grassy patio and a standard, closed, residential unit for wandering residents and nonwandering ones. The wanderers achieved a greater range of physical movement on the ward with the patio; the nonwanderers on that without the patio. Neither group showed differential gains or losses in cognitive and social functioning dependent on living site, although wanderers did decline in social functioning over the 12 weeks they were observed. Unfortunately, there are no follow-up data.

Recreational Activities and Objects

The activity level of nursing home residents can be increased by providing puzzles, simple dexterity toys and games, and prompting their use (Jenkins, Felce, Lunt, & Powell, 1977). Bingo playing was encouraged among 43 psychiatrically impaired older people by awarding badges that could later be used for obtaining refreshments. In this reinforcing condition, the number of players in a session increased from 3 to 15 (Quilitch, 1974). Providing an opportunity for indoor gardening increased the participation of frail elderly residents (Powell, Felce, Jenkins, & Lunt, 1979). McClannahan and Risley (1975a) examined the nature of response to toys and objects among "gerry chair" residents, patients who were nonambulatory, often severely incapacitated, and incontinent. They found that by simply placing objects (shapes, keys, beads, building blocks) on the trays of the residents' chairs, residents increased their activities and conversation. In another study with ambulatory nursing home residents, McClannahan and Risley (1975b) pinpointed the value of prompting the use of recreational materials instead of just making them available to residents. There was an increased use of the materials available in lounges only in the prompting condition. In an earlier study, McClannahan and Risley (1974) found it was possible to increase residents' presence in a lounge area simply by paying them $.25 to respond to a few general questions while sitting there. They noted not only an increase in the number of lounge users, but an increase in mutual assistance among the residents as well. Newkirk, Feldman, Bickett, Gipson, and Lutzker (1976) substantiated this finding in a comparison of types of prompts. They found that attendance at activities was increased when a room was centrally located and when the residents were called by name to the activity. Simply announcing the activity over a loudspeaker was not as effective.

Examination of this body of literature once again reveals evidence that is suggestive rather than conclusive. The group studies of McClannahan and Risley provide basis for a statement about relationships between activity level and environmental richness, but even these studies are based on one residential setting examined over a relatively short time period. The investigators measured a limited range of behaviors and there was no follow-up information. Costs to the institution and the individuals also merit investigation, so that we may understand what choices we make when providing or failing to provide a particular environment to residents. McClannahan and Risley indicated that three of the ten residents in the 1975b study failed to utilize any of the materials. One of these was hostile to the study. Three patients had limited vision. Would auditory devices have been effective for these residents? We need to know more about the match between residents' particular specifications and the environmental factors which would facilitate interactions. Such points have been noted by McClannahan and Risley themselves, along with other matters relating to cost, equipment preferences among the residents, and the need to deal with disengagement among all residents, not merely the more disabled. The other studies describing successful "one-shot" modifications resulting in increased engagement are undeniably valuable in buttressing the general argument that inactivity is not a necessary condition of institutionalized elderly. They also demonstrate that the strategy of providing and reinforcing participation may work effectively in institutional settings. Such studies, however, do not provide the systematic data needed to understand how best to utilize limited resources to obtain the maximum participation.

Beverages and Food

Increased social interaction has been noted in studies where the independent variable has been a beverage. Blackman, Howe, and Pinkston (1976) observed that when juice and coffee were served before breakfast, the number of residents in the area increased, and there was more interaction among residents at those times. They designed a study in which juice and coffee were available on Monday, Wednesday, and Friday, but not on Tuesday and Thursday, allowing comparison of the numbers present during the different conditions. Their data show clear differentiation in the resident behaviors in the presence of juice and coffee.

Quattrochi-Tubin and Jason (1980) provided coffee to nursing home residents participating in a morning exercise program. In an ABAB design, they documented increases in the number of residents present in the lounge and the number of exercising residents above baseline levels. According to self-reports by residents and observations by nursing staff, the residents also increased their enjoyment of the social interactions.

Alcoholic beverages have also been utilized successfully. Alcohol not only has a mild medicinal value, but it is associated with recognition of residents' adult status and may evoke pleasant memories of previous social events in which the consumption of beer, wine, or liquor occurred. Kastenbaum and Slater (1964) found that sessions in which wine was offered lasted longer than those at which grape juice was available, produced more group involvement, and occasioned the development of a sort of social club among the male residents of a geriatric facility. In a later extension of this program, wine was offered over a 21-month period contingent upon earning tokens for self-care activities, helping on the ward after mealtimes, and talking with others, or noncontingently in an "enriched" control ward. Several benefits were observed in both conditions. Medication usage declined in both settings, but the decline was greater in the noncontingent enriched program; there was more socialization, particularly on the enriched ward. The token economy program was judged more valuable for the more active residents (Mishara & Kastenbaum, 1974), and staff seemed to prefer it because it maintained more self-care activities in residents (Mishara, 1978).

Carroll (1978) instituted a social hour at which residents of a mental health institution could request their own beverages (soft drink, wine, or liquor) and found that during the program regular and occasional drinkers steadily increased their participation in recreational, occupational, and musical activities.

As with the earlier group of studies, the reports on the use of beverages as reinforcers offer interesting and suggestive commentary, but lack the generality and systematization necessary to establish conditions in which the techniques will be most useful.

Overall, this body of behavioral literature has produced some systematic findings, obtained with large numbers of people, and by several investigators in diverse settings. It seems safe to conclude that social interaction level and frequency is influenced by the contingent use of several kinds of items, including beverages, social responses, and tokens exchangeable for a variety of items. In addition to more rigorous research, more extensive research is needed, however, to determine which residents are appropriate for which programs, ways to obtain maximum benefits with minimal costs, and what the long-term consequences are of such programs.

One study which specifically addresses the concern of cost-effectiveness was conducted by Frank, Klein, and Jacobs (1982). They examined the length of stay and recidivism rate in a Washington State Hospital program. A treatment program with four phases (a token economy, a therapeutic community, a transitional phase within the hospital in which residents received tokens exchangeable for privileges,

For a client living in the community:

Physical Environment   Yes   No

Is the client consistently warm and cool enough?   _____   _____
Are repairs to the house or living space needed?   _____   _____
Can the client make needed repairs or obtain the   _____   _____
   needed service?
Is the existing lighting adequate?   _____   _____
Are any of the following in need of adjustment or repair
   because they endanger the client's safety?
     Plumbing   _____   _____
     Appliances   _____   _____
     Electricity   _____   _____
     Furnishings   _____   _____
     Bathroom equipment   _____   _____
     Kitchen utensils   _____   _____
Does the client have a sense of security?
     Inside residence?   _____   _____
     Outside residence?   _____   _____
Is emergency communication and assistance available   _____   _____
   and known to the client?
Is there access from residence to outside community?   _____   _____
Is transportation available?   _____   _____

Social Environment   Yes   No

Does the client feel comfortable in social network?   _____   _____
What is the composition of the social network?
     Family members   _____   _____
     Friends   _____   _____
     Neighbors   _____   _____
Does the client belong to clubs or social groups?   _____   _____
Does the client belong to a religious organization?   _____   _____
Is the client receiving enough support to be as socially   _____   _____
   and physically involved as desired?

Relocation Prospects

Does the client need to move?   _____   _____
Does the client want to move?   _____   _____

Describe any plans already made and those which need
   to be made. What changes in living can be
   anticipated and planned for?
Are choices in residences:
            Available?   _____   _____
            Feasible?   _____   _____

For a client living in an institutional residence:

Physical Environment	Yes	No
Are the physical arrangements suitable?	_____	_____
Is there sufficient privacy?	_____	_____
Does the client have the opportunity to personalize living space?	_____	_____
Is the client given enough information about the facility to feel secure and comfortable?	_____	_____
Can the client move through the facility with ease and security?	_____	_____
Is the environment free of barriers to movement?	_____	_____
Are furnishings within the client's private space comfortable?	_____	_____
Does the client have sufficient opportunity to make meaningful choices about schedules, activities, and his or her participation?	_____	_____
Is there maximum allowance for independence and self-management?	_____	_____
Are the public areas comfortable and facilitative of socialization?	_____	_____
Is there opportunity for and encouragement of social relationships?		
Within the institution?	_____	_____
Outside the institution?	_____	_____
Describe what else might be done for this client.		

FIGURE 1.   A checklist for evaluating residential factors important to an elderly client's functional level.

and a halfway house) was compared with the standard program of institutionalization. The investigators found a savings of $20 for each $1 spent since the length of stay was shortened in the treatment group as compared with the control group. Recidivism over the time of follow-up was not significantly different for the two groups. Such an analysis can be used to evaluate the effectiveness and efficiency of programs, and with sufficient detail, can evaluate intervention strategies in terms of their outcomes, costs, and savings.

CLINICAL RELEVANCE

The clinician can make use of the information in this chapter in several ways. He or she can first evaluate a client's living arrangements and make suggestions, if necessary, for improvement or change in the physical environment. The checklist presented in Figure 1 was designed for such an evaluation.

As client and clinician work together with this checklist, targets for behavioral intervention will become apparent. For example, one client may need to acquire a more effective way of interacting with repair people. Another client may need to reduce his or her anxiety about using public transportation. A third client may need to relocate into a less independent residence, and some desensitization of fears about alternative methods of living may be helpful.

The clinician may also use this information in consulting with residential planners or staff in institutions. When therapeutic goals are specified by staff, particularly in the areas of independent self-management or socialization, information on residential factors may be incorporated into well-structured treatment programs.

Clinicians need, at least, to recognize the value of these residential factors and consider how they might be causing or maintaining some behavior problems, or inhibiting positive development or independence. The physical conditions of a residence may also restrict some treatment recommendations, especially in the areas of socialization and recreation. The clinician must know how to use effectively the existing facilities and how to make a setting more productive or enhancing for maintaining a person's self-control, self-management, and life satisfaction.

SUMMARY

Both physical and interpersonal characteristics of the residential environment of the elderly can be influential in supporting independence and a level of maximal functioning. While many questions remain concerning the mechanisms of those influences and the most effective approaches to overcoming deficits in the environment, it is already clear that continued attention to factors such as building design and environmental artifacts will be fruitful. Sufficient evidence exists to support the argument that physical features of a residence and the larger community in which the elderly live should be arranged in such a way as to make possible independent execution of the activities of daily life. In cases in which elderly people require support and assistance of some kind, experimental and observational evidence indicates that independence is maintained at the highest level of competence when only the necessary assistance is provided, when skills which may have been lost are retaught, and when independent behavior is encouraged and reinforced.

REFERENCES

Aranyl, L., & Goldman, L. L. (1980). *Design of long-term care facilities*. New York: Van Nostrand Reinhold.
Arling, G. (1976). The elderly widow and her family, neighbors and friends. *Journal of Marriage and the Family, 38*, 757–768.

Ast, G. D. (1977). Moline, Illinois: Planning a barrier-free environment for the elderly and handicapped. In M. J. Bednar (Ed.), *Barrier-free environments* (pp. 106–131). Stroudsburg, PA: Dowden, Hutchinson, and Ross.

Atchley, R. C., & Miller, S. J. (1979). Housing and households of the rural aged. In T. O. Byerts, S. C. Howell, & L. A. Pastalan (Ed.), *Environmental context of aging: Lifestyles, environmental quality and living arrangements* (pp. 62–79). New York: Garstad STPM Press.

Avorn, J., & Langer, R. E. (1982). Induced disability in nursing home patients: A controlled trial. *Journal of the American Geriatrics Society, 30,* 397–400.

Baltes, M. M. (1982). Environmental factors in dependency among nursing home residents. In T. A. Wills (Ed.), *Basic processes in helping relationships* (pp. 405–425). New York: Academic Press.

Banziger, G., & Roush, S. (1983). Nursing homes for the birds: A control-relevant intervention with bird feeders. *The Gerontologist, 23,* 527–531.

Barton, C. M., Baltes, M. M., & Orzeck, M. J. (1980). On the etiology of older nursing home residents during morning care: The role of staff behavior. *Journal of Personality and Social Psychology, 38,* 423–431.

Baum, D. J. (1977). *Warehouses for death: The nursing home industry.* Don Mills, Ontario: Bunes & MacEachern.

Bayne, J. R. (1971). Environmental modification for the older person. *The Gerontologist, 11,* 314–317.

Blackman, D. K., Howe, M., & Pinkston, E. M. (1976). Increasing participation in social interaction of the institutionalized elderly. *The Gerontologist, 16,* 69–76.

Blazer, D. G. (1982). *Depression in late life.* St. Louis: C. V. Mosby.

Brody, E. M. (1978). Community housing for the elderly. The program, the people, the decision-making process and the research. *The Gerontologist, 18,* 121–128.

Brody, E. M., & Lang, A. M. (1982). They can't do it all: Aging daughters with their aging mothers. *Generations, 7,* 18–20.

Bultena, G. (1969). Rural–urban differences in the familial interaction of the aged. *Rural Sociology, 39,* 5–15.

Burby, R. J., & Weiss, S. F. (1967). *New communities USA.* Lexington, MA: D. C. Health.

Carp, F. M. (1966). Housing and living environments of older people. In R. C. Binstock & E. Shanas (Eds.), *Handbook of aging and the social sciences* (pp. 244–271). New York: Van Nostrand Reinhold.

Carp, F. M. (1976). User evaluation of housing for the elderly. *The Gerontologist, 16,* 102–111.

Carroll, P. J. (1978). The social hour for geropsychiatric patients. *Journal of the American Geriatrics Society, 26,* 32–35.

Cheek, F. E., Maxwell, R., & Weisman, R. (1971). Carpeting the ward: An exploratory study in environmental psychiatry. *Mental Hygiene, 55,* 109–118.

Coffman, T. L. (1981). Relocation and survival of institutionalized aged: A reexamination of the evidence. *The Gerontologist, 21,* 483–500.

Cohen, C. I., & Sokolovsky, J. (1980). Social engagement versus isolation: The case of the aged in single room occupancy hotels. *The Gerontologist, 20,* 36–44.

Cornbleth, T. (1977). Effects of a protected hospital ward on wandering and nonwandering geriatric patients. *Journal of Gerontology, 32,* 573–577.

Coward, R. T. (1979). Planning community services for the rural elderly: Implications from research. *The Gerontologist, 19,* 275–282.

Cunningham, C. L. (1976). Pattern and effect of crime against the aging: The Kansas City study. In J. Goldsmith & S. S. Goldsmith (Eds.), *Crime and the elderly* (pp. 31–56). Lexington, MA: Lexington Books.

Devlin, A. S. (1980). Housing for the elderly: Cognitive considerations. *Environment and Behavior, 14,* 451–466.

DiGiovanni, L. (1978). The elderly retarded: A little known group. *The Gerontologist, 18,* 262–265.

Dowd, J. J. (1975). Aging as exchange: A preface to theory. *Journal of Gerontology, 30,* 584–594.

Dunkle, R. E. (1983). Adult foster care: Its tenuous position on the care continuum. *Journal of Sociology and Social Welfare, 10,* 56–77.

Eckert, J. K., & Murray, M. I. (1984). Alternative modes of living for the elderly. In I. Altman, M. P. Lawton, & J. Wohlwill (Eds.), *Elderly people and the environment: Human behavior and environment* (pp. 95–128). New York: Plenum.

Frank, P. J., Klein, S., & Jacobs, J. (1982). Cost-benefit analysis of a behavioral program for geriatric impatients. *Hospital and Community Psychiatry, 33,* 374–377.

Gelwichs, L. E., & Newcomer, R. J. (1974). *Planning housing environments for the elderly.* Washington, DC: National Council on the Aging.

Golant, S. M. (1972). *The residential location and spatial behavior of the elderly* (Research Paper No. 43). Chicago: University of Chicago Press.

Golant, S. M. (1984). The effects of residential and activity behaviors on old people's environmental experiences. In I. Altman, M. P. Lawton, & J. Wohlwill (Eds.), *Elderly people and the environment: Human behavior and environment* (pp. 239–278). New York: Plenum.

Gottesman, L. E. (1971). The institutionalized elderly: A new challenge. In G. L. Maddox (Ed.), *The future of aging and the aged* (pp. 54–68). Atlanta: SNPA Foundation Seminar Books.

Gottesman, L. E., & Bourestom, N. C. (1974). Why nursing homes do what they do. *The Gerontologist, 14,* 501–506.

Gutman, G. M. (1978). Issues and findings relating to multilevel accommodations for seniors. *Journal of Gerontology, 33,* 592–600.

Harris, L. (1975). *The myth and reality of aging in America.* Washington, DC: National Council on Aging.

Hayslip, B., Ritter, M. L., Poltman, R. M., & McDonnell, C. (1980). Homecare services and the rural elderly. *The Gerontologist, 20,* 192–199.

Howell, S. C. (1980a). *Designing for aging.* Cambridge, MA: MIT Press.

Howell, S. C. (1980b). Environments and aging. In C. Eisdorfer (Ed.), *Annual review of gerontology and geriatrics* (pp. 237–260). New York: Springer.

Jasnau, K. F. (1967). Individualized versus mass transfer of nonpsychotic geriatric patients from mental hospitals to nursing homes, with special reference to the death rate. *Journal of the American Geriatrics Society, 15,* 280–284.

Jenkins, J., Felce, D., Lunt, B., & Powell, L. (1977). Increasing engagement in activity of residents in old people's homes by providing recreational materials. *Behaviors Research and Therapy, 15,* 429–434.

Kalish, R. A., & Knudtson, F. W. (1976). Attachment vs. disengagement: A life-span conceptualization. *Human Development, 19,* 171–181.

Kasl, S. V., & Rosenfield, S. (1980). The residential environment and its impact on the mental health of the aged. In J. Birren & R. Sloane (Eds.), *Handbook of mental health and aging* (pp. 468–498). Englewood Cliffs, NJ: Prentice-Hall.

Kastenbaum, R., & Slater, P. E. (1964). Effects of wine on the interpersonal behavior of geriatric patients: An exploratory study. In R. Kastenbaum (Ed.), *New thoughts on old age* (pp. 191–204). New York: Springer.

Kastler, J. M., Gray, R. M., & Carruth, M. L. (1968). Involuntary relocation of the elderly. *Gerontologist, 8,* 276–279.

Kennedy, S. M., & DeJong, F. (1977). Aged in cities. Residential segregation in 10 USA central cities. *Journal of Gerontology, 32,* 97–102.

Kivett, V. R. (1979). Discriminators of loneliness among the rural elderly: Implications for intervention. *The Gerontologist, 19,* 108–115.

Lally, M., Black, E., Thornock, M., & Hawkins, J. D. (1979). Older women in single room occupancy hotels: A Seattle profile. *The Gerontologist, 19,* 67–73.

Langer, E. J., & Rodin, J. (1976). The effects of choice and enhanced personal responsibility for the aged: A field experiment in an institutional setting. *Journal of Personality and Social Psychology, 34,* 191–198.

Langer, E. J., Rodin, J., Beck, P., Weinman, C., & Spitzer, L. (1979). Environmental determinants of memory improvement in late adulthood. *Journal of Personality and Social Psychology, 37,* 2003–2013.

Lawton, M. P. (1972). Assessing the competencies of older people. In D. Kent, R. Kastenbaum, & S. Sherman (Eds.), *Research planning and action for the elderly* (pp. 122–143). New York: Behavioral Publications.

Lawton, M. P. (1975). *Planning and managing housing for the elderly.* New York: Wiley and Sons.

Lawton, M. P. (1976). The relative impact of congregate and traditional housing on elderly tenants. *The Gerontologist, 16,* 237–242.

Lawton, M. P. (1979). Therapeutic environments for the aged. In D. Canter & S. Canter (Eds.), *Designing for therapeutic environments* (pp. 233–276). New York: Wiley & Sons.

Lawton, M. P. (1980). Psychosocial and environmental approaches to the care of the senile dementia patient. In J. O. Cole & J. E. Barrett (Eds.), *Psychopathology in the aged* (pp. 265–278). New York: Raven Press.

Lawton, M. P., & Bader, J. (1970). Wish for privacy by young and old. *Journal of Gerontology, 25,* 48–54.

Lawton, M. P., & Cohen, J. (1974). The generality of housing impact on the well-being of older people. *Journal of Gerontology, 29,* 194–204.

Lawton, M. P., Liebowitz, B., & Charon, H. (1970). Physical structure and the behavior of senile patients following ward remodeling. *Aging and Human Development, 1,* 231–239.

Lawton, M. P., Nahemov, L., Yaffe, S., & Feldman, S. (1976). Psychological impact of crime and fear of crime: The elderly and public housing. In J. Goldsmith & S. Goldsmith (Eds.), *Crime and the elderly: Challenge and response.* New York: D. C. Heath.

Lawton, M. P., Greenbaum, M., & Liebowitz, B. (1980). The lifespan of housing environments for the aging. *The Gerontologist, 20,* 56–64.

Lee, G. R., & Lassey, M. L. (1980). Rural–urban differences among the elderly: Economic, social, and subjective factors. *Journal of Social Issues, 36,* 62–74.

Lemke, S., & Moos, R. H. (1981). The suprapersonal environments of sheltered care settings. *Journal of Gerontology, 36,* 233–243.

Lester, P. B., & Baltes, M. M. (1978). Functional interdependence of the social environment and the behavior of the institutionalized aged. *Journal of Gerontological Nursing, 4,* 23–27.

Lieberman, M. A. (1974). Relocation research and social policy. *The Gerontologist, 14,* 494–501.

Lipman, A., & Slater, R. (1977). Status and spatial appropriation in eight homes for older people. *The Gerontologist, 17,* 250–255.

Lozier, J., & Althouse, R. (1975). Retirement to the porch in Appalachia. *International Journal of Aging and Human Development, 6,* 7–15.

Marans, R. W., Hunt, M. E., & Vakalo, K. L. (1984). Retirement communities. In I. Altman, M. P. Lawton, & J. Wohlwill (Eds.), *Elderly people and the environment: Human behavior and environment* (pp. 57–93). New York: Plenum.

McClannahan, L. E., & Risley, T. R. (1975a). Materials for severely disturbed geriatric patients. *Nursing Homes, 24,* 10–13.

McClannahan, L. E., & Risley, T. R. (1975b). Design of living environments for nursing home residents: Increasing participation in recreation activities. *Journal of Applied Behavior Analysis, 8,* 261–268.

McConnell, E. E. (1984). A note on the lifetime risk of nursing home residency. *The Gerontologist, 24,* 193–198.

Melin, L., & Gotestam, K. G. (1981). The effects of rearranging ward routines on communication and eating behaviors of psychogeriatric patients. *Journal of Applied Behavioral Analysis, 14,* 47–52.

Mikulic, M. A. (1971). Reinforcement of independent and dependent patient behavior by nursing personnel: An exploratory study. *Nursing Research, 20,* 162–169.

Mishara, B. L. (1978). Geriatric patients who improve in token economy and general treatment programs: A multivariate analysis. *Journal of Clinical and Consulting Psychology, 46,* 1340–1348.

Mishara, B. L., & Kastenbaum, R. (1972). Self-injurious behavior and environmental change in the institutionalized elderly. *International Journal of Aging and Human Development, 4,* 133–145.

Mishara, B. L., & Kastenbaum, R. (1974). Wine in the treatment of long-term geriatric patients in mental institutions. *Journal of the American Geriatrics Society, 22,* 88–94.

Mishara, B. L., Robertson, B., & Kastenbaum, R. (1973). Self-injurious behavior in the elderly. *The Gerontologist, 13,* 311–314.

Montgomery, J. T., Stubbs, A. C., & Day, S. S. (1980). The housing environment of the rural elderly. *The Gerontologist, 20,* 444–451.

Moss, F. E., & Halamandaris, V. J. (1977). *Too old, too sick, too bad: Nursing homes in America.* Germantown, MD: Aspen Systems.

Moos, R. H. (1981). Environmental choice and control settings for older people. *Journal of Applied Social Psychology, 11,* 23–43.

Moos, R. H., & Lemke, S. (1980). Assessing the physical and architectural features of sheltered care settings. *Journal of Gerontology, 35,* 571–583.

Moos, R. H., & Lemke, S. (1984). Suggestive residential settings for older people. In I. Altman, M. P. Lawton, & J. Wohlwill (Eds.), *Elderly people and the environment: Human behavior and environment* (pp. 159–190). New York: Plenum.

Myers, P. (1982). *Aging in place: Strategies to help elderly stay in revitalizing neighborhoods.* Washington, DC: The Conservation Foundation.

Nahemov, L., Lawton, M. P., & Howell, S. C. (1972). Elderly people in tall buildings: A nationwide study. In D. J. Conway (Ed.), *Human response to tall buildings* (pp. 175–181). Stroudsburg, PA: Dowden, Hutchinson and Ross.

National Institute of Mental Health. (1983). *Mental health, United States 1983* (DHHS ADM Rockville, MD).

Newkirk, J., Feldman, S., Bickett, A., Gipson, M., & Lutzker, J. (1976). Increasing extended care facility residents' attendance at recreational events with convenient locations and personal invitations. *Journal of Applied Behavior Analysis, 9,* 207.

Newman, S., Morgan, J., Marans, S., & Pastalan, L. (1976). *Housing adjustments of older people.* Ann Arbor, MI: Institute for Social Research.

Newman, S. J., Zais, J., & Struyk, R. (1984). Housing older Americans. In I. Altman, M. P. Lawton, & J. Wohlwill (Eds.), *Elderly people and the environment: Human behavior and environment* (pp. 17–55). New York: Plenum.

Nursing Homes and Hostels with Care Services for the Elderly. (1979). Ottawa, Canada: Mortage and Housing Corporation.

Peterson, R. F., Knapp, T. J., Rosen, J. C., & Pitcher, B. F. (1977). The effects of furniture arrangement on the behavior of geriatric patients. *Behavior Therapy, 8,* 464–467.

Philblad, C. T. (1975). Culture, life style and social environment of the small town. In R. C. Atchley & T. O. Byerts (Eds.), *Rural environments and aging* (pp. 47–52). Washington, DC: Gerontological Society.

Powell, L., Felce, D., Jenkins, J., & Lunt, B. (1979). Increasing engagement in a home for the elderly by providing an indoor gardening activity. *Behaviour Research and Therapy, 17,* 127–135.

Power, C. A., & McCaron, L. T. (1975). Treatment of depression in persons residing in homes for the aged. *The Gerontologist, 15,* 132–135.

Powers, E. A., Keith, P., & Goudy, W. J. (1979). Family relationships and friendships among the rural aged. In T. O. Byerts, S. C. Howell, & L. A. Pastalan (Eds.), *Environmental context of aging: Lifestyles, environmental quality and living arrangements* (pp. 80–101). New York: Garland–STPM Press.

Quattrochi-Tubin, S., & Jason, L. A. (1980). Enhancing social interactions and activity among the elderly through stimulus control. *Journal of Applied Behavior Analysis, 13,* 159–1653.

Quilitch, H. R. (1974). Purposeful activity increased on a geriatric ward through programmed recreation. *Journal of the American Geriatrics Society, 22,* 226–229.

Regnier, V. A. (1974). Matching older person's cognition with their use of neighborhood areas. In D. H. Carson (Ed.), *Man–environment interactions,* Vol. III (pp. 19–40). New York: Halstead.

Reid, D. W., & Ziegler, M. (1980). Validity and stability of a new desired control measure pertaining to psychological adjustment of the elderly. *Journal of Gerontology, 35,* 395–402.

Risley, T. R., & Edwards, K. A. (1978). *Behavioral technology for nursing home care: Toward a system of nursing home organization and management.* Paper presented at Nova Behavioral Conference on Aging. Port St. Lucie, FL.

Rodin, J., & Langer, E. J. (1977). Long-term effects of a control-relevant intervention with the institutionalized aged. *Journal of Personality and Social Psychology, 35,* 897–902.

Rose, E. (1978). *Housing for the aged.* Westwood, England: Saxon House.

Rowles, G. D. (1980). Growing old "inside": Aging and attachment to place in an Appalachian community. In N. Datan & N. Lohmann (Eds.), *Transitions of aging* (pp. 153–170). New York: Academic Press.

Rowles, G. D. (1981). The surveillance zone and meaningful space for the aged. *The Gerontologist, 21,* 304–311.

Rowles, C. D. (1984). Aging in rural environments. In I. Altman, M. D. Lawton, & J. Wohlwill (Eds.), *Elderly people and the environment: Human behavior and environment* (pp. 129–157). New York: Plenum.

Schooler, K. K. (1976). Environmental change and the elderly. In I. Altman & J. Wohlwill (Eds.), *Environment and behavior* (pp. 265–298). New York: Plenum.

Schultz, R., & Brenner, G. (1977). Relocation of the aged: A review and theoretical analysis. *Journal of Gerontology, 32,* 323–333.

Schultz, R., & Hanusa, B. (1978). Long-term effects of control and predictability-enhancing interventions: Findings and ethical issues. *Journal of Social and Personality Psychology, 36,* 1194–1201.

Sherman, S. R. (1975). Provision of on-site services in retirement housing. *International Journal of Aging and Human Development, 6*, 229–247.

Sherwood, S., Greer, D. S., Morris, J. N., & Mor, V. (1979). *An alternative to institutionalization: The Highland Heights experiment.* Cambridge, MA: Ballinger.

Simpson, S., Woods, R., & Britton, P. (1981). Depression and engagement in a residential home for the elderly. *Behaviour Research and Therapy, 19*, 435–438.

Sommer, R., & Ross, H. (1985). Social interaction on a geriatrics ward. *International Journal of Social Psychology, 4*, 128–133.

Strieb, C. F. (1978). An alternative family form for older persons: Need and social context. *The Family Coordinator, 27*, 413–420.

Taietz, P., & Milton, S. (1979). Rural–urban differences in the structure of services for the elderly in upstate New York counties. *Journal of Gerontology, 34*, 429–437.

Teski, M. (1981). Environment, crime and the elderly. In D. Lester (Ed.), *The elderly victim of crime* (pp. 45–60). Springfield, IL: Charles C Thomas.

Troll, L., Miller, S., & Atchley, R. (1977). *Families in later life.* Belmont, CA: Wadsworth.

Vincente, L., Wiley, J. A., & Carrington, R. A. (1979). The risk of institutionalization before death. *The Gerontologist, 19*, 361–36.

Wack, J., & Rodin, J., (1978). Nursing homes for the aged: The human consequences of legislation-shaped environments. *Journal of Social Issues, 34*(4), 7–21.

Walsh, D. A., Krauss, I. K., & Regnier, V. A. (1981). Spatial ability, environmental knowledge and environmental use: The elderly. In L. S. Liben, A. H. Patterson, & N. Newcombe (Eds.), *Spatial representation and behavior across the life-span: Theory and application* (pp. 321–357). New York: Academic Press.

Weinicke, I. (1973). The appeal of age-segregated housing to the elderly poor. *International Journal of Aging and Human Development, 4*, 293–306.

Weisz, J. R. (1983). Can I control it? In P. B. Baltes & O. G. Brim (Eds.), *Life-span development and behavior* (pp. 233–300). New York: Academic Press.

Windley, P. G., & Scheidt, R. J. (1982). An ecological model of mental health among small-town rural elderly. *Journal of Gerontology, 37*, 235–242.

Wisocki, P. A., & Mosher, P. (1982). The elderly: An understudied population in behavioral research. *International Journal of Behavioral Geriatrics, 1*, 5–14.

Ziegler, M., & Reid, B. W. (1983). Correlates of changes in desired control scores and in life satisfaction among elderly persons. *International Journal of Aging and Human Development, 16*, 135–146.

Zube, M. (1974). *Community of peers: Private and public lives of residents in housing for the elderly.* Unpublished doctoral dissertation, University of Massachusetts, Amherst.

5

The Influence of Social Support Factors on the Well-Being of the Elderly

BENJAMIN L. HANDEN

INTRODUCTION

Social support has received considerable attention in the literature as researchers have noted its influence upon both psychological well-being and physical health. Nowhere is the influence of social support more strongly felt than among the elderly population. This group typically experiences a gradual (and sometimes sudden) decline in both support systems and health status over time. Therefore, if social support can, indeed, influence health and well-being, it may be that this population has the most to gain from research findings in this area. This chapter focuses upon the influence of social support factors on both the psychological and physical health of the elderly, two interrelated and overlapping subareas. I will first describe definitional and measurement issues related to social support and health. Next, I will present various theories relating social support to physical and psychological health. In the subsequent sections, I will review demographic variables, which may be useful in identifying individuals at risk for succumbing to stressful life events, and I will discuss adverse effects of social support and make some clinical recommendations of ways to use this information.

There is considerable literature relating the positive effects of social support to health among both animal and human populations. Early work in animal laboratories sought to document the effects of social support on the development of disease (e.g., Andervont, 1984; Conger, Sawrey, & Turrel, 1958; Henry & Cassel, 1969). More recently, the literature has shown relationships between the positive effects of social support and psychological and physical health among humans, from pregnancy through life transitions and old age. For example, Nuckolls, Cassel, and Kaplan (1972) have shown that women with low social support and a large number of life changes or stresses had significantly more complications of pregnancy. Others have

BENJAMIN L. HANDEN • Children's Hospital of Pittsburgh, Pittsburgh, Pennsylvania 15213-3417.

found negative correlations between social support and treatment dropout (Backeland & Lundwell, 1975), depression in women facing severe life events (Brown, Bhrolchain, & Harris, 1975), and increased rates of tuberculosis (Holmes, 1956). Lack of social support has been implicated in increased suicide rates among single and divorced men following the death of their mothers (Burch, 1972) and increased incidence of psychiatric symptoms among Asian Americans (Lin, Ensel, Simeone, & Kuo, 1979). Syme, Hyman, and Enterline (1971) demonstrated a strong correlation between both cultural and social mobility and coronary heart disease, while Berkman and Syme (1979) found increases in mortality rates among those who lacked social and community ties such as marriage, social contact, and church membership.

A number of researchers have focused upon the association between social support and health among elderly subjects. For example, Carp (1966) found that those members of an elderly housing project who were rated as unpopular (and, therefore, might be expected to have fewer or less satisfactory social supports) had a significantly greater number of nervous symptoms, such as sleeplessness, headaches, and indigestion. Lowenthal and Haven (1968) found that the presence of just one confidant separated elderly subjects who could or could not cope in the community. They also identified a strong correlation between lack of social interaction and depression. More recently, Ward, Sherman, and LaGory (1984) studied a sample of 1,185 elderly and noted that subjective assessments of social ties and support were significantly associated with well-being. Liang, Dvorkin, Kahana, and Mazian (1980) also found a relationship between social support and morale among a group of 4,863 elderly subjects. Wood and Robertson (1978) found that interactions with friends were consistently related to psychological well-being among elderly patients. However, some researchers have emphasized that the evidence regarding the contribution of social support to well-being in this population has been inconsistent (Ward *et al.*, 1984). For example, Larson's (1978) review of 30 years of research on the subjective well-being of older Americans found little association between frequency of family interactions and subjective well-being. Hoyt, Kaiser, Peters, and Babchuk (1980) noted no significant relationship between interactions with relatives or household size and the total score of a life satisfaction scale using a random sample of 124 elderly respondents. Despite findings to the contrary, social support as a factor seems to explain between 8% and 13% of the variance in physical and psychological health measures in a number of studies involving elderly subjects (e.g., Lin *et al.*, 1979; Liang *et al.*, 1980; Schooler, Pastorello, Comen, & Clark, 1981; Ward *et al.*, 1984) and, thus, appears to have a significant impact upon the overall health of this population.

DEFINITIONAL AND MEASUREMENT ISSUES

Prior to examining the clinical implications of the social support literature, one must consider a number of definitional and measurement issues that have permeated the research in this area. To some extent, these issues will limit the conclusions drawn and usefulness of the research findings to applied settings.

Definition of Social Support

Basic to an understanding of the influence of social support upon physical health and well-being is a consistent and workable definition of social support. While numerous definitions have been proposed, all have been controversial. One of the first widely accepted definitions was proposed by Cobb in 1976, as "information leading the subject to believe that he is cared for and loved, esteemed, and a member of a network of mutual obligations" (p. 300). A more recent definition was proposed by Thoits (1982), who described social support as, "the degree to which a person's basic social needs are gratified through interactions with others" (p. 147). Wallston, Alagna, DeVellis, and DeVellis (1983) defined social support as, "comfort, assistance, and/or information one receives through formal or informal contacts with individuals or groups" (p. 369). Unfortunately, these definitions cover such a wide range of situations and events that they are essentially useless from a research standpoint. Wallston *et al.* (1983) point out that social support may be considered a unitary construct only if the widely varying events subsumed within its definition have a common psychosocial impact. To the extent that such events cover numerous and diverse phenomena, social support should be considered a complex group of constructs that have only some elements in common. Thus, there is no generally accepted universal definition of social support, leaving researchers to select measurements from a rather diverse and often unrelated group of variables.

In an attempt to solve the measurement issue, most researchers have divided social support into a variety of factors that can typically be placed along one of two broad dimensions: instrumental and expressive support. Instrumental support refers to the provision of material aid, assistance, or information. Expressive support refers to more emotional aspects of support, such as serving as a confidant. For example, Lopata (1975) identified three social support factors: emotional (expressive support involving empathy, love, and caring); informational (instrumental support involving nontangible aid or help); and material (instrumental support consisting of tangible aid or help). Kahn (1979) used the terms *affect* (emotional support), *instrumental* (material and information), and *affirmation* (information that is relevant to self-evaluation) to delineate the various forms of social support. House (1981) identified four factors that appear to combine those of Kahn and Lopata: emotional (involving empathy, love, and caring); appraisal (information relevant to self-evaluation); informational (nontangible aid or coping); and instrumental (tangible aid or help). Finally, Wills (1984) proposed six factors to describe the various forms and functions of social supports: (1) esteem support (emotional support or a confidant relationship); (2) status support (marital status, membership in organizations, belongingness); (3) informational support (process through which others provide information, advice, and guidance); (4) instrumental support (tangible or material aid); (5) social companionship (involvement in social activities); and (6) motivational support (encouraging the individual to persist in problem-solving efforts).

Antonucci (1985) identified three factors that may have more research utility than the two-factor model described previously. The first factor is individual perceptions, which involves a subjective assessment of social support and may be related to what House labels as "appraisal." The inclusion of individual perceptions as a component of social support is a significant contribution for, as will be discussed in a later section, there is some evidence that this factor may be far more important than the actual level of social support (e.g., Ward *et al.*, 1984). The second factor, type, defines social support in terms of the kinds of support offered, similar to the factors emotional, informational, and instrumental used previously. Finally, Antonucci introduced outcome (the effect of social support on health status) as a major factor of social support, for while the research on social support has been grounded upon the assumption of a positive relationship between social support and health, there is some evidence that social support may be detrimental to a number of individuals under certain conditions (e.g., Baltes, 1984; Garrity, 1973).

Measurement of Social Support

While the instrumental–expressive dimensions are useful in categorizing the various factors researchers have developed to define social support, attempts at measuring social support usually fall within either a quantitative or qualitative dimension. Quantitative measures typically refer to the frequency of social contacts or interactions, while qualitative measures refer to the perception or judgment of the accessibility or adequacy of social support. Measurement of social support has varied from fairly basic and limited conceptualizations, such as membership in a church or other organization (e.g., Berkman & Syme, 1979), to the mapping of complex social networks (e.g., Levitt, Antonucci, Clark, Rotton, & Finley, 1985–1986). Yet the tendency has been to measure rather limited constructs in a unitary rather than a multidimensional fashion.

To address this measurement problem, a number of researchers have proposed more extensive approaches to the quantification of social support. Turner (1983), for example, suggested that researchers utilize three types of measurement: social integration, which involves frequency-based information on an individual's connections with others (e.g., frequency of contacts, group membership); social network analysis, the description of an individual's network based upon its size, strength of ties, density, homogeneity of membership, and dispersion of membership; and a social-psychological or perceptual approach that focuses upon perceived emotional support, need satisfaction, etc. Antonucci (1985) also introduced a tridimensional measurement approach to social support. Like Turner, she utilized subjective data about the quality of relationships (perceptual approach) as well as what she termed categorical membership, or quantitative measures of social contacts. To gain an understanding of an individual's support network, Antonucci asked respondents to identify those people who perform certain activities or functions for them and vice versa (e.g., Who would take care of the individual if he or she were sick? Who would watch the individual's house if he or she were on a trip?). Both Turner and Antonucci have opted for a measurement system that utilizes quantitative, qualitative, and descriptive data in attempting to understand an individual's level of social support.

While the majority of social support measures are quantitative ones (Ward *et al.*, 1984), it has been suggested that qualitative measures may be more strongly related to psychological and physical health than quantitative measures (House, 1981; Turner, 1983; Wills, 1984). A number of researchers who have used multiple measures of social support have typically included measures of perceived support. For example, Lin, Dean, and Ensel (1981) identified a social support factor in which subjects rated how much they had been bothered by lack of close companionship, too few close friends, and the absence of an affectionate or loving relationship. Hussiani, Neff, Newbrough, and Moore (1982) assessed perceived satisfaction and happiness with spouse and marriage, and how well the spouse was perceived as understanding one's problems. Aneshensel and Frerichs (1982) used a Sense of Support Scale in their evaluation of the relationship between stress, support, and depression. Finally, Henderson, Duncan-Jones, Adcock, Scott, and Steele (1978) developed the Interview Schedule for Social Interaction (ISSI), which measured both actual conditions of the social environment and the adequacy of the environment as perceived by the subject.

The evidence from a number of studies measuring subjective levels of social support indicates the importance of this variable. For example, Blazer (1982) found that levels of perceived social support were more strongly related (inversely) to mortality rates than frequency of contacts and availability of attachments. Heltsley and Powers (1975) demonstrated that among a group of rural elderly, perceived adequacy of social interactions was significantly correlated with marital status, age, income, housing quality, perceived health, and a rated health score. Remarkably, the subjects' perceptions of the frequency of contacts and the actual number of contacts were not significantly correlated. Ward *et al.* (1984) found that among a sample of 1,185 elderly, subjective assessments of social ties and supports were more strongly associated with well-being than objective assessment. Handen (1985) has also reported significant correlations between measures of physical and psychological health and perceived social support in a sample of 70 community-active and 47 homebound elderly.

Conversely, Schooler *et al.* (1981) and Moriwaki (1973) found that subjective measures of support had little association with morale or well-being. In fact, in both studies objective measures proved more important. Finally, Sherman (1975) compared the relationship between perceived support and social contact in a group of elderly in retired housing with those in the community. While subjects in retired housing had fewer interactions with their families and younger people, those in the community had fewer interactions with neighbors and older people. Despite these differences, both groups perceived the same sufficiency of involvement with family, neighbors, older, and younger people. Sherman's study emphasizes the importance of examining perceived support from a variety of sources, for deficits in one area may be more than compensated by strong support in another.

In summary, perceived social support appears to be significantly associated with both psychological well-being and physical health. Contradictory findings are likely due to differences and variations in the definition of social support and health, measurement tools, and population sampling techniques. The overall results of research in this area may have implications for the development of clinical interventions for the elderly. In this regard, there appears to be differences in support needs across different age groups that must be considered. Even more importantly, perceived support and actual level of social contacts are not necessarily correlated, suggesting that increasing the frequency of social interactions alone may have limited impact upon health.

Definition of Health

As with social support, defining health is often an extremely subjective and value-laden task. The possible measures of health available to the researcher are numerous. Objective measures may include life span, disease, disability, health behavior, and compliance with medical regimen. Subjective measures of health may focus upon discomfort with an illness, interpersonal relations, or life satisfaction. The measures chosen for use may reflect the norms and standards established by previous investigators as well as the personal values of the individual researcher. Research in the area of social support provides a classic example of these definitional problems. As few standards have been established, many researchers attempt to redefine health to meet their particular needs and consequently utilize unique measurement tools. Conducting research with the elderly population only adds to these difficulties. For this population especially, health is often viewed in relative terms. In many cases, it is the subjective experience of physical illness of disability that impacts most upon subsequent physical and psychological functioning. While the normal physical and psychological functioning of an elderly individual may be quite different from that of an adolescent or young adult, separate norms for the elderly population are the exception.

Measurement of Health

Investigators studying social support and health have examined both physical health (perceived and objective) and psychological health and well-being (perceived and objective). Physical health measures have typically been more straight-forward than psychological health measures. They have often consisted of counts of chronic health problems taken from lists (e.g., Antonucci & House, 1983) or indications of functional health such as an ability to walk stairs or keep house (Antonucci & House, 1983; Shanas, 1982). Subjective measures of physical health have typically involved requests to respondents to rate their general health along a three- or four-point continuum from excellent to poor (e.g., Berkman & Syme, 1979). Such measures are extremely limited and are heavily influenced by cognitive factors.

Objective measures often consist of ratings of physical illness in a dichotomous fashion (e.g., Do you have arthritis? _____ Yes _____ No) and apply equal weight to conditions that may vary considerably in the effect they have upon one's health. Chronicity, threat to survival, level of pain or disability, and psychological import have rarely been considered and may be extremely important in an examination of the relationship between social support and physical health (DiMatteo & Hays, 1981).

Measures of psychological health or well-being have also been quite controversial. Horley (1984) identified two major problems with the use of subjective well-being indicators: a need for better conceptual clarity and consistency, and a need for developing levels of well-being assessment (on both a day-to-day basis and overall life domain levels). Assessment of day-to-day well-being has all but been ignored in the literature. Many scales combine overall life and present life domain questions (e.g., "Overall, my life has been as good as I expected," and "There are times when I feel like there's no one to talk to"). The assumption that overall life outlook is as important as more immediate measures of well-being may be faulty.

In measuring well-being, researchers have used either self-report scales comprising items about perceived support (e.g., Wood, Wylie, & Sheafor, 1969) or questionnaires completed by professionals following a number of interviews with a subject (e.g., Neugarten, Havighurst, & Tobin, 1961). Some researchers have used scales that measure more specific psychological functioning or mood, such as depression or anxiety (e.g., Derogatis, Rickels, & Rock, 1976). One problem with the use of such scales is that most have been developed and validated with younger populations, and it is not known whether the results can be extrapolated to elderly individuals (Himmelfarb & Murrell, 1983). There is also some question about whether or not it is appropriate to have a single definition for a term such as *well-being* (Horley, 1984).

THEORIES OF SOCIAL SUPPORT AND HEALTH

Despite a considerable number of studies indicating that social support reduces or buffers the impact of stressful life events, only a few writers have tried to explain how social support works, and particularly why it should be related to physical and psychological health. For example, Pearlin, Lieberman, Menaghan, and Mullan (1981) suggest that social support increases self-esteem and feelings of mastery over one's environment. Consequently, positive affect is enhanced and the effect of environmental stressors is lessened. Langlie (1977) proposed two hypotheses about the relationship of social group characteristics and the prevention of poor health: (1) norms regarding health promotion vary across social groups and, therefore, affect the way in which each group exerts pressure to conform to those norms; and (2) the provision of information on health maintenance and illness prevention is related to the interactional patterns of each social group. While Langlie demonstrated the importance of both social-psychological characteristics (e.g., perceived benefits, perceived barriers, and attitudes about health prevention) and characteristics of one's social milieu (e.g., socioeconomic status, religion, contact with kin and nonkin) in predicting the level of health prevention behavior, she was unable to determine the characteristics of social support that actually influence such behavior. Lin *et al.* (1979) suggest that if social support is to have an impact upon health, it may act as an antecedent to reduce the onset of illness as well as a buffer to reduce the effects of an illness. Thus, social support serves a coping function against a potential stress–illness relationship.

Major proponents of this theory (i.e., Antonovsky, 1980; Cobb, 1976) argue that we should not expect dramatic main effects from social support. Instead, social support probably moderates the effects of major transitions in life and of unexpected crises. Therefore, individuals with strong social supports should be better able to cope with stressful life events than individuals with poor support. In the absence of such events, the amount of social support should have little or no significant influence upon one's state of health or well-being (Gore, 1978; Nuckolls *et al.*, 1972).

Thoits (1982) contended that life events themselves may lead to changes in social support. She suggested that one must first examine the interaction between changes in life events and changes in social support. Life events are typically measured by counting the number of significant events experienced by an individual over the past 6 to 12 months that resulted in a change in behavior (e.g., Holmes & Rahe, 1967; Masuda & Holmes, 1967). Many of the life events scales used in social support research contain items that will result in either direct or indirect changes in social support itself. For example, loss of a spouse through death or divorce will result in a direct change in social support, while illness or demotion at work may have more indirect effects on an individual's support system. Since many studies measure social support only during or after the occurrence of a life event (e.g., Dean, Lin, & Ensel, 1980), it is difficult to evaluate the effect of a stressor on the availability of social support. Therefore, life events may be stressful both because they require some adjustment on the part of the individual and because they deprive the individual of important support resources. The effect of life events upon the availability of social support may have a far greater impact upon health and well-being than any moderating effect of social support upon the effects of stressful life events.

Thoits (1982) recommended testing the buffering hypothesis by obtaining support levels before a life event has occurred and then holding them constant during the analysis. Utilizing data from Myers, Lindenthal, and Pepper (1971), Thoits analyzed the buffering effects of marriage on psychological distress following a number of life events. She found that undesirable life events had a significant positive effect on psychological distress measures for both married and unmarried persons, but the effect was three times larger for unmarried individuals (a difference significant at the .001 level), thereby supporting the buffering hypothesis. However, when data were analyzed from those individuals whose marital status was unchanged before and after the life events (comprising 94% of the sample), unmarried individuals had only twice the effect as married individuals, a difference that was not significant. Further analysis also indicated that initial status and subsequent number of experienced life events were unrelated, removing this as a possible confound.

More recently, Thoits (1986) has suggested that social support functions as a form of coping assistance. Coping assistance is conceptualized as falling into one of four categories: behavior problem-focused coping, cognitive problem-solving coping, behavior emotion-focused coping, and cognitive emotion-focused coping. It is the ability of significant others to provide guidance in stress management that results in the effectiveness of social support. Thoits theorized that other conditions must be met for such guidance to be helpful. This includes support from persons who are socially similar and the ability of such persons to provide empathic understanding. The proliferation of volunteer self-help groups is considered an example of the need for support from socially similar individuals. Coyne and DeLongis (1986) suggest that social support is increasingly being viewed as a "personal experience" and is based very much on a cognitive appraisal model. Therefore, objective circumstances or interactional variables are less important from a theoretical (and subsequently clinical) basis.

A number of other investigators (e.g., Berkman & Syme, 1979; Miller & Ingham, 1976; Roy, 1978) have demonstrated a relationship between social support and psychological well-being in the absence of major life events. Others who included life events in their analyses found a main effect between social support and well-being, but no buffering effect on life events (Andrews, Tennant, Hewson, & Vaillant, 1978; Lin et al., 1981).

When social support is viewed as a function of cognitive appraisal or as cognitive assessment, there are considerable implications for clinical interventions. It has been generally accepted that social support buffers the adverse psychological impact of stressful life events. The myriad definitional and measurement problems make it difficult to assess accurately the level of social support available to an individual and, subsequently, to determine who may be at risk should stressful life events occur. In the following section the author reviews the sometimes confounding effects of demographic variables that may help identify those individuals who may be at risk.

CONFOUNDING EFFECTS OF DEMOGRAPHIC VARIABLES

Sex, marital status, age, and socioeconomic status may modulate the relationship of social support and health, especially among the elderly. In fact, demographic variables often have a more significant relationship to health measures than many measures of social support (e.g., Funch & Mettlin, 1982). In this section we will examine the relationship between the most commonly researched demographic variables and health.

Sex Differences

Among elderly populations, sex differences have been particularly striking. Women have larger, more multifaceted social networks available to them in old age than men. Several studies have indicated that older women have more friends outside of the family than do older men (e.g., Bengston, Kasschau, & Ragan, 1977; Troll, Miller, & Atchley, 1978) and that elderly men have fewer social support figures in general (Levitt *et al.*, 1985– 1986). In a study of 280 elderly subjects, Lowenthal and Haven (1968) found that women were more likely to have a confidant than men. For married older women, husbands were least often mentioned as confidants, while the reverse was true for older men. The evidence indicates that women typically turn to other women, siblings, or children for social support (Troll *et al.*, 1978), while men turn to their wives (Antonucci, 1985). A number of researchers account for this difference by suggesting that women have better interpersonal skills than men. With old age, these skills become significantly more useful in expanding and strengthening social support networks (Troll *et al.*, 1979). Elderly women also appear to make better use of organized social institutions. For example, women of all ages attend church more often than men and report that religion is more important to them (Bengston *et al.*, 1977; Britton & Britton, 1972). Social ties among elderly women are strongest between mother and daughter (with whom widows tend to live) or sister and sister, a relationship that often eclipses the marital relationship in terms of closeness later in life (Troll, 1971). Cumming and Schneider (1961) report that for both older men and women, morale is higher when siblings live nearby.

Marital Status

Marriage is positively correlated with improved health status and morale. Glenn and Weaver (1981) found that married subjects have more overall life satisfaction than unmarried subjects. This may be due in part to the fact that married people have larger social networks than people who are single, divorced, or widowed (Babchuck, 1978–1979). Among the elderly, in particular, it has been reported that marriage protects against low morale (Blau, 1973). However, there is some evidence that adults of all ages who are unhappily married have poorer physical and psychological health than unmarried individuals. Additionally, while individuals who have never been married usually report less life satisfaction or happiness than those who are married, they report higher life satisfaction or happiness than widowed or divorced individuals (Gove, Hughes, & Style, 1983).

Mortality and morbidity rates seem affected by marital status. Berkman and Syme (1979) found a positive correlation between marriage and decreased mortality rates among adults between the ages of 30 and 69. Prior to that study, Kraus and Lilienfeld (1959) observed not only lower mortality rates from all causes among married subjects versus single, divorced, or widowed subjects, but also that widowers had three to five times the death rate of married men of all ages. In examining incidence of psychopathology among elderly, Pfeiffer (1973) found greatest prevalence among the separated and divorced, followed by the widowed. Married subjects had the lowest rates of psychopathology.

There may be some important sex differences in the relationship between marriage and social support. Cumming and Schneider (1961) found morale for older women to be highest among widows and lowest among married women. Since women apparently act as primary sources of social support for their husbands, they may simultaneously deprive themselves of outside sources of support so important to them (Troll *et al.*, 1978).

Age Differences

The widespread assumption that people become more socially isolated as they age is not substantiated by research evidence. In fact, most elderly have fairly adequate social support networks (Harris, 1975). The difference between young and old age groups seems to lie less in the size of the network than in the number of confidants each group possesses (Campbell, 1980). While younger adults have more nonkin in their networks than older adults (Babchuck, 1978–1979; Fischer, 1982), the number of primary and confidant relatives tends to be the same across age groups (Babchuck, 1978–1979). In examining a national sample of subjects over 21 years of age, Varoff, Douvan, and Kulka (1981) found that older respondents had less interest in acquiring additional friends and social support and reported better feelings of network adequacy than the younger subjects. In a more recent study of 719 noninstitutionalized adults comprising three age groups, 50–64, 65–74, and 75–95, Kahn and Antonucci (1983) found no differences in network size across the groups and no differences in amount of social support received. However, younger respondents provided significantly more support to others and desired more support than was available.

A strong positive relationship between age and physical illness is both self-evident and confirmed by recent statistics indicating that elderly Americans are twice as likely to face activity limitations due to chronic medical conditions as Americans between the ages of 45 and 64 years of age, and seven times as likely to be physically limited as those under 35 years of age (U.S. Department of Commerce, U.S. Bureau of the Census, 1983). The incidence of chronic conditions such as coronary heart disease, hypertension, bronchitis, arthritis, rheumatism, and diabetes is significantly higher among those over 65 years of age (U.S. Department of Commerce, 1983).

Socioeconomic Status

Decreases in socioeconomic status, education, and income are each correlated with smaller social networks, while the reverse is true for higher socioeconomic levels, education, and income (Antonucci, 1985). Fischer (1982) found that people of all age groups with higher educational levels reported more diverse and broad support networks and that those who reported higher income levels had a larger number of nonkin network members. The elderly are no exception (Babchuck, 1978–1979; Lopata, 1979). In a study of a national sample of elderly conducted by Harris (1975), elderly with reduced incomes and educational levels expressed more feelings of loneliness than elderly individuals with financial resources and higher educational attainment. Interestingly, the relationship of sex and marital status to social support may be moderated by the effects of socioeconomic status. For example, Lopata (1979) found that widows with higher levels of education were more socially integrated than those with more limited educational backgrounds.

Not surprisingly, evidence indicating differences in rates of physical and psychological illness across socioeconomic groups is also available. Lower social class is positively correlated with the incidence of mental illness (Hollingshead & Redlich, 1958) and a limited educational level is positively related to increased reports of physical illness (Christenson & Hinkle, 1961). The United States Census Bureau (U.S. Department of Commerce, 1983) has documented that a significantly higher percentage of people in lower income brackets have physical activity limitations and that lower income is also associated with higher incidence of diabetes, coronary heart disease, and hypertension.

Overall, the effect of various demographic variables on the well-being and physical health of the elderly is impressive. The evidence to date indicates that elderly women have significantly greater social networks and support figures than elderly men. Marriage also appears to be correlated with physical and psychological health across all age groups. Yet, it is possible that some widows actually have more social support than married elderly women, who often serve as the primary support source for their husbands (which may result in increased isolation for these women). It is self-evident that age is correlated with increased physical health risk, but age alone is not necessarily indicative of a decrease in psychological health. Smaller social networks may be perceived as adequate by many elderly individuals. Finally, socioeconomic status clearly affects physical health among the elderly and is positively correlated with social network size, which is felt to impinge upon psychological health in this population as well.

ADVERSE EFFECTS OF SOCIAL SUPPORT

Not all researchers conducting work in this area agree upon the importance of social support and its effect upon the health of elderly individuals. For example, Lowenthal and Boler (1965) indicated that voluntary reduction in social activity (versus involuntary reduction due to widowhood, forced retirement, or physical problems) did not necessarily affect morale or mental health status in negative ways. In their study, those subjects who had suffered losses, retirement, or physical problems had much lower morale than subjects who had not had such experiences, regardless of whether or not there was a subsequent change in social interactions. They concluded that decreased morale and poorer mental health status were due to negative life events rather than loss of social support *per se*. Other researchers have found that elderly individuals who always lived alone fared better than those elderly who had had close relationships that were eventually lost (Clark & Anderson, 1967) and better than those who failed in attempts to establish social relations (Lowenthal, 1964).

The assumption that all forms of social support are helpful has also been challenged by a number of researchers. Fiore, Becker, and Coppel (1983) studied interactions between spouses of Alzheimer patients and their social networks. They found that depression scores on the Beck Depression Inventory were unrelated to perceived supportiveness of the social network. However, depression was related to the extent of upset with the social network, either as a result of unmet expectations of support or of negative input from important others. Baltes (1984) also found that nursing home residents were less apt to engage in independent self-care if loved ones or staff punished attempts at independence.

The family therapy literature has proposed a curvilinear relationship between social support and individual functioning (Coyne & Holroyd, 1982). Family members who are worrisome, intrusive, and overprotective may discourage autonomy and personal responsibility. Conversely, underinvolvement by family members may have detrimental effects on the psychological health of the stressed individual.

The negative impact of social support upon physical and mental health status affects more than just elderly populations. Hyman (1972) examined a sample of patients with a variety of medical conditions and found that perceived preferential treatment from the family was correlated with the level of subsequent disability at work, at home, and among friends. Garrity (1973) and Lewis (1966) both reported that the more a patient's family worried or was overprotective, the less likely he or she was to return to work.

DiMatteo and Hays (1981) discussed some possible reasons that social support may be counterproductive following a serious illness. First, they hypothesized that serious illness can severely disrupt family functioning, especially if the patient requires and receives considerable support. Second, social support may undermine the patient's self-esteem, as he or she must now be viewed as an "impaired person." As a result, the patient may feel distressed at being a "burden" and infringing upon his or her loved ones' time. Also, patients may resent or be ashamed of their new status and seek to hide their feelings and concerns with others. Ironically, in an attempt to limit the amount of attention received from their social support group (in order to preserve self-esteem and not be a burden), patients may actually further detach themselves from the very sources of support they seek to keep. Finally, compliance with medical regimens is often dependent upon social support in that families who question or have concerns about the patient's treatment are less apt to encourage him or her to follow a physician's recommendations.

The research indicating potential negative effects of social support suggests that clinical interventions in this area must be well thought out. Simply providing additional support to elderly individuals as a means of improving well-being and physical health may not only be naive, but may also produce the opposite effect. In fact, the above literature suggests that some individuals receive too much social *contact*, under the guise of social *support*. Clearly, the clinician must discriminate between increased social interaction and increased social support if interventions aimed at facilitating health are to be effective. Identifying the goal associated with support (e.g., promoting independence vs. providing more contacts upon whom an individual can depend) may, in many cases, determine the type of intervention chosen.

Clinical Recommendations

The use of social support in the clinical treatment of elderly individuals is not yet well understood. Given an overall lack of understanding regarding the definition and measurement of social support, few clear-cut guidelines are available. Identifying those elderly individuals at risk for physical–psychological health problems due to exposure to stressful life events and lack of social support may be an important first step. In terms of treatment options, working with a client's cognitions and teaching a client ways to cope with stress are two key factors in the appropriate use of social support. I will discuss each of these points below.

In identifying those elderly individuals who may be at risk for increased physical and psychological health problems due to lack of social support, it is important to remember that the elderly population is not any more at risk for increased psychological difficulties than any other population. Age is not a factor. However, elderly individuals who face negative environmental stressors may be at risk for subsequent physical–psychological problems, especially if they are unmarried or in an unhappy relationship. Such stressors may be of even more concern if the stressor is forced upon the individual (e.g., forced retirement, loss of spouse). Elderly men in general appear to be at greater risk than elderly women, due to weaker social support systems. Finally, lower socioeconomic status, education, and income seem to be factors that place elderly individuals at risk. Assessing these risk factors may help to determine the degree of clinical intervention required. If social support is viewed as coping assistance, increased involvement in support groups and increased contact with individuals who are "socially similar" may be an important consideration. It may be helpful to meet with members of an elderly individual's support system to discuss appropriate support-giving strategies. Thoits (1986) stresses the importance of empathic understanding and a number of ways in which coping assistance might be provided. For example, the clinician may recommend that an individual be removed from a difficult situation (e.g., by providing a loan, locating a job). Conversely, an individual may need to learn ways of reinterpreting or reframing his or her existing circumstances so that they are less threatening. A client's therapy may focus on learning ways of affecting physiological sensations that accompany emotional states by the use of stimulants, depressants, exercise, or relaxation, for example. Or, with the use of biofeedback, a person may learn to alter his or her physiological sensations at a cognitive level.

Lehman, Ellard, and Wortman (1986) have identified types of supportive statements and behaviors that were considered helpful or unhelpful to individuals who have lost a spouse or a child. Helpful behaviors included being more available to listen or just "being there," involving the individual in social activities, and contact with similar others. Unhelpful behaviors included minimizing the individual's loss or making statements such as "I know how you feel," if the speaker had never experienced a similar loss. Such interventions should be considered for elderly individuals who may have not only lost a loved one, but may have recently retired, moved to a smaller home or apartment, or experienced physical disabilities.

The clinician may also need to focus upon attaining an appropriate balance regarding family support. This may include reducing potential secondary gain from a family who is overprotective and fostering increased independence. Ironically, such interventions may involve actually working to decrease what is perceived by the family and friends as supportive behavior.

The area of preventive interventions provides even greater opportunity to influence large groups of elderly individuals. The literature suggests that simply increasing social contact in and of itself does not necessarily improve morale, nor buffer against the negative effect of future stressful events. Instead, improving the elderly individual's subjective–cognitive assessment of available social support may be a more appropriate area of focus. A person may improve his or her perceptions about levels of support by receiving regular visits from a social worker or nurse in which assistance and support are offered. Similar results might be accomplished by providing a 24-hour on-call staff person who could be easily reached in case of emergency. Regular phone calls to homebound individuals might also decrease feelings of isolation and lack of support. Organizing groups of elderly individuals in housing projects to check on neighbors regularly with offers of instrumental support (e.g., buying groceries for a neighbor) could also increase one's perception that assistance is available if needed. Even the structure of buildings may have a profound effect on social interactions (Lawton, 1977). In addition, elderly support programs such as Meals-on-Wheels, senior citizen centers, and community meal programs can prevent the negative effects of stressful events through facilitating the perception that assistance is available if needed.

Finally, providing clinical services to an elderly individual is likely to be a short-term endeavor. Consequently, goals should focus upon obtaining appropriate social support within the community rather than having the clinician serve as a primary support source. This may require more of a family therapy approach or a community psychology form of intervention where a number of potential support sources are brought together and enlisted to assist the client.

SUMMARY

While the relationship between social support and health has received considerable empirical support, research in this area has been characterized by definitional and conceptual problems. There is little agreement about a concise, yet all-encompassing, definition of social support. Health, too, is an extremely subjective concept, and most attempts to define it have been inadequate. This lack of consistency among both social support and health measures has made it difficult to organize and compare findings across studies, to understand conflicting results, and to develop appropriate clinical interventions based upon the literature in this area.

A number of theories have been proposed to explain the positive effects of social support upon health. Some view social support as a buffer against the adverse effects of stress, while others suggest a main effect of social support on health. Some have suggested that social support prevents the onset of health problems (by providing reinforcement for healthy behavior), increases compliance with medical regimens, or improves self-esteem. Others have theorized that social support is mainly a form of coping assistance for those facing stressful life events. Whatever the mechanism, the relationship between social support and health is further complicated by demographic variables such as sex, marital status, age, and socioeconomic status. In a number of studies, more variation in individual health is explained by those confounding variables than by social support itself.

The large number of retrospective studies in the literature has made it difficult to infer a causal role for social support. In those few studies that are prospective in nature, assistance from others is often confounded with the ability of the subject to elicit and make use of social support. Numerous researchers have treated social support as a unitary rather than a multidimensional construct. Yet, even when investigators use multidimensional approaches to the measurement of social support, they rarely distinguish among the various types of social support.

Despite these difficulties, the social support literature does provide some guidance toward developing clinical interventions. We are now better able to identify those individuals who are at risk for physical or psychological health problems following stressful life events. It is understood that simply increasing social contacts does not necessarily result in higher-quality social support. The perception of available social support may be a key factor, and interventions designed to enhance such perceptions should prove more productive. Conceptualizing the process of social support as coping assistance provides the clinician with therapeutic options such as cognitive-behavioral strategies as well as traditional behavioral interventions. Finally, examining the potential negative aspects of social support also suggests clinical interventions such as limiting secondary gain and training sources of support in more appropriate ways to interact with elderly individuals facing adverse life events.

REFERENCES

Andervont, H. B. (1944). Influence of environment on mammary cancer in mice. *Journal of the National Cancer Institute, 4,* 579–581.

Andrews, G., Tennant, C., Hewson, D. M., & Vaillant, G. E. (1978). Life event stress, social support, coping style, and risk of psychological impairment. *Journal of Nervous and Mental Diseases, 166,* 307–316.

Aneshensel, C., & Frerichs, R. (1982). Stress, support, and depression: A longitudinal causal model. *Journal of Community Psychology, 10,* 363–376.

Antonovsky, A. (1980). *Health, stress, and coping.* San Francisco: Jossey-Bass.

Antonucci, T. C. (1985). Personal characteristics, social support, and social behavior. In R. H. Binstock & E. Shanas (Eds.), *Handbook of aging and the social sciences* (pp. 94–128). New York: Van Nostrand Reinhold.

Antonucci, T., & House, J. (1983). *Health and social support among the elderly.* Paper presented at the annual meeting of the American Sociological Society, Detroit, MI.

Babchuck, N. (1978–1979). Aging and primary relations. *International Journal of Aging and Human Development, 9,* 139–152.

Backeland, F., & Lundwell, L. (1975). Dropping out of treatment: A critical review. *Psychological Bulletin, 82,* 738–783.

Bailer, C. (1968). Les états névrotiques chez les personnes agées. *Gazette Medicale de France, 75,* 3415–3420.

Baltes, M. (1984). *Dependent behavior of elderly in nursing homes.* Paper presented at the annual meeting of the Association for Behavior Analysis, Nashville, TN.

Bengston, V., Kasschau, P. K., & Ragan, P. (1977). The impact of social structure on aging individuals. In J. E. Birren & K. Schaie (Eds.), *Handbook of the psychology of aging* (pp. 327–347). New York: Van Nostrand Reinhold.

Berkman, L. R., & Syme, L. (1979). Social networks, host resistance, and mortality: A nine-year follow-up study of Alamada County residents. *American Journal of Epidemiology, 109*, 186–204.

Blau, Z. (1973). *Old age in a changing society*. New York: New Viewpoints.

Blazer, D. G. (1982). Social support and mortality in an elderly population. *American Journal of Epidemiology, 115*, 684–94.

Britton, J., & Britton, J. O. (1972). *Personality changes in aging: A longitudinal study of community residents*. New York: Springer.

Brown, G. W., Bhrolchain, M. N., & Harris, T. (1975). Social class and psychiatric disturbance among women in an urban population. *Sociology, 9*, 225–254.

Burch, J. (1972). Recent bereavement in relation to suicide. *Journal of Psychosomatic Research, 16*, 361–366.

Campbell, A. (1980). *A sense of well-being in America*. New York: McGraw-Hill.

Carp, F. M. (1966). *A future for the aged*. Austin: University of Texas Press.

Christenson, W. N., & Hinkle, L. E. (1961). Differences in illness and prognostic signs in two groups of young men. *Journal of the American Medical Association, 177*, 247–253.

Clark, M., & Anderson, B. (1967). *Culture and aging*. Springfield, IL: Charles C Thomas.

Cobb, S. (1976). Social support as a moderator of life stress. *Journal of Psychosomatic Medicine, 38*, 300–314.

Conger, J. C., Sawrey, W., & Turrel, E. S. (1958). The role of social experience in the production of gastric ulcers in hooded rats placed in a conflict situation. *Journal of Abnormal Psychology, 57*, 214–220.

Coyne, J. C., & DeLongis, A. (1986). Going beyond social support: The role of social relationships in adaptation. *Journal of Consulting and Clinical Psychology, 54*, 454–460.

Coyne, J. C., & Holroyd, K. (1982). Stress, coping, and illness: A transactional perspective. In T. Millon, C. Green, & R. Meagher (Eds.), *Handbook of health care psychology* (pp. 103–28). New York: Plenum.

Cumming, E., & Schneider, D. (1961). Sibling solidarity: A property of American kinship. *American Anthropology, 63*, 498–507.

Dean, A., Lin, N., & Ensel, W. (1980). The epidemiological significance of social support in depression. In R. Simmons (Ed.), *Research in community and mental health* (pp. 77–109). New York: JAI Press.

Derogatis, L., Rickels, K., & Rock, A. (1976). The SCL-90 and the MMPI: A step in the validation of a new self-report scale. *British Journal of Psychology, 128*, 280–289.

DiMatteo, M. R., & Hays, R. (1981). Social support and serious illness. In B. H. Gottlieb (Ed.), *Social networks and social support, Vol. 4* (pp. 117–148). Beverly Hills: Sage Publications.

Fiore, J., Becker, J., & Coppel, D. B. (1983). Social network interaction: A buffer or a stress? *American Journal of Community Psychology, 11*, 423–440.

Fischer, C. (1982). *To dwell among friends: Personal networks in town and city*. Chicago: Chicago University Press.

Funch, D., & Mettlin, C. (1982). The role of support in relation to recovery from breast surgery. *Social Science and Medicine, 16*, 91–98.

Garrity, T. (1973). Vocational adjustment after first myocardial infarction: Comparative assessment of several variables suggested in the literature. *Social Science and Medicine, 7*, 705–717.

Glenn, N. D., & Weaver, C. N. (1981). The contribution of marital happiness to global happiness. *Journal of Marriage and Family, 43*, 161–168.

Gore, S. (1978). The effect of social support in moderating the health consequences of unemployment. *Journal of Health and Social Behavior, 19*, 157–165.

Gove, W. R., Hughes, M., & Style, C. B. (1983). Does marriage have positive effects on the well-being of the individual? *Journal of Health and Social Behavior, 24*, 122–131.

Handen, B. L. (1985). The effect of social support and stress on the health of community-living elderly. (Doctoral dissertation, University of Massachusetts, Amherst, 1985). *Dissertation Abstracts International, 45*, 961B.

Harris, L. (1975). *The myth and reality of aging in America*. Washington, DC: The National Council on Aging.

Heltsley, M., & Powers, R. (1975). Social interaction and perceived adequacy of interaction of the rural aged. *The Gerontologist, 15*, 533–536.

Henderson, S., Duncan-Jones, P., Adcock, S., Scott, R., & Steele, G. (1978). Social bonds in the epidemiology of neurosis: A preliminary communication. *British Journal of Psychology, 132*, 463–466.

Henry, J. P., & Cassel, J. P. (1969). Psychosocial factors in essential hypertension. *Journal of Epidemiology, 90*, 171–200.

Himmelfarb, S., & Murrell, S. (1983). Reliability and validity of five mental health scales in older people. *Journal of Gerontology, 38*, 333–339.

Hollingshead, A. B., & Redlich, F. C. (1958). *Social class and mental illness.* New York: John Wiley and Sons.

Holmes, T. (1956). Multidiscipline study of tuberculosis. In P. J. Sparer (Ed.), *Personality, stress, and tuberculosis* (pp. 65–152). New York: International Universities Press.

Holmes, T. H., & Rahe, R. H. (1967). The social readjustment rating scale. *Journal of Psychosomatic Medicine, 11*, 213–218.

Horley, J. (1984). Life satisfaction, happiness, and morale: Two problems with the use of subjective well-being indicators. *The Gerontologist, 2*, 124–127.

House, J. S. (1981). *Work stress and social support.* Reading, MA: Addison-Wesley.

Hoyt, D., Kaiser, M., Peters, G., & Babchuk, N. (1980). Life satisfaction and activity theory: A multi-dimensional approach. *Journal of Gerontology, 43*, 409–421.

Hussiani, B., Neff, J., Newbrough, J., & Moore, M. (1982). The stress-buffering role of social support and personal competence among the rural married. *Journal of Community Psychology, 10*, 409–426.

Hyman, M. D. (1972). Social isolation and performance in rehabilitation. *Journal of Chronic Diseases, 25*, 85–97.

Kahn, R. (1979). Aging and social support. In M. W. Riley (Ed.), *Aging from birth to death* (pp. 77–91). Washington, DC: American Association for the Advancement of Science.

Kahn, R., & Antonucci, T. (1983). Convoys of social support: A life-course approach. In R. H. Binstock & E. Shanas (Eds.), *Handbook of aging and the social sciences* (2nd ed., pp. 383–405). New York: Van Nostrand Reinhold.

Kraus, A. S., & Lilienfeld, A. M. (1959). Some epidemiologic aspects of the high mortality rates in the young widowed group. *Journal of Chronic Diseases, 10*, 207–217.

Langlie, J. (1977). Social networks, health beliefs, and preventive health behavior. *Journal of Health and Social Behavior, 18*, 244–260.

Larson, R. (1978). Thirty years of research on the subjective well-being of older Americans. *Journal of Gerontology, 33*, 109–125.

Lawton, M. P. (1977). The impact of the environment on aging and behavior. In J. E. Birren & W. Schaie (Eds.), *Handbook of the psychology of aging* (pp. 276–295). New York: Van Nostrand Reinhold.

Lehman, D. R., Ellard, J. H., & Wortman, C. (1986). Social support for the bereaved: Recipients' and providers' perspectives on what is helpful. *Journal of Consulting and Clinical Psychology, 54*, 436–438.

Levitt, M., Antonucci, T., Clark, M., Rotton, J., & Finley, G. (1985–1986). Social support and well-being: Preliminary indicators on two samples of the elderly. *International Journal of Aging and Human Development, 21*, 61–78.

Lewis, C. E. (1966). Factors influencing the return to work of men with congestive heart failure. *Journal of Chronic Diseases, 19*, 1193–1209.

Liang, J., Dvorkin, L., Kahana, E., & Mazian, F. (1980). Social integration and morale: A re-examination. *Journal of Gerontology, 35*, 746–757.

Lin, N., Ensel, W., Simeone, R., & Kuo, W. (1979). Social support, stressful life events, and illness: A model and empirical test. *Journal of Health and Social Behavior, 20*, 108–119.

Lin, N., Dean, A., & Ensel, W. (1981). Social support scales: A methodological note. *Schizophrenia Bulletin, 7*, 73–87.

Lopata, H. Z. (1975). Support systems of elderly urbanites: Chicago of the 1970s. *The Gerontologist, 15*, 35–41.

Lopata, H. Z. (1979). *Women and widows: Support systems.* New York: Elsvier North Holland.

Lowenthal, M. F. (1964). Social isolation and mental illness in old age. *American Sociology Review, 29*, 54–70.

Lowenthal, M. F., & Boler, D. (1965). Voluntary vs. involuntary social withdrawal. *Journal of Gerontology, 20*, 54–70.

Lowenthal, M. F., & Haven, C. (1968). Interaction and adaptation: Intimacy as a critical variable. *American Sociology Review*, *33*, 20–30.

Masuda, M., & Holmes, T. H. (1967). Magnitude estimations of social readjustments. *Journal of Psychosomatic Research*, *11*, 219–225.

Miller, P., & Ingham, J. G. (1976). Friends, confidants, and symptoms. *Social Psychology*, *11*, 51–58.

Moriwaki, S. (1973). Self-disclosure, significant others, and psychological well-being in old age. *Journal of Health and Social Behavior*, *14*, 226–232.

Myers, J., Lindenthal, J., & Pepper, M. (1971). Life events and psychiatric impairment. *Journal of Nervous and Mental Disease*, *152*, 149–157.

Neugarten, B., Havighurst, R., & Tobin, S. (1961). The measurement of life satisfaction. *Journal of Gerontology*, *16*, 134–143.

Nuckolls, K. B., Cassel, J. C., & Kaplan, B. H. (1972). Psychosocial assets, life crisis, and the prognosis of pregnancy. *American Journal of Epidemiology*, *95*, 431–441.

Pearlin, L. L., Lieberman, M. A., Menaghan, E. G., & Mullan, J. T. (1981). The stress process. *Journal of Health and Social Behavior*, *22*, 337–356.

Pfeiffer, E. (1973). *Multidimensional quantitative assessment of three populations of elderly*. Paper presented at Annual Meeting of the Gerontological Society, Miami Beach.

Roy, A. (1978). Vulnerability factors and depression in women. *British Journal of Psychology*, *133*, 106–110.

Schooler, K., Pastorello, T., Comen, A., & Clark, C. (1981). The relative impact of objective and subjective social integration on morale: A replication. *The Gerontologist*, *21*, 292 (Abstract).

Shanas, E. (1982). *National survey of the aged* (DHHS Publication No. OHDS 83-20425). Washington, DC: U.S. Government Printing Office.

Sherman, S. (1975). Patterns of contacts for residents of age-segregated and age integrated housing. *Journal of Gerontology*, *30*, 103–107.

Syme, S. L., Hyman, M. M., & Enterline, P. E. (1971). Some social and cultural factors associated with the occurrence of coronary heart disease. *Journal of Chronic Diseases*, *19*, 277–289.

Thoits, P. A. (1982). Conceptual, methodological, and theoretical problems in studying support as a buffer against life stress. *Journal of Health and Social Behavior*, *23*, 145–159.

Thoits, P. A. (1986). Social support as coping assistance. *Journal of Consulting and Clinical Psychology*, *54*, 416–423.

Troll, L. (1971). The family of later life: A decade review. *Journal of Marriage and Family*, *33*, 263–290.

Troll, L., Miller, S., & Atchley, R. (1978). *Families of later life*. Belmont, CA: Wadsworth.

Turner, R. J. (1983). Direct, indirect, and moderating effects of social support on psychological distress and associated conditions. In H. B. Kaplan (Ed.), *Psychosocial stress: Trends, theory, and research* (pp. 105–155). New York: Academic Press.

U.S. Department of Commerce, Bureau of the Census. (1983). *Statistical abstract of the United States, 1984 (104th edition)*. Washington, DC: U.S. Bureau of the Census.

Varoff, J., Douvan, E., & Kulka, R. (1981). *The inner American*. New York: Basic Books.

Wallston, B. S., Alagna, S. W., DeVellis, B. M., & DeVellis, R. F. (1983). Social support and physical health. *Health Psychology*, *2*, 367–391.

Wad, R., Sherman, S., & LaGory, M. (1984). Subjective network assessments and subjective well-being. *Journal of Gerontology*, *39*, 358–366.

Wills, T. A. (1984). Supportive functions of interpersonal relationships. In S. Cohen & L. Syme (Eds.), *Social support and health* (pp. 61–82). New York: Academic Press.

Wood, V., & Robertson, J. (1978). Friendship and kinship interaction: Differential effect on the morale of the elderly. *Journal of Marriage and Family*, *40*, 367–373.

Wood, V., Wylie, M., & Sheafor, B. (1969). Analysis of a short self-report measure of life satisfaction: Correlation with rater judgments. *Journal of Gerontology*, *24*, 465–469.

6

The Complexities of Cognitive Impairment and the Process of Aging

Brad Crenshaw

Introduction

The topic of this chapter is cognitive impairment among elderly men and women. My attempt has been first to introduce some of the complexities involved in conceptualizing cognitive deficits in this population, and then to proceed systematically to identify the prominent categories of intellectual disturbances. In general, there are two broad divisions: those cognitive disorders that are reversible, such as pseudodementia or the effects of treatable medical conditions, and those cognitive disorders that are irreversible, such as Alzheimer's disease or Korsakoff's syndrome.

Once the categories are outlined, the specific disorders identified, and their salient characteristics discussed, the next step is to survey the assessments available by which cognitive functioning can be evaluated. Naturally, the nature of these assessments varies considerably. There are screening tests that provide a quick differential diagnosis between organic and psychiatric dysfunction. There are tests of general intellectual ability, tests of specific mental capacities, and comprehensive neuropsychological batteries—all of which merit some attention. The chapter concludes with a brief look at the uncertainties of both diagnosis and treatment that are endemic to any evaluation of cognitive disturbance among elders.

The concept itself, cognitive impairment among aged men and women, is complicated by recent shifts in theoretical emphasis. Current research in the neurology of the brain, and heightened sensitivity to the socio-historical context in which elders are embedded, have made us revise the concepts by which we understand the aging of intellectual functions. Consequently, what once were essential ideas defining our notions of aging have been decisively challenged and,

BRAD CRENSHAW • Department of Psychology, University of Massachusetts, Amherst, Massachusetts 01003.

in many instances, have lost their power to persuade. For example, the prominent notion that cognitive ability peaks in young adulthood, and forever after descends significantly into senescence (Jones, 1959; Spearman, 1927), is now thought an inadequate description of the pattern of intellectual decline. It is much too crude, presuming among other things that intelligence is a unitary phenomenon the power of which uniformly leaks away. The conceptual atom of intelligence has long since been split into many composite factors (see Cattell, 1963; Guilford, 1967; Horn & Cattell, 1966). Further, many researchers have observed that the rates of decline among the elderly are not uniform at all, but are differential (Botwinick, 1977; Cornelius, 1984; Craik, 1977; Labouvie-Vief, 1985; McCarty, Siegler, & Logue, 1982; Salthouse, 1988; Sattler, 1982). In particular, the elderly typically perform well on tests measuring stored memory, and perform poorly on tests requiring the integration of novel information and high degrees of abstract thinking (Cornelius & Caspi, 1987; Horn, 1970; Horn & Donaldson, 1980; Whitbourne & Weinstock, 1986). Hence, though no one seems to dispute the decline *per se* of cognitive ability (Bondareff, 1985; Hertzog & Schaie, 1988; Willis & Baltes, 1980)[1], the decrements are selective: primary deficits are thought to lie in the hierarchical integration of functions and the power of logical thought (Denney, 1981; Hooper, Fitzgerald, & Papalia, 1971; Horn, 1982), whereas faculties that rely on experiential learning, such as the ability to find relationships or to analyze problems and devise strategies for solving them, may increase in power throughout adulthood (Horn, 1970; Horn, 1982; Whitbourne, 1985; Whitbourne & Weinstock, 1986).

Further, such declines as there are appear to occur much later in life than previously believed. The image of aging that now is swimming into focus is one of a vigorous, relatively stable adult life span concluded by a dramatic and precipitous senescence (Labouvie-Vief, 1985). By retrospectively examining the changes in performance of elders as they neared death, several longitudinal studies (Eisdorfer & Wilkie, 1973; Riegel & Riegel, 1972) have convincingly shown that decrements in cognitive ability are correlated with the distance from death, not with the distance from birth (Baltes & Labouvie, 1973; Riegel & Riegel, 1972). These studies point out that earlier correlations of cognitive deficits with age, obtained by group-average data, are confounded by the increasing incidence of pathology among aging populations (Labouvie-Vief, 1985). Intellectual declines are not necessarily intrinsic to the aging process *per se*—which is to say that the biological causation of cognitive losses is not strictly deterministic, but is a feature of the life-ecology of the individual (Fries, 1980). Aging can be influenced by diet, exercise (Brunner & Meshulam, 1970; Haskel, 1984; Plowman, Drinkwater, & Horvath, 1979; Rose & Cohen, 1977), job category, and so on. In short, a person does not passively age according to his or her genetic timetable, but rather he or she influences the process by means of his or her behaviors and decisions.

A third revision in the current literature regarding cognitive impairment of the elderly must be made because of the confounds and limitations of the data obtained

---

[1] Stankov (1988) is a dissenting voice. In a recent study he has found that declines in fluid intelligence with increasing age disappear if three attentional factors—Search, Concentration, and Attentional Flexibility—are partialed out. He finds as well that improvements in crystalized intelligence with increasing age are greater if these same attentional factors are controlled for.

by experimenters. Most investigations are either cross-sectional studies that compared two or more age groups, or studies that are limited to the elderly, but whose findings are interpreted in light of previous research of younger adults (LaRue, Dessonville, & Jarvik, 1985). Schaie and his colleagues (Nesselroade, Schaie, & Baltes, 1972; Schaie & Labouvie-Vief, 1974; Schaie & Strother, 1968) have argued persuasively that the dramatic differences obtained in cross-sectional studies, which were interpreted to mean that elders suffer significant cognitive declines, are in fact largely functions of cohort variance. Specifically, the performance of younger subjects profited significantly by the greater incidence among them of advanced education and professional training relative to the elder subjects. What were measured were cultural differences in education between the two groups, and not the effects of aging.

Even in those instances in which the detection of cognitive deficits appears relatively straightforward, it can be tricky to sort through the contributions to the decline made by the chronic illnesses, multiple medications, traumatic life stresses, and consequent depressions that often complicate the case histories. Though such complications are frequently characteristic of elders, they nonetheless are contingent pathologies, events that are secondary to the process of aging. These factors, in combination with the heterogeneity of symptoms possible when there is physiological damage within the brain, all mean that elders who suffer cognitive impairments are not a homogeneous group. That impaired elders have been thought a homogeneous population seems in part the consequence of poor communication between clinical psychology and neurology. Neuropsychology, which is a relatively recent blend of the two disciplines, now emphasizes the need to identify clinical syndromes and correlate them with specific sites of brain damage, with similar types of destructive disease processes, or with the nature and extent of functional impairment.

For example, disorders of language among elders involve the interaction of faculties responsible for sensory integration (We make sense out of verbal speech that we hear), symbolic association (We make sense out of what we read), motor skills (We form speech sounds), learned syntactic patterns, and verbal memory (Kolb & Whishaw, 1985). Damage to different areas of the brain can interrupt any one or more of these faculties to induce a complicated pattern of dysfunction. Of the aphasias, which are disorders of language apparent in speech, reading (alexia), or writing (agraphia), the symptoms can vary significantly. Broca's aphasia, for instance, is caused by lesions in the left hemisphere of the frontal lobe anterior to the central gyrus. Symptoms center on the patient's inability to talk. This inability may include a motor component, which is to say that the patient may not be able to coordinate the peripheral parts of the vocal apparatus, but more importantly the patient cannot seem to find the correct programs for articulating the words that he or she knows but cannot say. The typical Broca's patient will have adequate content to his or her speech, but poor grammar, and poor use of function words such as prepositions, conjunctions, and articles. Verbs are commonly kept to the present tense, and sentence structure is simple (Carlson, 1981).

Wernicke's aphasia, on the other hand, is a language disorder so severe that it includes forms of dementia. It is caused by lesions in the area of the first temporal gyrus in the left hemisphere, where it appears that the sound images of objects are retained. The Wernicke's patient cannot comprehend words, either written or spoken, or arrange sounds into coherent speech. In order to comprehend, the patient must be able to identify the many sounds of speech, the phonemes, and the systems of phonemes, that are the basic units of speech in a given language (Carlson, 1981). A patient, for example, may call a toothbrush a "rockdreen," which has the same number of syllables as the correct word, but obviously has different— and in this case nonsensical—phonemes. Because the Wernicke's patient cannot identify the meaningful phonemic characteristics in his or her language, and cannot arrange them into significant patterns of verbal expression, he or she speaks a "word salad": fluent verbal sounds that make no sense.

Although both disorders involve disruptions of language, their etiologies, patterns of symptoms, and the consequent disabilities to the patient are significantly different. Whereas the Broca's patient has a disorder of production (he or she can comprehend spoken and written language but has difficulty producing grammatical verbal expressions), the Wernicke's patient has a disorder of comprehension (Kolb & Whishaw, 1985). He or she can neither comprehend nor produce spoken or written language, and therefore appears demented. The impairment in effect amounts to a thought disorder. Clearly it is important to clarify the differences between two patients suffering from the two different aphasias, and important as well to distinguish Wernicke's aphasia from other pathologies, such as Korsakoff's syndrome or even severe depression. Treatments will naturally depend on diagnoses, and can vary dramatically according to the impairments they are to remediate. Further, it often is important not only to be given the appropriate treatment, but *not* to be given the inappropriate one (Boll, 1981), particularly when treatments require medications. Finally, prognoses for recovery, which may influence the further course of treatment, depend on accurate estimations of the type and extent of impairment.

A look at the array of symptoms occurring from lesions in the frontal lobes can provide a last example of the complexities attending diagnosis of cognitive impairment. The difficulty begins with the lack of homogeneity among the frontal lobes— a term that simply designates all the brain tissue in front of the central sulcus. The frontal lobes contain areas that are both functionally and anatomically distinct, and include the primary motor cortex, the premotor cortex, Broca's area, the medial cortex, and the prefrontal cortex. The prefrontal cortex itself has three regions that are functionally distinct: the dorsolateral cortex (Brodmann's areas 9, 10, 44, 45, and 46), the orbital frontal cortex (areas 11, 12, & 47), and the frontal eye fields (areas 8 and 9). Further, the frontal lobes receive projections from the visual, auditory, and somatosensory association areas by way of the parietal cortex, and from such subcortical areas as the dorsomedial nucleus of the thalamus, the caudate nucleus, and the amygdala. They send projections to the parietal and temporal association cortex, the cingulate cortex, and such subcortical structures as the basal ganglia, hippocampus, hypothalamus, the amygdala, the dorsomedial thalamus, and the brain stem (Kolb & Whishaw, 1985).

In short, the "wiring" of the frontal lobes is extraordinarily complex, and the executive functions they provide mediate activities from many other areas of the brain. Depending on the area of the trauma, the symptoms can range from disruptions in the motor programs that oversee the fine movements of the fingers, to loss of flexibility in devising mental strategies and plans for behavior. Lesions that interfere with projections to and from the dorsomedial thalamus can interfere with the patient's ability to remember temporal sequences, and to discriminate among different contexts. For example, I park my car in the same parking lot every day at the University of Massachusetts campus. My ability to remember where I parked this morning, and distinguish it from where I parked every other morning this week, depends upon my skill at discriminating the details of today's context from those of yesterday's context, even though the vast majority of those details will be identical. I park in the same lot, drive to the university along the same route, walk to my office on the identical sidewalk, in similar weather from day to day, and so forth.

Finally, trauma to the orbital frontal cortical areas alters the "highest" level of control of affective behavior, and so can cause basic alterations of personality (Carlson, 1981). Sexual behavior can change drastically: lesions in the orbital frontal cortex can reduce sexual inhibition; damage to the dorsolateral cortex can reduce sexual drive. Similarly, social behaviors may be altered significantly if the patient descends into a "pseudodepression" (Blumer & Benson, 1975), in which there is a loss of initiative, gross reductions in sexual drive, general apathy, and impoverished verbal behavior. Naturally these symptoms, and the other sorts of deficits mentioned previously, all are distressing to the patient as he or she contends with the decrements that suddenly handicap his or her ability to think, act, regulate attention, converse, love, and work. The success with which the patient surmounts the impairments, and the strategies with which the patient tries to cope, are as variable as the individual differences that distinguish one patient from another.

It is seldom very useful to reduce behavioral problems to mere tissue damage, even when the physiological damage is clearly designated. The course of behavior of brain-damaged patients is a complex function of such factors as the site and extent of actual brain damage, the individual's efforts to contend with his or her deficits, and the environmental context in which the behavior occurs (Butler & Lewis, 1977; Hussian, 1981; Kolb & Whishaw, 1985; Lezak, 1983; Sloane, 1980). Verwoerdt (1976) suggests that cognitive impairments be considered as sociopsychosomatic in nature and origin since, by doing so, the clinician arms himself or herself with an appropriate, flexible model with which to design a comprehensive, multimodal treatment to address the behavioral and emotional problems that beset the patient.

PATTERNS OF COGNITIVE IMPAIRMENT

At present, the *Diagnostic and Statistical Manual of Mental Disorders* (3rd ed., revised) (American Psychiatric Association, 1987) provides the most commonly used system for classifying the disorders and syndromes of cognitive impairment. The authors of the manual have made conceptual distinctions between a syndrome, which designates a constellation of psychological and/or behavioral signs without reference to etiology, and a disorder, which designates a particular organic mental syndrome in which the etiology is either known or presumed. Further, there is a distinction between the pathological process itself and the psychological impairment that it causes. For example, Korsakoff's syndrome is caused by a deficiency in vitamin B_1. The treatment by which, in some instances, the course of the disease is remediated—resupplying Vitamin B_1—does not address the psychological treatment needs for impaired long-term memory.

In reviewing the patterns of cognitive impairment, the DSM-III-R terminology will be used where applicable.

Reversible Disorders

It has been estimated that 10–20% of patients with cognitive impairments may have reversible causes of their intellectual deficits, or reversible components that aggravate the deficits (LaRue *et al.*, 1985; Pfeiffer, 1977). Consequently, an initial goal during the evaluation of a patient is to determine whether he or she is suffering from a disorder whose process can be reversed or halted, thereby allowing a recovery of mental function. A large number of treatable medical diseases, conditions, and medications may have profound effects on intellectual functions. For example, patients with cardiovascular diseases may have ischemic or hemorrhagic strokes, or chronically poor oxygenation of the brain, either of which may induce memory disturbances, impairments in judgment and abstract thinking, or deficits in arousal and attention (Kolb & Whishaw, 1985; Pfeiffer, 1977; Sloane, 1980). Remedy the vascular disease, and the clinician may secondarily improve the patient's mental functioning as edematous tissue reduces its swelling or hypoxic regions are reoxygenated (Pfeiffer, 1977). Similarly, infections of the central nervous system (cerebral vasculitis, fungal meningitis, viral encephalitis, neurosyphilis) may have reversible intellectual impairments (Sloane, 1980). Further, the list of metabolic intoxications that can induce reversible impairment is immense, including diabetes, hypoglycemia, vitamin deficiencies (especially thiamine), and renal toxicity, to mention a few of the more prominent disorders.

Some functions may spontaneously recover, depending on the pathology that induced the impairment. Stroke victims, for instance, may experience a gradual, if not complete, return of function (Carlson, 1981; Kolb & Whishaw, 1985; Sloane, 1980). A Broca's patient may find that his or her language skills improve over time, or a patient suffering from an amnestic syndrome may gradually reorganize and recoup his or her memory. Further, in the case of cerebral tumors, intellectual functions and characteristic features of personality can recover after surgical interventions, chemotherapy, radiation, or other medical treatments excise or shrink the tumor. Such recoveries do not necessarily happen, of course, but the point is that there are treatable causes of dementia (Freeman, 1976), and that when they are identified, the decline of mental ability may be arrested or even reversed (American Psychiatric Association, 1987).

The effects of a major depressive episode are a particular case in point. A severely depressed patient can report memory impairments, poor concentration, difficulty in thinking, and general diminishment in intellectual functioning (LaRue et al., 1985; Sloane, 1980). The patient may likewise perform poorly on neuropsychological evaluations, and intelligence tests, and thus imitate the salient features of dementia. This phenomenon has been so prevalent (Breen, Larson, Reifler, Vitaliano, & Lawrence, 1984) that it has been given a label of its own: pseudo-dementia (American Psychiatric Association, 1987; Kwentus, Hart, Lingon, Taylor, Silverman, 1986; LaRue et al., 1985). Unlike true organic dementia, however, in which little can be done to ameliorate the impairments, depression often is responsive to treatments such as antidepressive medications, psychotherapy, or ECT. In this instance, knowledge of clinical history can aid in making a differential diagnosis. It is also likely that the differential diagnosis of reversible organic brain disorders is not a task solely for a psychologist or psychiatrist alone, but should involve personnel trained in general internal medicine, particularly in the diseases likely to beset an aged population (Pfeiffer, 1977).

Irreversible Disorders

Dementia

Dementia is the most frequently used term to designate irreversible global deterioration of mental functioning. According to the DSM-III-R (American Psychiatric Association, 1987), the preeminent feature of dementia is the impairment of long- and short-term memory. Associated with these impairments are deficits in abstract thinking, poor judgment, personality changes, and decrements in such higher cortical functions as language skills and constructional ability. Aphasias, agnosias, and apraxias may also be present. The frequency of dementia is highly correlated with age: of the American population over 65 years old, anywhere between 5–15% suffer from dementia, depending on the severity of the symptoms being counted (Arie, 1986; Gottfries, 1985; LaRue et al., 1985; Powers & Doughtery, Jr., 1985; Rogers, Meyer, Mortel, Mahurin, & Judd, 1986; Winogrond & Fisk, 1983). Further, within that population, less than 1% of the dementias occur in the age group around 65 years, while 48% occur in the age group above 95 (Gottfries, 1985). At present, over 50% of nursing home residents have been diagnosed for dementia.

Cerebrovascular Disorders. There are two main groups of dementias: those caused by cerebrovascular disorders and those caused by primary degenerative disorders (Gottfries, 1985). Cerebrovascular diseases in the central nervous system may be caused by thromboses, emboli, infarctions, angiomas, cerebral hemorrhage, and hypertensive encephalopathy (Gottfries, 1985; Kolb & Whishaw, 1985). The effects of the disease are strokes, or cerebral vascular accidents (CVAs), of which there are two types. An *ischemic stroke* is caused by the interruption, such as by thrombus, embolus, or tumor, of the blood flow irrigating a portion of the brain, which deprives tissues of oxygen, nutrients, and the ability to carry away the waste products of metabolism. Lack of oxygen for even a few minutes may produce an infarct: an area of dead or dying brain tissue. A *hemorrhagic stroke* is caused by the rupture of a blood vessel, which allows open bleeding into brain tissue. As in the ischemic stroke, brain tissue is deprived of oxygen and nutrients and may suffer from the toxicity of its own waste products that accumulate. Further, the bleeding may cause hematomas that compress surrounding brain tissue, disrupt the fibers of passage from other regions of the brain, or become focal sites for seizures. If the rupture is large enough, it may also induce an ischemic stroke in the area posterior to the rupture since adequate blood flow may be impeded by the leakage (Carlson, 1981).

Damage done by the CVA depends on several factors, not the least of which is the size of the vessel that is affected: the larger the vessel, the greater the effects. The health of the remaining vessels is also important. If, for instance, the rupture occurs in an area of unusual weakness, such as an aneurysm, then the prognosis may be better than if the event occurs in a generally weak, diseased system. The presence of preexisting vascular lesions similarly influences the extent of impairment since the sum of several small lesions could be serious. Multi-infarction dementia (MID) is a particular syndrome caused by multiple strokes that occur in a weakened vascular network and cause diffuse impairments the global effects of which in sum are dementing. Further, the location of the lesion would naturally be an important determinant of the nature of the mental deficits. And finally, the presence of anastomoses can be a determining factor influencing both the nature and extent of brain functioning. Anastomoses are connections of parallel blood vessels that allow the intercommunication of blood supply between them. If one vessel is blocked, the other artery could continue to supply blood to the affected area. The presence and pattern of anastomoses are highly individualized and contribute to the singular patterns of dysfunction that may distinguish one patient from another, even though each has lesions in roughly similar areas of the brain (Carlson, 1981; Kolb & Whishaw, 1985; Rogers *et al.*, 1986).

The cerebrovascular disorder that is most likely to produce a dementia-type illness is *multi-infarct dementia*, the clinical features of which are characteristically variable. The onset of the disease is stepwise rather than insidious, and the result typically is of many lacunar infarcts rather than one large stroke (Rogers *et al.*, 1986; Sloane, 1980). Mental deficits tend to be patchy: some functions remain intact, while others are significantly and rapidly impaired. Decrements may remit over time to such an extent that only by careful testing can residual intellectual deficits be detected (Sloane, 1980). Given the repeating nature of the disease, intellectual deterioration occurs over time, affecting memory, concentration, and comprehension.

There is no specific treatment for cerebrovascular disease, though the most common remedies include anticoagulants to dissolve blood clots, drugs to produce vasodilation, medicines to reduce blood pressure, and agents to reduce cerebral edema (Kolb & Whishaw, 1985). It should be noted that there is no evidence that arteriosclerosis causes chronic dementia (Rogers *et al.*, 1986; Tomlinson, Blessed, & Roth, 1970), although the disease does increase the likelihood of cerebral hemorrhages, emboli, and thromboses (Kolb & Whishaw, 1985). The buildup of layers of plaque within the vessels reduces their flexibility, the result of which increases the pounding effect of the heart as it pumps blood. This loss of elasticity, which tends to damp out the surge of pressure, means that the pressure is smoothed further and further downstream among the smaller, more fragile capillaries.

Primary Degenerative Disorders. The primary degenerative disorders are *senile dementia* and *Alzheimer's disease*, also known as dementia of the Alzheimer's type or senile dementia of the Alzheimer's type. Currently there is debate regarding the proper classification of the primary degenerative disorders, a debate made all the more tentative since at present it is not possible to distinguish mental impairment caused by dementia-type illness from the mental dilapidation found in the "normal" aging process as it eventually erodes the reserve neural capacities of the brain. The chief reason for grouping senile dementia and dementia of the Alzheimer's type is that the structural changes in the brain are of the same kind. Senile plaques and neurofibrillary tangles are characteristic of both, as they are of normal aging as well (Dodson, 1984; Gottfries, 1985; Kwentus *et al.*, 1986). However, dementia of the Alzheimer's type is a presenile disorder and has a different hereditary pattern than senile dementia, which occurs with the onset of advanced age. The former disorder is present among an homogeneous population, whereas the latter occurs among a heterogeneous group. There also are neurochemical characteristics that separate the two disorders (Fisher, 1986; Gottfries *et al.*, 1983; Rossor, Iverson, Reynolds, Mountjoy, & Roth, 1984).

The clinical features of senile dementia have a gradual, progressive onset beginning after the age of 70. These typically include forgetfulness, apathy, preoccupation with the past, and physical enfeeblement. Loss of urinary and fecal continence is also common. There can be instances of aphasia or apraxia, but the more notable symptoms are the patient's fatigue and lack of attention span (American Psychiatric Association, 1987; Pfeiffer, 1977; Sloane, 1980).

The clinical features of senile dementia of the Alzheimer's type closely resemble those of senile dementia, though typically its onset is believed to begin among patients in their 40s or 50s. Alzheimer himself first observed senile behavior in a 51-year-old woman. The course of the disease is thought to have three stages of development corresponding to behavioral signs that emerge as the disease progresses (Dodson, 1984; Kwentus *et al.*, 1986), though not all patients follow the classical evolution of symptoms. In the initial stage the individual suffers memory losses for which he or she may try to compensate with logic or judgment. For example, the individual may keep lists of usual routines, or calendars to remind him or her of appointments. The patient may complain of difficulties in finding the right word, or show mild versions of aphasia. Spatial relationships may deteriorate initially, so that he or she gets lost easily, and constructional apraxia is also common in the early stage. Symptoms of depression and fatigue may appear, along with subtle changes in personality, such as increasing social isolation, emotional outbursts, or an uncharacteristic dependency on family members to make decisions. (Dodson, 1984; Gottfries, 1985; Kwentus *et al.*, 1986; Pfeiffer, 1977).

In the second stage, there is global impairment in the higher cortical functions. Deteriorations in language, spatial relationships, and problem-solving abilities become more pronounced, so that the patient appears confused, bewildered, and manifests gross disorientation regarding time and place (Dodson, 1984; Pfeiffer, 1977). Often the overt denial of the first stage is replaced by anxiety and restlessness. In the final stage the patient is incontinent, often exhibits abnormal neurologic reflexes, and eventually descends into mutism. Death frequently results from infections such as pneumonia or decubitous ulcers (Dodson, 1984; Kwentus *et al.*, 1986; Sloane, 1980).

In general, the search for genetic factors related to senile dementia of the Alzheimer's type has been inconclusive. Several researchers have reported familial cases that tend to be autosomal dominant (Gustafson, & Nilsson, 1982; Kwentus *et al.*, 1986; Sloane, 1980; Wurtman, 1985), and there is some familial clustering in families without dominant inheritance (Kay, 1986; Kwentus *et al.*, 1986; Wurtman, 1985). According to Kokmen (1984), family clusters may account for as much as 5–10% of senile dementia of the Alzheimer's type. Further, there is an apparent link between Down's syndrome and dementia of the Alzheimer's type: patients with Down's syndrome, particularly if they survive beyond 40, tend to develop neuro-pathological symptoms characteristic of senile dementia of the Alzheimer's type (Ball, Schapiro, & Rapoport, 1986; Burger & Vogel, 1973; Kay, 1986; Kwentus *et al.*, 1986; Sloane, 1980; Wurtman, 1985). Some investigators have proposed that the common factor between these two diseases is an inherited microtubular abnormality that contributes to the mitotic changes of Down's syndrome and the neurofibrillary abnormalities in Alzheimer's disease (Heston, Masri, & Anderson, 1981; Kwentus *et al.*, 1986). Other etiologies that have been proposed include an autoimmune response, toxin, or virus (Kwentus *et al.*, 1986; Winblad *et al.*, 1985; Wisniewski, 1978).

Several pharmacological treatments of both senile dementia and dementia of the Alzheimer's type have been attempted, though none has shown much promise. According to Gottfries (1985), disturbances in the acetylcholine system may account for many of the intellectual symptoms of dementia, and disruptions in the dopaminergic system may explain the parkinsonian symptoms. However, treatments designed to stimulate cholinergic function have given little or no benefit to the patients treated. Nor has treatment with L-dopa elicited improvement of cognitive and motor disfunctions (Gottfries, 1985; Sloane, 1980; Soininen, Koskinen, Helkala, Pigache, & Riekkinen, 1985; Winblad *et al.*, 1985; Wurtman, 1985). Finally, in one study, treatment with piracetam, a nootropic drug believed to activate mental functions, did not significantly affect cognition among patients with senile dementia of the Alzheimer's type (Growdon, Corkin, Huff, & Rosen, 1986).

Other Causes. There are several other significant organic pathologies that impair cognitive functioning, though none are as prevalent as either senile dementia or senile dementia of the Alzheimer's type. Of these pathologies, perhaps the most important is *Pick's disease*, the clinical features of which are hard to distinguish from those of the two most common forms of dementia already discussed (Kolb & Whishaw, 1985; Pfeiffer, 1977; Sloane, 1980), though Gustafson and Nilsson (1982) have completed a rating-scale study that found distinctly different clinical symptoms that may be related to the differences in the neuropathological features of the two diseases. Amnestic aphasia, apraxia, and agraphia may also be somewhat less frequent in Pick's disease than in Alzheimer's disease.

Nonetheless, the most accurate means to date of distinguishing between the two etiologies involves autopsy of diseased brains. In general, Pick's disease is characterized by a distribution of brain lesions localized in the frontal and temporal lobes, whereas senile dementia of the Alzheimer's type is a diffuse brain disease with primary lesions in the frontal cortex, temporal cortex, and hippocampus (Kolb & Whishaw, 1985; Meier-Ruge, Iwangoff, & Reichlmeier, 1984; Sloane, 1980). Although there are neurochemical differences distinguishing Pick's and Alzheimer's disease, they are quantitative, not differences in kind. In both pathologies there are reductions in glycolytic enzymes, compared to levels in healthy brains, but in Pick's disease the decreases are slightly more pronounced, which suggests a more dramatic degenerative process in the brain than that found in Alzheimer's disease (Meier-Ruge et al., 1984).

Creutzfeldt–Jacob disease is another important dementing disease of later life. The cause of this encephalopathy is thought to be a slow virus (Beck, Matthews, & Stevens, 1969; Pfeiffer, 1977), the progress of which typically is much more rapid than the course of the other presenile dementias (Kolb & Whishaw, 1985; Pfeiffer, 1977). The neuropathology consists of general cortical atrophy. Deterioration of memory capacity is marked from the outset, and declines can almost be measured daily. In a matter of months the patient can descend from normal arousal to stupor, coma, and death (Kolb & Whishaw, 1985).

Korsakoff's syndrome is a further source of dementia that bears mentioning. The symptoms include anterograde amnesia, retrograde amnesia, confabulation, apathy, meager content in conversation, and a lack of insight into the nature of the disorder (Carlson, 1981; Kolb & Whishaw, 1985). The cause of the syndrome is a deficiency of thiamine most commonly produced by chronic alcoholism, especially when accompanied by malnutrition. Thiamine is necessary for the proper metabolism of carbohydrates; without it there is a toxic intercellular accumulation of pyruvate, the effects of which are irreparable cell damage (Carlson, 1981). Alcohol provides carbohydrates to be metabolized, but because it does not also provide thiamine, and because it inhibits as well the intestinal absorption of the vitamin as it is obtained from other nutritional sources, the consequent deficiency causes irreparable brain impairment. Currently it is thought that damage is severest in the medial thalamus and the mammillary bodies of the hypothalamus, though there may be some general cerebral atrophy as well (Kolb & Whishaw, 1985). The impairment is permanent, though the progress of the syndrome can be arrested by resupplying thiamine.

Finally, there are subcortical dementias, two significant causes of which are Huntington's chorea and Parkinson's disease (Kwentus et al., 1986). *Huntington's chorea* is a progressive degenerative disease transmitted as an autosomal dominant with complete penetrance (Kolb & Whishaw, 1985; Sloane, 1980). The most salient symptoms, from which the pathology takes its name, are the agitated, involuntary movements that involve whole muscle groups or limbs, and not single muscles. At the onset the movements resemble a restless fidgiting, and as the disease progresses they become more pronounced and incessant (Carlson, 1981; Kolb & Whishaw, 1985; Sloane, 1980). The psychiatric symptoms include depression, anxiety, and eventually psychosis. Personality changes may involve impairments in recent memory, apathy, attention deficits, and a slowing of the mental processing of information (Kolb & Whishaw, 1985; Kwentus *et al.*, 1986; Sloane, 1980). Ultimately, the mental deterioration concludes in death. Upon autopsy, the brains of patients with Huntington's chorea show marked cortical atrophy. The basal ganglia likewise show an immense degeneration of their intrinsic neurons, which is the neuropathology most likely responsible for the disorders of movement that characterize the chorea. There is some evidence that in Huntington's chorea the rates of metabolism in the caudate nucleus are depressed as compared to those of age-matched controls (Metter, Riege, Kameyama, Kuhl, & Phelps, 1984).

Parkinson's disease is another subcortical disorder that manifests as dysfunctions of movement. Marttila & Rinne (1976) estimate that dementia occurs in 20–40% of patients with Parkinson's disease, the symptoms of which show the characteristic subcortical pattern of depression, memory deficits, and slowed thinking (Knight, Godfrey, & Shelton, 1988; Kwentus *et al.*, 1986). The disease appears to be related to the degeneration of the substantia nigra, particularly to the loss of the neurotransmitter dopamine (Carlson, 1981; Kolb & Whishaw, 1985). Pharmacological treatments involve prescribing the drug L-dopa, which is converted to dopamine in the brain. The aim is to activate the dopamine synapses that remain functional. Other drugs, such as amantadine, amphetamine, monoamine oxydase inhibitors, and tricyclic antidepressants, have also been used to potentiate the transmission of dopamine (Kolb & Whishaw, 1985).

ASSESSMENT OF COGNITIVE DYSFUNCTION

Despite the increasing sophistication of neurodiagnostic procedures, the assessment of cognitive impairment, particularly that of the primary degenerative dementias, remains equivocal, and requires a combination of clinical and objective assessments (Gauthier, 1985; LaRue *et al.*, 1985; Marquez, 1983). Many of the symptoms of dementia occur in common among several different etiologies, the distinguishing features of which can be identified only in postmortem studies. Further, the technology involved in these diagnostic techniques—CT scans, Positron Emission Tomography (PET), Magnetic Resonance Imaging (MRI), Single Photon Emission Computed Tomography (SPECT) (Cohen *et al.*, 1986)—is highly specialized and extremely expensive, and therefore has limited availability. And finally, in several instances there is as yet no clear distinction between necessary and sufficient criteria for diagnoses when assessing senile dementia, senile dementia of the Alzheimer's type, Pick's disease, and normal aging (Masters, 1984).

Mental Status Exam

Diagnoses commonly are made by exclusion, which requires a careful and precise description of pathological features. Typically the first step in this process is the mental status exam, which is a structured clinical interview that in its most prevalent form has eight parts (see Fig. 1).

Outline of the Mental Status Exam

I. History

    a. Symptoms
    b. Type of onset
    c. Duration
    d. Family history

II. Insight

III. Orientation

    a. Person
       1. Name
       2. Identity
    b. Place
    c. Time
       1. Time of day
       2. Date
       3. Season

IV. Memory

    a. Recent
       1. Personal
       2. Historical past
    b. Remote
       1. Today
       2. Last night
    c. Learning
       1. Short-term memory
       2. Long-term memory

V. General information

VI. Capacity for sustained mental activity

    a. Calculation
    b. Abstract thinking

VII. General behavior

Figure 1.   Outline of the Mental Status Exam.

The exam begins as the clinician takes a history of the disorder (Gauthier, 1985). This often is done twice: once with the patient, and again with the spouse, friends, or other family members. Of particular interest in this portion of the exam is the nature of the symptoms and the type of onset. It is important to know, for instance, whether the symptoms appeared suddenly, as in a stroke, or insidiously, as in one of the progressive degenerating dementias. It is also important to learn of the duration of the symptoms. Do they come and go? Do they appear stable? Have they seemed to remit in severity? Finally, a family history is taken in order to learn of the prevalence of similar patterns of impairment among relatives. Not only are hereditary patterns important to identify, but a history of alcohol abuse or recurrent depressions would be significant information to obtain about the patient.

The second objective of the exam is to investigate the patient's insight into his or her dysfunction. The patient may not complain about any impairment at all, which of course can be the consequence of anxiety or mere stoicism, but in some instances such silences may indicate a lack of awareness even of serious impairments. Patients with parietal lesions, for example, or Korsakoff's syndrome, often will not perceive their symptoms. Particularly in the latter pathology, the patient is likely to become defensive when discrepancies in his or her story are pointed out, and will then offer confabulations in an attempt to justify the disparities.

Third, the clinician tests the patient's orientation to person, place and time. Does the patient know *who* he or she is, *where* he or she is, and know the time of day, the date, and the season of the year?

Fourth, the patient's memory is examined to detect retrograde amnesia. Recent memory is interrogated by having the patient answer questions regarding his or her immediate past: How long has he or she been in the hospital? What was he or she doing just prior to beginning the mental status exam? Remote memory is tested by questions regarding events that transpired in the patient's life earlier in the day or last night, such as asking about the last meal eaten, the last television program seen, and so forth. Finally, both short-term and long-term memory are inspected by having the patient repeat sequences of numbers, something on the order of the Digit Span subtest in the WAIS-R (or WISC-R).

The fifth section of the exam assesses the patient's accessible levels of general information, which naturally must be adjusted to the patient's own educational background and experience. For instance, the questions asked of an 85-year-old New England farmer to determine his general level of competence would necessarily be different than those asked of a 65-year-old female accountant. Cohort differences in professional training, gender differences, and education contribute to the particular content of an individual's general store of information.

The patient's capacity for sustained mental activity is investigated by having him or her perform mental calculations, such as subtracting by 7s from 100. Another common test is to have the patient interpret proverbs, though special caution needs to be exercised in assessing the patient's performance, since neither previous levels of comprehension nor abilities for abstract thinking are likely to be available to the examining clinician. Consequently, determinations of impairment often are founded on the clinician's judgment of how well the patient might be expected to perform.

Throughout all of the ensuing examinations, the patient's general behavior must be observed. Salient aspects of behavior include his or her vocabulary, in which an inappropriate use of words or impoverished diction is to be noted. Rate of speech, mispronunciations, and slurring are likewise worth notice. Grooming, or the lack of it, may give indications of apathy. Further, the patient's attentiveness should be investigated: Can he or she narrate a story? Does he or she follow complete sentences, or do the speech patterns follow stream of consciousness?

Finally, there are tests of localized cerebral function, two of which are important for assessing cognitive impairments. The first involves assessments for aphasia, which include tests of auditory and visual comprehension; oral and written expression with particular attention paid to repetitions, fluency, the ability to name familiar objects, and reading; and conversational speech (Kolb & Whishaw, 1985). The second functional test investigates possible apraxias. A quick, on-the-spot clinical exam includes having the patient use his or her hand to show the examiner how to use scissors, brush his or her teeth, comb his or her hair, clap hands, and snap fingers.

Screening Tests

In recent years there has been a notable surge in the development of mental status questionnaires (Lesher & Whelihan, 1986), whose design has been to aid in the diagnosis of intellectual dysfunction. These tests have brevity in common and are used most appropriately in combination with the clinical mental status exam to reduce the misclassification of normal elders as demented (LaRue et al., 1985; Pfeiffer, 1977). The tests are screening instruments, and are not intended to distinguish either different types or the causes of cognitive impairment. Several are commonly in use, perhaps the most notable of which are the Mental Status Questionnaire (MSQ; Kahn, Goldfarb, Pollack, & Peck, 1960), the Short Portable Mental Status Questionnaire (SPMSQ; Pfeiffer, 1975), and the Information–Memory–Concentration Test (IMCT; Blessed et al., 1968). Only the IMCT has been validated against postmortem findings (LaRue et al., 1985). However, the MSQ has a pedigree that includes both a long history of use and a well-documented validity of its psychometric properties (Eastwood, Lautenschlaeger, & Corbin, 1983). Similarly, the psychometric properties of the SPMSQ have been investigated (Pfeiffer, 1975; Wolber, Romaniuk, Eastman, & Robinson, 1984), and the results have indicated good diagnostic precision (Wolber et al., 1984).

Lesher and Whelihan (1986) have completed a study in which they employed test–retest, split-half, and internal consistency methods to determine the reliability of eight mental status questionnaires. Along with the MSQ, the SPMSQ, and the IMCT, the Extended Mental Status Questionnaire (EMSQ; Whelihan, Lesher, Kleban, & Granick, 1984), the Simplified Mental Status Questionnaire (SMSQ; Isaacs & Walkey, 1963), the Orientation Scale (OS; Kastenbaum & Sherwood, 1972), the Information–Orientation Section (IOS: Pattie & Gilleard, 1975), and the Short Orientation–Memory–Concentration Test (SOMCT: Katzman et al., 1983) were administered to a single sample of nursing home elderly.

The results suggested that the reliability of most of the tests was roughly equivalent in their ability to identify correctly cognitively impaired elders, and to distinguish them from elders free of impairment. The Orientation Scale was a notable exception to this success. Lesher and Whelihan found that, with regard to test–retest reliability, performance on this instrument had poor stability over time. Similarly, the correlations they obtained on their split-half reliability test indicated that the questionnaire did not have equivalent halves. Finally, the OS demonstrated only marginal internal consistency.

An assessment instrument commonly used in the United Kingdom, the Kendrick Battery for the Detection of Dementia in the Elderly (KBDDE; Gibson & Kendrick, 1979), has been attracting attention recently in the United States (Fish & Hayslip, 1983; Fish, Hayslip, Marcus, & Haynes, 1986). The battery consists of two subtests: the Object Learning Test and the Digit Copying Test. The former investigates short-term memory, and the latter assesses psychomotor skills. Fish and Hayslip (1983) report that the validity of the KBDDE is substantial: it yields 100% accuracy in distinguishing normal from demented elders, but drops to 77.7% when distinguishing among normal, depressed, and demented elders. However, the use of terms indigenous to British subjects represents at present an important limitation to its use in the United States. Many of these terms are not used in the United States, and conversely many common American terms are not listed as acceptable alternative responses. Consequently, the use of existing norms for the KBDDE are somewhat limited (Fish & Hayslip, 1983).

Tests of General Intellectual Functioning

The *Wechsler Adult Intelligence Scale* (WAIS) was the most commonly used test of general intellectual functioning until it was superseded in 1981 by the *Wechsler Adult Intelligence Scale-Revised* (WAIS-R). Like the WAIS before it, the WAIS-R consists of 11 subtests that examine different aspects of intellectual performance. The revisions include updated content among the items of the various subtests, the specifics of which Wechsler annotates in the WAIS-R manual (Wechsler, 1981). Similarly, the norms have been restandardized so that presently the test scores of current subjects are compared not only to those of their age peers (at least up to the age of 74, which is the uppermost age in the standardization sample), but also to those of their own generation.

This restandardization addresses at least one of the significant problems that Schaie and others have raised regarding the interpretation of cognitive declines among the elderly: the confound of educational differences among younger and older cohorts (Nesselroade *et al.*, 1972; Schaie & Labouvie-Vief, 1974; Schaie & Strother, 1968). Matarazzo and Herman (1984) have analyzed the standardization sample of the WAIS-R to identify the correlations between years of education and IQ. They found that of the subjects between the ages of 65 and 74, 41.55% had less than 9 years of formal education, and only 9.65% had at least a college education. Of the subjects between the years of 25 and 44, 40.85% had completed high school, and 20.85% had 16 or more years of schooling. In short, there are substantial differences in educational preparation between cohorts.

Regarding the relationship between years of schooling and Full Scale IQ (FSIQ), Matarazzo and Herman (1984) computed a correlation coefficient of .63 for subjects between the ages of 25 and 44, and .65 for those between 45 and 74. These are respectable correlations, and suggest that, at least as measured by the WAIS-R, the fewer the number of years of education, the lower the FSIQ. Since elders in general have completed less formal schooling, their FSIQ scores will likely be lower in comparison with those of younger subjects. Naturally, correlations do not imply causality, but rather point up the difficulty in interpreting levels of intellectual performance among the elderly. Concomitant physical illnesses, for instance, may contribute to poor test performance (LaRue, 1984). Similarly, decreases in visual acuity among older subjects may slow reading speed or hamper performance on certain specific subtests, such as the Picture Completion subtest (Popkin, Schaie, & Krauss, 1983). On the other hand, as Matarazzo and Herman (1984) suggest, the correlations may provide a rough estimate of premorbid cognitive functioning of those elders for whom there is no other information available.

Memory Tests

The *Wechsler Memory Scale* (WMS) (Wechsler, 1945) appears to be the test most commonly in use to evaluate memory (Brinkman, Largen, Gerganoff, & Pomara, 1983; Crosson, Hughes, Roth, & Monkowski, 1984), which makes its limitations all the more obvious. Chief among these limitations has been the lack of a systematically developed body of normative data (Brinkman *et al.*, 1983; Prigatano, 1978). Since Hulicka (1966) first published norms for 141 additional elderly subjects, there have been several investigators who have included further normative data for subjects over 60 (Bak & Greene, 1980; Brinkman *et al.*, 1983; Cauthen, 1977; McCarty, Logue, Power, Ziesat, & Rosenstiel, 1980). Further, Russell (1975) modified the original administration procedures of the WMS into a system that currently is widely used, whereby memory retention over time can be calculated separately for semantic and figural memory, and he likewise demonstrated that the differences between semantic and figural memory scores can be sensitive to the lateralization of brain impairment among patients (Brinkman *et al.*, 1983; Crosson *et al.*, 1984).

Nonetheless, despite the usefulness of Russell's system, normative data are still inadequate. Crosson and colleagues (1984) show that Russell's impairment ratings are too stringent to distinguish reliably between impaired and nonimpaired subjects: starting with age 30, 84% of Hulicka's (1966) and Wechsler's (1945) normative samples would be classified by Russell's norms as impaired. To provide interim, alternative norms until a body of data can be systematically developed, Crosson *et al.* (1984) pooled the scores from several studies to derive a composite mean, a standard deviation, and a table of T scores for Logical Memory and Visual Reproduction. They represent improvements on Russell's impairment ratings, but their clinical application should be made with caution, particularly since they apply only to immediate, and not delayed, recall.

A second popular test of memory function is the *Fuld Object Memory Test* (Fuld, 1978), which tests for memory of 10 common objects that the subject draws with alternating hands from a bag that screens the objects from view. The subject is given five trials to recall the objects, with a reminder after each recall attempt. The Fuld test offers several advantages. It guarantees the patient's attention to the stimuli and leaves no question that he or she is familiar with the objects. It also allows the investigator to observe the patient's right–left orientation, his or her ability to name the objects, and his or her word fluency. Also, there are norms for both community-dwelling and institutionalized elderly. Finally, it distinguishes between memory storage and retrieval (Masur & Fuld, 1982).

Comprehensive Neuropsychological Test Batteries

Large, comprehensive batteries of neuropsychological tests typically have two general purposes that inform their design: they aim to increase the accuracy of prediction in diagnosis, and they propose to collect information that contributes to the understanding of the nature of organic disabilities (Lezak, 1983). Because these batteries provide norm-referenced accounts of the subject's cognitive performance, they allow the clinician to compare an individual patient's scores with those of the normative sample, thereby allowing him or her to make statistically educated assumptions about the patient's dysfunction. They may also provide a baseline performance against which the patient's subsequent behavior can be measured. Likewise, they may be used to evaluate the effectiveness of various treatment and rehabilitation strategies (LaRue, 1984).

Of course, there are significant limitations that offset the advantages of using set batteries for neuropsychological assessments. As we have seen, there is at present no generally accepted necessary criteria by which a differential diagnosis can be made among several of the progressive degenerative dementias. Consequently, there is small likelihood that one battery of tests will be able to provide adequate specification of an individual patient's characteristic dysfunctions (Smith, 1983). Similarly, it is unlikely that one battery will amply satisfy the particular purposes of every referral. And finally, the cost in time and money to administer these batteries can be prohibitive. The Halstead–Reitan Battery, for instance, commonly takes 6 to 8 hours to administer, which can simply become an ordeal impossible for an elderly, infirm neurological patient to manage.

There are numerous tests designed to assess particular abilities, such as tests of motor performance; of orientation and attention; and of verbal, perceptual, constructional, conceptual, and executive functions. Often a neuropsychological assessment comprises a selection among the subtests of one of the larger neuropsychological batteries, and a sampling of the specific tests that the clinician may choose according to the requirements of the referral. An adequate discussion of these tests of specific functions is well beyond the scope of this chapter; the reader may wish to consult Muriel Lezak's (1983) classic text, *Neuropsychological Assessment (2nd ed.)*.

Of the representative neuropsychological batteries, the *Halstead–Reitan Battery* is the most prominent. The core tests include the Category Test, the Tactile Performance Test, the Rhythm Test, the Speech Sounds Perception Test, and the Finger Oscillation Test. To these are added the Trail Making Test and the Aphasia Screening Test; a sensory examination that tests for finger agnosia and skin writing recognition; either the WAIS-R or the WISC-R, depending on the age of the patient; a measure of hand grip strength; and the MMPI (Lezak, 1983).

Although this battery is one of the most reliable in its ability to identify patients with brain damage (Goldstein & Shelly, 1984; Lezak, 1983), there are significant limitations to its diagnostic efficiency. Goldstein and Shelly (1984) have found the Halstead–Reitan to have a higher discriminative validity among a general neuropsychological population (77.4% correct classifications) than the WAIS-R (65.5% correct classifications), and to be comparable to the Luria–Nebraska battery (79.8% correct classifications). Lezak (1983), however, cites investigators who find the battery inconsistent in its ability to discriminate left–right differences in its localization of lesions (Klove & Matthews, 1974; Reitan, 1955). Further, she reports that its impairment scales are not highly reliable (Dodrill & Troupin, 1975; Matarazzo, Weins, Matarazzo, & Goldstein, 1974), and points out that the normalization sample is based on a young group, which reduces its applicability to an elder population (Lezak, 1983).

The *Luria–Nebraska Neuropsychological Battery* (Golden, 1981; Golden, Hammeke, & Purisch, 1980) is perhaps the second most popular of the set batteries for neuropsychological evaluation. The test is designed according to Luria's clinical methods of assessment, and founded on the assumed scientific validity of Luria's theories regarding the functional organization of the brain (Smith, 1983). Because the battery is relatively new, and because its design is grounded on a conceptual scheme that, regardless of its clinical brilliance, remains unvalidated at present, the Luria–Nebraska battery has invited considerable critical debate (Mittenberg, Kasprisin, & Farage, 1985; Smith, 1983).

Lezak (1983) criticizes the battery for unsoundness in both its theoretical and psychometric bases, and cites several investigators who discovered lapses in its diagnostic accuracy. Adams and Brown (1980) found that the test critically overestimated the degree of pathology in their patient sample, and left other focal deficits undiagnosed. Delis and Kaplan (1982) similarly found that the battery misidentified the site of a lesion in a patient with a left posterior temporal lesion that was documented with a CT scan. Further, Brown, Adams, Rourke, Mehta, and Daly (1981) report that in their study the results of the Luria–Nebraska scales failed to confirm their hypothesis that the 35 patients with verified brain lesions would perform significantly poorer than the 18 normal controls.

However, other investigators have found the Luria–Nebraska battery to be an effective diagnostic tool. Mittenberg *et al.* (1985) found the L–N scales to be sensitive to core symptoms of aphasia when tested on a sample of patients diagnosed with Broca's, Wernicke's, mixed, anomic, or conductive aphasia. Goldstein and Shelley (1984) found the "hit-rate"—that is, the ability of the battery to discriminate between normals and brain-damaged subjects—of the Luria–Nebraska to be somewhat higher (79.8% correct classifications) than that of both the WAIS-R (65.5% correct classifications) and the Halstead–Reitan (77.4% correct classifications). Data obtained in a study by Sears, Hirt, and Hall (1984) similarly indicate that the battery is effective in discriminating brain-damaged from non-brain-damaged patients. None of these investigators, however, found the battery to be effective in localizing the site of the lesion.

CONCLUSIONS AND IMPLICATIONS

This review of current data regarding cognitive impairment among the elderly has had as its initial objective to identify some of the theoretical shifts among investigators that are revising our concepts of old age. Certain popular ideas about the aging intellect have lost prominence, and in their place have risen new expectations that are shaping research questions, redefining appropriate methodology, and guiding interpretation. Cognitive function in old age remains largely a terra incognita, though perhaps its expanse has been delimited somewhat, a few of its landmarks properly charted. The declines of intellect associated with old age, for instance, are better specified; intellectual ability is not a unitary phenomena, and decrements are neither widespread among the components of intellectual performance, nor do they progress at a uniform rate. Decrements in fact appear to be correlated with nearness to death rather than with distance from birth, which suggests that in the developmental life span an individual's cognitive ability normally remains relatively constant throughout his or her adult years until its precipitous decline at the conclusion of life.

Among those instances in which declines seem evident, there is considerable uncertainty in the process by which their etiologies are identified. Diagnoses are critical but difficult at the current level of knowledge. It can be an arduous task to separate cohort differences from pathological symptomology, and even among pathologies it can be guesswork to distinguish the contributions of chronic illnesses, multiple medications, depression, and enduring life stresses. Goldstein and Shelly's study (1984) indicated that there is nearly one chance in three of misclassifying a general neuropsychological patient as normal. Hence, one of the first responsibilities of neuropsychological assessment is to discriminate between reversible and irreversible disorders. Cognitive failures can be iatrogenic, the consequence among other things of prescribed medications, as well as the product of a host of remediable, common medical disturbances. The irreversible disorders themselves likewise pose diagnostic conundrums that at present require post mortem studies to unravel with any degree of certainty. Further, current levels of expertise are yet unable to distinguish the neurological deficits of normal aging from those of the most common progressive dementias. What is needed is continued focused research on the processes and cures of dementing illnesses. Investigation is proceeding, of course, but the present state of understanding and treatment is cautionary. Few real advances have been produced.

REFERENCES

Adams, K. M., & Brown, S. J. (1980). *Standardized behavioral neurology: Useful concept, mixed metaphor, or commercial enterprise?* Paper presented at the American Psychological Association Convention, Montreal, Quebec, Canada.

0American Psychiatric Association. (1987). *Diagnostic and statistical manual of mental disorders* (3rd ed., revised). Washington, DC: Author.

Arie, T. (1986). Management of dementia: A review. *British Medical Bulletin, 42*, 91–96.

Bak, J. S., & Greene, R. L. (1980). Changes in neuropsychological functioning in an aging population. *Journal of Consulting and Clinical Psychology, 48*, 395–399.

Ball, M. J., Schapiro, M. B., & Rapoport, S. I. (1986). Neuropathological relationships between Down syndrome and senile dementia Alzheimer type. In C. J. Epstein (Ed.), *The neurobiology of Down's syndrome* (pp. 45–58). New York: Raven Press.

Baltes, P. B., & Labouvie, G. V. (1973). Adult development of intellectual performance: Description, explanation, and modification. In C. Eisdorfer & M. P. Lawton (Eds.), *The psychology of adult development and aging* (pp. 157–219). Washington, DC: American Psychological Association.

Beck, E., Matthews, W. B., & Stevens, D. L. (1969). Creutzfeld–Jacob disease: The neuropathology of a transmission experiment. *Brain, 92*, 699.

Blessed, G., Tomlinson, B. E., & Roth, M. (1968). The association between quantitative measures of dementia and of senile change in the cerebral grey matter of elderly subjects. *British Journal of Psychiatry, 114*, 797–811.

Blumer, D., & Benson, D. F. (1975). Personality changes with frontal and temporal lobe lesions. In D. F. Benson & D. Blumer (Eds.), *Psychiatric aspects of neurological disease* (pp. 151–170). New York: Grune & Stratton.

Boll, T. J. (1981). Assessment of neuropsychological disorders. In D. H. Barlow, (Ed.), *Behavioral assessment of adult disorders* (pp. 45–86). New York: Guilford Press.

Bondareff, W. (1985). The neural basis of aging. In J. E. Birren & K. W. Schaie (Eds.), *Handbook of the psychology of aging* (2nd ed., pp. 95–112). New York: Van Nostrand Reinhold.

Botwinick, J. (1977). Intellectual abilities. In J. E. Birren & K. W. Schaie (Eds.), *Handbook of the psychology of aging* (pp. 580–605). New York: Van Nostrand Reinhold.

Breen, A. R., Larson, E. B., Reifler, B. V., Vitaliano, P. P., & Lawrence, G. L. (1984). Cognitive performance and functional competence in coexisting dementia and depression. *Journal of the American Geriatrics Society, 32*, 132–137.

Brinkman, S. D., Largen, J. W., Jr., Gerganoff, S., & Pomara, N. (1983). Russell's revised Wechsler Memory Scale in the evaluation of dementia. *Journal of Clinical Psychology, 39*, 989–993.

Brown, S., Adams, K., Rourke, B., Mehta, B., & Daly, R. (1981). Predictive utility of the Luria–Nebraska Scales in brain-damaged and non-brain-damaged groups. *International Neuropsychological Society Abstracts, 13*.

Brunner, D., & Meshulam, N. (1970). Physical fitness of trained elderly. In D. Brunner & E. Jokl (Eds.), *Physical activity and aging* (Medicine and Sport, Vol. 4, pp. 80–88). Baltimore: University Park Press.

Burger, P. C., & Vogel, F. S. (1973). The development of the pathologic changes of Alzheimer's disease and senile dementia in patients with Down's syndrome. *American Journal of Pathology, 73*, 457–476.

Butler, D. M., & Lewis, M. I. (1977). *Aging and mental health: Positive psychosocial approaches.* St. Louis: C. V. Mosby.

Carlson, N. R. (1981). *Physiology of behavior* (2nd ed.). Boston: Allyn & Bacon.

Cattell, R. B. (1963). Theory of fluid and crystallized intelligence: A critical experiment. *Journal of Educational Psychology, 54*, 1–22.

Cauthen, N. R. (1977). Extension of the Wechsler Memory Scale norms to older age groups. *Journal of Clinical Psychology, 33*, 208–211.

Cohen, M. B., Graham, L. S., Lake, R., Metter, E. J., Fitten, J., Kulkarni, M., Sevrin, R., Yamada, L., Chang, C. C., Woodruff, N., & Kling, A. S. (1986). Diagnosis of Alzheimer's disease and multiple infarct dementia by tomographic imaging of iodine-123 IMP. *The Journal of Nuclear Medicine, 27*, 769–774.

Cornelius, S. W. (1984). Classic pattern of intellectual aging: test familiarity, difficulty & performance. *Journal of Gerontology, 39*, 201–206.

Cornelius, S. W., & Caspi, A. (1987). Everyday problem solving in adulthood and old age. *Psychology and Aging, 2*, 144–153.

Craik, F. I. M. (1977). Age differences in human memory. In J. E. Birren & K. W. Schaie (Eds.), *Handbook of the psychology of aging* (pp. 384–420). New York: Van Nostrand Reinhold.

Crosson, B., Hughes, C. W., Roth, D. L., & Monkowski, P. G. (1984). Review of Russell's norms for the logical memory and visual reproduction subtests of the Wechsler Memory Scale. *Journal of Consulting and Clinical Psychology, 52,* 635–641.

Delis, D., & Kaplan, E. F. (1982). The assessment of aphasia with the Luria–Nebraska Neuropsychological Battery: A test case. *Journal of Consulting and Clinical Psychology, 50,* 32–39.

Denney, N. W. (1981). Adult cognitive development. In D. S. Beasley & G. A. Davis (Eds.), *Aging, communications processes and disorders* (pp. 123–137). New York: Grune & Stratton.

Dodrill, C. B., & Troupin, A. S. (1975). Effects of repeated administrations of a comprehensive neuropsychological battery among chronic epileptics. *Journal of Nervous and Mental Disease, 161,* 185–190.

Dodson, J. (1984). The slow death: Alzheimer's disease. *Journal of Neurosurgical Nursing, 16,* 270–274.

Eastwood, M. R., Lautenschlaeger, E., & Corbin, S. (1983). A comparison of clinical methods for assessing dementia. *Journal of the American Geriatrics Society, 31,* 342–347.

Eisdorfer, C., & Wilkie, F. (1973). Intellectual changes with advancing age. In L. F. Jarvik, C. Eisdorfer, & J. C. Blum (Eds.), *Intellectual functioning in adults* (pp. 21–29). New York: Springer.

Fish, M., & Hayslip, B., Jr., (1983). The clinical use of the Kendrick battery in differentiating dementia and depression in the elderly. *Clinical Gerontologist, 5,* 54–56.

Fish, M., Hayslip, B., Jr., Marcus, S., & Haynes, J. R. (1986). Construct validity of the Kendrick battery with institutionalized aged. *The Journal of Psychology, 120,* 335–343.

Fisher, A. (1986). Potential animal models for senile dementia of Alzheimer's type, with emphasis on AF64A-induced cholinotoxicity. *Annual Review of Pharmacological Toxicology, 26,* 161–181.

Freeman, F. R. (1976). Evaluation of patients with progressive intellectual deterioration. *Archives of Neurology, 33,* 658–659.

Fries, J. F. (1980). Aging, natural death, and the compression of morbidity. *New England Journal of Medicine, 303,* 130–135.

Fuld, P. A. (1978). Psychological testing in the differential diagnosis of dementia. In R. Katzman, R. D. Terry, & K. L. Blik (Eds.), *Alzheimer's disease: Senile dementia and related disorders* (pp. 185–193). New York: Raven Press.

Gauthier, S. (1985). Practical guidelines for the antemortem diagnosis of senile dementia of the Alzheimer's type. *Progress in Neuro-Psychopharmacology and Biological Psychiatry, 9,* 491–495.

Gibson, A., & Kendrick, D. (1979). *The Kendrick battery for the detection of dementia in the elderly.* Windsor, Great Britain: NFER Publishing.

Golden, C. J. (1981). A standardized version of Luria's neuropsychological tests. In S. Filskov & T. J. Boll (Eds.), *Handbook of clinical neuropsychology* (pp. 608–642). New York: Wiley–Interscience.

Golden, C. J., Hammeke, T. A., & Purisch, A. D. (1980). *Manual for the Luria-Nebraska neuropsychological battery.* Los Angeles: Western Psychological Services.

Goldstein, G., & Shelly, C. (1984). Discriminative validity of various intelligence and neuropsychological tests. *Journal of Consulting and Clinical Psychology, 52,* 383–389.

Gottfries, C. G. (1985). Alzheimer's disease and senile dementia: Biochemical characteristics and aspects of treatment. *Psychopharmacology, 86,* 245–252.

Gottfries, C. G., Adolfsson, R., Aquilonius, S. M., Carlsson, A., Eckernas, S. A., Nordberg, A., Oreland, L., Svennerholm, L., Wiberg, A., & Winblad, B. (1983). Biochemical changes in dementia disorders of Alzheimer type (AD/SDAT). *Neurobiology of Aging, 4,* 261–271.

Growdon, J. H., Corkin, S., Huff, F. J., & Rosen, T. J. (1986). Piracetam combined with lecithin in the treatment of Alzheimer's disease. *Neurobiology of Aging, 7,* 269–276.

Guilford, J. P. (1967). *The nature of human intelligence.* New York: McGraw-Hill.

Gustafson, L., & Nilsson, L. (1982). Differential diagnosis of presenile dementia on clinical grounds. *Acta Psychiatrica Scandinavia, 65,* 194–209.

Haskel, W. L. (1984). The influence of exercise in the concentrations of tryglyceride and cholesterol in human plasma. *Exercise and Sport Science Reviews, 12,* 205–244.

Hertzog, C., & Schaie, K. W. (1988). Stability and change in adult intelligence: 2. Simultaneous analysis of longitudinal means and covariance structures. *Psychology and Aging, 3,* 122–130.

Heston, L. L., Masri, A. R., & Anderson, E. (1981). Dementia of the Alzheimer's type: Clinical genetics, natural history, and associated conditions. *Archives of General Psychiatry, 38,* 1085–1090.

Hooper, F., Fitzgerald, J., & Papalia, D. (1971). Piagetian theory and the aging process: Extensions and speculations. *Aging and Human Development, 2,* 3–20.

Horn, J. L. (1970). Organization of data on life-span development of human abilities. In L. R. Goulet &

P. B. Baltes (Eds.), *Life-span developmental psychology: Research and theory*, (pp. 424–466). New York: Academic Press.

Horn, J. L. (1982). The theory of fluid and crystallized intelligence in relation to concepts of cognitive psychology and aging in adulthood. In F. I. M. Craik & S. Trehub (Eds.), *Aging and cognitive process* (pp. 237–278). New York: Plenum.

Horn, J. L., & Cattell, R. B. (1966). Refinement and test of the theory of fluid and crystallized intelligence. *Journal of Educational Psychology, 57,* 253–270.

Horn, J. L., & Donaldson, G. (1980). Cognitive development in adulthood. In D. G. Brim & J. Kagan (Eds.), *Constancy and change in human development* (pp. 445–529). Cambridge, MA: Harvard University Press.

Hulicka, I. M. (1966). Age differences on Wechsler Memory Scale scores. *Journal of Genetic Psychology, 109,* 135–145.

Hussian, R. A. (1981). *Geriatric psychology: A behavioral perspective.* New York: Van Nostrand.

Isaacs, B., & Walkey, F. A. (1963). The assessment of the mental state of elderly hospital patients using a simple questionnaire. *American Journal of Psychiatry, 120,* 173–174.

Jones, H. E. (1959). Intelligence and problem solving. In J. E. Birren (Ed.), *Handbook of aging and the individual* (pp. 700–738). Chicago: University of Chicago Press.

Kahn, R. L., Goldfarb, A. I., Pollack, M., & Peck, A. (1960). Brief objective measures for the determination of mental status in the aged. *American Journal of Psychiatry, 117,* 326–328.

Kastenbaum, R., & Sherwood, S. (1972). VIRO: A scale for assessing the interview behavior of elderly people. In D. P. Kent, R. Kastenbaum, & S. Sherwood (Eds.), *Research planning and action for the elderly* (pp. 166–200). New York: Behavioral Publications.

Katzman, R., Brown, T., Fuld, P., Peck, A., Schecter, R., & Schimmel, H. (1983). Validation of a short orientation–memory–concentration test of cognitive impairment. *American Journal of Psychiatry, 140,* 734–739.

Kay, D. W. K., (1986). The genetics of Alzheimer's disease. *British Medical Bulletin, 42,* 19–23.

Klove, H., & Matthews, C. G. (1974). Neuropsychological studies of patients with epilepsy. In R. M. Reitan & L. A. Davison (Eds.), *Clinical Neuropsychology* (pp. 175–226). Washington, DC: Hemisphere.

Knight, R. G., Godfrey, H. P. D., & Shelton, E. J. (1988). The psychological deficits associated with Parkinson's disease. *Clinical Psychology Review, 8,* 391–410.

Kokmen, E. (1984). Dementia: Alzheimer type. *Mayo Clinic Proceedings, 59,* 35–42.

Kolb, B., & Whishaw, I. Q. (1985). *Fundamentals of human neuropsychology* (2nd ed.). New York: W. H. Freeman.

Kwentus, J. A., Hart, R., Lingon, N., Taylor, J., & Silverman, J. J. (1986). Alzheimer's disease: A review. *American Journal of Medicine, 81,* 91–96.

Labouvie-Vief, G. (1985). Intelligence and cognition. In J. E. Birren & K. W. Schaie (Eds.), *Handbook of the psychology of aging* (2nd ed., pp. 500–530). New York: Van Nostrand Reinhold.

LaRue, A. (1984). Neuropsychological testing. *Psychiatric Annals, 14,* 201–204.

LaRue, A., Dessonville, C., & Jarvik, L. F. (1985). Aging and mental disorders. In J. E. Birren & K. W. Schaie (Eds.), *Handbook of the psychology of aging* (2nd ed., pp. 664–702). New York: Van Nostrand Reinhold.

Lesher, E. L., & Whelihan, W. M. (1986). Reliability of mental status instruments administered to nursing home residents. *Journal of Consulting and Clinical Psychology, 54,* 726–727.

Lezak, M. D. (1983). *Neuropsychological assessment* (2nd ed.). New York: Oxford University Press.

Marquez, J. A. (1983). Computerized tomography and neuropsychological tests in dementia. *Clinical Gerontologist, 2,* 13–22.

Marttila, R. J., & Rinne, U. K. (1976). Dementia in Parkinson's disease. *Acta Neurologica Scandinavia, 54,* 431–441.

Masters, C. L. (1984). Etiology and pathogenesis of Alzheimer's disease. *Pathology, 16,* 233–234.

Masur, D. M., & Fuld, P. A. (1982). The neuropsychological evaluation of dementia: Two case studies. *Clinical Gerontologist, 1,* 23–28.

Matarazzo, J. D., & Herman, D. O. (1984). Relationship of education and IQ in the WAIS-Q standardization sample. *Journal of Consulting and Clinical Psychology, 52,* 631–634.

Matarazzo, J. D., Weins, A. N., Matarazzo, R. N., & Goldstein, S. G. (1974). Psychometric and clinical test–retest reliability of the Halstead Impairment Index in a sample of healthy, young, normal men. *Journal of Nervous and Mental Disease, 158,* 37–49.

McCarty, S. M., Logue, P. E., Power, D. G., Ziesat, H. A., & Rosenstiel, A. K. (1980). Alternate-form reliability and age-related scores for Russell's Revised Wechsler Memory Scale. *Journal of Consulting and Clinical Psychology, 48,* 296–298.

McCarty, S. M., Siegler, I. C., & Logue, P. E. (1982). Cross-sectional and longitudinal patterns of three Wechsler Memory Scale subtests. *Journal of Gerontology, 37,* 169–175.

Meier-Ruge, W., Iwangoff, P., & Reichlmeier, K. (1984). Neurochemical enzyme changes in Alzheimer's and Pick's disease. *Archives of Gerontology and Geriatrics, 3,* 161–165.

Metter, E. J., Riege, W. H., Kameyama, M., Kuhl, D. E., & Phelps, M. E. (1984). Cerebral metabolic relationships for selected brain regions in Alzheimer's, Huntington's, and Parkinson's diseases. *Journal of Cerebral Blood Flow and Metabolism, 4,* 500–506.

Mittenberg, W., Kasprisin, A., & Farage, C. (1985). Localization and diagnosis in aphasia with the Luria–Nebraska Neuropsychological Battery. *Journal of Consulting and Clinical Psychology, 53,* 386–392.

Nesselroade, J. R., Schaie, K. W., & Baltes, P. B. (1972). Ontogenetic and generational components of structural and quantitative change in adult cognitive behavior. *Journal of Gerontology, 27,* 222–228.

Pattie, A. H., & Gilleard, C. J. (1975). A brief psychogeriatric assessment schedule. *British Journal of Psychiatry, 127,* 489–493.

Pfeiffer, E. (1975). A short portable mental status questionnaire for the assessment of organic brain deficit in elderly patients. *Journal of the American Geriatrics Society, 23,* 433–441.

Pfeiffer, E. (1977). Psychopathology and social pathology. In J. E. Birren & K. W. Schaie (Eds.), *Handbook of the psychology of aging* (pp. 650–671). New York: Van Nostrand.

Plowman, S. A., Drinkwater, B. L., & Horvath, S. (1979). Age and aerobic power in women: A longitudinal study. *Journal of Gerontology, 34,* 512–520.

Popkin, S. J., Schaie, K. W., & Krauss, I. K. (1983). Age-fair assessment of psychometric intelligence. *Educational Gerontology, 9,* 47–55.

Powers, L. B., & Doughtery, J. H., Jr. (1985). Dementia of the Alzheimer's type: Clinical overview. *Journal of the Tennessee Medical Association, 78,* 13–15.

Prigatano, G. P. (1978). Wechsler Memory Scale: A selective review of the literature. *Journal of Clinical Psychology, 34,* 816–832.

Reitan, R. M. (1955). Certain differential effects of left and right cerebral lesions in human adults. *Journal of Comparative and Physiological Psychology, 48,* 474–477.

Riegel, K. F., & Riegel, R. M. (1972). Development, drop, and death. *Developmental Psychology, 6,* 306–319.

Rogers, R. L., Meyer, J. S., Mortel, K F., Mahurin, R. K., & Judd, B. W. (1986). Decreased cerebral blood flow precedes multi-infarct dementia, but follows senile dementia of Alzheimer type. *Neurology, 36,* 1–6.

Rose, C. L., & Cohen, M. L. (1977). Relative importance of physical activity for longevity. *Annals of New York Academy of Science, 301,* 671–697.

Rossor, M. N., Iverson, L. L., Reynolds, G. P., Mountjoy, C. Q., & Roth, M. (1984). Neurochemical characteristics of early and late onset types of Alzheimer's disease. *British Medical Journal, 288,* 961–964.

Russell, F. W. (1975). A multiple scoring method for assessment of complex memory functions. *Journal of Consulting and Clinical Psychology, 43,* 800–809.

Salthouse, T. (1988). Initiating the formalization of theories of cognitive aging. *Psychology and Aging, 3,* 3–16.

Sattler, J. M. (1982). Age effects on Wechsler Adult Intelligence Scale-Revised tests. *Journal of Consulting and Clinical Psychology, 50,* 785–786.

Schaie, K. W., & Labouvie-Vief, G. (1974). Generational versus ontogenetic components of change in adult cognitive behavior: A fourteen-year cross sequential study. *Developmental Psychology, 10,* 305–320.

Schaie, K. W., & Strother, C. R. (1968). A cross-sectional study of age changes in cognitive behavior. *Psychological Bulletin, 70,* 671–680.

Sears, J. D., Hirt, M. L., & Hall, R. W. (1984). A cross-validation of the Luria–Nebraska Neuropsychological Battery. *Journal of Consulting and Clinical Psychology, 52,* 309–310.

Sloane, R. B. (1980). Organic brain syndrome. In J. E. Birren & R. B. Sloane, (Eds.), *Handbook of mental health and aging* (pp. 554–590). Englewood Cliffs, NJ: Prentice-Hall.

Smith, A. (1983). Clinical psychological practice and principles of neuropsychological assessment. In C. E. Walker (Ed.), *Handbook of clinical psychology: Theory, research and practice* (pp. 445–500). Homewood, IL: Dorsey Press.

Soininen, H., Koskinen, T., Helkala, E.-L., Pigache, R., & Riekkinen, P. J. (1985). Treatment of Alzheimer's disease with a synthetic ACTH 4–9 analog. *Neurology, 35*, 1348–1351.

Spearman, C. (1927). *The abilities of man*. New York: Macmillan.

Stankov, L. (1988). Aging, attention, and intelligence. *Psychology and Aging, 3*, 59–74.

Tomlinson, B. E., Blessed, G., & Roth, M. (1970). Observations on the brains of demented old people. *Journal of Neurological Science, 11*, 205–242.

Verwoerdt, A. (1976). *A clinical geropsychiatry*. Baltimore: Williams and Wilkins.

Wechsler, D. (1945). *WAIS manual*. The Psychological Corporation. New York: Harcourt Brace Jovanovich.

Wechsler, D. (1981). *WAIS–R manual*. The Psychological Corporation. New York: Harcourt Brace Jovanovich.

Whelihan, W. N., Lesher, E. L., Kleban, M. H., & Granick, S. (1984). Mental status and memory assessment as predictors of dementia. *Journal of Gerontology, 39*, 572–576.

Whitbourne, S. K. (1985). *The aging body: Physiological changes and psychological consequences*. New York: Springer–Verlag.

Whitbourne, S. K., & Weinstock, C. S. (1986). *Adult development* (2nd ed.). New York: Praeger.

Willis, S. L., & Baltes, P. B. (1980). Intelligence in adulthood and aging: Contemporary issues. In L. W. Poon (Ed.), *Aging in the 1980's: Psychological issues* (pp. 260–272). Washington, DC: American Psychological Association.

Winblad, B., Adolfsson, R., Alafuzoff, I., Almqvist, P., Bixo, M., Bucht, G., Hardy, J., Marcusson, J., Nyberg, P., Viitanen, M., Wester, P., & Osterlind, P. O. (1985). Transmitter deficits in Alzheimer's disease. *Annals of the New York Academy of Sciences, 444*, 255–268.

Winogrond, I. R., & Fisk, A. A. (1983). Alzheimer's disease: Assessment of functional status. *Journal of the American Geriatrics Society, 31*, 780–785.

Wisniewski, H. M. (1978). Possible viral etiology of neurofibrillary changes and neuritic plaques. In R. Katsman, R. D. Terry, & K. L. Beck (Eds.), *Alzheimer's disease: Senile dementia and related disorders* (pp. 355–358). New York: Raven Press.

Wolber, G., Romaniuk, M., Eastman, E., & Robinson, C. (1984). Validity of the short portable mental status questionnaire with elderly psychiatric patients. *Journal of Consulting and Clinical Psychology, 52*, 712–713.

Wurtman, R. J. (1985). Alzheimer's disease. *Scientific American, 252*, 62–66; 71–74.

Wurtman, R. J. (1986). Activation of neurotransmitters in the brain: strategies in the treatment of AD/SDAT. *Clinical Neuropharmacology, 9*, 53–57.

III

Treatment Applications

7

Stress and Stress Management with the Elderly

BENJAMIN L. HANDEN

INTRODUCTION

The relationship of stress to psychological functioning and health has been examined for some time by both basic and applied researchers. Stress has been associated with the onset and/or course of a number of physical and psychological conditions. Consequently, stress reduction procedures have been increasingly utilized with children and adults in both primary and adjunctive treatment. Such procedures have been used successfully to treat a range of anxiety disorders such as phobias, obsessive–compulsive behavior, and generalized anxiety. They have also been used in the treatment of other psychological disorders in which anxiety plays an important role, such as somatic complaints, paranoid ideation, depression, and in the treatment of psychophysiological dysfunctions such as high blood pressure, lower-back pain, headache pain, and the aversive side effects of cancer treatment. Despite relatively high rates of both psychological disorders and psychophysiological conditions, the elderly have been systematically neglected in the stress management literature. These individuals face a number of potentially stressful situations that are unique to this age group and place them at risk for developing stress-related disorders. This chapter will focus upon the use of stress management procedures with the elderly. First, there will be a brief examination of conceptual issues in stress research. This will be followed by a discussion of reported problems in generalizing stress management procedures to the elderly population. Finally, there will be a review of the literature on stress reduction procedures involving elderly individuals and recommendations for future research needs.

BENJAMIN L. HANDEN • Children's Hospital of Pittsburgh, Pittsburgh, Pennsylvania 15213-3417.

Conceptual Issues in Stress Research

Despite wide acceptance of the negative impact of stress upon both psychological and physical health, research has been hindered by disparity in conceptual and methodological areas. Moss (1973) reviewed models of stress and placed them into three categories: (1) stress as a psychological response to physical, chemical, and organic agents (based upon Selye's General Adaptation Syndrome), (2) stress as a physiological response to social and psychological stimuli (viewing stress as an interaction between the external environment and the organism), and (3) stress as a behavioral response to social psychological stimuli (viewing stress from a cognitive perspective). These differing perspectives on stress have resulted in a range of research endeavors and subsequent treatment approaches that can be used individually or in combination. Specific treatment approaches will be addressed in more detail in a later section.

Were it possible to develop a conceptualization of stress that encompassed the variety of perspectives identified above, research in this area would nonetheless remain problematic. A primary difficulty is the observation that laboratory stressors may not be consistently perceived as stressful by all subjects or even by the same subject over time (Averill, 1979). Consequently, the designation of a stimulus as stressful as well as an individual's response to that stimulus may be extremely idiosyncratic. Yet despite such observations, a wide consensus seems to exist among researchers as to the types of stimuli that may be perceived as stressful (Antonovsky, 1980), hence, the well-accepted use of stress rating scales (e.g., Holmes & Rahe, 1967), which consist of lists of potentially stressful life events and assume a certain universality in individual responses to these stimuli. It is important to note that such scales provide information about the relationship between exposure to a presumed stressful event and subsequent development of maladaptive responses among a large group of subjects. Despite statistically significant associations, these findings do not allow for the prediction of individual responses to such stimuli and cannot necessarily be used for clinical purposes.

The treatment focus for stress-related disorders is often based upon a clinician's conceptualization of both stressful stimuli and subsequent responses. Individual responses to stress have typically been divided into three categories: physiological responses, behavioral responses, and the reporting of subjective states. As will be seen, the treatment of elderly individuals often requires that the clinician address the entire range of possible stress responses.

Generalizing Stress Management Techniques to the Elderly

There are indications that standard behavior therapy procedures may need to be modified for use with an elderly population. For example, there is some research evidence that older individuals require longer periods of time to acquire new skills than younger subjects (cf. review by Botwinick, 1970). Such findings may have implications for the methods used to instruct elderly clients in self-management techniques. Cautela (1967) provided some anecdotal evidence for this when he reported that elderly patients in his clinical practice required considerably more therapy sessions to learn progressive muscle relaxation than other adults. Linoff and West (1982) described a similar problem in their treatment of an 89-year-old male nursing home resident. A relaxation tape alone was inadequate, but soothing background music was helpful in producing the desired effect. A number of biobehavioral studies indicate differential results for subjects over and under the age of 60 (e.g., Barlow, O'Brien, & Last, 1984; Blanchard *et al.*, 1985; Lammers, Naliboff, & Straatmeyer, 1984). These studies are described later in the chapter.

Williamson and Ascione (1983) suggest that the effectiveness of behavioral procedures with the elderly has been well established and that the elderly should not be considered as a unique population in this regard. They reviewed 36 studies involving elderly subjects in which contingency management and stimulus control procedures were utilized. While elderly subjects were, indeed, amenable to behavior change, Williamson and Ascione did not evaluate the literature on self-control procedures (e.g., reciprocal inhibition, cognitive behavior therapy), where more apparent differences may be found. In summary, given the relative paucity of literature on behavior therapy and the elderly population, it is difficult to discern whether the elderly will require procedural modifications for effective therapy or if these few simple findings represent individual client differences, which one would expect to observe with any population.

STRESS REDUCTION PROCEDURES WITH THE ELDERLY

The forthcoming discussion of stress reduction procedures is divided into three sections: studies involving the individual treatment of anxiety disorders, including phobias, generalized anxiety, paranoia, somatic complaints, obsessive–compulsive behavior; studies describing group therapy for anxiety disorders; and studies involving the treatment of psychophysiological dysfunctions. In general, stress reduction procedures involve the use of reciprocal inhibition, response prevention, and cognitive-behavioral techniques. Operant procedures such as stimulus control or contingency management have occasionally been included in treatment protocols in which family, friends, or staff try to enhance the effectiveness of self-management procedures. In a few of the studies, operant procedures alone were used to treat anxiety disorders.

Individual Treatment of Anxiety Disorders

Phobias

Anxiety problems in the form of phobias and generalized anxiety are the most frequently studied of all the stress-related disorders among elderly patients. The psychological literature is replete with case studies of the treatment of dog phobias, agoraphobia, and anxiety in social situations. Progressive muscle relaxation has been the primary treatment of choice for such disorders. It is often combined with systematic desensitization or more cognitively oriented procedures. In one of the earliest reported case studies, Friedman (1966) successfully used pictures to desensitize a 66-year-old deaf and mute man to a disabling fear of dogs. He used intravenous injections of a short-acting barbiturate anesthetic to assist the client to achieve a relaxed state. Six treatment sessions were required, and a 6-month follow-up found the client to be symptom-free. Another early case study was reported by Wander (1972), who used systematic desensitization and thought stopping in the treatment of a 60-year-old man who was described as acrophobic, aerophobic, and chronically depressed with a history of suicide attempts. Following 23 sessions of therapy, the client showed considerable improvement. At a 3-year follow-up, the client reported that he had traveled around the world, gone to the top of tall buildings, decreased his frequency of negative thoughts, and increased the number of positive self-evaluations.

More recent reports have continued to demonstrate the efficacy of self-management procedures for the treatment of phobias among elderly clients. Garrison (1978) published a case study summarizing the results of 7 weeks of relaxation training with a 65-year-old man presenting a 10-year history of agoraphobia. Following his last "attack" he had taken early retirement and spent most of his time at home. In addition to progressive muscle relaxation, the patient went through a graduated hierarchy of *in vivo* steps, taking him further from his home for increasingly longer periods of time. At the end of treatment and at a 1-year follow-up, the man reported that he could independently walk around the neighborhood and could go to the center of town if accompanied by another family member. Hussian (1981) described the treatment of four, elderly institutionalized men who were unable to use elevators. An informal relaxation procedure was used in conjunction with education around the working of elevators, practice of positive verbalizations, and guided *in vivo* exposure to elevators. Treatment required 10 sessions. At a 2-month follow-up, all four residents were riding on elevators several times a day with minimal anxiety, according to self-report ratings. Finally, Thyer (1981) reported the successful treatment of a 70-year-old woman who had a dog phobia. He conducted five hour-long sessions of prolonged *in vivo* exposure to dogs, beginning with small dogs and gradually introducing larger dogs such as Doberman pinschers, an 80-pound Afghan, and finally a 95-pound Great Dane. Telephone follow-ups at 3 and 6 months indicated that therapeutic gains had been maintained, as the client was able to go about her day without the sound or sight of dogs causing her fear.

Generalized Anxiety

Self-management procedures have also been successfully used to treat generalized anxiety. Garfinkel (1979) reported the successful treatment of a 75-year-old woman with a 35-year history of restricted activity due to feelings of tightness in her chest, choking, and a feeling that she couldn't breathe. Progressive muscle relaxation and graduated *in vivo* exposure to anxiety-producing situations in the community were successfully used over a 5-month period. In a follow-up conversation some months after treatment, the patient reported that she had remained symptom-free. Garfinkel related that six to eight sessions were necessary to teach the client progressive muscle relaxation in comparison with two to three sessions for younger clients. This finding is similar to that of Cautela (1967).

Falloon (1975) described the treatment of two depressed elderly clients who exhibited a number of anxieties, fears, and sleeping problems. *In vivo* desensitization and social-skills training were used in conjunction with anti-anxiety medications and sedatives. In addition, nursing staff were taught to reinforce differentially appropriate verbalizations and motor responses. In both cases, scores on a depression rating scale significantly decreased from the depressed to nondepressed range with similar improvement noted on an anxiety subscale of the same instrument. A 3-month follow-up with one patient indicated continued improvement, especially in social spheres and independent living. No follow-up was reported for the second patient.

It is not always possible to teach progressive muscle relaxation to clients who have physical disabilities. Other methods may be required. Hussian (1981) described such a case involving an 83-year-old institutionalized woman who felt anxious among other residents and consequently exhibited "strange" behavior. Because the client was confined to a wheelchair and was unable to tense and release her muscles, Hussian substituted rational self-statements as responses incompatible with anxiety. Systematic desensitization was successfully used over five 1-hour sessions combining both imagery-based and *in vivo* situations of the client sitting in common areas with other residents. The client was soon able to handle these social situations with only minimal anxiety. At 3 weeks and 6 months after treatment, progress had been maintained.

Paranoia

Paranoia is another prevalent psychological disorder that has been treated by behavioral methods. Most paranoid clients exhibit poor memory, decreased acuity of sense organs, confusion, and anxiety. While not generally considered an anxiety disorder, anxiety reduction is typically a primary treatment objective. This is often achieved through the teaching of self-management procedures in combination with operant conditioning interventions carried out by institutional staff or family members. For example, Brink (1980) described the case of an 81-year-old community-dwelling woman who frequently accused neighbors of taking her belongings and replacing them with poorer-quality items. Complaints about her neighbors had become the focus of all of her conversations with family members. A form of reality therapy was used in which the patient was asked to stop accusing her neighbors of stealing. The therapist explained that he understood that she was not intentionally lying, but that her memory was not reliable in these situations. In fact, continued accusations against her neighbors would lead to a deterioration of her relationship with them and might lead to lawsuits. The client reluctantly agreed to comply. Extinction was also an important component of the treatment. The client's daughter (who spoke by phone to her mother daily) was instructed to ignore all references to what the neighbors had done and to redirect the conversation. Follow-up reports at 3 months indicated that all paranoid behaviors had disappeared and the client continued to engage in appropriate conversations with relatives and community members.

Carstensen and Fremouw (1981) treated the paranoia of an elderly woman residing in a nursing home. The client was moderately depressed as well, and her refusal to take her cardiac medication had resulted in a myocardial infarction. Treatment involved one-to-one supportive therapy in which the therapist provided positive reinforcement for appropriate verbal behavior and expressed sincere concern over the patient's problems. The patient was also asked to keep a diary of her helping behavior so that she could focus upon positive rather than negative events. In addition, staff were told to ignore paranoid statements and to reinforce a range of appropriate behaviors. Within 2 weeks, paranoid verbalizations and fears were eliminated.

Hussian (1981) described two case reports in which progressive muscle relaxation was used with two institutionalized elderly clients presenting with paranoid thoughts. The first was a 67-year-old woman who was in constant fear that someone would kill her while she slept. Consequently, she slept less than 2 hours a night. The client was trained in progressive muscle relaxation and cognitive restructuring, in which she substituted more rational statements for paranoid ones. The client was also asked to keep a diary of paranoid statements. Four weeks after treatment began, the patient reported no longer hearing voices and was sleeping a total of 6 hours nightly.

The second patient described by Hussian (1981) was a 62-year-old woman who thought that someone was attempting to poison her. She spent much of her day in her room and had become extremely weak and anemic due to low consumption of food. Medical treatment, while initially helpful, had not alleviated the problem. Hussian taught the client progressive muscle relaxation and a form of systematic desensitization. While relaxing during sessions, the patient was instructed to imagine the feared situation (being poisoned) and to counter her anxiety with more rational, positive statements. After six sessions, the patient's appetite returned to normal, and she no longer reported hearing voices saying that she was to be poisoned. Medication was terminated 6-weeks later and progress was maintained at a 2-month follow-up.

Finally, Haley (1983) reported the successful treatment of a 71-year-old woman with a history of psychiatric hospitalizations and paranoid schizophrenia. The subject had frequent conflicts with both staff and residents. Eight sessions of cognitive behavior therapy were conducted, including role playing appropriate responses, assertiveness training, use of self-disclosure and feeling statements, as well as progressive muscle relaxation and deep-breathing exercises. The therapist also suggested to staff that the subject's behavior be relabeled as healthy assertiveness. Incidents of conflict and agitation decreased from four per month during baseline to zero to two per month following treatment. Daily doses of chlorpromazine were changed to PRN.

Somatic Complaints

In describing commonly observed neuroses of the elderly, Kral (1982) notes that somatic complaints and hypochondriacal fears are more frequently observed in elderly than in younger populations. There have been a few cases of behavioral treatment for this problem published in the literature. Flannery (1974) described the treatment of a 77-year-old man with agitated depression and grief following the death of his sister. The client reported frequent headaches and insomnia and had a history of collecting prescriptions from several different clinics and overmedicating himself. A behavioral contract was written specifying at which agency the client would seek medical services, the disposal of all other medications, and daily attendance at the elderly drop-in center. Therapy was made contingent upon abiding by the agreement. Anecdotal reports indicated that the client met the terms of the contract and decreased his depressive behaviors and somatic complaints. The number of treatment sessions required was unspecified. Gains were maintained during a follow-up period of unknown duration.

Williamson (1984) worked with a 73-year-old institutionalized woman who had a history of depression and complained of agitation and anxiety over her physical well-being. She also issued a high rate of somatic complaints. The client was seen for thirty-three 20- to 40-minute sessions in which she was reinforced with time to talk of her somatic complaints as she gradually engaged in longer periods of appropriate conversation. Initially, 1 minute of appropriate conversation was required for 4 minutes of "somatic conversation." This ratio was gradually increased to 5 minutes of appropriate conversation in order to earn 1 minute of somatic talk. The therapist dealt with somatic talk during periods of appropriate conversation by turning away from the client and restarting the timing of the period. Data collected during sessions indicated that the percent of somatic talk decreased from about 65% of 20 one minute intervals during baseline to about 20% during the final seven intervention sessions. The patient was discharged at the end of the therapy. This study was somewhat unusual in that an ABAB single-subject design was used, demonstrating the functional relationship between the intervention and the rate of somatic complaints.

Obsessive-Compulsive Behavior

Obsessive-compulsive behavior has been treated somewhat differently from the behaviors described previously. O'Brien (1978) developed an unusual treatment for a 70-year-old woman with a 30-year history of obsessive-compulsive handwashing and a fear of contracting smallpox. Instead of using relaxation, he selected reading and writing as incompatible responses to the client's frequent handwashing. Other components of the treatment included assertiveness training for both the client and her husband and the use of contingent extinction (following inappropriate behavior) and reinforcement (following appropriate behavior) by the husband. The client was symptom-free after 16 one-hour sessions and continued to do well at a 24-month follow-up.

One of two clients treated by Rowan, Holborn, Walker, and Siddiqui (1984) was a 67-year-old woman with a fear of contamination, resulting in frequent handwashing and the disposal of items she believed were contaminated. Treatment involved *in vivo* exposure to contaminated items using modeling, guided modeling, and finally the fading of guidance. Response prevention was used, and relatives and friends were asked not to throw out items if the client requested it. As homework assignments, the client was required to wear "contaminated" garments. At the end of the treatment, the patient was able to make prolonged contact with 44 previously "contaminated" items. Additionally, the significant improvement in depressive symptomatology was accompanied by eventual discontinuation of medication. Treatment gains were maintained at 6-, 12-, and 18-month follow-ups.

A third case was reported by Junginger and Ditto (1984). Following the death of her sister, a 65-year-old woman began asking neighbors to check things around her home. This behavior became so severe that the patient was placed in a nursing home. Subsequently, she became afraid that she might accidently hurt someone and experienced a number of panic attacks, leading to hospitalization. Treatment was conducted in the hospital. It consisted of Imipramine, response prevention, and the exaggerated description of her fears. Nurses were instructed to ask the client periodically if she had hurt anyone, and then they asked the client to hit a nurse on the back with a rolled-up paper a number of times daily. Treatment continued for 47 days. At the end of that time, checking behavior decreased from a baseline frequency of five to fourteen per day, to zero to one per day. A 7-month follow-up revealed the same low figure.

In summary, the use of stress management procedures to treat elderly individuals with a variety of anxiety disorders has begun to appear more frequently in the literature. Yet, the vast majority of the published studies have been single case reports. Many do not involve the use of appropriate single-subject research designs to demonstrate a functional relationship between intervention and target response. None of the reviewed studies utilized well-controlled group designs, and there has been little emphasis on generalization and maintenance. Issues of reliability, often the hallmark of behavioral research, are rarely addressed in this literature. Instead, progress is more typically assessed using self-report measures or general observations by staff or family members. Finally, many of the stress management interventions involved the use of treatment packages. A number of studies included the use of psychotropic medications. Little attempt has been made to conduct component analyses of the various behavioral and/or medical procedures utilized in these studies. If work in this area is to progress beyond the case report format, well-controlled studies utilizing appropriate research designs and addressing issues of generalization are necessary.

Group Therapy for Anxiety Disorders

There have been a few studies in which elderly clients were treated for anxiety in group therapy. Keller, Croake, and Brooking (1975) examined the effects of a 4-week educational program about rational emotive therapy principles with 15 community-dwelling elderly. The treatment group showed significant increases in rational thinking and decreases in trait anxiety over a control group given no treatment. A follow-up assessment was not conducted. Toseland and Rose (1978) compared three training methods designed to increase assertiveness and decrease anxiety using small groups of community-dwelling elderly. The three methods involved were behavioral role playing, problem solving, and social group work involving six 90-minute sessions. The groups given behavioral role playing and problem solving demonstrated significantly improved performances on a role-play test conducted immediately after training. At a 3-month follow-up, however, all groups, including those receiving social group work, had increased in their performance to the same level. Interestingly, no decrease was evident on the response anxiety and response probability scales of the Gambrill–Richey Assessment Interview and Group Evaluation Inventory or self-report questionnaire that was completed by each client. Toseland and Rose reported that these results were similar to those of other studies that used role-play measures and self-report inventories. They hypothesized that the delayed effectiveness of the social group work method was due to a practice effect from posttraining to follow-up (social work group members had not been encouraged to practice newly acquired skills during group meetings).

Ingersoll and Silverman (1978) compared the effect of two types of group therapy on self-esteem, anxiety, and somatic behavior in community-dwelling elderly. The first group focused on ways to cope with anxiety due to recent life events. They were taught progressive muscle relaxation and modeling, reinforcement, and role playing as coping skills. The second group received guidance in establishing a bridge between past and present. They focused on reminiscing and a life review process. In general, self-esteem increased and anxiety decreased for participants in both groups, but these changes were not statistically significant. The second group, however, reported a significantly greater decrease in somatic complaints than the group using behavioral techniques. The reasons for these results are unclear. The number of participants in each group was small (8 and 9) and both groups had inconsistent attendance and high attrition rates. Additionally, it was hypothesized that there may have been insufficient time for members of the first group to become facile with the behavioral procedures. No follow-up assessments were conducted.

Weldon and Yesavage (1982) introduced progressive muscle relaxation, self-hypnosis techniques, shifting attention (learning to attend to different areas of the body while relaxed), and imagery to a group of 25 subjects with senile dementia (Alzheimer's type) or multi-infarct dementia. A matched group of 25 control subjects participated only in a discussion of current events. The subjects ranged in age from 52 to 93 years. Both groups met three times a week for 1-hour sessions over a 3-month period. Significant improvement on measures of psychiatric symptoms, self-help skills, communication, and social interaction skills was noted in the treatment group. Ten subjects no longer needed sleep medication. Follow-up assessments were not conducted.

It is difficult to draw conclusions about the efficacy of group interventions from the small number of stress-reduction studies conducted with groups of elderly. In fact, in half of the studies, the experimental group was no better than the control group on dependent measures of anxiety. In one case the results from the experimental group were worse than those of the control group. The most significant weaknesses in this group of studies were the lack of long-term follow-up and the lack of an assessment of generalization to the natural environment. Use of role playing or self-report checklists do not adequately address these needs. Weldon and Yesavage's (1982) use of a behavioral rating scale begins to provide a more adequate measure, although we are not told who completed the observations and whether these observers were blind about group membership or were lacking information about the study.

Treatment of Psychophysiological Dysfunctions

Stress reduction procedures are frequently used in the psychophysiological treatment of chronic health problems in both children and adults. The literature includes studies of the treatment of cardiovascular heart disease, high blood pressure, pain from chronic disorders or diseases (e.g., headache pain, back pain, cancer pain), and pain associated with invasive medical procedures or the iatrogenic effects of treatment. Even though the elderly have the highest percentage of chronic health problems in the U.S. population, few studies have included them as subjects. When people over the age of 60 have been included, the findings for those subjects have not generally been analyzed separately.

This section will begin with a description of five studies involving the treatment of adults with psychophysiological conditions. Elderly subjects were included in these studies and their data were analyzed separately. This will be followed by a review of single case studies involving elderly subjects who suffer from a variety of chronic medical conditions.

The five studies presented are interesting in that they provide data contrasting the ways older and younger subjects respond to behavioral treatment. Lammers, Naliboff, and Straatmeyer (1984) described the effect of progressive muscle relaxation on stress ratings and blood glucose levels in four diabetic patients (one of whom was 64 years old). An ABAB single-subject design was used. Two subjects evidenced significant decreases in blood glucose levels, but there were no effects on stress levels during the treatment phases. The remaining two patients, including the elderly subject, demonstrated no significant decreases in blood glucose. They exhibited gradual decreases in stress levels across all four phases of the study that were not functionally related to the use of progressive muscle relaxation. Barlow, O'Brien, and Last (1984) evaluated the efficacy of couples treatment of agoraphobia in which 14 women received group treatment with their husbands and 14 received group treatment without their spouses. The treatment format included cognitive restructuring and graduated exposure to fearful situations. Only 5 of the 28 subjects did not respond to treatment and improved little on clinical rating scales. One of the five was the only elderly subject (63 years of age) included in the sample.

Blanchard et al. (1985) reported the results of a clinical replication series with 250 chronic headache patients who had received behavioral treatment. Treatment initially involved progressive muscle relaxation only. Of those who failed to show improvement, tension headache sufferers were given EMG frontalis biofeedback, while migraine headache sufferers and those subjects with combined headache type were given thermal biofeedback. The analysis was conducted by dividing the sample across age groups. Across all three headache types, the oldest group consistently reported less improvement with progressive muscle relaxation alone. For example, 77.8% of those subjects over the age of 55 with tension headaches were unimproved (versus 35.8% of those subjects between 32 and 39 years of age),

66.7% of those subjects over the age of 44 with migraine headaches were unimproved (versus 33.3% for those subjects between 36 and 39 years of age), and 85.7% of those subjects over the age of 50 with combined headache type were unimproved (versus 41.7% for those subjects 39 years of age and less). The addition of biofeedback (for those subjects who failed to improve) did little to change the disparity between the age groups with the exception of those subjects with combined headache type. The subjects over 40 years of age in this group reported only a 14.3% unimproved rate, while 41.7% of subjects less than 39 years of age were unimproved.

Benson, Alexander, and Feldman (1975) taught a relaxation response to patients with stable ischemic heart disease. Five of the eleven patients were over 60 years of age. Following 4 weeks of relaxation training, which consisted of two 20-minute practice sessions a day, premature ventricular contractions (PVCs) were measured at rest, during sleep, and following exercise. Three of the five elderly subjects demonstrated striking decreases in PVCs at rest. Two of the three had lowered PVCs in the recovery period following exercise. The mean for the entire group of eleven subjects was significantly lower during sleeping hours. However, there was no long-term follow-up and no control group in this study.

The remaining group of studies are single case reports and are confined solely to elderly subjects. Levendusky and Pankratz (1975) utilized relaxation, covert imagery, and cognitive relabeling to treat a 65-year-old man who had a history of abdominal operations, intense abdominal pain, loss of weight, and social withdrawal. Using an approach similar to that developed by Fordyce, Fowler, Lehman, and Delateur (1968), Levendusky and Pankratz successfully decreased the use of pain medication and the awkward and embarrassing posturing that had developed as a result of the pain. The pain medication was gradually withdrawn by diluting it with saline. No experimental design was used and the results were based on the client's self-report. A 6-month follow-up indicated that the client was still using the relaxation technique, planning a summer vacation, and had returned to club activities and part-time teaching. Because the medication was withdrawn without the client's knowledge, the study is a controversial one.

Two additional case reports describe the use of stress reduction procedures to control pain. Czirr and Gallagher (1983) treated a 62-year-old man suffering from painful rheumatoid arthritis and depression. His score on the Beck Depression Inventory (BDI) was 17, an indication of moderate depression. The investigators implemented a program of progressive muscle relaxation, imagery, and suggestions to increase his active engagement in pleasant events. Following 7 weeks of treatment, the depression had subsided (BDI of 4), and self-reports of pain had decreased in intensity by almost half. Progress was maintained at a 3-month follow-up.

Taped relaxation instructions were combined with soothing background music by Linoff and West (1982) for the treatment of an 89-year-old male nursing home resident with a 20-year history of headache pain. Following 19 treatment sessions, the patient reported few headaches, had significantly decreased the number of somatic complaints, and requested pain medication only once in 3 weeks (after previously being on constant pain medication). There was no follow-up.

There are three studies which explored the use of stress reduction procedures to treat elderly patients with a variety of medical problems. Hamberger (1982) found that progressive muscle relaxation was an effective coping skill for a 68-year-old cancer patient when used to control gastric upset. The patient's problem began 3 years prior to treatment, during radiation therapy, and continued in the form of intense stomach pain, nausea, and vomiting whenever she felt anxious, angry, or tense. Before treatment the patient spent an average of 4.5 days per month in bed. Immediately after treatment and at a 12-month follow-up, she spent no days in bed. Kolko (1984) also found relaxation useful in treating a 61-year-old women who exhibited excessive daytime sleepiness, periodic cataplexy, and nocturnal urinary frequency. Along with learning progressive muscle relaxation, the client's fluid intake was restricted and she wore a rubberband on her wrist, which she snapped whenever she felt sleepy to increase daytime arousal. Following 18 weeks of treatment, sleep attacks and cataplectic episodes had been eliminated; nocturnal urinary frequency decreased by about 50%. At 6- and 12-month follow-ups there were further gains.

Tauber (1982) used biofeedback to treat a 64-year-old woman who had a history of alcoholism, insomnia, neck pain, high blood pressure, bruxism, ruminating thoughts, and depression. He conducted seven biofeedback sessions that consisted of progressive muscle relaxation and autogenic training. The patient was also involved in group therapy. Anecdotal reports indicated that the patient had improved sleep, a decrease in bruxism, and had eliminated the need for blood pressure medication. Data from the biofeedback sessions indicated that the patient successfully relaxed. Frontalis EMG readings decreased from 10 microvolts during baseline to 2 to 3 microvolts during training. Treatment gains were maintained at a 2-month follow-up, and blood pressure medication was discontinued.

The studies reviewed in this section suffer from some of the same deficiencies described for previous work. Most of the studies failed to use appropriate research designs with which to demonstrate a functional relationship between intervention and treatment outcome. Additionally, interventions typically included a range of procedures, making it difficult to determine the relative efficacy of the various treatment components. The possible exceptions are those studies in which elderly individuals comprised only a subgroup of the total number of subjects. Those studies were well controlled and used appropriate research designs. The results of individual elderly subjects, however, were not always distinguished from the remaining subjects in the sample. Perhaps the most important finding among this group of studies was the differential response of older and younger patients to behavioral interventions, but due to the relatively small number of studies, it is difficult to draw a definitive conclusion in this matter. It will be necessary for future researchers to conduct methodologically sound studies of stress management and chronic illness among the elderly if work in this area is to progress.

SUMMARY

Until recently, the use of behavioral techniques with the elderly has been limited to operant-based procedures that focused upon antecedent control and contingency management. The population of interest has generally been confined to nursing homes or chronic care hospitals. Stress management procedures to treat elderly individuals with anxiety disorders have begun to appear with greater frequency in the literature. Most of these studies have lacked methodological rigor, however.

A second body of literature involving stress reduction procedures and elderly subjects is found in the psychophysiological research. While few studies have been focused exclusively on elderly subjects, several have included one or more elderly individuals in their subject samples. Unfortunately, data from those subjects have not always been analyzed separately. An important advantage of this literature is that the research tends to be well controlled and utilizes both valid and reliable measures. A small group of studies involving elderly subjects suffering from pain and related disorders does appear in the literature, but these are single-case designs with many of the same methodological inadequacies noted in the anxiety disorders research.

There are still a number of unanswered questions about the use of stress reduction procedures with the elderly. Are there differences in the way in which elderly patients respond to stress reduction procedures? Must some procedures be modified or revised for this population, and can a clinician expect the same response to treatment as he or she achieves with young and middle-aged adults? What are the limits of behavioral techniques, especially stress reduction procedures, in the treatment of conditions that were previously thought to be due to the irreversible biological declines that accompany aging?

In general, the literature on the treatment of anxiety disorders among the elderly is at an extremely basic level. Few investigators have used single-subject designs, and few have demonstrated functional control of treatment methods. These are badly needed. Research on the treatment of anxiety disorders among the elderly must include the use of well-controlled group designs that seek to demonstrate the efficacy of treatment packages and their individual components. The use of anecdotal reports and subjective data to demonstrate treatment gains must be augmented by more objective measures of both overt behavior and physiological correlates where possible. Researchers need to address issues of generalization and maintenance of treatment gains. Research on the behavioral treatment of elderly patients should expand the focus upon community-dwelling individuals who comprise the largest percentage of elderly in the country. Many of the problems facing this population have not been considered by behavioral researchers. The most important role for behavioral technology may be to enable elderly individuals to maintain an independent lifestyle and decrease the need for residential services.

References

Antonovsky, A. (1980). *Health, stress, and coping.* San Francisco: Jossey-Bass.

Averill, J. R. (1979). A selective review of cognitive and behavioral factors involved in the regulation of stress. In R. A. Depue (Ed.), *The psychobiology of the depressive disorders: Implications for the effects of stress* (pp. 365–387). New York: Academic Press.

Barlow, D., O'Brien, G., & Last, C. (1984). Couples treatment of agoraphobia. *Behavior Therapy, 15*, 41–58.

Benson, H., Alexander, J., & Feldman, C. L. (1975). Decreased premature ventricular contractions through use of the relaxation response in patients with stable ischaemic heart-disease. *Lancet, 2*, 380–382.

Blanchard, E., Andrasik, F., Evans, D., Neff, D., Appelbaum, K., & Rodichok, L. (1985). Behavioral treatment of 250 chronic headache patients: A clinical replication series. *Behavior Therapy, 16*, 308–327.

Botwinick, J. (1970). Geropsychology. *Annual Review of Psychology, 21*, 234–272.

Brink. T. L. (1980). Geriatric paranoia: Case report illustrating behavioral management. *Journal of the American Geriatrics Society, 28*, 519–522.

Carstensen, L. L., & Fremouw, W. J. (1981). The demonstration of a behavioral intervention for late paranoia. *The Gerontologist, 21*, 329–333.

Cautela, J. R. (1967). *Behavior therapy with the aged*. Paper presented at the meeting of the Eastern Psychological Association, Boston.

Czirr, R., & Gallagher, D. (1983). Case report: Behavioral treatment of depression and somatic complaints in rheumatoid arthritis. *Clinical Gerontologist, 2*, 63–66.

Falloon, I. (1975). The therapy of depression: A behavioral approach. *Psychotherapy and Psychosomatics, 25*, 69–75.

Flannery, R. B. (1974). Behavior modification of geriatric grief: A transactional perspective. *International Journal of Aging and Human Development, 5*, 192–203.

Fordyce, W. E., Fowler, R. S., Lehman, J. F., & Delateur, B. (1968). Some implications of learning in problems of chronic pain. *Journal of Chronic Disease, 21*, 179–190.

Friedman, D. (1966). Treatment of a case of dog phobia in a deaf mute by behavior therapy. *Behavior Research and Therapy, 4*, 141.

Garfinkel, R. (1979). Brief behavior therapy with an elderly patient: A case study. *Journal of Geriatric Psychiatry, 12*, 101–109.

Garrison, J. W. (1978). Stress management training for the elderly. A psychoeducational approach. *Journal of the American Geriatrics Society, 26*, 397–403.

Haley, W. E. (1983). Behavioral self-management application to a case of agitation in an elderly chronic psychiatric patient. *Clinical Gerontologist, 1*, 45–52.

Hamberger, L. K. (1982). Reduction of generalized adversive responding in a post treatment cancer patient: Relaxation as an active coping skill. *Journal of Behavior Therapy and Experimental Psychiatry, 13*, 229–233.

Holmes, T. H., & Rahe, R. H. (1967). The social readjustment rating scale. *Journal of Psychosomatic Research, 11*, 213–218.

Hussian, R. A. (1981). *Geriatric psychology: A behavioral perspective*. New York: Van Nostrand Reinhold.

Ingersoll, B., & Silverman, A. (1978). Comparative group psychotherapy for the aged. *The Gerontologist, 18*, 201–206.

Junginger, J., & Ditto, B. (1984). Multitreatment of obsessive-compulsive checking in a geriatric patient. *Behavior Modification, 8*, 379–390.

Keller, J. F., Croake, J. W., & Brooking, J. Y. (1975). Effects of a program in rational thinking and anxieties in older persons. *Journal of Counseling Psychology, 22*, 54–57.

Kolko, D. (1984). Behavioral treatment of excessive daytime sleepiness in an elderly woman with multiple medical problems. *Journal of Behavior Therapy and Experimental Psychiatry, 15*, 341–345.

Kral, V. A. (1982). Neuroses of the aged: A neglected area. *Clinical Gerontologist, 1*, 29–35.

Lammers, C., Naliboff, B., & Straatmeyer, J. (1984). The effects of progressive relaxation on stress and diabetic control. *Behavior Research and Therapy, 22*, 641–650.

Levendusky, P., & Pankratz, L. (1975). Self-control techniques as alternatives to pain medication. *Journal of Abnormal Psychology, 84*, 165–168.

Linoff, M. G., & West, C. M. (1982). Relaxation training systematically combined with music: Treatment of tension headaches in a geriatric patient. *International Journal of Behavioral Geriatrics, 1*, 11–16.

Moss, G. E. (1973). *Illness, immunity, and social interaction*. New York: Wiley & Sons.

O'Brien, J. S. (1978). The behavioral treatment of a thirty year smallpox obsession and handwashing compulsion. *Journal of Behavior Therapy and Experimental Psychiatry, 9*, 365–368.

Rowan, V., Holborn, S., Walker, J., & Siddiqui, A. (1984). A rapid multi-component treatment for an obsessive–compulsive disorder. *Journal of Behavior Therapy and Experimental Psychiatry, 15,* 347–352.

Tauber, L. (1982). Biofeedback as an adjunct in treating elders. *Clinical Gerontologist, 11,* 72–73.

Thyer, B. A. (1981). Prolonged *in vivo* exposure therapy with a 70-year-old woman. *Journal of Behavior Therapy and Experimental Psychiatry, 12,* 69–71.

Toseland, R., & Rose, S. D. (1978). Evaluating social skills training for older adults in groups. *Social Work Research Abstracts, 14,* 25–33.

Wander, T. W. (1972). Existential depression treated by desensitization of phobias: Strategy and transcript. *Journal of Behavior Therapy and Experimental Psychiatry, 3,* 111–116.

Weldon, S., & Yesavage, J. (1982). Behavioral improvement with relaxation training in senile dementia. *Clinical Gerontologist, 1,* 43–49.

Williamson, P. N. (1984). An intervention for hypochondriacal complaints. *Clinical Gerontologist, 3,* 64–68.

Williamson, P. N., & Ascione, F. R. (1983). Behavioral treatment of the elderly: Implications for theory and therapy. *Behavior Modification, 7,* 583–611.

8

The Promotion of Positive Social Interaction through Social Skills Training

MARY-LOUISE ENGELS

INTRODUCTION

Training programs in assertion and social skills typically encourage people to increase the frequency of their social interactions and to behave in more expressive, assertive, and adaptive ways. Although such programs have been widely used among diverse population groups (Bellack & Hersen, 1979), little training of such complex interpersonal behaviors has been undertaken in older people. The present chapter, written from the standpoint of the practising clinician, covers the following subjects: the changes that occur in social interaction patterns in later life, and their possible consequences for personal adjustment; the relevance of social skills and assertion training in promoting more frequent, effective, and positive social interactions; and a training program in social skills for elderly clients, along with illustrative case study descriptions. The chapter concludes with special considerations for implementing training with the elderly and suggestions for additional research.

CHANGES IN SOCIAL INTERACTION IN LATER LIFE

The observation that many elderly people are relatively isolated and socially inactive requires little documentation. Many elderly experience widowhood and diminished contact with their children. For most men, and for an increasing number of women, the loss of the job role at retirement brings with it the loss of many important social contacts that may never be satisfactorily replaced. The death of peers progressively constricts the range of friendships, at a time when the elderly have fewer opportunities to make new friends.

MARY-LOUISE ENGELS • Behavior Therapy Unit, Douglas Hospital Center, Verdun, Quebec, Canada H4H IR3.

Despite the inevitable changes and losses in their social worlds, many older people, perhaps the majority, are able to develop new social attachments and interests and deepen old ones. A significant percentage, however, seem to lack the ability to restructure a social world and to gain emotional support from others (Levy, 1981). For those elderly who confront multiple stressors at a time when social contacts and support are diminished or unavailable, high rates of personal distress, psychiatric symptomatology, and illness might be predicted. The importance of social support for the health and well-being of the elderly has been discussed elsewhere in this volume (see Chapter 5). A community survey of psychological distress among older people has highlighted the negative psychological impact of role loss and constricted social interactions (Abrahams & Patterson, 1979). The survey found that the ability to take social initiatives, organize a pattern of varied daily activity, and maintain social relationships outside the home was strongly associated with psychological health in the elderly. On the other hand, it found that vulnerability to the stresses of aging increased under conditions of habitual dependency, social passivity, and inadequate interpersonal skills. In particular, many older women have been socialized in relatively dependent and compliant styles of interpersonal behavior (Maccoby & Jacklin, 1974) and precluded from learning ways to construct social networks and develop assertive social skills (Levy, 1981). Levy has therefore recommended the benefits of social skills training and linkage into community networks. Other writers have similarly urged the development of social skills programs to help older people cope with the negative effects of social isolation and loneliness (Corby, 1975; Welford, 1980).

More frequent and rewarding interactions with others are likely to have a beneficial impact on overall personal adjustment in older people, as suggested by the Social Reconstruction Model of successful aging (Kuypers & Bengston, 1973). In this formulation, increased competence leads to a self-reinforcing process characterized by the buildup and maintenance of coping skills; an internalized view of the self as effective; increased self-confidence and self-reliance; a labeling of oneself as able; and the internalization of one's self-view as effective. Kuypers and Bengston suggest that the social reconstruction process may be set in motion by providing beneficial inputs into the older person's environment. Programs to promote competence in social interactions would constitute one such positive input. It is therefore appropriate to consider in more detail the relevance of social skills training for the elderly.

RELEVANCE OF SOCIAL SKILLS TRAINING FOR THE ELDERLY

Social skills training comprises a set of principles and procedures derived from social learning theory. The major focus of treatment is on observable behavior. Modeling, direct instruction, coaching, and repeated practice are typically employed to improve client performance in a range of interpersonal situations. To date, few empirical studies have examined the effects of social skills training on the community-dwelling elderly. There are reasons to believe, however, that such training may well offer an effective way of teaching specific competencies and promoting personal adjustment in this population group, and of enhancing mood and cognitive function.

A particularly important category of psychological dysfunction in later life for which social skills training may have remedial or preventive value is depression. This mood disturbance is the most commonly diagnosed of old age (Blazer, 1982). Blazer, who has outlined a social stress– social support model of etiology in the onset and maintenance of late-life depression, noted the contribution of the following components: roles and available attachments; frequency of social interactions; and perceived social support. Each of these parameters was found to predict 30-month mortality in a group of elderly community patients (Blazer, 1980). Interventions designed to buffer the depressogenic effects of social stressors by enhancing social attachments, interactions, and supports would therefore seem to have important therapeutic potential.

The amount and quality of social interaction have been linked to cognitive functioning in the elderly as well as to mood disturbance. Dolen and Bearison (1982) reported a positive and significant relation between social interaction and social cognitive abilities in a group of community-dwelling subjects. Levels of social interaction were a more significant predictor of cognitive decline than age. Ernst and colleagues have proposed a circular relation between social isolation and decrements leading to cognitive dysfunction (Ernst, Beran, Safford, & Kleinhauz, 1978). The authors of both papers recommended an increase in treatments designed to counteract social isolation and to support and extend social competence.

Numerous suggestions regarding suitable targets for social skills training with the elderly have been advanced, including initiating friendships, increasing social contacts, and making effective requests and refusals. Corby (1975) recommends training in self-disclosure to assist older women in developing intimate relations with confidantes. She also considers skills training desirable in the initiation of new relationships and in the reduction of such aversive behaviors as complaining, which may alienate actual or potential members of the elderly person's support network. In the same vein, Welford (1980) predicts that social skills training will become a powerful means of reducing the interpersonal problems of old people. An important target for training is suggested by Wheeler (1980), whose descriptive report on the conduct of assertion groups with the elderly recommends the development of skills in handling ageist encounters. According to this author, the older person is at risk for incorporating the unduly restrictive and negative assumptions of age-based stereotyping into his or her self-image. The ability to counter derogatory remarks and slights in an assertive manner is said to enhance feelings of self-esteem and self-efficacy.

The literature just reviewed offers at least indirect encouragement for the belief that social skills training may have beneficial effects in promoting personal adjustment, remediating or forestalling impairments in mood and cognitive functioning, and improving specific deficits. There is impressionistic support for the probable benefits of social skills training with the elderly, and anecdotal descriptions of program offerings (Corby, 1975; Wheeler, 1980). Welford, who pioneered studies of sensorimotor skills in the elderly, predicted that explicit training in social skills would be a primary focus in applied gerontology during the 1980s. As yet, however, little social skills research has appeared documenting the efficacy of social skills training programs for achieving specific goals with this population group. The majority of published studies to date has been restricted primarily to psycho-geriatric subjects (Berger & Rose, 1977; Lopez, Hoyer, Goldstein, Gershaw, & Sprafkin, 1980; Patterson, 1982). Although these studies reported improvements of specific skills at the end of training, limitations in respect to maintenance and generalization of treatment gains were noted. The modest impact of these skills training programs may be primarily a function of subject sampling, since reports have featured delimited response patterns in relatively frail and dependent sub-jects. A more extensive review of research on social skills training for the institu-tionalized elderly is contained in Chapter 19. However, such studies do not speak directly to the issue of whether complex repertoires of socially skilled behavior can be acquired or reinstated in older people outside of institutional settings. Further investigation is therefore required before the potential value of social skills training programs for elderly subjects living in the community can be determined with confidence.

SOCIAL SKILLS TRAINING PROGRAM

In the following sections, I will outline a training program based on a research study of social skills training with community-living elderly, using single-case methodology and multiple outcome measures (Engels & Poser, 1987). The section on assessment indicates how role playing, goal setting, and questionnaires may be used for initial evaluation and treatment planning. The section on treatment de-scribes how a brief intervention of 10–12 sessions can use role playing, modeling, cognitive training, and homework in helping clients to improve specific social skills. Finally, three case studies illustrate the problems and treatment progress of three clients who participated in the program.

Assessment

Assessment may be usefully divided into two phases: initial screening and the assessment interview.

Initial Screening

The purpose of an initial screening interview, which may take place by tele-phone or in person, is to determine whether social skills training is an appropriate form of intervention for the individual client. The presence of relatively clear-cut and potentially modifiable social skills deficits that are significantly impairing the client's current life adjustment is sufficient to include clients in a treatment pro-gram. Factors that might exclude clients from social skills training are: significant cognitive impairment; major depressive disorder or psychosis; significant stressor not appropriate for treatment by social skills training (e.g., recent bereavement, intractable pain or illness, imminent marital breakdown, severe sensory or physical handicap). If it is clear that social skills training is not the treatment of choice, the clinician should be prepared to suggest alternative treatment resources. During this initial contact, the therapist discusses the problem-focused nature of the intervention and the rationale for homework assignments that will be given throughout the training program.

Assessment Interview(s)

In this phase of assessment, which may well require two sessions, the clinician acquires relevant information about the client's personal history and circumstances, pinpoints target behaviors for modification, and establishes treatment goals. There are a number of assessment tools that may be useful in facilitating individual assessment, setting the stage for treatment, and monitoring treatment efficacy. These are described below.

Behavioral Role-Play Tests. Behavioral role playing, while not without its problems (Bellack, 1979), remains a useful way of assessing response style and identifying specific deficits in a client's repertoire. Inventories of role-play situations, such as those devised by Hersen, Bellack, and Turner (1978), may be adapted for older people, and they should be constructed so as to assess clients' capacities to produce appropriate positive responses (praise, favorable comment), and negative responses (refusal, complaints, disagreement). Typically, the clinician/researcher describes a specific social situation, and plays the part of the other person in the scene, as in the following examples.

You go into a restaurant at noon with a reservation. You are given a table in a rather dark and noisy corner, near the kitchen, by a hurried, unsmiling waitress.
She says: "Here's your table, Madame."
You'd say: _____
You are a member of a group where people have been discussing their views and habits on physical exercise. Someone turns to you and says:
"What do you do to keep fit?"
You'd say: _____
You have been standing near a cash register in a store, waiting to pay for a purchase and have it wrapped. The clerk turns to a man beside you who arrived after you did.
She says: "May I help you, Sir?"
You'd say: _____
At the center where you do volunteer work, one of the volunteers comes in wearing an attractive new suit.
She says: "Good morning!"
You'd say: _____

Clients should be told that the purpose of the role-playing exercise is to see where they are *now*, with respect to their response styles in certain social situations. They should respond *as they actually would* in such a situation at the present time, and not in what they feel is the "right" or the "best possible" way. Early in the assessment session, before the actual role-play assessment takes place, clients should be given an outline of the scenes that will subsequently be played, so that they will be familiar with the general nature of the situations. More characteristic responses will likely be forthcoming, and the possibly stressful nature of the procedure reduced (Bellack, 1979). Audiotaping or videotaping of role-playing responses is recommended during assessment and training, if possible, in order to help the client become more aware of his or her response style and to monitor progress. On the basis of the role-play assessment and other information provided by the client, a few (perhaps two to four) specific target behaviors may then be selected for training (e.g., expressing opinions in groups; initiating conversations; responding to put-downs).

Goal Setting. The purpose of this assessment strategy is to identify three or four specific goals that the client would like to achieve in his or her social environment by the end of treatment. The use of goal attainment scaling (Smith, 1981) is especially helpful in this process. Table 1 provides an example of goal attainment scaling (GAS) devised for a client who was less active than she wished to be, in both group and one-to-one social situations. She also complained of frequent arguments with her sister. Under each of the three scales are five behavioral descriptions of the anticipated status of the client with respect to each goal at the end of treatment. Outcomes both more or less favorable than the expected outcome are described. All five are nonoverlapping and plausible, with the expected level being the most likely to occur after successful treatment. Numerical values are assigned to outcome levels, with the best expected outcome scored 2, the outcome more favorable than anticipated scored 1, and the expected level scored 0. In similar fashion, the worst expected outcome is −2, and a less favorable than expected outcome −1.

It is not essential to use a formalized measurement device such as GAS. The primary feature of the goal-setting exercise is to invite clients to define clear treatment goals at the outset of treatment related to specific changes they would like to bring about in their social situations, and to describe where they would expect to be with respect to each goal by the time treatment ends. Clients can be assisted in reformulating vague goals in more operational terms. For example, "getting along better with my husband" might be defined as "unpleasant interaction (more than 10 minutes) every 2 weeks"; "pleasant interaction (more than 15 minutes) two to three times a month." When the client expresses goals related to subjective states, such as "not feeling lonely," or "being more self-confident," these can again be recast in behavioral terms (e.g., "outing every second week; one weekly telephone visit"; "express opinions 75% of the time in group settings"). Goal setting not only establishes an outcome measure that focuses on the client's behavior in the natural environment but also facilitates treatment planning and implementation. The experience of operationally defining goals provides something tangible for the client to work toward and thus has a motivational impact (McLean & Hakstian, 1979). It teaches clients to become sensitive to daily self-monitoring, helps to link homework assignments to treatment goals and procedures, and offers the client a model of a broad, general approach to problem solving.

TABLE 1
Goal Attainment Follow-up Guide

Levels of attainment	Scale 1: Choral group	Scale 2: Social contacts with persons her own age	Scale 3: Relationship with sister
−2 (Much less than expected level)	Withdraw from group.	Goes out with friends every 6 weeks.	Deteriorated situation; 2–3 arguments weekly, pervasive preoccupation.
−1 (Somewhat less than expected level)	Attendance unchanged, attends about ¾ of meetings.	Goes out with friend(s) once a month.	Weekly argument (10+ minutes).
0 (Expected level of outcome)	Regular attendance, more enjoyment.	Goes out every 2 weeks, plus 1 phone visit.	Argument twice a month; pleasant interactions (10 min.) 2–3 times a month.
1 (Somewhat more than expected level)	Executive position in group.	Weekly outings or entertaining.	Pleasant interaction weekly, argument once a month.
2 (Much more than expected level)	Executive position plus greater use and recognition by others of musical training.	Weekly outings plus one new friend.	Stabilized, cooperative situation; arguments less than once a month, pleasant interactions 2+ times weekly.

Assessment of Cognitions. The clinician must pay particular attention to clients' "thinking styles" during assessment. Clients must examine their characteristic beliefs about themselves and others; to whom they attribute responsibility for successes and setbacks; whether or not they anticipate disappointment, frustration, or rejection in interpersonal situations. Past research has indicated that cognitions including expectations, attributions, and self-evaluations may strongly affect performance in interpersonal situations (Eisler, Hersen, Miller, & Blanchard, 1975; Fielder & Beach, 1978). During the course of treatment, clients should be given opportunities to become aware of, and to modify, the kinds of erroneous expectations and negative self-evaluations that may be inhibiting effective interpersonal behavior. Typically, such cognitive modification can be employed to determine what the client's reasonable rights are; to examine fears of being rejected or ignored, and to rehearse adaptive self-talk should rejection occur; to assess feelings of being culpable or disagreeable in refusal situations, or of being "nosy," or "pushy," when asking open-ended questions, paying compliments, or initiating conversations with strangers.

Self Report Measures. Depending on the requirements of the client, setting, and therapist, the clinician may wish to use some self-report measures during assessment in order to gain further information for treatment planning and as ancillary outcome measures. Among questionnaires containing item content appropriate for elderly groups (Levy, Derogatis, Gallagher, & Gatz, 1980) are those that assess such relevant variables as self-esteem (Rosenberg, 1979), depression, anxiety, and social introversion (Derogatis, Lipman, Rickels, Uhlenhuth, & Covi, 1974).

Treatment Program

The following program may be presented in 10 weekly sessions, followed by three booster sessions a month apart. It is also possible to conduct the program twice weekly, or for a longer time period. Three target behaviors may be systematically trained with this particular format. Time is available for discussion of homework and for evaluating the client's progress towards goal attainment. It also permits the therapist to attend to changing negative cognitions in social situations. The clinician may, of course, adapt the number of behaviors trained and sessions provided to the requirements of the client and the therapy setting. Clinical judgment is indispensable in determining those target behaviors likely to be amenable to brief therapeutic intervention. The fundamental clinical question is: with this client, in this particular time period, what feasible changes in behavior and cognitions will help him or her to engage the environment in more productive and enjoyable ways?

The First Treatment Session

In this session the therapist finalizes the client's treatment goals and discusses the rationale and treatment program in a more detailed fashion. For example, the therapist may inform the client that skills in expressing both positive and negative feelings directly and appropriately and a reasonable level of social interaction are correlated with psychological well-being. He or she may say that the treatment the client is about to undergo is an educational program to develop more rewarding methods of interacting with others in the client's social environment. The intent of the time-limited intervention is not to reconstruct the "personality," but to change specific behaviors or verbal interaction patterns with others, primarily through modeling, role play and rehearsal. Clients are asked to examine the kinds of thoughts and expectations that might be impeding effective behavior. The therapist assures them that they will receive help in achieving their social goals by breaking them down into small, component steps.

Following this initial session, the training program focuses on the target behaviors chosen for modification, with three sessions allotted for each behavior. In our program, subjects then received three "booster" sessions over a 3-month maintenance period, for a total of 13 individual sessions. Following a further 3 months during which no contact occurred, final assessment measures were taken.

Session Format

Each treatment session lasts between 60 and 90 minutes. Older people require adequate time for the repetitive practice involved in learning new behaviors, and they appreciate the chance to air concerns that may be unrelated to the agenda of a particular session. A flexible and unhurried stance is always valuable for those engaged in educational and therapeutic endeavors with the elderly. The general format of the sessions, emphasizing focused behavioral training in more effective, expressive verbal responses, is an adaptation of the model outlined in a recent social skills training manual (Bellack, Hersen, & Himmelhoch, 1980).

The outline of a session is presented below, using the sample target problem of "dealing with difficult people."

15 min.	Review homework; reinforce effort; conversation regarding occurrences in client's life since previous session.
15 min.	Train client on first interaction, e.g., respond to waitress who has been abrupt.
10–15 min.	Train on second interaction, e.g., respond to friend who has been unreasonable.
10–15 min.	Train on third interaction, e.g., respond to authority figure who has been unjust.
15 min.	Cognitive modification.
10–15 min.	Summarize; assign homework related to goal attainment.

Training Format

Four social contexts are considered in designing practice role plays for training sessions: friends and relatives, strangers, work or volunteer settings, group (church or social organization). As indicated in the session format outlined above, repeated role plays of specific interactions are the heart of the treatment program. These role-played scenes should be based primarily on examples from the client's current or recent experience, or on potentially difficult encounters in the near future. Two or three such interactions, in ascending order of difficulty, can be role played during each session, in accordance with the following training format.

1. Role play to assess response style. Encourage clients to attend to what they say, and to how they say it; i.e., to vocal tone, inflection and pitch, speech latency and fluency.
2. Rationale for behavior change.
3. Instructions and modeling. Here the therapist can give suggestions and present possible response sequences. It should be emphasized that these are illustrative only, and that the training program aims to help the individual develop his or her own style of handling situations more adaptively. Invite clients to try out alternative responses, and to select and practice what they feel comfortable with.
4. Feedback, positive reinforcement from therapist.
5. Repeated role play.

Homework

Homework is an indispensable part of the treatment program. The therapist should regularly instruct clients to practice in the natural environment the target behavior on which they are currently working. Specific assignments used to facilitate practice of the target behaviors can be adapted from suggestions found in current popular self-help manuals on the topics of assertion and shyness (e.g., Alberti & Emmons, 1975; Fensterheim & Baer, 1975; Zimbardo, 1977). Examples include renewing previous social contacts by making phone calls to old friends and acquaintances; introducing oneself to a new person in apartment block, church, or senior group; conversing with strangers in line at the bank or grocery store; inviting an acquaintance over for dessert and coffee; expressing disagreement with another person's confidently delivered opinion; taking back an article one has purchased; paying two compliments each day. "Analogue" assignments can also be given. Clients who are improving conversational skills can be advised to write a number of brief stories about interesting things that have happened to them, either recently or in the past, or accounts of articles that they have read in the newspaper. They can then practice narrating these in front of a mirror until they develop fluency. In view of the importance of nonverbal communication, clients can practice adopting a more animated and expressive facial expression and vocal tone, or adopting a more "engaged" bodily posture while talking in front of a mirror. One of our clients was assigned to construct harsh put-down situations, to which she then prepared and rehearsed devastating rejoinders. Homework assignments also include encouraging clients to take steps toward goal attainment: e.g., to telephone the university to get a copy of course listings offered in the coming semester; to buy a small gift for a relative; to plan a dinner party.

CASE STUDIES

In this section the author presents case studies of clients who followed the social skills training program just described. They were recruited, as were all participants, through announcements placed in churches and in the mass media. They resembled other clients in their physical health status, level of education, socioeconomic status, and presenting complaints. These particular cases were selected to illustrate outcomes that were superior (Miss A), roughly typical (Mrs. N), and somewhat less successful (Ms. R) than those obtained by program participants as a whole.

Miss A was a 69-year-old former insurance company office worker, who had been retired for 7 years. She lived in an apartment building for senior citizens and attended the monthly tenants' committee meetings, but otherwise spoke rarely to the other residents. Her only family connections were two married nieces, whom she saw three or four times a year. Her contacts with friends from her working days had become infrequent (six to eight times a year). She attended church every Sunday and went to a seniors' group once a month, but had initiated few social interactions in these settings and expressed relatively few comments and opinions. A talented needlewoman, she sold her handcrafted items to a suburban boutique. She told the therapist that she was especially concerned that she was beginning to withdraw from people, was afraid of being rejected by others, and was losing interest in social activities.

Her facial expression was serious to the point of sternness, and she frequently frowned, even when recounting positive events. Her speech was clipped and businesslike. Although moderately overweight, she exercised daily, and reported her health as good, apart from intermittent bouts of arthritis. She had been insomniac since her mother's death 12 years before. Her pension income was adequate to maintain a modest standard of living, which included regular vacations.

Her goals for treatment included: participating in more planned activities where others were involved, and increasing her contacts with neighbors and acquaintances. Target behaviors to reach these goals were: paying compliments, initiating conversations, and expressing opinions.

During treatment this client manifested the same conscientiousness in practicing her new verbal behaviors, carrying out homework assignments, and following up informal suggestions that had presumably served her well during her working life. At the end of the maintenance period (3 months after the end of regular treatment sessions), Miss A reported frequent and pleasurable interactions with the neighbors in her apartment. She helped distribute the monthly apartment newspaper and attended a regular exercise class. She took part in regular outings with friends and relatives and attended weekly meetings of a senior group with new acquaintances from the apartment. She spent several hours each month in genealogical research, which had opened up new contacts with others. Miss A had expanded and placed on a more businesslike basis her production and sales of handicrafts. Moreover, during the summer months, she had returned to the insurance company to work part time. Finally, although this issue had not been addressed in treatment, she lost 20 pounds through systematic diet and exercise. After a further 3 months, she reported that these improvements were maintained or further enhanced, to her considerable satisfaction.

In view of Miss A's restricted lifestyle when treatment began, and her stated concerns about her growing social withdrawal and indifference, the rapid and extensive gains she made during and after treatment were an agreeable surprise to the therapist. She impressed the therapist as an energetic, competent, and determined woman who was able to mobilize her considerable resources after a few sessions of training and encouragement. Following initial successes in targeted behaviors, she appeared ready and eager to undertake new initiatives and carry them through to satisfactory conclusions.

Mrs. N.

Mrs. N was a 70-year-old woman, widowed for 10 years, who described feelings of social inferiority and moderate depression. She reported occasional crying spells, and periods of feeling discouraged and hopeless. However, she denied having ever contemplated suicide, which was against her strongly held religious convictions. At the time treatment began, Mrs. N had minimal contact with her daughter, who was "living in sin" in another province. Her son lived in a nearby suburb with his wife and two young children, but meetings with them were also infrequent (three or four per year). Mrs. N's life revolved around her church, where she attended the Women's Guild, sang in the choir, and worked for Meals-On-Wheels. Relationships with other churchwomen were not wholly satisfactory, since Mrs. N often found it difficult to initiate conversations with others, to handle rude or critical comments, or to insure that her opinions were heard. As a result, she often felt put down and ignored. She had a few friends of long-standing, but found that it was often "too much effort" to get in touch with them, following their moves to distant parts of the city (she saw a friend once every 6–8 weeks). Apart from her church activities, therefore, Mrs. N spent most of her time cleaning her small apartment and watching television. At 185 pounds, she was at least 50 pounds overweight, which she attributed in part to hypothyroidism, a condition for which she had been receiving medication for 30 years. Her major concerns were the inadequacy of her interpersonal relations and her overweight.

Together, the therapist and client established the following treatment goals: to increase her contacts with relatives, to increase her frequency of interaction with friends, and to speak up more effectively in groups. Target behaviors consisted of initiating conversations, expressing opinions, and responding to put downs. At her request, a behavioral weight reduction plan, involving regular weigh-ins and recordkeeping of food intake, became an ancillary part of her program.

Treatment centered on repeated role plays of difficult situations, and graduated assignments to increase the variety and frequency of her social interactions. Mrs. N encountered the most resistance in respect to her wish for more frequent contact with her son's family, apparently because of her daughter-in-law's reluctance to see her more often. At the end of maintenance treatment, however, she was seeing and telephoning her grandchildren more frequently than when treatment began. She had increased without difficulty the frequency of her interactions with friends and acquaintances, and reported an improvement in her ability to hold her own comfortably in the group settings she frequented. She had also maintained the weight loss of nine pounds that had occurred during the phase of active treatment. At 6-months follow-up, however, her contacts with her family had declined to their previous level, and Mrs. N felt unwilling to make further overtures, in view of her daughter-in-law's continuing coolness. She had also regained most of the weight she had lost. However, the improvements previously registered in respect to social contacts and speaking out comfortably in group settings continued, and Mrs. N described positive changes in mood and self-concept.

Ms. R

This 63-year-old divorcée had been on her own for 6 years and had experienced intense feelings of depression, anxiety, and resentment about having to "start all over again" after 37 years of marriage. Three major tasks had confronted her following the divorce: to become self-supporting, to develop a satisfying pattern of activities, and to create a new set of social relationships. At the time treatment began, she worked full-time as an aide in a nursing home, and had reactivated an interest in music by joining a women's choral group. She had weekly contacts with her two adult daughters and paid frequent visits to the home of her sister, who cared for their demented mother. Arguments with her sister, who resented her "burden" but refused to relinquish it, occurred at every meeting. Ms. R was unhappy about her social "isolation," reporting that she saw people her own age only every 4–6 weeks. Her major reported concerns were sporadic periods of depression, intermittent strain in coping with the demands of family members, and loneliness. Specific deficits related to initiating and sustaining conversations, and in responding to criticisms and put downs. She had considered leaving the choral group, for example, because of difficulty in dealing with the rudeness of a few of its members.

The goals that she chose to work on related to greater involvement in her choral group, more frequent contacts with persons her own age, and an improved relationship with her sister (her goal attainment scaling follow-up guide was presented in Table 1). Target behaviors were dealing with criticisms and put downs; starting conversations with others, and positive reinforcement of others.

Her course of treatment was complicated by the multiple stresses that arose in addition to her presenting problems. These included financial difficulties, relocation to a smaller apartment, an exhausting work schedule, concerns about the precarious life circumstances of her daughters, and the prolonged illness of her granddaughter. Role playing of difficult interpersonal situations was carried out adequately during treatment sessions, but homework assignments were sometimes not completed, particularly those related to increasing the frequency of her social contacts. However, she remained in her choral group, and by the end of the maintenance period she had been appointed group librarian. She also reported responding more sympathetically to her sister's frustrations as caregiver. Ms. R and her sister were able to explore together the possibility of institutionalization, an alternative that the sister had previously refused to consider. The client's level of social interaction remained unchanged. At 6-months follow-up, Ms. R reported that she had developed further activities in her choral society, but her social contacts were even less frequent than when treatment began. She and her sister engaged in more mutual problem solving and support, and had placed their mother's name on the waiting list for an institution. Overall, however, Mrs. R described an increase in subjective distress over the previous assessment period, owing to financial setbacks, long hours of shift work, and continuing worry about her daughters and granddaughter.

In general, the results of this training program were encouraging. For the most part, measurable improvements in target behaviors occurred, along with progress toward the realization of clients' goals, and enhanced subjective well-being. Improvement was less marked in cases where clients developed physical health problems during the course of treatment or, as in the case of Ms. R, experienced unusual personal difficulties.

SPECIAL CONSIDERATIONS AND RECOMMENDATIONS

Among the important characteristics of training programs such as the one described in this chapter are the following: the presentation of a preliminary rationale; specific goal setting; opportunities for repeated practice; and stepwise, sequential learning (Rosenthal & Bandura, 1978). These characteristics are consistent with experimental findings regarding optimal learning conditions for the elderly. These include concreteness (Botwinick, 1978) high degrees of structure and predictability (Schulz, 1976) and appropriate repetition and pacing (Arenberg & Robertson-Tchabo, 1977). They are also in accordance with anecdotal clinical reports suggesting that therapists of widely differing persuasions favor focused, goal-oriented, problem-solving techniques in the psychological treatment of older people (Brink, 1979; Lehmann, 1980).

It is never easy to isolate the elements of a complex treatment program that are the most important in promoting change. To cast light on this issue, we asked clients who participated in the intervention to rank order the perceived usefulness of these six components of treatment: "understanding why I was experiencing certain difficulties; practicing different ways of handling real-life situations; having someone encourage me; role playing difficult situations; discussing problems with a sympathetic person; someone helping me plan the practice and discussing the results." The highest overall rating was assigned by participants to the second item: "practicing different ways of handling real-life situations." Interestingly, half the subjects ranked "encouragement" and/or "sympathy" as the "most helpful," and half ranked these items as the 'least helpful" components of treatment, suggesting that therapist characteristics cannot be ignored in planning interventions of this nature with elderly individuals. For some clients the presence of a therapist who is perceived as sympathetic and encouraging may be of paramount importance. However, the high rank assigned to "practice," as anticipated, suggested that the behavioral focus of treatment was indeed found uniquely helpful in facilitating desired change.

It is worth mentioning that some older clients found the role-play exercises an unfamiliar task, and initially were reluctant and embarrassed to "play act." When they were told that some awkwardness is natural in any novel situation, and that "perfect" responses were not demanded, they were usually able to enter into the spirit of the exercises, gaining assurance as they acquired more skills through repeated practice with the therapist. When they began to put these skills into practice in their daily encounters, their confidence was further enhanced, and the relevance and utility of role-play procedures confirmed. *In vivo* assignments should be carefully graduated, so that new behaviors are tried out in the natural environment only after successful practice in the clinical setting. It is useful, however, for clients to realize in advance that some "failures" will occur. For example, a waitress may not give them the better table they request, or a friendly overture may be ignored. Such experiences should not be viewed as catastrophes. Rather, they may indicate that further practice is required, or simply that social interactions for everyone are accompanied at times by setbacks, difficulties, and disappointments, which need not cause a drastic loss in self-esteem (cf. Ellis, 1977).

On the whole, homework assignments were well done. Clients, for the most part, collaborated effectively in selecting their assignments and relating these tasks to their personal goals. However, in cases like that of Ms. R, whose relative noncompliance with homework appeared to be related to severe life stressors, much less overall progress took place.

The goal-setting exercise in this program seemed to have an immediate impact by engaging clients from the beginning in a collaborative process. The focus on specific treatment goals has been ranked by others as one of the major strengths of GAS and similar procedures (Mintz & Kiesler, 1982). The forward-looking emphasis on movement toward goals also appears to be a welcome feature to the elderly clients. Two of them in our study commented that in applying for psychological treatment, they had dreaded the prospect of exhaustively rehearsing their perceived present inadequacies and past infelicities. The emphasis on concrete, observable, short-range goals was also well accepted, and is in accordance with clinical lore regarding desirable treatment methods in gerontological psychotherapy (Brink, 1979). The existence of well-defined endpoints of treatment also provided a yardstick of treatment progress and a marker of achievement. One client who experienced setbacks during the follow-up period referred to the specific goal achievements that she had nonetheless maintained as "consolation prizes." From the outset, treatment was focused not only on practicing new verbal behaviors in the treatment setting, but also on working toward specific aims outside it. Thus, by the time treatment ended, the specific skills acquired through practice had to some extent been integrated into new patterns of behavior in the clients' daily lives.

Social skills training has been successfully used in the past with many different target populations in both individual and group formats. In practice, the clinician/ program planner rarely enjoys complete freedom as to whether an intervention will be on a group or individual basis, and will select one or the other in accordance with the demands of the work setting, the client, and his or her own skills and preferences. In social skills training, a group may often be more desirable because it is less costly and provides richer opportunities for modeling, role play, and feedback. The group format need not preclude individualization of treatment goals, although it is likely that group members will find many common difficulties to work on together (e.g., standing up for their rights more effectively, initiating conversations, complimenting others.) The mutual support and sharing that a group affords, along with opportunities for social enjoyment and new friendships, are further reasons why group social skills training with the community-dwelling elderly merits further empirical investigation. A point to be kept in mind when offering such groups is the "rose by any other name" caveat. Those who have developed assertiveness training groups for older people in the past caution that one must label with care (Wheeler, 1980; Corby, 1975). Programs in "personal effectiveness" or "communications training" are more acceptable to those who tend to confuse assertiveness with abrasiveness or aggressiveness.

Further clinical investigation needs to be conducted with respect to the kinds of elderly subjects for whom social skills training may be beneficial. Those who participated in our program were all females who had completed an average of 10.5 years of schooling. They were representative of many older women in that they were unattached (single, divorced, widowed, or separated), unimpaired, and, with one exception, of modest means. In view of the wide range of population groups with which social skills training has been successfully employed, there is no a priori reason to believe that such training would not be useful with more disadvantaged older women, or with older men, provided the intervention were structured to their particular needs. Social skills training may also be serviceable with community-dwelling elderly suffering from mild cognitive impairment.

A final important question for further research is whether social skills training may be useful in work with elderly depressed subjects. As already noted, depression is widespread among the elderly, and psychopharmacology is neither the only treatment nor always the most appropriate form of treatment for it. Structured behavioral and cognitive treatments have already been found useful with some elderly depressed clients (Steuer, Mintz, Hammen, Hill, & Jarvik, 1984; Chapter 10, this volume). Since social skills training has been successful in alleviating depression among younger people, research into its efficacy with the elderly appears timely. As an appropriate research strategy I would recommend a series of single-case design studies, selecting initially those depressed individuals most likely to benefit from social skills interventions, such as those who manifest little or no endogenous depression (Gallagher & Thompson, 1983) those who manifest specific deficits in social skills, and those whose environments offer realistic possibilities for increased social activity, support, and pleasure.

Clearly, clinical practitioners have only begun to address the need for brief, effective treatments for older adults facing changing life demands. Social skills training appears to be a promising form of intervention that can assist the elderly in acquiring or improving the kinds of competencies that facilitate coping and adaptation in later life.

SUMMARY

Numerous writers have advocated the development of social skills training programs for the elderly. Such interventions, it has been suggested, could well convey specific competencies and promote personal adjustment among those elderly suffering from isolation, loneliness, and inadequate social support.

In the present chapter, a social skills training program for community-dwelling elderly was described. In the assessment phase, social skills deficits (target behaviors) were selected for training. Clients also chose objectives, related to their interpersonal relations, which they wished to achieve during the course of treatment. They completed questionnaires measuring self-esteem, depression, anxiety, and social introversion. Treatment consisted of 10 weekly sessions and three "booster" sessions a month apart. Training emphasized role playing of effective, expressive verbal responses in a variety of social contexts. Homework assignments involved practice of target behaviors in the natural environment, and specific assignments related to the attainment of the clients' social goals. Clients also learned how to attend to the negative expectations and self-appraisals that were often inhibiting their interpersonal dealings. Results at the end of treatment and at follow-up for the most part indicated a pattern of positive change. Possible areas of future research include: group social skills training, and programs for the depressed elderly.

REFERENCES

Abrahams, R., & Patterson, R. (1979). Psychological distress among the community elderly. Prevalence, characteristics and implications for service. *International Journal of Aging and Human Development, 1*, 1–18.

Alberti, R., & Emmons, M. (1975). *Stand up, speak out, talk back!* New York: Pocket Books.

Arenberg, D., & Robertson-Tchabo, E. (1977). Learning and aging. In J. Birren & K. Schaie (Eds.), *Handbook of the psychology of aging* (pp. 421–449). New York: Van Nostrand Reinhold.

Bellack, A. (1979). A critical appraisal of strategies for assessing social skill. *Behavioral Assessment, 1*, 157–176.

Bellack, A., & Hersen, M. (Eds.). (1979). *Research and practice in social skills training.* New York: Plenum.

Bellack, A., Hersen, M., & Himmelhoch, J. (1980). Social skills training for depression, a treatment manual. *JSAS: Catalogue of Selected Documents in Psychology, 10*, 4 (Ms. No. 2156).

Berger, R., & Rose, S. (1977). Interpersonal skill training with institutionalized elderly patients. *Journal of Gerontology, 32*(3), 346–353.

Blazer, D. (1980). Life events, mental health functioning, and the use of health care services by the elderly. *American Journal of Public Health, 70*, 1174.

Blazer, D. (1982). *Depression in late life.* St. Louis: C. V. Mosby.

Botwinick, J. (1978). *Aging and behavior* (2nd ed.). New York: Springer.

Brink, T. (1979). *Geriatric psychotherapy.* New York: Human Sciences Press.

Corby, N. (1975). Assertion training with aged populations. *Counseling Psychologist, 5* (4), 69–74.

Derogatis, L., Lipman, R., Rickels, K., Uhlenhuth, E., & Covi, L. (1974). The Hopkins Symptom Checklist (HSCL): A self-report symptom inventory. *Behavioral Science, 19*, 1–15.

Dolen, L., & Bearison, D. (1982). Social interaction and social cognition in aging. *Human Development, 25*, 430–442.

Eisler, R., Hersen, M., Miller, P., & Blanchard, E. (1975). Situational determinants of assertive behaviors. *Journal of Consulting and Clinical Psychology*, *43*, 330–340.

Ellis, A. (1977). The basic clinical theory of rational-emotive therapy. In A. Ellis & R. Grieger (Eds.), *Handbook of rational-emotive therapy* (pp. 3–34). New York: Springer.

Engels, M-L., & Poser, E. (1987). Social skills training with older women. *Clinical Gerontologist*, *6*(4), 70–73.

Ernst, R., Beran, B., Safford, F., & Kleinhauz, M. (1978). Isolation and the symptoms of organic brain syndrome. *Gerontologist*, *18*, 468–474.

Fensterheim, H., & Baer, J. (1975). *Don't say yes when you want to say no*. New York: Dell Publishing.

Fiedler, D., & Beach, L. (1978). On the decision to be assertive. *Journal of Consulting and Clinical Psychology*, *46*, 537–546.

Gallagher, D., & Thompson, L. (1983). Effectiveness of psychotherapy for both endogenous and non-endogenous depression in older adult outpatients. *Journal of Gerontology*, *38*(6), 707–712.

Hersen, M., Bellack, A., & Turner, S. (1978). Assessment of assertiveness in female psychiatric patients: Motor and autonomic measures. *Journal of Behavior Therapy and Experimental Psychiatry*, *9*, 11–16.

Kuypers, J., & Bengston, V. (1973). Competence and social breakdown. A social-psychological view of aging. *Human Development*, *16*, 37–49.

Lehmann, H. (1980). Recognition and treatment of depression in geriatric patients. In F. Ayd (Ed.), *Clinical depressions: Diagnostic and therapeutic challenges* (pp. 57–69). Baltimore, MD: Ayd Medical Communications.

Levy, S. (1981). The aging woman: Developmental issues and mental health needs. *Professional Psychology*, *12*(1), 92–102.

Levy, S., Derogatis, L., Gallagher, D., & Gatz, M. (1980). Intervention with older adults and the evaluation of outcome. In L. Poon (Ed.), *Aging in the 1980's: Psychological Issues* (pp. 41–61). Washington, DC: American Psychological Association.

Lopez, M., Hoyer, W., Goldstein, A., Gershaw, N., & Sprafkin, R. (1980). Effects of overlearning and incentive on the acquisition and transfer of skills with institutionalized elderly. *Journal of Gerontology*, *35*(3), 403–408.

Maccoby, E., & Jacklin, C. (1974). *The psychology of sex differences*. Stanford, CA: Stanford University Press.

McLean, P., & Hakstian, R. (1979). Clinical depression: Comparative efficacy of outpatient treatments. *Journal of Consulting and Clinical Psychology*, *47*, 818–836.

Mintz, J., & Kiesler, D. (1982). Individualized measures of psychotherapy outcome. In P. Kendall & J. Butcher (Eds.), *Handbook of research methods in clinical psychology* (pp. 491–534). New York: J. Wiley.

Patterson, R. (1982). *Overcoming deficits of aging*. New York: Plenum.

Rosenberg, M. (1979). *Conceiving the self*. New York: Basic Books.

Rosenthal, J., & Bandura, A. (1978). Psychological modeling: Theory and practice. In S. Garfield & A. Bergin (Eds.), *Handbook of psychotherapy and behavior change* (2nd ed., pp. 621–658). New York: Wiley.

Schulz, R. (1976). Effects of control and predictability on the physical and psychological well-being of the institutionalized aged. *Journal of Personality and Social Psychology*, *33*, 563–573.

Smith, A. (1981). Goal attainment scaling: A method for evaluating the outcome of mental health treatment. In P. McReynolds (Ed.), *Advances in psychological assessment* (Vol. 5, pp. 424–459). San Francisco: Jossey-Bass.

Steuer, J., Mintz, J., Hammen, C., Hill, M., & Jarvik, L. (1984). Cognitive-behavioral and psychodynamic group psychotherapy in treatment of geriatric depression. *Journal of Consulting and Clinical Psychology*, *52*, 180–189.

Welford, A. (1980). Epilogue: Where do we go from here? In L. Poon (Ed.), *Aging in the 1980's: Psychological issues* (pp. 615–621). Washington: DC: American Psychological Association.

Wheeler, E. (1980). Assertive training groups for the aging. In S. Sargent (Ed.), *Nontraditional therapy and counseling with the aging* (pp. 15–29). New York: Springer.

Zimbardo, P. (1977). *Shyness*. New York: Jove.

9

Problems in (Really) Living
Behavioral Approaches to the Elderly's Goals Regarding Dating, Marriage, and Sex

Jane E. Fisher and William O'Donohue

In recent years behaviorists and behavior therapists have begun studying the behavior and treating the problems of the elderly (Baltes & Barton, 1977; Hussian, 1981; Skinner & Vaughn, 1983). These endeavors give rise to some important questions regarding the assumptions and the goals of what is often called "behavioral gerontology." For example: What can be a proper rationale for a behaviorally oriented clinician or researcher to demarcate a subset of the population (i.e., those over 65 years of age) for special study?; Is this consistent with the behavioral theoretical framework?; Are there any considerations that render the demarcation criterion (advanced chronological age) problematic?

In this chapter we will first examine these questions, because they are concerned with the foundations of behavioral approaches to the problems of the elderly. These must be properly and clearly considered because responses to these issues provide the general outline of the purposes and prospects of the field. The tentative responses that we make to these issues will provide the general structure for the behavioral approaches discussed in this chapter to problems the elderly encounter in dating, marriage, and sex—or to paraphrase Szasz (1960)—what the elderly find to be problems in really living.

Science and Senescence

Any science is confronted with two basic problems: (1) What are the basic elements in this field? and (2) What are the laws, i.e., the orderly ways in which these elements behave? Each question serves as a touchstone for the other—we believe that we have found the basic elements when we have discovered entities that behave lawfully, and we believe that we have discovered lawful relationships when

Jane E. Fisher and William O'Donohue • Department of Psychology, Northern Illinois University, DeKalb, Illinois 60115.

we have analyzed diverse ordinary objects to the same set of simple elements and we find that these fundamental elements behave in an orderly fashion.

The case for the legitimacy of distinguishing the elderly from others rests upon whether this distinction is relevant, indeed, the most relevant distinction to scientific explanation and prediction. The history of science is littered with failed attempts to identify fundamental elements and thereby to form sciences. For example, the ancient Greek cosmologist Anaximander proposed that everything could be analyzed into four basic elements of fire, earth, air, and water. However, this rudimentary theory of chemistry was abandoned because it failed to yield lawful relationships that could be used to predict and explain phenomena in which he was interested. We know now that this theory was bound to fail *because it was wrong in this attempt to identify fundamental elements*. The question becomes, "does behavioral gerontology rest upon a distinction—advanced age—that is the most relevant to scientific explanation and prediction?" In order to address this fundamental question we will now briefly review scientific explanation and prediction to see how a term might be relevant and whether advanced age is relevant to explanation and prediction in the behavioral approach.

SCIENTIFIC EXPLANATION

A term can be a part of scientific explanation in either of two ways. First, it can be part of the *explanandum*, the event to be explained. For example, the terms "copper" and "electricity" are part of the *explanandum* in, "Why does copper conduct electricity?" Second, terms can be a part of the *explanans*, the considerations brought forward to account for the *explanandum*. So, the question then becomes, Does "the elderly" or some equivalent term form a part of the *explanandum* or the *explanans* in explanation in the behavioral approach?

Deductive-Nomological Explanation

There are two kinds of lawful relationships and hence two kinds of scientific explanations in science (Hempel, 1970). One type is known as "deductive-nomological explanation" (DN explanation), because (1) the explanation has the form of a valid deductive argument with the *explanandum* as the conclusion and the *explanans* as the premise, and (2) the *explanans* contains at least one universal law. More precisely, DN scientific explanations are of the following form:

$$\frac{\begin{array}{l}C1, C2, \ldots Ci \\ L1, L2, \ldots Ln\end{array}}{E}$$

where $C1$ to Ci are statements of initial conditions, $L1$ to Ln are statements of laws, and E is the *explanandum*, a deductive logical consequence of the initial condition(s) and general law(s). Here is an example of a DN explanation that attempts to give an account of the *explanandum* "Why does this piece of matter conduct electricity?"

> This is a piece of copper.
> All copper conducts electricity.

> (Therefore) This piece of matter conducts electricity.

This model of scientific explanation is sometimes referred to as the covering law model because it subsumes the *explanandum* under principles that have the form of general laws. Also notice that this type of explanation can be used to explain laws. In this case a law occurs as the *explanandum*. Here's an example:

> Copper is an element whose outermost electrons are loosely held.
> All elements whose outermost electrons are loosely held conduct electricity.

> (Therefore) All copper conducts electricity.

Does "the Elderly" Appear in the Explanans in DN Explanation?

At the core of the behavioral approach are psychological principles such as classical conditioning and operant conditioning that function as the nomologicals in DN explanations. The response to the question above, then, is a function of two important open and empirical questions, viz., (1) Does advanced age serve as a parameter in these nomologicals? and (2) Are there other nomologicals, as a stage theorist might believe, that only emerge with advanced chronological age? That is, is advanced age an initial condition for any nomological?

To date the research literature is consistent with a negative response to both of these questions. First, there is no evidence that suggests that advanced chronological age is a variable that affects the psychological principles that are currently known. (Even if advanced age is shown to be related to, say, the speed of operant conditioning, one needs to ask is it age *per se*, or is age only correlated with the real causal variable, e.g., a certain physiological change?) Moreover, because behaviorists tend to look for functional relationships and this requires that the explanatory variables be manipulable, and because age is not a variable that can be manipulated, it is unlikely that age will play a role in behavioral principles.

Finally, there is no indication that in behavioral theory there are any laws of the form: When someone is 65 years of age, then this (hitherto inoperative) psychological principle obtains. That is, there is no empirical evidence that there are psychological principles that emerge with the passage of time.

However, it must be emphasized that these are open, empirical questions: it is empirically possible that further research will reveal that chronological age *per se* is a parameter or an initial condition in psychology.

The Statistical Relevance (SR) Model of Scientific Explanation

The second type of scientific explanation is a collection of facts that are statistically relevant to the *explanandum*. A factor is statistically relevant to the occurrence of the *explanandum* if it makes a difference to the probability of occurrence of the event to be explained.

Let us consider the following example. Suppose we are wondering why our Brazilian friend, Senhor Citizen, gets into very few traffic accidents. Salmon (1971) suggests that *explananda* have the general form, "Why is this individual, X, who is A, also B?" And explanations have the general form, "Because this X is also C." So our question more precisely put is, "Why does this individual, Senhor Citizen, who is a driver (A) also someone who gets into few accidents (B)?" And our answer is of the form, "Because this individual who is a driver is also C." We are then looking for a factor C such that

$$P (A.C, B) \neq P (A, B)$$

This reads "The probability of B, given A and intersect C, is not equal to the probability of B given A. Where P denotes probability, A denotes the reference class, B the attribute class, and C a partition of A, i.e., a property that divides A into two mutually exclusive and exhaustive subclasses. If a C can be found that satisfies this equation, then this C is said to be statistically relevant to B and is to be used in the *explanans*.

Let us see how this works with our question concerning Senhor Citizen. Suppose we propose to explain Senhor Citizen's safe driving by appealing to the fact that he is also elderly. Further suppose we find the following probabilities:

P (given that one is a driver, having an accident) = .09
P (given that one is a driver and elderly, having an accident) = .01

Since the probability of having an accident when one is a driver and elderly is different than the probability of having an accident for drivers in general, then the property of being elderly is relevant to explanations of safe driving. After all, it gives us information that influences our expectations.

The best explanation is the explanation that assigns the individual case to the broadest homogeneous reference class to which it belongs. If there is no property C by which a statistically relevant partition of A can be made with respect to the occurrence of B, then A is homogeneous with respect to B. In other words, we are interested in making the partition(s) that most accurately divides the reference group into relevant cases and irrelevant cases. For example, suppose that the situation is that when people are over 65 years of age they get into fewer traffic accidents. But further suppose that someone who only had an inkling of this relationship claimed, instead, that the relevant partition was having grey hair. Although the researcher would find that grey hair is indeed a statistically relevant partition, it is not as homogeneous as our original partition because of the irrelevant cases it includes, i.e., young individuals who are prematurely grey, and the safe driving elderly who for one reason or another are not grey.

The *broadest* homogeneous reference group is desired because we do not want to exclude relevant cases so that we can maximize the number of cases for our inductive generalization. Thus, if the partition 75 years or older has the same probability as the partition of 65 years or older, then this second partition is to be used because it is broader: it includes more relevant cases.

Now it seems that we have found a legitimate role for advanced age in the *explanans* in scientific explanation—it can serve as a partition that is the broadest homogeneous reference class that is statistically relevant to the attribute class. However, it is always the case that *causal* explanations (or more causally proximate explanations) provide more homogeneous reference classes than explanations that involve only correlated variables. So let us suppose that it's not the fact of being old that results in fewer traffic accidents, but slow, cautious driving is the causal factor and being elderly is positively correlated with slow, cautious driving. Again, the partition 65 years or older produces a statistically relevant partition (because of the correlation with slow, cautious driving), but this partition, slow, cautious drivers, produces a more homogeneous reference class, since after all it excludes the little old lady from Pasadena and includes young parents driving Volvos. Formally, we say that slow, cautious drivers *screens off* being 65 years old from having accidents in the reference class of people who drive if and only if:

$$P\,(A.\ C.\ D,\ B) = P\,(A.\ D,\ B) \neq P\,(A.\ C,\ B)$$

where D is the new partition of being a slow, cautious driver. The property that is screened off becomes irrelevant and no longer has any explanatory value.

Thus, we can see that every explanation that attempts to use the elderly in the *explanans* will fall into one of these five cases:

1. The elderly will *not* be a statistically relevant partition of the reference class relative to the attribute class, and therefore ought not to be part of the *explanans*.
2. The elderly will be a statistically significant partition but will be *screened off* by broader or more homogeneous partitions, especially partitions that are causal, and thereby ought not to be part of the *explanans*.
3. At any point in time our ignorance of better partitions, especially those involving causal factors, will make the elderly the partition that is the *epistemically most homogeneous*. Because at the current time we don't know of more homogeneous statistically relevant partitions, for the time being "the elderly" will appear in the *explanans*.
4. Because of limited resources, the elderly might comprise a partition that is the *practically most homogeneous* partition—it is a partition that is so cheap and easy to make relative to others that it will be used in the *explanans*.
5. The mere passage of a significant period of time (e.g., 65 years) causes certain changes such as an entropy-like physiological deterioration. When these causal relationships are found, then the elderly will be the most homogeneous partition and will appear in the *explanans*.

Now we are ready to make a few important points. First, it is important to know precisely into which of the five categories above an explanation involving advanced age fits. Currently, we suggest that many extant explanations in the behavioral sciences appealing to advanced chronological age are not of type 5, but rather of type 1–4. Second, if the above is true, then because behaviorists tend to be interested in causal explanations they will tend to be only sanguine about current explanations involving the elderly of type 1–4. Finally, a theoretical point: If the passage of time affects behavior only indirectly, i.e., through a mediating factor (for example, if time causes certain physiological deterioration which in turn causes certain behavior change—e.g., tremors—and if there are other changes—e.g., some disease state—that produce the deterioration, or if time alone is not a sufficient condition for these physiological changes) then time will not be the most homogeneous partition, but will be screened off by the more proximate causal factor, viz., the physiological change.

Does "the Elderly" Appear in the Explanda in Scientific Explanations?

Thus far we have discussed the role of advanced chronological age in the *explanans* in scientific explanation. However, we said that another way that advanced chronological age can have a role in science is by having a role in the *explanadum*, the phenomenon to be explained. We turn now to a discussion of this issue.

How is this elderly person's sexual performance anxiety to be treated? Do the elderly have different moral beliefs concerning dating, marriage, and sexuality? Why do the elderly have fewer traffic accidents? Surely, one might reply, doesn't each of these examples show that advanced age can play a role in the *explanandum* in scientific explanations? And even more broadly, doesn't the mere existence of questions such as these that ask if advanced age isn't systematically related to something not only demonstrate the actuality of gerontology, but also demonstrate its legitimacy?

The answer to these questions is no. The *explanada* must be described in a way that is apt from a scientific point of view. For example, if the following request for an explanation were to be posed to a physicist, "Why do individuals that are 65 years old or older fall to the center of the earth?" the physicist would of course reply, "Well, because these people have mass, and masses are attracted to each other by a gravitational force such that . . . And the fact that these things are people of a certain age is not at all relevant. What's relevant is that they have mass."

As previously stated, whether we have identified fundamental elements is answered by whether we find that these elements behave in lawful relationships so that these laws can be used to explain phenomena in which we are interested. Thus, the question of whether advanced age is a proper distinction in *explanada* rests upon whether this property is a part of the *explanans* in scientific explanation. The mere ability to pose the question "Why do elderly things fall to the center of the earth?" is not a sufficient condition for establishing the ultimate scientific legitimacy of the question.

However, it must also be noted that in the human sciences a distinction can become relevant simply because we make the distinction and employ it. Thus, "65 years or older" can become relevant to explanation because it is a property that through various social mechanisms becomes systematically related to such things as employment, social security eligibility, and certain social roles. Thus, through certain social decisions, the property of being 65 years of age can determine contingencies (e.g., the schedule of rewards given for retirement, and for other behaviors) and thereby be systematically related to behavior.

It is not our purpose to rain on the behavioral gerontology picnic. Rather we wish simply to be as clear as possible about some very basic issues involved in behavior therapy with the elderly. Whether researchers will find that advanced age *per se* serves as a parameter or a boundary condition to extant psychological principles, such as operant conditioning, or whether principles that only emerge with advanced age will be found are open, empirical, questions—and indeed, important questions. However, to date, the research literature provides no support that advanced age *per se* has these roles. The extent to which advanced age serves to be the broadest possible reference group for the attribute class in SR explanation is also an important, open, empirical question. Behaviorists for a variety of reasons are primarily interested in causal explanation and therefore will be only slightly satisfied with explanations that use advanced age as a partition that is only practically or epistemically relevant to the attribute class. Moreover, whether advanced age is a property that can serve as a component of a meaningful request for explanation depends upon whether we find it to be relevant to the *explanans*.

MAKING THE ELDERLY NORMAL: THE CASE AGAINST DISCRIMINATION

One desirable consequence of this cautious approach to the use of advanced age is that it is quite inconsistent with ageism. Prejudicial practices can be characterized as the use of irrelevant or less relevant factors (especially demographic factors) in explanations. Thus we typically would regard someone as sexist who attempts to explain Laura's change of mind by referring to her gender. We may actually find that women change their minds more often and that therefore gender is statistically relevant. However, it is also likely that this is not a causal relationship but rather women change their minds more often because, say, women *tend* to be better users of novel information. Then, of course, if we partition by this criterion, gender will be screened off. Similarly, as professionals concerned with human welfare we do not want to make invidious distinctions regarding age. We can unintentionally promote age discrimination by the incautious use of age in our attempts to question and explain. Doesn't gerontology imply that there is something special, something unordinary, something abnormal about those of advanced age? The cautious approach we propose here will tend to allow attributions to advanced age only when advanced age has passed the tough test of being shown empirically that this property is a relevant property, indeed the *most* relevant property, to the description and explanation of some phenomenon.

The general points stated above will provide the structure of our discussion of dating, marriage, and sex. We will see that: (1) There is reason to believe that the behavior, including the social, marital, and sexual behavior, of the elderly can be understood and modified by the same psychological principles that are operative in the behavior of the nonelderly. (2) Advanced chronological age often serves only as an epistemically homogeneous or practically homogeneous partition. Thus, in many cases, for pragmatic purposes, we may speak of advanced age as a factor that is relevant to assessment and treatment, but more precisely, the most relevant factor is actually something that is only correlated with advanced age. (3) In some cases, due to, for example, various social factors, advanced age *per se* has become a causal variable that is directly implicated in assessment and treatment. One way that this may occur is because people treat the elderly differently, the elderly come to behave differently.

DATING AND MARRIAGE

Living to old age often results in the experience of a number of changes not usually encountered in earlier adulthood. These include retirement, widowhood, and declines in health. All of these events influence the social behavior of an individual. For the most part researchers of relationships among the aged have concentrated on the study of bereavement, widowhood, and caregiving. Marital problems, dating, and sexuality have largely been ignored by gerontological researchers.

Based on the lack of published research, one could claim that the elderly are underserved. This brings up some interesting possibilities that should be evaluated, because different interpretations of the lack of published research in this area suggest different courses of action. It may be the case, for example, that the current cohort of older adults are not dissatisfied with their dating, marital, and social activities and so they are not actually underserved because they do not desire any service. To evaluate this possibility, the elderly's satisfaction with their dating, marital, and/or social activity needs to be investigated. It is also possible that there are significant incidences of problems in these areas and older adults are not being adequately helped by mental health professionals. This view seems to be popular (Brink, 1979; Butler & Lewis, 1983). Epidemiological research would provide answers to the questions surrounding these possibilities.

Perhaps older adults are not seeking the help of mental health professionals because they are not properly informed of the available services. Or, they may not want help because they hold irrational beliefs, such as old people shouldn't care about dating. Research is needed in order to determine the prevalence of irrational ideas that might be impeding the attainment of satisfying social experiences of older adults. Such irrational ideas may be the products of ageist cultural values. If this is the case, what are we to do as behavior therapists? We believe there are two options. We can respect a decision even when the decision is made under suboptimal conditions. The price of this approach is that we allow individuals to experience negative consequences that are preventable. Alternatively, we can challenge the decision because we believe it is not a properly informed one (e.g., it is based on an ageist premise). It is clear that more data regarding the incidence and prevalence of problems in social relationships among older adults are needed before we can make informed decisions regarding intervention.

Before addressing questions regarding the application of behavioral assessment and therapy techniques for the marital and courtship problems of older adults, we will review some relevant demographic characteristics.

Demographics

According to the report of U.S. Senate Special Committee on Aging (U.S. Senate, 1982), over half of the individuals over the age of 65 are married. Most men (81%) aged 65–74 are married, while only half of the women are married. For men aged 75 and over nearly 70% are married, while the proportion of married women drops to 23%. Nearly 7 out of 10 women aged 75 and over are widows, while less than one-quarter are married. For all age groups only a small percentage (2–4%) are divorced. For both sexes the percentage of the divorced decreases with age.

When marital status and gender are categorized by their relative frequencies we find that married men are most numerous (7,590,000), followed by widowed women (7,121,000), married women (5,546,000), widowed men (1,333,000), single women (824,000), single men (499,000), divorced women (468,000), and divorced men (361,000) (U.S. Senate, 1982). The statistics on male–female ratios suggest that for some who want a monogamous intimate relationship, opportunity may be limited in later life.

Figures from the 1981 U.S. Census indicate that the rate of divorce has increased over the last 20 years. In 1960 there were 44 divorced older women per 1,000 married persons. By 1981 the proportion of divorced women had more than doubled (95 per 1,000). In 1960 there were 24 divorced men per 1,000. In 1981 the ratio for older men was 44 per 1,000. Although only a small minority of older people have experienced divorce, the size of the minority has more than doubled in the past 20 years.

It has been suggested that the increased incidence of divorce and continued increases in the proportion of the never-married may lead to a preponderance of nonmarried older people in the future (Cargan & Melko, 1982). These changes will occur while the proportion of widowed older adults will remain relatively stable. At present it is unclear how this situation will impact on the social behavior of older adults. Further research should investigate the impact of marital status on psychological health among older adults.

Marital Relationships

Estimates of the duration of marriages among the aged vary widely. Parron and Troll (1978) estimated that fewer than 3% of all marriages endure past the 50th anniversary. In contrast, Glick and Norton (1977) suggest that one in five first marriages lasts for 50 years. Changes in the character of long marriages rarely have been studied longitudinally. Ade-Ridder and Brubaker (1983) reviewed studies of the quality of long-term marriages and found many inconsistencies. Differences in the measures of marital quality and methodologies employed make comparisons difficult. These authors report that earlier studies generally found declines in marital quality following an initial period of happiness. These studies for the most part did not include adequate samples of older adults, however. Later studies (e.g., Anderson, Russell, & Schumm, 1983) tended to find an initial period of satisfaction followed by a decline during the child-rearing years and an increase in the postchild years.

At present we do not have any evidence that suggests that the treatment of marital problems among aged individuals should deviate from the approaches applied with younger individuals. This assertion is unfortunately based on an absence of information rather than on empirical findings. There is currently a dearth of research examining the prevalence of specific marital problems among the aged. Further, no studies have systematically investigated the application of marital therapy techniques with aged couples. Given this state of affairs, we will present a distillation of behavioral assessment and treatment techniques, hoping that the reader will be mindful of the fact that these approaches have not been tested with older married couples.

ASSESSMENT OF MARITAL PROBLEMS

Behavioral marital assessment often involves a number of different techniques including direct observation of marital interaction using structured interactional coding systems, self- and spouse monitoring (using either individualized or standardized measures), self-reporting questionnaires, and interviews. These techniques are used to assess both individual and relationship characteristics. According to Weiss and Margolin (1986), the most important areas to assess that are relevant to the individual include: satisfaction, interest in staying in the relationship, the changes being requested, and their individual skills and resources. The assessment of relationship factors focuses on both moment-to-moment interactions as well as the identification of patterns over weeks, months, or years.

When first confronted with a couple in distress, the therapist must assess whether the goals of the individuals are compatible. Determining whether both individuals are interested in staying in the relationship is of primary importance. Divorce is often a discomforting topic for therapists to approach with clients. Addressing this issue may be particularly intimidating for the therapist working with a couple that has been married for over 50 years. It is, however, very important to assess how committed each spouse is to staying in the relationship, as this will impact on the mode of therapy. Marital therapy requires that both spouses be willing to invest time and energy toward the goal of improving their relationship. If they are seriously contemplating divorce it may be more useful to focus on helping them to adjust to separation.

When considering the histories of problems within older marriages it is clear that there is potential for much variability in the severity and the timing of problems. For many couples there may be a long history of difficulties, while others may be experiencing severe problems for the first time. Retirement, chronic physical ailments, and declining health are age-associated phenomena that may precipitate marital problems within older marriages, as these events often require major adjustments of roles and responsibilities within a marriage (Beckman & Giordano, 1986).

Several researchers have suggested that health is one of the most important variables affecting the family and marital relationships of older people (Atchley & Miller, 1983; Beckman & Giordano, 1986). Therefore, it seems important that therapists working with elderly couples carefully assess the physical functioning of each spouse as well as the relationship factors. Beckman and Giordano (1986) presented a number of issues therapists should investigate when trying to understand the relationship between illness and marital difficulties in an elderly couple. For example, illness in either spouse may reduce interest in sexual activity, ability to work, and interest in formerly shared social activities. Such changes may have a great impact on the couple's functioning. The stress of these changes may be exacerbated if the couple also has a history of poor communication.

Information regarding health, satisfaction, and commitment to the relationship can be gathered through an interview. We will now review various assessment techniques developed by behavioral marital therapists. Caution should be exercised when using these techniques with older couples because researchers have not investigated the validity of their application with this age group. However, to date we do not have any information that suggests they would not be valid.

Self-Report Questionnaires

Behavioral marital therapists often use self-report questionnaires in the assessment of marital dysfunction. Presented below is a brief description of some easily administered self-report measures that might prove useful in the assessment of marital problems among elderly couples. The various questionnaires target a variety of variables including marital satisfaction, change, stability, and conflict.

The Marital Adjustment Scale (MAS; Locke & Wallace, 1959) and the Dyadic Adjustment Scale (DAS; Spanier, 1976) are the most widely used marital satisfaction questionnaires in behavioral marital assessment and are useful for screening marital distress and adjustment. Both of these questionnaires are brief and easily administered. The MAS contains 15 items that provide ratings on overall satisfaction, amount of disagreement between spouses in eight areas of marriage, and extent of spouses' mutual activity and decision making. The Dyadic Adjustment Scale is an updated version of the Marital Adjustment Scale. The items of the DAS overlap approximately 75% with the MAS. It contains 32 items that form four factors, including dyadic satisfaction, dyadic cohesion, dyadic consensus, and expression of affection. According to Spanier (1976), each item of the DAS discriminates between happily married and divorced samples.

The Marital Satisfaction Inventory (MSI; Snyder, Wills, & Keisler, 1981) is a 280-item measure designed to assess several dimensions of marital satisfaction including problem solving, communication, quality and quantity of leisure time activity, and sexual dissatisfaction. Some of the items are probably less relevant for older couples (e.g., those dealing with conflict over childrearing) than they are for younger couples.

The Areas of Change Questionnaire (AC; Weiss & Birchler, 1978) is useful for assessing the specific behaviors that each spouse would like to see changed and the magnitude of the desired change. The AC also includes items asking each spouse to predict the changes the other spouse desires, thereby providing a measure of the quality of communication between the spouses. The AC comprises two parts, each of which contains identical listings of 34 behaviors. In Part I, the client indicates whether he or she wants the spouse to increase, decrease, or maintain the rate of each behavior. In Part II, the client indicates whether the increase, decrease, or maintenance of a behavior will be pleasing to the spouse. The AC has been found to discriminate between distressed and nondistressed couples and to correlate with the MAS (Weiss, Hops, & Patterson, 1973). According to Weiss and Margolin (1986), because of its comprehensiveness and ease of administration, the AC is a useful instrument for assessing change over the course of therapy.

The Cost–Benefit Analysis (Weiss & Perry, 1979) is another questionnaire that is useful for measuring change. Using a 6-point scale, spouses rate potentially pleasing behaviors on degree of benefit should their spouse engage in the behavior. Spouses then rate each behavior on the dimension of cost to themselves if they were to provide the behavior for their partners. The Cost–Benefit Analysis provides data on spouses' views regarding the value of specific changes and the time, effort, or hassle involved in providing those changes. This information is useful in the determination of treatment goals because it suggests which types of change are most important for the couple.

Self- and Spouse Monitoring

Self- and spouse monitoring are means of obtaining observational data in a standardized manner. The procedures used to obtain this information vary with regard to the length of the observation interval, time between observation and recording, and complexity of the behavior being recorded. Within this approach, the participant observer receives training in the recording of specific behaviors. In contrast with some types of self-report measures, an emphasis is placed on current behaviors that occur during a circumscribed period. Self- and spouse monitoring procedures are often tailored to meet the needs of an individual couple. There are, however, a number of standardized measures that may be useful for the behavior therapist working with elderly couples.

The Spouse Observation Checklist (SOC) is a self-report measure that is very useful in assessing change in behavioral marital therapy (Weiss & Margolin, 1986). It is the most widely used self-report measure of marital relationship characteristics. It can be used solely during the assessment phase of therapy, throughout treatment, or as a posttreatment change measure. The SOC contains a list of pleasing and displeasing relationship behaviors. The list includes approximately 400 items that represent 12 relationship dimensions: companionship, affection, consideration, sex, communication process, coupling activities, household management, financial decision making, education–employment, childrearing, personal habits, and self and spouse independence. Spouses complete the SOC every evening by making a check next to each behavior that occurred that day. They then tally the subtotals for each of the categories and produce a profile of the pleasing and displeasing behavior that occurred that day. They also rate their satisfaction with their marriage for that day on a 9-point scale and thus are able to compare the relationship between marital satisfaction and the frequencies of specific behaviors.

Overall scores on the SOC have been found to discriminate between distressed and nondistressed couples. Some of the individual dimensions are more robust discriminators than others (Margolin & Jacobson, 1981). Instructing couples to examine each other's SOC can be therapeutic in and of itself (Jacobson, 1981).

Interactional Coding Systems

For the most part, interactional coding systems have been used only by researchers. These systems are not a practical choice for the clinician as they tend to be fairly complex and time consuming. Markman, Notarius, Stephen, and Smith (1981) provide a summary of four observational coding systems used for describing marital interaction. These include: Marital Interaction Coding System (Hops, Wills, Weiss, & Patterson, 1972; Weiss & Summers, 1983), the Coding Scheme for Interpersonal Conflict (Rausch, Barry, Hertel, & Swain, 1974), the Marital and Family Interaction Coding System (Olson & Ryder, 1973, 1975), and the Couples Interaction Coding System (Gottman, Notarius, Gonso, & Markman, 1976; Notarius & Markman, 1981). These systems were designed for assessment of conflict-resolving interactions. Descriptive and evaluative reviews of these systems are available elsewhere (Margolin & Jacobson, 1981; Weiss & Summers, 1983; Weiss & Margolin, 1986) and therefore will not be presented here. To date, behavioral researchers have not used interactional coding systems to study the marital interactions of elderly couples. Such systems could be very useful in describing the changes that occur in interaction patterns among married couples over the life span and in delineating differences in the types of problems encountered in old, middle-aged, and young couples.

BEHAVIORAL MARITAL THERAPY

Behavioral marital therapy focuses on changing thoughts and feelings within the context of modifying interaction patterns. This may be accomplished through a variety of different strategies including: (1) changing moment-to-moment interactions through communication skills training; (2) changing daily patterns through behavioral exchange, increasing shared pleasurable activities, and decreasing negative exchanges; and (3) changing long-term patterns by improving coping skills. These strategies are presented in more detail below.

Changing Communication Patterns

The modification of communication patterns often begins with the patterns that are observed within the therapy session. Communication training is a term that is used to describe a variety of strategies that vary in their foci. Some approaches are directed at the listener, while others focus on the speaker. The goal of all approaches, however, is to reduce listener–speaker discrepancies (Gottman *et al.*, 1976).

Listener deficits include tuning out too quickly, focusing on only part of a message, or generating a rebuttal before the message is finished (Weiss & Margolin, 1986). Intervention involves teaching listening skills that stress active listening strategies, such as paraphrasing, reflecting, and summarizing, in an atmosphere of support and appreciation (Jacobson & Margolin, 1979).

Speaker deficits include being long-winded, expressing dissatisfaction in a blaming manner, and making demands rather than requests (Weiss & Margolin, 1986). Interventions designed to modify speaker deficits focus first on clarifying the content of the speaker's statement. The nonverbal affective components as well as the content of the message are addressed here. The therapist helps the speaker examine whether the content of a statement communicates the desired meaning and whether the affect expressed matches the intended message.

Problem-solving skills is an area of communication training that has received the most attention by behavioral marital therapists. Using the listening and speaking skills they have learned, the couple attempts to resolve a specific conflict-ridden issue. Jacobson and Margolin (1979) developed a manual that describes a variety of skills that are associated with conflict resolution and positive communication. The model of problem solving that they present is fairly extensive and requires that the couple adopt a collaborative approach, accepting that both spouses are responsible, in part, for their conflicts.

When attempting communication and problem-solving skills training with elderly couples it is important that the therapist be active and directive and be able to interrupt destructive patterns and present alternatives. This may be difficult for the young or inexperienced therapist who is not accustomed to interrupting and correcting older adults.

Changing Daily Behavior Patterns

After the couple has gained experience in applying the communication and problem-solving skills within the safety of the therapy setting, it is time to direct change toward the home environment. One common approach to changing daily patterns is to instruct each spouse to engage in activities that are pleasing to his or her partner. In the past, behavioral marital therapists attempted to increase the number of pleasant exchanges by engaging couples in quid pro quo contracting. This did not prove effective because spouses tended to attribute their partners behavior to an external source (e.g., "He only did it because I asked, not because he wanted to.") (Jacobson, 1981). A more effective approach is to instruct spouses to generate their own ideas about how to please their partners. Rather than being told directly to engage in specific behaviors, they are encouraged to devote energy toward pleasing their spouse, for example, over the next week.

We have observed that this approach can be effective among older couples who have been married for several years because it renews the appreciation the spouses feel for one another. An older couple that was referred to the first author for marital therapy found the assignment to "surprise one another" challenging yet very enjoyable. They had been married for 62 years and reported that they had stopped sleeping in the same bed 14 years earlier because the husband was a "loud snorer." As one of their surprises, each spouse decided to crawl in bed with the other and enjoyed laughing when they bumped into one another in the dark hallway.

Increasing the number of shared activities between partners is effective in increasing intimacy and improving marital satisfaction. This strategy is appropriate because of the conflicts and hostilities that have been built up over time. According to Weiss and Margolin (1986) this approach can increase the salience of positive feelings and reduce overgeneralizations about the negative aspects of the marriage.

As is the case with behavioral assessment techniques, the application of behavioral marital therapy to the problems of older couples has not been studied systematically. The emphasis on continuous assessment of effectiveness is a characteristic of behavior therapy that makes it especially appealing when working with this population. Because our treatments cannot be directly data-based at present we should rely on data-generating methods.

DATING IN LATE LIFE

For the most part, researchers interested in dating and courtship have not studied these activities among elderly adults. This is somewhat surprising given the large number of nonmarried older adults. Studies of changes in friendship patterns over the life course (Brown, 1981; Tesch, 1983) indicate that old people are at risk for losing friends because of factors such as declining health, income loss due to retirement, and widowhood. For the most part, however, studies of friendship among older adults have been cross-sectional, comparing older adults with middle-aged individuals. It may be that the observed differences were due to cohort membership and the older people studied may always have had fewer friends. As Carstensen (1987) suggests, social activity in old age should be compared with levels of interactions earlier in life on an intraindividual basis. This suggestion is particularly pertinent for clinicians working with older adults because, as Carstensen (1987) points out, there are no norms of optimal social activity level for this or any age group.

A survey of elderly women's friendship patterns (Adams, 1985) found that few of the women reported having a current relationship with a man. Of the friendships described by the 70 participants, 90.6% were with women, 6.1% were with couples, and only 3.6% were with men. Almost all (95.7%) of the women were able to name at least one female friend, while only 17.1% named at least one male friend. An obvious explanation for the scarcity of cross-sex relationships among older women is the limited opportunity of elderly women to meet older men. Adams (1987) suggested that other factors also impact on the prevalence of male–female relationships. Almost all of the women interviewed indicated that they viewed these relationships as courting relationships. Several of those who reported having no male friends indicated that they were concerned that their children or friends would disapprove of such a relationship. Adams suggested that these attitudes are probably associated with cohort membership. The women in this study were probably not exposed to nonromantic male–female relationships in young adulthood and, therefore, according to Adams, did not view men as potential candidates for nonromantic relationships. This study raises some interesting questions about cross-sex relationships in old age, but the design does not allow for the assessment of the relative contributions of aging and cohort effects. The friendship patterns of older men also deserve investigation. Given the large number of older nonmarried women, the social environments of older men are very likely quite different than those of older women.

When determining the treatment goals of an elderly individual who is expressing dissatisfaction with his or her heterosocial relationships, the behavior therapist should collect information about the client's description of the problem, the onset and course of the problem, the magnitude and nature of the distress caused by the problem, and any past attempts made by the client to deal with the problem.

In addition, we believe the following information is important and should be sought when trying to develop a treatment program for an elderly individual who is dissatisfied with his or her social life: (1) A description of current social activity, including the frequency and quality of interactions. Is dissatisfaction due to a lack of opportunity to engage in interactions with the opposite sex or is it a result of anxiety? (2) An indication of cognitions, including defeating self-statements (e.g., "I'm too old to be attractive to anyone") and irrational beliefs ("People will think I'm a hussy"). (3) Feelings regarding physical appearance. (4) Quality of social skills and assertiveness skills. Does it appear that a skills deficit might be impeding success in developing relationships? (5) Relationship history. Has the client ever had a satisfying intimate relationship? If so, how long ago was it? How did it end? If he or she is widowed, what was the marriage like? How have attitudes and behavior toward the opposite sex changed since the death of the spouse?

SEX

The major purposes of assessment in behavior therapy are to determine what are the individual's goals and to understand the causal nexus of these goals. This is not different when the client is elderly and the goals are sexual ones.

In addressing the question of which goal(s) the elderly individual or couple wishes to pursue, the therapist should strive to allow the client(s) to make an uncoerced, informed choice (O'Donohue, Fisher, & Krasner, 1987). The behavior therapist may need to provide information about the existence of alternative goals or factual information about the probable consequences of each choice, so that the elderly client(s) can make an informed choice. Many individuals hold false beliefs concerning sex. For example, some believe that masturbation causes mental illness. Individuals who hold false beliefs face an artificially constrained set of alternatives. Second, the behavior therapist must also assess the extent to which the individual has been coerced to seek therapy for a particular sexual concern. Many are made uncomfortable by the sexual behavior or interest of the elderly and may pressure the elderly individual to seek therapy for what they consider inappropriate sexual behavior. It may be more important to train the client in assertion skills and problem-solving skills or to advocate for the client than to conduct sex therapy.

Therefore, the first set of questions is: What are the elderly client(s) goals? Is this an informed choice? Is this an uncoerced choice?

The second set of assessment questions involve understanding the causal forces that are related to the goals of the client(s). As in any therapy case one needs to ascertain information about: (1) what the client sees as the problem; (2) the onset and course of the problem (age, gradual or sudden, precipitating events, contingencies, changes over time); (3) the magnitude and nature of the distress caused by the problem; (4) past attempts to change and the outcome of these attempts (including self-help, medical evaluation and treatment, and previous psychological treatment); (5) the presence of other sexual or nonsexual problems. It is also useful to inquire about the client's current sex life, including the frequency and quality of intercourse, the nature, length, and quality of foreplay, the frequency and quality of noncoital activities, the male's latency to ejaculation and the female's orgasmic potential, the individual's and/or couple's use and nature of sexual fantasies. The therapist should get information about any traumatic sexual experiences, the range of sexual interests (e.g., homosexual contacts or fantasies), the client's knowledge of basic sexual physiology and effective sexual techniques, misperceptions about sexuality, past and present attitudes toward sex, the real and perceived attitudes of past and present significant others, and religious attitudes and training. The client should describe his or her cognitions, particularly any defeating self-statements and irrational beliefs and relate concerns about anxiety or fears. It is important to determine the quality of the current relationship, the presence or absence of marital discord, the level of intimacy experienced by the clients, whether or not there is any generalized hostility toward the opposite sex, the history of interactions with people in general, and quality of one's social skills and assertiveness skills. The therapist must observe and inquire about the quality of communication in the relationship, particularly regarding sexual likes and dislikes, messages about current sexual problems, and the client's feelings about his or her own physical appearance. Information should be gathered about the client's current lifestyle and sex roles, the availability of a partner or partners, the opportunity (time and place) to have sex, the priority placed on having sex, and any difficulties the client may experience due to his or her sex roles. Finally, the clinician should be aware of two inventories that appear useful in assessing relevant matters. These are the Aging Sexuality Knowledge and Attitudes Scales (White, 1982), and the Sexual Interaction Inventory (LoPiccolo & Steger, 1974).

Treatment of Sexual Problems

There are two studies relevant to the treatment of the elderly's sexual problems. Kaas and Rousseau (1983) reported a case study of a 65-year-old male treated through the use of Annon's (1976) four stage behavioral model of permission, limited information, specific suggestions, and intensive therapy. The client described himself as impotent and attributed his impotence to age and hypertensive medication. He was divorced and reported only limited social contact. During a visit to a senior's drop-in medical clinic, verbal and nonverbal permission to discuss sexual concerns were provided by asking the client if he had sexual concerns and by having several books on sexuality in the office. After complaining of impotence, the client was invited to join a group on sexuality and aging. In addition, during individual counseling he received information on the sexual response cycle and was informed that the antihypertensive medication that he was taking did not affect the sexual response cycle. Self-pleasuring behaviors (including masturbation and sexual fantasizing) were encouraged, while the intake of alcohol prior to sexual activity was discouraged. During the 1-month treatment period the client's social contacts and self-pleasuring behaviors increased. He resumed having wet dreams, and his ability to achieve erections during masturbation improved the possibility of pursuing a sexual relationship.

Rowland and Haynes (1978) described a sexual enhancement program designed to improve the elderly's communication and to increase enjoyment of sexual contact. The subjects were 10 married couples ranging in age from 51 to 71 years. Length of marriage ranged from 3 to 45 years with a mean duration of 30.3 years. The 6-week program began by providing information on human sexual functioning, particularly in older adults. During group discussion sessions, topics covered included: attitudes about sexual interest and activity in old people, body image, and health concerns and sexual functioning. Educational reading material was also provided. Following this, communication exercises and training in sexual techniques were presented. In addition to receiving homework assignments to practice pleasuring techniques, participants were encouraged to increase their physical attractiveness and relearn flirtation techniques. The program resulted in increased sexual satisfaction, frequency of certain sexual activities, and improved attitudes toward marriage and life in general.

The two studies described above are the only published reports of treatment studies for sexual problems of the elderly. This lack of research directly concerned with the elderly's sexual problems may not be serious. Many studies have shown that sexual behavior can be changed by modifying factors that are not in themselves manifestly sexual (Annon, 1976). Communication training, social skills training, systematic desensitization of anxiety, thought stopping, and rational restructuring are all techniques that effectively alter the conditions that are functionally related to targeted sexual behaviors. As these techniques are present in the behavior therapist's repertoire, he or she should have the general skills necessary to treat many of the sexual problems of the elderly, which are basically no different from the sexual problems of any other age population.

It is beyond the scope of this chapter to review behavioral treatments that are unique to the treatment of sexual problems. Annon (1976), Fischer and Cochros (1977), and LoPiccolo and LoPiccolo (1978) are three excellent general sources for this information. Some of the techniques described in these books, however, may need some modification. Felstein (1983), for example, suggests that the use of the squeeze technique with the elderly male may cause a local petechial effect in the penile skin.

O'Donohue (1987) has reviewed evidence that the elderly and others believe that the elderly are not sexually desirable, desirous, or capable. These are myths, widely held, but nonetheless false beliefs. The clinician needs to determine if these are held by the client or significant others, and whether modifying these beliefs by cognitive restructuring might have a beneficial effect.

Some elderly individuals are institutionalized. It is the rare institution that is accepting of the sexual behavior of the elderly. Nursing homes are often segregated by gender and do not provide places that are private, much less romantic. It might be necessary for the clinician to consider educating the staff and management of these institutions regarding the sexual interests and abilities of the elderly. It seems plausible that if an institution would allow more outlets for appropriate sexual behavior, inappropriate sexual behavior would decrease.

Kassel (1983) recounts a story about two elderly residents of a nursing home that illustrates the problems presented by institutions and the truth of the maxim "Where there's a will, there's a way."

> They visited an understanding physician and requested that he oversee, from his professional viewpoint, their lovemaking. He was to determine whether they were indulging in sexual intercourse properly. He agreed. After they completed the act, he told them that it was perfect, and then charged them $10 for the office visit. They returned weekly for 8 weeks, and each time they paid $10 for the office visit. Finally the doctor told them the continuation of their visits was senseless because he repeatedly confirmed that their sex life was perfect. The couple then confided that they were residents of the Shady Nook Nursing Home, and that they could find no privacy for themselves. They could not go to their children's homes, and they could not afford $20 for a motel room. On the other hand, the doctor visits cost $10, and they received $8 refunds from Medicare. (p. 179)

A satisfactory sex life is important for a variety of reasons. Butler and Lewis (1978) have suggested that for older individuals sex may serve as a means of expressing passion, affection, admiration, and loyalty; affirming one's body and its functioning; asserting oneself; protecting oneself from anxiety; defying the stereotypes of the elderly; creating a sense of romance; affirming life; and experiencing pleasure through touch. It seems fair to say that sex can be very important for the young *and* the old. Therefore, it is certainly a worthy end for behavior therapists to attempt to understand the roles of sex in the lives of the elderly, and to assist them in achieving their goals regarding sex.

REFERENCES

Adams, R.G. (1985). People would talk: Normative barriers to cross-sex friendships for elderly women. *The Gerontologist*, *25*, 605–611.

Adams, R. G. (1987). Patterns of network change: A longitudinal study of friendships of elderly women. *The Gerontologist*, *27*, 222–227.

Ade-Ridder, L., & Brubaker, T. H., (1983). The quality of long-term marriages. In T. H. Brubaker (Ed.), *Family relationships in later life* (pp. 21–30). London: Sage Publications.

Anderson, S. A., Russell, C. S., & Schumm, W. A. (1983). Perceived marital quality and family life-cycle categories: A further analysis. *Journal of Marriage and the Family*, *95*, 127–139.

Annon, J. S. (1976). *Behavioral treatment of sexual problems*. Hagerstown, MD: Harper & Row.

Atchley, R. C., & Miller, S. J. (1983). Types of elderly couples. In T. H. Brubaker (Ed.), *Family relationships in later life* (pp. 77–90). Beverly Hills, CA: Sage Publications.

Baltes, M. M. & Barton, E. M. (1977). New approaches toward aging: A case for the operant model. *Educational Gerontology, 2*, 383–405.

Beckman, K., & Giordano, J. A. (1986). Illness and impairment in elderly couples: Implications for marital therapy. *Family Relations, 35*, 257–264.

Brink, T. L. (1979). Geriatric rigidity and its psychotherapeutic implications. *Journal of the American Geriatrics Society, 26*, 274–277.

Brown, B. B. (1981). A life-span approach to friendship: Age-related dimensions of an ageless relationship. In H. Lopata and D. Maines (Eds.), *Research in the interweave of social roles: Friendship* (pp. 23–50). New York: JAI Press.

Butler, R. N., & Lewis, M. I. (1978). The second language of sex. In R. Solnick (Ed.), *Sexuality and aging* (pp. 176–183). Los Angeles: University of Southern California Press.

Butler, R. N., & Lewis, M. I. (1983). *Aging and mental health.* New York: New American Library.

Cargan, L., & Melko, Y. M. (1982). Singles: Myths and realities. Beverly Hills, CA: Sage Publications.

Carstensen, L. L. (1987). Age-related changes in social activity. In L. L. Carstensen & B. A. Edelstein (Eds.), *Handbook of clinical gerontology* (pp. 222–237). New York: Pergamon Press.

Felstein, I. (1983). Dysfunction: Origins and therapeutic approaches. In R. Weg (Ed.), *Sexuality in the later years* (pp. 223–247). New York: Academic Press.

Fischer, J., & Cochros, H. L. (1977). *Handbook of behavior therapy with sexual problems.* New York: Pergamon Press.

Glick, P., & Norton, A. J. (1977). *Population reports.* Washington, DC: U.S. Bureau of the Census.

Gottman, J., Notarius, C., Gonso, J., & Markman, H. J. (1976). *A couple's guide to communication.* Champaign, IL: Research Press.

Hempel, C. (1970). *Aspects of scientific explanation.* New York: The Free Press.

Hops, H., Wills, T. A., Weiss, R. L., & Patterson, G. R. (1972). *Marital interaction coding system.* Eugene, OR: University of Oregon and Oregon Research Institute.

Hussian, R. A. (1981). *Geriatric psychology: A behavioral perspective.* New York: Van Nostrand Reinhold.

Jacobson, N. S. (1981). Behavioral marital therapy. In A. S. Gurman & D. P. Knishern (Eds.), *Handbook of family therapy* (pp. 35–52). New York: Brunner/Mazel.

Jacobson, N. S., & Margolin, G. (1979). *Marital therapy: Strategies based on social learning and behavior exchange principles.* New York: Brunner/Mazel.

Kaas, M. J., & Rousseau, G. K. (1983). Geriatric sexual conformity: Assessment and intervention. *Clinical Gerontologist, 2*, 31–34.

Kassel, V. (1983). Long term care institutions. In R. Weg (Ed.), *Sexuality in the later years* (pp. 167–184). New York: Academic Press.

Locke, H. J., & Wallace, K. M. (1959). Short-term marital adjustment and predictia tests: Their reliability and validity. *Journal of Marriage and Family Living, 21*, 251–255.

LoPiccolo, J., & LoPiccolo, L. (1978). *Handbook of sex therapy.* New York: Plenum.

LoPiccolo, J., & Steger, J. C. (1974). The sexual interaction inventory: A new instrument for assessment of sexual dysfunction. *Archives of Sexual Behavior, 3*, 585–595.

Margolin, G., & Jacobson, N. S. (1981). The assessment of marital dysfunction. In M. Hersen & A. S. Bellack (Eds.), *Behavioral assessment: A practical handbook* (pp. 389–426). New York: Pergamon Press.

Markman, H. J., Notarius, C. I., Stephen, T., & Smith, R. J. (1981). Behavioral observation systems for couples: The current status. In E. E. Filsinger & R. A. Lewis (Eds.), *Assessing marriage: New behavioral approaches* (pp. 234–262). Beverly Hills, CA: Sage Publications.

Notarius, C. F., & Markman, H. J. (1981). The couples interaction scoring system. In E. E. Filsinger & R. A. Lewis (Eds.), *Assessing marriage: New behavioral approaches* (pp. 112–127). Beverly Hills, CA: Sage Publications.

O'Donohue, W. (1987). The sexual behavior and problems of the elderly. In L. Carstensen & B. Edelstein (Eds.), *Handbook of clinical gerontology* (pp. 66–75). New York: Pergamon Press.

O'Donohue, W., Fisher, J. E., & Krasner, L. (1987). Ethics and the elderly. In L. Carstensen & B. Edelstein (Eds.), *Handbook of clinical gerontology* (pp. 387–399). New York: Pergamon Press.

Olson, D. H., & Ryder, R. G. (1973). *The IMC coding system.* Unpublished manuscript, University of Minnesota.

Olson, D. H., & Ryder, R. G. (1975). *Marital and family interaction coding system (MFICS).* Unpublished manuscript, University of Minnesota.

Parron, E. A., & Troll, L. E. (1978). Golden wedding couples: Effects of retirement on intimacy in long-standing marriages. *Alternate Lifestyles, 1,* 447–464.

Raush, H. L., Barry, W. A., Hertel, R. K., & Swain, M. A. (1974). Communication, conflict, and marriage. San Francisco: Jossey Bass.

Rowland, K. F., & Haynes, S. N. (1978). A sexual enhancement program for elderly couples. *Journal of Sex and Marital Therapy, 4,* 91–113.

Salmon, W. C. (1971). *Statistical explanation and statistical relevance.* Pittsburgh: University of Pittsburgh Press.

Skinner, B. F., & Vaughn, M. E. (1983). *Enjoy old age.* New York: W. W. Norton.

Snyder, D. K., Wills, R. M., & Keisler, T. W. (1981). Empirical validation of the Marital Satisfaction Inventory: An actuarial approach. *Journal of Consulting and Clinical Psychology, 49,* 262–268.

Spanier, G. B. (1976). Measuring dyadic adjustment: New scales for assessing the quality of marriage and similar dyads. *Journal of Marriage and the Family, 38,* 15–28.

Szasz, T. S. (1960). The myth of mental illness. *American Psychologist, 15,* 113–118.

Tesch, S. A. (1983). Review of friendship development across the life span. *Human Development, 26,* 266–276.

U. S. Senate (1982). *Special committee on aging report.* Report 97–314, Vol. 1. U. S. Government Printing Office: Washington, DC.

Weiss, R. L., & Birchler, G. R. (1978). Adults with marital dysfunction. In M. Hersen & A. Bellak (Eds.), *Behavior therapy in the psychiatric setting* (pp. 331–364). Baltimore: Williams & Wilkins.

Weiss, R. L., & Margolin, G. (1986). Assessment of marital conflict and accord. In A. R. Ciminero, K. S. Calhoun, & H. E. Adams (Eds.), *Handbook of behavioral assessment* (2nd ed., pp. 561–600). New York: John Wiley & Sons.

Weiss, R. L., & Perry, B. A. (1979). *Assessment and treatment of marital dysfunction.* Eugene, OR: Oregon Marital Studies Program.

Weiss, R. L., & Summers, K. J. (1983). Marital interaction coding system-III. In E. E. Filsinger (Ed.), *A source book of marriage and family assessment* (pp. 85–115). Beverly Hills, CA: Sage.

Weiss, R. L., Hops, H., & Patterson, G. R. (1973). A framework for conceptualizing marital conflict, a technology for altering it, some data for evaluating it. In L. A. Hamerlynck, L. C. Handy, & E. J. Mash (Eds.), *Behavior change: Methodology, concepts, and practice* (pp. 309–342). Champaign, IL: Research Press.

White, C. B. (1982). A scale for the assessment of attitudes and knowledge regarding sexuality in the aged. *Archives of Sexual Behavior, 11,* 491–502.

10

Behavioral Assessment and Treatment of Depression in Older Adults

Linda Teri

This chapter will provide an overview of the literature on behavioral assessment and treatment of depression in older adults. It will begin with a discussion of generally accepted and well-established definitions of depression and the behavioral theory of depression development and maintenance. It will then survey the available methods for assessing depression in older adults, discuss strategies for intervention, and conclude with a case presentation illustrating the behavioral treatment of a depressed older adult.

Definition of Depression

Clinical depression is most often defined by the DSM-III diagnostic criteria (American Psychiatric Association, 1980) or the Research Diagnostic Criteria (RDC; Spitzer, Endicott, & Robins, 1978). The former is often used in clinical settings, the latter in research protocols. Each relates easily to the other and both are presented in Table 1. As can be seen, depression is a multifaceted disorder, characterized by affective distress (dysphoria), behavioral difficulties (sleep and appetite disturbance, complaints of fatigue, social withdrawal) and cognitive dysfunction (thoughts of death and suicide, problems of concentration). Both DSM-III and RDC criteria require that dysphoric mood and a minimum of four symptoms be present for at least 2 weeks. While it is not necessary for a depressed patient to have all of these symptoms, most depressed patients display the majority of them to some degree. To date, there have been no additional or alternative diagnostic criteria systematically employed to define depression in older adults.

Linda Teri • Department of Psychiatry and Behavioral Sciences, University of Washington Medical School, Seattle, Washington 98195.

Table 1
Diagnostic Criteria for Depression

RDC: Major Depressive Disorder	DSM-III: Major Depressive Disorder
A. Dysphoria	Same
B. Symptoms	
At least four symptoms for probable	At least four symptoms
1. Loss of appetite	
2. Sleep difficulties	
3. Psychomotor agitation or retardation	
4. Loss of energy	
5. Loss of interest or pleasure	
6. Feelings of worthlessness, self-reproach, or guilt	
7. Complaints or evidence of concentration difficulties	
8. Recurrent thoughts of death or suicide or suicidal behavior	
C. Duration: 2 weeks	Same
D. Exclusionary criteria (simplified for this table)	
1. Schizophrenia	
2. Presence of mood-incongruent delusion or hallucination	
E. Evidence of impaired functioning	Not specified

Behavioral Theory of Depression

The behavioral view of depression has been primarily advanced by Lewinsohn and his colleagues (Lewinsohn, Antonuccio, Steinmetz, & Teri, 1984; Lewinsohn, Teri, Hoberman, & Hautzinger, 1985b), who have argued that, among other factors, depression results from too few pleasant and too many negative person-environment interactions. These interactions are governed by the same laws of learning that govern normal behavior (cf. Bandura, 1977). Thus, depressive behaviors are viewed as maladaptive learned phenomena that can be changed by altering the person-environment interactions sustaining them, enabling new learning to occur and be maintained. Although formulated on middle-aged adults, this theory may generalize to older adults as well. One may hypothesize that many of the factors that contribute to a decrease in pleasant events and/or an increase in aversive events may occur in the lives of older individuals. For example, older adults experience a high rate of health problems that have been consistently associated with increased depression (Radloff & Teri, 1986). Such diminished health status may inhibit the older adult's ability to engage in activities they once enjoyed (decreased pleasant events) and may expose the older adult to pain and decreased function (increased unpleasant events). A similar scenario can be constructed for social interactions that are affected by the physical conditions of friends and loved ones. When these people become ill and die, the survivor may have less opportunity to engage in pleasant interactions (decreased pleasant events), and may be required to live in more unpleasant situations (increased unpleasant events).

ASSESSMENT

Lewinsohn, Teri, and Wasserman (1982) have identified three major goals for the assessment of depressed adults: (1) accurate and early differential diagnoses; (2) formulation of functional diagnoses and identification of targets for intervention; and (3) evaluation of treatment effectiveness through ongoing assessment of target behaviors. Each of these goals as they relate to older adults will be discussed in the following section.

Differential Diagnosis

The clinician must evaluate whether depression is present, whether or not it is the most prominent problem experienced by the client, and/or whether it is one of many difficulties reported. If depression is present, a comprehensive physical examination that includes a good medical history, an analysis of current medication, and laboratory tests is essential to determine whether the depression is caused or exacerbated by a physical disorder. Not only do health problems contribute significantly to depression, they can mimic depression and, if undetected, can further jeopardize health status. Depression may occur secondary to organic problems, be a prodromal indicator to the onset of physical disease, or be concurrently superimposed on physical disease. Depression may also occur as a side effect to certain medications. Thus, it is critical for clinicians to identify (if not disentangle) the role of health status in the older adult's presentation of depression. (For further review, the reader is referred to Salzman & Shader, 1979).

Depression can coexist and/or be confused with dementia. A careful cognitive evaluation should be an integral part of the diagnostic evaluation. It is beyond the scope of this chapter to discuss the evaluation of dementia in older adults in any detail. Chapter 6 of this text contains such information. It should be noted here, however, that many of the symptoms of depression (such as cognitive disturbance, impairment in functioning, and loss of interest or pleasure in usual activities) may be misinterpreted as symptoms of dementia, and vice versa. The danger of labeling a treatable disorder as a nontreatable disorder and the danger of expecting unrealistic levels of performance from patients with significantly diminished cognitive capacity cannot be overemphasized. For more detailed discussion of these issues, readers are referred to recent reviews by Teri and Keller (1987), Teri and Reifler (1987), and Zarit and Zarit (1983).

Functional Assessment

The purpose of a functional assessment is to identify the individual constellation of depressive behaviors present in each patient and to clarify the unique personal and environmental factors that shaped and maintain those behaviors. Each of the symptoms of depression should be assessed to determine the degree to which each contributes to observable dysfunction. Depressed patients often report that they are unaware of the events that trigger their depressed affect and are unable to describe situational factors. Thus, it is helpful for the interviewer to have an array of questions to which the patient can respond. Since the hallmark of depression is dysphoric mood, mood should be carefully evaluated. The rate and nature of behavioral and cognitive activity should also be evaluated to determine the degree to which training in different behavioral and cognitive skills will be useful to the individual patient. For example, asking patients whether they experience each of the depression symptoms listed in Table 1 can help clarify the individual constellation of depression symptoms. Asking patients what activities they currently engage in, enjoy, and participated in and enjoyed in the past may help clarify what skills and deficits they possess. Providing patients with a preestablished list of activities, such as the Pleasant Events Schedule, described below, will avoid the often negativistic answers to open-ended questions that characterize depressed patients (such as "I don't know" and "nothing"). More detailed strategies for assessment are discussed next.

Strategies for Assessment

A wide variety of assessment methods have been used to evaluate depression. The most common include: (1) an interview with the patient; (2) self-report symptom checklists; and (3) behavioral observations. Each strategy can complement the other to form a complete picture of the individual patient's unique constellation of depressive behaviors and cognitions. Each of these methods will now be discussed.

Interviews

Unstructured clinical interviews or structured interview schedules have been employed in clinical and research settings to assess the range of depressive symptoms discussed earlier. Such interviews frequently focus on the presence or absence of specific depressive symptoms, the history and cause of such symptoms, the associated difficulties reported, and the presence, absence, and nature of other psychiatric or psychosocial disturbance. Structured interview schedules have the advantage of providing a clear format with which clinicians can obtain information germane to diagnosis and treatment. The success of unstructured interviews relies heavily on the level of experience of the clinician and may not offer a reliable source from which to evaluate patients. Important questions may be omitted and thus important factors may not be assessed. The goal of a structured interview is to provide a methodical and reliable method of assessing all symptoms relevant to depression, including those important to differential or exclusionary diagnoses. One structured clinical interview is the Schedule for Affective Disorders and Schizophrenia (SADS; Endicott & Spitzer, 1978), which allows a clinician to evaluate a wide range of psychiatric symptoms. Information from the SADS can be used to derive diagnoses based upon the RDC discussed earlier. Investigators have found that the SADS differentiates between older adults with major depression and normal, healthy older adults (Dessonville, Gallagher, Thompson, Finnel, & Lewinsohn, 1982), and it may be used reliably by trained nonprofessional interviewers (Teri & Lewinsohn, 1982). There are several versions of the SADS, each designed to evaluate something different, including the presence of any lifetime psychiatric disturbance (SADS-L), the presence of current psychiatric disturbance (SADS-R), and change occurring in psychiatric status over time (SADS-C).

The Hamilton Rating Scale for Depression (HRS-D; Hamilton, 1967) has been used in a number of studies with older adults to evaluate change in depression. As such, it may be helpful as a pre-post treatment index for therapeutic improvement. Salzman and Shader (1979) report good reliability and validity for this scale with the elderly, although it has certain problems. For example, Sarteschi, Cassano, Castrogiovanni, and Conti (1973) reported that older adults endorsed more frequent and severe symptoms than younger adults. On the other hand, Schnurr, Hoaken, and Jarret (1976) reported that the HRS-D was unaffected by age, sex, or educational factors. Most likely, the difference in findings reflect differences in sampling. But, until the effects of age and education on the scale are better understood, the HRS-D should be interpreted cautiously with older adults. Scores on the HRS-D have also been associated with health status and therefore might be problematic for use with medically ill older adults (Gallagher, Slife, Rose, & Okarma, 1982; Yesavage, Brink, Rose, Lum, Huang, Adey, & Leirer, 1983).

There are many other geriatric rating scales that are based partially upon interview data or are designed to allow multidimensional comprehensive assessment of older adults rather than the specific assessment of geriatric depression. Examples of these scales are the Comprehensive Assessment and Referral Evaluation (Gurland, Kuriansky, Sharpe, Simon, Stiller, & Birkett, 1977), the Philadelphia Geriatric Center's Multilevel Assessment Instrument (Lawton, Moss, Fulcomer, & Kleban, 1982), and the Older Americans' Resources and Services Questionnaire (Fillenbaum & Pfeiffer, 1976).

Self-Report Inventories

Self-report of depression depends on the older adult's perception and report of his or her current status. Concerns have been voiced about the use of self-report depression inventories with older adults because they may give socially desirable or limited responses; they may conceptualize events in nonpsychological terms; or they may have negative attitudes toward mental health (Lawton, 1979). Although these tendencies can bias responses to self-report inventories, recent empirical data suggest that they are not sufficient to prevent the use of depression inventories in older adults (cf. Radloff & Teri, 1986; Teri & Lewinsohn, 1986). Several self-report measures of depression are reliable and valid with a geriatric population and will be discussed next.

The Beck Depression Inventory (BDI) was developed by Beck, Ward, Mendelson, Mock, and Erbaugh (1961). It contains 21 items rated on a scale of increasing frequency and severity. The BDI has good psychometric properties with older adults, accurately and reliably classifying subjects who did and did not meet RDC for Depression (Gallagher, Nies, & Thompson, 1982; Gallagher, Breckenridge, Steinmetz, & Thompson, 1983).

The Center for Epidemiological Studies—Depression Scale (CES-D) was developed by Radloff (1977) and requires subjects to rate the frequency of occurrence in the past week of 20 depressive symptoms on a 4-point scale. A recent review of the use of the CES-D with older adults (Radloff & Teri, 1986) indicated that this scale is reliable and valid for older adults and yields a stable factor structure tapping positive and negative affect, interpersonal difficulties, and somatic and retarded activity. Like other measures of depression, the CES-D consistently correlates to measures of health status and should be interpreted cautiously with physically ill populations (Radloff & Teri, 1986).

The Geriatric Depression Scale (GDS) was developed by Brink, Yesavage, Lum, Heersema, Adey, and Rose (1982) specifically for use with geriatric populations. It requires only a "yes" or "no" response to items and is not heavily weighted with physical symptom items. If future research supports initial estimates of its validity and reliability (Yesavage et al., 1983), the GDS could be a useful measure for self-report of depression in a geriatric population.

The Minnesota Multiphasic Personality Inventory—Depression Scale (MMPI-DS) was originally normed and developed for younger adults (Dahlstrom, Welsh, & Dahlstrom, 1975). Because response patterns to the MMPI-DS are considerably different for older adults, the factor structure may not be stable across different age spans (Harmatz & Shader, 1975). In addition, longitudinal studies indicate that MMPI-DS scores increase with age (Leon, Kamp, Gillum, & Gillum, 1981; Swenson, 1961). A similar rise in scale scores has been noted on the shortened MMPI, the Mini-Mult (Kincannon, 1968), with demographic variables further confounding results (Fillenbaum & Pfeiffer, 1976). Thus, the MMPI-DS should be carefully interpreted with older adults.

The Zung Self-Rating Depression Scale (Zung, 1965) is similar to the CES-D in response format, requiring respondents to indicate the frequency of the occurrence of depression symptoms on a 4-point scale. This scale has been widely used with younger populations, but there is considerable controversy over its utility with older adults (Gallagher, McGarvey, Zelinski, & Thompson, 1978; Murkofsky, Conte, Plutchik, & Karasu, 1978). A large proportion of the items are related to physical symptoms and do not correlate well with other indications of mood disorder in the aged (Blumenthal, 1975; Gallagher et al., 1978). Further, the factor structure is unstable for adults over 70 years of age (Gallagher et al., 1978).

The Pleasant Events Schedule for the Elderly and the Unpleasant Events Schedule for the Elderly (PES-E and UES-E) evaluate the rate and nature of behavioral activity (Teri & Lewinsohn, 1982). The 114-item PES-E is a modification of the original PES (MacPhillamy & Lewinsohn, 1982), a checklist in which activities are rated for frequency and perceived pleasantness. For example, the behavior "being with family" is rated for its frequency of occurrence within the past month on a 3-point scale: 0 = has not happened at all in the past 30 days; 1 = has happened a few times (one to six times); 2 = has happened often (seven or more times). That same behavior is then rated for its pleasantness on a 3-point scale (O = not pleasant, 1 = somewhat pleasant, 2 = very pleasant). The UES-E is a 131-item modification of the original UES (Lewinsohn, Mermelstein, Alexander, & MacPhillamy, 1985a), a checklist similar to the PES, in which activities are rated for frequency and perceived aversiveness. For example, the behavior "being alone" is first rated for its frequency of occurrence, and then rated for its aversiveness on a 3-point scale (0 = not unpleasant, 1 = somewhat unpleasant, 2 = very unpleasant). These inventories are different from the depression inventories discussed thus far in that they do not assess depression symptoms, but rely on the individual's self-report of activity. Consequently, they may be considered a hybrid between self-report and behavioral observation. They require patients to report on how often they engage in each activity (frequency) and how much pleasure (enjoyability) or displeasure (aversiveness) is derived from each activity. Providing a list to which patients can react often takes the burden of initiation away and reduces the frequency of responses such as "nothing" or "I don't know" in answer to direct questions about what enjoyable activities exist. Patients can be encouraged to add, change, or omit whatever items they wish. Often the process of completing the PES-E will raise patients' awareness of how little they do that they enjoy. The original PES and UES are widely used and well developed with younger adults. The inventories modified for older adult patients are briefer, easy to read, and have age-relevant items. They correlate highly with the original measures and have normative data available (Teri & Lewinsohn, 1982). Rapp and Jarrett (1984) have successfully used the PES-E with their older patients. They have added a rating of "accessibility" whereby the respondent indicates if he or she is unable to engage in activities due to physical or environmental limitations. Another modification of the PES and UES for older adults was made by Hedlund and Gilewski (1980).

Behavioral Observations

There is no paucity of direct observational techniques that can be used with depressed older adults. Behavioral approaches to the assessment of depression typically include measures of overt verbal and motor behaviors on both a macro level (e.g., "social skills") and a micro level (e.g., smiling and eye contact). (For more detailed information, see reviews by Rehm and Kornblith, 1979, and Lewinsohn and Lee, 1981.) In using these observational approaches, investigators should remember that normative data are not readily available for geriatric populations. These measures, however, are typically used to monitor changes over time rather than to compare specific patients to others.

There are many other geriatric rating scales based upon observational data (e.g., PAMIE: Gurel, Linn, & Linn, 1972; OARS: Fillenbaum, 1978; CARE: Gurland *et al.*, 1977; SCAG: Shader, Harmatz, & Salzman, 1974), and although they do not specifically assess geriatric depression they may be helpful in providing a global assessment of behavior and behavioral change.

A common observational technique is to have patients observe their own behavior by keeping a diary or daily log of their day's activities, thoughts, and affect. Obviously, involving another person (such as a spouse or an adult child) who has knowledge of the depressed person's activities is also quite useful.

In summary, there are a number of diverse methods for evaluating depression in the older patient. Recommended methods include (1) using a structured interview schedule, such as the SADS, which would permit diagnostic decisions based upon either the RDC or DSM-III; (2) complementing the interview with a self-report inventory such as the BDI that is reliable with older adults and provides an overview of the patient's perceptions of his or her symptoms; and (3) using a behavioral inventory such as the PES-E to individualize treatment to the patient's unique depressive experience.

Because depression is multifactorial, involving affect, cognition, and behaviors, the strongest assessment approach is multifactorial. Diagnostic interviews, self-report inventories, and behavioral observations by the patient and others all contribute to developing a complete picture of the depressed patient and to providing necessary information for diagnosis and treatment planning.

TREATMENT OF DEPRESSION

Once accurate diagnosis has been established, the treatment of the depressed older adult can begin. While there is little empirical information available to guide the clinician in the use of behavioral techniques with this population, accumulating research lends support to the utility of behavioral interventions. This section will provide an overview of the behavioral treatment of depression in older adults and an outline to facilitate effective treatment. This outline is taken from the Coping with Depression Course, formulated and developed for younger adults by Lewinsohn *et al.* (1984) and adapted to older adults by a number of investigators (Gallagher, 1981; Steinmetz, Zeiss, & Thompson, 1983; Teri, 1985). This is a rapidly growing area, and therapists must keep abreast of the literature to maintain their effectiveness.

Recall that Lewinsohn *et al.* (1985b) argued that depression is caused and maintained by person-environment interactions. Depressed adults are often socially isolated and withdrawn; their conversation is often marred by depressive statements; their ideations are often negative and deprecatory; and they often lack the skills to enhance their lives. Treatment, therefore, focuses on increasing pleasant interactions, decreasing negative interactions, and providing the individual with the appropriate skills to influence his or her environment in order to produce the desired positive outcome. Consistent with a behavioral view of psychopathology, depression is viewed as a syndrome of learned maladaptive patterns that can be altered. The symptoms of depression are viewed as important problems in their own right and are addressed directly. Because depression is an affective, cognitive, and behavioral disorder that presents with a great deal of individual variability, the treatment of depression is often tailored to the individual and structured to evaluate and effect each of the important domains.

Treatment may be offered on a group or individual basis. Thus far, little empirical information is available to suggest that one modality is better or worse than the other. In one study with younger depressives (mean age 35), Teri and

Lewinsohn (1986) compared group and individual social-learning approaches and found both approaches equally effective. They suggested that unless there are extenuating circumstances, the group intervention should be considered because it is more cost-effective. Gallagher and her colleagues report successes with both group and individual treatment for cognitively intact older adults. Their work is described in greater detail in recent reviews (Gallagher & Thompson, 1983; Steinmetz, Thompson, Breckenridge, & Gallagher, 1984) and in a manual that presents session-by-session outlines of their intervention procedures (Gallagher, Thompson, Baffa, Piatt, Ringering, & Stone, 1981). When treating older depressed adults, the presence and the degree of cognitive impairment must be noted and factored into intervention plans. Teri (1985) developed a program for treating older depressed adults with considerable cognitive impairment. Patients diagnosed with dementia of the Alzheimer's type as well as major depressive disorder were successfully treated for their depression with the involvement of their caregivers. A case illustration of this procedure is provided later in this chapter and additional detail is available in Teri and Uomoto (1986).

Stages of Treatment

Behavioral treatment of the depressed older adult may be conceptualized as occurring in three stages. The first stage consists of orienting patients to the behavioral framework for depression treatment. The second stage is one of skill building, in which patients are taught the prerequisite skills necessary to alleviate their depression. The third stage involves maintenance and generalization. During this time, patients are trained to employ their skills independent of the therapy session. The bulk of therapy time is spent in the middle skill-building stage, but the first and last stages are no less important to the successful outcome of therapy. Each of these stages is discussed in detail below.

Stage 1. Orienting the Patient

Patients often view depression as something imposed either by some internal weakness (e.g., "I'm just no good") or uncontrollable external circumstances (e.g., "Things just go wrong"). Patients should be encouraged to think of depression as a skill deficit that they can overcome with new, effective skills. In taking this view, patients are better able to dispel the notion that depressed people are sick, crazy, or diseased. Older patients may consider depression as "normal" for their age or something they must tolerate. They may make comments such as "What can you expect? I'm 85" or "I'm too old to change now." Patients should be encouraged to think of themselves as having a legitimate right to happiness and as having the capability to change.

In the beginning of therapy it is especially important that patients understand and agree with the social-learning rationale in order to engage in the activities of therapy. Many of the suggestions for behavior change are difficult for depressed patients to hear. When therapists encourage them to be proactive, optimistic, and motivated, patients wonder how to achieve those goals in their depressed condition. Therefore, these ideas must be presented carefully and with a great deal of support.

As part of the patient's orientation to therapy, both therapist and patient should arrive at goals that are pragmatic and clearly defined. For example, while the goal "to be happy" is certainly understandable, it is not readily definable. More specific goals might include increasing activities, especially those that are enjoyable; learning to cope better in interactions that are distressing; and decreasing negative thoughts and statements. Each of these goals can be further delineated into even smaller, more definable subgoals.

Stage 2. Teaching Necessary Skills

The cornerstone of behavioral intervention is teaching patients the necessary skills to overcome their depression. The following skills are often useful.

Developing a Self-Change Plan. Patients must learn how to design, implement, and evaluate a self-change plan that includes: (1) targeting a clearly defined and reasonable behavior for change; (2) monitoring the behavior to identify baseline levels; (3) identifying stimuli that precede and follow the behavior (antecedents and consequences); (4) establishing realistic goals for behavior change; (5) defining strategies for reinforcing achieved goals; and (6) evaluating the self-change process for modifications as needed. Obviously, these skills will be useful in developing other skills.

Increasing Pleasant Activities. Once activities are identified, a reasonable schedule for increasing them should be determined. "Reasonable" in this regard has a number of dimensions: the number of activities should not be too large; the types of activities selected should not be too difficult; activities should be accessible; and they should be time limited. For example, a patient who has spent the last 3 months at home alone, sitting on the couch, and staring into space is not being realistic in promising daily attendance at the Senior Center. A more realistic plan would be for the patient to meet this goal by participating in a series of steps: first, telephoning the Senior Center to find out what they offer; next, walking over to the Senior Center to obtain a copy of their schedule of activities; then reviewing the schedule and selecting one activity for participation. If the patient is not yet ready to participate, she could choose to attend the activity as a passive observer until she feels comfortable in participation. Gradually, the number of activities, the frequency of attendance, and the sites of activities could be increased. Devising an activity schedule should be carefully negotiated between patient and therapist. Both should feel confident that the patient *can* do what she says she *will* do.

As much as feasible, when an activity is planned, the entire scenario should be carefully spelled out and role-played in the therapy session. From the previous example, points of clarification might include the time the patient plans to call the Senior Center; the way the patient intends to get the telephone number; the way to handle a busy signal; the dialogue between the patient and whoever answers the phone; etc. The therapist can model effective problem-solving strategies for the patient and encourage the patient to think through many possible situations. Role-playing these situations helps the patient avoid failure experiences. Because one can never fully anticipate setbacks, patients should be encouraged to see the activity as an experiment in which there is no success or failure. If something goes "wrong" or "right," patients should consider it an opportunity to learn. Patients and therapists should always be challenged to explain in behavioral terms *why* something did or did not work. In addition to providing patients with information about their behavior, this process encourages them to perceive themselves as in control and capable of formulating and executing plans to affect their behavior.

Relaxation Training. When patients begin to engage in activities not previously a part of their lives, or from which they have withdrawn, they may often feel anxious. At these times, training in stress reduction techniques can be very useful. While there are many relaxation training programs available, progressive muscle relaxation, based on Jacobson's work (1938), is one commonly employed. With this procedure, patients alternately tense and relax different muscle groups. For older patients, particularly those with muscle pain, it may be helpful to use a guided imagery procedure in which a pleasant scene (often taken from their responses to the PES-E schedule) is imagined while taking regular deep breaths and telling oneself to be calm. Patients are encouraged to practice relaxation in nonthreatening situations first and then, once the procedure is learned, to use it in stressful situations. Patients learn to identify and monitor times when they feel tense or uncomfortable and evaluate the degree of their relaxation at those times.

Combating Negative Cognitions. Depressed patients often evaluate themselves or their situations in very negative terms. Beck and Greenberg (1974) describe a number of techniques used to combat negative cognitions. Primary among them are thought stopping and thought challenging. Thought stopping is a straightforward procedure that has been used clinically even with cognitively impaired depressed adults. It consists of identifying the negative thought and pairing it with an abrupt aversive stimulus, such as the verbal shout "stop" or the pop of a rubber band on the wrist. Each time a particular negative thought is experienced (e.g., "I can't do anything right"), the negative consequence of "stop!" or "pop!" is enacted. The thought challenging procedure requires that patients challenge their negative cognitions with rational, optimistic inquiry. It requires an ability to think logically and calmly. Therapists can model this technique by asking patients about their negative cognitions and challenging them during the therapy session.

Social Skills. Some patients must learn (or relearn) ways to engage in prosocial (nondepressive) conversation, initiate positive interactions, and contend with difficult social situations. Assertion training can be useful in this area.

Patients may have progressed far enough in therapy at this point to believe they can resolve long-standing conflicts or engage in social interactions quite different from their usual routines. As in the earlier example, a patient who never attended one Senior Center activity may say she is going to visit the center everyday. It is important to select realistic and clear goals, at this stage as well. Patients should develop a hierarchy of social situations and test their developing skills in each one, step by step, slowly and experimentally. They can "try on" or "experiment" with different responses until they find one they can use in the actual situation. Finally, patients can learn how to continually evaluate, monitor, and learn from their endeavors.

Stage 3. Maintenance and Generalization

Up to this point in therapy, there has been an emphasis on teaching patients to practice their skills outside the therapy session. During the final stage of therapy, this emphasis becomes more explicit as patients are encouraged to plan for situations that are likely to occur once therapy ends. The goal is to maintain the gains made in therapy and to generalize their new skills to different situations. Therapist and patient review the skills that were most valuable to the patient, ways of maintaining those skills once therapy ends, methods for monitoring the patient's mood, and strategies to use if the patient begins feeling depressed again. The goal is to develop pragmatic approaches to potential problems rather than "hope" the problems will not recur.

CASE ILLUSTRATION

Description of Client

In this section the ideas discussed in this chapter will be illustrated by describing the details of a case actually treated at the Geriatric and Family Services Clinic at the University of Washington Hospital. Mrs. B. was an 84-year-old woman referred by her family. They expressed concern over her behavior, which suggested to them that she was "giving up on life." The family also reported that Mrs. B. seemed to be having more and more problems with memory. Mrs. B. was given a comprehensive geriatric evaluation, including intake, psychometric tests, social work report, and physical work-up with laboratory tests. (For a more detailed discussion of this evaluation, the reader is referred to Reifler, Larson, and Teri, 1987).

Mrs. B. lived by herself in her own home. She cooked her own meals and cleaned her own house, albeit irregularly. Her children, one daughter and two sons, lived within 25 minutes of her home. Mrs. B.'s physical problems included hypertension that was under control and rheumatoid arthritis. Her physical exam failed to reveal any additional medical problems.

Mrs. B.'s family was quite concerned about her cognitive status. She often forgot things, misplaced objects, and was confused in new situations. They reported that these problems had been evident for 4 years, and they noted a "slow, but steady" progressive loss. Mrs. B. herself complained about an inability to remember things and difficulty with concentration, but she believed that these problems had developed only over the previous few months.

Mrs. B. evidenced definite cognitive impairment on psychometric testing and in the diagnostic interview. When given a mental status screening exam, she was oriented and was able to perform simple cognitive tasks (such as repeating phrases, writing a sentence, copying two geometric shapes, and carrying out a simple 3-step command), but she had trouble completing more complex tasks requiring sustained attention and cognitive flexibility (e.g., the instruction to subtract 7 from 100 consecutively for a set number of serials) and abstract concept formation (e.g., interpreting proverbs). On more detailed psychometric evaluation, she showed considerable memory difficulties and had problems with complex tasks, especially those requiring new learning. This performance was significantly poorer than one would expect from her prior level of independent function and her educational level. As a result of these evaluations, Mrs. B. was given a diagnosis of dementia of the Alzheimer's type.

As a widow of 15 years, Mrs. B. reported that "her life ended" at her husband's death. She said that although she was "close" to her family, they were "too busy with their own lives to worry about an old burden like me." During the intake interview, Mrs. B. was often tearful, apologetic, and self-deprecatory. She rarely engaged in eye contact and generally looked down at her hands. During the 1½-hour interview, she smiled only once, when she spoke about her family in the past, when her husband was alive and her children were younger. She spoke quite calmly about wanting to die and was tearful when discussing her feelings of loneliness and worthlessness that she said were "always" with her. After recounting a tale of unhappiness and isolation, she observed, "Well, what can I expect, after all I'm an old lady."

Mrs. B. met DSM-III criteria for major depressive disorder. Her scores on the Beck Depression Inventory and the Hamilton Depression Rating Scale were 32 and 28 respectively, indicating that she was "severely depressed." Functionally, Mrs. B.'s depression seemed to be maintained by four factors: infrequent engagement in pleasant events, considerable social isolation, negative cognitions, and unwitting reinforcement by her family. She spent the majority of her time alone in her home with the blinds down and lights out, doing nothing. The only time she saw her family was when they visited and tried to "entice" her to be happy. She shopped for food only when her children took her or if a neighbor invited her to go. She initiated little activity and viewed herself as a burden to family and friends.

Treatment

Orientation to Treatment

At the end of the evaluation, the diagnoses of depression and dementia of the Alzheimer's type were discussed with Mrs. B. and her family. Mrs. B. was assured that "just because she was 84," she need not be depressed and that she could learn to feel better than she was currently feeling. The therapist stressed that although little could be done for her memory, a good deal could be done for her depression. The therapist took time to explain the relationship between depression and memory loss and the association between pleasant events and depressed mood to Mrs. B. and her family. Although Mrs. B. consistently made disparaging remarks about her inability to engage in activity, she acknowledged that the ideas made sense and that she could understand how "someone" could feel better if "they" did more. She could not, however, imagine *herself* doing more than she was currently doing.

The possibility of medication was also discussed with Mrs. B., her family, and the clinic psychiatrist. On the basis of the behavioral assessment, all agreed that a behavioral approach seemed hopeful and would be tried first. Although not optimistic, Mrs. B. agreed to try treatment for six sessions to see if her mood would improve. Mrs. B.'s family was quite eager to pursue treatment, and Mrs. B.'s older daughter agreed to accompany Mrs. B. to each appointment. Other family members offered to help as needed.

Mrs. B. was then asked to complete a PES-E and was given a behavioral diary in which to record her actual activities, and a mood rating scale for charting her daily mood levels. Her daughter agreed to help her complete the forms.

Skill Building

Self-Change. Mrs. B. and her daughter were taught to pinpoint behaviors, establish baseline, identify antecedents and consequences, establish goals, and choose reinforcers. Both Mrs. B. and her daughter were asked to monitor Mrs. B.'s mood each day by rating her mood on a 0–10 scale, with zero representing the worst she has ever felt (very unhappy) and 10 representing the best she has ever felt (very happy). Examples of situations in which she felt "0" and "10" were discussed. Mrs. B. and her daughter decided that early evening was the best time to evaluate her mood, and the daughter agreed to call once each evening to discuss the prior day with her mother, remind her to write down her mood score, and make her own rating of her mother's mood based on this telephone conversation.

Pleasant Events. The activity diary supported the information obtained in the intake interview. Mrs. B. spent most of her day alone, at home, sitting in a chair, inactive. During a small part of her day, the TV set was on. On the basis of the intake interview and the completed PES-E, three activities were identified that might provide Mrs. B. with pleasant experiences. One activity was a community-based program for older adults that was open from 11:30 a.m. to 2:30 p.m. and offered lunch, group activities, and special events. The program was located about two blocks from Mrs. B.'s home and was easily accessible although she had never visited it. The second activity involved a friend with whom Mrs. B. had once enjoyed a close relationship but whom she had not seen in the last year. According to her daughter, Mrs. B.'s friend had occasionally called and invited Mrs. B. to join her, but Mrs. B. had refused the invitations and the friend had gradually stopped calling. Mrs. B. was sure her friend would not want to be "bothered" with her. The third activity involved family. Mrs. B. greatly enjoyed her family's attention. Although she saw them often, she and they reported that these times had become difficult. When they were together the family spent most of their time trying to cheer her; she spent most of the time complaining. Each of these activities was discussed with Mrs. B. and her daughter, and specific plans were made for scheduling these activities.

Additional Skills. In each of the activities planned, Mrs. B. needed assistance. In order to attend the community association, she had to cope with her discomfort about going into new situations, meeting new people, and being out of her home on her own. To achieve this goal, Mrs. B. and the therapist role-played her behavior in these situations. A hierarchy of steps was developed that progressed from walking into the community center, introducing herself, initiating conversation, and arranging for continued involvement. Topics of "conversational chatter" were discussed and practiced. This hierarchy spanned a number of sessions, and Mrs. B.'s out-of-session homework paralleled her in-session hierarchy. That is, Mrs. B. was encouraged to carry out in real life whatever items on the hierarchy she had imagined during the therapy session. For example, after the session in which she practiced going into the agency for the first time, she was expected to go. After the session in which she practiced initiating conversation, she was expected to speak with someone she met, and so forth. A similar approach was taken with the second activity. Mrs. B. rehearsed making a telephone call to her old friend, practiced what she would say, and planned how she would handle her feelings at the time. In each of these situations, relaxation training helped Mrs. B. stay calm prior to embarking on the goal behavior. She was learning new behaviors and relearning old behaviors that had dropped out of her repertory.

Mrs. B.'s daughter learned how to decrease the attention she gave to depressive behaviors and increase her attention to incompatible (nondepressive) behaviors. For example, when Mrs. B.'s daughter was shown how to initiate and maintain conversations that would focus on nondepressive topics (such as what activities Mrs. B. enjoyed, positive reminiscences, etc.), she was also shown how to divert depressive topics and keep her responses to the absolute minimum. The daughter was responsible for relaying these skills to the other members of her family so as to maintain consistency in reinforcing nondepressive behaviors.

In teaching Mrs. B. and her daughter these behavioral skills, it became apparent that both engaged in cognitive self-statements that hindered their progress. Mrs. B. was convinced that she was a bother to everyone around her and had to be taught to decrease her negative statements (those she made covertly to herself and those she made overtly to whomever she met). Mrs. B. also learned to confront her negative opinions and evaluate herself more optimistically. Mrs. B.'s daughter was fearful of not being a "good daughter" and was very involved in "helping" Mrs. B. She learned to redefine "good daughter" and to encourage Mrs. B.'s independent activity.

Maintenance and Generalization

Prior to terminating therapy, Mrs. B. and her daughter were encouraged to think of ways in which they could maintain the gains they both had made in therapy. Mrs. B. believed she could continue to go to the community center. She found that she actually looked forward to it. She enjoyed seeing her friend and discussed some other friends she was thinking of "looking up."

Mrs. B.'s daughter felt it was vital that she speak to Mrs. B. each day to be certain she was continuing her activities. She acknowledged the role she and her family played in maintaining the depression and seemed knowledgeable about how to avoid that role in the future. She believed she would continue to monitor her mother's mood, although she doubted whether she would write down each activity because that was "such a big job."

Following treatment, Mrs. B. was seen 1 month, 3 months, 6 months, and 1 year after her last session. Mrs. B. continued to have cognitive difficulties, and many of her problems increased. She continued to visit the community center and her friends, saying, "It's a habit I enjoy." Her daughter continued daily contact. In the intervening months, Mrs. B.'s close friend died and that was a difficult time for her. She spoke of it with emotion but concluded by saying, "Death is death. She enjoyed her life. That's what's important." Mrs. B. and her daughter began discussing a retirement home, which Mrs. B. insisted should have "a lot of activity to keep me busy."

CONCLUSION

At this time, there is an assumption that teaching depressed older adults skills to combat their depression will decrease their depression. This assumption has been empirically validated with younger depressed adults (Lewinsohn *et al.*, 1984) and with older depressed adults (cf. Gallagher *et al.*, 1981), although the latter body of empirical work is much less extensive. As has been illustrated with the preceding case example, clinical strategies used with younger patients can be successfully adapted to older adults. The degree to which this adaptation is successful depends, in part, upon the therapists' ability to utilize the very skills they are teaching their patients, namely, to focus on progress, keep steps small and realistic, reinforce success, and to avoid focusing on what is yet to be done, trying to accomplish unrealistic goals, or attending to failure in nonconstructive ways. The more the therapist is successful in implementing and encouraging patients to implement behavior change strategies, the more successful treatment will be.

REFERENCES

American Psychiatric Association. (1980). *Diagnostic and statistical manual of mental disorders* (3rd ed., revised). Washington, DC.

Bandura, A. (1977). *Social learning theory*. Englewood Cliffs, NJ: Prentice-Hall.

Beck, A. T., & Greenberg, R. (1974). *Coping with depression*. Philadelphia: Center for Cognitive Therapy.

Beck, A. T., Ward, C. H., Mendelson, M., Mock, J., & Erbaugh, J. (1961). An inventory for measuring depression. *Archives of General Psychiatry, 4,* 561–571.

Blumenthal, M. (1975). Measuring depressive symptomatology in a general population. *Archives of General Psychiatry, 32,* 971–978.

Brink, T. L., Yesavage, J. A., Lum, O., Heersema, P., Adey, M., & Rose, T. L. (1982). Screening tests for geriatric depression. *Clinical Gerontologist, 1,* 37–43.

Dahlstrom, W. G., Welsh, G. S., & Dahlstrom, L. E. (1975). *An MMPI handbook.* Minneapolis, MN: University of Minnesota Press.

Dessonville, C., Gallagher, D., Thompson, L. W., Finnell, K., & Lewinsohn, P. M. (1982). Relation of age and health status of depressive symptoms in normal and depressed adults. *Essence, 5,* 99–117.

Endicott, J. E., & Spitzer, R. L. (1978). A diagnostic interview, the Schedule for Affective Disorders and Schizophrenia. *Archives of General Psychiatry, 35,* 837–844.

Fillenbaum, G. G. (1978). Validity and reliability of multi-dimensional functional assessment questionnaire. In *Multi-dimensional functional assessment: The OARS methodology.* Durham, NC: Duke University.

Fillenbaum, G. G., & Pfeiffer, E. (1976). The mini-mult: A cautionary note. *Journal of Consulting and Clinical Psychology, 44,* 698–703.

Gallagher, D. (1981). Behavioral group therapy with elderly depressives: An experimental study. In D. Upper & S. Ross (Eds.), *Behavioral group therapy* (Vol 3, pp. 187–224). Champaign, IL: Research Press.

Gallagher, D., & Thompson, L. W. (1983). Depression. In P. M. Lewinsohn & L. Teri (Eds.), *Clinical geropsychology* (pp. 7–37). Elmsford NY: Pergamon Press.

Gallagher, D., McGarvey, W., Zelinski, W., & Thompson, L. W. (1978). *Age as a factor structure of the Zung Depression Scale.* Paper presented at the 31st annual meeting of the Gerontological Society. Dallas, TX.

Gallagher, D., Thompson, L., Baffa, G., Piatt, C., Ringering, L., & Stone, V. (1981). *Depression in the elderly: A behavioral treatment manual.* Los Angeles: University of Southern California.

Gallagher, D., Nies, G., & Thompson, L. (1982). Reliability of the Beck Depression Inventory with older adults. *Journal of Consulting and Clinical Psychology, 50,* 152–153.

Gallagher, D., Slife, B., Rose, T., & Okarma, T. (1982). Psychological correlates of immunologic disease in older adults. *Clinical Gerontologist, 1,* 51–58.

Gallagher, D., Breckenridge, J., Steinmetz, J., & Thompson, L. W. (1983). The Beck Depression Inventory and Research Diagnostic Criteria: Congruence in an older population. *Journal of Consulting and Clinical Psychology, 51,* 933–4.

Gurel, L., Linn, M. W., & Linn, B. S. (1972). Physical and mental impairment of function evaluation in the aged: The PAMIE Scale. *Journal of Gerontology, 27,* 83–90.

Gurland, B., & Kuriansky, J., Sharpe, L., Simon, R., Stiller, P., & Birkett, P. (1977). The Comprehensive Assessment and Referral Evaluation (CARE), rationale, development and reliability, *International Journal of Aging and Human Development, 8,* 9–42.

Hamilton, M. (1967). Development of a rating scale for primary depressive illness. *British Journal of Social and Clinical Psychology, 6,* 278–296.

Harmatz, J. S., & Shader, R. I. (1975). Psychopharmacologic investigation in healthy elderly volunteers: MMPI Depression Scale. *Journal of the American Geriatric Society, 23,* 350–354.

Hedlund, B., & Gilewski, M. (1980). *Development of pleasant and unpleasant events schedules for older adults: A validation study of short forms for use with elderly individuals.* Unpublished paper, University of Southern California, Los Angeles.

Jacobson, E. (1938). *Progressive relaxation.* Chicago: University of Chicago Press.

Kincannon, J. C. (1968). Prediction of the standard MMPI scale score from 71 items: The mini-mult. *Journal of Consulting and Clinical Psychology, 32,* 319–25.

Lawton, M. P. (1979). Clinical geropsychology. Problems and prospects. *Master Lectures on the Psychology of Aging.* Washington, DC: American Psychological Association.

Lawton, M. P., Moss, M., Fulcomer, M., & Kleban, M. H. (1982). A research and service-oriented multilevel assessment instrument. *Journal of Gerontology, 37,* 91–99.

Leon, G. R., Kamp, J., Gillum, R., & Gillum, B. (1981). Life stress and dimension of functioning in old age. *Journal of Gerontology, 36,* 66–69.

Lewinsohn, P. M., & Lee, W. M. L. (1981). Assessment of affective disorders. In D. H. Barlow (Ed.), *Behavioral assessment of adult disorders* (pp. 129–170). New York: Guilford Press.

Lewinsohn, P., Teri, L., & Wasserman, D. (1982). Behavioral treatment of depression. In M. Hersen (Ed.), *Outpatient behavior therapy: A clinical guide* (pp. 81–108). New York: Grune & Stratton.

Lewinsohn, P. M., Antonuccio, D. O., Steinmetz, J. L., & Teri, L. (1984). *The coping with depression course*. Eugene, OR: Castalia Publishing.

Lewinsohn, P. M., Mermelstein, R. M., Alexander, C., & MacPhillamy, D. J. (1985a). The Unpleasant Events Schedule: A scale for the measurement of aversive events. *Journal of Clinical Psychology, 41*, 483–498.

Lewinsohn, P., Teri, L., Hoberman, H., & Hautzinger, M. (1985b). An integrative theory of depression. In S. Reiss & R. Bootzin (Eds.), *Theoretical issues in behavior therapy* (pp. 331–359). New York: Academic Press.

MacPhillamy, D. J., & Lewinsohn, P. M. (1982). The pleasant events schedule: Studies on reliability, validity, and scale intercorrelation. *Journal of Consulting and Clinical Psychology, 50*, 363–380.

Murkofsky, C., Conte, H. R., Plutchik, R., & Karasu, T. B. (1978). Clinical utility of a rapid diagnosis test series for elderly psychiatric outpatients. *Journal of American Geriatric Society, 26*, 22–26.

Radloff, L. W. (1977). The CES-D scale: A self-report depression scale for research in the general population. *Applied Psychological Measurement, 1*, 385–401.

Radloff, L. W., & Teri, L. (1986). Assessing depression in older adults: The CES-D scale. *Clinical Gerontologist, 5*, 119–137.

Rapp, S., & Jarrett, R. B. (1984). *Depression and pleasant events in the elderly: The relationship of frequency, enjoyability, availability, and ability*. Paper presented at the 18th annual meeting of the Association for the Advancement of Behavior Therapy, Philadelphia, PA.

Rehm, L. P., & Kornblith, S. J. (1979). Behavior therapy for depression: A review of recent developments. In M. Hersen, R. M. Eisler, & P. M. Miller (Eds.), *Progress in behavior modification* (pp. 277–318). New York: Academic Press.

Reifler, B. V., Larson, E., & Teri, L. (1987). An outpatient geriatric psychiatry assessment and treatment service. *Clinics in Geriatric Medicine, 3*, 203–209.

Salzman, C., & Shader, R. I. (1979). Clinical evaluation of depression in the elderly. In A. Raskin & L. F. Jarvik (Eds.), *Psychiatric symptoms and cognitive loss in the elderly* (pp. 39–72). Washington, DC: Hemisphere.

Sarteschi, P., Cassano, G., Castrogiovanni, P., & Conti, L. (1973). Use of rating-scales for computer analysis of affective symptoms in older age. *Comprehensive Psychiatry, 14*, 371–379.

Schnurr, R., Hoaken, P. C. S., & Jarrett, F. J. (1976). Comparison of depression inventories in a clinical population. *Canadian Journal of Psychology, 21*, 473–476.

Shader, R. I., Harmatz, J. S., & Salzman, C. (1974). A new scale for clinical assessment in geriatric populations: Sandoz Clinical Assessment—Geriatric (SCAG). *Journal of the American Geriatric Society, 22*, 107–113.

Spitzer, R. L., Endicott, J., & Robins, E. (1978). Research diagnostic criteria: Rationale and reliability. *Archives of General Psychiatry, 35*, 773–782.

Steinmetz, J. L., Zeiss, A. M., & Thompson, L. W. (1983). *The life satisfaction course: An intervention for the elderly*. San Francisco: NIMH Conference.

Steinmetz, J. L., Thompson, L. W., Breckenridge, J. N., & Gallagher, D. (1984). Behavioral group therapy with the elderly. In D. Upper & S. Ross (Eds.), *Handbook of behavioral group therapy* (pp. 275–299). New York: Plenum.

Swenson, W. (1961). Structured personality testing in the aged: An MMPI study of the gerontological population. *Journal of Clinical Psychology, 17*, 302–304.

Teri, L. (1985). *Depression in dementia patients*. Paper presented to the Society of Behavioral Medicine, New Orleans.

Teri, L., & Keller, L. (1987). Multimodal assessment of the cognitively impaired older adult. In E. Borgatta (Ed.), *Alzheimer's caregivers: Strategies for support* (pp. 40–64). Seattle: University of Washington Press.

Teri, L., & Lewinsohn, P. M. (1982). Modification of the pleasant and unpleasant events schedules for use with the elderly. *Journal of Consulting and Clinical Psychology, 50*, 444–445.

Teri, L., & Lewinsohn, P. M. (1986). Individual and group treatment of unipolar depression: Comparison of treatment outcome and identification of predictors of successful treatment outcome. *Behavior Therapy, 17*, 215–228.

Teri, L., & Reifler, B. V. (1987). Depression and dementia. In L. Carstensen & B. Edelstein (Eds.), *Handbook of clinical gerontology* (pp. 112–119). New York: Pergamon Press.

Teri, L., & Uomoto, J. (1986). *Pleasant events and depression in Alzheimer's patients*. Unpublished manuscript, University of Washington, Seattle.

Yesavage, J., Brink, T., Rose, T., Lum, O., Huang, O., Adey, V., & Leirer, V. (1983). Development and validation of a geriatric depression screening scale: A preliminary report. *Journal of Psychiatric Research* , *17*, 215–228.

Zarit, S., & Zarit, J. (1983). Cognitive impairment. In P. Lewinsohn & L. Teri (Eds.), *Clinical geropsychology* (pp. 38–80). New York: Pergamon Press.

Zung, W. (1965). A self-rating depression scale. *Archives of General Psychiatry*, *12*, 63–70.

11

Cognitive-Behavioral Interventions for Age-Related Memory Impairment

Linda Warren Duke, William E. Haley, and Thomas F. Bergquist

Introduction to Age-Related Memory Impairment

Annie Smith is a 72-year-old widowed woman who responded to an advertisement for volunteers interested in learning skills to improve their memory functions. Although she continues to live an active and independent life, managing all of her own household and financial affairs and volunteering two days per week at a local hospital, she reports a number of memory problems that are sources of embarrassment and inconvenience in her daily life. Most of these problems are focused around several situations that are important to her. First, at church, she finds herself having difficulty remembering the names of some of the other members of her congregation. When in a crowd of people, she often has trouble remembering what people have told her; she may lose her train of thought or have trouble finding the right words. On several occasions, she has forgotten to put her money into her purse before going to church, and has been embarrassed at being unable to give her offering. Mrs. Smith has played bridge with a small group of women on a weekly basis over the past 12 years. Lately, she notes that she forgets the cards which have been played, and has occasionally even forgotten the bid. While she used to take pride in her ability to do her grocery shopping completely from memory, lately she has relied on making hurried lists on scraps of paper, which she frequently cannot find in her purse. She also misplaces important objects, such as her eyeglasses or purse, while at home. Sometimes she spends hours looking for lost bills or objects. She is also distressed that she is unable to remember friends' telephone numbers, and relies on her address book for all of this information. Mrs. Smith is in good health and denies significant depression or anxiety, but she admits some fear that she is developing Alzheimer's disease.

Linda Warren Duke, William E. Haley, and Thomas F. Bergquist • Department of Psychology, University of Alabama at Birmingham, Birmingham, Alabama 35294.

A review of recent research reflects a growing awareness that substantial memory problems and other cognitive deficits can be reliably associated with *normal* aging. In a survey of crossectional and longitudinal studies, Yesavage (1985) estimated a magnitude of decline of function by age 70 of approximately 15–40% of raw scores on a range of tests of intelligence, memory, and attention. Older adults readily complain about memory deficits when asked. Lowenthal *et al.* (1967) reported that two-thirds of a sample of community-dwelling people over age 60 complained of memory loss. Nevertheless, community-dwelling elderly tend to deny that memory or cognitive deficits cause them serious problems in their daily lives (Sunderland, Watts, Baddeley, & Harris, 1986). Probably because both professionals and the elderly themselves recognize age-related memory decline as primarily an inconvenience, and not a serious functional impairment, this decline is considered "normal." It is often referred to as "minimal memory impairment" or "benign senescent forgetfulness" by clinicians and is distinguished from deficits associated with the dementias or other organic conditions. As in the prototypical case described above, however, relatively mild cognitive impairment can be a source of distress and may interfere with optimal functioning.

With the more widespread recognition of the nature of age-related memory impairment has come the realization that cognitive-behavioral assessment and treatment approaches may be particularly useful to the elderly (Gouvier, Webster, & Blanton, 1986; Nolan, Swihart, & Pirozzolo, 1986). These approaches are currently being used in a number of clinical and research settings (Wilson & Moffat, 1984) and are being marketed in workshops and self-help books (Lapp, 1987; Skinner & Vaughan, 1983). The purposes of this chapter are to review the evidence for the effectiveness of these interventions for the memory problems of the elderly, to present some strategies for implementing cognitive memory training with the elderly, and to suggest some ways to increase the availability of clinically relevant research designed to evaluate the effectiveness of such training.

GENERAL OBLIGATIONS TO THE ELDERLY CLIENT

Professionals in the aging field frequently suggest that close attention to individual differences and tailoring of training goals to take those differences into account are critical in ensuring the success of training programs with the elderly (Costa & Fozard, 1978; Treat, Poon, Fozard, Popkin, & Popkin, 1978). In attempting to assess and treat memory and cognitive deficits, it is particularly important to recognize that a wide range of physical and psychological variables can exert profound influences on cognition in the elderly (Avorn, 1982) and that without adequate assessment, fundamental problems may be ignored. When offering memory rehabilitation and training services to the elderly, the practitioner has a special obligation to insure that: (1) the *client* has sufficient information, and appropriate referral resources, to rule out other treatable sources of memory impairment; and (2) the *practitioner* has sufficient information to tailor the treatment to the particular individual's pattern of functional abilities. Avorn (1982) recommends that every older person who complains of memory impairment be first referred for a thorough physical evaluation. The physical evaluation should include an eye examination and hearing tests and thus may require referral beyond the primary care physician. Thorough psychological assessment, as described below, is also important to determine the potential contribution of such diverse problems as anxiety, depression, stress-related disorders, and the nature and stage of cognitive impairment.

AGE-RELATED CHANGES IN COGNITIVE PROCESSES— THE TARGETS OF INTERVENTION

What are the age-related changes in memory and cognitive function that the elderly client and the practitioner should consider "normal," yet that may benefit from cognitive-behavioral treatment? Aging has two components: a primary nonpathological aging process and secondary, pathological processes (such as arthritis and hypertension) that are frequently associated with aging (Nolan *et al.*, 1986). Rarely is an elderly person free from such secondary processes. Thus, in this section primary and secondary age changes in memory and cognitive function that neither seriously impair daily functioning nor are readily associated with a dementing disease will be considered.

A number of recent and extensive reviews of research on age changes in cognitive functioning (Birren & Schaie, 1977, 1985; Botwinick, 1984; Craik & Trehub, 1982; Kausler, 1982) can serve as references for the practitioner. Probably the elderly client should also have at least a general acquaintance with this information, with particular emphasis on the practical aspects. The popular books by Lapp (1987) and Skinner and Vaughan (1983) present basic information in lay language that can be supplemented by the practitioner. Changes commonly found in normal aging will be briefly reviewed in order to clarify the typical targets of treatment.

Sensory Processes

In the elderly as a group, age-related declines in function have been noted within each sensory modality (Corso, 1981; Kausler, 1982). In the visual system, many individuals experience a reduction in acuity and increased need for corrective lens; a need for increased illumination in work areas or while reading; a greater susceptibility to glare; an increase in the time needed to adapt to change in illumination, such as when entering or leaving a movie or when getting up in the night; a constricted visual field with reduced peripheral sensitivity to low spatial frequencies (such as oncoming vehicles); decreased depth perception; and reductions in ocular motility (Cohen & Lessell, 1984; Fozard, Wolf, Bell, McFarland, & Podolsky, 1977).

In the auditory system, losses in binaural processes and insensitivity to high-frequency sounds can result in difficulties in speech perception, particularly in a noisy area; difficulties in localizing the source of sounds; and a general hearing loss due to reduction in amplitude sensitivity (Corso, 1981).

Other age-related changes in somatosensory, vestibular, and kinesthetic systems can lead to changes in sensitivity to touch and pain, alterations in balance and motor control, and changes in the chemical sense systems that affect smell and taste. Because changes in the sensory systems frequently occur slowly and imperceptibly, they may contribute to feelings that one's general intellectual abilities are failing and to feelings of malaise, anxiety, or depression. Sensory deficits also influence information processing and thus may have a direct negative effect on everyday memory functioning.

General Intellectual Processes

There are also age-related declines in general intellectual functioning. Most individuals will show greater declines in some cognitive skills than in others. The "classic aging pattern" refers to the general tendency of scores on the verbal subtests of the Wechsler Adult Intelligence Scale (WAIS) (Wechsler, 1955) to remain relatively stable with increasing age, while scores on the performance subtests decline (Botwinick, 1984). Most of the verbal subtests require a set of cognitive skills that are necessary for the appropriate use of language. Such skills are dependent on educational and cultural knowledge. They are acquired gradually over the life span, are highly overlearned, and are used relatively automatically. These skills remain fairly stable into old age and have been referred to as "crystalized" intelligence (Horn, 1982). The performance subtests of the WAIS all require sustained attention and active, effortful problem-solving skills, including strategic planning; cognitive manipulation, as in perceiving relations and reasoning; perceptual motor manipulation, as in hand–eye coordination and manipulation of objects; and speeded performance (Baltes & Willis, 1982). These skills, referred to as "fluid" intelligence by Horn (1982), are thought to develop early in the life span and to begin a gradual decline in early adulthood. The elderly are able to substantially improve performance on a variety of tests of "fluid" intelligence with training based on instruction, practice, and feedback (Beres & Baron, 1981; Plemons, Willis, & Baltes, 1978; Schultz & Hoyer, 1976). These studies suggest that the elderly are often able to perform the mental operations required for active problem solving when they are guided in doing so, but they may not efficiently carry out the relevant mental operations spontaneously.

Memory Processes: Objective Impairment

Age-related deficits on memory tasks are well documented, but they are less apparent on some memory tasks than on others (Craik, 1977, 1984). For example, age differences on recall tasks are typically larger than those on recognition tasks. Age differences on secondary memory tasks (retrieving information acquired in the past) are typically larger than those on primary memory tasks (maintaining information in conscious awareness).

Perhaps the most comprehensive and influential attempt to account for the differential deficits observed on different memory tasks is that of Hasher and Zacks (1979). They conceptualize a broad range of memory phenomena as varying in terms of their attentional requirements. Memory operations that require minimal energy from the limited capacity attentional mechanism are called *automatic*. Certain aspects of perceptual information related to time, space, and frequency of occurrence are assumed to be encoded relatively automatically in memory. Automatic encoding processes are expected to show limited changes with normal aging. Contrasted with automatic processes are *effortful* memory operations. Effortful processes require attention and are only initiated intentionally. Effortful processes have also been labelled *conscious* processes (Posner & Snyder, 1975) and *controlled* processes (Shiffrin & Schneider, 1977). Processes such as forming mental images, rehearsing, organizing, and using strategies to remember are considered effortful. When memory tasks require these activities for successful performance, age deficits are likely to occur.

A variety of specific age-related deficits in the intentional components of effortful controlled processing have been proposed. Several investigators have noted that the elderly select inefficient memory encoding strategies (Craik, 1977; Perlmutter & Mitchell, 1982; Smith, 1980). Others have identified a "production" deficiency, similar to that observed on fluid intelligence tests. The elderly appear capable of carrying out more effective memory encoding and retrieval operations but do not spontaneously do so (Craik & Byrd, 1982; Perlmutter & Mitchell, 1982). The elderly can engage in more effective processing when induced by task conditions to do so, but they are most deficient on tasks that provide little guidance or that require active, novel manipulation of information (Craik & Rabinowitz, 1984). An important consequence of this decreased efficiency in memory operations is less elaborate memory encodings (Sanders, Murphy, Schmitt, & Walsh, 1980). Semantic encodings are more general, prototypical, global, and they neglect specific features of the current situation that differentiate one experience from another (Rabinowitz & Ackerman, 1982). In general, the elderly seem less able to assess a memory task so as to develop and execute a plan of action (Welford, 1980) and to elaborate minimal retrieval cues to guide retrieval and reconstruct the original experience (Craik, 1984).

A range of explanations for these age-related encoding and retrieval deficits has been offered. The elderly may not have enough energy available for processing (Craik & Byrd, 1982), or their capacity to store information may be limited (Welford, 1980), or they might be reluctant to encode information considered insignificant, unimportant, or incoherent (Waugh & Barr, 1982). Another possibility is that encoding habits do not really change with age, but rather that the young can get by with low-effort encoding because the memory system of the young is simply more efficient.

The attentional component of controlled processing is another likely source of the age-related memory deficit. Schonfield (1982) has noted that the elderly may have less attentional resource, while Fager (cited in Schonfield, 1982) contends that they have greater difficulty dividing and switching attention among tasks. These attentional deficits may create difficulties in preparing sequences of intended mental or behavioral actions. In any type of active, strategic processing, attention must be divided between processing current information and preparing future steps. A difficulty in dividing attention may also result in greater disruption of ongoing activities following distraction (Lapp, 1987).

Memory Processes: Subjective Assessment

Subjective assessment of everyday memory functioning by the elderly has provided additional, but sometimes perplexing, information about the nature of the age-related memory deficit. The memory failures that normal elderly adults report as occurring most often are similar to those reported by normal young adults and young head-injured amnesic patients (Sunderland, Harris, & Gleave, 1984). These memory complaints include word-finding problems, misplacing personal possessions, forgetting to carry out intentions or whether they have been carried out, forgetting what someone said, forgetting when something happened, and losing one's train of thought when speaking (Sunderland, et al., 1986). While such failures are reported more frequently by older adults than younger adults (Lowenthal et al., 1967; Perlmutter, 1978), subjective assessments of everyday memory failures by the elderly and their performance on laboratory memory tests are only slightly correlated (Kahn, Zarit, Hilbert, & Niederehe, 1975; Permutter, 1978.

In studies that included clinically depressed elderly, ratings of memory complaints correlated with ratings of depression, but not with performance on memory tests (Kahn et al., 1975). However, Scogin, Storandt, and Lott (1985) found no difference in depression ratings for a group of elderly with high complaints about memory failure who were specifically seeking memory treatment and the depression ratings of an elderly community group with a low rate of memory complaints. As in previous studies, the high complainers and low complainers did not differ in performance on memory tests. Thus, it is not yet clear what subjective complaints of memory deficits represent. Subjective ratings may be complexly determined, not only by affective status, but by the demands of the person's lifestyle, and the effort a person is willing to make to avoid memory failure (Zelinski, Gilewski, & Thompson, 1980). A major difference between objective and subjective assessments, which has been largely overlooked, is the different types of memory tasks assessed in the laboratory or in everyday life. A low correlation exists among different laboratory memory tasks (Underwood, Boruch, & Malmi, 1978), and it seems likely that the retention problems mentioned most often on subjective assessments (forgetting of autobiographical experiences and intentional behaviors, and language access difficulties) may be due to different skills and abilities than is the retention of the kinds of factual, and usually personally irrelevant, information typically found in laboratory memory tasks. Thus, it is certainly possible that subjective memory complaints reflect memory deficits that are difficult to detect with current objective assessment instruments.

What Can Be Learned from Studies of Memory Skills Training in the Elderly?

In a comprehensive review of cognitive-behavioral treatments for memory impairment with normal aging, Yesavage (1985) has argued that training programs have improved performance on a variety of memory tasks to about the same degree that such performance declines with age. It has been apparent since the early work of Hultsch (1969, 1971) and Hulicka and Grossman (1967) that the elderly can improve their ability to memorize unrelated verbal items when instructed to use organizational methods or appropriate visual and verbal mediators. Subsequent research demonstrated that elderly subjects could also learn a formal mnemonic technique (the method of loci) that involves visualizing objects to be remembered in familiar locations. Using it, they increased their recall of a list of unrelated words to levels comparable to that of untrained young subjects (Robertson-Tchabo, Hausman, & Arenberg, 1976; Rose & Yesavage, 1983). Other investigators have demonstrated that elderly subjects could improve their performance on a face–name recall task by using a standard mnemonic procedure, based on identifying a distinctive facial feature, making a concrete verbal association to the name, and then forming an interacting visual image relating the facial feature and the verbal associate (Yesavage, Rose & Bower, 1983). Performance using this face–name mnemonic was improved even more if the elderly were pretrained in techniques to improve visual imagery ability (Yesavage, 1983) or if instructed to elaborate the processing of the visual image by making a semantic judgment (Yesavage et al., 1983). Arenberg (1977) reported improved retention of visual designs in a group of elderly men who were given verbal descriptions of the designs to guide visual processing.

Not all attempts to improve memory performance of the elderly with mnemonic training have been completely successful. In a series of studies, Smith (1975) and Mason and Smith (1977) failed to find facilitating effects of either imagery instructions or the rhyming-peg mnemonic (one is a bun, two is a shoe) on list recall in the elderly, even though the recall of younger subjects did benefit from the technique. Other research suggested that facilitating effects of such mnemonics may occur only if the elderly are practiced in constructing visual images (Yesavage, 1983) and if they have sufficient time both to construct and to recall their images at test (Treat & Reese, 1976). In addition, Robertson-Tchabo et al. (1976) reported that their subjects did not spontaneously use the just-learned mnemonic, the method of loci, if not specifically instructed to do so.

All of the above mentioned studies were attempts to determine whether specific mnemonic techniques would aid the elderly on specific memory tasks. Only a few studies have attempted to determine whether such memory skills training has any practical impact on subjective evaluations or other aspects of memory performance. In a group-training study, Zarit, Cole, and Gardner (1981) compared the effects of specific memory training (teaching four memory strategies) with the effects of studying current events on recall performance and subjective memory complaints. The specific memory training group improved their memory performance on the trained tasks more than the current events group, but both groups had comparable reductions in memory complaints. In another study, Zarit, Gallagher, and Kramer (1981) taught a wider range of memory strategies to one group of subjects. Their results were compared to those of a personal growth group that dealt with interpersonal and affective issues. In this study, memory performance improved and memory complaints declined as a function of participation in the study (pre–post), but there was no difference in the effectiveness of the specific memory training and the personal growth instruction.

Scogin et al. (1985) explored the effectiveness of a self-taught program of memory skills training in the elderly. Participants worked through training materials at home at their own pace. They found improvement on 6 of 11 different measures of memory, compared with a wait-list control group, but there were no effects of memory training on subjective complaints or on a measure of depression. Treatment gains were maintained at a one month follow-up. Although these training studies may be considered modestly successful, there is no objective evidence, as yet, that any generalization of training occurs from laboratory or clinic training to everyday memory problems. Also, nonspecific treatment factors may affect both memory performance and subjective memory complaints. Thus, the clinical utility of memory training remains an open question.

TOWARD A THEORY OF AGE-RELATED MEMORY IMPAIRMENT AND ITS TREATMENT

In this section, we will attempt to integrate some of the features of current conceptions of memory processes based primarily on laboratory research (Hasher & Zacks, 1979; Shiffrin & Schneider, 1977) with conceptions derived primarily from the analysis of everyday memory problems and failures (Norman, 1981; Reason, 1984). While acknowledging that we have borrowed ideas from these authors, our conceptualization may not in all respects be consistent with theirs. Our aim is to present a framework for understanding age-related memory impairment that can guide the development and evaluation of memory training procedures that lead to generalized improvements in everyday memory.

Automatic versus Controlled Processing

Some of our cognitive processes occur without direct conscious control. These automatic processes tend to be driven, or determined, by the current internal and external stimulus environment and are less affected by attentional and intentional processes. Ordinary perceptual processes and the access of general semantic knowledge, including language processes and motor programs for familiar activities, are all relatively automatic cognitive processes. It has been assumed that automatic processes are relatively immune to normal age changes, and when they do fail due to disease or injury, they may be both difficult and slow to remediate.

Other cognitive operations are relatively effortful and are under more direct cognitive control. These operations *do* depend on attentional and intentional processes. Since there is presumably a limited processing capacity for these activities, only a limited amount of cognitively controlled mental "work" can be carried out at a time. The major culprit in poor performance on laboratory memory tasks and in everyday lapses of memory by older adults appears to be the cognitively controlled processing system. This is the system that also seems most susceptible to age-related processing deficits. The elderly do not appear to lose the *ability* to carry out cognitively controlled processing operations, but rather they are less likely to attempt to do so. This may be due to reductions in the rates or capacity for processing, leading to fewer surplus processing resources. Subjectively, controlled processing may involve more "work" as one ages, and ideas may not flow as freely and naturally as before. Whatever the reason for failing to do spontaneously what one is still capable of doing, the implication for remediation is positive. If the elderly can be trained to mobilize the controlled processing system appropriately in situations in which they are motivated to do so, then substantial improvement in memory should occur.

The controlled processing system consists of three subsystems. The most important target for intervention is the *executive*, or *intentional, system*. This is the system that activates the appropriate memory information necessary to carry out plans for internal and external behaviors and monitors whether the behavioral goals or objectives are met. This is the system that selects appropriate mnemonic strategies and that implements plans for the effective encoding and retrieval of information. It is the failure to select and use appropriate strategies, and to monitor the implementation of these strategies, that accounts for much of the decline in performance on laboratory memory tasks and for much of everyday absentmindedness.

The success of the executive system clearly depends upon the second subsystem: the *attentional system*. This is the guidance, or energy, system necessary for carrying out the executive's plans. If attention is not sufficient for carrying out a cognitive plan, or if one's attention is prematurely distracted from the plan, potentially successful plans for processing information will fail. In many situations, conscious attempts to increase attention to a task will improve subsequent memory.

The third subsystem of the cognitively controlled processing system is the *memory system*. It is the least "controlled" component of the entire system. Both automatic and controlled cognitive operations are assumed to access a common permanent memory store. Once encoding and retrieval strategies have been selected by the executive system, the implementation of memory storage and retrieval is a relatively automatic process and is assumed to be least affected by memory-training interventions.

In summary, this model suggests that intervention to improve everyday memory should be aimed at improving the effectiveness of controlled processing. In particular, clinical intervention aimed at the executive subsystem may be more powerful and lead to greater generalization of treatment than relatively narrow treatments focused only on improving the efficiency of the memory system. For example, some clients may benefit from efforts to plan ways to use reduced attentional resources more efficiently or to use external prosthetic memory aids as a way of adapting to reduced capacity, rather than direct training to increase memory capacity.

Stages and Types of Memory

Memory can be thought of as a process of encoding and retrieving information. Although people think of memory problems as problems in retaining information, this is somewhat misleading. We assume that memory storage is a relatively automatic process and that information stored in memory is relatively permanent. Probably everything we perceive or think about is stored in memory. However, some types of information are more readily retrieved from memory than others. Thus, it is important to *encode* information in a way that makes it more readily *retrievable*.

To be most useful, information in memory should become available when we need it, and stay unobtrusively in storage when we don't need it. Our memory system has solved this problem by requiring that a memory cue be present either externally or internally in order for a target memory to be activated or retrieved. A memory cue is some piece of information that was connected with the target information at the time of storage and would have effectively activated the target information at that time. Memory encoding is the process of connecting memory cues to target information. The fundamental mechanism for improving memory is to encode more effective memory cues, via effortful, controlled processing. Sometimes a memory cue occurs in the environment. We notice it and automatically a target memory is activated. We see a person, and his name springs spontaneously to mind. At times, one memory serves as a cue for another, and we reminisce about past events. And at other times we consciously, and perhaps with great effort, control the search for a memory cue, trying one thing and then another, until the sought-for information finally comes to mind.

The actual storage and activation of memory information occurs outside our conscious awareness, and outside of our conscious control. It is automatic. The only direct way we have of influencing memory storage and retrieval is by controlling our thoughts (i.e., using controlled processing to think of effective memory cues during storage and at retrieval) and by controlling the environment so that we will attend to external memory cues when they are needed for recall.

What makes a memory cue effective, other than its presence at both storage and retrieval? We assume that the effectiveness of a particular type of memory cue will depend upon the content of the target information. For purposes of understanding memory impairment and rehabilitation, three broad categories of memory information seem relevant: autobiographical, factual, and intentional.

Autobiographical memory refers to memory for the events and activities of one's daily life. This class of information is also referred to as episodic memory (Tulving, 1972). Memory problems frequently result not only from forgetting *what* happened, but *whether* something happened. Because this type of memory information is so dependent on the relations among perceptual experiences, recall and recognition will depend upon the availability of situational and temporal cues as memory cues. Memory aids will focus on the strategies for providing such cues.

Factual information always occurs in some episodic–autobiographical context, but it is considered to be relevant as knowledge, independent of the time and place in which one learned it. If such information is organized or meaningfully related, the critical memory cues for retrieval will be those that relate to the structure and organization of the information or to the relation of the information to prior knowledge. Memory aids will focus on using or enhancing these cues. If the factual information is less meaningful or arbitrary, such as names, dates, phone numbers, lists of chores, etc., there are several alternatives for developing effective memory cues. One approach is to recode the information into a more meaningful form. A second is to focus on surface-structure sensory cues such as the visual, auditory, or graphic features. And a third is to avoid encoding the information into memory by using external storage devices. Which strategy is most appropriate will depend on the associated memory-processing demands, such as when and how often the information must be retrieved.

Intentional memory is frequently referred to as prospective memory because it refers to one's plans for future activities and behaviors. Memory problems associated with intentional information may relate to retrieving the content of the intention ("What was it that I needed to do?"), in which case the appropriate memory cues for retrieval will depend on whether the content of the intent is primarily autobiographical ("Oh, call the hardware store") or has embedded factual information ("Now, what is the hardware store number?"). However, the relatively unique aspect of intentional memory is that the intent must be retrieved during a predetermined time interval and/or at a predetermined place. One is aware of retrieval failure not at the time it occurred, but later, when one finally retrieves the intent ("Oh, I forgot to call the hardware store"), or not at all ("Are you sure I said I would pick up the milk?"). The major focus of memory strategies for remembering intentional behavior is on the provision of effective memory cues at the appropriate future time and place. Such cues will almost always involve external memory aids, except for highly routine or sequential behaviors.

Memory fails either because no effective memory cue was encoded at storage or because a previously encoded memory cue is not currently available. A memory problem occurs at retrieval when a person is actively trying to remember, momentarily without success, and is seeking a way to recover the information that he or she assumes or hopes is still in memory. The only way to aid memory when retrieval fails is to reinstate effective memory cues. Obviously this is not an ideal situation, since, if one could remember the cues, there would have been no failure in retrieval.

There are certain guidelines for selecting memory aids that may be effective following retrieval failure, but their success is far from assured. Thus, one major goal of memory training is to minimize the need for such aids, by converting memory problems into *anticipated*, rather than *actual*, retrieval problems. However, since retrieval failure will be the common theme among presented memory problems, and since no preventive training program will be perfect, specific strategies for dealing with retrieval failure will be necessary for most memory problems targeted for remediation.

Anticipated memory problems are memory problems that have not yet occurred. For these problems it is still possible, via a strategy for memory encoding, to enhance, supplement, or replace memory storage, and to insure that effective retrieval cues will be available when needed. The strategy selected should be appropriate to the content of the memory. Also, because it is assumed that the person does, in fact, intend to retrieve the information at some later time and place, it is very important when selecting the most effective memory aid to know the length of the anticipated retention interval, and how often and under what conditions the person wants to be able to retrieve the information. For example, very different aids will be best for remembering a particular grocery list once, after a brief retention interval, and for remembering the details of an important event for a lifetime. Thus, the focus of memory training is to teach the person to anticipate memory problems and to prevent them. To do this effectively, a person must understand what type of memory strategy is most likely to help, and must be motivated to use the strategy at the appropriate time and place.

In the following section, we will describe clinical assessment and treatment procedures for age-related memory problems. Where possible, we will integrate these procedures with the model described above.

TRAINING STRATEGIES FOR THE TREATMENT OF AGE-RELATED MEMORY IMPAIRMENT

Assessment of Age-Related Memory Impairment

The literature on assessment of memory and intellectual functioning in the elderly is voluminous and has been summarized in a number of reviews (e.g., Albert, 1981; Erickson, Poon, & Walsh-Sweeney, 1980; Poon, 1985; Zarit, Eiler, & Hassinger, 1985) and a recently published book (Poon, 1986). Ideally, clinical assessment is multifaceted and includes the following areas.

Screening for Dementia and Medical Exclusion Criteria. Since a number of reversible medical problems and medications may produce cognitive impairment in older individuals, screening should include efforts to ensure that such medically treatable problems have not been overlooked. In addition, because there is little evidence that older patients with dementia significantly benefit from memory retraining (Zarit, Zarit, & Reever, 1982), exclusion of such patients is recommended for memory-training studies.

Assessment of Depression and Anxiety. Depression and anxiety may be related to problems in self-reported and objective memory performance. For individuals with memory problems and anxiety or depression, some clinicians have targeted primary intervention at the affective disturbance in hope of improving memory (e.g., Yesavage, 1984), while others have utilized memory-training strategies and assessed potential changes in depression or anxiety (e.g., Scogin et al., 1985).

Standardized Psychometric Laboratory Assessment. Psychometric laboratory assessments of memory performance are potentially useful in identifying the presence of objective performance deficits and individuals' relative strengths and weaknesses in performance, and in documenting posttreatment effects of intervention. Unfortunately, commonly used laboratory tasks or clinical memory batteries have been widely criticized for failing to assess theoretically significant components of memory and for lack of validity as predictors or everyday functioning (Poon, 1985). These tests are reviewed more thoroughly in the review articles cited at the beginning of this section.

Self-Report Measures of Memory Impairment. Subjective reports of memory functioning have been assessed by a variety of methods, including questionnaires and diaries (Herrmann, 1984; Reason & Lucas, 1984). The validity of these techniques has been criticized, and little relationship has been established between self-reports of memory problems and performance on objective tests.

Individualized Cognitive-Behavioral Assessment. The literature includes few examples of the use of individualized cognitive-behavioral assessment for the purpose of planning memory enhancement intervention. We believe memory skills training will be of greatest practical benefit in actually changing memory encoding and retrieval behaviors in everyday life when it is based on this type of practical, individualized assessment. Once specific problems have been identified, an analysis of the antecedent and consequent conditions, as well as an analysis of the specific type of memory problem, will guide the selection of appropriate strategies for intervention. For example, in the prototypic case described earlier in the chapter, different interventions (e.g., reassurance, use of external memory aids) might be appropriate for each of the elderly patient's unique problems. Hanley (1986) has argued for the importance of such an individualized approach to assessment and intervention, and he has presented several examples of the use of behavioral methods in the treatment of patients with severe cognitive impairment.

In summary, behavioral intervention is most likely to be successful when based on a thorough assessment, leading to an individualized treatment plan. This strategy, combined with single-case experimental methods, deserves more widespread utilization.

General Strategies

Three general components of treatment that can be included in any treatment plan are: education about normal age changes, reduction of anxiety and depression, and training in self-management of memory behaviors. The first two treatment components are typically not intended to improve memory directly, but they are likely to facilitate assessment, affect motivation for more specific treatment, and may, in fact, affect ability to attend to and concentrate on specific treatment, thereby improving performance. The third treatment component is likely to serve a key role in the effective teaching and use of all of the specific memory aids. We will discuss each of these components in more detail.

Education about Normal Age Changes in Memory

Poor self-image and stereotypes of the elderly as having poor memory may contribute to poor memory performance (Kinsbourne, 1980). Fear that memory impairment may be a precursor to dementia is common and can contribute to anxiety and depression (Hulicka, 1982). The direct effects of educational interventions on memory performance remain unexplored. However, introductory information of the sort presented in this chapter, provided in oral or written form and serving as a basis for further discussion, seems both a natural, and potentially therapeutic, way to initiate any treatment plan. Reassurance about the normalcy of occasional memory failures may be an important intervention in its own right.

Techniques for Reduction of Anxiety and Depression

Studies by Yesavage (1984) and Yesavage, Rose, and Spiegel (1982) suggest that relaxation training is one effective way to reduce performance anxiety in elderly individuals who receive cognitive training. Results indicated that only those subjects with high initial levels of anxiety benefited from relaxation training, but that the amount of reduction in anxiety scores was correlated with improved performance after memory training. Other studies demonstrated that anxiety reduction techniques alone were as effective as specific mnemonics or a problem-solving approach in improving cognitive function in the elderly (Labouvie-Vief, 1976; Labouvie-Vief & Gonda, 1976).

There is considerable evidence that depression is related to increased subjective complaints about memory; it remains a point of controversy whether depression is objectively related to poorer memory functioning (Wells, 1979). A number of cognitive-behavioral techniques currently used in reducing depression in the elderly could be readily incorporated into a memory treatment plan. Zarit, Gallagher, and Kramer (1981) reported that group therapy to reduce depression in the elderly was effective in reducing both depression and memory complaints and in improving memory performance. However, it was no more effective than a memory training group not specifically intended to reduce depression. In another study, self-administered individual memory skills training improved memory performance but did not reduce depression or subjective memory complaints (Scogin *et al.*, 1985). Thus memory training *per se* is probably not an effective treatment for depression. However, reducing depression may be an effective treatment for memory impairment. Evidence, comparable to the studies on anxiety reduction (Yesavage *et al.*, 1982) is needed to show that treating depression improves the effectiveness of *concurrent* memory training.

Self-Management Strategies

The most important goal in any training program is to transfer treatment gains into the natural environment. One major focus of memory training with the elderly is to teach and make readily available appropriate strategies for remembering. But such training will be of no practical benefit if it is not used at the critical time and place. Virtually no research exists on the application of such techniques as self-monitoring, self-cueing, self-instructions, self-reinforcement, and covert conditioning as ways to assist memory functioning directly (as opposed to treating associated conditions such as depression). However, such techniques have been used effectively to improve problem-solving ability (Labouvie-Vief & Gonda, 1976; Meichenbaum, 1974) and seem the most likely way to deal with the problem of transfer of training. They can also be used to teach the elderly how to select and implement appropriate mnemonic techniques.

A natural way to begin to teach "planning to remember" is as a by-product of individualized cognitive-behavioral assessment. Memory training starts, whether in a group or individual setting, with targeting of a particular real-world memory problem selected and elaborated upon by each participant. Next the participants are guided in an analysis of the problem, focusing on *motivation* (why is it important to improve this memory-related behavior problem?), *strategy selection* (what type of strategy is most likely to help?), and *strategy use* (what is the best way to incorporate the strategy into the behavioral repertoire?). When conceptualized this way, it becomes clear that selecting and teaching an appropriate mnemonic strategy is only part, and usually the easier part, of memory training. Using the strategy at the appropriate time and place is accomplished with the more traditional techniques of behavior therapy. For example, the client may be taught to visualize the relevant situation(s), experience the actual environmental context, rehearse the reason for using the strategy, plan to use the strategy by talking through it out loud, anticipate how it might work, and reinforce himself or herself for success. An obvious advantage of this type of training is that it is more readily generalized to new target memory problems than are particular memory aids.

Case Study Example. Mrs. Smith ranked her problem in remembering the names of the members of her church congregation as her most important concern. She was asked to list reasons why she wanted to improve this skill. Then she selected from among the strategies described those that she thought she would use. Initially, she selected external strategies (writing down names of new members when they joined the church and referring to the church directory on Saturday night). Next she developed a plan for actually using the strategies at home and at church. She was encouraged to include in her plan frequent review of her motivations for improvement and self-reinforcement for using appropriate strategies. Later in training, Mrs. Smith spontaneously generalized her plan to include an appropriate strategy for the intentional behavior of remembering to put her offering in her purse.

Mrs. Smith also reported increased memory problems when in a crowd. She reported losing her train of thought and forgetting what people told her. Relaxation training, which helped her calm herself and focus her attention in anxiety-provoking situations, may have consequently improved her memory.

Specific Aids to Memory

All effective memory aids share one or both of these features: they enhance, supplement, or replace memory storage, and they provide effective cues for retrieval. Memory aids are either internal or external. Internal aids are most like, and not always distinguishable from, natural encoding and retrieval activities that people may engage in spontaneously, either as by-products of perceptual analysis, or as intentional thinking processes that are considered by the individual to aid memory. External aids are most like naturally occurring cues in the environment that elicit certain memories spontaneously. Both old and young people report greater use of external than internal memory aids in the natural environment (Cavanaugh, Grady, & Perlmutter, 1983; Harris, 1980; Intons-Peterson & Fournier, 1986), but this may be because many internal aids are not clearly distinguishable from normal "thinking." Internal aids are frequently categorized into predominantly verbal, predominantly visual/spatial, or both. Cermak (1980) has suggested that the elderly may benefit more from verbal than visual internal aids. However, a more general issue is whether the memory aid fits the memory problem. A "good" memory aid is not only one that works, but one which is readily available at the right time, is specific to the task, is not much trouble to use, and is reinforcing to use.

Below is a description of specific memory aids, some of which have been suggested for memory therapy primarily with the brain-injured (Moffat, 1984), some of which normal adults say they actually use (Intons-Peterson & Fournier, 1986), and a very few of which have been investigated in memory-training research reviewed in this chapter. Only a few of the techniques have been researched with elderly subjects, and most have not been systematically investigated at all. We have organized the description of memory aids according to the time of first use (at encoding or at retrieval) and the type of memory problem they are most likely to help (recall of autobiographical details, impersonal factual information, or intentional behaviors), using the analysis of Morris (1978). It should be apparent that the distinctions between types of memory problems are somewhat arbitrary. Actual memory problems may contain elements of all three types. In the following sections, we will suggest specific interventions for each of these classes of memory failure.

Remembering Autobiographical Information

As mentioned earlier in this chapter, we think that effective memory aids for encoding autobiographical experiences are those that will serve as retrieval cues for the details of time, place, people, or events. Memory aids for encoding autobiographical information can be divided into three categories: those which elaborate on, or enrich, the information encoded in memory and increase the availability and effectiveness of internal retrieval cues; those which structure the environment to provide more effective external memory cues; and those which provide external storage sources for information and external cues for retrieval.

Elaborating on Experiences. Reality orientation, a technique used primarily with dementia patients, involves forcing or encouraging increased attention to details of date, time, and place (Woods & Holden, 1982). It may be useful for the normal aged as well as the severely impaired. Any behavior that serves to increase the perceptual processing of situational cues related to time and place is likely to improve autobiographical memory. Examples of such strategies are searching the environment for distinctive cues; mentally rehearsing the current situation; talking out loud to oneself or others about relevant details of a situation; self-testing for relevant information ("Where am I right now?" "What does the waitress look like?"); and then attending to missing information. For example, a woman who was afraid to go shopping because she became confused and disoriented in department stores learned to orient herself immediately upon entering the store. She noted and rehearsed obvious and clearly visible details that she used both to reassure herself and to guide her in finding the exit.

Structuring the Environment. The idea of the prosthetic environment is common to most rehabilitation efforts. Fowler, Hart, and Sheehan (1972) have argued that the idea of the prosthetic memory can probably be applied with some success to improving memory functioning. Many common, vexing memory problems involve misplaced personal items, an inability to locate places or things, and confusion or forgetfulness about the details of one's environment. One approach to this problem is to make constant what is variable and to make distinctive what is constant but confusing. Thus, establishing fixed places for frequently misplaced objects is a useful strategy, as is color coding, labeling, organizing, or physically separating confusable containers, articles of clothing, etc. For example, a large red ribbon attached to a car antenna can eliminate the need to remember a parking place in a crowded parking lot. Harris (1980) described a decrease in the rate of incontinence on a geriatric unit when the restroom doors were painted a distinctive color. Drawing a simple map is an obvious external aid for learning and remembering distinctive details of a new physical environment or a new route.

External Storage Devices. In many situations where it is important to remember, it makes good sense to supplement memory with external storage devices. Pocket tape recorders, instant cameras, maps, sketches, and notes are all ways of supplementing memory. External storage is not only a highly effective way of preserving information, but it is an effective means of stimulating retrieval. For example, taking Polaroid shots of significant, but infrequently seen, people (such as doctors, lawyers, or professional acquaintances) and labeling them with appropriate names and other identifying information may be a much more effective strategy for remembering than relying on internal information. Likewise, recording instructions from physicians, lawyers, etc. on a pocket tape recorder is a useful habit for those with impaired memory.

Retrieval Aids. Despite one's best intentions, encoding is frequently haphazard, retrieval cues are often ineffective, and memory fails. The best strategies for recovering forgotten autobiographical information are likely to be those that attempt to reinstate temporal and situational cues. Actual retracing of one's steps, mental retracing or reconstruction of events, and consulting external records, including asking other people, are the strategies most often suggested.

Case Study Example. Mrs. Smith considered misplacing personal articles, especially her eyeglasses and mail, as her main problem with autobiographical memory. She agreed that structuring her environment and guiding her attentional behavior with self-statements would probably help. She rejected the suggestion that she use a neck cord for her eyeglasses because it was "too bothersome." Instead she decided to try to pay more attention to where she placed her glasses, noting their location and rewarding herself for doing so. She saw this as a game and enjoyed the challenge of overcoming this minor annoyance with an internal strategy. She saw the mail problem, however, as more serious. On several occasions she had misplaced a bill and had to pay late charges. She readily agreed to identify a fixed location for mail and to develop a self-management plan to insure that all mail was placed there.

Remembering Impersonal Factual Information

Most memory training studies have focused on memory aids for encoding impersonal factual information. These aids can be divided into those that are most appropriate for remembering highly meaningful (organized, coherent, thematic) information, such as current events, educational materials, movies, plays, TV shows, jokes, narrative accounts, book plots, etc; and those most appropriate for encoding less meaningful, more arbitrary, factual information, such as names, dates, numbers, lists, etc.

Encoding Aids for Coherent Factual Information. Effective memory aids are those that increase the association or connection between organizational cues and the information to be recalled, and those that enhance the availability of these organizational cues.

Internal strategies include formal study techniques for written material, such as those suggested by Rowntree (1970) under the acronyms S.Q. 3R (survey, question, read, recall, review) and PQRST (preview, questions, read, state, test), and less formal organizational techniques that can be adapted to a variety of source media. An example of an informal organizational memory aid is giving a descriptive or summarizing title to information. A title works as an organizational memory aid because it requires that the person attend to thematic content and it also makes that thematic content more available as a retrieval cue. This verbal strategy of attending to theme may especially enhance memory for visual media such as movies, plays, and TV shows. Another informal organizational strategy is to place verbally presented information into a mental visual–spatial context and to imagine the described action or interaction. This visual strategy also facilitates organization and retrieval and works well for verbal information such as current events, jokes, narrative conversations, and book plots. For factual information that is not perceptually coherent and that does not readily come to mind with a few effective retrieval cues, more extensive organizational processing may be needed. This processing occurs in the following stages: (1) dividing the information into meaningful subunits; (2) arranging subunits according to a logical, hierarchical, or temporal sequence; and (3) connecting each subunit to an organizational cue using the strategies described above. Active rehearsal and self-testing for the effectiveness of these organizational cues will also help.

External strategies for remembering meaningful, factual information usually involve external storage of the information. Hence, external strategies are frequently more effective than internal strategies. For example, taking and organizing notes, writing out instructions, or recording important information on tape or with photocopies will often save both the time and the energy invested in internal memory aids and result in more accurate storage of information.

Retrieval Aids for Coherent Factual Information. Internal strategies for recalling meaningful factual information, once encoded, generally depend on reinstating organizational cues, either by generating the topic or the theme, generating relevant parts, or generating related ideas. Occasionally, generating the autobiographical context in which the factual information occurred will also help, particularly if there was active rehearsal, discussion, or other interaction with the information at the time of storage. For example, trying to remember when and with whom you saw a particular movie may help recall the details of the film, but only if you actually discussed the film, or if your reaction to the film depended on the situation or companion. When internal strategies for recall fail, external records or other persons may still provide effective memory cues.

Encoding Aids for Arbitrary Factual Information. Most memory-training research has focused on the internal strategies (commonly referred to as "mnemonics") that are effective for remembering arbitrary factual information, such as names of people, products, businesses, and places; remembering lists; remembering numbers or letter–number combinations, such as street addresses, phone numbers, dates, etc. Two recent reviews of mnemonic devices describe their use in some detail (Moffat, 1984; Wilson & Moffat, 1984). Mnemonics supplement the target information to be remembered with additional information that both can be readily associated with the target information and is itself more easily recalled, thus serving as an effective retrieval cue. Many of these techniques also aid in recalling the correct amount of information in the correct order, by adding a set of retrieval cues of the appropriate length and order. Some of these techniques require minimal instruction (e.g., stringing together information by forming mediating verbal associations, incorporating information into a rhyme, singing information to the tune of a familiar melody, forming bizarre or interacting images, noting the first letters of verbal items and using them to form acronyms, making up a sentence or story including the target information, and associating motor movements to the target information). Other more formal mnemonic techniques, such as the face–name association method, the rhyming-peg method, the phonetic-peg method, and the method of loci, involve more time to learn. The use of such devices requires some creativity to generate appropriate, effective associations. As reviewed earlier in the chapter, the lack of spontaneous generation of associated thoughts and images during memory encoding seems to underly much of the age-related memory deficit. This difficulty in generating one's own images, as opposed to imagining familiar locations, may explain why the elderly appear to benefit less from the rhyming-peg mnemonic (one is a bun) than from the method of loci (e.g., pairing an object with a familiar location) (Poon, Walsh-Sweeney, & Fozard, 1980). Another major drawback to the use of the formal mnemonic techniques is that the elderly may not spontaneously generalize their use to other appropriate situations (Robertson-Tchabo *et al.*, 1976).

As mentioned earlier, the available research suggests that the elderly are able to improve recall of unrelated word lists with at least some of these mnemonic techniques. However, we view this research as demonstrative of the immediate gains that can result from appropriate encoding and retrieval strategies, rather than as a model for treatment. Many of the classic mnemonic devices will have an occasional use in memory training, but as a practical memory strategy they seem most appropriate for information that is important enough to be needed both frequently and for a long time. For arbitrary factual information that is likely to be used infrequently, it is both more efficient and more effective to use external storage devices such as taking notes, making lists, using date books, or referring to address or telephone directories. A memory-impaired elderly person, who may have tremendous difficulty with the weekly grocery shopping, should probably not try to memorize the grocery list using a mnemonic device, especially if that same time might be used organizing a written list so that items are grouped according to where they are located in the store.

Retrieval Aids for Arbitrary Factual Information. Strategies for recalling arbitrary or nonmeaningful information, once retrieval has failed, depend on reinstating the effective retrieval cues. For the internal mnemonic devices to work they must be recalled. If the encoding device cannot be recalled or if none was used, the best retrieval cue will probably be one related to the sound of verbal information. Alphabetic searching and first-letter cueing of verbal information are methods used by people and may in fact be effective (Gruneberg & Sykes, 1978). In recalling forgotten numbers, such as a house address or zip code, generating likely alternatives and recognizing the correct sequence may work if the information was well learned initially. But we suspect that people have limited success with such methods.

Case Study Example. As her two most embarrassing, and personally most important, memory problems, Mrs. Smith identified her difficulties in recalling people's names at church and in remembering the bid and the cards played during bridge.

Many memory problems begin with inattention during encoding. Mrs. Smith was encouraged to use external aids to facilitate encoding (i.e., writing down the names of new church members, and referring to an already available church directory). She decided to make this a regular Saturday night activity. She reviewed familiar names, tested herself for recall of faces, and each week tried to rehearse the names and faces of several new members. After learning a face–name association technique (Yesavage *et al.*, 1983), she attempted to use it when new members were introduced to the church congregation.

Mrs. Smith's problems playing bridge were addressed in two different ways. An external aid was identified to help her remember the bidding. Mrs. Smith unobtrusively rearranged the order of the suits in her hand to reflect the order of the bidding. However, Mrs. Smith agreed that the task of trying to encode internally all of the cards played had probably become too difficult for her, even with extensive training. She was encouraged to acknowledge to her friends that her memory wasn't quite what it used to be. If she still felt her occasional lapses affected her own or others' enjoyment of the game, she was encouraged to seek new bridge partners who would be more accepting of her memory limitations or to consider alternative recreations.

Remembering Intentions

The key to remembering intentions is identifying a retrieval cue that effectively recalls the intention *and* that effectively captures attention at the intended future time and place for performing the intended behavior. These two important jobs of an effective intentional retrieval cue are approximately equivalent to what Norman (1981) refers to as the activation function and the triggering function. An intention must be effectively "activated" or else we may know we intended to do *something*, but we will forget what it was. An intention must be effectively "triggered" or else the intended time and place for the intended action or activity will pass without the deed being done. We may also not carry out an intention because the intention itself was poorly integrated at encoding. Norman (1981) considers this problem an "incomplete description" of the intention. Thus, a fleeting thought in the morning that you need to go to the store after work may be a sufficient activation to trigger the response to turn in when driving by the store that evening. Upon arriving, however, you may have little idea of why you came.

Strategies that are appropriate for encoding a more complete description of intentions or for activating intentions are the same as those already described for autobiographical or factual information. The unique part of the strategy for retrieving intentions is the focus on a trigger cue, a cue that will capture attention at the intended time and place. A trigger cue, or reminder, will typically be external and at best, should be active (i.e., captivating, noticeable), timely (i.e., occurring at the intended time and place), and task specific (i.e., it will tend to activate the appropriate intention) (Harris, 1984). One of the advantages of training a person to solve an intentional memory problem is that, in order to develop and identify a good trigger cue, a person must plan to remember. Thus, the learning of general self-management skills for remembering is an integral part of successful intentional memory training. Intentional memory is trained by identifying the future time and place where the intention needs to be retrieved. The trigger cue should then occur as closely as possible to that identified time and place. Hence, the trigger cue must be placed *now* so that it will occur at the *later* intended time. One way of placing a trigger cue is to identify an object that will necessarily be seen or heard at the intended time and place. This insures timeliness. The object may be one's body, a piece of furniture, a door, a clock or alarm timer, an appointment book, a calendar, an electronic schedule planner, etc. Next, the selected object must be made distinctive so that an attentional response of "What is it?" or "Why is that there?" will occur. This insures that the trigger will be active. Alarm timers are excellent cues in this respect because they cannot be ignored. Placing an umbrella by the door is good, but placing the umbrella on the door knob, so that the door can't be opened until the umbrella is removed, is better (Skinner & Vaughn, 1983). The same goes for notes to oneself. A note placed so that one must move it to do a routine task is better than a note placed where you think you will see it. Making a trigger cue impossible to ignore is good insurance against habituation. Habituation will occur if the cue is encountered frequently before it is needed or if the same cue is used repeatedly. And finally, the trigger cue should be task specific. An ideal trigger cue will itself activate the intention, i.e., it will be an effective retrieval cue. Thus, a note to oneself or an entry on a calendar or appointment book has the advantage of cueing *what* was intended as well as *when* it was intended. Simple pictures, drawings, and tangible objects can often replace thoughts, notes, or verbal cues as trigger cues for intentions. For example, taping a pill to the bathroom cup may be a more effective reminder to take a pill than placing a note on the mirror, because it is more timely, active, and task specific. In our experience, the elderly can more readily think of creative and effective external trigger cues than they can generate the internal verbal or visual imagery cues associated with the use of the internal mnemonic strategies.

As mentioned before, once an intentional behavior has been forgotten, there is often little to be done about it, because the time and place for the action have passed. However, because forgetting intentions typically involves some negative consequences or inconvenience, most people can be easily motivated to improve intentional memory. Hence, a good place to start memory training is with intentional memory.

Case Study Example. Mrs. Smith reported that she had difficulty remembering to put her money into her purse before going to church. She was embarrassed at being unable to make her intended offering. Mrs. Smith never left the house without her purse or with insufficient funds for other activities. Further analysis revealed two sources of her problem. On Sunday morning, she dressed up, which involved selecting a purse different from her usual one. Also, for safekeeping, Mrs. Smith kept her church money in a box, separate from her other operating funds. She could not remember to take her offering from her offering box and place it in the selected purse just before leaving to go to church. This was usually a hurried time for Mrs. Smith because she had a number of other things on her mind.

Mrs. Smith identified her bible as her "trigger" object, because she had never forgotten to take her bible to church. She taped an old church offering envelope to the front of the bible. When she picked up the bible, she saw the envelope and remembered to get her offering. This trigger cue was task specific and timely, but unfortunately was not sufficiently active. It worked the first Sunday, but the second Sunday she picked up the bible without looking at it and failed to notice the offering envelope. Mrs. Smith spontaneously devised a better alternative. She placed her bible, her bible study materials, her church offering box, and the church directory all in a drawer beside her reading chair. On Saturday nights, she studied her bible lesson, reviewed the names of church members, and placed her offering in an envelope inside her bible. Her trigger cues were then embedded in a well-planned sequence of behaviors, and she carried out her intentions without error.

WORD-FINDING DIFFICULTY—A NEGLECTED PROBLEM

A most vexing and common memory problem for the elderly is "word finding" or "information finding." This memory retrieval problem is associated with the ongoing, everyday use of well-learned language-dependent semantic information. In earlier years the information was readily available, but with age it becomes stubbornly unresponsive to formerly effective retrieval cues. Hence, the elderly frequently find themselves in a T-O-T (tip of the tongue) state (Gruneberg & Sykes, 1978). They may feel sure that they know the word or name they are trying to say, but it "just will not come." Little research has been done on the extent of this is memory-related language impairment in the elderly, although it is their most frequently reported memory problem (Sunderland *et al.*, 1986). Apparently, there is little problem in lexical access *per se* (Waugh & Barr, 1982). The elderly can read words as quickly as the young, and they can generate instances of a given category as quickly (Eysenck, 1975; Drachman & Leavitt, 1972). However, when generating labels for pictures (Thomas, Fozard, & Waugh, 1977), generating words that begin with a particular letter or sound (Albert, 1981), or naming objects (Obler & Albert, 1984), the elderly are slower than the young. It is not really clear whether these tasks are an appropriate laboratory analogue for the word-finding problem that the elderly experience in everyday speech (Lachman & Lachman, 1980); nor is it clear how to approach remediation. Since word-finding difficulty seems to reflect periodic retrieval failure for an already well-learned but vast store of information, it may be particularly difficult to remediate.

SUMMARY AND CONCLUSIONS

Clearly, older individuals experience a variety of problems in memory functioning that are apparent on self-report, with psychometric testing, and in laboratory studies of memory. There is also considerable evidence that older individuals can improve memory functioning in laboratory settings through a variety of psychological interventions. However, the clinical utility of behavioral intervention for age-related memory decline has not yet been determined. There is little evidence that commonly used interventions, such as imagery and mnemonics, are used outside of the training environment, or lead to significant improvements in older patients' everyday memory functioning. The results of many of the research studies of memory training we reviewed have been primarily useful in developing basic theories of memory processing in aging. There has been little effort to assess standard clinical research questions (e.g., Kazdin, 1980), such as generalization of training, clinical significance of the magnitude of change, and whether results are generalizable to clinical populations. More careful research scrutiny of clinically focused descriptions of comprehensive memory enhancement packages (e.g., Wilson & Moffat, 1984) are needed.

In this review, we suggest a number of changes necessary to develop clinically effective programs for enhancing memory functioning in older individuals. Individualized assessment and treatment, based on an integration of the cognitive psychology of memory and cognitive-behavioral training procedures, are important. Future intervention should focus more on common, functionally significant daily memory problems and on the development of techniques that can be readily used in real-world situations. Research methods incorporating single-case designs will be helpful in addressing the unique nature of individuals' specific daily memory impairments.

There are particular everyday memory problems that need further study. Memory for lists has been the most widely studied memory phenomenon, but more common self-reported deficits, such as word finding, remembering appointments, and misplacing objects, have received little attention.

Several treatment techniques also deserve greater development. While both younger and older adults report using external memory aids much more frequently than internal strategies (Cavanaugh et al., 1983), there has been little work on the development of efficient and practical environmental aids, such as lists. We have argued that internal aids should be aimed at higher-level, controlled, executive functions, rather than simply at the learning of memory storage and retrieval strategies. In some instances, everyday memory problems may require intervention aimed at acceptance of limitations, rather than amelioration of deficits. While intervention with the older individual should not be based on nihilism or pessimism, unrealistically positive expectations about the benefits of memory training may also blind the clinician to the necessity of helping the older patient develop new activities or interests when former abilities cannot be retained.

ACKNOWLEDGMENT

The authors wish to thank Robert L. Duke, Jr., for his careful review of and editorial comments on this chapter.

REFERENCES

Albert, M. L. (1981). Changes in language with aging. Seminars in Neurology, 1, 43–46.

Arenberg, D. (1977). The effects of auditory augmentation on visual retention for young and old adults. Journal of Gerontology, 32, 193–195.

Avron, J. (1982). Studying cognitive performance in the elderly: A biopsychosocial approach. In F. I. M. Craik & S. Trehub (Eds.), Aging and cognitive processes (pp. 317–330). New York: Plenum.

Baltes, P. B., & Willis, S. L. (1982). Plasticity and enhancement of intellectual functioning in old age: Penn State's Adult Development and Enrichment Project (ADEPT). In F. I. M. Craik & S. Trehub (Eds.), Aging and cognitive processes (pp. 353–390). New York: Plenum.

Beres, C. A., & Baron, A. (1981). Improved digit symbol substitution by older women as a result of extended practice. Journal of Gerontology, 36, 591–597.

Birren, J. E., & Schaie, K. W. (Eds.). (1977). Handbook of the psychology of aging. New York: Van Nostrand Reinhold.

Birren, J. E., & Shaie, K. W. (Eds.). (1985). Handbook of the psychology of aging (2nd ed.). New York: Van Nostrand Reinhold.

Botwinick, J. (1984). Aging and behavior: A comprehensive integration of research findings (3rd ed.). New York: Springer.

Cavanaugh, J. C., Grady, J. G., & Perlmutter, M. P. (1983). Forgetting and the use of memory aids in 20- and 70-year olds' everyday life. *International Journal of Aging and Human Development, 17,* 113–122.

Cermak, L. S. (1980). Comments on imagery as a therapeutic mnemonic. In L. W. Poon, J. L. Fozard, L. S. Cermak, D. Arenberg, & L. W. Thompson (Eds.), *New directions in memory and aging: Proceedings of the George A. Talland memorial conference* (pp. 507–510). Hillsdale, NJ: Lawrence Erlbaum.

Cohen, M. M., & Lessell, S. (1984). Neuro-opthalmology of aging. In M. L. Albert (Ed.), *Clinical neurology of aging* (pp. 219–230). New York: Oxford University Press.

Corso, J. F. (1981). *Aging sensory systems and perception.* New York: Praeger.

Costa, P. T., & Fozard, J. L. (1978). Remembering the person: Relations of individual difference variables to memory. *Experimental Aging Research, 4,* 291–304.

Craik, F. I. M. (1977). Age differences in human memory. In J. E. Birren & K. W. Schaie (Eds.), *Handbook of the psychology of aging* (pp. 384–420). New York: Van Nostrand Reinhold.

Craik, F. I. M. (1984). Age differences in remembering. In L. R. Squire & N. Butters (Eds.), *Neuropsychology of memory* (pp. 3–12). New York: Guilford Press.

Craik, F. I. M., & Byrd, M. (1982). Aging and cognitive deficits. The role of attentional resources. In F. I. M. Craik & S. Trehub (Eds.), *Aging and cognitive processes* (pp. 191–212). New York: Plenum.

Craik, F. I. M., & Rabinowitz, J. C. (1984). Age differences in the acquisition and use of verbal information. In H. Bouma & D. G. Boushuiz (Eds.), *Attention and performance X: Control of language processes* (pp. 471–500). Hillsdale, NJ: Lawrence Erlbaum.

Craik, F. I. M., & Trehub, A. (Eds.) (1982). *Aging and cognitive processes.* New York: Plenum.

Drachman, D. A., & Leavitt, J. (1972). Memory impairment in the aged: Storage versus retrieval deficit. *Journal of Experimental Psychology, 93,* 302–308.

Erickson, R. C., Poon, L. W., & Walsh-Sweeney, L. (1980). Clinical memory testing of the elderly. In L. W. Poon, J. L. Fozard, L. S. Cermalt, D. Arenberg, & L. W. Thompson (Eds.), *New directions in memory and aging: Proceedings of the George A. Talland memorial conference* (pp. 379–402). Hillsdale, NJ: Lawrence Erlbaum.

Eysenck, M. W. (1975). Retrieval from semantic memory as a function of age. *Journal of Gerontology, 30,* 174–180.

Fowler, R., Hart, J., & Sheehan, M. (1972). A prosthetic memory: An application of the prosthetic memory concept. *Rehabilitation Counseling Bulletin, 16,* 80–85.

Fozard, J. L., Wolf, E., Bell, B., McFarland, R. A., & Podolsky, S. (1977). Visual perception and communication. In J. E. Birren & K. W. Schaie (Eds.), *Handbook of the psychology of aging* (pp. 497–534). New York: Van Nostrand Reinhold.

Gouvier, W. D., Webster, J. S., & Blanton, P. D. (1986). Cognitive retraining with brain-damaged patients. In D. Wedding, A. M. Horton, Jr., & J. Webster (Eds.), *The neuropsychology handbook: Behavioral and clinical perspectives* (pp. 278–324). New York: Springer.

Gruneberg, M. M., & Sykes, R. N. (1978). Knowledge and memory: The feeling of knowing and reminiscence. In M. M. Gruneberg, P. E. Morris, & R. N. Sykes (Eds.), *Practical aspects of memory* (pp. 189–198). New York: Academic Press.

Hanley, I., (1986). Reality orientation in the care of the elderly patient with dementia—three case studies. In I. Hanley & M. Gilhooly (Eds.), *Psychological therapies for the elderly* (pp. 65–79). Washington Square, NY: New York University Press.

Harris, J. E. (1980). Memory aids people use: Two interview studies. *Memory and Cognition, 8,* 31–38.

Harris, J. E. (1984). Remembering to do things: A forgotten topic. In J. E. Harris & P. E. Morris (Eds.), *Everyday memory, actions and absent-mindedness* (pp. 71–92). New York: Academic Press.

Hasher, L., & Zacks, R. T. (1979). Automatic and effortful process in memory. *Journal of Experimental Psychology: General. 108,* 356–388.

Herrmann, D. J. (1984). Questionnaires about memory. In J. E. Harris & P. E. Morris (Eds.), *Everyday memory, actions, and absent-mindedness* (pp. 133–151). London: Academic Press.

Horn, J. L. (1982). The theory of fluid and crystallized intelligence in relation to the concepts of cognitive psychology and aging in adulthood. In F. I. M. Craik & S. Trehub (Eds.), *Aging and cognitive processes* (pp. 237–278). New York: Plenum.

Hulicka, I. M. (1982). Memory functioning in late adulthood. In F. I. M. Craik & S. Trehub (Eds.), *Aging and cognitive processes* (pp. 331–352). New York: Plenum.

Hulicka, I. M., & Grossman, J. L. (1967). Age-group comparisons for the use of mediators in paired-associate learning. *Journal of Gerontology, 22,* 46–51.

Hultsch, D. F. (1969). Age differences in the organization of free recall. *Developmental Psychology, 1,* 673–678.

Hultsch, D. F. (1971). Organization and memory in adulthood. *Human Development, 14,* 16–29.

Intons-Peterson, M. J., & Fournier, J. (1986). External and internal memory aids: When and how often do we use them? *Journal of Experimental Psychology: General, 115,* 267–280.

Kahn, R. L., Zarit, S. H., Hilbert, N. M., & Niederehe, G. (1975). Memory complaint and impairment in the aged. *Archives of General Psychiatry, 32,* 1569–1573.

Kausler, D. H. (1982). *Experimental psychology and human aging.* New York: John Wiley & Sons.

Kazdin, A. E. (1980). *Research design in clinical psychology.* New York: Harper & Row.

Kinsbourne, M. (1980). Attentional dysfunctions and the elderly: Theoretical models and research perspectives. In L. W. Poon, J. L. Fozard, L. S. Cermak, D. Arenberg, & L. W. Thompson (Eds.), *New directions in memory and aging: Proceedings of the George A. Talland memorial conference* (pp. 113–130). Hillsdale, NJ: Lawrence Erlbaum.

Labouvie-Vief, G. (1976). Toward optimizing cognitive competence. *Educational Gerontology, 1,* 75–92.

Labouvie-Vief, G., & Gonda, J. N. (1976). Cognitive strategy training and intellectual performance in the elderly. *Journal of Gerontology, 31,* 327–332.

Lachman, R., & Lachman, J. L. (1980). Picture naming: Retrieval and activation of long-term memory. In L. W. Poon, J. L. Fozard, L. S. Cermak, D. Arenberg, & L. W. Thomson (Eds.), *New directions in memory and aging: Proceedings of the George A. Talland memorial conference* (pp. 285–312). Hillsdale, NJ: Lawrence Erlbaum.

Lapp, D. C. (1987). *Don't forget! Easy exercises for a better memory at any age.* New York: McGraw-Hill.

Lowenthal, M. F., Berkman, P. L., Buehler, J. A., Pierce, R. C., Robinson, B. C. & Trier, M. L. (1967). *Aging and mental disorder in San Francisco.* San Francisco: Jossey-Bass.

Mason, S. E., & Smith, A. D. (1977). Imagery in the aged. *Experimental Aging Research, 3,* 17–32.

Meichenbaum, D. (1974). Self-instructional strategy training: A cognitive prosthesis for the aged. *Human Development, 17,* 273–280.

Moffat, N. (1984). Strategies of memory therapy. In B. Wilson & N. Moffat (Eds.), *Clinical management of memory problems* (pp. 63–88). London: Aspen.

Morris, P. E. (1978). Sense and nonsense in traditional mnemonics. In M. M. Gruneberg, P. E. Morris, & R. N. Sykes (Eds.), *Practical aspects of memory* (pp. 155–163). New York: Academic Press.

Nolan, B. H., Swihart, A. A., & Pirozzolo, F. J. (1986). The neuropsychology of normal aging and dementia: An introduction. In D. Wedding, A. M. Horton, Jr., & J. Webster (Eds.), *The neuropsychology handbook: Behavioral and clinical perspectives* (pp. 410–440). New York: Springer.

Norman, D. A. (1981). Categorization of action slips. *Psychological Review, 88,* 1–15.

Obler, L. K., & Albert, M. L. (1984). Language in aging. In M. L. Albert (Ed.), *Clinical neurology of aging* (pp. 245–253). New York: Oxford University Press.

Perlmutter, M. (1978). What is memory aging the aging of? *Developmental Psychology, 14,* 330–345.

Perlmutter, M., & Mitchell, D. B. (1982). The appearance and disappearance of age differences in adult memory. In F. I. M. Craik & S. Trehub (Eds.), *Aging and cognitive processes* (pp. 127–144). New York: Plenum.

Plemons, J. K., Willis, S. L., & Baltes, P. B. (1978). Modifiability of fluid intelligence in aging: A short-term longitudinal training approach. *Journal of Gerontology, 33,* 224–231.

Poon, L. W. (1985). Differences in human memory with aging: Nature, causes, and clinical implications. In J. E. Birren & K. W. Schaie (Eds.), *Handbook of the psychology of aging* (2nd ed., pp. 427–462). New York: Van Nostrand Reinhold.

Poon, L. W. (Ed.) (1986). *Handbook for clinical memory assessment of older adults.* Washington, DC: American Psychological Association.

Poon, L. W., Walsh-Sweeney, L., & Fozard, J. L. (1980). Memory skill training in the elderly: Salient issues on the use of imagery mnemonics. In L. W. Poon, J. L. Fozard, L. S. Cermak, D. Arenberg, & L. W. Thompson (Eds.), *New directions in memory and aging: Proceedings of the George A. Talland memorial conference* (pp. 461–484). Hillsdale, NJ: Lawrence Erlbaum.

Posner, M. I., & Snyder, C. R. R. (1975). Attention and cognitive control. In R. L. Solso (Ed.), *Information processing and cognition: The Loyola symposium* (pp. 55–86). Hillsdale, NJ: Lawrence Erlbaum.

Rabinowitz, J. C., & Ackerman, B. P. (1982). General encoding of episodic events by elderly adults. In F. I. M. Craik & S. Trehub (Eds.), *Aging and cognitive processes* (pp. 145–155). New York: Plenum.

Reason, J. T. (1984). Absent-mindedness and cognitive control. In J. E. Harris & P. E. Morris (Eds.), *Everyday memory, actions and absent-mindedness* (pp. 113–132). New York: Academic Press.

Reason, J. T., & Lucas, D. (1984). Using cognitive diaries to investigate naturally occurring memory blocks. In J. E. Harris & P. E. Morris (Eds.), *Everyday memory, actions and absent-mindedness* (pp. 53–70). New York: Academic Press.

Robertson-Tchabo, E. A. Hausman, C. P., & Arenberg, D. (1976). A classical mnemonic for older learners: A trip that works! *Educational Gerontology*, *1*, 215–226.

Rose, T. L., & Yesavage, J. A. (1983). Differential effects of a list-learning mnemonic in three age groups. *Gerontology*, *29*, 293–298.

Rowntree, D. (1970). *Learn how to study*. London: MacDonald.

Sanders, R. E., Murphy, M. D., Schmitt, F. A., & Walsh, K. K. (1980). Age differences in free recall rehearsal strategies. *Journal of Gerontology*, *35*, 550–558.

Schonfield, D. (1982). Attention switching in higher mental processes. In F. I. M. Craik & S. Trehub (Eds.), *Aging and cognitive processes* (pp. 309–316). New York: Plenum.

Schultz, N. R., & Hoyer, W. J. (1976). Feedback effects on spatial egocentrism in old age. *Journal of Gerontology*, *31*, 72–75.

Scogin, F., Storandt, M., & Lott, L. (1985). Memory-skills training, memory complaints, and depression in older adults. *Journal of Gerontology*, *40*, 562–568.

Shiffrin, R. M., & Schneider, W. (1977). Controlled and automatic human information processing II: Perceptual learning, automatic attending, and a general theory. *Psychological Review*, *84*, 127–190.

Skinner, B. F., & Vaughan, M. E., (1983). *Enjoy old age: A program of self-management*. New York: W. W. Norton.

Smith, A. D. (1975). *Interaction between human aging and memory* (Technical Report No. 2). Washington, DC: National Institute of Child Health and Development.

Smith, A. D (1980). Age differences in encoding, storage and retrieval. In L. W. Poon, J. L. Fozard, L. S. Cermak, D., Arenberg, & L. W. Thompson (Eds.), *New directions in memory and aging: Proceedings of the George A. Talland memorial conference* (pp. 23–46). Hillsdale, NJ: Lawrence Erlbaum

Sunderland, A., Harris, J. E., & Gleave, J. (1984). Memory failures in everyday life following severe head injury. *Journal of Clinical Neuropsychology*, *6*, 127–142.

Sunderland, A., Watts, K., Baddeley, A. D., & Harris, J. E. (1986). Subjective memory assessment and test performance in elderly adults. *Journal of Gerontology*, *41*, 376–384.

Thomas, J. C., Fozard, J. L., & Waugh, N. E. (1977). Age-related differences in naming latency. *American Journal of Psychology*, *90*, 499–509.

Treat, N. J., & Reese, H. W. (1976). Age, pacing and imagery in paired-associate learning. *Developmental Psychology*, *12*, 119–124.

Treat, N. J., Poon, L. W., Fozard, J. L., Popkin, J. L., & Popkin, S. J. (1978). Toward applying cognitive skill training to memory problems. *Experimental Aging Research*, *4*, 305–319.

Tulving, E. (1972). Episodic and semantic memory. In E. Tulving & W. Donaldson (Eds.), *Organization of memory* (pp. 382–404). New York: Academic Press.

Underwood, B. J., Boruch, R. F., & Malmi, R. (1978). Composition of episodic memory. *Journal of Experimental Psychology: General*, *107*, 393–419.

Waugh, N. C., & Barr, R. A. (1982). Encoding deficits in aging. In F. I. M. Craik & S. Trehub (Eds.), *Aging and cognitive processes* (pp. 183–190). New York: Plenum.

Wechsler, D. (1955). *Manual for the Wechsler Adult Intelligence Scale*. New York: Psychological Corporation.

Welford, A. T. (1980). Memory and age: A perspective view. In L. W. Poon, J. L. Fozard, L. S. Cermak, D. Arenberg, & L. W. Thompson (Eds.), *New directions in memory and aging: Proceedings of the George A. Talland memorial conference* (pp. 1–15). Hillsdale, NJ: Lawrence Erlbaum.

Wells, C. E. (1979). Pseudodementia. *American Journal of Psychiatry*, *136*, 895–900.

Wilson, B. A., & Moffat, N. (1984). *Clinical management of memory problems*. London: Aspen.

Winocur, G. (1982). Learning and memory deficits in institutionalized and noninstitutionalized old people: An analysis of interference effects. In F. I. M. Craik & S. Trehub (Eds.), *Aging and cognitive processes* (pp. 155–182). New York: Plenum.

Woods. R. T., & Holden, V. P. (1982). Reality orientation. In B. Isaacs (Ed.), *Recent advances in geriatric medicine* (pp. 181–199). Livingston: Churchill.

Yesavage, J. A. (1983). Imagery pretraining and memory training in the elderly. *Gerontology, 29,* 271–275.

Yesavage, J. A. (1984). Relaxation and memory training in 39 elderly patients. *American Journal of Psychiatry, 141,* 778–781.

Yesavage, J. A. (1985). Nonpharmacologic treatments for memory loss with normal aging. *American Journal of Psychiatry, 142,* 600–605.

Yesavage, J. A., Rose, T. A., & Spiegel, D. (1982). Relaxation training and memory improvement in elderly normals. *Experimental Aging Research, 8,* 195–198.

Yesavage, J. A., Rose, T. L., & Bower, C. H. (1983). Interactive imagery and affective judgements improve face–name learning in the elderly. *Journal of Gerontology, 38,* 197–203.

Zarit, S. H., Cole, K. D., & Gardner, R. L. (1981). Memory training strategies and subjective complaints of memory in the aged. *The Gerontologist, 21,* 158–164.

Zarit, S. H., Gallagher, D., & Kramer, N. (1981). Memory training in the community aged: Effects on depression, memory complaint, and memory performance. *Educational Gerontology, 6,* 11–27.

Zarit, S. H., Zarit, J. M., & Reever, K. E. (1982). Memory training for severe memory loss: Effects on senile dementia patients and their families. *The Gerontologist, 22,* 373–377.

Zarit, S. H., Eiler, J., & Hassinger, M. (1985). Clinical assessment. In J. E. Birren & K. W. Schaie (Eds.), *Handbook of the psychology of aging* (2nd ed., pp. 725–754). New York: Van Nostrand Reinhold.

Zelinski, E. M., Gilewski, M. J., & Thompson, L. W. (1980). Do laboratory tests relate to self-assessment of memory ability in the young and old? In L. W. Poon, J. L. Fozard, L. S. Cermak, D. Arenberg, & L. W. Thompson (Eds.), *New directions in memory and aging: Proceedings of the George A. Tallard memorial conference* (pp. 519–544). Hillsdale, NJ: Lawrence Erlbaum.

12

Insomnia as a Problem for the Elderly

MINDY ENGLE-FRIEDMAN AND RICHARD R. BOOTZIN

INTRODUCTION

The report of sleep problems, particularly insomnia, is frequent among older adults. The careful assessment and treatment of sleep problems for older adults is important not only for their sense of well-being but for their physical health and ability to function during the day. A complete understanding of the insomnia experienced by the older adult requires a working knowledge of the structure of sleep and general overview of sleep characteristics, knowledge of how the sleep of the older adult differs from that of younger individuals, and comprehension of the factors that contribute to insomnia. In this chapter, we will provide a brief overview of sleep, with a focus on changes in sleep as one ages. In addition, we will explore the multiple causes of sleep disturbance and report on current behavioral techniques used in the treatment of insomnia. Finally, we will recommend a progression of steps used in the identification of factors impacting on sleep.

MEASURES AND STAGES OF SLEEP

Sleep can be measured in a number of ways. The most reliable and valid measure is polysomnography (Bootzin & Engle-Friedman, 1981), which consists of the all-night recording of the electroencephalogram (EEG), a measure of brain activity; electrooculogram (EOG), a measure of eye movements; and the electromyogram (EMG), a measure of muscle tension. Other measures, such as respiration and heart rate, are often taken for special purposes. With the use of criteria developed by Rechtschaffen and Kales (1968), the polysomnographic record can be scored visually to discriminate sleep from wakefulness and between different

MINDY ENGLE-FRIEDMAN • Baruch College, City University of New York, New York, New York 10010.   RICHARD R. BOOTZIN • Department of Psychology, University of Arizona, Tucson, Arizona 85721.

stages of sleep. This method permits the designation of stage-wake, stage-1, stage-2, stage-3, stage-4, and rapid eye movement (REM) sleep.

Stage-1 sleep is a brief stage that indicates that the sleeper is in transition from wakefulness to sleep. The EEG pattern is typically of a low-voltage, mixed frequency pattern. It accounts for about 5% of the total night's sleep, and people usually describe themselves as being awake when aroused out of this stage. Stage 2 usually comprises 40–60% of the night's sleep. It is characterized by EEG events known as sleep spindles and K-complexes. The appearance of either of these wave forms signals sleep onset, and sleepers usually describe themselves as asleep once they have demonstrated this stage for about 5 minutes. Stages 3 and 4 are often called deep sleep because it is most difficult to awaken a person while in these stages, especially early in the sleep process. Stages 3 and 4 are distinguished by delta waves, which are high-amplitude slow waves. Young adults typically experience stages 3 and 4 in the first 3 hours of the night. These stages constitute 20% of total sleep. Rapid eye movement sleep is marked by cortical activation indicated by mixed frequency, low-voltage EEG pattern. Low muscle tone is continuous or tonic throughout this stage, while the rapid eye movements, which give the stage its name, are intermittent or phasic. Awakening sleepers out of REM sleep is as difficult as awakening them out of stage 2. In this stage, sleepers usually report dream activity, and it comprises 20–25% of a night's sleep. This stage appears at regularly spaced intervals that begin at about 70 to 100 minutes after sleep onset. Thereafter, REM periods occur at intervals of approximately 90 minutes from the onset of one REM period to the onset of the next REM period.

CHANGES IN SLEEP WITH AGING

In a national survey conducted in 1979 (Mellinger, Balter, & Uhlenhuth, 1985), the prevalence of "serious" insomnia (defined as a lot of trouble falling asleep or staying asleep within the last 12 months) increased over the life span from 14% for the 18–34 year age group to 25% for the 65–79 year age group. The number of individuals with "less severe" insomnia also rose with increasing age. All told, 45% of those people aged 65–79 years had some difficulty with insomnia in the previous 12 months. Since approximately 22 million Americans are over age 65, it appears that a tremendous number of people are having trouble sleeping.

Polysomnographic Changes

Aging results in changes in sleep that have been documented through polysomnography. Increased fragmentation of sleep is among the most consistent and disturbing of these changes. This increase in fragmentation results from an increase in the frequency of awakenings, particularly during the last half of the night (Agnew, Webb, & Williams, 1967; Feinberg, Koresko, & Heller, 1967; Hayashi & Endo, 1982; Kahn & Fisher, 1969; Kales, Wilson, Kales, Johnson, Paulson, Kollar, &

Walter, 1967; Webb, 1982a; Williams, Karacan, & Hursch, 1974). Once awakened, older adults have more difficulty falling back to sleep than do younger sleepers. Webb and Campbell (1980) found that individuals 50 to 60 years old took longer to fall asleep when awakened after the first 80 minutes of the night than subjects 21 to 23 years old. This increased difficulty in falling back to sleep later in the night may, in part, account for the increased frequency of early morning awakenings among the elderly.

Another change seen with aging is increased difficulty in falling asleep initially (Feinberg et al., 1967; Hayashi & Endo, 1982; Webb, 1982a; Williams et al., 1974). Webb (1982a) found that sleep latency was more than twice as long in women aged 50–60 than in women aged 20–30 years.

Sleep onset latency and awakenings are reflected in a commonly used measure–sleep efficiency. Sleep efficiency is the total amount of time asleep divided by the total time in bed after the lights are turned off. With increased awakenings and longer sleep onset latencies, sleep becomes substantially less efficient with age. For example, mean sleep efficiency was 80% in individuals 30–54 years old, while it was only 67% in individuals 60–85 years old (Coleman, Miles, Guilleminault, Zarcone, van den Hoed, & Dement, 1981).

Older adults get less total sleep at night than younger adults, apparently as a direct consequence of increased time awake and difficulty returning to sleep once awakened (Hauri, 1977). But daytime naps increase in frequency with age (Zepelin, 1973), often making the total amount of sleep of the elderly during the entire 24-hour day approximately equivalent to the total sleep of younger subjects (Webb & Swinburne, 1971; Zepelin, 1973).

Components of the sleep stages themselves also undergo changes with age. Sleep spindles, most frequently associated with non-REM sleep (stages 2, 3, 4) and particularly stage-2 sleep, show reductions in spindle density (bursts of spindles per minute) in normal and senile aging (Feinberg, 1976; Feinberg et al., 1967), along with spindle duration and amplitude of the spindle waves (Guazelli, Feinberg, Aminoff, Fein, Floyd, & Maggini, 1986). Guazelli et al. (1986) also found that unlike the younger subjects, the older subjects had neither increased frequency of spindles across non-REM periods nor increased density and duration across non-REM periods. It is important to note, however, that the reduction in spindling found in older people shows considerable variability and is not consistent within an age range. Some older people show spindle densities as high as those found in younger people, while in others spindling is virtually absent (Guazelli et al., 1986). Although spindle activity has been hypothesized to reflect processes that keep the person asleep, the absence of significant correlations between measures of sleep and arousal within the elderly group caused these researchers to conclude that decreased spindle activity is not the cause of increased arousals found in the older group.

Slow-wave sleep (stages 3 and 4) is greatly reduced with aging (Coleman et al., 1981; Hayashi & Endo, 1982; Reynolds, Kupfer, Taska, Hoch, Sewitch, & Spiker, 1985). One-fourth of the population over the age of 60 may have little or no stage-4 sleep. This deficit is much more likely to occur in males than in females (Williams et al., 1974). The decrease in slow-wave sleep is due to the fact that there is a reduction in amplitude of the slow waves that does not meet the established amplitude criterion and, therefore, cannot be scored as slow-wave sleep (Agnew *et al.*, 1967; Feinberg *et al.*, 1967; Kales, 1975; Miles & Dement, 1980; Prinz, Obrist, & Wang, 1975; Webb & Debrow, 1982). When the amplitude criterion is modified, older adults have the same amount of slow-wave sleep as younger adults (Feinberg, Fein, Floyd, & Aminoff, 1983; Smith, Karacan, & Yang, 1977; Webb, 1982b). The functional significance of the amplitude reduction in older adult slow-wave sleep is not presently known, although EEG amplitude has been hypothesized to reflect the physical integrity of the organism.

Rapid eye movement (REM) sleep is the stage typically associated with dreaming. Normally, the largest proportion of REM sleep occurs in the last half of the night, since REM periods tend to increase in duration throughout the night. There are small decreases in REM sleep with aging (Coleman *et al.*, 1981; Williams *et al.*, 1974). Unlike younger individuals, older adults have REM periods that remain uniform or decrease in duration during the night (Hayashi & Endo, 1982; Reynolds *et al.*, 1985). Increased REM early in a night's sleep is often associated with depression. Shortened latency to REM sleep and lower amounts of REM have been associated with intellectual decline (Feinberg *et al.*, 1967).

Variability in a number of sleep parameters, including time in bed, total sleep time, sleep latency, number of awakenings, and time awake after sleep onset, increases with age (Williams *et al.*, 1974). In documenting the wide range of sleep patterns of persons aged 50–70, Webb (1982b) showed that some subjects had short sleep latencies with uninterrupted sleep, while others showed fragmented and disorganized sleep. These older adults included the full gamut of individual differences in sleep, including long and short sleepers, nappers and nonnappers, and light and deep sleepers. The reasons why some people develop sleep fragmentation and intrastage sleep changes and why others do not are currently unknown. The ability to predict who will have particular sleep patterns is not yet available. While the sleep of the older person shows marked changes in comparison with a younger counterpart, it is important to be aware that marked individual differences still exist within age ranges. This is especially true in the older adult age range and, in fact, there are older persons without any sleep problems whatsoever.

Subjective Changes

The most frequent sleep complaints of older adults are increased frequency and duration of nocturnal awakenings, frequent early morning awakenings, increased latency to sleep onset, and excessive daytime sleepiness (Dement, Miles, & Carskadon, 1982; Gerard, Collins, & Dore, 1978; Karacan, Thornby, Anch, Holzer, Warheit, Schwab, & Williams, 1976; McGhie & Russell, 1962; Miles & Dement, 1980; Strauch & Wollschlaeger, 1973). They also report next-day effects on mood, performance, fatigue, and motivation. Webb and Levy (1982) found that in comparison with 18- to 22-year-olds, 40- to 49-year olds showed significantly poorer performance on auditory vigilance, addition tasks, and mood scales following two nights of sleep deprivation.

The multiple sleep latency test (MSLT) is a measure of ability to fall asleep during the day. It can be used to determine how sleepy a person is as a result of the previous night's sleep. Sleep onset latency is calculated five or six times a day by asking subjects to attempt to sleep in a controlled environment. Using this measure, Carskadon, Brown, and Dement (1982) have found that in older people the speed at which a person will fall asleep during the day is related to the number of arousals from sleep and the number of apneas and respiratory pauses experienced the night before.

Sleepiness can also be assessed with pupillary measures (Pressman, DiPhillipo, & Fry, 1986). As alertness decreases, pupillary size becomes smaller and less stable and pupillary reflexes decrease (Yoss, Moyer, & Ogle, 1969). When older persons were studied, this measure of sleepiness was correlated with the fragmentation of sleep the night before. The authors suggested that small pupil size in otherwise healthy persons could be a marker of daytime sleepiness and disordered sleep.

It should be noted that while there are substantial changes in sleep associated with aging, these changes do not always result in a subjective complaint of sleep disturbance. For example, frequent awakenings influence judgments about the quality of sleep, while changes in slow-wave sleep and REM sleep do not (Bonnet & Johnson, 1978). Despite the lack of subjective complaints, some researchers suggest that the changes are not trivial. They suggest that the observed changes in sleep parameters reflect degradation of the central nervous system, including deceases in neurons, metabolic rate, and blood flow. These organic changes may impact on both sleep and intellectual performance (Prinz, 1977). For example, there are striking changes in the sleep of people with dementia, including frequent nocturnal awakenings, time spent awake, sleep latency, and decreased REM sleep. These changes parallel, but exceed in magnitude, the changes corresponding to "normal aging" (Prinz, Reskind, Vitalino, Raskind, Eisendorfer, Zemcuznikov, & Gerber, 1982). People experiencing senile dementia of the Alzheimer type (SDAT) show abnormalities in both the waking and sleeping EEG, similar to the pattern of normal older people, but they also show a decrease in slow-wave sleep substantially different from that of normal older adults. An extreme decrease in slow-wave sleep has been positively and significantly correlated with the Wechsler Memory Quotient Score (Loewenstein, Weingartner, Gillin, Kaye, Ebert, & Mendelson, 1982) and when combined with decreased REM percentage and decreased dominant occipital frequency, Prinz, Reskind, and colleagues (1982) have demonstrated that patients could be classified into nondemented and mildly demented categories based on sleep activity.

CAUSES OF SLEEP DISTURBANCE

A number of factors contribute to sleep disturbance: physical pathology, inactivity, one's personal circadian rhythm, the sleep environment, one's sleep habits, the reinforcement of sleep complaints (Bootzin, Engle-Friedman, & Hazlewood, 1983), prescription and nonprescription medication, alcohol, caffeine and nicotine, stress and anxiety, and psychopathology. A thorough assessment of each factor is required in order to implement effective interventions. In the following section we have elaborated on each of these factors.

Physical Disorders

Sleep-related respiratory disturbance is the most common physical disorder that affects sleep. These disturbances include sleep apnea (a cessation of airflow for 10 seconds or longer) and hypopnea (50% or greater reduction of airflow for 10 seconds or longer). Sleep-related respiratory disturbance is considered abnormal when it exceeds 5 apneas per hour. During sleep, most cortical influences on sleep are eliminated, and the brainstem becomes the major regulator of respiration as it responds to the inputs of central and peripheral chemical and neuroreceptors (Smith & Bleeker, 1986). During non-REM, there is a relaxation of the upper airway musculature that results in narrowing of the airway, which thereby limits ventilation. During REM, upper airway muscle tone becomes atonic and respiration becomes irregular. A blockage of the airway and consequent increases in carbon dioxide from the respiratory pause stimulates an electroencephalographic arousal. Respiration during sleep is likely to be compromised in people with obstructive lung disease as well. However, people with primary disorders of nocturnal respiration must be evaluated by means of sleep monitoring (Smith & Bleeker, 1986), since the disturbance would not be seen in waking behavior.

A 1981 survey was done of 16 sleep disorder centers and more than 4,000 patients. The results indicated that over 6% of the subjects complaining of insomnia had a sleep apnea syndrome (Coleman, 1982). More recently, Hoch, Reynolds, Kupfer, Houck, Berman, and Stack (1986) found that 5.4% of the normal elderly they studied and 41.7% of the Alzheimer's patients studied had sleep apnea. Respiratory pauses and sleep apnea increase with age (Ancoli-Israel, Kripke, Mason, & Messin, 1981; Carskadon, Brown, & Dement, 1980; Krieger, Turlot, Mangin, & Kurtz, 1983). In fact, sleep apnea is the most common diagnosis of older adult patients seen in sleep disorder clinics, accounting for 39% of older patients (Coleman et al., 1981). Pack and Millman (1986) suggest that between 18–40% of well, elderly subjects experience frequent apnea. Respiratory disturbances have been found in both asymptomatic (McGinty, Littner, Beahm, Ruiz-Primo, Young, & Saver, 1982) and symptomatic (Ancoli-Israel et al., 1981) older adults. When oxygen consumption was measured, investigators found that nocturnal respiration became increasingly more irregular with increasing age. A rare longitudinal study found that sleep apnea increases as the individual ages (Bliwise, Carskadon, Carey, & Dement, 1984). Of particular relevance to the sleep process are the arousals that must occur for a respiratory pause or apnea to be terminated. In older adults the increase in respiratory pauses and apneas can produce repetitive arousals from sleep (Smith & Bleeker, 1986). Thus, as one ages, there is likely to be an increase in arousals to terminate apneas. In addition to producing frequent arousals, sleep-related respiratory disturbances produce excessive daytime tiredness, headaches, dry mouth, and cognitive and perceptual–motor deficits (Guilleminault & Dement, 1978; Yesavage, Bliwise, Guilleminault, Carskadon, & Dement, 1985). They have also been implicated in pulmonary decompensation of impaired cardiovascular systems, which may lead to death (Dement *et al.*, 1982). Interestingly, Lorrain, De Koninck, Dionne, and Goupil (1986) found that older adults were more likely to sleep on their right side and not their stomachs, possibly because they require physical assistance for respiratory and cardiovascular functions.

Two muscular disorders, nocturnal myoclonus and restless legs, can also impair sleep. In nocturnal myoclonus, leg twitches occur repeatedly throughout the night (Lugaresi, Coccagna, Berti-Ceroni, & Ambrosetto, 1968). A person who experiences restless leg syndrome feels deep itching in the legs and tries to stop the itching by moving the legs. Both disorders increase with age and account for between 18% and 25% of diagnoses of older adults in sleep disorders clinics (Ancoli-Israel *et al.*, 1981; Coleman *et al.*, 1981; Roehrs, Zorick, Sicklesteel, Wittig, & Roth, 1983). Bliwise, Petta, Seidel, and Dement (1985) found that polysomnographic sleep latencies were unrelated to the number of leg movements of their subjects.

A number of other physical disorders can interfere with sleep. Physical illness, such as back, abdominal, or chest pain, may cause such discomfort that sleep is disrupted. The experience of pain, especially that associated with arthritis, constitutes one of the most frequent sleep disruptions among older adults (Prinz & Raskind, 1978). Sleep patterns may also be disrupted by diabetes when the under-regulation of blood sugar results in glycosuria and nocturia or when the over-regulation of blood sugar leads to hypoglycemia (Prinz & Raskind, 1978). Cardiovascular disease, particularly angina pectoris, increases arousals, sleep latency, and time spent in stages 1 and 2, and decreases sleep efficiency and time spent in stages 3 and 4 (Karacan & Williams, 1983).

Organic brain syndromes produce an increase in wakefulness and a decrease in total sleep, stage-4 sleep, REM sleep, and eye movements during REM. "Sundown syndrome," which sometimes results from organic brain syndrome, can include behaviors before and during the sleep period, such as delirium and hallucinations during the night and disorientation and wandering during sleep (Karacan & Williams, 1983). Some researchers suggest that these sleep-related changes reflect degenerative changes in the brain evidenced by decreased cerebral blood flow and slowed frequency of the alpha background rhythm in the EEG. They further suggest that on a continuum, normal sleep in the elderly signifies or mimics minor damage, while sundown syndrome represents severe impairment.

Inactivity and Daytime Naps

An inactive lifestyle may have considerable effects on the sleep of older adults. This is particularly true for the institutionalized elderly, but it is also true of many healthy, adaptive, noninstitutionalized elderly individuals. Oftentimes, a less than active lifestyle provides increased opportunity to nap. Older adults frequently nap during the day, an activity that can have adverse effects on nighttime sleep. Sleep onset latency, for example, is inversely related to the length of time since the individual last slept (Webb, 1975). Specifically, the shorter the time from the end of the last sleep period (in this case, a nap) to the beginning of the next sleep period (in this case, nighttime sleep), the more difficult it will be for a person to fall asleep quickly. Afternoon and evening naps contain more deep and less REM sleep than morning naps. The night's sleep following an afternoon or evening nap continues as if the nap were part of the night's sleep. Therefore, the entire night's sleep is similar to the last half of a typical night's sleep, with more light and REM sleep and more frequent awakenings (Webb, 1975). A morning nap, on the other hand, is a continuation of the previous night's sleep and has minimal effect on the structure of the subsequent night's sleep.

Circadian Rhythm Alterations

The effect of napping on subsequent sleep has much to do with a person's circadian rhythm of sleep, the patterning of the sleep–wake schedule within the 24-hour day. This daily sleep–wake pattern may serve as the pacemaker for other important daily physiological changes, including the timing of temperature and hormonal secretions. These other physiological fluctuations feed back to and impact on the circadian rhythm of sleep. The circadian rhythm of sleep and fluctuations in temperature are highly interrelated in normal conditions. In younger adults, temperature rises upon awakening. Among the elderly, temperature rises before awakening and may account for early morning awakening. The temperature of the older adult is lower at wake time, however, suggesting that the arousal process at the final awakening in the morning may not be as intense for the older adult as it is for the younger adult. Some investigators (Weitzman, Moline, Czeisler, & Zimmerman, 1982) have suggested that the lower amplitude in body temperature results from the increased arousals and decreases in stages 3 and 4 for the older adult. It is unclear whether changes in temperature rhythm impact on and cause sleep disturbance, whether disturbances in sleep cause temperature rhythm alterations, or whether another variable is responsible for these changes. In any event, the circadian control of body temperature and the circadian control of sleep undergo significant change with age.

Hauri (1970) has noted that insomniacs who fall into the habit of sleeping late in the morning or taking naps whenever fatigue overwhelms them are likely to develop circadian rhythm disturbances. If circadian cycles become desynchronized, there may never be an optimal time for sleeping. Webb (1974) pointed out that with aging there is a breakdown in the biphasic pattern of sleep and wakefulness. Older adults appear to return to the polyphasic alteration of sleep and wakefulness of infancy.

Disruptions of circadian wake–sleep schedules are particularly common in institutionalized elderly (Wessler, Rubin, & Solberger, 1976) and may be caused by a variety of factors. First, noise is more disruptive for older adults (Karacan &

Williams, 1983), and institutions can be especially noisy and unsettling for the sleeper. Second, the patient's natural sleep–wake schedule may be very different from the institution's schedule. Third, when outside of the institution, the patient experiences natural cues or zeitgebers (discriminative stimuli or time keepers) that set the timing of sleep and wake. These include sunrise and sunset, clock time, alarms, the regular social behaviors of spouses or roommates, and meal time, to name a few. These zeitgebers, however, may be unavailable in the institutional setting. Instead, factors that are not as salient or meaningful for the patient may be related to the patient's bedtime, such as changes in nursing staff shifts or time of medication distribution.

Circadian rhythm disturbances may result from physical impairment as well. Persons who suffer from blindness experience alterations in circadian rhythm and have complaints about their sleep. Sewitch and her colleagues (1986) reported a case study of a 77-year-old legally blind man who had developed a polyphasic sleep–wake rhythm and spent 14% of his day sleeping, almost three times as much daytime sleep as that found in members of his age group. This phenomenon was similar to that seen in people subjected to constant conditions of light or dark. In multiple sleep latency tests throughout the day, this client showed an abnormal proportion of slow-wave sleep occurring in the morning, at the time REM would ordinarily occur. The authors suggested that the lack of sufficient cues (i.e., zeitgebers of light and dark) impaired his ability to maintain the natural 24-hour sleep–wake rhythm.

Sleep Environment

There are many sleep environment factors that may influence the quality of an individual's sleep, such as the temperature of the room, firmness of the mattress, noise, and whether or not another person shares the bed or bedroom. People can learn to sleep comfortably in a wide range of temperatures and on many different surfaces. There is no ideal room temperature or degree of mattress firmness. However, individuals may develop strong preferences for sleep conditions. People sleeping in a new environment or moving to a new location often experience sleep disruption due to a lack of familiarity with the new setting.

Noise affects sleep by decreasing the amount of deep sleep and increasing the frequency of awakenings. Even people who habitually sleep in noisy environments do not fully adapt to noise (Sanchez & Bootzin, 1985). Since the elderly are more easily awakened (Zepelin, McDonald, & Zammit, 1984) and have more difficulty falling back to sleep once awakened (Webb & Campbell, 1980), noisy environments are likely to be particularly troublesome for them.

Sleep Habits

Insomniacs may engage in activities at bedtime that are incompatible with falling asleep (Bootzin, 1972, 1976, 1977; Bootzin & Nicassio, 1978). Insomniacs may, for example, use their bedroom for reading, talking on the telephone, watching television, snacking, and listening to music. The result is that the bed is no longer a cue just for sleeping, but it becomes a cue for physiological arousal and a variety of other behaviors incompatible with sleep. Insomniacs often sleep well in places other than their own beds. For example, they often sleep better in a sleep laboratory than they do at home (de la Pena, Flickinger, & Mayfield, 1977). In contrast, people who have no difficulty falling asleep in their own beds often have difficulty doing so in strange surroundings.

Cognitive intrusions may be particularly disruptive. Worries and concerns are often accomplished by emotional upset, yet they may appear in the absence of excessive physiological arousal (Starker & Hasenfeld, 1976). The content of the insomniac's concerns may shift from the general pressures of current and future problems to the more specific concerns about his or her ability to fall asleep or to get enough sleep during the night (Hauri, 1977) and the effect of sleep loss on the next day's performance. Therefore, the bedroom can become a cue for the anxiety and frustration associated with trying to fall asleep.

If physical illness or situational stress was the initial cause of sleeping difficulties and insomnia, the resultant poor sleeping habits may help maintain insomnia. For the chronic insomniac, sleeping difficulties usually continue long after the initial causes have disappeared.

Reinforcement

Sleep complaints may be reinforced by their consequences, such as the attention of sympathetic listeners. Some insomniacs may find that others are more tolerant of their shortcomings when they appear fatigued, groggy, and irritable as a result of sleeping poorly. The inadvertent reinforcement of "sick" behavior has been found to play a prominent role in other disorders as well (Fordyce, 1976).

Medication

Medication taken for a variety of medical conditions can negatively affect sleep. According to an assessment by the *Statistical Bulletin of the Metropolitan Life Insurance Company* (1978), almost half of the people 65 years old and older were limited in their daily activities due to a chronic disease. Of this group, 20% was disabled by cardiovascular disease or arthritis. The medications prescribed to alleviate these disorders can often have major effects on sleep. Diuretics and beta-adrenoreceptor blockers, drugs which affect the central nervous system, are the most frequently prescribed antihypertensive medications. Nightmares have been associated with the beta-blocker medications in particular (Bengtsson, Lennartsson, Lindquist, Noppa, & Sigurdsson, 1980). Diuretics can increase nighttime urination and may cause the individual to awaken more frequently. Guilleminault and Silvestri (1982) reported that nightmares and night terrors may result from antiarrhythmic drugs such as quinidine and drugs with quinidine-like effects. Patients have reported feeling very disoriented, frightened, or confused upon awakening from sleep. In some instances, these sleep-related disturbances did not disappear with time, and it was necessary to withdraw some patients from the drugs. The sleep disturbance of Parkinson's disease includes nocturnal disorientation and is sometimes associated with nightmares or confusion. The medications used to relieve the Parkinson symptoms, such as LevoDOPA with DOPA-decarboxylase inhibitors (Sinemet), may induce nightmares, night terrors and toxic reactions that include nocturnal confusion and wandering (Guilleminault & Silvestri, 1982). Asthma medication (e.g., theophylline) acts as a stimulant and can interfere with sleep if taken at night. Tricyclic antidepressants suppress REM sleep and can exacerbate nocturnal myoclonus. The hypnotics, which are used to alleviate poor sleep, can be detrimental for the older person. Sedatives and hypnotics will be discussed further in a later section on treatment modalities.

Alcohol

Like other depressants, alcohol deprives a person of REM sleep. Habitual heavy drinking results in fragmented sleep with frequent awakenings. Withdrawal from alcohol produces increased arousals and stage changes (Lester, Rundell, Cowden, & Williams, 1973). Stage-1 sleep is frequently increased, often requiring a person to need more time to get to sleep (Gross, Goodenough, Nagarajan, & Hastey, 1973). Fitful sleep and nightmares bring about REM rebound. Alcohol also potentiates the effects of hypnotics and other depressants. Thus, the combination of alcohol and sleeping pills may intensify and prolong deleterious side effects, thereby producing lethal levels of overdose (Institute of Medicine, 1979). It is likely, too, that alcohol will be less tolerated by the older than the younger adult since toxic substances remain in the aging body for extended periods of time.

Caffeine and Nicotine

Caffeine and nicotine are central nervous system stimulants that produce lighter and more fragmented sleep (Bonnet, Webb, & Barnard, 1979; Soldatos, Kales, Scharf, Bixler, & Kales, 1980). Caffeine is contained in many foods and beverages, including coffee, tea, soft drinks, and chocolate. Since caffeine has a plasma half-life of approximately 6 hours, the older adult might continue to experience its effect long after ingestion. Reducing or eliminating the intake of caffeine, particularly in the afternoon and evening, and quitting smoking can lead to substantial improvement in sleep.

Stress

Sleeping difficulties not caused by physical disorder are usually seen as the symptom of some psychological problem. People who ordinarily have no trouble sleeping often develop insomnia during periods of stress (Healy, Kales, Monroe, Bixler, Chamberlin, & Soldatos, 1981). As a person ages, he or she may have trouble adjusting to many important life events and thus sleep may be affected. For example, a spouse may die, living arrangements may change, or the individual may become aware of changes in his or her physical and intellectual functioning. Retirement itself has not been associated with a worsening of sleep quality, although the years before retirement have been linked to more frequent sleep complaints (Kronholm & Hyyppa, 1985).

Psychopathology

The relationship between psychopathology and sleep disturbance has been studied extensively, particularly with regard to anxiety and depression. On self-report personality inventories, insomniacs appear as more introverted, anxious, neurotic, and depressed than normal sleepers (e.g., Costello & Smith, 1963; Coursey, Buchsbaum, & Frankel, 1975; Haynes, Follingstad, & McGowan, 1974; Kales, Caldwell, Preston, Healy, & Kales, 1976; Nicassio & Bootzin, 1974). Older insomniacs, however, appear less depressed and anxious than their younger insomniac counterparts (Roehrs et al., 1983).

A number of studies have focused specifically on the sleep of patients diagnosed as depressed (Kupfer & Foster, 1978). In nearly all studies of depressed patients, investigators have determined that slow-wave sleep is reduced (Mendelson, Gillin, & Wyatt, 1977), a finding that has led many to suggest that shortened REM latency and increased REM sleep percentage is symptomatic of major depression (e.g., Hartmann, 1968; Kupfer, Reynolds, Ulrich, Shaw, & Coble, 1982; Snyder, 1966). Kales and Kales (1970) recommended prescribing antidepressant medication for those patients whose insomnia is diagnosed as *resulting from* depression. It is difficult, if not impossible, however, to determine that depression (or anxiety) is directly causing insomnia since it is observed in covariation (Bootzin & Nicassio, 1978). In cases where psychological problems accompany sleep disturbance, separate therapeutic attention should be given to each. The therapist should not assume that improvement in one will automatically produce improvement in the other.

TREATMENTS FOR INSOMNIA

Pharmacological Treatment of Insomnia

The disproportionate use of sleep medication in older adults corroborates the survey reports of sleep disturbances. Of those taking prescription medication for sleep, 69% were individuals aged 50–79 (Melinger et al., 1985). The use of hypnotics is even greater among the institutionalized elderly. For example, a U.S. Public Health Service (1976) survey of prescribing patterns in skilled nursing facilities found that prescriptions for hypnotics had been written for 94.2% of the 98,505 patients studied. In an intensive study of 180 nursing home residents, 39% received hypnotics daily (Cohen, Eisendorfer, Prinz, Breen, Davis, & Gadsby, 1983). An examination of the patients' charts revealed that no notations had been made concerning either a diagnosis of sleep disturbance or the type of sleep problem. In addition, there was no relationship between the use of hypnotics and the occurrence of sleep problems as rated by either the patients or the nurses. Thus, it appears that older adults consume disproportionate amounts of sleep medication, and people living in institutions may be using these medications without an antecedent sleep disturbance.

Despite the heavy reliance on sleep medication, the use of hypnotics is both ineffective and potentially dangerous for the chronic insomniac. Most hypnotics lose their effectiveness within 2 weeks of continuous use (Kales, Allen, Scharf, & Kales, 1970). Tolerance to hypnotics develops rapidly, so larger and larger doses are required to have any effect. Continuous use results in less deep sleep and more light, fragmented sleep. In addition, most hypnotics deprive a person of REM sleep and produce a marked REM rebound on subsequent nights. REM-rebound nights are often spent in restless dreaming, nightmares, and fitful sleep. The insomniac may conclude that the hypnotics are needed to avoid the rebound effect and, thus, may become drug dependent (Kales, Scharf, & Kales, 1978).

Besides their disruptive effect on sleep, hypnotics have a number of deleterious side effects. As central nervous system depressants, they affect respiration (Carskadon et al., 1980; Dolly & Block, 1982). They also produce drug hangover and can affect functioning the next day. In comparison with young adults, older adults are more vulnerable to the negative side effects of sedative–hypnotic drugs, including confusional states (Evans & Jarvis, 1972), psychomotor performance deficits (Castleden, George, Marcer, & Hallet, 1977), and nocturnal falls (MacDonald & Mac-Donald, 1977). Dysphoric moods, impaired motor and intellectual functioning, and daytime sleepiness have all been reported as daytime side effects of hypnotics. These daytime effects are probably due to the fact that most hypnotics have long elimination half-lives and may be observed for days or weeks after the individual has stopped taking sleep medication. For example, flurazepam has a plasma half-life of 50–100 hours. Thus, the daytime side effects are evidence of continued pharmacological action of a central nervous system depressant.

Recently, hypnotics with short-elimination half-lives (less than 5 hours), such as triazolam (Halcyon), have been introduced. These hypnotics are effective for transient and short-term sleep onset problems, but they are REM depriving and produce more wakefulness in the last third of the night, i.e., rebound insomnia the very same night the medication was taken. In addition, continuous use has resulted in memory deficits and daytime anxiety (Morgan & Oswald, 1981; Soldatos, Bixler, & Kales, 1985). There are drugs that have intermediate half-lives of 9–12 hours, such as temazepam (Restoril), which appear effective for sleep maintenance and early morning awakening problems with less evidence of daytime hangover (*Physicians' Desk Reference*, 1987).

The elderly are particularly vulnerable to deleterious side effects because they are more likely to have disorders aggravated by hypnotics such as pulmonary, hepatic, renal, or cardiac dysfunction (Institute of Medicine, 1979). Benzodiazepines are central nervous system depressants, which, for persons with sleep apnea, may interact with the control of breathing in sleep by leading to respiratory depression and by increasing the threshold needed for arousal. Flurazepam, a benzodiazepine, increases the frequency and duration of apneic events in healthy elderly subjects (ages 66–75 years), but for individuals experiencing sleep apnea prior to drug use the respiratory response is even more profound (Dement *et al.*, 1982).

The age-associated decreases in protein-binding ability, circulation time, and kidney and liver metabolism lengthen the time drugs remain in the body, extending the period of potential toxicity (Albert, 1981). The elderly are also likely to have increased risk of toxic interactions from multiple drug use (Miles & Dement, 1980), exacerbated by the habits older people have in substituting one drug for another, exchanging drugs with friends, obtaining drugs from a number of physicians, and using drugs beyond their expiration date (Hemminki & Heikkila, 1975).

In a National Institutes of Health (1983) consensus conference, experts recommended that hypnotics not be used for chronic sleep disturbances. The effects of sleeping pills on nighttime alertness, performance in response to an emergency, and a person's well-being and performance the day following the administration of the medication on both short- and long-term use have not been evaluated. Performance is most frequently evaluated with young male adults who are not representative of the majority of sleeping pill users, i.e., postmenopausal elderly women (Guilleminault & Silvestri, 1982).

The hazardous effects of hypnotics, therefore, include hangover effects that impact on nighttime and next-day functioning, additive toxicity when combined with alcohol or other central nervous system depressants, development of dependence on drugs to sleep, disruption of normal sleep stages, drug-dependent insomnia, increase in the number of sleep apneas, dysphoric mood, impaired motor and intellectual functioning, daytime sleepiness, and an impact on physiological systems already made vulnerable through disease and aging. The same side effects, multiple drug interactions, and disrupted sleep that are associated with hypnotics also apply to tranquilizers such as diazepam (Valium). Neither hypnotics nor tranquilizers are an appropriate treatment for chronic sleep disturbance.

The active ingredient in most over-the-counter sleep medication is an antihistamine, which has a side effect of drowsiness and may lead the user to believe it will effectively facilitate the onset of sleep. However, polysomnographic investigations of these medications have equated their effects with those of placebos (e.g., Kales, Tan, Searingen, & Kales, 1971). In addition to their ineffectiveness, over-the-counter sleep medications are associated with a number of hazards. As depressants, they potentiate the effect of alcohol, hypnotics, and tranquilizers. In addition, they can produce side effects of confusion, disorientation, and memory disturbance (Institute of Medicine, 1979).

There is now considerable consensus that sleep medication is not the appropriate treatment for the chronic insomniac of any age. If hypnotics are to be replaced in treating elderly insomniacs, viable short-term alternatives must be utilized and evaluated.

Behavioral Treatment of Insomnia

A number of short-term nonpharmacological interventions for insomnia have been evaluated during the past 15 years (for reviews see Bootzin & Nicassio, 1978; Borkovec, 1982; Youkilis & Bootzin, 1981). Only recently, however, has there been any systematic attempt to evaluate the effectiveness of such treatments with older adults. Because of the marked changes in sleep associated with aging and the large variety of factors that can interfere with sleep, many professionals have assumed that psychological interventions would be ineffective. This is a common attitude about many problems experienced by the elderly, resulting in a lack of treatment for many treatable problems (Rowe, 1985; Zarit & Zarit, 1983).

Prior to these evaluations, elderly were advised to accept reassurance by the physician (Prinz & Raskind, 1978), decrease the noise and increase the privacy of the bedroom (Miles & Dement, 1980), establish prebed rituals (Butler & Lewis), use nonsleeping time at night for unfinished business (Raskind, 1977), and to undergo psychotherapy (Berlin, 1985). Pfeiffer (1977) went so far as to recommend nonintervention in the sleep of the older adult.

There are three kinds of psychological interventions for the treatment of insomnia. Two of them, progressive relaxation training (Bernstein & Borkovec, 1973) and stimulus control instructions (Bootzin, 1972, 1976, 1977), have been thoroughly evaluated previously with younger adults and therefore are quite promising for use with the elderly. The third treatment, information and support, is usually a component of all forms of treatment. We will next discuss each of these treatments in some detail, beginning with the one element common to most treatments.

Information and Support

An important component of effective therapy for a variety of problems is the extent to which the individual stops perceiving himself or herself as a victim of the problem and begins to believe that he or she can cope with it (Bootzin, 1985). The insomniac's appraisal of the problem is often an important component in its maintenance. Perseverant worry about why one cannot sleep, as well as preoccupation with one's inability to sleep and the consequences of sleeplessness are likely to intensify any existing problem (Youkilis & Bootzin, 1981). The goal of the information and support treatment is to reverse the cycle by helping the insomniac change his or her appraisal of the problem.

With this type of treatment, subjects are informed about sleep stages and the developmental changes that occur with age. They are appraised of the effects on sleep of physical illness, prescription and nonprescription medication, alcohol, caffeine, nicotine, stress, inactivity, naps, sleep environment factors, and reinforcement for sleeplessness.

Two additional points are stressed (Bootzin, Engle-Friedman, & Hazlewood, 1983). First, there are large individual differences in sleep needs. Some people have lived long, productive, satisfying lives getting less than 2 hours of sleep a night for as long as they can remember (Meddis, 1977). In general, the body will get the amount of sleep that it needs. People may not need as much sleep as they believe necessary. Second, it is not a calamity to go without sleep. There is very little performance deficit following prolonged periods of reduced sleep (Friedman, Globus, Huntley, Mulaney, Naitch, & Johnson, 1977; Webb & Agnew, 1974) or even following total sleep deprivation for as long as 8 days (Pasnau, Naitch, Stier, & Kollar, 1968). Even studies of sleep deprivation with the elderly indicate that the effects on performance are small (Bonnet, 1984). Older adults show responses to 64 hours of sleep deprivation similar to that of their younger counterparts, including increased sleep efficiency and increase in slow-wave sleep on their first recovery night.

The major effects of sleep deprivation are fatigue and irritability. However, even if the individual goes without sleep entirely, fatigue follows a daily circadian rhythm (Kleitman, 1963). A person will be fatigued and have a low body temperature at times when he or she would ordinarily be asleep. On the other hand, the individual will be alert even after sleep deprivation at times when he or she is ordinarily awake. Thus, the day's performance is not as dependent on the previous night's sleep as many patients expect.

The goal of the information and support treatment is to help the insomniac put the problem in a coping context. The therapist explores with the patient the nature and severity of the problem, possible causes, and alternative solutions.

Stimulus Control Instructions

In giving stimulus control instructions, the therapist's goals are to help the insomniac acquire a consistent sleep rhythm, to strengthen the bed as a cue for sleep, and to weaken it as a cue for activities that might interfere with sleep. The following stimulus control instructions are given to each insomniac client (after Bootzin, 1972, 1976, 1977).

1. Lie down intending to go to sleep only when you are sleepy.
2. Do not use your bed for anything except sleep. That is, do not read, watch television, eat, or worry in bed. Sexual activity is the only exception to this rule. On such occasions, the instructions are to be followed afterward when you intend to go to sleep.
3. If you find yourself unable to fall asleep, get up and go into another room. Stay up as long as you wish and then return to the bedroom to sleep. Although we do not want you to watch the clock, we want you to get out of bed if you do not fall asleep immediately. Remember the goal is to associate your bed with falling asleep quickly! If you are in bed more than about 10 minutes without falling asleep and have not gotten up, you are not following this instruction.
4. If you still cannot fall asleep, repeat Step 3. Do this as often as is necessary throughout the night.
5. Set your alarm and get up at the same time every morning regardless of how much sleep you had during the night. This will help your body acquire a consistent sleep rhythm.

6. Do not nap during the day.

Stimulus control instructions have been proven highly effective in case studies and controlled evaluations (e.g., Bootzin, 1972, 1975; Haynes, Price, & Simons, 1975; Lacks, Bertelson, Gans, & Kunkel, 1983; Turner & Ascher, 1979, 1982). Although the focus of most evaluations has been on sleep onset latency, there have been reports of improvement in total sleep (Bootzin, 1975) and number and duration of arousals (Lacks, Bertelson, Sugerman, & Kunkel, 1983; Toler, 1978). Of the six studies comparing stimulus control instructions and progressive relaxation training, four of them demonstrated superior effects for the stimulus control instructions (Bootzin, 1975; Lacks, Bertelson, Gans, & Kunkel, 1983; Lawrence & Tokarz, 1976; Slama, 1975). The other two studies reported no significant differences between the two treatments (Turner & Ascher, 1979, 1982). At present, stimulus control instructions appear to be the most effective psychological intervention for insomnia (Borkovec, 1982). Thus, it holds considerable promise as a treatment for the elderly. In the only published study of stimulus control with elderly insomniacs, Puder, Lacks, Bertelson, and Storandt (1983) found stimulus control instructions effective in a between-subjects multiple-baseline design with 16 sleep onset insomniacs over the age of 60.

In our study of the various treatments (Bootzin *et al.*, 1983), clients received support and sleep hygiene information in addition to stimulus control instructions through weekly discussions. Some of the problems clients had in carrying out the instructions included disturbing the spouse's sleep when the insomniac got out of bed and a reluctance to leave the warmth of their beds, especially during the winter. For the first problem, the spouse's cooperation was often insured by direct discussion of the importance of the treatment. For the second problem, suggestions for keeping warm robes near the bed and keeping an additional room warm through the night, along with encouragement to try to follow the instructions, were usually effective in promoting compliance.

Progressive Relaxation Training

The most frequently recommended nonpharmacological treatment for insomnia is some type of relaxation training (Bootzin & Nicassio, 1978). This includes a variety of training procedures such as progressive relaxation, autogenic training, transcendental meditation, yoga, hypnosis, and EMG biofeedback. As treatments for insomnia, all of these procedures are based on the same premise: if people can learn to be relaxed at bedtime, they will fall asleep faster. The different types of relaxation procedures have all achieved about the same degree of effectiveness.

Prolonged relaxation, developed by Edmund Jacobson (1938, 1964), has been the most thoroughly evaluated relaxation method for treating insomnia. A number of studies provide evidence for the superior effectiveness of progressive relaxation when compared with placebo and nontreatment conditions (see review by Borkovec, 1982). As with stimulus control instructions, most evaluations have focused on sleep onset insomnia. Coates and Thorensen (1979), however, reported a case study in which relaxation training was effective with sleep maintenance problems.

Other investigators have reported improvement in total sleep or number of awakenings (e.g., Borkovec & Fowles, 1973; Lick & Heffler, 1977).

One common problem in using relaxation with the elderly is that the client may experience arthritic pain as a result of tensing and releasing particular muscle groups (Bootzin et al., 1983). When a client does have arthritis, he or she is instructed not to tense that muscle group, but to just release the tension from whatever level of tension is already present. In our study, we discouraged the use of tape-recorded relaxation instructions to prevent dependence on the tape recorder. The goal of relaxation training is to teach the patient a new coping skill that can be available whenever it is needed.

Since many insomniacs are aroused and anxious, relaxation training may provide a double benefit. First, it is helpful in inducing sleep and, second, it may be used as a general coping skill for dealing effectively with the stresses of the day.

The first controlled evaluation of all three of these interventions in the treatment of insomnia in the elderly has been reported in two sources (Bootzin et al., 1983; Engle-Friedman, 1985). In this study, 53 insomniacs, ranging in age from 47 to 76, were randomly assigned to one of the following groups: support and sleep hygiene information alone (SI); support and information plus progressive relaxation training (PR); support and information plus stimulus control instructions (SC); and no treatment. Participants received 2 weeks of baseline, 4 weeks of weekly individual treatment sessions, and 2 weeks of follow-up. All three treatments resulted in significant improvement ($p < .05$). Participants reported fewer awakenings, almost 50% less nap taking, increased feelings of being refreshed in the morning, increased self-efficacy with respect to sleep, decreased concern about being able to fall asleep, and decreased depression, according to the Beck Depression Inventory (Engle-Friedman, 1985).

It is particularly noteworthy that awakenings were reduced by treatment, since increased awakenings are among the sleep changes most often associated with aging (Hayashi & Endo, 1982; Webb & Campbell, 1980). The finding of reduced nap taking also runs counter to the general findings associated with advancing age (Miles & Dement, 1980) and certainly indicates that these patterns may be reversible. Particularly encouraging were the results of increased self-efficacy and decreased concern regarding sleep.

The finding of decreased depression following treatment of sleep disturbance is also intriguing. Of older adults, 15–20% experience depression of sufficient severity to seek psychological or psychiatric intervention (Shamoian, 1983). Our results indicated that treatment for insomnia not only improved the sleep process but improved mood as well. It is also possible that improvement in sleep generalized to improved mood. In either case, improved mood may be a benefit of effectively treating sleep disturbance.

All treatments studied in this investigation were effective, but some differential effects did emerge. The amount of improvement from baseline to the end of treatment on reported sleep latency was 35% for SC, 23% for SI, and 8% for PR ($p < .10$). An analysis of covariance of the posttherapy polysomnographic assessment, with the baseline as a covariate, indicated that the addition of either stimulus control or relaxation training to support and information resulted in improved sleep efficiency ($p = .10$). The adjusted sleep efficiency means were 78.6% for PR, 77.3% for SC, and 60.3% for SI. This result is due to a reduction of almost 50% of time spent in stage wake for both SC and PR, with no reduction for SI. These sleep efficiency results are impressive, since sleep efficiency was found to average 67% in 60- to 85-year-old noninsomniacs (Coleman *et al.*, 1981).

To evaluate whether the results were maintained, a 2-year follow-up using telephone interviews and sleep diaries was conducted (Tsao, Bootzin, Hazlewood, & Engle-Friedman, 1985) with 42 of the 53 participants. Half of these participants completed sleep diaries for 1 week. The results showed that clients had maintained or improved upon the results obtained in treatment on measures of total sleep and sleep onset latency. Again, there were few differential treatment effects. Insomniacs who received stimulus control instructions, however, reported that they continued to use components of the treatment more than did those receiving other treatments ($p < .01$); they reported the most improvement on sleep onset latency in their diaries ($p < .01$); and they reported that their sleep was least affected negatively by changing life events ($p < .01$). Thus, while all treatments were effective immediately after treatment and 2 years later, stimulus control instructions were more effective than other treatments on those few measures on which differential effects emerged.

The possibility of improving the sleep of older persons has been demonstrated despite the myriad of factors that may impact on and disrupt sleep, not the least of which is the developmental trend toward sleep disturbance with aging. The most successful treatment outcomes are likely to be those in which the clinician has evaluated the contribution of many variables that could result in sleep disturbance. Once the clinician has eliminated factors that do not play a role in the person's sleep problem, he or she will be able to help the person focus on those factors that may truly interfere with the sleep process. The clinician should remember, however, that the etiological factors in sleep disturbance may not be the factors that maintain it.

CLINICAL RECOMMENDATIONS

In evaluating the sleep disturbance of a client, we recommend that the clinician consider the following points:

1. For the person to have true insomnia, the client himself or herself must report sleep disturbance. If the source of the report of poor sleep is someone else's (e.g., a husband reports that his wife does not get a full 8 hours of sleep), the investigation should go further, because there are vast individual differences in sleep requirements.
2. It is valuable to collect sleep information in a daily sleep diary before instituting treatment. A diary serves as a daily indication of the magnitude of the sleep problem and its variability. Before keeping daily records, clients are often unaware of the frequency and severity of their problems.
3. The duration of sleep disturbance is an important element. A person who reports sleep disturbance for a very short time because of an unusual and time-limited circumstance may be experiencing transient disturbance that

may result in a spontaneous recovery. On the other hand, a person with a considerable duration of sleep disturbance (a month or more) may not show the same ease of resolution. In either case, it is important for the person to maintain good sleep hygiene in order to insure that the sleep disturbance does not become even more troublesome.

4. It is important to evaluate physical problems that could exacerbate sleep disturbance.

5. It is necessary to evaluate the use of prescription and nonprescription medications. Important medications for physical ailments can negatively affect sleep. Clients may be appraised of the contributions the medications have on their sleep. Discussions with the client's physician may lead to a substitution of a less sleep-disrupting medication. Sleep medications themselves have deleterious effects on sleep and a wide range of functions in the older adult. The older adult, the physician, and the clinician can work toward the careful withdrawal of the client from the hypnotic, which may by itself be sufficient to restore good sleep and next-day functioning.

6. It is imperative to evaluate the substances ingested by the older person during the day. Alcohol, a CNS depressant, will impact negatively on respiration during sleep and will cause increased awakenings during the night. A patient who reports drinking wine or brandy to induce sleep should be discouraged from continuing that practice. Stimulants such as caffeine and nicotine are poorly excreted by the older person and will cause nighttime stimulation as well, even if ingested several hours before bedtime.

7. Client reports of functional problems during the day should be evaluated with care. The clinician must inquire about the hangover effects of medication and the occurrence of sleep apnea, restless legs, physical ailments, or sleep deprivation.

8. The clinician should ask about the client's participation in daily stimulating activities. The lack of activities and interests may affect the sleep–wake cycle by making it likely the person will nap intermittently during the day.

9. It is possible that an institutional setting may promote sleep disturbance and therefore institutional factors should be included in the evaluation.

Conclusions

The most important outcome of work done to date on the sleep of older adults indicates that insomnia in the elderly can be effectively treated with short-term nonpharmacological therapy. The magnitude of the effect, particularly on the polysomnographic measures, has not been as large as that obtained with younger insomniacs. Nevertheless, the effects have been substantial and have been shown to impact on some measures (such as awakenings) that are commonly associated with aging and should be difficult to treat. Older insomniacs may benefit from booster sessions to maintain the improvements made during the treatment period.

The majority of research studies presented here evaluated single-treatment components. While such work is essential, a multicomponent treatment combining sleep hygiene information, relaxation training, and stimulus control instructions may be particularly appropriate for some clients. Because many insomniacs lack the skills to deal effectively with the stresses of their environment, training in coping skills such as cognitive restructuring, social skills training, and stress management may be important supplements to the direct treatment of the sleep disorder.

The improved sleep of the older person depends on comprehensive evaluation and the utilization of new treatment approaches. We have a good understanding of the treatment of sleep disturbance in younger populations, and the work presented in this chapter indicates that the same procedures hold considerable promise for the elderly.

REFERENCES

Agnew, H., Webb, W., & Williams, R. L. (1967). Sleep patterns in late middle-aged males: An EEG study. *Electroencephalography and Clinical Neurophysiology, 23,* 168–171.

Albert, M. S. (1981). Geriatric neuropsychology. *Journal of Consulting and Clinical Psychology, 49,* 835–850.

Ancoli-Israel, S., Kripke, D. F., Mason, W., & Messin, S. (1981). Sleep apnea and nocturnal myoclonus in a senior population. *Sleep, 41,* 349–358.

Bengtsson, C., Lennartsson, J., Lindquist, O., Noppa, H., & Sigurdsson, J. (1980). Sleep disturbances, nightmares and other possible central nervous disturbances in a population sample of women, with special reference to those on antihypertensive drugs. *European Journal of Clinical Pharmacology, 17,* 173–177.

Berlin, R. M. (1985). Psychotherapeutic treatment of chronic insomnia. *American Journal of Psychotherapy, 39,* 68–74.

Bernstein, D. S., & Borkovec, T. D. (1973). *Progressive relaxation training.* Champaign, IL: Research Press.

Bliwise, D., Carskadon, M., Carey, E., & Dement, W. (1984). Longitudinal development of sleep-related respiratory disturbance in adult humans. *Journal of Gerontology, 39,* 290–293.

Bliwise, D., Petta, D., Seidel, W., & Dement, W. (1985). Periodic leg movements during sleep in the elderly. *Archives of Gerontology and Geriatrics, 4,* 273–281.

Bonnet, M. H. (1984). The restoration of performance following sleep deprivation in geriatric normal and insomniac subjects. *Sleep Research, 13,* 188.

Bonnet, M. H., & Johnson, L. C. (1978). Relationship of arousal threshold to sleep stage disturbance and subjective estimates of depth and quality of sleep. *Sleep, 1,* 161–168.

Bonnet, M. H., Webb, W. B., & Barnard, G. (1979). Effect of flurazepam, pentobarbital and caffeine on arousal threshold. *Sleep, 1,* 217–219.

Bootzin, R. R. (1972). *Stimulus control treatment of insomnia.* Paper presented at the meeting of the American Psychological Association, Honolulu, HI.

Bootzin, R. R. (1975). *A comparison of stimulus control instructions and progressive relaxation training in the treatment of sleep onset insomnia.* Unpublished manuscript, Northwestern University, Evanston, IL.

Bootzin, R. R. (1976). Self-help techniques for controlling insomnia. In C. M. Franks (Ed.), *Behavior therapy: Techniques, principles, and patient aids.* New York: Bimonitoring Applications.

Bootzin, R. R. (1977). Effects of self-control procedures for insomnia. In R. B. Stuart (Ed.), *Behavioral self-management: Strategies, techniques and outcomes* (pp. 176–195). New York: Brunner-Mazel.

Bootzin, R. R. (1985). The role of expectancy in behavior change. In L. White, G. Schwartz, & B. Tursky (Eds.), *Placebo: Clinical phenomena and new insights* (pp. 196–210). New York: Guilford Press.

Bootzin, R. R., & Engle-Friedman, M. (1981). The assessment of insomnia. *Behavioral Assessment, 3,* 107–126.

Bootzin, R. R., & Nicassio, P. M. (1978). Behavioral treatment for insomnia. In M. Hersen, R. M. Eisler, & P. M. Miller (Eds.), *Progress in behavior modification* (Vol. 6, pp. 1–45). New York: Academic Press.

Bootzin, R. R., Engle-Friedman, M., & Hazlewood, L. (1983). Insomnia. In P. M. Lewinsohn & L. Teri (Eds.), *Clinical geropsychology: New directions in assessment and treatment* (pp. 81–115). New York: Pergamon Press.

Borkovec, T. D. (1982). Insomnia. *Journal of Consulting and Clinical Psychology, 50,* 880–895.

Borkovec, T. D., & Fowles, D. (1973). Controlled investigation of the effects of progressive relaxation and hypnotic relaxation on insomnia. *Journal of Abnormal Psychology, 82,* 153–158.

Butler, R., & Louis, M. (1973). *Aging and mental health: Positive psychosocial approaches.* St. Louis: Mosby.

Carskadon, M. A., Brown, E. D., & Dement, W. C. (1980). Respiration during sleep in the elderly. *Sleep Research, 9,* 99.

Carskadon, M. A., Brown, E. D., & Dement, W. C. (1982). Sleep fragmentation in the elderly: Relationship to daytime sleep tendency. *Neurobiology of Aging, 3,* 321–327.

Castelden, C. M., George, C. F., Marcer, D., & Hallet, C. (1977). Increased sensitivity to nitrazepam in old age. *British Medical Journal, 1,* 10–12.

Coates, T. J., & Thorensen, C. E. (1979). Treating arousals during sleep using behavioral self management. *Journal of Clinical and Consulting Psychology, 47,* 603–605.

Cohen, D., Eisdorfer, C., Prinz, P., Breen, A., Davis, M., & Gadsby, A. (1983). Sleep disturbances in the institutionalized aged. *Journal of the American Geriatric Society, 31,* 79–82.

Coleman, R. M. (1982). Periodic movements in sleep (nocturnal myoclonus) and restless legs syndrome. In C. Guilleminault (Ed.), *Sleeping and waking disorders: Indications and techniques* (pp. 265–295). Menlo Park: Addison-Wesley.

Coleman, R. M., Miles, L. E., Guilleminault, C. C., Zarcone, V. P., van den Hoed, J., & Dement, W. C. (1981). Sleep–wake disorders in the elderly: A polysomnographic analysis. *Journal of the American Geriatric Society, 29,* 289–296.

Costello, C. G., & Smith, C. M. (1963). The relationships between personality, sleep and the effect of sedatives. *British Journal of Psychiatry, 109,* 568–571.

Coursey, R. D., Buchsbaum, M., & Frankel, B. C. (1975). Personality measures and evoked responses in chronic insomniacs. *Journal of Abnormal Psychology, 84,* 239–249.

de la Pena, A., Flickinger, R., & Mayfield, D. (1977). *Reverse first night effect in chronic poor sleepers.* Paper presented at the Association for Psychophysiological Study of Sleep, Houston, TX.

Dement, W. C., Miles, L. E., & Carskadon, M. A. (1982). "White paper" on sleep and aging. *Journal of the American Geriatric Society, 30,* 25–50.

Dolly, F. R., & Block, A. J. (1982). Effect of flurazepam on sleep disoriented breathing and nocturnal oxygen desaturation in asymptomatic subjects. *American Journal of Medicine, 73,* 239–243.

Engle-Friedman, M. (1985). *An evaluation of behavioral treatments for insomnia in the older adult.* Unpublished Ph.D. dissertation, Northwestern University, Evanston, IL.

Evans, J. G., & Jarvis, E. H. (1972). *British Medical Journal, 4,* 487.

Feinberg, I. (1976). Functional implications of change in sleep physiology with age. In R. D. Terry & S. Gershon (Eds.), *Neurobiology of aging* (pp. 23–41). New York: Raven Press.

Feinberg, I., Koresko, R., & Heller, N. (1967). EEG sleep patterns as a function of normal and pathological aging in man. *Journal of Psychiatric Research, 5,* 107–144.

Feinberg, I., Fein, E., Floyd, T. C., & Aminoff, M. J. (1983). Delta (0.5–3 Hz) EEG waveforms during sleep in young and elderly normal subjects. In M. H. Chase (Ed.), *Sleep disorders: Basic and clinical research* (pp. 449–462). New York: Spectrum.

Fordyce, W. F. (1976). *Behavioral methods for chronic pain and illness.* St. Louis: Mosby.

Friedmann, J., Globus, G., Huntley, A., Mulaney, D., Naitch, P., & Johnson, L. (1977). Performance and mood during and after gradual sleep reduction. *Psychophysiology, 14,* 245–250.

Gerard, P., Collins, K., & Dore, C. (1978). Subjective characteristics of sleep in the elderly. *Age and Aging, 7,* 55.

Gross, M. M., Goodenough, D. R., Nagarajan, M., & Hastey, J. M. (1973). Sleep changes induced by four and six days of experimental alcoholization and withdrawal in humans. In M. M. Gross (Ed.), *Alcohol intoxication and withdrawal: Experimental studies* (pp. 291–304). New York: Plenum.

Guazelli, M., Feinberg, I., Aminoff, M., Fein, G., Floyd, T. C., & Maggini, C. (1986). Sleep spindles in normal elderly: Comparison with young adult patterns and relation to nocturnal awakening, cognitive functioning and brain atrophy. *Electroencephalography and Clinical Neurophysiology, 63,* 526–539.

Guilleminault, C., & Dement, W. C. (1978). Sleep apnea syndromes and related sleep disorders. In R. L. Williams & I. Karacan (Eds.), *Sleep disorders: Diagnosis and treatment* (pp. 9–28). New York: Wiley.

Guilleminault, C., & Silvestri, R. (1982). Aging, drugs and sleep. *Neurobiology of Aging, 3,* 379–386.

Hartmann, E. (1968). Longitudinal studies of sleep and dream patterns in manic–depressive patients. *Archives of General Psychiatry, 19,* 321–329.

Hauri, P. (1970). Evening activity, sleep mentation and subjective sleep quality. *Journal of Abnormal Psychology, 76,* 270–275.

Hauri, P. (1977). *The sleep disorders.* Kalamazoo, MI: Upjohn.

Hayashi, Y., & Endo, S. (1982). All night sleep polygraphic recordings of healthy aged persons: REM and slow wave sleep. *Sleep, 5,* 277–283.

Haynes, S. N., Follingstad, D. K., & McGowan, W. T. (1974). Insomnia: Sleep patterns and anxiety level. *Journal of Psychosomatic Research, 18,* 69–74.

Haynes, S. N., Price, M. G., & Simons, J. B. (1975). Stimulus control treatment of insomnia. *Journal of Behavior Therapy and Experimental Psychiatry, 6,* 279–282.

Healy, E. S., Kales, A., Monroe, L. J., Bixler, E. O., Chamberlin, K., & Soldatos, C. R. (1981). Onset of insomnia: Role of life-stress events. *Psychosomatic Medicine, 43,* 439–451.

Hemminki, E., & Heikkila, J. (1975). Elderly people's compliance with prescriptions and quality of medication. *Scandanavian Journal of Social Medicine, 3,* 87–92.

Hoch, C. C., Reynolds, C. F., III, Kupfer, D. J., Houck, P. R., Berman, S. R., & Stack, J. A. (1986). Sleep disordered breathing in normal and pathological aging. *Journal of Clinical Psychiatry, 47,* 499–503.

Institute of Medicine (1979). *Sleeping pills, insomnia and medical practice.* Washington, DC: National Academy of Science.

Jacobson, E. (1938). *Progressive relaxation.* Chicago: University of Chicago Press.

Jacobson, E. (1964). *Anxiety and tension control.* Philadelphia: Lippincott.

Kahn, E., & Fisher, C. (1969). The sleep characteristics of the normal aged male. *Journal of Nervous and Mental Disease, 148,* 474–494.

Kales, A., & Kales, J. D. (1970). Evaluation, diagnosis and treatment of clinical conditions related to sleep. *Journal of the American Medical Association, 213,* 2229–2234.

Kales, A., Wilson, T., Kales, J. D., Jacobson, A., Paulson, M., Kollar, E., & Walter, R. O. (1967). Measurement of all-night sleep in normal elderly persons: Effects of aging. *Journal of the American Geriatric Society, 15,* 405–415.

Kales, A., Allen, W. C., Scharf, M. B., & Kales, J. D. (1970). Hypnotic drugs and effectiveness: All-night EEG studies of insomniac subjects. *Archives of General Psychiatry, 23,* 226–232.

Kales, A., Caldwell, A. B., Preston, T. A., Healey, S., & Kales, J. D. (1976). Personality patterns in insomnia. *Archives of General Psychiatry, 33,* 1128–1134.

Kales, A., Scharf, M. B., & Kales, J. D. (1978). Rebound insomnia: A new clinical syndrome. *Science, 201,* 1039–1040.

Kales, J. (1975). Aging and sleep. In R. Goldman & M. Rickstein (Eds.), *Symposium of the psychology and pathology of aging* (pp. 187–202). New York: Academic Press.

Kales, J., Tan, T., Searingen, C., & Kales, A. (1971). Are over-the-counter sleep medications effective? All night EEG studies. *Current Therapeutic Research, 13,* 143–151.

Karacan, I., & Williams, R. L. (1983). Sleep disorders in the elderly. *American Family Physician, 27,* 143–152.

Karacan, I., Thornby, J., Anch, M., Holzer, C. E., Warheit, G. J., Schwab, J. J., & Williams, R. L. (1976). Prevalence of sleep disturbance in a primarily urban Florida county. *Social Science Medicine, 10,* 239–244.

Kleitman, N. (1963). *Sleep and wakefulness.* Chicago: University of Chicago Press.

Krieger, J., Turlot, J., Mangin, P., & Kurtz, D. (1983). Breathing during sleep in normal young and elderly subjects: Hyponeas, apneas and correlated factors. *Sleep, 6,* 108–120.

Kronholm, E., & Hyyppa, M. T. (1985). Age-related sleep habits and retirement. *Annals of Clinical Research, 17,* 257–264.

Kupfer, D. J., & Foster, F. G. (1978). EEG sleep and depression. In R. L. Williams & I. Karacan (Eds.), *Sleep disorders: Diagnosis and treatment* (pp. 163–204). New York: Wiley.

Kupfer, D. J., Reynolds, C. F., III, Ulrich, R. F., Shaw, D. H., & Coble, P. A. (1982). EEG sleep, depression, and aging. *Neurobiology of Aging, 3,* 351–360.

Lacks, P., Bertelsen, A. D., Gans, L., & Kunkel, J. (1983). The effectiveness of three behavioral treatments for different degrees of sleep onset insomnia. *Behavioral Therapy, 14,* 593–605.

Lacks, P., Bertelson, A. D., Sugerman, J., & Kunkel, J. (1983). The treatment of sleep-maintenance insomnia with stimulus control techniques. *Behavior Research and Therapy, 21,* 291–295.

Lawrence, P. S., & Tokarz, T. (1976). *A comparison of relaxation training and stimulus control.* Paper presented at the Association for the Advancement of Behavior Therapy, New York.

Lester, B. K., Rundell, O. H., Cowden, L. C., & Williams, H. L. (1973). Chronic alcoholism, alcohol and sleep. In M. M. Gross (Ed.), *Alcohol intoxication and withdrawal: Experimental studies.* New York: Plenum.

Lick, J. P., & Heffler, D. (1977). Relaxation training and attention placebo in the treatment of severe insomnia. *Journal of Clinical and Consulting Psychology, 45,* 153–161.

Lorrain, D., De Koninck, J., Dionne, H., & Goupil, G. (1986). Sleep positions and postural shifts in elderly persons. *Perceptual and Motor Skills, 63,* 352–354.

Lowenstein, R. J., Weingartner, H., Gillin, J. C., Kaye, W., Ebert, M., & Mendelson, W. B. (1982). Disturbances of sleep and cognitive functioning in patients with dementia. *Neurobiology of Aging, 3,* 371–377.

Lugaresi, E., Coccagna, G., Berti-Ceroni, G., & Ambrosetta, C. (1968). Restless legs and nocturnal myoclonus. In H. Gastant, E. Lugaresi, G. Berti-Ceroni, & G. Coccagna (Eds.), *The abnormalities of sleep in man* (pp. 285–294). Bologna, Italy: Aulogaggi.

MacDonald, J. B., & MacDonald, E. T. (1977). Nocturnal femoral fracture and continuing widespread use of barbiturate hypnotics. *British Medical Journal, 2,* 483–485.

McGhie, A., & Russel, S. (1962). The subjective assessment of normal sleep patterns. *Journal of Mental Science, 108,* 642–654.

McGinty, D., Littner, M., Beahm, E., Ruiz-Primo, E., Young, E., & Saver, J. (1982). Sleep related breathing disorders in older men: A search for underlying mechanisms. *Neurobiology of Aging, 3,* 337–350.

Meddis, R. (1977). *The sleep instinct.* London: Routledge & Kegan Paul.

Mellinger, G. D., Balter, M. B., & Uhlenhuth, E. H. (1985). Insomnia and its treatment. *Archives of General Psychiatry, 42,* 225–232.

Mendelson, W. B., Gillin, J. C., & Wyatt, R. J. (1977). *Human sleep and its disorders.* New York: Plenum.

Miles, L. E., & Dement, W. C. (1980). Sleep and aging. *Sleep, 3,* 119–120.

Morgan, K., & Oswald, I. (1981). Anxiety caused by a short-life hypnotic. *British Medical Journal, 284,* 942.

National Institutes of Health. (1983). *Consensus development conference summary: Drugs and insomnia, 4,* Bethesda, MD: Office of Medical Applications Research.

Nicassio, P. M., & Bootzin, R. R. (1974). A comparison of progressive relaxation training and autogenic training as treatment for insomnia. *Journal of Abnormal Psychology, 83,* 253–260.

Pack, A. I., & Millman, R. P. (1986). Changes in control of ventilation, awake and asleep in the elderly. *Journal of the American Geriatrics Society, 34,* 533–544.

Pasnau, R. O., Naitch, P., Stier, S., & Kollar, E. J. (1968). The psychological effects of 205 hours of sleep deprivation. *Archives of General Psychiatry, 18,* 496–505.

Pfeiffer, E. (1977). The patients of geriatric psychiatry. *Career Directions, 5,* 20–38.

Physicians' desk reference. (1987). Oradell, NJ: Edward R. Barnhart, Medical Economics.

Pressman, M. R., DiPhillipo, M. A., & Fry, J. M. (1986). Senile miosis: The possible contribution of disordered sleep and daytime sleepiness. *Journal of Gerontology, 41,* 629–634.

Prinz, P., (1977). Sleep patterns in the healthy aged: Relationship with intellectual function. *Journal of Gerontology, 32,* 179–186.

Prinz, P., & Raskind, M. (1978). Aging and sleep disorders. In R. Williams & I. Karacan (Eds.), *Sleep Disorders: Diagnosis and treatment* (pp. 303–321). New York: Wiley.

Prinz, P., Obrist, W., & Wang, H. (1975). Sleep patterns in healthy elderly subjects: Individual differences as related to other neurological variables. *Sleep Research, 4,* 132.

Prinz, P. N., Reskind, E. R., Vitaliano, P. P., Raskind, M. A., Eisdorfer, C., Zemcuznikov, N., & Gerber, C. J. (1982). Changes in the sleep and waking EEGs of nondemented and demented elderly subjects. *Journal of the American Geriatric Society, 30,* 86–93.

Prinz, P. N., Vitaliano, P. P., Vitiello, M. V., Bokan, J., Raskind, M., Peskind, E., & Gerber, C. (1982). Sleep,

EEG and mental function changes in senile dementia of the Alzheimer's type. *Neurobiology of Aging, 3,* 361–370.

Puder, R., Lacks, P., Bertelsen, A. D., & Storandt, M. (1983). Short-term stimulus control treatment of insomnia in older adults. *Behavior Therapy, 14,* 424–429.

Raskind, M. (1977). Why don't you sleep like you used to? *Drug Therapy, 7,* 51–52.

Rechtschaffen, A., & Kales, A (Eds.). (1968). *A manual of standardized terminology, techniques and scoring system for sleep stages of human subjects.* Washington, DC: U.S. Government Printing Office.

Reynolds, C. F., Kupfer, D. J., Taska, L. S., Hoch, C. C., Sewitch, D. E., & Spiker, D. G. (1985). Sleep and healthy seniors: A revisit. *Sleep, 8,* 20–29.

Roehrs, T., Zorick, F., Sicklesteel, J., Wittig, R., & Roth, T. (1983). Age related sleep–wake disorders at a sleep disorder center. *Journal of the American Geriatric Society, 31,* 364–369.

Rowe, J. W. (1985). Health care of the elderly. *New England Journal of Medicine, 312,* 827–835.

Sanchez, R., & Bootzin, R. R. (1985). A comparison of white noise and music: Effects of predictable and unpredictable sounds on sleep. *Sleep Research, 14,* 121.

Sewitch, D. E., Kupfer, D. J., & Reynolds, C. F., III. (1986). Alpha-NREM sleep distributed across the 24-hour day in a legally blind, elderly male. *Biological Psychiatry, 21,* 201–207.

Shamoian, C. A. (1983). Psychogeriatrics. *Medical Clinics of North America, 67,* 361–378.

Slama, K. (1975). *Stimulus control and progressive relaxation procedures in the treatment of sleep onset disturbance.* Unpublished master's thesis, University of Iowa, Iowa City.

Smith, J., Karacan, I., & Yang, M. (1977). Ontogeny of delta activity during human sleep. *Electroencephalography and Clinical Neurophysiology, 43,* 229–237.

Smith, P. L., & Bleecker, E. R. (1986). Ventilatory control during sleep in the elderly. *Geriatric Clinics of North America, 2,* 227–240.

Snyder, F. (1966). Toward an evolutional theory of dreaming. *American Journal of Psychiatry, 123,* 121–126.

Soldatos, C. R., Kales, J. D., Scharf, M. B., Bixler, E. O., & Kales, A. (1980). Cigarette smoking associated with sleep difficulty. *Science, 207,* 551–553.

Soldatos, C. R., Bixler, E. O., & Kales, A. (1985). *Behavioral side-effects of benzodiazepine hypnotics.* Paper presented at the IVth World Congress of Biological Psychiatry, Philadelphia.

Starker, S., & Hasenfeld, R., (1976). Daydream styles and sleep disturbance. *Journal of Nervous and Mental Disease, 163,* 391–400.

Statistical bulletin of the metropolitan life insurance company. (1978).

Strauch, I., & Wollschlaeger, M. (1973). Sleep behavior in the aged. In U. Jovanovic (Ed.), *The nature of sleep* (pp. 129–131). Stuttgart: Fischer.

Toler, H. C. (1978). The treatment of insomnia with relaxation and stimulus control instructions among incarcerated males. *Criminal Justice and Behavior, 5,* 117–130.

Tsao, C., Bootzin, R. R., Hazlewood, L., & Engle-Friedman, M. (1985). Long-term follow-up of the effectiveness of several behavioral treatments for older adult insomniacs. Unpublished paper, Northwestern University, Evanston, IL.

Turner, R. M., & Ascher, M. (1979). Controlled comparison of progressive relaxation, stimulus control and paradoxical intention therapies for insomnia. *Journal of Consulting and Clinical Psychology, 49,* 500–508.

Turner, R. M., & Ascher, L. M. (1982). Therapist factor in the treatment of insomnia. *Behaviour Research and Therapy, 17,* 107–112.

U.S. Public Health Service. (1976). *Physicians' drug prescribing patterns in skilled nursing facilities.* Washington, DC: U.S. Department of Health, Education and Welfare.

Webb, W. B. (1975). *Sleep: The gentle tyrant.* Englewood Cliffs, NJ: Spectrum.

Webb, W. B. (1982a). Sleep in older persons: Sleep structures of 50 to 60 year old men and women. *Journal of Gerontology, 37,* 581–586.

Webb, W. B. (1982b). The measurement and characteristics of sleep in older persons. *Neurobiology of Aging, 3,* 311–319.

Webb, W. B., & Agnew, H. W., Jr. (1974). The effects of a chronic limitation of sleep length. *Psychophysiology, 11,* 265–274.

Webb, W. B., & Campbell, S. S. (1980). Awakenings and the return to sleep in an older population. *Sleep, 3,* 41–46.

Webb, W. B., & Debrow, L. M. (1982). A modified method for scoring slow wave sleep of older subjects. *Sleep, 5*, 195–199.

Webb, W. B., & Levy, C. M. (1982). Age, sleep deprivation and performance. *Psychophysiology, 19*, 272–276.

Webb, W. B., & Swinburne, H. (1971). An observational study of sleep in the aged. *Perceptual Motor Skills, 32*, 895–898.

Weitzman, E. D., Moline, M. L., Czeisler, C. A., & Zimmerman, J. C. (1982). Chronobiology of aging: Temperature, sleep–wake rhythms and entrainment. *Neurobiology of Aging, 3*, 299–309.

Wessler, R., Rubin, M., & Sollberger, A. (1976). Circadian rhythm of activity of sleep–wakefulness in elderly institutionalized patients. *Journal of Interdisciplinary Cycle Research, 7*, 333.

Williams, R. L., Karacan, I., & Hursch, C. J. (1974). *EEG of human sleep: Clinical applications.* New York: Wiley.

Yesavage, J., Bliwise, D., Guilleminault, C., Carskadon, M., & Dement, W. (1985). Preliminary communication: Intellectual deficit and sleep related respiratory disturbance in the elderly. *Sleep, 8*, 30–33.

Yoss, R. E., Moyer, N., & Ogle, K. (1969). The pupillogram and narcolepsy: A method to measure decreased levels of wakefulness. *Neurology, 19*, 921–928.

Youkilis, H. D., & Bootzin, R. R. (1981). A psychophysiological perspective on the etiology and treatment of insomnia. In S. N. Haynes, & L. A. Gannon (Eds.), *Psychosomatic disorders: A psychophysiological approach in etiology and treatment* (pp. 179–221). New York: Praeger.

Zarit, S. H., & Zarit, J. M. (1983). Cognitive impairment. In P. M. Lewinsohn, & L. Teri (Eds.), *Clinical geropsychology: New directions in assessment and treatment* (pp. 38–80). New York: Pergammon Press.

Zepelin, H. (1973). A survey of age differences in sleep patterns and dream recall among well-educated men and women. *Sleep Research, 2*, 81.

Zepelin, H., McDonald, C. S., & Zammit, G. K. (1984). Effects of age on auditory awakening thresholds. *Journal of Gerontology, 39*, 294–300.

13

Behavioral Treatment of Aged Alcoholics and Drug Addicts

ARTHUR MACNEILL HORTON, JR.
AND CHARLES J. FOGELMAN

From earliest recorded time, individuals have used substances to change their moods, perceptions, and behaviors. Primitive people used naturally available substances from plants, such as peyote from the cactus, marijuana leaves, or opium from the poppy plant. More developed cultures processed raw materials to produce alcohol, heroin, and cocaine. Modern times have brought technological advances in chemistry that have included methadone, LSD, and PCP, among others.

Substance abuse problems are long standing and worldwide. In the early 1600s, tobacco, introduced to Europeans by Columbus, was opposed by the government of King James I. In the 1700s to 1800s, the use of opium was vigorously opposed in China by the Emperor. Perhaps the most inglorious chapter of British imperialism was that which details the two Opium Wars, which ended in a treaty legalizing the drug. In 1920 the United States prohibited alcohol, only to allow it again in 1933.

DEFINITIONS

It is well known that societal norms play a role in determining if the use of a particular substance is maladaptive behavior. For example, some American Indian tribes in the southwest use peyote as part of their religious ceremonies; the Roman Catholic Church and Judaism include the use of alcohol in their rites.

In the United States, the most commonly accepted definitions of substance

ARTHUR MACNEILL HORTON, JR. • Department of Psychiatry, University of Maryland Medical School, Baltimore, Maryland 21218.   CHARLES J. FOGELMAN • The Baltimore Psychologists, Baltimore, Maryland 21420.   Dr. Horton's contribution was made in his capacity as a private citizen and was neither reported or endorsed by the federal government.

abuse and dependence are given in the third edition of the *Diagnostic and Statistical Manual of Mental Disorders* (DSM-III; APA, 1980) in the category of "Substance Use Disorders." DSM-III asserts that this group of disorders, ". . . deals with behavioral changes associated with more or less regular use of substances that affect the central nervous system" (p. 163). Behavioral changes include impairment in the ability to interact socially or to work productively; failure to regulate or terminate substance use; and, in some cases, physical or psychological withdrawal symptoms after lessened or interrupted substance intake. These sorts of behavioral changes are considered maladaptive by most segments of American society. Nonpathological use for recreational or medical purposes is, of course, distinguished from the above by the severity of the behavioral changes.

The revised third edition of the *Diagnostic and Statistical Manual of the American Psychiatric Association* (DSM-III-R; APA, 1987) includes some dramatic changes. The concept of a psychoactive substance disorder has been introduced, with this crucial element: "a cluster of cognitive, behavioral, and physiologic symptoms that indicate that the person has impaired control of psychoactive substance use and continues use of the substance despite adverse consequences" (p. 166).

Essentially, the range of symptoms that might classify a person as suffering from a psychoactive substance abuse disorder has been extended beyond the physiological to the cognitive and behavioral realms. In addition, dependence is seen as having degrees of severity, and DSM III-R provides specific guidelines for assessing if a person's dependence is mild, moderate, or severe or is in partial or full remission.

In the general diagnosis of psychoactive substance dependence there are two major criteria. First, the person must have at least three of nine symptoms of dependence from the following list (APA, 1987, pp. 167–168): (1) the substance is often taken in large amounts or over a longer period than the person intended; (2) the person has a persistent desire or has made one or more unsuccessful efforts to cut down or control substance use; (3) the person spends a great deal of time in activities necessary to obtain the substance, take or recover from its effects; (4) the person experiences frequent intoxication or withdrawal symptoms when expected to fulfill major role obligations at work, school, or home or when the substance makes some activity (e.g., driving) physically hazardous; (5) the person gives up or reduces participation in important social, occupational, or recreational activities because of substance use; (6) the person continues to use the harmful substance despite knowledge of having a persistent or recurrent social, psychological, or physical problem that is caused or exacerbated by the use of the substance; (7) the person has a marked tolerance for the substance and a need for markedly increased amounts of the substance (i.e., at least 50% increase) in order to achieve intoxication or the desired effect, or has a markedly diminished effect with the continued use of the same amount of the substance; (8) there are characteristic withdrawal symptoms; and (9) the person often takes the substance to relieve or avoid withdrawal symptoms. (These last two items may not apply to cannabis, hallucinogens, or phencyclidine.)

The second major criterion is that some of the symptoms must have lasted 1 month or have occurred more than once over a longer period of time.

Substances Abused

DSM-III-R (APA, 1987) classified nine substances associated with both abuse and dependence. These are alcohol, cocaine, hallucinogens, inhalants, phencyclidine (PCP) or similarly acting arylcyclohexylamines, opioids, amphetamines or similarly acting sympathomimetics, cannabis, and sedatives, hypnotics, or xiolytics.

Many of these substances can produce associated substance-induced organic mental disorder. The direct acute and/or chronic effects of some of the above substances on the central nervous system may be classified as an intoxication, withdrawal or delirium, delusional disorder, mood disorder, or other syndromes.

Aging and Substance Use Disorder

Aging affects different substance use disorders in different ways. Perhaps most dramatic is opioid dependence. With an annual death rate of 1% (10 per 1,000) or higher each year, and an age of onset in the late teens or early 20s, many opioid-dependent persons do not survive into old age. The violent and criminal lifestyle associated with the drug, as well as medical complications, are responsible for the deaths of many. Many others end usage with increasing years.

The use of other substances, such as cocaine, PCP, or amphetamines, are either of unknown course or completely unstudied in the elderly. This chapter will focus upon the particular substances for which some information is available about elderly citizens. These are alcohol and barbiturates or similarly acting sedatives and opioids. Tobacco, while clearly a substance for which a dependency can be demonstrated, is not associated with impairment of social or occupational functioning and is therefore excluded from further consideration. This omission should in no way be considered an endorsement of tobacco use in any form or condition.

In this chapter we will first discuss the assessment and behavioral treatment of elderly alcoholics and then devote attention to what little is known about treating elderly persons who abuse barbiturates or similarly acting sedatives or hypnotics. Due to admittedly large gaps in the empirical literature regarding the treatment of the elderly for inappropriate alcohol and drug use, some sections will be primarily based upon personal clinical experience with these patients, which we hope will spark empirical efforts in these areas.

Although this chapter focuses on behavioral treatment approaches, we do not mean to devalue nonbehavioral approaches. It is, of course, important to make available to the clinician as much information as possible. A comparison of various treatment approaches is a fruitful enterprise and prevents the development of parochial viewpoints. Unfortunately, a recent methodological review of the various modalities of alcoholism treatment (Civiello & Horton, 1988) revealed such problems with outcome measures as to preclude the drawing of conclusions regarding the relative values of any treatment approaches. At present, theoretical preferences rest on clinical biases rather than empirical data.

AGING ALCOHOLICS

In this section we will first survey some relevant epidemiological facts regarding the elderly who abuse alcohol. Next, we will present a case for subtypes among the aging alcoholic population. And finally, we will consider definitional problems and treatment settings for the elderly alcoholic.

Epidemiology

The fact that health problems associated with aging will be *the* major public health issue of the next half century is well known (Horton, 1982). The explosive growth rate of the aging population in the United States can only be appreciated if one recalls that in 1920, only 5% of the population was above age 65; by 1980, the figure doubled. By the year 2000, 20% of the U.S. population or 40,000,000 people, will be above age 65.

Alcoholism is the major mental health problem of the century. Over 10 million Americans of all ages either abuse or are addicted to alcohol (Mendelson & Mello, 1985). Alcohol has been implicated in many health problems, including heart disease, hepatitis, cirrhosis of the liver, and cancers of the mouth, esophagus, larynx, liver, and other organs. The economic costs of alcohol abuse are substantial. When lost productivity at work is added to property damage and health care bills, the associated costs of alcohol abuse are estimated to exceed 100 billion dollars.

Less well known are the mental health effects of alcoholism. Estimates suggest that 86% of homicide cases involve alcohol and that 50% of rapes and automobile accidents are alcohol related. Particularly startling data regarding the prevalence of alcoholism were published in the October 1984 issue of *Archives of General Psychiatry*. These data suggest that 19% of the U.S. population have mental disorders, and that the most frequent mental disorder for males of all ages was alcohol abuse. Alcohol abuse was the most common diagnosis for males from 18 to 64 and the third most common disorder for those over age 65.

The best available data suggest that 10–20% of the elderly are alcoholic. Interestingly, prevalence estimates often appear to covary with treatment settings (Schuckit & Pastor, 1978). For example, in nursing home populations about 20% of the residents have been diagnosed as alcoholics (Graux, 1969). Surveys of general medical wards show similar rates, but provide a range between 15% and 20% (Barchha, Stewart, & Guze, 1968; McCusker, Cherubin, & Zimberg, 1971). Community-dwelling samples show prevalence rates of approximately 10% (Glatt, 1961; Rosen & Glatt, 1968). The possible cause for the covariance of higher rates by alcoholism and more structured and intensive treatment settings could be that as alcoholics drink they become more mentally and physically impaired and thus make up a larger portion of the elderly in medical wards and nursing homes.

Subtypes

A wealth of data suggest that there are two distinct and reliable subtypes of aging alcoholics (Gaitz & Baer, 1971; Rosen & Glatt, 1968; Simon, Epstein, &

Reynolds, 1968; Zimberg, 1978). These subtypes can be differentiated in terms of age of onset. Those who began drinking at an early age (before or during their early 20s) constitute about two-thirds of the aged alcoholic population (Zimberg, 1978). By contrast, one-third of elderly alcoholics began to drink during or after their middle 50s (Zimberg, 1978). While it is true that people become alcoholics between the ages of 20 and 50, the onset of heavy drinking is early or late. Due to their physiological vigor, people who begin heavy drinking at age 20 often do not show the social, emotional, occupational, and neuropsychological effects of alcoholism for 20 to 30 years. Individuals over age 50 are more likely to show less delay between the onset of heavy drinking and the beginning of problems related to drinking.

There are a number of factors that appear to characterize each subgroup. Early-onset elderly alcoholics are more likely to demonstrate a lifelong personality pattern of addiction (Zimberg, 1978). The late-onset alcoholic is thought to drink in response to external stresses associated with aging rather than personality or internal factors. These late-onset alcoholics are likely to drink less alcohol than early-onset alcoholics, but are more likely to drink on a daily basis. Unfortunately, there is so little research on subtypes of elderly alcoholics that it is not possible to offer even an educated hypothesis about gender differences, socioeconomic status, the effects of rural or urban settings, and so forth.

Stresses Associated with Aging

There is no doubt that old age is a time of loss and declining resources. As one grows older, social opportunities diminish. Children grow up and have their own interests. Neighbors move away and coworkers take different jobs. Spouses may become ill and pass away. The elderly are often in poor health and are more likely to have a debilitating medical illness. Financial status declines. With retirement, most pension plans provide only a fraction of one's former income. At the same time, expenses remain relatively constant or increase with inflation. The result is "golden years" on very little "silver," much less "gold."

Any or all of these conditions may contribute to excessive drinking among elderly. The wonder is that, if these factors are truly stressful, there are not more elderly who use alcohol as a way to cope. The current research literature is inadequate to address the issue of whether or not alcoholism among the elderly is a growing or static problem. Nor is it possible to say why these stresses appear to pay a role in the drinking of some elderly people and not others.

TREATING THE ELDERLY ALCOHOLIC

At this point, some attention should be devoted to treatment considerations regarding the elderly alcoholic. In order to provide a conceptual framework, we will first address definitional problems and some problems generated by various treatment settings. Then we will discuss methods of assessment, treatment studies, and guidelines for treatment of the alcoholic.

Problems of Identification

The first consideration in the initiation of treatment for elderly alcoholics is the identification of these patients. This can be something of a problem. While the *Diagnostic and Statistical Manual* (DSM-III-R) of the American Psychiatric Association (1987) provides a definition of alcohol abuse, there are difficulties in applying this definition to the elderly alcoholic of the late-onset type. In younger alcoholics, work performance and family relations provide a standard of measurement. Elderly alcoholics of the late-onset type are often retired and live alone. They hide their drinking from others and often refuse to admit that they have problems. If one cannot rely upon the patient's self-report and there is no opportunity for observation, it is difficult to detect alcohol abuse problems.

Problems with Treatment Settings

An issue of some concern relates to the setting most appropriate for initiating treatment with elderly alcoholics. Each of the more traditional settings has some benefits for treating aging alcoholics, along with some problems. One setting is an alcohol treatment facility in which elderly alcoholics are treated along with younger alcoholics. Such a setting provides considerable expertise and experience in diagnosing and treating alcoholics, but it is often biased toward younger clients who can be returned to gainful employment. Young, attractive, verbal, and intelligent patients are preferred to elderly patients who may be unattractive, nonverbal, and demented. Negative attitudes toward the elderly are common in nonaging-focused treatment settings and can be expected in alcoholism treatment settings as well. By contrast, facilities for the elderly have a different set of strengths and weaknesses. They have a wealth of expertise in treating elderly individuals, but often do not know how to deal effectively with the difficult problems of the alcoholic population. Such facilities may have negative attitudes toward the alcoholic. There is no way to resolve the issue of which setting is better until an empirical test is made between them.

Behavioral Assessment of Aging Alcholics

In order to discuss the behavioral assessment of aging alcoholics, it is necessary first to distinguish between general and specific behavioral assessment following John D. Cone's (1978) conceptualization of the behavioral assessment funnel. Cone distinguishes between the utilization of broad-based screening instruments that enable one to make comparisons with normative data for large populations and the more specific, individual, and flexible assessment tools that enable one to make interindividual comparisons over time to demonstrate individual behavior change. For example, the Minnesota Multiphasic Personality Inventory (MMPI) is sometimes used by behaviorists to screen for general psychopathology in alcoholic populations because of its empirical research base. In this context, the MMPI is an example of general behavioral assessment. Examples of specific behavioral assessments include self-monitoring of urges to drink in specific situations and in the company of certain types of people. These assessment formats are used in a complementary manner, beginning with a general behavioral assessment and followed by specific behavioral measures. The permutations of general and specific behavioral assessments that can be demanded by various single-subject research designs are virtually endless.

Second, it is necessary to distinguish between diagnosis and assessment. Diagnosis requires the assignment of the patient to a specific group or category (Horton & Wedding, 1984). It is simply a question of placing a label on the subject. In the best of worlds (not always the present one), a label has straightforward treatment implications. By contrast, the process of assessment requires the description of the patient on a specific dimension of functioning. The description can be quite dynamic and flexible with respect to a number of varied parameters at the same time.

It is important to underscore the point that *often* assessments focus on specific behavioral measures while diagnoses focus on general behavioral measures. The word "often" is especially emphasized because these relationships are not hard and fast.

The functional ability of elderly alcoholics is determined along a number of dimensions. Miller and Hester (1980) have identified the following as most important: the amount of alcohol and drugs used; neuropsychological effects of alcohol; existing psychopathology; and specific behavioral assessment. We will examine each of these areas in the following section.

Alcohol and Drug Use

The Comprehensive Drinker Profile (CDP; Marlatt & Miller, 1984) is a structured intake interview widely used to assess alcohol and drug use. It normally requires 1–2 hours to complete, and it can be administered by paraprofessionals after appropriate training and experience. The CDP is organized in three major sections. In the first section demographic information is elicited, including data on age, residence, family status, employment and income information, and educational history. In the second section the client reports on his or her drinking history, covering subareas on the development of the drinking problem, drinking settings, associated behaviors, beverage preferences, and relevant medical history. In the third section information on motivation is gathered. A person describes reasons for drinking, the effects of drinking, other life problems, and motivation for treatment.

While it is clearly the most comprehensive structured clinical interview for the behavioral assessment of alcoholism, the CDP is flawed for use with elderly alcoholics because it lacks age-specific normative data. Like all self-report measures, it is useful to supplement the information gained from it with reports from significant others and official records (e.g., arrest records, driving records, paycheck stubs, etc.). Research on alcoholics' self-reports indicates that they are often accurate on major life events related to alcohol, but sometimes they unduly minimize current drinking behaviors (Polich, 1982).

Neuropsychological Effects

Elderly alcoholics generally score in the range associated with brain damage on the Halstead–Reitan Neuropsychological Test Battery (Parsons & Farr, 1981). In terms of general ability patterns, elderly alcoholics show relatively well-preserved verbal abilities and general psychometric intelligence. Yet they consistently show deficits in abstract thinking and problem solving involving integration of novel materials, particularly of a visual–spatial nature (Chelune & Parker, 1981). Specific tests of the Halstead–Reitan on which alcoholics have consistently demonstrated impaired neuropsychological abilities include the category test (a measure of abstract reasoning), Part B of the trail marking test (a measure of cognitive flexibility), and the tactual performance test (a measure of tactual–spatial psychomotor problem solving) (Chelune & Parker, 1981). On the Wechsler Adult Intelligence Scale (WAIS), which is often considered part of the Halstead–Reitan Battery, alcoholics show significant impairment in block design (a measure of visual–spatial problem solving), object assembly (a measure of visual problem solving), and digit symbol (a measure of visual–motor problem solving) (Parsons & Farr, 1981). In an attempt to summarize the general patterns of test performance obtained by alcoholics as a group on the Halstead–Reitan Battery, Chelune and Parker (1981) have said, "Alcoholics have particular difficulty on higher-order cognitive tasks that require integration of new information in the immediate setting" (p. 196).

The work of Butters and colleagues (Butters, 1985; Butters & Cermak, 1980; Ryan & Butters, 1986) on the memory disorders of alcoholics has filled an important gap in the research utilizing the Halstead–Reitan. They have demonstrated continuities in memory deficits between alcoholic Korsakoff patients and long-term non-Korsakoff alcoholics. Combined with the findings of Parker and Noble (1972), who found alcoholic consumption-related cognitive deficits in social drinkers, this evidence completes the picture of progressive neurotoxic effects associated with alcohol use.

An important moderator variable in both quantitative and qualitative studies of the neuropsychological effects of alcoholism is length of time a person abstains from alcohol. Kleinknecht and Goldstein (1972) demonstrated that there are three types of cerebral dysfunction associated with alcoholism: short-term reversible; intermediate-term reversible; and permanent. Maximal recovery from the intermediate cognitive effects of alcohol abuse occurs between 15 and 21 days of abstinence (Kish, Hagan, Woody, & Harvey, 1980).

At this point we will attempt to draw some clinical implications for treatment from the neuropsychological literature on alcoholics. First, a clinician should realize that alcoholics have impaired cognitive functioning, despite an absence of clinically obvious or organic mental impairment, when setting counseling goals and making vocational decisions (Chelune & Parker, 1981). Second, given the temporal course of cognitive recovery from the mental effects of alcohol abuse, it is best to delay intensive psychotherapeutic intervention until 3 weeks following detoxification (Kish *et al.*, 1980). Indeed, failures to find differential outcome for varying amounts of psychotherapeutic treatment of alcoholics (Mosher, Davis, Mulligan, & Iber, 1975) could be due to the intermediate-reversible effects of alcohol abuse. Third, the prognosis of treatment appears to be inversely related to the degree of deterioration in neuro-psychological functioning (Miller, 1982).

Many of these most sensitive tests of the neurotoxic effects of alcoholism are also particularly sensitive to the effects of aging (Miller & Saucedo, 1983). One possible solution to this problem is afforded by the Brain Age Quotient (BAQ), devised by Ralph M. Reitan (1973). The BAQ is an actuarial combination of six neuropsychological test scores (in the categories of test-errors, tactual performance, test-total time and location, trail marking test-part B, time and block density, and the digit symbol subtest from the WAIS) that Reitan initially proposed as a means of studying age-correlated brain deterioration. The BAQ score is independent of the subject's age (Schau & O'Leary, 1977). Because of the inclusion of tests sensitive to alcoholism and its independence of age effects, the BAQ appears to be a particularly suitable measure of neuropsychological effects in elderly alcoholics. A short form of the BAQ, based on either a three-subtest set (trails-B, block design, digit symbol) or simply trails-B, may serve as an acceptable substitute for the long form BAQ (Horton & Anilane, 1986). The short form of the BAQ is especially useful in time series experimental designs.

Measure of Psychopathology

When screening for psychopathology, perhaps no single measure is more valuable than the MMPI. Although it is not considered a behavioral assessment tool, the wealth of research data attesting to its clinical value argues for its use. The MMPI is useful for identifying patients who need specialized mental health services and for identifying patients with extreme antisocial personality disorders.

The Alcohol Use Inventory (AUI; Wanberg, Horn, & Foster, 1977) was developed to exemplify a multidimensional model of alcohol abuse, but its clinical utility has not yet been demonstrated. Of the more specific behavioral assessment strategies, perhaps the most time honored is self-monitoring (Miller & Mastria, 1977). Depending upon the clinician's intent, the self-monitoring can focus upon any aspect of the patient's drinking, including time, type of beverage, place where drinking occurs, persons involved, antecedent and consequent events to drinking, as well as pre- or postcognitions and effects. Analysis of self-monitoring records can be helpful in conducting a functional analysis of the patient's alcohol abuse. Usually preprinted 3×5 cards facilitate data collection. Like all direct self-report measures, however, self-monitoring is vulnerable to intentional or unintentional bias. There is no practical way to validate self-monitoring data of daily alcohol intake. More often self-monitoring information is supplemented by direct observation or collateral reports from significant others (Maisto, Sobell, & Sobell, 1979; Rosenbluth, Nathan, & Lawson, 1978).

The use of breath-testing instruments on a daily or random basis is an alternative to self-monitoring, but there are many practical difficulties with those instruments because they are dependent on the patient's cooperation. Patients may simply fail to appear for the test, for example. In institutional settings, however, patient access is under a measure of control since they are usually available for breath testing (Horton & Howe, 1982).

Behavioral Treatment Studies of Elderly Alcoholics

While there are volumes on the treatment of alcoholism and volumes on aging, the treatment literature on aging alcoholics is scarce. The extant research literature on the behavioral treatment of aging alcoholics is even more rare. After a computer search of the available research literature on both MEDLINE and PSYCH ABSTRACTS, the authors identified only three papers that described behavioral treatment programs. In this section, each of these papers will be examined in chronological order to clarify the current state of the research literature.

Horton and Howe (1982) described the behavioral treatment of a 68-year-old white male who had completed 8 years of education and was diagnosed as a chronic alcoholic with chronic brain syndrome. The nursing home in which the patient was a resident had very strict regulations concerning alcohol use, and the patient was in danger of being discharged because of his repeated drinking. Assessment of the problem behavior included both neuropsychological and behavioral strategies. Neuropsychological assessment demonstrated both short- and long-term memory problems, but reading and math skills were relatively intact. Moreover, the patient was able to utilize feedback and formulate reasonable expectations. There was an absence of self-reported or observed depressive affect or behaviors. Behavioral assessment consisted of daily observations of the patient's free operant behavior in the nursing home and adjacent medical center. Of particular interest was the patient's entrepreneurial activities. On a daily basis the patient made deals with bedridden nursing home residents to buy them various articles from the medical center canteen (approximately a quarter mile from the nursing home). He charged a fee for these services and recorded his transactions in a small notebook to compensate for his memory deficit.

A behavioral treatment plan based on response cost was formulated in conjunction with administrative and clinical staff. At first the therapist discussed the rules of the nursing home regarding alcohol use. Next, the therapist and patient negotiated the following contingencies: (1) The client would be breathalized after every meal; (2) in event of a breathalizer reading >.10 at any meal, the patient would be confined to his room until the next meal; (3) in event of a breathalizer reading >.10 for two consecutive days, the patient would be restricted to his room until the next day.

The results of this program were dramatic. After one restriction, the patient's drinking ceased to be a problem. We felt that the loss of income from his daily enterprise was sufficient to control his drinking behavior.

After approximately 6 months, the patient was referred again for alcoholic problems. Careful investigation of the patient's chart revealed that there were no drinking problems until the nursing home staff became lax in their enforcement of the response–cost contingencies after the initial success. The patient quite naturally relapsed into his old behaviors. We decided to cue the nursing home staff to enforce the response–cost contingencies by attaching the behavioral data recording form to the patient's medication record. This strategy improved nursing home staff compliance, and the patient's behavior again improved.

In contrast to this case study, the two other papers dealt with programmatic interventions. Dupree, Broskowski, and Schonfeld (1984) conducted research on the location, description, and treatment of later-life onset alcohol abusers. Later-life onset alcohol abusers were defined by the researchers as persons who began abusing alcohol after age 49 and who were at least 55 years old. This study was conducted through the Gerontology Alcohol Project (GAP), a pilot day-treatment program (Dupree, 1982) which utilized an A-B-C (antecedents, behaviors, consequences) model to guide assessment and intervention strategies. The program emphasized the functional analysis of drinking behaviors, acquisition of self-management skills, and reestablishment of viable social support networks.

The treatment methodology was rather sophisticated. Specific treatment modules were standardized in formal procedure manuals and delivered to patients in 45-minute group sessions. The five modules dealt with the following areas: (1) analysis of drinking behavior in terms of its antecedents and consequences; (2) self-management in high-risk situations, which dealt with ways of coping with the antecedents associated with drinking, such as anger, depression, and peer pressure; (3) alcohol information and education in which patients were taught the medical, psychological, and social aspects of alcohol abuse; (4) general problem-solving skills, which focused upon methods of defining problems, generating solutions, and making decisions; (5) social support networks in which patients were taught ways of expanding their social contacts and activities.

The first module was taught for 12 sessions. The other four modules were taught for 10–15 sessions each. A year after completing the program, 14 (82%) of the 17 subjects successfully abstained from alcohol. It is important to note that the above study had a small sample size and a high dropout rate (Dupree, 1982). While the entire study contained a number of ancillary data analyses, the major findings supported the contention that a behaviorally oriented self-management program can be devised for elderly alcohol abusers with results as good as, or better than, the results of behavioral treatment programs with other populations of alcoholics (see review by Miller, 1976, for the results of other treatment programs).

More positive results were found in a long-term follow-up study of the behavioral treatment of geriatric alcoholics by Carstensen, Rychtarik, and Prue (1985). These investigators examined a sample of patients who were over the age of 60, when they participated in a 28-day alcoholism inpatient treatment program at the Veterans Administration Medical Center in Jackson, Mississippi. They contacted patients 2 to 4 years after discharge. The Jackson VA Medical Center's program follows a social learning model of treatment (Miller & Mastria, 1977). Program elements include medical care, individual treatment by alcoholism counselors, alcoholism education classes, and self-management and problem-solving training. As needed, marital therapy and vocational rehabilitation were also available. The study attempted to determine three things: the abstention rate of elderly alcoholics at least 2 years after inpatient treatment; the differences, if any, between late- and early-onset elderly alcoholics; and if demographic and/or daily activity variables could distinguish successfully abstinent from relapsing elderly alcoholics. Sixteen subjects and their collateral significant others were interviewed.

When the results were analyzed, the investigators found that 50% of the sample had been abstinent for 2 years, and another 12% had significantly decreased their alcohol intake. They found that the majority of late-onset elderly alcoholics began drinking when they retired. There was no significant differentiation between groups of early- and late-onset alcoholics on the demographic and daily activity variables.

The total number of subjects treated in this brief review of the literature on the behavioral treatment of elderly alcoholics is a grand total of 34. The results are encouraging, however, and they support the idea that further research with this population is worthwhile.

Behavioral Treatment Guidelines

How one translates the results of these few studies into clinically effective behavioral treatment strategies is problematic. It is usual clinical practice to tailor the treatment plan to the specific problems of the individual patient. That is to say, if the patient is anxious, use relaxation training; if unassertive, then assertive training. If he or she is having marital problems, then behavioral marital therapy, emphasizing the behavior contracting and problem solving, is recommended. In the Horton and Howe (1982) case study, the subject, an institutionalized patient in a nursing home, responded well to a response–cost contingency program, *as long as it was consistently applied*. In the study by Dupree *et al.* (1984), outpatients benefited significantly from a series of treatment sessions oriented toward the functional analysis of drinking behavior, acquisition of self-management skills, and reestablishment of social networks.

In line with these findings, the first decision point in the treatment of an elderly alcoholic may depend on whether or not the patient is in an institution. If he or she is an inpatient, then an operant approach might be initiated utilizing response–cost procedures. If the patient can be treated outside the hospital, the approach might better focus upon the functional analysis of drinking behavior, acquisition of self-management skills, and reestablishment of social support networks. Of course, the other social, medical, recreational, intellectual, vocational, and psychological needs of the patient must be addressed along with the behavioral treatment program. The primary goal, however, is to decrease the behavior of excessive drinking.

DRUG USE AMONG THE ELDERLY

Unfortunately, there are few empirical research studies concerning drug use among the elderly and virtually no treatment research for this population. We will present the little that is known regarding elderly drug users, however, in two sections. In the first section we will discuss the abuse of drugs that are legal (prescription or over-the-counter medications), and in the second section we will discuss the abuse of drugs that are illegal, mainly opioids.

Most of the literature on drug use in the elderly is over a decade old. While at first glance this finding seems most surprising, some points become more clear on further reflection. First, high-quality clinical research in the United States is to a large measure driven by federal funding. There are such difficulties in studying drug abuse that it is likely that only federally approved investigators will be working in this field. Second, federal research dollars are allocated according to perceived social needs, as determined by the Congress and the federal research establishments. Third, the late 1960s and early 1970s were a time of particular social unrest, with the antiwar movement and psychedelic drug usage vying for supremacy as the primary social issue. It appears that the attention paid to elderly drug use in the 1970s was a spillover effect from the major focus upon drug use in the American society. With the recent upsurge of interest in the use of drugs among athletes and school children, we can expect to see increased research dollars and attention devoted to the drug abuse problem, and some of these efforts will again be focused upon drug abuse among the elderly.

Use of Legal Drugs among the Elderly

Relative to younger individuals, there is greater per person legal drug use among the elderly (Task Force on Prescription Drugs, 1968). Approximately one-fourth of all drugs prescribed go to the elderly, which comprise only one-tenth of the U.S. population. Moreover, these elderly use more kinds of legal drugs and spend more for them than younger people (Task Force on Prescription Drugs, 1968). The most common legal drugs used are heart medications, tranquilizers, diuretics, and sedative-hypnotics (Peterson & Wittington, 1977).

It is commonly believed that the elderly misuse legal drugs at a high rate. According to Petersen and Thomas (1975), essentially all elderly patients admitted to hospitals for drug overdoses had acute reactions to legal drugs, and the majority of those who sought emergency medical care had misused a sedative or tranquilizer.

The aging process itself contributes to the misuse of legal drugs among the elderly. As documented by Keuthen in Chapter 2 of this volume, there are very specific effects of medications on the aging organism. These issues will not be further discussed here except to highlight briefly problems of drug interactions and side effects (Davis & Smith, 1973; Fann & Maddox, 1974; Lamy & Kitler, 1971). Many elderly people have multiple chronic medical conditions for which they take different drugs. As the elderly metabolize drugs more slowly than younger people, they are at greater risk for drug toxicity. Moreover, many drugs produce psychological and physical side effects, which the elderly are more prone to experience in severe degrees because of their slower metabolism (Lamy & Kitler, 1971).

It is not uncommon to see a plastic bag filled with medication pass from one neighbor to another as one dies. "Norma would want you to have these, I know, since you and she had some of the same illnesses," the story goes. And so, in the face of high expense for medication and a common reluctance to see a physician, outdated drugs are made available to more people. One thing to correct in new patients is inappropriate prescribing for insufficiently or inaccurately diagnosed psychological conditions. Many people, especially older women, have been taking tranquilizers for many years to quiet their "nerves." Often they were originally prescribed at the time of a funeral, and the prescription was simply renewed automatically thereafter. Antidepressants are prescribed in inappropriate doses, without sufficient monitoring, and without regard to whether the patient needs them. Often a patient's experience of sadness is misdiagnosed as depression, and antidepressants are prescribed. Therapy is a more appropriate strategy in such cases. This is not a discourse on others' errors, but an attempt to emphasize that educating physicians and pharmacists, as well as patients, is a necessary step in fighting intentional or unintentional pharmaceutical abuse.

Use of Illegal Drugs among the Elderly

Beliefs about the elderly narcotic addict have been undergoing a radical change. In earlier times it was thought that the problem of drug addiction decreased dramatically after age 45 (Capel & Peppers, 1978). The available evidence (O'Donnell, 1969) appeared to support the "maturing out" theory proposed by Winick (1962), which stated that the aging narcotic addict learned the error of his or her ways as age and/or years of substance abuse increased and that, therefore, drug addiction was of little relevance to gerontologists (Capel, Goldsmith, Waddell, & Stewart, 1972).

More recent research, however, has demonstrated that this notion was premature and apparently incorrect. One of the factors that contributed to the earlier illusionary conclusion was the source of the statistics on the elderly addict. Researchers used the enrolled population of the Federal Bureau of Narcotics "active addict" list to estimate the prevalence of elderly narcotic addicts (Winick, 1964). Later research demonstrated that many active addicts were not on the Federal Bureau of Narcotics list (O'Donnell, 1969).

Data from a study by Capel *et al.* (1972) further disputed earlier findings. These investigators identified about 60 elderly addicts involved in a methadone maintenance program and 38 additional narcotic addicts who were not in any sort of treatment program. In direct conflict with the "maturing out" hypothesis, these elderly narcotic addicts continued their drug abuse, but were able to avoid official attention by making a number of changes in their drug-taking behavior. These changes included switching from heroin to a cheaper, more easily obtainable drug such as Diaudid, depending almost exclusively on the neighborhood pusher, and decreasing their usual dose or substituting alcohol or a barbiturate for their most commonly used drug.

In a follow-up study, Capel and Peppers (1978) found that after 7 years there were increasing numbers in the elderly narcotic addict population. Of the 38 elderly narcotic addicts who had not been in any treatment program in the Capel *et al.* (1972) study, 11 were located and interviewed. All were still using drugs in approximately the same amount as they had 7 years before. Of the rest, 6 had died of natural causes and 20 could not be located. As they stated:

> No abnormal mortality rates were detected at least not over this relatively short span of years, and there is reason to believe that past mortality figures attributed to narcotics may have been more a result of drug impurities, irregular life-styles, harassment by the law and the like rather than the drugs per se. (Capel & Peppers, 1978, p. 431)

It is possible to conclude from these few studies that the elderly narcotic addict population is increasing and that many of these addicts do not come to the attention of the legal authorities for a number of reasons.

Treatment for this problem is undoubtedly difficult. We were unable to find a single treatment study relevant to the elderly narcotic addict in the research literature. Perhaps the model used to treat elderly alcoholics has some merit for the elderly drug addict.

CONCLUSION

In this chapter we have reviewed the available literature on elderly alcohol and drug addicts and made some suggestions regarding their assessment and treatment. It has been obvious that there is little research on the elderly alcoholic and virtually none on the elderly drug addict. At this point, all suggestions for behavioral treatment of these populations rest more on clinical lore than on empirical practice. There is an urgent need for greatly expanded research efforts on these particularly needy populations. Research efforts will contribute significantly to the development of empirical behavioral treatment of elderly alcoholics and drug addicts.

REFERENCES

American Psychiatric Association. (1980). *Diagnostic and statistical manual of mental disorders* (3rd ed.). Washington, DC: Task Force on Nomenclature and Statistics of the American Psychiatric Association.

American Psychiatric Association. (1987). *Diagnostic and statistical manual of mental disorders* (3rd ed., revised). Washington, DC: Task Force on Nomenclature and Statistics of the American Psychiatric Association.

Barchha, R., Stewart, M. A., & Guze, S. (1968). The prevalence of alcoholism among general hospital ward staff. *American Journal of Psychiatry, 125,* 681–684.

Butters, N. (1985). Alcohol Korsakoff's syndrome 2: Some unresolved issues concerning etiology, neuropsychology, and cognitive deficits. *Journal of Clinical and Experimental Neuropsychology, 7,* 181–210.

Butters, N., & Cermak, L. S. (1980). *Alcoholic Korsakoff's syndrome.* New York: Academic Press.

Capel, W. C., & Peppers, G. T. (1978). The aging addict: A longitudinal study of known abuses. *Addictive Diseases, 3,* 389–402.

Capel, W. C., Goldsmith, B. M., Waddell, K. J., & Stewart, G. T. (1972). The aging narcotic addict: An increasing problem for the next decades. *Journal of Gerontology, 27,* 102–108.

Carstensen, L. L., Rychtarik, R. G., & Prue, D. M. (1985). Behavioral treatment of the geriatric alcohol abuser: A long term follow-up study. *Addictive Behaviors, 10,* 307–311.

Chelune, C. J., & Parker, J. B. (1981). Neuropsychological deficits associated with chronic alcohol abuse. *Clinical Psychology Review, 4,* 181–195.

Civiello, C. L., & Horton, A. M., Jr. (1988). *Effectiveness of various alcoholism treatment modalities: A critical review* Unpublished manuscript, Veteran's Administration Medical Center, Baltimore.

Cone, J. D. (1978). The behavioral assessment grid (BAG): A conceptual framework and taxonomy. *Behavior Therapy, 1,* 882–888.

Davis, R. H., & Smith, W. K. (1973). *Drugs and the elderly.* Los Angeles: University of Southern California, Ethel Percy Andrus Gerontology Center.

Dupree, L. W. (1982). Gerontology alcohol project; Characteristics of treatment program graduates versus dropouts. *The Gerontologist, 22,* 258–259.

Dupree, L. W., Broskowski, H., & Schonfeld, L. (1984). The gerontology alcohol project: The behavioral treatment program for elderly alcohol abusers. *The Gerontologist, 24,* 510–516.

Fann, W. C., & Maddox, G. L. (1974). *Drug issues in geropsychiatry.* Baltimore: Williams & Wilkins.

Gaitz, C. M., & Baer, P. E. (1971). Characteristics of elderly patients with alcoholism. *Archives of General Psychiatry, 24,* 327–378.

Glatt, M. M. (1961). Drinking habits of English alcoholics. *Acta Psychiatrica Scandinavica, 37,* 88–113.

Graux, P. (1969). Alcoholism of the elderly. *Review of Alcoholism, 15,* 61–63.

Horton, A. M., Jr. (1982). Introduction to the psychotherapy of the aging. In A. M. Horton, Jr. (Ed.), *Mental health interventions for the aging* (pp. 1–17). New York: Praeger.

Horton, A. M., Jr., & Anilane, J. (1986). Relationships of trail marking test-part B and brain age quotient— long and short forms. *Psychotherapy in Private Practice, 4,* 39–43.

Horton, A. M., Jr., & Howe, N. (1982). Behavior therapy with an aged alcoholic: A case study. *International Journal of Behavioral Geriatrics, 1,* 17–18.

Horton, A. M., Jr., & Wedding, D. (1984). *Clinical and behavioral neuropsychology.* New York: Praeger.

Kish, G. B., Hagen, J. M., Woody, M. M., & Harvey, H. L. (1980). Alcoholic's recovery from cerebral impairment as a function of duration of abstinence. *Journal of Clinical Psychology, 36,* 584–589.

Kleinknecht, R. A., & Goldstein, S. G. (1972). Neuropsychological deficits associated with alcoholism. *Quarterly Journal of Studies in Alcoholism, 33,* 999–1019.

Lamy, P. P., & Kitler, M. E. (1971). Drugs and the geriatric patient. *Journal of the American Geriatrics Society, 19,* 23–33.

Maisto, S. A., Sobell, L. C., & Sobell, M. B. (1979). Comparison of alcoholics' self-reports of drinking behavior with reports of collateral informants. *Journal of Consulting and Clinical Psychology, 47,* 106–112.

Marlett, G. A., & Miller, W. R. (1984). *Comprehensive drinker profile.* Odessa, FL: Psychological Assessment Resources.

McCusker, J., Jr., Cherubin, C. E., & Zimberg, S. (1971). Prevalence of alcoholism in general municipal hospital population. *New York State Journal of Medicine, 71,* 751–754.

Mendelson, J. H., & Mello, N. K. (Eds.). (1985). *Diagnosis and treatment of alcoholism* (2nd ed.). New York: McGraw-Hill.

Miller, P. M. (1976). *Behavioral treatment of alcoholism.* New York: Pergamon Press.

Miller, P. M., & Mastria, M. A. (1977). *Alternatives to alcohol abuse: A social learning model.* Champaign, IL: Research Press.

Miller, W. R. (1982). Treating problem drinkers: What works. *The Behavior Therapist, 5,* 15–18.

Miller, W. R., & Hester, R. K. (1980). Treating the problem drinker: Modern approach. In W. P. Miller (Ed.), *The addictive behavior: Treatment of alcoholism, drug abuse, smoking, and obesity* (pp. 11–141). New York: Pergamon Press.

Miller, W. R., & Saucedo, C. E. (1983). Assessment of neuropsychological impairment and brain damage in problem drinkers. In C. J. Golden, J. A. Moses, Jr., J. A. Coffman, W. R. Miller, & F. D. Strider (Eds.), *Clinical neuropsychology: Interface with neurological and psychiatric disorders* (pp. 141–195). New York: Grune & Stratton.

Mosher, V., Davis, J., Mulligan, D., & Iber, F. L. (1975). Comparison of outcome in a 9-day and 30-day alcoholism treatment program. *Journal of Studies on Alcohol, 36,* 1277–1281.

O'Donnell, J. A. (1969). *Narcotic addicts in Kentucky,* (Public Health Service Publication No. 1881). Washington, DC: National Institute of Drug Abuse.

Parker, E. S., & Noble, E. P. (1972). Alcohol consumption and cognitive functioning in social drinkers. *Journal of Studies on Alcohol, 34,* 1224–1232.

Parsons, O. A., & Farr, S. P. (1981). The neuropsychology of alcohol and drug use. In S. B. Filskov, & T. J. Boll (Eds.), *Handbook of clinical neuropsychology* (pp. 320–325). New York: John Wiley & Sons.

Petersen, D. M., & Thomas, C. W. (1975). Acute drug reactions among the elderly. *Journal of Gerontology, 30,* 552–556.

Petersen, D. M., & Whittington, F. J. (1977). Drug use among the elderly: A review. *Journal of Psychedelic Drugs, 9,* 25–37.

Polich, J. M. (1982). The validity of self-reports in alcohol research. *Addictive Behaviors, 1,* 123–132.

Reitan, R. (1973). *Behavioral manifestations of impaired brain function in aging*. Paper presented at the Annual Meeting of the American Psychological Association, Montreal, Canada.

Rosen, J. J., & Glatt, M. W. (1968). Alcohol excess in the elderly. *Quarterly Journal of Studies on Alcohol, 32*, 125–131.

Rosenbluth, J., Nathan, P. E., & Lawson, D. N. (1978). Environmental influences on drinking by college students in a college pub: Behavioral observations in the natural environment. *Addictive Behaviors, 3*, 117–121.

Ryan, C., & Butters, N. (1986). Neuropsychology of alcoholism. In D. Wedding, A. M. Horton, Jr., & J. S. Webster (Eds.), *Handbook of clinical and behavioral neuropsychology* (pp. 376–409). New York: Springer.

Schau, E. J., & O'Leary, M. R. (1977). Adaptive abilities of hospitalized alcoholics and matched controls: The brain-age quotient. *Journal of Studies on Alcohol, 38*, 403–409.

Schuckit, M. A., & Pastor, P. A. (1978). The elderly is a unique population: Alcoholics. *Alcoholism: Clinical and Experimental Research, 2*, 31–38.

Simon, A., Epstein, L. J., & Reynolds, L. (1968). Alcoholism in the geriatrically mentally ill. *Geriatrics, 23*, 125–131.

Task Force on Prescription Drugs. (1968). *The drug users*. Washington, DC: U.S. Government Printing Office.

Wanberg, K. W., Horn, J. L., & Foster, F. M. (1977). A differential assessment model for alcoholism: The scales of the alcohol use inventory. *Journal of Studies on Alcoholism, 38*, 512–543.

Winick, C. (1962). Maturing out of narcotic addiction. *United Nations Bulletin on Narcotics, 14*, 1–7.

Winick, C. (1964). The life cycle of the narcotic addict and of addiction. *United Nations Bulletin on Narcotics, 16*, 1–11.

Zimberg, S. (1978). Diagnosis and treatment of the elderly alcoholic. *Alcoholism: Clinical and Experimental Research, 2*, 27–29.

14

The Problem of Urinary Incontinence

KATHRYN LARSEN BURGIO AND LOUIS D. BURGIO

INTRODUCTION

Urinary incontinence is a disorder that is seen in individuals of every age but is most prevalent among people 65 years of age and older. A significant number of otherwise healthy men and women develop difficulties with bladder control as they grow older. Studies of community populations report that 6–15% of elderly men and 11–50% of elderly women experience urinary incontinence (Feneley, Shepherd, Powell, & Blannin, 1979; Yarnell, Voyle, Richards, & Stephenson, 1981). Incontinence is even more common in nursing homes, where 38–56% of residents have uncontrolled urine loss (Jewett, Fernie, Holliday, & Pim, 1981; U.S. DHEW, 1975).

The consequences of mild incontinence may be overcome with only minor accommodations of lifestyle, but moderate or severe incontinence has more serious implications. It predisposes patients to other health problems (e.g., decubitus ulcers, urinary tract infections) and contributes to depression, anxiety, and social isolation. Incontinence is a significant source of dependency among the elderly and a widely cited factor in nursing homes admissions. The costs of incontinence are very high, with an estimated expenditure of $0.5–1.5 billion each year in U.S. nursing homes (Ouslander & Kane, 1984).

Because incontinence is most common among the elderly, it is often mistakenly attributed to aging. While the elderly are more likely to have conditions that predispose them to incontinence or contribute to the causes of incontinence, many of these conditions may be controlled if properly identified. Urinary incontinence is not a normal aspect of aging, nor is it irreversible. Elderly patients should be treated with the same effort afforded to younger patients with incontinence.

Traditionally, the treatment of incontinence has been the realm of medicine and nursing. Several surgical procedures have achieved acceptance as standard treatments for certain types of incontinence, and pharmacological therapies have also

KATHRYN LARSEN BURGIO AND LOUIS D. BURGIO • University of Pittsburgh School of Medicine, Pittsburgh, Pennsylvania 15213.

proven successful, although their effectiveness with the elderly has not yet been adequately tested. Nursing interventions usually consist of programs of timed voiding, which modify overt toileting behavior through antecedent control (prompts). With the field of behavioral medicine rapidly expanding, there is increased involvement of behaviorally trained professionals in the assessment and treatment of incontinence and the development of new methods of modifying bladder function. Behavioral interventions are relevant for the elderly for two reasons. First, surgery is often unacceptable to elderly patients or inadvisable due to other medical conditions. Second, pharmacological therapy often produces side effects that can limit its usefulness. Existing behavioral interventions offer a potentially effective means of improving incontinence without these risks or side effects. The purpose of this chapter is to describe behavioral approaches to the assessment and treatment of urinary incontinence and to present a model for the collaboration of health professionals that will facilitate the delivery of behavioral services to those with problems of bladder control.

PHYSIOLOGY OF CONTINENCE AND INCONTINENCE

Normal bladder control involves a complex set of interacting physiological responses that have been described in depth by Bradley, Timm, and Scott (1974). Stretch receptors located in the bladder wall detect bladder filling, and afferents from these receptors enter the spinal cord at the level of the sacrum. At a critical threshold volume, a spinal cord reflex (the micturition reflex) stimulates the bladder to empty. This is accomplished by rhythmic contractions of the detrusor muscle, a smooth muscle that surrounds the bladder wall, and relaxation of the external urinary sphincter, a striated muscle that surrounds the urethra. Voluntary control over urination is accomplished via neural circuits from the cerebral cortex that allow inhibition and disinhibition of the micturition reflex. Continence requires that the individual anticipate the threshold for bladder emptying and avoid incontinence by emptying the bladder before the threshold is reached, or more commonly, by sensing bladder distention and inhibiting reflex contractions until an appropriate setting for urination is found. One must also be able to occlude the urethra to prevent incontinence during uninhibited bladder contraction or sudden pressure rises associated with physical activities such as coughing or sneezing. Thus, the maintenance of continence requires that one be able to empty the bladder voluntarily as well as to inhibit emptying.

Failure to emit these physiological responses at the appropriate times results in three common types of incontinence, which are described in Table 1. They include (1) urge incontinence, in which bladder contractions are not inhibited; (2) stress incontinence, in which the outflow is not effectively prevented during transient rises in pressure; and (3) overflow incontinence, in which urine is lost from a chronically full bladder because the bladder does not fully empty. A fourth type of incontinence (functional incontinence) can occur in individuals who have normal physiological responses, but, for other reasons such as cognitive or mobility impair-

TABLE 1
Types and Causes of Persistent Urinary Incontinence

Type	Definition	Mechanism	Causes
Urge	Urine loss associated with sensation of bladder fullness or urgency and inability to inhibit bladder contractions.	Increased bladder pressure due to bladder contraction.	Central nervous system disorder, e.g., stroke; local irritation, e.g., bladder infection.
Stress	Urine loss associated with increased intra-abdominal pressure brought on by physical activities, e.g., coughing, exercising.	Increased abdominal pressure overcomes inadequate urethral resistance.	Damage to pelvic floor tissues, e.g., perinatal damage; weak or uncoordinated muscles.
Overflow	Urine loss when pressure in chronically full bladder exceeds urethral resistance.	Increased bladder pressure due to inability to empty bladder.	Atonic bladder, e.g., with diabetes mellitus; Obstruction, e.g., due to enlarged prostate, fecal impaction, or stricture.
Functional	Urine loss resulting from inability or unwillingness to use the toilet appropriately.	Lack of appropriate toileting.	Cognitive impairment; mobility impairment; depression.

ment, do not reach or use the toilet reliably. It is not uncommon to find more than one type of incontinence in a patient.

TYPES AND CAUSES OF INCONTINENCE

Urge Incontinence

The category "urge incontinence" encompasses a group of diagnoses including bladder instability, detrusor hyperreflexia, spastic bladder, neurogenic bladder, and uninhibited bladder. Urine loss is associated with uncontrolled contractions of the smooth detrusor muscle of the bladder wall.

The inability to inhibit detrusor contraction can be caused by neurologic disorders or injuries that impair central nervous system control: cerebrovascular accident, brain tumor, dementia, parkinsonism, multiple sclerosis, or spinal cord injury. Bladder dysfunction can also be produced by local inflammation or irritation of the bladder or urethra due to such conditions as urinary tract infection, fecal impaction, benign prostatic hypertrophy, uterine prolapse, or bladder carcinoma.

Bladder instability can also result from poor bladder habits such as frequent voiding. Since the bladder is elastic, it tends to accommodate to repeated filling and stretching. Repeated low-volume voiding prevents the bladder from accommodating normal urine volume, which decreases bladder capacity, resulting in increased urinary frequency and urgency (Frewen, 1978, 1980).

The primary interventions for urge incontinence are medications that inhibit bladder contractions and behavioral procedures such as bladder training, habit training, or biofeedback. Two pharmacological agents, oxybutinin chloride and imipramine, have been tested in a very small number of elderly patients, with 60–70% improvement rates (Castleden, George, Renwick, & Asher, 1981; Moisey, Stephenson, & Brendler, 1980). Behavioral procedures for urge incontinence are described later in this chapter.

Stress Incontinence

Stress urinary incontinence is the involuntary loss of urine that results from a sudden rise in intra-abdominal pressure produced by physical activities such as coughing, sneezing, exercising, or lifting. Incontinence results when a corresponding rise in bladder pressure exceeds urethral resistance in the absence of a bladder contraction. Stress incontinence is due to a defect of the bladder outlet (sphincter insufficiency, incompetent sphincter) such that the resistance provided by the urethra is inadequate to prevent leakage during the activity.

In our clinical experience, stress incontinence occurs so commonly in women that mild incontinence is accepted as normal by many women and a surprising number are content to wear protective pads rather than be treated. In a study of college-aged, nulliparous women, Wolin (1969) reported that 51% experienced stress incontinence, although only 16% had daily leakage. Among men, stress incontinence is rare and is usually associated with urologic surgery such as prostatectomy.

One commonly accepted etiologic factor in female stress incontinence is perinatal damage to the supporting tissues of the pelvic floor. The precise mechanism of urine loss is a topic of debate. Anatomical explanations emphasize the loss of the vesico-urethral angle due to overstretched or damaged pelvic floor tissues. A normal angle between the bladder floor and urethra provides transmission of pressure to the urethra and bladder simultaneously during physical activities. Thus, urethral pressure is increased during transient rises in bladder pressure and prevents leakage. When the position of the urethra is altered by loss of urethral support, sudden increases in abdominal pressure are transmitted to the bladder, leaving urethral pressure unaltered and incontinence results. The usual treatment for stress incontinence is surgical restoration of a normal vesico-urethral angle by repositioning the urethra and improving support to the bladder. Surgical approaches are known to be effective in properly selected patients, but study patients have predominantly been younger women. Thus little is known about the effectiveness of surgery for elderly patients.

Functional explanations of stress incontinence attribute urinary leakage to a lack of awareness or control over pelvic floor muscles (Kegel, 1948, 1956) or a failure of the striated muscle of the distal urethral sphincter to contract during transient rises in intra-abdominal pressure. The usual method for improving weak muscles is physiotherapy. Behavioral methods for training patients to exercise pelvic floor muscles are described in detail later in this chapter.

Overflow Incontinence

Overflow incontinence is the leaking of urine when pressure in a chronically full bladder exceeds urethral resistance. This may be due to an atonic (acontractile) bladder or to a functional or mechanical obstruction of the bladder outlet. Atonic bladder usually results from spinal cord trauma, multiple sclerosis, or diabetes mellitus. In an elderly person, outlet obstruction is often due to fecal impaction (Willington, 1980). Other sources of obstruction are benign prostatic hypertrophy, carcinoma of the prostate, and bladder-sphincter dyssynergia, in which the sphincter contracts simultaneously with bladder contraction.

Functional Incontinence

Functional incontinence refers to urine loss resulting from inability or unwillingness to use the toilet appropriately. In a person with normal bladder function, incontinence can be precipitated by limitations that prevent reaching the toilet in time. Factors that contribute to functional incontinence may be classified as deficits of mobility, mental status, or motivation, or environmental barriers.

Normal use of the toilet can be limited by physical conditions such as arthritic pain, muscle weakness, disorders of balance, joint abnormalities, fractures, or fatigue. Ouslander, Kane, and Abrass (1982) studied 299 elderly nursing home patients with frequent incontinence and reported that only 15% were ambulatory. The other 85% suffered severe impairments of mobility, which caused them to be wheelchair bound or bed bound. They describe the predicament of many patients who are able to sense bladder fullness, but are unable to postpone urination until staff assistance is available. Continence in patients with mobility impairment will depend upon their ability to perform toileting skills, the availability of caregivers to assist toileting on a regular schedule, or upon the promptness with which caregivers respond to the patients' requests for assistance.

In patients with significant cognitive impairment, incontinence may be related to memory deficits, confusion, depression, or fears that interfere with appropriate voiding. Using the Short Portable Mental Status Questionnaire (Pfeiffer, 1976), Ouslander et al. (1982) showed that most elderly incontinent nursing home patients have some degree of cognitive impairment, and that the severity of this impairment was related to the degree of incontinence.

Incontinence is occasionally used to elicit attention. Or it may be the result of indifference to or the absence of social consequences. It is not unusual in institutional or home settings for incontinence to elicit more attention than dryness. Environmental factors such as lack of privacy, uncomfortable toilet facilities, poor lighting, and physical barriers can also contribute to functional incontinence.

Conditions that facilitate functional incontinence are crucial variables in nursing home patients whose incontinence is often secondary to the disabilities that required institutional care. Intervention for functional incontinence aims to improve the functional level of the patient and depends entirely on the nature of the deficit. Treatment aims to reverse the conditions that impair the patient's functional level either by removing environmental barriers, introducing stimuli or devices that facilitate function, improving performance through training, or introducing contingencies that encourage appropriate voiding habits.

ASSESSMENT

Incontinence is a medical and nursing problem, but it is also a behavioral problem. Collaboration among these professions is needed for optimal diagnosis and management of incontinence. Before a behavioral intervention is planned, incontinence should first be evaluated medically. Medical screening includes a history and physical examination to detect conditions that may not be apparent otherwise, and to exclude conditions that are inappropriate for behavioral intervention. Examination of urine to detect urinary tract infection is an indispensable component of the routine medical evaluation. Postvoid catheterization for residual urine will detect overflow incontinence, which usually requires medical or surgical intervention. Physical examination will reveal the presence of fecal impaction, benign prostatic hypertrophy, atrophic vaginitis, and other conditions that are reversible causes of incontinence. Following medical evaluation, a decision to intervene behaviorally should be reached concurrently by physician and behavior therapist.

Incontinence, like any other behavior, can be viewed as a function of its antecedents and its consequences. Antecedents of incontinence can be external stimuli, such as the sight of a bathroom, which signals that it is appropriate to void once positioned properly on the toilet. They can also be internal stimuli, such as a feeling of urgency, which is an interoceptive stimulus indicating bladder fullness and a cue that one should find an appropriate place for bladder emptying. If it is not possible to void immediately, urgency is a cue to postpone urination by inhibiting detrusor contractions or by contracting peri-urethral muscles to prevent urine loss.

Consequences are also important for urinary control. One reason that continence is maintained in most people is that incontinence usually meets with social disapproval, and maintaining bladder control avoids this aversive consequence. In elderly patients, confusion or depression can result in indifference to the social consequences of incontinence, and this affects the punishing value of the consequences.

The goal of a behavioral assessment is to analyze the individual antecedents and consequences of incontinence. In the following pages the authors describe the primary components of a behavioral assessment.

The Interview

Behavioral assessment of incontinence begins with an interview with the patient or a caregiver if the patient is unable to participate. The interviewer can elicit information that in many cases will give a clear picture of the behavioral mechanisms (or correlates) of the incontinence and formulate a preliminary diagnosis. The interviewer should also determine if the client has age-related deficits, such as impaired mobility, diminished vision, or deficits in mental status.

Patients with urge incontinence usually give a clear description of accidents that occur in the presence of a strong sensation of urge to void and an inability to reach the toilet in time. Typical antecedents of urge incontinence are the sounds of running water, thinking about going to the toilet, the sight of a toilet, or cold weather. A common report is the occurrence of accidents as one returns home and unlocks the door of the house. This difficulty, termed "key in the door syndrome," is partially the result of classical conditioning in which arriving home has been repeatedly paired with bladder emptying.

Patients with stress incontinence are usually able to identify specific physical activities that precipitate incontinence. Common among these are coughing, sneezing, lifting, bending, or stooping. One must be alert to identify cases in which the physical activity is subtle. Patients occasionally report the absence of physical activity when in fact they are walking, turning, or standing up from a sitting position. Incontinence can occur in response to slight jarring movements (climbing stairs) or changes in position. Sometimes, the patient is not aware of the relationship between these behaviors and urine loss.

Bladder Records

Bladder records are used by the patient or caregiver to document voiding habits and patterns of incontinence on a daily basis. The records have two purposes. First, they provide detailed information about patient behavior that can be used together with the interview to identify the causes of incontinence and formulate a rational treatment plan. Second, they function as a vehicle for evaluating progress during treatment. Bladder records complement retrospective verbal reports by providing *in vivo* data at the time incontinence occurs. It is difficult for patients to judge frequency or patterns of incontinence retrospectively, especially if their pattern is irregular. Home recording over a period of 2 to 4 weeks will often document patterns of variability that the patient finds difficult to discriminate. Frequently, patients are surprised to find that they had so many or so few accidents once they are required to record them. Home records are important for averting the tendency of some patients to report positively on their progress in order to please the therapist. We have seen patients who claim improvement although their diaries showed no change in the size or frequency of accidents.

A variety of record forms have been developed for documentation of bladder habits (e.g., Clay, 1980). Most have been designed for use by nurses and most are complex. If patients or caregivers are expected to keep meaningful records, a simple bladder form is crucial. A form used by Whitehead, Burgio, and Engel (1984) to document the most necessary information is presented in Figure 1. In this form space is provided to record time of voiding, time of incontinent episodes, and whether the accident was large or small based on whether the outer clothing was wet. Finally, comments on the reason for incontinence are elicited, which help to identify the antecedents of incontinence.

Observation of Mobility and Toileting Skills

The ability to reach and use the toilet appropriately is a basic skill for the maintenance of continence. Direct observation of one or more toileting episodes is the best way to determine these skills. One can measure the patient's ability to locate the toilet, and the time needed to reach the toilet, to undress, and to position appropriately for voiding. If any of these behaviors cannot be performed independently, the observer notes the amount of assistance required and its availability in the patient's natural environment. The type of clothing worn is also of interest if it might be modified to make undressing less cumbersome. In physically handicapped patients, one can use behavioral observation to define skill deficits, such as inadequate transfer skills, which might be overcome with training.

Mental Status Evaluation

While cognitive deficits may surface in other areas of assessment, it is often useful to evaluate them using standardized tests. The Mini-Mental State Examination (Folstein, Folstein, & McHugh, 1975) is a brief test of mental status that includes assessment of orientation, memory, attention, and concentration. Since it was designed for rapid assessment of acutely ill patients, it does not fully evaluate the range of cognition, and when indicated, it should be supplemented by more elaborate neuropsychological instruments.

Urodynamics

Physiological measurement of bladder pressure and sphincter activity are routine methods for assessing bladder or sphincter function. The cystometrogram measures bladder pressure during rapid bladder filling and is standard in urology clinics. It often is complemented by measurement of intra-urethral pressures (urethral pressure profile) or a measure of pelvic floor activity such as sphincter electromyography. With modification, the cystometrogram provides a useful behavioral evaluation of incontinence.

During a cystometrogram the patient's report of bladder sensation during filling provides critical information about the presence or absence of cues that signal bladder fullness and voluntary inhibition of bladder contractions. For urge incontinent patients, it is important to determine not only the sensory threshold for bladder filling, but the amount of time between the onset of sensation and the threshold for uninhibited bladder contractions. This is the amount of time the patient has to reach a toilet or to implement bladder inhibition before incontinence

Bladder Record

Name: _____ Date: _____

Instructions: 1. In the 1st column, mark the time every time you void.
2. In the 2nd or 3rd column, mark every time you accidentally leaked urine.
3. Write "dry" if no accident occurred in the 2-hour interval.

Time interval	Urinated in toilet	Leaking accident	or	Large accident	Reason for accident
6–8 AM					
8–10 AM					
10–12 AM					
12–2 PM					
2–4 PM					
4–6 PM					
6–8 PM					
8–10 PM					
10–12 PM					
Overnight					

Number of pads used today: _____
Comments: _____
_____
_____
Exercises: _____
_____
_____
_____

FIGURE 1.   Bladder record form used by patients to document voiding, incontinent episodes, volume of accidents, and antecedents of incontinence.

occurs. Once the patient reports bladder sensation, the response to this sensation can be observed. Specifically, one can observe the patient's ability to inhibit bladder contractions voluntarily and his or her use of peri-urethral muscles to occlude the urethra.

Voluntary contractions of the peri-urethral muscles can be measured in a variety of ways. One which is relatively comfortable for the patient involves placing an air-filled balloon at the external anal sphincter. Because the innervation of the external urethral sphincter is similar to that of the external anal sphincter, this balloon provides an indirect index of urethral sphincter activity.

Testing should also include a measure of intra-abdominal pressure such as rectal pressure. The purpose of this measure is to identify increases in bladder pressure that are attributable to increases in intra-abdominal pressure, and to detect inappropriate response to the desire to void. Many incontinent patients respond to the sensation of urgency by tensing abdominal muscles in an effort to prevent incontinence (Burgio, Whitehead, & Engel, 1985). This response increases bladder pressure and, thus, makes an accident more likely.

Urodynamic testing in patients with cognitive impairment poses a serious problem. With this form of testing it is necessary that patients understand that they should make every effort to inhibit urine loss and they must be motivated to do so. If neither criterion is met, the mechanism of an uninhibited detrusor contraction may be uninterpretable.

INTERVENTION

Behavioral interventions are a diverse group of procedures that involve the modification of incontinence through the systematic alteration of antecedent or consequent stimuli or both. If a patient displays a deficit that can be attributed to insufficient antecedent stimuli (e.g., loss of bladder sensation), new antecedents such as reminders to void regularly can be employed to compensate for lost cues. In this case, the patient avoids urinary accidents by urinating on a schedule instead of in response to bladder fullness. Instructions to patients, reminders to void, assistance in toileting, and contraction of the pelvic floor muscles are all examples of antecedent stimuli used in behavioral treatment of incontinence.

If the behavioral assessment suggests that the current consequences of incontinence are inadequate or inappropriately applied, environmental changes might take the form of positive attention for a period of dryness, thus rewarding continence instead of incontinence. Other examples of consequent control are material rewards or privileges for periods of dryness or mild social disapproval for incontinence.

The primary behavioral interventions for incontinence are described in Table 2.

TABLE 2
Behavioral Interventions for Urinary Incontinence

Intervention	Description	Types of incontinence
Habit training	Fixed or flexible toileting schedule, adjusted to accommodate patient's pattern of incontinence.	Urge; functional
Bladder retraining	Toileting interval is gradually increased or decreased to normal.	Urge; neurogenic
Contingency management	Systematic reinforcement of appropriate toileting; inappropriate toileting ignored or punished.	Functional
Staff management	Systematic structuring and reinforcement of appropriate implementation of treatment by staff.	Functional
Biofeedback	Feedback of physiological responses used to teach sphincter contraction (pelvic floor exercise), bladder inhibition, or abdominal relaxation.	Stress; urge

The choice of a behavioral technique depends upon the type of incontinence, the mental and physical abilities and limitations of the individual patient, and the setting in which the patient resides.

Generally, patients will fall into one of two groups: those who are capable of learning self-management procedures and who will control the antecedents and consequences of this program, or those who require ongoing intervention from a caregiver. Usually, but not necessarily, the former will be community-dwelling elderly and the latter will be institutionalized elderly. Community-dwelling patients usually have demonstrable bladder or sphincter dysfunction but are other wise functional in terms of self-care. They often have minimal or no cognitive impairment, and frequently are capable of independent living. They can be managed in an outpatient setting where they receive training in self-management skills in the clinic and implement prescribed practice at home.

Institutionalized patients are often characterized by functional dependency, typically significant cognitive and/or mobility impairment, and require assistance from staff in the management of incontinence. Some of these will be unaware of, or indifferent to, their incontinence. Treatment requires that the community caregivers or institutional staff implement treatment procedures that involve the control of environmental factors. In such cases the focus of intervention may be staff behavior. Systematic procedures exist for teaching staff how to help incontinent patients, and for maintaining new patterns of caring for them. Interventions for institutionalized and community-dwelling eldery are described in the pages that follow.

Habit Training

Habit training, or the use of voiding schedules, is the most frequently used behavioral method of managing incontinence in nursing homes. The objective of habit training is not to modify bladder function but to keep the patient dry. The procedure focuses on changing antecedent conditions by instituting frequent scheduled toileting. Treatment consists of the establishment of a voiding routine, usually within 2–4 hour intervals, whether or not a sensation to void is present. Both fixed and flexible schedules have been used (Clay, 1980; Sogbein & Awad, 1982). Habit training may be individualized by adjusting the voiding schedule to the needs of the patient. The voiding interval is shortened if incontinence persists and lengthened when the patient is consistently dry at a certain interval (Clay, 1980). In addition to the voiding routine, habit-training programs usually involve careful control of fluid intake and medications. Habit training is often combined with contingency management procedures in which appropriate toileting is rewarded and inappropriate voiding or incontinence is discouraged.

These procedures, though widely adopted and advocated, have not been tested extensively with the elderly. Sogbein and Awad (1982) used a fixed 2-hour voiding schedule to treat 20 elderly men with bladder hyperreflexia. Eighty-five percent achieved the criterion for improvement (reduction of incontinence to less than 20% of the time). Spangler, Risley, and Bilyew (1984) implemented a fixed 1.5-hour toileting schedule for 16 nonambulatory geriatric nursing home patients. In addition, staff were instructed to remind the patients after every scheduled toileting event that he or she would return in 1.5 hours to give the patient another opportunity for toileting. Results showed a significant decrease in incontinence, with eight patients (50%) displaying no toileting accidents following treatment.

Clay (1978) reported the results of habit training with adjustment of the voiding schedule to "catch the patient" before incontinence occurred. Among 20 male patients in an assessment and rehabilitation ward, 63% were successfully managed. Habit training was successful for 73% of a group of 11 female patients on a continuous care and rehabilitation ward. These patients were apparently less impaired physically than those in other studies, and several of them were discharged following training. Among four patients who were "mentally disoriented," one improved to a satisfactory extent, and two others showed improvement.

When the goal is to keep the patient dry, temporal voiding routines have proven successful, even with physically and mentally debilitated patients. Habit training may be self-administered by capable patients or caretaker-administered for the patient with functional disabilities. In most instances, it is clear that continence is not a result of relearning on the part of the patient. Continence results from alterations in the habits of the caregiver, and continued continence depends upon continued and consistent involvement of the caregiver.

Bladder Retraining

Bladder retraining (also termed bladder training or bladder drill) is also an intervention that focuses on the manipulation of antecedent conditions. The primary objective of this procedure is to restore a normal pattern of voiding and normal bladder function. Rather than adjusting the voiding schedule to the needs of the patient, bladder retraining encourages the patient to adopt an expanded voiding interval. By gradually increasing the voiding intervals, the patient corrects the bad habit of frequent voiding, improves his or her ability to suppress bladder instability, and eventually diminishes urgency.

Frewen (1978, 1980) provides the rationale for this approach. He proposed that urinary frequency is a precursor and a precipitant of bladder instability, and that urgency is not only a symptom of detrusor instability but an initiating factor because it increases frequency of urination, which contributes to decreased bladder capacity. The Frewen bladder drill program requires patients to resist the sensation of urgency, to postpone voiding, and to urinate by the clock rather than in response to an urge. The aim is to increase bladder capacity gradually. Frewen advocates admission to a hospital for 7–10 days for a combination of bladder drill, supportive therapy, anticholinergic medication, and sedatives. Using this regime with women aged 15–77 years, Frewen (1978, 1979) reported an 82–86% cure rate (i.e., patients were free of abnormal symptoms and showed normal cystometrogram results). Unfortunately, the contribution of the medication was not assessed independently of the behavioral procedure in these studies. A later assessment by Frewen (1982) of bladder retraining without medications in an outpatient setting, however, resulted in 97% of patients achieving continence.

Jarvis tested the bladder drill procedure without adjunctive medication in the treatment of women aged 17–79 with urge incontinence. He reported 61–90% cure rates (Jarvis, 1981, 1982; Jarvis & Millar, 1980). Other researchers have reported lower, but still impressive, success rates. Of their patients, 44–52% were cured, and an additional 25–34% showed improvement with bladder drill alone or in combination with other treatment (Elder & Stephenson, 1980; Pengally & Booth, 1980; Svigos & Matthews, 1977).

Bladder retraining, like habit training, has had no documented side effects, and the procedures are easy to implement. Research on bladder retraining indicates that incontinence can be reduced and bladder function altered through the modification of toileting habits. Bladder retraining requires the cooperation of a motivated patient who is mentally and physically capable of participating. Thus, it is more demanding than habit retraining, which emphasizes caregiver management.

Contingency Management

Contingency management procedures involve the systematic and consistent application of rewards and punishments to improve continence. They are most appropriate in institutional settings but can also be used with elderly people in the community who require the assistance of a caregiver. Although these procedures have usually been combined with habit training or bladder retraining, independent applications have been reported with mixed results.

Grosicki (1968) reported an unsuccessful attempt to reduce incontinence using contingent tokens and social interactions with 20 ambulatory men (aged 63–85) in a psychiatric unit of a veterans' hospital. Many had "genito-urinary system impairments." Patients were checked hourly and given 3 minutes of social attention if dry. In a separate trial, tokens were awarded for proper elimination and withdrawn if the patient was found incontinent. The experimental subjects showed no significant change, but the control subjects showed a significant reduction in incontinence. It is difficult to interpret these findings since subjects were not randomly assigned to groups.

Another unsuccessful application of contingency management was reported by Pollock and Liberman (1974) with six demented, ambulatory men, aged 61–79 years. During 1 week, patients were required to mop up following an incontinent episode and were not changed unless they requested it. For an additional 3 weeks, dry checks were rewarded with social interaction including praise and material rewards (e.g., candy, cigarettes). The authors note that the patients had memory deficits, and two were unable to locate the toilet. They suggest that the training may have been more effective if it had included physical guidance to the toilet and shaping of appropriate toileting behavior. One cannot expect to achieve continence unless appropriate voiding habits are established.

Wagner and Paul (1970) observed positive results from a stringent program for 19 psychotic male patients, aged 25–66. Dry checks were rewarded with candy, cigarettes, social approval, and progressively more comfortable sleeping conditions. Incontinence was punished by withholding up to two meals. All patients improved following 22 weeks of training. Six were completely continent, eight more were incontinent only at night, and five were improved, but not completely continent.

Multicomponent Behavioral Interventions

The most sophisticated application of behavioral procedures combines both antecedent and consequent manipulations into multicomponent treatment packages.

In the earliest multicomponent study, Carpenter and Simon (1960) compared two contingency management procedures with habit training and usual institutional care for 94 hospitalized, psychotic patients between the ages of 33 and 84. Patients were ambulatory and without known urinary tract abnormalities. Groups received either habit training alone (regular visits to the toilet every 2 hours), habit training plus verbal approval for successful toileting and disapproval for accidents, or habit training plus permission to wear a clean suit of personal clothing (instead of hospital fatigues) as long as they remained continent. Unfortunately, subjects were not randomly assigned to treatment groups. The nurses in charge of the experimental groups each chose their own patients, and the remaining patients served as controls. As a result, only the within-group comparisons are interpretable. The group receiving clothing privileges showed a rapid, sustained decrease in frequency of incontinence from 4.6 to 0.5 incontinent episodes per week within the first month of training. The verbal approval–disapproval group also showed significant reductions, from 4.5 to less than 0.5 accidents per week, but required more than 2 months of training. Neither the habit training alone nor the control group showed consistent decreases in incontinence.

In a carefully controlled study of incontinence in two nursing homes, Schnelle et al. (1983) implemented hourly checks for incontinence followed by prompts (reminders to void). Habit training was accomplished by contingency management procedures: social approval contingent on dry checks or patient requests for toileting assistance, and mild social disapproval for incontinence. In 11 geriatric patients, most of whom were diagnosed with senile dementia or organic brain syndrome and none of whom were independently ambulatory, correct toileting increased by 45% and incontinence was reduced by 49%. A large clinical trial of this procedure was cosponsored by the National Institute on Aging (1985) and the Division of Nursing of the Health Resources and Services Administration. Data from the study can be obtained from the authors.

A comprehensive approach to toilet-training retarded adults, aged 20–62, was described by Azrin and Foxx (1971). They conceptualized continence as a complex chain of behaviors, each of which must be taught. By encouraging a patient to drink excessive amounts of fluids, they artificially increased the frequency of urinations and intensively trained each patient 8 hours per day. The first step involved teaching the patient to walk to the commode, remove clothing, and sit on the commode. They immediately rewarded the patient with a snack food and praise for each successive approximation and they physically guided the patient's hands and body when necessary. They gave prompts to go to the toilet every 30 minutes and the patient received a reward for every 5 minutes with dry clothes (detected by means of a urine detector in the patient's pants). Urination in the toilet was also rewarded. Gradually they eliminated prompts and rewarded self-initiated toileting. When self-initiation occurred at a high frequency, the patient was moved farther and farther from the toilet, and the interval between pants checks was increased from every 5 minutes to several hours. Throughout this procedure, the patient was required to clean up following incontinent episodes and to practice going to, and sitting on, the commode several times. This program resulted in at least an 80% reduction in the frequency of accidents in an average of 6 days of training, and results were well maintained at follow-up 5 months later.

The Azrin and Foxx procedure was developed for retarded patients who had no history of successful toileting. Its appropriateness for demented geriatric patients who are not retarded, but have a different type of cognitive impairment and a history of continence, has not been established. It is probable that the procedure in its original form would be impractical in institutional settings for the elderly because families or nursing staff would object to the punishment components of the program. Moreover, many geriatric patients may lack the stamina required for such an intensive program. There are anecdotal reports that fluid loading in elderly incontinent patients is counterproductive. Empirical testing may indicate that, with modifications, the Azrin and Foxx method is useful for the elderly. For example, Sanavio (1981) reported achieving continence with a 60-year-old with urinary incontinence and a 77-year-old with fecal incontinence, using a modified form of this procedure.

Biofeedback

In the interventions described above, toileting habits are the primary targets of behavioral change. Biofeedback is a form of behavioral training that aims to reverse incontinence by altering physiological responses of the bladder and pelvic floor muscles that mediate incontinence. The targets of the intervention are the striated muscles of the pelvic floor or abdominal wall and the smooth detrusor muscles, which mediate bladder emptying.

Using biofeedback, physiological change is possible by means of operant conditioning through which suitably motivated patients can learn to control bladder and sphincter responses voluntarily by observing the results of their efforts. Intra-urethral resistance can be increased by training patients to contract periurethral muscles, and voluntary inhibition of bladder contractions can be relearned. Although biofeedback combines both antecedent and consequent conditions and thus can be considered a multicomponent procedure, due to the technical sophistication of this treatment it will be discussed separately for urge, stress, and overflow incontinence.

Urge Incontinence

The earliest reported use of a biofeedback procedure for urge incontinence was reported in 1948 by Wilson. He reported that 10 of 23 elderly patients with precipitancy or incontinence improved or became completely continent, and 5 others were somewhat improved following a diagnostic cystometrogram. During cystometrograms, bladder pressure readings were available to his patients and may have served as a mechanism for feedback that allowed them to acquire better control. Wilson referred to his method as inhibitory reeducative training, but he clearly described a form of intervention that would now be termed biofeedback.

Willington (1980) has also described a method of biofeedback in which a patient's catheter is attached to a vertical tube in which the fluid level is visible to the patient. The fluid level remains low as long as the bladder remains relaxed, but rises noticeably when bladder contractions occur.

Cardozo and her colleagues (Cardozo, Abrams, Stanton, & Feneley, 1978; Cardozo, Stanton, Hafner, & Allan, 1978) described a bladder pressure biofeedback procedure for treating urge incontinence. This method provides both auditory and visual feedback of bladder pressure during repeated bladder filling. Twenty-seven women aged 18–64 with bladder instability were treated in four to eight 1-hour sessions at weekly intervals. Of these women, 81% were improved, including 41% who were judged cured.

Investigators at the National Institute on Aging developed a procedure that provides simultaneous feedback of bladder pressure, anal sphincter activity, and intra-abdominal pressure (Burgio *et al.*, 1985). The third component, intra-abdominal pressure, was added because many patients exhibit a tendency to tense abdominal muscles while trying to prevent incontinence. This behavior is counterproductive because it increases bladder pressure and consequently increases the probability of urine loss. Simultaneous feedback of the three pressures provides a mechanism for operant conditioning of bladder, sphincter, and abdominal muscle responses. Specifically, patients acquire selective responses: bladder inhibition (relaxation) or active contraction of pelvic floor muscles coupled with abdominal relaxation. The procedure was tested as an integral component in a behavioral training program for treating urinary incontinence in an outpatient clinic. After incontinence was not resolved by a 2-hour voiding schedule, 18 elderly patients aged 60–86 (mean=72 years) with urge incontinence were given biofeedback. Patients achieved 39–100% reductions of incontinence following an average of four training sessions. This study demonstrated that biofeedback is a practical and effective approach to treating urge incontinence in older patients.

Stress Incontinence

The first report of feedback for stress incontinence was published by A. H. Kegel (1948), a gynecologist who asserted that stress-incontinent women lack awareness of function and coordination of pelvic floor muscle function. He developed what is now regarded as a biofeedback device, the perineometer, which was used by his patients to monitor the strength of pelvic floor muscle contractions during daily exercises. The perineometer consisted of an intravaginal balloon attached to an external pressure gauge that registered the strength of vaginal muscle contractions. Kegel (1956) reported 90% improvement among 455 women who were trained with this method.

Over the years, Kegel exercises have continued to be prescribed, but typically without the benefit of the perineometer. Instead, the patient is instructed to squeeze her vaginal muscles around the examiner's fingers to learn the correct technique, and she is instructed to practice contracting these muscles at home without feedback. She also may be asked to practice interrupting the urinary stream. Under these conditions, the exercises are apparently less effective, and their use has waned.

Burgio *et al.* (1985) used feedback of bladder pressure, abdominal pressure, and sphincter activity to teach elderly patients ways of selectively contracting and relaxing pelvic floor muscles without increasing bladder pressure or abdominal pressure. Following acquisition of this skill, they were instructed in the daily exercise of these muscles at home and the active contraction of these muscles to prevent leakage during physical activities that were known to produce incontinence. Nineteen patients aged 65–86 (mean=74 years) were trained in an average of three and one-half 1-hour sessions. These patients achieved an average 82% reduction in the frequency of urinary accidents.

Two studies investigated the importance of feedback in the treatment of stress incontinence. Shepherd, Montgomery, and Anderson (1983) trained voluntary contraction of pelvic floor muscles in 22 stress-incontinent women aged 29–64. One group of patients were trained using a vaginal perineometer similar to Kegel's. The control group was taught without the perineometer. Ninety-one percent of biofeedback patients, but only 55% of control patients, were cured or improved. Burgio, Robinson, and Engel (1986) treated 24 stress-incontinent women aged 29–64 using simultaneous bladder, sphincter, and abdominal pressure feedback. Results were similar to those of Shepherd *et al.* (1983). Ninety-two percent of biofeedback patients and 55% of control patients were cured or at least 50% improved. These studies indicate that feedback improves the patient's ability to learn appropriate pelvic floor contraction and increases the likelihood of successful physiotherapy.

Overflow Incontinence

There is one report of bladder pressure biofeedback used in the successful treatment of a child with atonic (acontractile) bladder secondary to traumatic cord injury (Schneider, 1972). Biofeedback has also been used in the treatment of bladder-sphincter dyssynergia (Maizels, King, & Firlet, 1979; Wear, Wear, & Cleeland, 1979). These disorders are not common among the elderly, but biofeedback may hold promise for this group of patients as well.

PRACTICAL APPLICATIONS

It is clear that more extensive research is needed on the efficacy of behavioral treatments for urinary incontinence in the elderly. In particular, studies are needed of the relative contributions of behavioral procedures and other interventions, as well as their combined effectiveness. Current data on the application of these procedures is sufficient, however, to justify their application in clinical practice. In the United States, behavior therapy for incontinence is not currently available to most institutionalized or community-dwelling elderly. This situation is changing, however, and behavior therapists can promote such change in several ways.

First, they can initiate the establishment of continence services. Second, as consultants, they can train care providers to implement behavioral interventions. Third, as teachers they can educate future care providers. In all these roles the behavior therapist has the opportunity to disseminate information that will help to dispel the many myths about incontinence.

Incontinence clinics are well established in Great Britain, where nurse continence advisors have professional status. In the United States, continence clinics that offer behavior therapies are far less common and exist primarily in research settings. Outpatient services can be administered by behavior therapists or by appropriately trained nurses provided that patients are medically screened. Such interdisciplinary services might be situated in hospitals, health maintenance organizations, behavioral medicine clinics, or the offices of geriatricians, gynecologists, or family practice physicians.

The success of behavioral interventions in these settings is largely dependent upon the abilities of the behavior therapist and the physician or nurse to form a successful collaboration. The behavior therapist has special knowledge of the behavioral principles underlying incontinence. Nurses can offer an abundance of practical information derived from their experience as care providers in institutions, day-care settings, and community service facilities. The expertise of the physician in the diagnostic phase is critical in determining the causes of incontinence and the appropriateness of behavioral intervention.

Behavioral programs to treat incontinence in the institutionalized elderly will also benefit from interdisciplinary collaboration. Nurses in these settings usually have little or no formal training in behavioral principles, yet they play a critical role in the successful management of incontinent patients. Treatment of the institutionalized patient usually requires external management as opposed to self-management procedures. Thus, the intervention is likely to be time-consuming and intensive. It will be necessary to change the behavior of the care provider. A staff-administered habit-training and contingency management program for impaired nursing home patients requires training of the staff who will apply the procedures, regular and continued involvement of the staff, and systematic monitoring by supervisors to ensure that the procedures are maintained over time.

In essence, the success of such an inpatient program relies on procedures that teach staff how to implement treatments for their patients. Of equal importance, though often neglected, are staff management procedures that provide direct care staff with the structure and incentives needed to ensure that their skills are consistently performed over time. Systematic procedures for training and managing staff behavior can be developed by behavior therapists who function as consultants to nursing homes.

In addition to initiating clinics and serving as consultants, behavior therapists can influence the practice of behavioral medicine through teaching roles in nursing or medical schools. As faculty members, behavioral scientists could provide medical or nursing students with specialized training in biofeedback and a variety of other behavioral interventions. While they acquire their basic education, students would have the opportunity to develop skills not only for treating incontinence, but for the management of other clinical problems of the elderly. Formal training in the principles of human behavior will promote systematic application of behavioral techniques with the potential for improving health care and preventing institutionalization of many older adults.

REFERENCES

Azrin, N. H., & Foxx, R. M. (1971). A rapid method of toilet training the institutionalized retarded. *Journal of Applied Behavior Analysis, 4*, 89–99.

Bradley, W. E., Timm, G. W., & Scott, F. B. (1974). Innervation of the detrusor muscle and urethra. In J. Lapides (Ed.), *Symposium on neurogenic bladder, urologic clinics of North America* (pp. 3–27). Philadelphia: W. B. Saunders.

Burgio, K. L., Whitehead, W. E., & Engel, B. T. (1985). Urinary incontinence in the elderly: Bladder-sphincter biofeedback and toileting skills training. *Annals of Internal Medicine, 103*, 507–515.

Burgio, K. L., Robinson, J. C., & Engel, B. T. (1986). The role of biofeedback in Kegel exercise training for stress urinary incontinence. *American Journal of Obstetrics and Gynecology, 154*, 58–64.

Cardozo, L. D., Abrams, P. D., Stanton, S. L., & Feneley, R. C. L. (1978). Idiopathic bladder instability treated by biofeedback. *British Journal of Urology, 50*, 27–30.

Cardozo, L. D., Stanton, S. L., Hafner, J., & Allan, V. (1978). Biofeedback in the treatment of detrusor instability. *British Journal of Urology, 50*, 250–254.

Carpenter, H. A., & Simon, R. (1960). Effect of several methods of training on long-term incontinent, behaviorally regressed hospitalized patients. *Nursing Research, 9*, 17–22.

Castleden, C. M., George, C. F., Renwick, A. G., & Asher, M. J. (1981). Imipramine—a possible alternative to current therapy for urinary incontinence in the elderly. *Journal of Urology, 125*, 318–320.

Clay, E. C. (1978). Incontinence of urine: A regime for retraining. *Nursing Mirror, 146*, 23–24.

Clay, E. C. (1980). Promoting urine control in older adults: Habit retraining. *Geriatric Nursing, 1*, 252–254.

Elder, D. D., & Stephenson, T. P. (1980). An assessment of the Frewen regime in the treatment of detrusor dysfunction in females. *British Journal of Urology, 52*, 467–471.

Feneley, R. C. L., Shepherd, A. M., Powell, P. H., & Blannin, J. (1979). Urinary incontinence: Prevalence and needs. *British Journal of Urology, 51*, 493–496.

Folstein, M. F., Folstein, S. E., & McHugh, P. R. (1975). "Mini-mental state". A practical method for grading the cognitive state of patients for the clinician. *Journal of Psychiatric Research, 12*, 189–198.

Frewen, W. K. (1978). An objective assessment of the unstable bladder of psychosomatic origin. *British Journal of Urology, 50*, 246–249.

Frewen, W. K. (1979). Role of bladder training in the treatment of the unstable bladder in the female. *Urologic Clinics of North America, 6*, 273–277.

Frewen, W. K. (1980). The management of urgency and frequency of micturition. *British Journal of Urology, 52*, 367–369.

Frewen, W. K. (1982). A reassessment of bladder training in detrusor dysfunction in the female. *British Journal of Urology, 54*, 372–373.

Grosicki, J. P. (1968). Effect of operant conditioning on incontinence in neuropsychiatric geriatric patients. *Nursing Research, 17*, 304–311.

Jarvis, G. J. (1981). A controlled trial of bladder drill and drug therapy in the management of detrusor instability. *Journal of Urology, 53*, 565–566.

Jarvis, G. J. (1982). The management of urinary incontinence due to primary vesical sensory urgency by bladder drill. *British Journal of Urology, 54*, 374–376.

Jarvis, G. J., & Millar, D. R. (1980). Controlled trial of bladder drill for detrusor instability. *British Medical Journal, 281*, 1322–1323.

Jewett, M. A. S., Fernie, G. R., Holliday, P. J., & Pim, M. E. (1981). Urinary dysfunction in a geriatric long-term care population: Prevalence and patterns. *Journal of the American Geriatrics Society, 29,* 211–214.

Kegel, A. H. (1948). Progressive resistance exercise in the functional restoration of the perineal muscles. *American Journal of Obstetrics and Gynecology, 56,* 238–248.

Kegel, A. H. (1956). Stress incontinence of urine in women: Physiologic treatment. *Journal of the International College of Surgeons, 25,* 487–499.

Maizels, M., King, L. R., & Firlet, C. F. (1979). Urodynamic biofeedback: A new approach to treat vesical sphincter dyssynergia. *Journal of Urology, 122,* 205–209.

Moisey, C. U., Stephenson, T. P., & Brendler, C. B. (1980). The urodynamic and subjective results of treatment of detrusor instability with oxybutinin chloride. *British Journal of Urology, 52,* 472–475.

National Institute on Aging (1985). *Seventh Report to Council on Program.* Bethesda, MD: Author.

Ouslander, J. G., & Kane, R. L. (1984). The costs of urinary incontinence in nursing homes. *Medical Care, 22,* 69–79.

Ouslander, J. G., Kane, R. L., & Abrass, I. B. (1982). Urinary incontinence in elderly nursing home patients. *Journal of the American Medical Association, 248,* 1194–1198.

Pengelly, A. W., & Booth, C. M. (1980). A prospective trial of bladder training as treatment for detrusor instability. *British Journal of Urology, 52,* 463–466.

Pfeiffer, E. (1976). A short portable mental status questionnaire for the assessment of organic brain deficit in elderly patients. *Journal of the American Geriatrics Society, 23,* 433–437.

Pollack, D. D., & Liberman, R. P. (1974). Behavior therapy of incontinence in demented inpatients. *The Gerontologist, 14,* 488–491.

Sanavio, E. (1981). Toilet training psychogeriatric residents. *Behavior Modification, 5,* 417–427.

Schneider, R. D. (1972). Adjuvant bladder-pressure biofeedback in treating neurogenic bladder dysfunction: A case report. *Behavior Therapist, 2,* 29.

Schnelle, J. F., Traughber, B., Morgan, D. B., Embry, J. E., Binion, A. F., & Coleman, A. (1983). Management of geriatric incontinence in nursing homes. *Journal of Applied Behavior Analysis, 16,* 235–241.

Shepherd, A. M., Montgomery, E., & Anderson, R. S. (1983). Treatment of genuine stress incontinence with a new perineometer. *Physiotherapy, 69,* 113.

Sogbein, S. K., & Awad, S. A. (1982). Behavioral treatment of urinary incontinence in geriatric patients. *Canadian Medical Association Journal, 127,* 863–864.

Spangler, P. F., Risley, T. R., & Bilyew, D. P. (1984). The management of dehydration and incontinence in nonambulatory geriatric patients. *Journal of Applied Behavior Analysis, 17,* 397–401.

Svigos, J. M., & Matthews, C. D. (1977). Assessment and treatment of female urinary incontinence by cystometrogram and bladder retraining programs. *Obstetrics and Gynecology, 50,* 9–12.

U.S. DHEW, PHS, Office of Nursing Home Affairs (1975). *Long-term care facility improvement study* (Pub. #PHS 588–459). Washington, DC: U.S. Government Printing Office.

Wagner, B. R., & Paul, G. L. (1970). Reduction of incontinence in chronic mental patients: A pilot project. *Journal of Behavior Therapy and Experimental Psychiatry, 1,* 29–38.

Wear, J. B., Jr., Wear, R. B., & Cleeland, C. (1979). Biofeedback in urology using urodynamics: Preliminary observations. *Journal of Urology, 121,* 464–468.

Whitehead, W. E., Burgio, K. L., & Engel, B. T. (1984). Behavioral methods in the assessment and treatment of urinary incontinence. In J. C. Brocklehurst (Ed.), *Urology in the elderly* (pp. 74–92). New York: Churchill Livingstone.

Willington, F. L. (1980). Urinary incontinence: A practical approach. *Geriatrics, 35,* 41–48.

Wilson, T. S. (1948). Incontinence of urine in the aged. *Lancet, 2,* 374–377.

Wolin, L. H. (1969). Stress incontinence in young, healthy nulliparous female subjects. *The Journal of Urology, 101,* 545–549.

Yarnell, J. W. G., Voyle, G. J., Richards, C. J., & Stephenson, T. P. (1981). The prevalence and severity of urinary incontinence in women. *Journal of Epidemiology and Community Health, 35,* 71–74.

15

Treatment Applications for Psychological and Behavioral Problems of the Elderly in Nursing Homes

Laura L. Carstensen and Jane E. Fisher

Introduction

About 1.3 million elderly people currently live in some 18,000 nursing homes in this country (Eustis, Greenberg, & Patten, 1984). Although this number represents only 5% of the population of elderly persons, it is misleading to think that nursing home placement is a concern for an insignificant portion of the aged population. Only 5% reside in nursing homes at any point in time, but the lifetime probability of placement in a nursing home is 25–30% (Lesnoff-Caravaglia, 1978–1979). That is, for those elderly who live into advanced old age, the odds of placement increase from 1 in 20 to 1 in 4. As the aging population steadily grows in size, with the "old-old" segment growing fastest, the absolute number of old people living in nursing homes will continue to increase well past the turn of the century. By 2050, if present trends continue, the number of institutionalized elderly people is expected to reach 5.2 million (Brody & Foley, 1985). There is no doubt that this group of physically frail elderly has psychological problems that demand our attention, problems that present significant economic, social, and ethical dilemmas for families, caregivers, and professionals involved in their care.

However misleading, the infamous 5% statistic is important because it begins to paint the picture of the population that resides in long-term care facilities. They are by no means representative of the elderly population at large. They are older

Laura L. Carstensen • Department of Psychology, Stanford University, Stanford, California 94131. Jane E. Fisher • Department of Psychology, Northern Illinois University, DeKalb, Illinois 60115. Work on this chapter was supported in part by a grant to the senior author from the National Institute on Aging R23 AG05592.

(35% of persons over 85 years live in nursing homes); they are more likely to be widowed; and they typically suffer from multiple medical problems. Psychological disorders also are abundant. Whanger (1980) estimated that 80% of nursing home residents suffer from significant psychiatric disturbance. In some studies, estimated prevalence of organic brain syndromes exceeds 60% among institutionalized populations, and 50% have prior psychiatric histories. Thus, these are the frailest of the frail elderly, many of whom have always functioned "on the edge" and in late life find preexisting problems compounded by yet another hardship—old age.

In spite of the clear evidence of need, treatment for emotional and behavior problems in nursing homes is virtually nonexistent. Few nursing homes employ psychiatrists, psychologists, or counselors. With the exception of a few model research nursing homes (e.g., The Philadelphia Geriatrics Center, Philadelphia, PA, and the Geriatric Research and Education Centers, GRECs, established by the Veteran's Administration), few nursing homes in this country have integrated mental health care into standard practice. Thus, while a good deal of clinical research on this population has been reported in the literature, it rarely reflects a treatment effort implemented by a nursing home.

In the following pages we discuss the brief but significant history of the nursing home industry, review the major psychological and behavioral problems common to the population of nursing home residents, overview theoretical issues relevant to behavioral treatment of the problems of residents in nursing homes, and selectively review behavioral treatment approaches for some common problems nursing home residents experience. (We have omitted the review of major psychological disorders that are the focus of specific chapters in this book, e.g., anxiety disorders, depression.) Finally, we consider the ethical implications of behavioral treatment and provide general treatment guidelines for interventions with the elderly in nursing homes.

HISTORICAL TRENDS AND CURRENT STATUS

The nursing home industry does not have a long history. In the late 1800s and early 1900s, care homes for the destitute were established at the community level. They were synonymous with poor houses and housed the down and out, mostly elderly individuals who lacked earning power. In 1935, the Social Security Act provided older people with a fixed income. Consequently, the nursing home industry evolved to meet the needs of this newly monied population.

Still, for many years nursing homes were relatively scarce, populated by older people suffering primarily from physical problems. In the 1960s, deinstitutionalization of patients from state mental hospitals dramatically changed the composition of nursing homes. Quickly and painfully it became apparent that people who had spent most of their lives in state mental hospitals had been discharged to communities unprepared to meet their needs. Many of these people were unable to function independently. Facing a dearth of community resources, 40% of those discharged entered nursing homes. Noble as were the sentiments that stimulated the deinstitutionalization movement, their impracticality soon became apparent. Virtually overnight, homes designed for the physically infirm aged became homes for a "needy" psychiatric population of varied ages.

The change was significant, not only for the discharged psychiatric patient, but also for the older person living in a nursing home. There were few psychiatric services: care was provided primarily by aides. The impact of the admission of these patients on the psychologically "normal" nursing home resident is rarely discussed, but it was, no doubt, profound. One can only speculate about the sudden change in social climate that must have occurred. Older people with even minor cognitive problems may have felt that they must be "crazy" too.

Today the nursing home population is highly diverse. A *minority* of residents, about 15%, have purely physical problems. Teeter, Garet, Miller, and Heiland (1976) reported that 85% of the nursing home residents in their samples had concomitant psychological and physical problems. Approximately one-third had primary diagnoses of mental disorders or senility. In a study of Chicago nursing homes, Shadish, Straw, McSweeny, Koller, and Bootzin (1981) found that 65% of nursing home residents in intermediate care facilities were former mental patients. Schmidt, Reinhardt, Kane, and Olsen (1977), in a survey of Utah facilities, reported that 35–70% of nursing home residents were diagnosed psychotic. Other studies report varying estimates, most likely reflecting differences in the composition of the groups of nursing homes surveyed. Some nursing homes have established admission policies that limit the percentage of psychiatric patients in residence at any point in time; others restrict the admission of demented patients. But, regardless of admission policy, nursing homes are places where old people suffering from significant psychological distress are protoytpical. The distress may have led them to the nursing home or it may have followed admission. But the psychologically healthy old person in a nursing home is the exception, not the rule.

What are the predisposing factors to nursing home placement? Not surprisingly, demographic factors are excellent predictors. The U.S. Bureau of Census (1976) reported the following statistics: half of the individuals living in nursing homes are childless; 20% never married; only 14% have a living spouse; most are women. The preponderance of women in nursing homes is due to some extent to the increased longevity of women over men, leaving more women widowed and without companionship or assistance than men. Clearly, being alone is a highly significant predictor of nursing home placement.

The largest percentage of old people admitted to nursing homes are transferred from hospitals for convalescence. Others enter directly from the community for a wide variety of reasons. Many, having had a close call with an accident, decide that they prefer the safety of a nursing home. Others who have lived for some time with their families are admitted to nursing homes after the family has exhausted their own personal and financial resources. Still others are placed because the adult caregivers, often elderly themselves, experience catastrophic illnesses. Some old people decide to enter because they view nursing homes as places where they will not be as isolated as they were in the community. Many are avid in contending that they do not want to live with their children, preferring a nursing home residence over one with a relative where they would feel burdened with the guilt of imposition. Yet few enter as a matter of preference. Even those who choose to enter typically view the choice as their only viable alternative. The vast majority of nursing home residents readily contend that they would rather be living in their own homes. Thus, entering a nursing home is almost always a difficult transition for the elderly individual and his or her family.

Chronic physical disability, more so than acute disability, places one at risk for nursing home care. Incontinence and impaired ambulation are two primary physical predisposing factors. For obvious practical reasons, these problems can lead to functional impairment that surpasses even more life-threatening diseases. Interestingly, however, psychological factors place one at even higher risk. Newman (1976) reported that impairment in psychological domains is four times more likely to lead to nursing home placement than physical disability.

As Brody (1986) has noted, however, "old age and disability in themselves do not account for institutionalization, since twice the number of severely impaired old people live in the community as live in institutions" (in Shanas, 1982, p. 239). Brody, Poulshock, and Masciocchi (1978) contend that the critical factor in determining entrance to a nursing home versus community residence is absence of social support from the family.

To recapitulate, the complexion of the nursing home industry has changed significantly since it's inception some 50 years ago. As the rates of psychiatric admissions to mental hospitals declined, rates of psychiatric admissions to nursing homes skyrocketed. Nursing homes, previously a place for the few elderly without families or income, have come to house over a million people in this country—a vastly heterogeneous population that includes expsychiatric and demented patients as well as old people suffering from significant physical disability.

PSYCHOLOGICAL PROBLEMS OF THE ELDERLY IN NURSING HOMES

The plethora of emotional and behavioral problems among nursing home residents is undeniable, but surprisingly little is known about the breakdown of specific psychological disorders in these settings. In part, this is due to poor or absent diagnostic practices for nonmedical problems. In a review of existing epidemiological data, however, Blazer (1980) reported the sobering finding that only 14% of the elderly in nursing homes are in good mental health. The rest of the population are plagued by the effects of alcohol abuse (approximately 20%, as contrasted with 2% to 10% of community elderly, according to the USDHEW, 1971); organic brain syndromes (in 35% to 70%, Schmidt et al., 1977); and schizophrenic and paranoid symptoms (in 11% of the residents according to Teeter et al., 1976). Rates of depression are assumed to be extremely high, but precise estimates are unknown because of the overlapping symptomatology with the senile dementias and subsequent misdiagnoses (Eustis et al., 1984). Rates of anxiety disorders among nursing home residents are also expected to be quite high, but again, an absence of formal diagnosis makes prevalence rates difficult to establish. Teeter et al. (1976) did report that 17% of subjects in their study displayed symptoms consonant with neurotic disorders. Rates of anxiety disorders *per se* were not reported.

Behavior problems common among nursing home residents include wandering, disorientation, social withdrawal, agitation, confusion, dependency, skill deficits in self-care, and a host of other problems consistent with the major psychological disorders noted above. In addition the pervasiveness of behavior problems and psychopathology among nursing home residents, there are a number of normal concerns that many nursing home residents acknowledge. These including wanting to return home, adjusting to the loss of privacy, problems associated with chronic illness, getting along with other nursing home residents, and infrequent contact with friends and relatives (Carstensen & Fisher, 1984).

PERTINENT THEORETICAL ISSUES

Several general methods of aging hold great relevance to the elderly in nursing homes. M. P. Lawton's theoretical model of competence, environmental press, and adaptation (Lawton & Nahemow, 1973; Lawton, 1975, 1977) holds particular significance for treatment of the aged in nursing homes. Expounding on Murray's (1938) notion of a need–press system, Lawton and his colleagues developed an ecological model of aging that takes into consideration the competence level of the individual and the level of environmental press in the individual's immediate surroundings. *Environmental press* refers to physical or social stressors that influence adaptation level. In Lawton's model, however, environmental press is defined in relation to the competence level of the individual. What functions as a weak stimulus to a highly competent individual may function as a potent stimulus to a less competent individual. A basic assumption in the model is that humans constantly orient toward neutral emotional and behavioral states, referred to as "adaptation level." Although mild deviations from one's adaptation level are experienced as pleasant, simulation beyond this optimal range is harmful, experienced as either deprivation or overload (Lawton, 1975). Figure 1 provides an visual representation of the model.

Lawton's model, then, would suggest that optimal environments are not stable across the life span nor consistent across individuals. Rather, an environment that could maximize positive affect and adaptive behavior in a physically healthy and productive worker at age 28 could function as behaviorally toxic for that same individual when she is 80 years old and arthritic. Social environments can be interpreted in a similar manner. A 40-year-old socially active woman with a large social network and myriad social obligations may experience that environment as maximizing her performance potential. Yet, in advanced age, she may find the same environment intolerable. In a similar vein, environments with too little stimulation can have deleterious effects. When an 80-year-old woman reaches a point in her life where her environment is void of social contacts, the result may be negative affect and maladaptive behavior.

The decision to enter a nursing home is often made on the realization that the demands of the existing environment exceed the competence of the individual. Unfortunately, nursing homes often provide so little stimulation that the affective

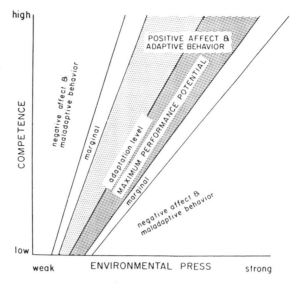

FIGURE 1.   Diagrammatic representation of the behavioral and affective outcomes of person–environment transaction. From Lawton and Nahemow, 1973. Copyright 1973 by the American Psychological Association. Reprinted by permission.

and behavioral consequences are as deleterious, in their own way, as the previous ones. Optimizing the individual's adaptation level requires a consideration of his or her level of competence in an environment designed to maximize utilization of the person's skills and minimize insurmountable obstacles.

Finding and maintaining that optimal level for each individual resident is a difficult goal to achieve. In fact, such a goal works directly against the principles by which institutions operate. One is reminded of Goffman's (1961) sociological analysis of total institutions. "Total" institutions, according to Goffman, are institutions in which all of one's physical and social needs are provided under the same roof by people without regard to individual differences. The result that Goffman predicts is a loss of prior identify, low self-esteem, and the perception that one is unable to care for oneself, a profile that is alarmingly consistent with the behavior of nursing home residents.

In recent years, behavioral researchers have offered explanations for the impoverished behavior of the institutionalized elderly based on learning theory. Although these behavioral interpretations focus more specifically on antecedents and consequences of maladaptive behaviors, they are in no way incompatible with Lawton's environmental model or Goffman's sociological analysis. Antecedent conditions can include social and psychological losses, as well as decrements in the individual's physical condition. Consequences of behavior also change as a function of age. Social reinforcement for a particular behavior may be qualitatively different, or in some cases absent, for the frail old person (see Sperbeck & Whitbourne, 1981). Baltes and her colleagues (Baltes, Burgess, & Steward, 1980; Barton, Baltes, & Orzech, 1980) have argued that the dependency for which nursing home residents are notorious is in fact reinforced by nursing home staff. In several studies, Baltes found that independent behavior was ignored by staff; only dependent behavior was reinforced. Thus, there appear to be clear changes in circumstances surrounding behaviors that accompany old age.

Regardless of the theoretical model one adopts, there is considerable evidence for the contention that behavioral deficits of the elderly in nursing homes exceed the functional limitations determined by physical infirmity. It is undeniable that for some individuals nursing home placement invokes powerful effects on psychological well-being. But one cannot forget that the elderly in nursing homes are the frailest of the frail, suffering from multiple psychological and physical problems. It is not the case that the problems of most nursing home residents would disappear outside of the institution. In fact, for many families, nursing home placement of an elder family member leads to an improvement of intergenerational family relations (Smith & Bengston, 1979). The benefits of providing 24-hour nursing care, emergency medical service, and adequate nutrition often go unacknowledged but should not be minimized. At this time, there are no obvious alternatives.

The task of the behavior therapist working with the elderly nursing home resident is to optimize the level of adaptation. For many, this will involve *increasing* the environmental demands of the environment so that existing skills (both physical and psychological) are maximized. For others, the task will involve the removal of obstacles that require skills beyond the individual's capabilities.

TREATMENT STRATEGIES FOR SELECTED PROBLEMS

In this section, we review the behavioral literature on treatment strategies for self-care skills, wandering, inappropriate sexual behavior, social behavior, and paranoia in an effort to elucidate treatment approaches for some problems common among nursing home elderly.

Maintenance of self-care skills such as bathing, eating, toothbrushing, dressing, and toileting is essential if one is to function as an acceptable member of society. Although the majority of these skills are learned early in life, the elderly in nursing homes often experience a depletion of the reinforcement contingencies that are necessary for their maintenance. Several studies of nursing home residents have identified poor environmental living conditions as responsible for the performance decrements of these skills (Baltes & Zerbe, 1976; Geiger & Johnson, 1974; Risely & Edwards, 1978). In a study of the self-help behaviors of residents in a nursing home, Baltes *et al.* (1978) found that although residents displayed independent self-help skills, these behaviors were usually ignored or discouraged by the staff. More frequently, residents received attention and support if they failed to exhibit self-help behaviors.

Various types of behavioral approaches have been utilized to increase the occurrence of self-help behaviors. Interventions designed to increase self-feeding, ambulation, and self-grooming have been successfully applied within nursing homes. A review of the treatment literature on self-care is provided below.

Eating

The utility of operant techniques for the reinstatement of self-feeding or correct eating behavior has been demonstrated in several studies. Risley and Edwards (1978) combined physical guidance and praise for successive feeding attempts in a sample of elderly nursing home residents. Self-feeding was successfully reestablished in a relatively short period of time by fading guided participation into self-directed motion and applying positive reinforcement in the form of praise and food on a contingent basis. Baltes and Zerbe (1976) utilized a reversal design to increase self-feeding in a 67-year-old woman who had not demonstrated self-maintenance behavior for a period of 5 months. The treatment program consisted of verbal prompting combined with stimulus control procedures, immediate reinforcement, and a time-out procedure for refusal to eat and such inappropriate behaviors as dropping food on the floor. During the treatment phases, self-feeding increased dramatically over a baseline frequency that was close to zero. Geiger and Johnson (1974) provided rewards contingent on correct eating behavior to elderly nursing home residents. Subjects who completed the training procedure displayed increases in correct eating behavior that ranged from 12% to 84%. Although the functional relationship between reinforcer administration and increases in correct eating was clearly demonstrated through a reversal design, no follow-up data were reported.

Before implementing a program to increase self-feeding, the therapist should determine whether physical problems such as arthritis, visual deficits, or hand tremors are preventing clients from eating independently. If clients have stopped feeding themselves because of physical limitations, it may not be possible for them to return to complete independence. Frequently, however, nursing home staff have taken over most or all of residents' self-feeding tasks because this requires less time than allowing residents to feed themselves. If this is the case, treatment may involve instructing the staff in ways to help residents remain as independent as possible and reinforcing them for attending to strategies that promote independence. For clients with manual dexterity problems, utensils can be modified by building up handles with foam rubber and tape. Bowls or plates with enlarged rims can also be used to facilitate food pick up. If there does not appear to be a physical disorder involved in the deficit, a functional analysis of eating behavior can identify precisely the troublesome behaviors, the conditions under which they occur, and the frequency of occurrence.

Operant procedures appear to be especially appropriate for teaching self-feeding skills because powerful reinforcers (viz., the food itself) are built into feeding programs (O'Brien, Bugle, & Azrin, 1972). Programs for clients who no longer display any self-feeding skills may need to begin with manual guidance. This fairly common procedure involves a staff member holding the client's hand closed around the spoon or fork, filling it, and bringing it to the client's mouth. As the client becomes more skilled, the staff member reduces the amount of assistance, possibly by shifting the manual guidance from the hand to the forearm, elbow, and finally the shoulder. For residents who have at least minimal self-feeding skills, the staff person may increase independence by combining instructions with an appropriate positive reinforcer contingent upon independent eating behavior.

In addition to teaching appropriate behavior, self-feeding programs occasionally include procedures for reducing inappropriate behaviors such as taking other patient's food, eating too fast, throwing food or utensils, and/or eating food that was spilled on tables or on the floor. A variety of procedures can be used to reduce inappropriate mealtime behaviors. Briefly withdrawing the client's chair from the table or removing the client's food for a short period of time (e.g., 15 seconds) while providing no attention can reduce the frequency of inappropriate behaviors.

Hussian and Davis (1985) suggest that differential reinforcement of other behavior (DRO) incompatible with a problem behavior is a useful technique for increasing correct eating behavior. A favorite food or drink is provided at intervals throughout the meals during which inappropriate behavior was not displayed. The length of the interval can be determined by assessing the maximal length of time a client naturally refrains from engaging in inappropriate behavior during a meal. For example, if a client can eat for 5 minutes without stealing food, then the DRO interval would be set at 3 or 4 minutes. This ensures that reinforcement occurs when the inappropriate response is absent.

Ambulation

A problem frequently observed among elderly nursing home residents is decline in mobility. This behavioral deficit has been associated with serious sequelae including urinary incontinence, muscle atrophy, hypostatic pneumonia, labile blood pressure, and decreases in bone mass (Hogue, 1985).

Reductions in mobility may be caused by physical limitations, environmental influences, or a combination of these. Cerebrovascular accident, for example, may impair motor functioning, while inadequate staff-to-resident ratios may preclude the implementation of adequate physical therapy. The architectural design of a nursing home can also influence mobility. For example, hand rails and nonglare flooring can facilitate ambulation, while poor lighting and slick flooring may hamper it. Staff behavior may also impact on ambulation, as Baltes, Honn, Barton, Orzech, and Lago (1983) have demonstrated. As with other types of independent behaviors, these authors documented that walking is rarely followed by staff attention, while requests for assistance are readily reinforced. Other reinforcement contingencies may also operate within nursing homes to reduce the motivation of residents to walk. We have observed, for example, that within some nursing homes wheelchairs are associated with certain privileges and become a status symbol that is sought after by residents who do not require a wheelchair for any medical reason. For example, residents in wheelchairs are often allowed into the dining room for meals and other activities before all other residents. Alternating the schedule for entering the dining room first would reduce the attractiveness of using a wheelchair for those who do not require one.

Several intervention studies have demonstrated the efficacy of reinforcement techniques for increasing walking among elderly nursing home residents. Sachs (1975) conducted two case studies in which tokens were given on a contingent basis to increase the number of minutes or the distance walked among two elderly nursing home residents. In the first case, an 88-year-old woman who was rarely observed out of her wheelchair or room earned points exchangeable for back-up reinforcers for every minute she walked. Time spent walking increased significantly. In the second case, a 64-year-old man with Parkinson's disease earned tokens for every 25 feet he walked. Following intervention this subject increased the distance he covered and decreased the time it took him to initiate walking. Although the results of these case studies are promising, the lack of information about the observation system used in the study and the reliability of the observations limit the conclusions that can be drawn. In addition, no follow-up data were reported.

MacDonald and Butler (1974) used a reversal design to increase independent walking in two nursing home residents. Verbal and physical prompts combined with contingent staff attention and praise resulted in increases in the target behavior for both residents. However, the opportunity for residents to walk during baseline was not specified and no follow-up data were reported.

A recently reported study by Burgio, Burgio, Engel, and Tice (1986) focused on increasing the degree of independence of ambulation as well as the distance walked during a meal in eight nursing home residents. Using a combination of praise and prompts similar to those used by MacDonald and Butler (1974), Burgio et al. demonstrated increases in the distances walked across six of eight subjects through a multiple-baseline across-subjects-and-settings design. Two of the subjects demonstrated ceiling levels of walking during baseline. Generalization was assessed by measuring distances walked during a different meal in which praise and prompts were not administered. Generalization to the second meal was observed in all subjects for whom it could be assessed. Walking in areas other than the dining room did not increase following intervention.

Data on independence of ambulation, assessed by observing the amount of assistance requested and the use of prosthetic devices such as canes and walkers, indicated that six of the eight subjects progressed to more independent means of ambulation following intervention. Follow-up data indicated maintenance or increases of the distances walked for all subjects for whom this could be measured as well as maintenance or increases in independence.

The findings reported above provide support for the role of environmental contingencies in the maintenance of independent ambulation. Again, we find that a common behavioral deficit among the elderly in nursing homes is due not to physical impairment or a skill deficit, but rather to environmental contingencies (Baltes et al., 1983). The finding that independent ambulation can be enhanced by rather simple techniques has implications not only for the effective use of staff time but also for the health of residents if the sequelae associated with inactivity can be prevented.

Grooming

To date, only a few studies have investigated the use of behavioral techniques for increasing self-grooming skills in the elderly. In one study, Rinke, Williams, Lloyd, and Smith-Scott (1978) reestablished self-bathing in six elderly nursing home residents through the use of prompts and reinforcement in the form of praise, visual feedback, and food items. The authors found that this combination increased self-care for several behavior categories involved in self-bathing, including undressing, soaping, rinsing, drying, and dressing.

Sachs (1975) used the behavioral techniques of shaping and reinforcement with tokens to improve oral hygiene in three elderly nursing home residents. The first phase of the program consisted simply of providing tokens to reinforce toothbrushing after meals. In the second phase, tokens were administered contingent upon clients picking up their toothbrushes from the nursing station, brushing their teeth, and returning the toothbrushes within 30 minutes after completing the task. The program effectively increased the frequency of toothbrushing in two of the residents, but when the treatment required picking up and returning the toothbrush, the third subject decreased the rate at which he successfully completed the task. It is possible that this subject had too many demands placed on him too quickly or that he was not competent in carrying out the extended chain of behaviors.

Prior to designing and implementing a program to improve self-grooming skills, the therapist should identify the physical and social factors contributing to the deficits. These may include such problems as arthritis or poor vision, memory deficits that interfere with the clients' recall of the need to groom, or nursing home staff who take over grooming tasks in order to save time.

As with self-feeding, if physical limitations are the primary cause of a client's failure to groom, it may not be possible for that individual to return to full independence. Grooming instruments can be modified to facilitate the acquisition of at least partial independence. For residents suffering from arthritis or hand tremors, large combs may facilitate grasp. As with eating utensils, the handles of hair and toothbrushes can be enlarged with foam rubber and tape so that they can be held more comfortably. Prosthetic grooming devices are available through hospital supply companies.

Prompting and daily charts that are checked off after a task is completed may be useful for residents with memory problems. Hussian and Davis (1985) suggest that stimulus control techniques are useful for clients with very severe memory impairments for whom verbal prompts prove ineffective. These authors note that grooming activities should be carried out in a maximally consistent manner. Grooming tasks should be scheduled to occur at the same time of day, in the same area, with the same materials.

The following rules may be useful in teaching grooming behaviors: (1) the task should be divided into small steps; (2) to maximize stimulus control, training should occur daily at the same time, in the same area, with the same materials; (3) initially, task performance should be reinforced for each correct step in the chain of behaviors needed to complete the task; (4) and reinforcement should be gradually delayed until the entire behavior sequence has been completed.

As with any self-care task, correct grooming responses and cooperation should be reinforced with praise and, if necessary, primary reinforcers such as food or drink. If residents are not grooming themselves independently because the nursing home staff has taken the responsibility away from them, the staff should be instructed to require the residents to complete tasks as independently as possible. Unfortunately, modifications in staff behavior may not be easily achieved. Research has suggested that institutional staff are unlikely to respond to in-service training and changes in scheduling without the addition of contingencies for staff behavior implemented at an administrative level (Whitman, Scibak, & Reid, 1983). To date, issues concerning staff training and management in nursing homes have not been adequately investigated. This is an area that requires further attention if optimal care of nursing home residents is to be realized.

Wandering

Wandering is a behavior that is highly correlated with organic impairment (Cornbleth, 1977). According to Hussian and Davis (1985) wandering refers to "ambulation that occurs independently of the usual environmental cues" (p. 85). It can have serious consequences, including physical injury, and requires constant vigilance by caregivers to protect the patient. Typically, modification of wandering has involved physical or chemical restraint, which unfortunately results in sensory deprivation and the further loss of control and independence.

Although wandering behavior appears to be a purposeless and random activity, results of a study by Hussian (1981) suggest that it does come under environmental control. Hussian studied the wandering patterns of residents of a long-term care facility and found that patients spent the greatest amount of time in geographic places that contained the highest density of stimuli and potential reinforcement, including areas where others were present, windows, drinking fountains, and untended food trays. In addition, mapping the routes of each wanderer over time indicated that consistent geographic patterns developed within subjects, further suggesting that wandering behavior is under some degree of stimulus control. Finally, it was observed that the duration and distance of wandering decreased significantly when periods of free ambulation were provided on a daily basis. Hussian suggested that alternatives designed to capitalize on the predictability of wandering patterns will prove superior to the use of physical restraints.

In a subsequent study, Hussian and Davis (1985) provided empirical support for the contention that wandering is not random. After conducting systematic observations of the wandering behavior of 13 residents of a geriatric unit of a state mental institution, they concluded that ambulation patterns could be classified in one of four ways:

1. *Akathesia*. Akathesia is motor restlessness with an inability to sit still. It is observed in patients receiving high doses of neuroleptic medication. These patients tend to ambulate at high rates and demonstrate little interest in leaving the unit or in self-stimulatory activity.
2. *Exit Seeking*. These behaviors tend to be exhibited by those most recently admitted to the unit and include frequent requests to leave the unit as well as attempts to open exit doors more often than other types of doors.
3. *Modeling*. Individuals demonstrating this behavior tend to ambulate only

in the presence of another ambulator. They touch door knobs briefly, and seldom exhibit self-stimulatory behavior.

4. *Self-Stimulation*. This ambulation pattern involves frequent touching and repeated turning of door knobs, which results in apparent auditory and tactile stimulation. Other forms of stereotypic behavior, including hand-clapping and rubbing objects, are also displayed by these patients.

According to Walker and Brodie (1980), akathesia usually develops within 5 to 40 days after the administration of antipsychotic medication is begun. Because it can be misdiagnosed as agitation, a physician may prescribe an increase in the dose of antipsychotic medication. For patients with akathesia such medication may make them even more restless or sedate and rigid. It is more appropriate for those patients to reduce, discontinue, or change the antipsychotic medication.

Before attempting to modify wandering behavior, clinicians should identify the ambulation pattern exhibited by the client. Hussian and Davis (1985) suggest that exit seeking can be eliminated through extinction, i.e., the consistent withdrawal of reinforcement at exit doors. Ambulation can also be shaped to containment within a specified area through stimulus control. Hussian and Davis (1983), for example, modified the wandering behavior of three residents of a long-term care facility by consistently pairing two colored stimuli with two different consequences, one positive and one negative. These different-colored stimuli were then posted on the ward; the one that had been associated with negative consequences in areas where ambulation was discouraged, the other in areas where ambulation was encouraged. Those who underwent this treatment continued to ambulate at approximately the same rate and duration, but made fewer entries into dangerous areas.

Hussian and Davis (1985) also recommend shaping of ambulation by stimulus control for patients who exhibit ambulation patterns consistent with modeling and self-stimulation. In addition, these authors suggest that the extinction of knob turning through the reduction of the sensory stimulation obtained by this activity and a DRO procedure may be effective for modifying the behavior of self-stimulators.

Inappropriate Sexual Behavior

Sexual behavior that occurs at inappropriate times and places can be due to a lack of stimulus control. It is frequently associated with significant organic brain impairment and typically involves a disoriented resident mistaking a public room for his or her private domain. Such behavior rarely presents a real danger to staff or other patients but can be highly distressing to staff, family, and residents who witness the behavior.

Decisions regarding treatment for such behaviors are difficult because they inevitably raise ethical questions. Since masturbatory behavior is not dangerous, and may present one of the few opportunities for pleasure among the institutionalized elderly, elimination of the behavior through treatment may be ethically indefensible. Rather than attempt to decrease overall rates of such behavior, treatment attempts may be best aimed at altering the contexts within which such behavior occurs. Through stimulus control training similar to that used to treat wandering, one can change the setting in which the behavior occurs. This will reduce the negative consequences the individual receives for engaging in the behavior while allowing him or her to continue to display the behavior.

Both qualitative aspects of the target behavior and level of client functioning are important considerations in the determination of the treatment goals and the type of treatment program for a particular client. Hussian (1981) reported a case study in which he demonstrated the successful use of a stimulus control program to reduce public masturbation in a 64-year-old male nursing home resident. The treatment involved interrupting the client's masturbation when it occurred in public areas and allowing it to reach its natural outcome when it occurred in the resident's bedroom. In addition, a bright orange symbol was placed above the client's bed in order to accentuate the distinction between the public and private setting. This procedure resulted in the elimination of public masturbatory acts and an increase in private masturbation.

Social Behavior

The social behavior of the elderly in nursing homes is depicted as lethargic, withdrawn, and apathetic. Anecdotal reports abound describing nursing home residents who are unaware of the names of their roommates and who refuse to eat meals in a central dining area or participate in scheduled activities. Cognitively impaired nursing home residents often lack the skills necessary for effective social interaction. Limited privacy and the vast heterogeneity of the resident population often contribute to the withdrawal of cognitively intact residents, a withdrawal that can be conceptualized as an avoidance response. The result is a social climate that tends to inhibit social interaction of any kind.

A great deal of research in gerontology has been directed at the modification of the social behavior of the institutionalized elderly. Both verbal assertiveness and participation in leisure activities have been frequent targets for change. Several studies have demonstrated the efficacy of reinforcement procedures for reinstating speech in older institutionalized psychiatric patients.

Mueller and Atlas (1972) implemented two treatments to increase verbal responding in a group of five asocial male geriatric clients. The use of primary reinforcers failed to increase participation in group discussion, but prompts and token reinforcers produced a dramatic increase. Although all five subjects demonstrated increases in participation in group discussions, the use of tokens was confounded with verbal prompts, making it impossible to separate the contributions of the treatment components. In addition, no reversal or follow-up data were reported. Hoyer, Kafer, Simpson, and Hoyer (1974) successfully reinstated speech by reinforcing verbalizations in a small-group context. Two of four subjects were given pennies contingent upon verbalizations. Increases in word frequency generalized across the subjects who were not directly reinforced. Using a reversal design, these authors also investigated an intervention designed to increase verbal interaction rather than word frequency. Responses were reinforced with either candy or cigarettes regardless of the length. An increase in the frequency of prompted and unprompted verbalizations occurred. Follow-up data were not reported. MacDonald (1978) utilized an ABAB design to increase social interaction at mealtime in three "lucid" but "chronically socially isolated" male nursing home residents. During the treatment phase, the experimenter sat with the three subjects and provided verbal reinforcement for social interaction. The manipulation resulted in the successful increase in participation in mealtime conversation among the subjects. The strength of the study lies in its focus on the establishment of interresident interaction. Unfortunately, however, the fact that conversation decreased during reversal conditions does not bode well for maintenance of treatment gains.

A variety of techniques have been applied in an attempt to increase attendance and interaction rates of social activities. For example, Blackman, Howe, and Pinkston (1976) utilized a reversal design to study the effects of providing refreshments on interaction rate among nursing home residents. The results indicated that refreshments served as reinforcers for attendance at the activity and were effective in increasing rates of interaction. This finding was replicated by Carroll (1978) and Quattrochi-Tubin and Jason (1980).

Although providing refreshments appears to be a simple and effective means of increasing interaction rates among nursing home residents, some caveats should be noted (see Carstensen, 1986). A study by Carstensen and Erickson (1986) indicates that such increases may not result in uniformly beneficial effects. These authors replicated the procedures used by Blackman *et al.* (1976) and Quattrochi-Tubin and Jason (1980) but also included an assessment of the qualitative content of vocal behavior emitted by the subjects. Results indicated that quantitative increases in the rates of interaction were accounted for by ineffective vocalizations, i.e., babbling or unreciprocated and incoherent speech. In this study, more appropriate vocal behaviors (e.g., questions, opinions) decreased during treatment phases. These findings suggest that future attempts to improve the social environment of nursing homes should address changes in qualitative aspects of interactions as well as the quantitative aspects.

Given that older adults are faced with a number of potentially stressful events as they age, several researchers (e.g., Berger & Rose, 1977; Toseland, 1977) have argued that competence in social interaction is essential if the elderly individual is to cope effectively. Changes involving negative stereotypes about old age, ambiguous societal expectations, the loss of roles, and decrements in problem solving may all contribute to elderly nursing home residents' diminished control over their environments as well as their effectiveness in interpersonal relationships. Nevertheless, although social skill training with children and adults has received a great deal of attention in the behavioral literature, relatively little has been written about the application of such training with the institutionalized elderly. What literature exists is reviewed below.

Berger and Rose (1977) utilized methods developed by Goldfried and D'Zurilla (1969) to assess and improve the social skills of nursing home residents. Through interviews they identified frequently occurring and difficult social situations that residents encountered. Appropriate responses to the situations were defined and rated by staff members. Half of the situations were used in training residents to apply effective responses; the remaining half were used to assess generalization of training. The investigators obtained direct behavioral measures of performance in social situations and self-ratings of satisfaction with performance. The residents were able to learn the skills taught. Those who received the training were significantly more effective than control subjects in responding to social situations for which effective responses had been taught. The skills were retained 2 months after training but did not generalize to situations that were not specifically targeted in training.

In an attempt to improve transfer of training of social skills, Lopez (1980) investigated the effects of overlearning and precounseling structuring combined with structured learning therapy (Goldstein, Sprafkin, & Gershaw, 1976) to teach 70 elderly psychiatric inpatients preparing to reenter the community how to express appreciation. Subjects were assigned to one of six experimental conditions and one control condition. The six experimental conditions included three groups that received precounseling training and either high, medium, or low overlearning and three groups that received either high, medium, or low overlearning without precounseling training. Control group subjects were provided a combination of attention and brief discussion about reentry into the community. The structured learning therapy combined modeling, role playing, and social reinforcement to teach small concrete steps involved in expressing appreciation in social situations.

All treatment groups acquired the skill. Medium overlearning enhanced skills transfer, while high overlearning decreased skill acquisition and transfer. Precounseling structuring had no effect on acquisition and transfer. Although skills did transfer to role-play situations that had not been specifically trained, they did not transfer to situations that occurred outside of the experimental setting. As Lopez (1980) states, "none of the treatment subjects changed their behavior in the units in which they resided" (p. 291).

In an attempt to improve generalization of skills to a broad range of social situations and to enhance transfer beyond the treatment setting, Fisher and Carstensen (1986) trained elderly nursing home residents in specific social skills *and* in the use of general behavioral principles. As in the Berger and Rose (1977) study, the subjects determined their own treatment goals by identifying the social situations in which they were most dissatisfied with their effectiveness. Results indicated that the residents were able to formulate their own treatment goals and to learn and apply the skills. Moreover, direct observation of their behavior on the ward indicated that the behavior change generalized beyond the treatment setting. The authors suggest that involving the elderly individual in the determination of treatment goals as well as providing training in general behavioral principles may improve treatment generalization.

We have much to learn about the significance of social interaction for the elderly. Prevailing sentiments among researchers and nursing home staff alike clearly reflect a tacit belief that the elderly "should" interact, and, further, that nursing home residents should interact with one another. In reality there exists little empirical evidence for this position. What is sorely needed at this time is a thoughtful examination of the social worlds of the institutionalized elderly and a better assessment of their goals for social interaction.

Paranoia

Although depression, anxiety, and paranoia are among the most common problems of the aged in nursing homes, they have received relatively little research attention. Rather, the vast majority of intervention research in nursing homes has targeted remediation of behavior problems and skills deficits. The focus of behavior therapists on overt "disturbing" behavior rather than subjective "disturbed" behavior is significant. A depressed nursing home resident rarely demands attention. Similarly, a resident who is paranoid may actively avoid contact for fear of being harmed by others. In contrast to skills deficits, which often demand attention, psychological distress may actually function to present fewer demands on health care staff. Thus, this type of problem may go unnoticed. There is little doubt that even among the organically impaired elderly, rates of subjective distress are high, but this kind of distress often fails to come to the attention of professionals.

For a discussion of the treatment of depression and anxiety, the reader is referred to chapters by Teri (Chapter 10) and Handen (Chapter 7), respectively, in this book. In the following pages we will discuss the treatment of paranoid behavior as displayed by the elderly in nursing homes.

Paranoia among the aged is somewhat different than that observed in younger people. Delusional beliefs tend to be less grandiose and target familiar persons rather than public figures or imaginary characters. Common delusional beliefs among younger people involve the FBI or "God." A prototypical delusion of an elderly individual, however, is the belief that his or her Social Security checks are being stolen by a neighbor. While the delusions themselves may be less toxic, the effects are not necessarily less so. Such beliefs can be highly troublesome to the individual and alienating to the accused. In severe instances, the individual may feel compelled to take self-defensive action that can place him or her in physical jeopardy, e.g., refusing to take life-sustaining medication due to a fear of being poisoned.

Paranoid ideas are substantially more common in the elderly, probably due to sensory and cognitive decrements associated with normal aging. According to Pfeiffer (1977), paranoid ideation in the elderly frequently represents an effort to "fill in" information that has been lost due to these deficits. For example, if an older person is in the vicinity of a conversation but cannot hear what is being said, he or she may imagine the unheard content. Also, if one is experiencing memory deficits and frequently misplaces items, the likelihood that one will attribute lost articles to thievery is increased.

The nursing home environment contains additional physical and social conditions that may precipitate paranoia or exacerbate the suspiciousness associated with sensory loss. For example, muffled sounds heard over a loudspeaker, nurses checking a pulse during the night, and clothing taken to the laundry room may be construed as evidence of malevolent action on the part of the staff or other "conspirators." The lack of personal control inherent in an institutional setting also may be a contributing factor. Limited access to friends and family and dependence on others to provide food, social contact, clothing, and money all may contribute to a heightening of anxiety and paranoid ideation.

Since loss of sensory acuity, particularly auditory loss, has been associated with paranoia, assessment of auditory functioning is essential when dealing with the problem. The use of hearing aids is a practical and important treatment approach for the restoration of auditory loss associated with paranoia. Hearing-aid use can be increased and maintained through various forms of reinforcement including praise, social contact, and music.

The centrality of memory and attention deficits in paranoia among the aged suggests that the remediation of these deficits may contribute to a remediation of the delusion. For example, difficulty in locating objects and the suspicion of theft may be alleviated through the utilization of aids for organizing possessions. In addition, staff and family members should be counseled about the nature of the problem in order to reduce tension and solicit their assistance in remediation. It is important to instruct staff and family members not to provide reinforcement for the paranoid beliefs through sympathetic reassurance and attention. Rather, they should be instructed to correct paranoid verbalizations calmly, without engaging in lengthy discussion about the verity of the allegation. If statements persist, subsequent allegations should be ignored. If an extinction approach is utilized, however, it is essential to provide increased attention to the individual when he or she is not verbalizing delusional beliefs. Most people have a tendency to provide comfort when they observe someone in fear. Unfortunately, such reassurance can serve as reinforcement for the fearful statements, and in the long run, work in opposition to the goal of calming the person.

Pharmacotherapy for this problem is usually not recommended because paranoid individuals are often suspicious of the medication given to them and the side effects of major tranquilizers are frequently contraindicated for medical reasons. For more severe cases of paranoid behavior when medication is indicated, Eisdorfer (1980) suggests that antianxiety medication, used for a short period of time in conjunction with other forms of treatment, is the treatment of choice. Still, for the patient who refuses medication this is a practical impossibility.

A case study by Carstensen and Fremouw (1981) demonstrated the effective application of behavioral strategies for the treatment of paranoid behaviors displayed by a 68-year-old female nursing home resident. In this report, a staff level intervention combined with individual therapy resulted in a significant reduction in the paranoid ideation of the client. Staff members were instructed to provide consistent feedback in response to the client's allegations. Specific client fears were addressed during individual sessions. After 14 weekly individual sessions and two staff training sessions, the client displayed minimal anxiety and ceased to talk about paranoid fears.

A final note—therapists working with the elderly in nursing homes should be mindful that the suspiciousness exhibited by the residents is not always unrealistic (Hussian & Davis, 1985; Pfeiffer, 1980). The possibility of valid accusations should always be considered when one is assessing paranoia. Indeed, it is not uncommon for nursing home staff to admit that staff or other patients have removed possessions belonging to a resident considered to be paranoid.

General Guidelines for Treatment

We have discussed treatment approaches for only a few of the myriad problems confronting nursing home residents. In large part, basic principles involved in psychological and/or behavioral interventions with nursing home residents are similar to the underlying principles involved in work with any other population or age group. There are several special considerations, however, unique to work with this group that should be taken into account to maximize the probability of successful outcome.

Many of these factors relate directly to defining characteristics of the staff and resident population. Staff characteristics are especially important to treatment. Of paramount importance is the fact that 90% of patient care is provided by untrained aides and orderlies who have a 75% annual turnover rate (Vladeck, 1980). Glasscote (1976) found that only 26% of nursing homes employed a full-time social worker, and more than half did not employ any social work staff at all. As noted above, only a paucity of nursing homes employ other professional psychology or psychiatry staff. As bleak a picture as this may paint at the onset, staff members can also be a therapist's greatest ally in a therapeutic effort. If the therapist is able to enlist the support of staff, interventions can be much more efficient than they would be if the individual client lived in the community or some other less structured setting. Thus, staff participation in interventions can substantially improve an intervention.

Moreover, in many cases, staff members are the primary social supports of nursing home residents and function in much the same way as family members. It is essential to understand, however, that workers in nursing homes are typically uneducated and always overworked and underpaid. Requests for time must be minimal and their genuine support must be enlisted. If a therapist can work with staff members toward a common goal—a goal that the staff values—success is likely. To work without the support of staff in a nursing home setting is much like working without the support of family members in family therapy.

Whenever possible, family members also should be involved in assessment and treatment. In fact, it has been suggested that the family be the *focus* of treatment (Brody, 1986). Brody pointed out that there is little truth in the stereotype of the nursing home resident as being "dumped" by the family. Not only do 9 out of 10 residents have a next-of-kin, nursing homes are usually selected because of proximity to a relative. She cites statistics from the Survey of Institutionalized Persons, which found that the majority of nursing home residents who had a spouse, child, or grandchild received at least weekly visits. Only a small percentage of nursing home residents had no family contact. Interestingly, Smith and Bengston (1979) found evidence for *improvement* in family relations after nursing home placement. These authors interviewed 100 institutionalized elderly parents and their children after the parent was placed in a nursing home. The majority expressed a continuation of close family ties or improvement in their relationships with relatives. Only 10% reported negative effects of placement on their relationships.

A consideration of the potential influence of social desirability on interview responses such as these is important; older people very likely want to paint a good picture of family relationships and may be reluctant to express negative feelings about their children. But, it is also important to acknowledge the positive aspects of nursing home placement, both for the elderly individual and family caregivers. There is a tendency to think of nursing home versus home care in black and white terms, with nursing homes being "bad" and home care being "good," but this is not the case. As mentioned earlier in this chapter, the strain of caregiving and care-receiving can create significant problems in family relationships. Smith and Bengston (1979) suggest that because institutions provide 24-hour technical care to frail family members they reduce the caregiving strain on the family, allowing relationships to be based on mutual interests and emotional support rather than instrumental care.

Involving family members in the development and implementation of treatment programs for nursing home residents may be an effective means of improving service delivery in this setting. In fact, a recent study by Carstensen and Fisher (1984) suggests that many nursing home residents prefer to speak to family and friends about personal problems instead of health care professionals. Ninety-two residents from 20 nursing homes named the following as people they spoke to about personal problems: relatives (30.9%), health care professionals (20.2%), friends (23.4%), physicians (9.6%), clergy (9.6%), no one (10.6%), and others (22.3%). Asked with whom they *preferred* to discuss problems, family members were clearly the most desired (51.6%), followed by friends (22.6%), clergy (17.2%), and physicians (7.5%). Mental health care professionals (e.g., social workers, psychologists, and psychiatrists) were identified as the least desirable persons with whom to discuss personal problems (4.3%). These statistics suggest that nursing home residents do not consider professional mental health services to be particularly desirable or that the professionals they have encountered have not been helpful. They may also be reflective of a lack of familiarity with such services or to an incompatibility with their personal values. Harel and Noelker (1983) reported that although the frail elderly desire social contact, they want it with family and friends. They do not desire social contact with strangers. Whatever the reason for the disinterest in professional services, these results do suggest that focusing on work with family and friends is a viable alternative to traditional forms of mental health services.

Treatment efforts obviously must be tailored to each particular resident and problem, but some general information about the characteristics of the resident population also bear mentioning. Most nursing home residents suffer from multiple physical problems. Physical disability not only relates directly to psychological–emotional well-being, it limits treatment approaches as well. For example, participation in scheduled activities may help to alleviate a depressed individual's mood, but if the activity is something that requires an extended effort, the activity may actually function to depress mood further. Not only does the individual become physically fatigued, he or she is faced with the fact that even previously reinforcing events are no longer pleasant, which leaves the client more depressed than ever.

Often treatment strategies have to be highly creative in order to exploit the individual's existing strengths. An illustrative example is an intervention reported by Wisocki and Mosher (1980) in which a socially isolated, aphasic nursing home resident was trained in sign language to facilitate communication with other residents.

As mentioned earlier, the nursing home population is also highly medicated, presenting yet another consideration for both assessment and treatment. Up to 75% of nursing home residents receive psychotropic drugs (Vestal, 1985). Many receive major psychotropic drugs, such as chlorpromazine or theoridazine, the effects of which are even more potent in the old than in the young. Not only are actions of some specific drugs different for old people (e.g., increased sensitivity of the benzodiazepines due to changes in pharmacokinetics), but the frail elderly are frequently on medication regimens that include multiple drugs. As Keuthen has pointed out (Chapter 2, this volume), interactions of drug effects, in combination with age-related changes in absorption and excretion of each specific drug, often present a complicated clinical picture. Moreover, decreased metabolic mechanisms that stem from the type of normal age-related change noted above may exacerbate relatively minor excesses of drug actions. In many cases, answers to questions about drug interactions in the elderly patient are simply not known and must be empirically determined for each individual client. Thus, we must underscore the importance of close contact with the resident's primary care physician in order to provide the patient with the most effective treatment.

ETHICAL ISSUES

There are a number of highly salient ethical issues that must be taken into consideration when working with a nursing home population. Elderly nursing home residents lead very dependent lives. They are dependent on relatives, nursing home staff, and social service agencies for the provision of most of their vital necessities. It is largely this dependence that raises several ethical questions when one is attempting to provide the institutionalized elderly with therapeutic services.

Because of their reduced autonomy some have suggested that it is impossible for elderly in nursing homes to give truly informed consent to treatment (Ratzan, 1980). In addition, mental competence, an essential precondition of informed consent, cannot be assumed in many of those with psychiatric diagnoses. For those who have been determined to be mentally incompetent, the process of informed consent is clearly inappropriate. Unfortunately, the mental competence of nursing home residents is rarely empirically verified. Rather, it is assumed. Controversial issues concerning treatment are inevitably raised (McCullough, 1984). On the one hand, treatment may result in improvement in the person's quality of life. On the other hand, in the absence of informed consent, tremendous assumptions about the "good" of the individual are tacitly made.

It is desirable that therapy be initiated only if the elderly nursing home resident or an appropriate proxy consents to treatment. This position is shared by various professional organizations including the Association for the Advancement of Behavior Therapy (AABT). The ethical guidelines contained in AABTs *Ethical Issues for Human Services* state that "ideal interventions would have the maximum involvement by the person whose behavior is to be changed, and the fullest possible consideration of societal pressures on that person. . ." (AABT, 1977). Several authors (Hoyer, 1973; Richards & Thorpe, 1977) have pointed out that nonelderly usually determine the target behaviors and reinforcement contingencies of the elderly. O'Donohue, Fisher, and Krasner (1986) present evidence to substantiate this point. In a review of 29 published reports of studies using a behavioral approach to clinical problems of the elderly, the elderly individual was involved in the determination of treatment goals in only three. This is an issue that requires thoughtful consideration by behavior therapists (see O'Donohue, Fisher, & Krasner, 1988, for further discussion).

Another issue concerns the types of behaviors targeted for change. Page, Caron, and Yates (1973) have questioned the ethics of applying behavior modification in institutions as a means to enforce traditional institutional values such as "cleanliness, order, punctuality, deference, and demeanor" (p. 28). Richards and Thorpe pointed out (1977) that the behaviors targeted for change among elderly nursing home residents typically have been those complained of by relatives and staff (e.g., incontinence, grooming behavior), rather than those presented by the elderly individuals themselves (e.g., anxiety and depression). Findings from the literature analysis conducted by O'Donohue *et al.* (1986) provide further support for such allegations. Behaviors such as participation in ward activities and the correct use of eating utensils were found to be frequent targets of change. While such targets are by no means inherently "wrong," they require a great deal of consideration before implementation. We cannot assume that the goals of the infirm elderly are the same as the goals of younger relatives or staff members of a nursing home. Approaches that ignore or minimize the elderly individual's input in the treatment process serve to enhance the power inequities that are inherent in the institutional setting and are ethically questionable.

In light of this small but sobering literature on ethics, one final comment is warranted. The functional values of what appear to be dysfunctional behaviors must be considered in order to employ effective interventions. This notion is certainly not new to behavior therapists, but there is sometimes a tendency to move too quickly to eliminate a behavior without teaching the client ways to gain access to the reinforcers it derived previously. Ethical questions are inevitably raised: Should the resident whose only contact with staff is being fed at mealtimes be taught to feed herself? Similarly, should the man who repeatedly disrupts mealtimes be removed from the situation if there are no alternatives to his gaining attention from others? In considering answers to these questions, it is imperative that the therapist consider the behavior in a broad context and be aware of the contingencies that operate in nursing home environments.

SUMMARY

Treatment of the elderly in nursing homes presents some unique challenges to the behavior therapist. Behavioral and psychological problems of the frail elderly are compounded by the effects of failing health, failures that also restrict plans for treatment. Behavioral and psychological improvement may occur for a time, only to be followed by deterioration and health decline. Moreover, social and psychological losses that members of this aged population face are often irreplaceable.

Yet, often we are able to bring about substantial behavior change after only minor environmental modifications. A great deal of functional impairment can be remedied through the design of a social and physical environment that utilizes the strengths of the individual and compensates for the weaknesses. Treatment efforts frequently can capitalize on the fact that many of the desired behaviors were present in the client's repertoire earlier in life and therefore can be reinstated quickly. Even those elderly who suffer from psychological problems related to irreversible organic deterioration may show dramatic effects from behavioral treatment.

There is every reason to expect that the number of older people living in nursing homes will increase dramatically in upcoming decades. It is essential that we begin to recognize the extensive problems faced by this needy population and to proceed with interventions in a thoughtful and ethical manner.

REFERENCES

Association for the Advancement of Behavior Therapy. (1977). *Ethical issues for human services*. New York: Author.

Baltes, M. M., & Zerbe, M. B. (1976). Re-establishment of self-feeding in a nursing home resident. *Nursing Research, 25*, 24–26.

Baltes, M. M., Burgess, R. L., & Stewart, R. B. (1980). Independence and dependence in nursing home residents: An operant ecological study. *International Journal of Behavioral Development, 3*, 489–500.

Baltes, M. M., Honn, S., Barton, E. M., Orzech, M., & Lago, D. (1983). On the social ecology of dependence and independence in elderly nursing home residents: A replication and extension. *Journal of Gerontology, 38*, 556–564.

Barton, E. M., Baltes, M. M., & Orzech, M. J. (1980). On the etiology of dependence in older nursing home residents during morning care: The role of staff behavior. *Journal of Personality and Social Psychology, 38*, 423–431.

Berger, R. M., & Rose, S. D. (1977). Interpersonal skill training with institutionalized patients. *Journal of Gerontology. 32*, 346–353.

Blackman, D., Howe, M., & Pinkston, E. M. (1976). Increasing participation in social interaction of the institutionalized elderly. *Gerontologist, 16*, 69–76.

Blazer, D. G. (1980). The epidemiology of mental illness in late life. In E. W. Busse & D. G. Blazer (Eds.), *Handbook of geriatric psychiatry* (pp. 3–27). New York: Van Nostrand Reinhold.

Brody, E. M. (1986). The role of the family in nursing homes: Implications for research and public policy. In N. Harper (Ed.), *Mental illness in nursing homes: Agenda for research* (pp. 159–179). Washington, DC: National Institute of Mental Health.

Brody, J. A., & Foley, D. J. (1985). Epidemiologic considerations. In E. L. Schneider (Ed.), *The teaching nursing home* (pp. 9–25). New York: Raven Press.

Brody, S. J., Poulshock, S. W., & Masciocchi, C. F. (1978). The family caring unit: A major consideration in the long-term support system. *The Gerontologist, 18*, 556–561.

Burgio, L. D., Burgio, K. L., Engel, B. T., & Tice, L. M. (1986). Increasing distance and independence of ambulation in elderly nursing home residents. *Journal of Applied Behavior Analysis, 19*, 357–366.

Carroll, P. S. (1978). The social hour for geropsychiatric patients. *Journal of the American Geriatrics Society, 11*, 32–35.

Carstensen, L. L. (1986). Social support among the elderly: Limitations of behavioral interventions. *The Behavior Therapist, 6*, 111–113.

Carstensen, L. L., & Erikson, R. J. (1986). Increasing rates of social interactions among nursing home residents: Are high rates enough? *Journal of Applied Behavioral Analysis, 19*, 349–355.

Carstensen, L. L., & Fisher, J. E. (1984). *Mental health needs of the elderly in nursing homes: Staff and resident perspectives.* Paper presented at the Association for the Advancement of Behavior Therapy, Philadelphia.

Carstensen, L. L., & Fremouw, W. J. (1981). The demonstration of behavioral intervention for late life paranoia. *The Gerontologist, 21*, 329–333.

Cornbleth, T. (1977). Effects of protected hospital ward area on wandering and nonwandering geriatric patients. *Journal of Gerontology, 32*, 573–577.

Eisdorfer, C. (1980). Paranoia and schizophrenic disorders in late life. In E. W. Busse & D. G. Blazer (Eds.), *Handbook of geriatric psychiatry* (pp. 329–337). New York: Van Nostrand Reinhold.

Eustis, N., Greenberg, J., & Patten, S. (1984). *Long-term care for older persons: A policy perspective.* Monterey, CA: Brooks/Cole.

Fisher, J. E., & Carstensen, L. L. (1988). *The elderly nursing home resident as contingency manager.* Unpublished manuscript, University of Indiana, Bloomington.

Geiger, G. O., & Johnson, L. A. (1974). Positive education for elderly persons, correct eating through reinforcement. *The Gerontologist, 14*, 488–491.

Glasscote, R. M. (1976). Old-folks at home: A field of nursing and board-and-care homes. Washington, DC: American Psychiatric Association and the National Association for Mental Health, Joint Information Service.

Goffman, E. (1961). *Asylums: Essays on the social situation of mental patients and other inmates.* Garden City, NY: Doubleday.

Goldfried, M. R., & D'Zurilla, T. J. (1969). A behavioral-analytic model for assessing competence. In C. D. Spielberger (Ed.), *current topics in clinical and community psychology* (Vol. 1, pp. 151–196). New York: Academic Press.

Goldstein, A. P., Sprafkin, R. P., & Gershaw, N. J. (1976). Structured learning therapy-training for community living. *Psychotherapy: Theory, Research, and Practice, 13*, 374–377.

Harel, Z., & Noelker, L. (1983). Social integration, health and choice: The impact of well-being on institutionalized aged. *Research on Aging, 4*, 97–111.

Hogue, C. C. (1985). Mobility. In E. Schneider (Ed.), *The teaching nursing home* (pp. 231–243). New York: Raven Press.

Hoyer, W. J. (1973). Application of operant techniques to the modification of elderly behavior. *The Gerontologist, 13*, 18–22.

Hoyer, W. J., Kafer, R. J., Simpson, S. C., & Hoyer, F. W. (1974). Reinforcement of verbal behavior in elderly mental patients using operant procedures. *The Gerontologist, 14*, 149–152.

Hussian, R. A. (1981). *Geriatric psychology: A behavioral perspective.* New York: Van Nostrand Reinhold.

Hussian, R. A., & Davis, R. L. (1985). *Responsive care: Behavioral interventions with elderly persons.* Champaign, IL: Research Press.

Lawton, M. P. (1975). Competence, environmental press and the adaptation of older people. In P. G. Windley & G. Ernst (Eds.), *Theory development in environment and aging* (pp. 13–70). Washington, DC: Gerontological Society of America.

Lawton, M. P. (1977). The impact of the environment on aging and behavior. In J. E. Birren & W. W. Schaie (Eds.), *Handbook of the psychology of aging* (pp. 276–301). New York: Van Nostrand Reinhold.

Lawton, M. P., & Nahemow, L. (1973). Ecology and the aging process. In C. Eisdorfer & M. P. Lawton (Eds.), *The psychology of adult development and aging* (pp. 619–674). Washington, DC: American Psychological Association.

Lesnoff-Caravaglia, G. (1978–1979). The five percent fallacy. *International Journal of Aging and Human Development, 79*, 187–192.

Lopez, M. A. (1980). Social-skills training with institutionalized elderly: Effects of pre-counseling structuring and over-learning on skill acquisitions and transfer. *Journal of Counseling Psychology, 27*, 286–293.

MacDonald, M. L. (1978). Environmental programming for the socially isolated aging. *Gerontologist, 18*, 350–354.

MacDonald, M. L., & Butler, A. K. (1974). Reversal of helplessness: Producing walking behavior in nursing home wheelchair residents using behavior modification procedures. *Journal of Gerontology*, *29*, 97–101.

McCullough, L. B. (1984). Medical care for elderly patients with diminished competence: An ethical analysis. *Journal of the American Geriatrics Society*, *32*, 150–153.

Mueller, D. J., & Atlas, L. (1972). Resocialization of depressed elderly residents: A behavioral management approach. *Journal of Gerontology*, *27*, 390–392.

Murray, H. (1938). *Explorations in personality*. New York: Oxford University Press.

Newman, S. J. (1976). *Housing adjustment of older people: A report from second phase*. Ann Arbor: University of Michigan, Institute for Social Research.

O'Brien, F., Bugle, C., & Azrin, N. H. (1972). Training and maintaining a retarded child's proper eating. *Journal of Applied Behavior Analysis*, *5*, 67–72.

O'Donohue, W. T., Fisher, J. E., & Krasner, L. (1986). Behavior therapy and the elderly: A conceptual and ethical analysis. *International Journal of Aging and Human Development*, *23*, 1–15.

O'Donohue, W. T., Fisher, J. E., & Krasner, L. (1988). Ethics and the elderly. In L. L. Carstensen & B. A. Edelstein (Eds.), *Handbook of clinical gerontology* (pp. 387–399). New York: Pergamon Press.

Page, S., Caron, P., & Yates, E. (1975). Behavior modification methods and institutional psychology. *Professional Psychology*, 175–181.

Pfeiffer, E. (1977). Psychopathology and social pathology. In J. E. Birren & W. K. Schaie (Eds.), *Handbook of the psychology of aging* (pp. 650–671). New York: Van Nostrand Reinhold.

Pfeiffer, E. (1980). The psychosocial evaluation of the elderly patient. In E. W. Busse & D. G. Blazer (Eds.), *Handbook of geriatric psychiatry* (pp. 275–284). New York: Van Nostrand Reinhold.

Quattrochi-Tubin, S. & Jason, L. A. (1980). Enhancing social interactions and activity among the elderly through stimulus control. *Journal of Applied Behavior Analysis*, *13*, 159–169.

Ratzan, R. M. (1980). 'Being old makes you different': The ethics of research with elderly subjects. *Hastings Center Report*, *10*, 32–42.

Richards, W. S., & Thorpe, G. L. (1977). Behavioral approaches to the problems of later life. In M. Storandt, I. C. Siegler, & M. F. Elias (Eds.), *The clinical psychology of aging* (pp. 253–269). New York: Plenum.

Rinke, C. L., Williams, J. J., Lloyd, K. L., & Smith-Scott, W. (1978). The effects of prompting and reinforcement on self-bathing by elderly residents of nursing homes. *Behavior Therapy*, *9*, 873–881.

Risely, T. R., & Edwards, K. A. (1978). *Behavioral technology for nursing home care: Toward a system of nursing home organization and management*. Paper presented at the Nova Behavioral Conference on Aging, Port St. Lucie, FL.

Sachs, D. A. (1975). Behavioral techniques in a residential nursing home facility. *Journal of Behavior Therapy and Experimental Psychiatry*, *6*, 123–127.

Schmidt, L. J., Reinhardt, A. M., Kane, A. L., & Olsen, D. M. (1977). The mentally ill in nursing homes. *Archives of General Psychiatry*, *34*, 687–691.

Shadish, W. R., Straw, R. B., McSweeny, A. J., Koller, D. L., & Bootzin, R. R. (1981). Nursing home care for mental patients: Descriptive data and some propositions. *American Journal of Community Psychology*, *9*, 617–633.

Shanas, E. (1982). *National survey of the aged* (Office of Human Development Services, DHHS Publication No. OHDS83-20425). Washington, D.C.: OHDS.

Smith, K. F., & Bengston, V. L. (1979). Positive consequences of institutionalization: Solidarity between elderly parents and their middle-aged children. *The Gerontologist*, *19*, 438–447.

Sperbeck, D. J., & Whitbourne, S. K. (1981). Dependency in the institutional setting: A behavioral training program for geriatric staff. *The Gerontologist*, *21*, 268–275.

Teeter, R. B., Garet, F. K., Miller, W. B., & Heiland, W. F. (1976). Psychiatric disturbances of aged in skilled nursing homes. *American Journal of Psychiatry*, *133*, 1430–1434.

Toseland, R. W. (1977). A comparison of three group methods to train social skills in older persons. *The Gerontologist*, *17*, 127.

U.S. Bureau of Census. (1976). *Survey of institutionalized persons. Current population reports* (Special Studies Series P-23, No. 69). Washington, DC: Author.

U.S. Department of Health, Education and Welfare. (1971). *First special report to U.S. Congress on alcohol and health* (pp. 23–26). Rockville, MD: National Institute of Alcohol Abuse and Alcoholism.

Vestal, R. E. (1985). Clinical pharmacology. In R. Andes, E. Bierman, & W. Hazzard (Eds.), *Principles of geriatric medicine* (pp. 424–443). New York: McGraw-Hill.

Vladeck, B. C. (1980). *Unloving care: The nursing home tragedy.* New York: Basic Books.

Walker, J. L., & Brodie, K. H. (1980). Neuropharmacology of aging. In E. W. Busse & D. G. Blazer (Eds.), *Handbook of geriatric psychiatry* (pp. 102–134). New York: Van Nostrand Reinhold.

Whanger, A. D. (1980). Treatment within the institutions. In E. W. Busse & D. G. Blazer (Eds.), *Handbook of geriatric psychiatry* (pp. 102–134). New York: Van Nostrand Reinhold.

Whitman, T. L., Scibak, J. W., & Reid, D. H. (1983). *Behavior modification with the severely and profoundly retarded: Research and applications.* New York: Academic Press.

Wisocki, P. A., & Mosher, P. M. (1980). Peer-facilitated sign language training for a geriatric stroke victim with chronic brain damage. *Journal of Geriatric Psychiatry, 13,* 89–102.

16

Behavioral Medicine for the Health Concerns of the Elderly

NANCY KEUTHEN AND PATRICIA A. WISOCKI

HEALTH STATUS OF THE ELDERLY

Good health is the key to a good life, a long life. "If you have your health, you have everything" is an old saw, often quoted. The attribute of physical health is often used as the primary index for denoting ourselves and others as aged. Health and longevity are inextricably tied.

Although they report few worries overall, the elderly worry more about their health than any other topic (Wisocki, Handen, & Morse, 1986). Health worries occur about one's own physical decline, the increased responsibility of caring for others, the costs of health care, failing memory, inability to make decisions, and the possibility of needing to be looked after away from home and family. It is with good reason that health is the primary concern of this age group. Of those over age 65, 85% have at least one chronic medical illness, and more than 50% have two or more medical conditions (cited in Shamoian, 1983). The elderly as a group have the highest overall rate of illness, disability, and activity restrictions. This group uses health care services more frequently and, consequently, incurs more health care expenses than any other age group. Hospital utilization is more than doubled for the elderly, and hospital stays are more prolonged. More than 15 years ago, Kimmel (1974) estimated that the amount of money expended on total health care for the elderly exceeds that spent on younger individuals by a factor of three. Not only are the current needs of this age group overwhelming, but they will grow further as this population increases in number.

Despite these statistics, older adults are less likely than younger adults to seek medical help, and when they do, it is likely to be much later in the course of an illness. They also underreport their symptoms and diseases (Besdine, 1981) and show less confidence in the medical profession than younger adults. They often ignore their medical care habits, mistakenly believing that illness and diseases are

NANCY KEUTHEN • Psychosomatic Medicine Unit, Massachusetts General Hospital, Boston, Massachusetts 02114.   PATRICIA A. WISOCKI • Department of Psychology, University of Massachusetts, Amherst, Massachusetts 01003.

inevitable and natural artifacts of aging. Thus, discomfort is expected and accepted as indicative of aging itself (Boyd & Oakes, 1969). Many elderly may avoid consulting a physician because they equate the pronouncement of disease with the verification of one's old age or impending death.

To some extent, of course, this state of affairs is attributable to medical doctors who have been trained to believe that aging is a natural disease process and that treatment attempts with the old are futile (Boyd & Oakes, 1969). Thus, the use of preventive medical procedures is less likely with the elderly than with other age groups. In general, a dislike for working with elderly patients has been documented (Field, 1970), which may in part be attributable to this belief that they profit minimally from professional interventions.

In this chapter we focus on a discussion of the health problems of elderly individuals and the ways behavioral technology may be applied to those problems. In the first part of the chapter we present an overview of the physiological changes one might expect in an aging body. In the second part we discuss the disease, chronic health problems, and health-related disorders most common to an aging population and the available behavioral research on treating and preventing those problems. Finally, we consider factors that contribute to health problems experienced by elderly men and women and make recommendations for good health practices based on current work in the field of behavioral health.

THE AGING BODY

As people age, they experience diminished efficiency on both physiological and behavioral levels. Normally these changes occur gradually and slowly with considerable individual differences. Tissues, body systems, and cells all age differently from person to person and within persons, perhaps following genetic mandates or perhaps due to health care routines established over a lifetime. Thus, it is important to remember that while we discuss averages for the elderly population, individual cases may vary substantially from the picture presented.

The changes occurring in the aging organism are many and varied. The performance of complex coordinated activities becomes more difficult than it was when one was younger. There is a decline in the overall functioning of the nervous system, resulting in decreased reaction time, speed, flexibility, and coordination. The cardiac system is also affected by age. The heart works harder, and diastolic and systolic blood pressures are likely to rise. In the pulmonary system, there is a reduction in breathing capacity, residual lung function, and basal oxygen consumption, all of which affect digestion, cell respiration, and assimilation. As all these changes occur, there is a corresponding decrease in body reserves for all functions, which, in turn, makes health maintenance more problematic. Environmental temperature changes, particularly heat stress, often pose a serious adjustment problem. When exposed to hot temperatures, older people experience significantly less water loss than younger people, which means it is more difficult for the aging body to cool itself by evaporation than it was in the past.

The skin of an elderly person loses its elasticity and moisture. It breaks easily, is irritated easily, and is more susceptible to sensations of cold. As calcium is withdrawn from cartilage and ligaments, bones become more porous and brittle. Many elderly experience calcification of cartilage and ligaments. A decrease in bone mass places extra stress on weight-bearing areas, and bones become predisposed to fracture. Muscle mass decreases. The degeneration of joint cartilage causes the experience of pain as people move about. The frame settles and often becomes 2 or 3 inches shorter in height. The walk slows.

Perhaps the most subjectively distressing changes are those which occur in the sensory system. Gradual declines in visual acuity, audition, olfaction, taste acuity, proprioception, and tactile sensitivity may produce a greater sensitivity to light stimuli, an inability to distinguish between some sounds, lack of interest in food, impaired coordination and balance, and decreased responsivity to environmental stimuli. Some researchers have reported that the elderly have a higher threshold of pain than younger adults (Samiy, 1983), a finding that suggests a lack of detection for medical problems that are normally signalled by pain. The work of other researchers, however, disputes this finding. Harkins and Chapman (1977), for example, did not find differences in pain experiences between young and old subjects.

The immunological system exhibits some decline in functioning with age. Immune responsivity on both the humoral and cellular levels decreases. These changes correlate with an elevated incidence of infection, malignancy, and autoimmune disease in the elderly, and it is assumed by many gerontologists that the former, in fact, causes the latter.

These physiological changes that accompany aging may certainly affect behavior, but they seldom mean a total loss of function. In a healthy person many of these changes may be delayed for a long time and have little effect on activity level.

SPECIFIC HEALTH PROBLEMS

According to figures cited by the U.S. Special Committee on Aging (1984), three out of every four individuals 65 years of age or older in the United States die from either cardiovascular disease, cancer, or stroke. The most common chronic conditions for elderly are osteoarthritis, hypertensive disease, and osteoporosis. In this section we will examine each of these problems in more detail.

Cardiovascular Disease

Cardiac disease is the primary cause of morbidity and mortality in the elderly. Mortality rates linked to this disease increase through successive age brackets as people age beyond 65 years, although lately a trend toward decreasing mortality from cardiac illness, in general, and from ischemic heart disease, in particular, has been recognized in those 55 years of age and older (National Center for Health Statistics, 1986).

Approximately 50% of those over 65 have some evidence of cardiac disease, including active angina, a prior myocardial infarction, symptoms or signs of congestive heart failure, or EKG abnormalities (Kennedy, Andrews, & Caird, 1977). Cardiac illness in this age group manifests itself with symptoms similar to those in younger patients, such as coronary heart disease, hypertensive heart disease, cardiomyopathy, and valvular heart disease. There are also subtypes of cardiac illness more characteristic of the elderly, such as calcific degenerative disorders or degeneration of the valves and conducting system.

Of the known cardiovascular risk factors, hypertension is the most treatable and most frequent contributor to coronary disease, heart attacks, and stroke (Kannel, 1976). Research to date does not suggest a blood pressure threshold for the establishment of such risk. (See the section on hypertension in this chapter for further information on the etiology and incidence of this disorder and for possible treatment interventions.) Leaverton, Havlik, and Ingster-Moore (1990) report that increased serum cholesterol levels and cigarette smoking may also have some ability to predict cardiac illness. Results from the National Health and Nutrition Examination Survey indicate the percent of individuals with high-risk serum cholesterol levels is nearly twice as high for elderly black and white women than for comparably aged black and white men (see National Center for Health Statistics, 1987, p. 38), although for all groups these levels are on the decline.

Cigarette smoking continues to be a problem for this age group, with 19.6% of elderly men smoking in 1985 (see National Center for Health Statistics, 1987), a percentage that has not changed since a 1979 survey of this subgroup. Excess weight has also been identified as a potential risk factor, although the relationship between excess weight and heart disease in unclear (Bray, 1984). Approximately one-fourth of men between 55 and 74 years of age are overweight. A greater proportion of females are overweight than males, and more black females are overweight than their white counterparts. Excess weight is also associated with blood pressure and glucose elevations and, thus, may be linked to heart disease via its involvement in hypertension.

While certain lifestyle variables (including smoking, excess weight, and dietary factors) have been statistically associated with heart disease and stroke, our understanding of the relationships among these variables, the aging process, and disease remains rudimentary. We should not assume that lowering or eliminating known risk factors will necessarily lower associated risk. There have been few investigations of the mutability of risk by alteration of risk factors (Arnold, Kane, & Kane, 1986). Studies to date have not systematically explored the outcome of weight reduction, smoking cessation, and diet alteration on cardiovascular risk in the elderly. Some initial studies, however, have reported positive benefits of increased physical activity on cardiac functioning. Kasch and Wallace (1986) demonstrated cardiovascular benefits of regular exercise in an aging adult over a period of 10 to 15 years. Sidney and Shepard (1978) cited improvements in general cardiovascular fitness in an older adult who exercised two to four times per week.

Furthermore, generalization of findings relevant to risk reduction from a younger-aged cohort to the elderly can be dangerous. For example, contrary to what one might expect extrapolating from research with younger samples, Sparacino (1979) reported that aggressive and competitive behavior in the elderly can actually have a positive effect on morbidity rates.

Behavioral interventions that address the modification of associated cardio-vascular risk factors may be particularly useful in determining whether or not the optimization of lifestyle variables will have an effect on morbidity and mortality. (Potential interventions are discussed later in this chapter in the section on hypertensive disease). Other areas ripe for contributions from behavioral researchers relevant to the treatment of cardiovascular disease include work on compliance with medical regimens, such as adherence to medication requirements, dietary changes, weight loss, and exercise programs. All of these possibilities are considered later in the chapter.

Cancer

Malignant neoplasms are ranked as the second leading cause of death for U.S. citizens in the 55–64, 65–74, and 75–84 year age brackets, and as the third leading cause of death for those 85 years of age and older (National Center for Health Statistics, 1986). More than 50% of cancers are diagnosed in those over 65 years of age (Surveillance, Epidemiology, & End Results, 1981) and approximately 60% of mortalities attributable to cancer occur in this age group (Horm & Cicero, 1984). While mortality from cardiac disease has declined in recent years, deaths attributable to cancer, especially respiratory tract cancer, have been increasing over the past 20 years (National Center for Health Statistics, 1987). The incidence of cancer is significantly greater among elderly men than elderly women, and the average annual changes in cancer mortality rates appear to have increased more for male than female elderly. Cancer incidence rises exponentially with age and, thus, as our population distribution changes with a greater representation by the elderly, proportionately more individuals will be at risk for cancer development every year.

Cancers of the prostate, lungs, colon, rectum, and bladder rank highest for elderly white males. Eighty percent of prostate cancers, 55% of lung cancers, and 68% of all colon cancers are first diagnosed in elderly males. For elderly females, leading cancer sites include the breast, colon, lungs, uterus, and rectum. Fifty percent of lung, breast, and uterine cancers as well as 70–75% of colorectal cancers in women occur among elderly citizens (Baranovsky & Myers, 1986).

Early cancer detection may be important in increasing the probability of identifying more localized, and possibly more treatable, disease. This still remains conjecture, however, as it has yet to be documented that early cancer detection yields lowered mortality rates in the elderly (Winawer, Baldwin, Herbert, & Sherlock, 1983). While studies show that cancers presented in the elderly are generally not more advanced than those diagnosed in middle-aged individuals, an estimated one-third to one-half of newly diagnosed cancers in the elderly are at an advanced stage for which the 5-year survival rates are poorer (Warnecke, Havlicek, & Manfredi, 1983). Cancer treatments are efficacious in the elderly; current data suggest comparable treatment response ratios between older and younger cohorts.

Kegeles and Grady (1982) propose that the elderly are less likely to avail themselves of services prerequisite for early cancer detection. Numerous factors may contribute to this situation. Reduced mobility, poor health insurance or limited finances, myths concerning cancer, and fear may hinder or prevent access to appropriate caregivers. In an investigation of beliefs concerning cancer endorsed by elderly citizens, Rimer, Jones, Wilson, Bennett, and Engstrom (1983) found that 30% to 60% of a sample of community elderly were unaware that their age group was at increased risk for the development of cancer. Furthermore, more than 50% of this sample believed that treatment for cancer was worse than the disease itself.

German (1981) has reported that the elderly are likely to ignore early symptoms of disease, and Howe (1981) has found them less likely to comply with prevention strategies and utilize assessment techniques for early detection. Decreased rates of breast self-examination among elderly females (Foster, Lang, Costanza, Worden, & Haines, 1978) may be of concern, as newly discovered lumps in elderly females are more likely to be malignant than in their younger counterparts (Mant, Vessey, Neil, McPherson, & Jones, 1987). In addition, early detection and treatment may be further limited, as medical caregivers may attribute early symptoms such as weight loss, fatigue, and weakness to alternative physical or psychological etiologies.

The importance of enhancing treatment interventions and facilitating earlier detection of cancers in the elderly is highlighted by the reality that many 65-year-old individuals in the United States can now expect to live an additional 20 years. The diagnosis of cancer evokes fears of protracted disability, chronic pain, dependence on others, and certain death. Nonpharmacological avenues of treatment are also crucial, as some cancer patients are unable to tolerate therapy or have adverse effects from the illness itself due to the use of other medications, concurrent illnesses, or age-related physical decrements. Pain is a major concern in about one-third of patients in cancer treatment (Payne & Foley, 1984), and approximately one-fifth of cancer patients experience pain that is not alleviated by normal doses of oral narcotics.

Variables that have been empirically linked to cancer development include cigarette smoking, unprotected sun exposure, diet, and alcohol. Tobacco use has been identified as the most common cause of cancer in the elderly, with associations established to cancer of the oral cavity, larynx, lungs, esophagus, pancreas, kidney, and bladder (Ewing, 1940). Cigarettes alone account for perhaps as much as 30% of all death attributable to cancer (cf. Rabin & Schnipper, 1988). The risk of lung cancer from smoking rapidly decreases upon cessation, yet many elderly continue to smoke.

Excessive exposure to the sun without adequate protection can cause skin cancer in individuals of all ages. As elderly citizens often have more leisure time and pursue hobbies that increase their exposure to the sun, they may be at greater risk for skin cancer than other age groups.

Diet has also been implicated to cancer development and prevention. High-fat diets and obesity have been related to increased risk for cancers of the breast, colon, endometrium, and prostate. High-fiber diets are associated with a decreased risk for colon cancer. There has been some speculation that consumption of foods rich in Vitamins A and C may decrease the risk for lung, larynx, and esophageal cancers, though this remains controversial. Alcohol may also act as a carcinogen in combination with tobacco in head, neck, and visceral cancers, though it is difficult to separate out the respective contributions of these two factors. The empirical research upon which these claims have been based has largely been conducted with subjects of all ages. It remains to be shown that the recommended lifestyle modifications in an elderly sample do, in fact, result in lowered risk.

The potential for substantive contributions by behavior therapists in this field is vast. Included among areas of opportunity are control of cancer pain, interventions for chemotherapy side effects, lifestyle modifications to lower cancer risk, and strategies to enhance compliance with medical recommendations (e.g., breast self-examination). Bonica and Ventafridda (1979) have recommended the use of hypnosis, acupuncture, and biofeedback in the treatment of cancer-related pain. While extensive data attest to the efficacy of behavioral interventions in chronic pain control (see Dolce & Dickerson, Chapter 17, this text), further research is needed to document the outcome of the application of similar interventions for elderly cancer patients. For example, relaxation training with this group may be beneficial for treating accompanying anxiety. Some data suggest the potential value of relaxation training in the control of pain intensity (Turk, Meichenbaum, & Genest, 1983) and enhancement of the patient's expectations of control during periods of pain and stress (Turk & Rennert, 1981).

Anticipatory nausea and vomiting is a commonly reported side effect associated with chemotherapy. Redd and Andersen (1981) have proposed that this behavior be understood as a conditioned response. Morrow and Morrell (1982) successfully utilized relaxation as an incompatible response to nausea and vomiting and demonstrated lowered occurrence of this side effect. In a single-subject reversal design, Greene and Seime (1987) used a taste-masking solution to lower anticipatory nausea in a 61-year-old female oncology patient. In this case study, maintenance of gains were documented even after treatment withdrawal.

Empirical studies of the prophylactic application of behavioral techniques for weight loss, diet modification, smoking cessation, and alcohol treatment in elderly cohorts are sorely needed. It remains to be seen whether variables associated with this age group (e.g., cognitive impairments, poor finances, limited social supports) may necessitate modification of intervention strategies proven effective for younger patient samples. Educational campaigns and instruction of elderly females in breast self-examination may improve early detection rates and early treatment. Mant *et al.* (1987) reported that women under 60 years of age who were taught breast self-examination techniques were more likely to discover localized, smaller tumors than those who self-examined without prior instruction. The outcomes of a few health education programs for elderly clients have demonstrated knowledge gain (Mettler & Fallcreek, 1981) as well as enhanced motivation to seek cancer screening (Elwood, Erickson, & Lieberman, 1978).

Stroke

While there has been a decline in the incidence of stroke over the past 20 years (Garraway, Whisnant, Furlan, Phillips, Kurland, & O'Fallon, 1979), and a 50% reduction in stroke mortality over the last 10 years, stroke and other neurologic diseases still account for a significant portion of disability in the elderly. Decreased incidence rates have at least partially been attributed to improvements in the treatment of hypertension. The Hypertension Detection and Follow-up Program Cooperative Group (1982) reported that long-term reductions in diastolic blood pressure to levels below 90 mm Hg were associated with significantly fewer strokes in elderly of both sexes. Lowered mortality attributable to stroke has been associated with decreased severity of strokes in all age groups (see Walshe, 1988).

Advanced age is the most consistent risk factor for stroke (Wolf, 1985). Dramatic increases in stroke incidence occur with age elevations. Twice as many strokes occur in people between 65 and 74 years of age as occur among people 54 to 64 years. Furthermore, between the ages of 75 and 84 years, the rates are nearly triple those of the earlier decade (see McDowell, 1986). It is widely believed that stroke occurrence is generally more common in males than females. Some researchers suggest that this difference continues into the later years (Weiss & Weinfeld, 1981), while others have reported that the incidence rates for females approximates those for males in advanced old age.

In addition to advancing age, hypertension, as well as other cardiac disease, cigarette smoking, and diabetes mellitus are recognized as risk factors for stroke. For the elderly, hypertension and cigarette smoking are associated with the highest rate of stroke incidence as well as the highest mortality rates.

Behavioral professionals may have some impact in both the areas of stroke prevention as well as rehabilitation of its victims. Risk reduction, either by smoking cessation or management of hypertension, may involve the expertise of a trained behavioral clinician. As behavioral techniques have empirically demonstrated efficacy in smoking cessation treatment, it is necessary to further evaluate them when applied to elderly individuals. While behavioral techniques, including relaxation training and biofeedback, have successfully lowered blood pressure in younger cohorts, further research is needed to examine outcomes when they are used with elderly hypertensives.

In the field of rehabilitation, age does not appear to be a relevant outcome factor, but associated medical conditions and depression have been implicated in outcome. Surveys report that nearly one-third of all stroke victims are depressed upon evaluation for rehabilitation after cerebral infarction (Reding, Orto, Willensky, Fortuna, Day, Steiner, Gehr, & McDowell, 1985). Unexplored terrain for behavioral researchers has been the treatment of depression in stroke victims and the application of behavioral contingency management and feedback mechanisms to improve compliance with rehabilitation programs. Considerable evidence exists to substantiate the efficacy of psychological treatments for depression in older individuals (Gallagher, 1981; Teri, Chapter 10, this text), and both the operant and cognitive-behavioral models have been adapted for use with the elderly (Emery, 1981; Gallagher, Thompson, Baffa, Piatt, Ringering, & Stone, 1981). Exploration of the value of such interventions in treatment of depressed stroke victims is warranted.

Osteoarthritis

An estimated 50 million Americans are diagnosed with arthritis, and approximately 600,000 new cases present each year (Arthritis Foundation, 1973). Of all individuals over age 60, 60–90% are affected by arthritis, and it ranks number one as a cause of disability in the elderly (Newacheck, Butler, Harper, Piontkowski, & Franks, 1981). In 1980 and 1985, limitations attributable to arthritis occurred in 26.5 and 29.7%, respectively, of the elderly. In all elderly age subgroups, rates of arthritis are higher in females than in males, with more than one-half of all women 65 years of age or older having it. The associated medical expenditures are high. Lubeck and Holman (1982) estimated that the annual cost for medical services and drugs for osteoarthritis patients older than 50 years of age can be $800 per person.

The diagnosis of arthritis encompasses nearly 100 conditions, with the most common forms being osteoarthritis, rheumatoid arthritis, ankylosing spondylitis, systemic lupus erythematosus, and gout. The role of stress in arthritis has been documented repeatedly (Schochet, Lisansky, Schubart, Fiocco, Kurland, & Pope, 1969; Wyatt, 1969), with many different stressors affecting disease status, including divorce, surgery, and financial concerns. While it has been postulated that stress may act as a triggering mechanism in autoimmune disorders, understanding of the pathophysiological mechanism is lacking (Weiner, 1977). As stress results in increased muscle tension in rheumatoid arthritis patients (Morrison, Short, Ludwig, & Schwab, 1947), some investigators have hypothesized that elevated muscle tension may be a mediating variable between stress and flare-ups in rheumatoid arthritis (Moos & Engel, 1962).

Treatment recommendations for arthritis patients often include exercise to strengthen supporting muscles and weight loss, if applicable, as well as anti-inflammatory drugs and bed rest. While numerous opportunities for behavioral intervention exist in the care of arthritis patients, few controlled treatment outcome studies have been conducted. Among these potential contributions are pain control interventions, relaxation procedures to decrease muscle tension, weight control techniques, and strategies to enhance compliance with medical recommendations (including exercise and medication use).

To date, a few preliminary investigations, largely utilizing small samples, have documented the positive effects of pain reduction, decreased muscle tension, and sleep improvements from relaxation techniques, biofeedback, and self-regulation strategies (Achterberg, McGraw, & Lawlis, 1981; Denver, Laveault, Girard, Lacourciere, Latulippe, Grove, Preve, & Doiron, 1979; Wickramasekera, 1976). Varni (1981a, 1981b) reported successful use of progressive muscle relaxation, meditative breathing, and guided imagery to decrease reported joint pain associated with three cases of hemophilia. Furthermore, he reported maintenance of the effect in 7- and 14-month follow-up periods. In a recent case study utilizing biofeedback treatment alone for an 80-year-old female suffering from arthritis, Boczkowski (1984) reported decreased pain and stiffness, as well as lowered medication use. In a self-management course for arthritis patients aged 55–94 years of age, Lorig, Laurin, and Holman (1984) found that instruction in relaxation training and problem solving, as well as exercise and education, resulted in fewer visits to physicians, lowered subjective reports of pain, and increased knowledge. This course was led by nonprofessionals. In light of the fact that the behavioral literature adequately documents the efficacy of behavioral techniques for pain control and stress management, it is striking that the application to elderly arthritic individuals has been so limited.

Compliance is a crucial issue for elderly patients in general, but may be especially difficult for arthritic individuals. Arthritis is a chronic degenerative illness; its treatment is lengthy and may involve adverse side effects. Treatment adherence in arthritis is not necessarily predictive of a positive treatment outcome. When exercise and dietary change are part of a recommended treatment program, elderly may not be amenable to such lifestyle modifications. Waggoner and LeLieuvre (1981) successfully utilized visual feedback displays to enhance compliance with exercise regiments in rheumatoid arthritis patients. Additional studies investigating the applicability of feedback mechanisms and contingent reinforcement to improve compliance in this patient population are warranted.

Hypertension

As defined by a systolic blood pressure greater than 160 mm Hg and a diastolic blood pressure greater than 95 mm Hg, hypertension occurs in about 45% of individuals older than 60 years of age (O'Malley & O'Brien, 1980; Simpson, 1980). Numerous studies in Western countries have reported increases in systolic blood pressure from approximately the age of 30 years into old age and smaller elevations in diastolic blood pressure, peaking in the mid-50s for males and mid-60s for females (Gordon & Shurtleff, 1974). (It is important to note that less developed countries fail to report similar blood pressure elevations in the elderly, suggesting that such changes are not inevitable sequelae of the aging process.) According to Hoy and Ponte (1984) this problem affects a higher percentage of elderly blacks (55%) than elderly whites (40%). It is also more common among elderly females than elderly males.

Historically, isolated systolic blood pressure elevations were viewed as a normal result of aging and were not treated. Within the past several years, however, several large-scale studies of elderly Americans with hypertension have underscored the significant risk associated with elevations in either component of blood pressure (Amery, Wasir, Bulpitt, Conway, Fagard, Lijnen, & Reybrouch, 1978; Osterfield, 1978; O'Malley & O'Brien, 1980). The same investigations have suggested that the risks of cardiovascular morbidity and mortality are more elevated the higher the blood pressure and the older the patient. Specific cardiovascular diseases associated with blood pressure elevations include cerebral infarction, myocardial infarction, renal insufficiency, congestive heart failure, retinopathy, and ischemic heart disease. Incidence of cardiovascular disease has been estimated to be three to four times greater in elderly hypertensives than in similar-aged cohorts without blood pressure abnormalities. The bulk of evidence suggests that elevated risk from hypertension continues well into old age and that current and past levels of systolic blood pressure are better predictors of risk than diastolic blood pressure levels. Similar levels of risk have been reported for elderly of both sexes with blood pressure elevations (Whelton, 1985).

Many internal and external factors have been implicated in the etiology of hypertension in the elderly. For example, decreased artery elasticity due to arteriosclerosis or calcification, and replacement of elastic tissue with fibrous tissue, can lead to increased peripheral vascular resistance. Arteriosclerosis appears to be the primary factor in elevated systolic blood pressure. In addition, reductions with age in the regulatory functioning of the kidneys may be contributory. Other changes, including net decreases in total body water as a percentage of total body weight, shrinking of plasma volume, and reductions in plasma renin activity, lead to a low-renin type of hypertension.

Factors intrinsic to the individual, including inadequate exercise levels, cigarette smoking, obesity, situational stress, and excessive salt intake are definitely implicated in the etiology of hypertension (see Hoy & Ponte, 1984). Harlan, Oberman, Mitchell, and Graybiel (1973) reported that initial blood pressure levels and weight gain maintain a stronger relationship to blood pressure changes in Western cultures than the factor of age. In a large cross-sectional study, Pan, Nanas, Dyer, Liu, McDonald, Schoenberger, Shekelle, Stamler, and Stamler (1986) cited higher blood pressure levels in all age categories with greater degrees of obesity. While middle-aged overweight hypertensives have evidenced significant blood pressure decreases with weight loss, similar empirical studies have not yet been done for elderly hypertensives. It has also been suggested that some changes in cardiac functioning accompanying old age may be more a reflection of sedentary lifestyles in the elderly than of the aging process itself. Barry, Daly, Pruett, Steinmetz, Page, Birkhead, and Rodahl (1966), DeVries (1970), and Sidney and Shephard (1977) have reported significant reductions in resting systolic and diastolic blood pressures when older adults have engaged in systematic exercise programs.

In the treatment of elderly hypertensives, both pharmacological and nonpharmacological interventions should be considered. Potential adverse side effects to antihypertensive medications include impotence, gout, postural hypotension, and impaired glucose tolerance (Oliver, 1982), as well as depression. Thus, it is important to investigate nondrug alternatives for this problem. However, as the predominant etiology of hypertension in the elderly differs from that in younger cohorts, it may be risky to use behavioral interventions, which have been effective with younger samples, indiscriminately with older samples. Empirical verification of blood pressure reductions in elderly patients with the same interventions is needed. Relaxation and biofeedback techniques, which have repeatedly been demonstrated to reduce blood pressure elevations in younger adults, should be explored. Behavioral weight reduction strategies, including stimulus control techniques, reduced caloric intake, self-reinforcement methods, social support, and cognitive interventions, should be examined for overweight elderly. Similarly, behavioral techniques for smoking cessation, including stimulus control strategies, graduated reduction, relaxation training, contracting, self-reinforcement, social support and cognitive restructuring, may be effective.

Contingency management and feedback mechanisms should be investigated to increase exercise programs and enhance compliance with reduced salt and low-fat diets. These suggested lifestyle modifications of long-term habits will require education, support, and repeated reinforcement, and they may be more difficult for the elderly men and women than other age groups. Lastly, educational efforts targeting this age population are imperative. A survey examining the elderly's awareness of etiological factors in hypertension revealed that only 18% endorsed obesity as a cause, 11% endorsed excess salt, 6% endorsed smoking, and 3% endorsed lack of exercise (Urban Behavioral Research Associates, 1981).

Osteoporosis

Osteoporosis is a disorder characterized by increased porousness in bone structures resulting in skeletal fragility. It is almost exclusively a problem of the elderly and occurs four times more often in women than in men. It has been hypothesized that estrogen withdrawal accounts for this gender differential. Epidemiological data estimating that approximately 14 million women in the United States meet minimal criteria for this diagnosis reflect the grave proportions of this disorder (Scileppi, 1983). By age 70 women may have lost approximately 30% of their bone, a factor that results in about 150,000 hip fractures a year and a death rate of about 45,000 women within a year (Smith, 1984). With moderate exercise and a diet that included significant amounts of calcium, Smith, Redden, and Smith (1981) reported positive gains in bone mineral of the radium midshaft among a group of elderly women who participated in a series of chair exercises over a 3-year period. A control group, on the other hand, experienced a decrease in the same bone area. Other investigators (Riggs, Seeman, & Hodgson, 1982) have demonstrated a reduction in the incidence of bone fractures and some efficacy in forming new bone (Scileppi, 1983). Current medical approaches include calcium and estrogen treatments to reduce further bone resorption. Estrogen, however, has been implicated in the occurrence of endometrial carcinoma, cholelithiasis, and hypertension when used for a prolonged time by postmenstrual women (Scileppi, 1983). Nutritional impoverishment in early life, particularly inadequate calcium and phosphorous intake, may be associated with later-life development of this disorder. It has also been shown that decreases in bone mass accompany reduction in physical activity (Donaldson, Halley, Voge, Hattner, Bayers, & MacMillan, 1970).

Treatment interventions for this problem would certainly include nutritional education. Behavioral techniques for pain control may be useful to enhance coping with fractures resulting from bone fragility or chronic back pain associated with this disorder.

FACTORS CONTRIBUTING TO HEALTH PROBLEMS

There are at least four factors that contribute significantly to the health problems of the elderly. These are nutritional practices, drug use, compliance patterns, and stress. These areas are addressed in detail in other chapters in this text and so will be mentioned only briefly here.

Nutritional Practices

Gershell (1981) has estimated that as many as one-half of the health problems experienced by the elderly are related in some way to nutritional deficiencies.

Because elderly require less food than younger people, they need a diet higher in nutrients. As caloric intake decreases, nutrient intake must remain at normal levels (or even increase). This is not the case, however. Recent surveys indicate that between 40% and 50% of the elderly are consuming fewer calories than recommended, with a probable diminution in nutrient levels at the same time.

Drug Use

As a group the elderly are more likely to take drugs, use several drugs at a time, and use them for longer periods. Estimates indicate that they use 25% of prescription drugs, including large amounts of barbiturates and tranquilizers. Over-the-counter medication, including aspirin and laxatives, are also used excessively. In addition, the elderly frequently decide on their own medication without consulting a physician (Lenhart, 1976); they save outdated medication, share prescriptions with friends (Gibson & O'Hare, 1968), and often combine drugs with alcohol (Capel & Stewart, 1971). Their normally decreased metabolism means that they are twice as likely to react negatively to even normal doses of medication (Cooper, 1975) and to suffer more side effects from drugs than younger populations (Morrant, 1975).

Alcohol is another substance that seriously endangers the health of elderly citizens (McCusker, Cherubin, & Zimberg, 1971). Alcoholism, which sometimes originates as a problem in middle age, may be a maladaptive response pattern for coping with stress brought on by loss, sickness, financial difficulties, housing problems, family tensions, and other problems. Alcohol has multiple adverse effects on the body, leading most often to cirrhosis of the liver, automobile fatalities, and severe cognitive changes. Alcohol also depletes nutritional resources, can effect changes in bone marrow and red blood cells, and is toxic to the pancreas.

Treatment Compliance

The elderly as a group have a poor record of adhering to treatment recommendations (Brand & Smith, 1974). To some extent the record is influenced by problems of memory impairment and sensory deficits, which are often present in this age group. A case study by Dapcich-Miura and Hovell (1979) demonstrated improved compliance with a complex medical regimen as a result of token reinforcement. Wandless and Davies (1977) found that their elderly subjects had significantly fewer errors in medication compliance when they used tear-off calendars or tablet identification cards than when they used standard instructions. Further studies along these lines are sorely needed.

Stress

Stress has often been implicated in a variety of diseases, and it may also decrease the body's ability to fight disease. It may be a major component in the onset of disease, or it may have an indirect effect by negatively influencing one's health care behavior. Research on the role of stress in the experience of various diseases has produced mixed results. However, most studies have demonstrated that stress predisposes the body to diseases associated with the immune system (e.g., cancers, rheumatoid arthritis, ulcerative colitis) by influencing the endocrine system. Stress is linked, of course, to other types of diseases including coronary heart disease and respiratory diseases, but the data on these mechanisms are less clear.

The ways in which individuals cope with stress is an important modifier of the effects of stress on disease. Coping behaviors are one element implicated in the modification of the stress–disease relationship. Cohen (1984) presents five ways in which coping strategies may affect the cause of disease and recovery from it. Coping strategies (1) may "increase hormonal levels, causing direct tissue damage or influencing bodily resistance to illness" (p. 265); (2) have a direct impact on health in that they involve habits that either promote good health (e.g., exercise) or reduce it (e.g., smoking); (3) may enhance recovery from illness or diminish its severity; and (4) affect the way a person interacts with a health professional and thus influence the type of treatment one receives. Lastly, (5), positive outlook "may trigger production of beta-endorphins which can reduce pain and may speed healing" (p. 265). Thus, people who are unable to cope may be more susceptible to disease, but the data implicating this relationship are not clear.

Stress management techniques may include relaxation training, desensitization to anxiety-provoking conditions, thought stopping for perseverative thoughts, various reinforcement methods to increase desired activities, "stress inoculation" procedures to address how one perceives the world, cognitive coping skills for processing information, cognitive restructuring for dealing with nonproductive negative self-statements, assertiveness training to encourage self-expression and defense of one's rights, biofeedback training to learn control over certain physiological mechanisms, reinforcer sampling to increase the number and variety of pleasurable events, and a variety of all-purpose imagery techniques. Stress management techniques are applicable to a person's day-to-day worries and anxieties and have as their goal improved coping ability and prevention of disease-enhancing factors. In addition, they are useful for helping people cope with pain and other effects from disability and disease.

Relationship of Lifestyle and Environment to Health

All of the health-related problems and specific diseases outlined earlier are related to lifestyle and environment. Heart disease is related to smoking, hypertension, elevated serum cholesterol, dietary factors, excess weight, lack of exercise, and stress. Cancer is related to smoking, worksite and environmental carcinogens, poor compliance with assessment and prevention strategies, alcohol and diet, and exposure to the sun. The incidence of strokes is related to hypertension, smoking, and diabetes. Arthritis is influenced by stress, exercise, and excess weight. Hypertension is influenced by arteriosclerosis, inadequate exercise, smoking, obesity, stress, and diet. The effects of osteoporosis may be modified by diet and exercise.

Thus, none of these problems are necessarily inevitable accompaniments of the aging process but derive to a large extent from our own health habits and the environmental conditions we allow to exist.

There are five good health practices recommended for maintaining health:

1. Monitor what enters the body, including food, alcohol, drugs and nicotine, and use each substance properly.
2. Maintain weight at prescribed levels.
3. Engage in physical exercise on a daily basis.
4. Learn to relax, enjoy life, deal effectively with stressful events, and rest as needed.
5. Take responsibility for one's own health.

While these recommendations make good sense, some experimental data exist to support them as well. A study by Belloc (1973) demonstrated that people who practice these habits plus other simple measures (including wearing seat belts and observing the speed limit) lived on the average 11 years longer than people who practiced none of them.

The field of behavioral medicine emerged in the mid-1970s as a partnership between behavioral scientists and biomedical health specialists. One of its primary goals was the application of behavioral and biomedical science knowledge and techniques to prevention, diagnosis, treatment, and rehabilitation (Schwartz & Weiss, 1978). More recently the term "behavioral health" has been coined to emphasize the promotion of a "philosophy of health that stresses individual responsibility in the application of behavioral and biomedical knowledge and techniques to the maintenance of health and the prevention of illness and dysfunction. . ." (Matarazzo, 1980, p. 813).

Research examining the differential efficacy of various behavioral interventions for health problems of the elderly has been scarce. Furthermore, it is unclear to what extent, if any, the age factor may warrant modifications in standard behavioral health interventions. Thus, many of the following recommendations are not unique to this age cohort. It is our hope, however, that in the next few years researchers in this burgeoning field will scientifically address these questions.

REFERENCES

Achterberg, J., McGraw, P., & Lawlis, G. F. (1981). Rheumatoid arthritis: A study of relaxation and temperature biofeedback as an adjunctive therapy. *Biofeedback and Self-Regulation, 6*, 207–233.

Amery, A., Wasir, H., Bulpitt, C., Conway, J., Fogard, R., Lijnen, P., & Reybrouck, T. (1978). Aging and the cardiovascular system. *Acta Cardiologica, 33*, 443–467.

Arnold, S., Kane, R. L., & Kane, R. A. (1986). Health promotion and the elderly: Evaluating the research. In W. K. Dychtwald & J. MacLean (Eds.), *Wellness and health promotion in the elderly* (pp. 327–344). Rockville, MD: Aspen Systems.

Arthritis Foundation. (1973). *Primer on the rheumatic diseases*. Washington, DC: Author.

Baranovsky, A., & Myers, M. H. (1986). Cancer incidence and survival in patients 65 years of age and older. *Cancer, 36*, 26–41.

Barry, A. J., Daly, J. W., Pruett, E. D. R., Steinmetz, J. R., Page, H. F., Birkhead, N. C., & Rodahl, K. (1966).

The effects of physical conditioning on older individuals: I. Work capacity, circulatory-respiratory function and electrocardiogram. *Journal of Gerontology, 21,* 182–191.

Belloc, N. (1973). Relationship of health practices and mortality. *Preventive Medicine, 2,* 67–81.

Besdine, R. (1981). Health and illness behavior in the elderly. In D. Parron, F. Solomn, J. Rodin (Eds.), *Health behavior and aging: A research agenda* (Interim report No. 5, pp. 15–24). Washington, DC: Division of Mental Health and Behavioral Medicine, National Academy Press.

Boczkowski, J. A. (1984). Biofeedback training for the treatment of chronic pain in an elderly arthritic female. *Clinical Gerontology, 2,* 39–46.

Bonica, J. J., & Ventafridda, V. (Eds.). (1979). *Advances in pain research and therapy* (Vol. 2). New York: Raven Press.

Boyd, R., & Oakes, C. (1969). *Foundations of practical gerontology.* Columbia: University of South Carolina Press.

Brand, F., & Smith, R. (1974). Life adjustment and relocation of the elderly. *Journal of Gerontology, 29,* 336–340.

Bray, G. (1984). The role of weight control in health promotion and disease prevention. In J. Matarrazzo, S. Weiss, J. Herd, N. Miller, & S. Weiss (Eds.), *Behavioral health* (pp. 632–656). New York: John Wiley & Sons.

Capel, W., & Stewart, G. (1971). The management of drug abuse in aging populations: New Orleans findings. *Journal of Drug Issues, 1,* 114–120.

Cohen, F. (1984). Coping. In J. Matarrazzo, S. Weiss, J. Heerd, N. Miller, and S. Weiss (Eds.), *Behavioral health* (pp. 261–274). New York: John Wiley & Sons.

Cooper, J. W. (1975). Implications of drug reaction: Recognition, incidences, and prevention. *Rhode Island Medical Journal, 58,* 274–280.

Dapcich-Miura, E., & Hovell, M. (1979). Contingency management of adherence to a complex medical regimen in an elderly heart patient. *Behavior Therapy, 10,* 193–201.

Denver, D. R., Daveault, D., Girard, F., Lacourciere, Y., Latulippe, L., Grove, R. N., Preve, M., & Doiron, N. (1979). Behavioral medicine: Biobehavioral effects of short-term thermal biofeedback and relaxation in rheumatoid arthritis patients. *Biofeedback and Self-Regulation, 4,* 245–246.

DeVries, H. A. (1970). Physiological effects of an exercise training regimen upon men aged 52–88. *Journal of Gerontology, 25,* 325–336.

Donaldson, C., Halley, S., Voge, J., Hattner, R., Bayers, J., & MacMillan, D. (1970). Effects of prolonged bedrest on bone mineral. *Metabolism, 19,* 1071–1084.

Elwood, T., Erickson, A., & Lieberman, S. (1978). Comparative educational approaches to screening for colorectal cancer. In J. Wakefield (Ed.), *Public education about cancer* (pp. 26–34). Geneva: UICC.

Emery, G. (1981). Cognitive therapy with the elderly. In G. Emery, S. Hollon, & R. Bedrosian (Eds.), *New directions in cognitive therapy* (pp. 84–88). New York: Guilford Press.

Ewing, J. (1940). *Neoplastic diseases.* Philadelphia: W. B. Saunders.

Field, M. (1970). *Depth and extent of the geriatric problem.* Springfield, IL: Charles C. Thomas.

Foster, R., Lang, S. P., Costanza, M. C., Worden, J., & Haines, C. (1978). Breast self-examination practices and breast cancer stage. *New England Journal of Medicine, 299,* 265–270.

Gallagher, D. (1981). Behavioral group therapy with elderly depressives: An experimental study. In D. Upper & S. Ross (Eds.), *Handbook of behavioral group therapy* (pp. 275–299). Champaign, IL: Research Press.

Gallagher, D. Thompson, L., Baffa, G., Piatt, C., Ringering, L., & Stone, V. (Eds.). (1981). *Depression in the elderly: A behavioral treatment manual.* Los Angeles: University of Southern California.

Garraway, M. N., Whisnant, J. P., Furlan, A. J., Phillips, L. H., Kurland, L. T., & O'Fallon, W. M. (1979). The declining incidence of stroke. *New England Journal of Medicine, 300,* 449–452.

German, P. (1981). *Delivery of care to older people: Issues and outlooks.* Rockville, MD: Aspen Systems.

Gershell, W. J. (1981). Psychiatric manifestations of nutritional deficiencies in the elderly. In A. J. Levenson & R. C. Wall (Eds.), *Neuropsychiatric manifestations of physical disease in the elderly* (pp. 119–132). New York: Raven Press.

Gibson, S., & O'Hare, M. (1968). Prescription of drugs for old people at home. *Gerontologica Clinica, 10,* 271–280.

Gordon, T., & Shurtleff, D. (1974). Means at each examination and inter-examination variation of specified characteristics: The Framingham study. In W. B. Kannel, & T. Gordon (Eds.), *The*

Framingham study: An epidemiologic investigation of cardiovascular disease (DHEW Publication No. NIH 74478, Section 29, pp. 1–53). Washington, DC: U.S. Government Printing Office.

Green, P. G., & Seime, R. J. (1987). Stimulus control of anticipatory nausea in cancer chemotherapy. *Journal of Behavior Therapy and Experimental Psychiatry, 18*, 61–64.

Harkins, S., & Chapman, C. (1977). Detection and decision factors in pain perception in young and elderly men. *Pain, 2*, 253–264.

Harlan, W. R., Oberman, A., Mitchell, R., & Graybiel, A. (1973). A thirty year study of blood pressure in a white male cohort. In G. Onesti, K. E. Kim, & J. H. Moyer (Eds.), *Hypertension: Mechanisms in management* (pp. 85–91). New York: Grune and Stratton.

Horm, J. W., & Cicero, J. (Eds.). (1984). *SEER Program: Cancer incidence and mortality in the United States, 1973–1981.* (NIH Publication No. 85–1837). Bethesda, MD: National Cancer Institute.

Howe, H. (1981). Social factors associated with breast self-examination among high risk women. *American Journal of Public Health, 71*, 251–253.

Hoy, R. H., & Ponte, C. D. (1984). Cardiovascular disorders. In T. R. Covington, & J. I Walker (Eds.), *Current geriatric therapy* (pp. 140–177). Philadelphia: W. B. Saunders.

Hypertension Detection and Follow-up Program Cooperative Group (1982). Five-year findings of the Hypertension Detection and Follow-up Program. *Journal of the American Medical Association, 247*, 633–638.

Kannel, W. B. (1976). Some lessons in cardiovascular epidemiology from Framingham. *American Journal of Cardiology, 37*, 269–282.

Kasch, F. W., & Wallace, J. P. (1986). Physiological variables during 10 years of endurance exercise. *Medicine and Science in Sports and Exercise, 8*, 5–8.

Kegeles, S., & Grady, K. (1982). Behavioral dimensions. In D. Shottenfeld & J. Fraumeni (Eds.), *Cancer epidemiology and prevention* (pp. 1049–1063). Philadelphia: W. B. Saunders.

Kennedy, R. D., Andrews, G. R., & Caird, F. I. (1977). Ischematic heart disease in the elderly. *British Heart Journal, 39*, 1121–1127.

Kimmel, D. (1974). *Adulthood and aging.* New York: John Wiley & Sons.

Leaverton, E., Havlik, R. J., & Ingster-Moore, L. (1990). Coronary heart disease and hypertension. In J. Cornoni-Huntley, R. R. Huntley, & J. J. Feldman (Eds.), *Health status and well-being of the elderly* (pp. 53–70). New York: Oxford University Press.

Lenhart, D. G. (1976). The use of medications in the elderly populations. *Nursing Clinics of North America, 11*, 135–143.

Lorig, K., Laurin, J., & Holman, H. R. (1984). Arthritis self-management: A study of the effectiveness of patient education for the elderly. *The Gerontologist, 24*, 455–457.

Lubeck, D. P., & Holman, H. R. (1982). *Health status, utilization, and satisfaction across the health care systems.* Paper presented at the Tenth Annual Meeting of the American Public Health Association, Montreal.

Mant, D., Vessey, M. P., Neil, A., McPherson, K., & Jones, L. (1987). Breast self-examination and breast cancer stage at diagnosis. *British Journal of Cancer, 55*, 207–211.

Matarazzo, J. (1980). Behavioral health and behavioral medicine: Frontiers for a new health psychology. *American Psychologist, 35*, 807–817.

McCusker, J., Cherubin, C., & Zimberg, S. (1971). Prevalence of alcoholism in general municipal hospital populations. *New York State Journal of Medicine, 71*, 751–754.

McDowell, F. H. (1986). Neurologic diseases: Stroke and other cerebrovascular conditions. In E. Calkins, P. J. Davis, & A. B. Ford (Eds.), *The practice of geriatrics* (pp. 214–224). Philadelphia: W. B. Saunders.

Mettler, M., & Fallcreek, S. (1981). *A healthy old age.* Seattle; University of Washington.

Moos, R. H., & Engel, B. T. (1962). Psychophysiologic reactions in hypertensive and arthritic patients. *Journal of Psychosomatic Research, 6*, 227.

Morrant J. (1975). Medicines and mental illness in old age. *Canadian Psychiatric Journal, 31*, 687–695.

Morrison, L., Short, C., Ludwig, A. O., & Schwab, R. (1947). The neuromuscular system in rheumatoid arthritis: Electro-myographic and histologic observations. *American Journal of Medical Science, 214*, 33–37.

Morrow, G. R., & Morrell, C. (1982). Behavioral treatment for anticipatory nausea and vomiting induced by cancer chemotherapy. *New England Journal of Medicine, 307*, 1476–1480.

National Center for Health Statistics. (1986). *Monthly vital statistics report.* (Vol. 35, No. 6, Supp. 2) (DHS Publication No. [PHS] 86-1120). Hyattsville, MD: Public Health Service.

National Center for Health Statistics. (1987). *Health statistics on older persons, United States, 1986.* (DHS Publication No. [PHS] 87-1409). Hyattsville, MD: Public Health Service.

Newacheck, P. W., Butler, L. H., Harper, A. K., Piontkowski, D. L., & Franks, P. (1987). Income and illness. *Medical Care, 18,* 1165–1176.

Oliver, M. F. (1982). Risk of correcting the risks of coronary disease and stroke with drugs. *New England Journal of Medicine, 306,* 297–298.

O'Malley, K., & O'Brien, E. (1980). Management of hypertension in the elderly. *New England Journal of Medicine, 302,* 1397–1401.

Osterfield, A. M. (1978). The elderly hypertensive patient: Epidemiologic review. *New York Journal of Medicine, 78,* 1125–1129.

Pan, W. H., Nanas, S., Dyer, A., Liu, K., McDonald, A., Schoenberger, J. A., Shekelle, R. B., Stamler, R., & Stamler, J. (1986). The role of weight in the positive association between age and blood pressure. *American Journal of Epidemiology, 124,* 612–623.

Payne, R., & Foley, K. (1984). Advances in the management of cancer pain. *Cancer Treatment Reports, 68,* 173–183.

Rabin, M. S., & Schnipper, L. E. (1988). Cancer in the elderly. In J. W. Rowe, & R. W. Besdine (Eds.), *Geriatric medicine* (2nd ed.) (pp. 324–333). Boston: Little, Brown.

Redd, W. H., & Andersen, G. V. (1981). Conditional aversion in cancer patients. *Behavior Therapy, 4,* 3–4.

Reding, M., Orto, L., Willensky, P., Fortuna, I., Day, N., Steiner, S. F., Gehr, L. R., & McDowell, F. (1985). The dexamethasone suppression test: An indication of depression in stroke. *Archives of Neurology, 42,* 209–212.

Riggs, B., Seeman, E., & Hodgson, S. (1982). Effect of the fluoride/calcium regimen in vertebral fracture occurrence in postmenopausal osteoporosis. *New England Journal of Medicine, 306,* 446–450.

Rimer, B., Jones, W., Wilson, C., Bennett, D., & Engstrom, P. (1983). Planning a cancer control program for older citizens. *The Gerontologist, 23,* 384–389.

Samiy, A. H. (1983). Clinical manifestations of disease in the elderly. *Medical Clinics of North America, 67,* 333–334.

Schochet, B. R., Lisansky, E. T., Schubart, A. F., Fiocco, V., Kurland, S., & Pope, M. (1969). A medical psychiatric study of patients with rheumatoid arthritis. *Psychosomatics, 10,* 271–279.

Schwartz, G., & Weiss, S. (1978). Yale Conference on Behavioral Medicine: A proposed definition and statement of goals. *Journal of Behavioral Medicine, 1,* 3–12.

Scileppi, K. P. (1983). Bone and joint disease in the elderly. *Medical Clinics of North America, 67,* 517–530.

Shamoian, C. A. (1983). Psychogeriatrics. *Medical Clinics of North America, 67,* 361–377.

Sidney, K. H., & Shephard, R. J. (1977). Perceptions of exertion in the elderly: Effects of aging, mode of exercise and physical training. *Perceptual and Motor Skills, 44,* 999–1010.

Sidney, K. H., & Shephard, R. J. (1978). Frequency and intensity of exercise training for elderly subjects. *Medicine and Science in Sports and Exercise, 10,* 125–131.

Simpson, F. O. (1980). Hypertensive disease. In G. S. Avery (Ed.), *Drug treatment: Principles and practice of clinical pharmacology and therapeutics* (pp. 638–682). New York: AIDS Press.

Smith, E. (1984). Special considerations in developing exercise programs for the older adult. In J. Matarrazzo, S. Weiss, J. Herd, N. Miller, & S. Weiss (Eds.), *Behavioral health* (pp. 525–548). New York: John Wiley & Sons.

Smith, E., Redden, W., & Smith, P. (1981). Physical activity and calcium modalities for bone mineral increase in aged women. *Medicine and Science in Sports and Exercise, 13,* 60–64.

Sparacino, J. (1979). The Type A (coronary prone) behavior pattern, aging, and mortality. *Journal of the American Geriatrics Society, 27,* 251–257.

Surveillance, Epidemiology, and End Results (SEER). (1981). *Incidence and mortality data, 1973–1977* (National Cancer Institute Monograph 57, NIH Publication No. 81–2330). Rockville, MD: National Institute of Health.

Turk, D. C., & Rennart, K. (1981). Pain and the terminally-ill cancer patient: A cognitive-social learning perspective. In H. J. Sobel (Ed.), *Behavior therapy in terminal care: A humanistic approach* (pp. 95–124). Cambridge, MA: Ballinger.

Turk, D. C., Meichenbaum, D., & Genest, J. (1983). *Pain and behavioral medicine: A cognitive-behavioral perspective.* New York: Guilford Press.

Urban Behavioral Research Associates. (1981). *The public and high blood pressure: Six-year follow-up survey of public knowledge and reported behavior* (NIH Publication No. 81–2118). Rockville, MD: National Institutes of Health.

U.S. Special Committee on Aging. (1984). *Aging America: Trends and projections.* Washington, D.C.: U.S. Department of Health and Human Service.

Varni, J. W. (1981a). Behavioral medicine in hemophilia arthritic pain management: Two case studies. *Archives of Physical Medicine and Rehabilitation, 62,* 183–187.

Varni, J. W. (1981b). Self-regulation techniques in the management of chronic arthritic pain in hemophilia. *Behavior Therapy, 12,* 185–194.

Waggoner, C., & Lelieuvre, R. (1981). A method to increase compliance to exercise regimens in rheumatoid arthritis patients. *Journal of Behavioral Medicine, 4,* 191–201.

Walshe, T. M. (1988). Stroke. In J. W. Rowe & R. W. Besdine (Eds.), *Geriatric medicine* (2nd ed., pp. 346–354). Boston: Little, Brown.

Wandless, I., & Davies, J. (1977). Can drug compliance in the elderly be improved? *British Journal of Medicine, 1,* 359–361.

Warnecke, R. B., Havlicek, P. L., & Manfredi, C. (1983). Awareness and use of screening by older-aged persons. In R. Yancik, P. P. Carbone, W. B. Patterson, K. Steel, & W. D. Terry (Eds.), *Perspectives on prevention and treatment of cancer in the elderly* (pp. 275–287). NY: Raven Press.

Weiner, H. M. (1977). *Psychobiology and human disease.* NY: Elsevier Press.

Weiss, W., & Weinfeld, F. D. (1981). The national survey of stroke. Introduction. *Stroke, 12,* (Supplement No. 1), 13–15.

Whelton, P. K. (1985). Hypertension in the elderly. In R. Andres, E. L. Biermon, & W. Hazzard (Eds.), *Principles of geriatric medicine* (pp. 536–551). New York: McGraw-Hill.

Wickramasekere, I. (1976). The management of rheumatoid arthritic pain: Preliminary observations. In I. Wickramasekera, S. T. Truong, M. Brush, & C. Orr (Eds.), *Biofeedback, behavior therapy, and hypnosis: Potentiating the verbal control of behavior for clinicians* (pp. 47–55). New York: Nelson-Hall.

Winawer, S. J., Baldwin, M., Herbert, E., & Sherlock, P. (1983). Screening experience with fecal occult blood testing as a function of age. In R. Yancik, P. P. Carbone, W. B. Patterson, K. Steel, & W. D. Terry (Eds.), *Perspectives in prevention and treatment of cancer in the elderly* (pp. 265–274). New York: Raven Press.

Wisocki, P. A., Handen, B., & Morse, C. (1986). The Worry Scale as a measure of anxiety among homebound and community active elderly. *The Behavior Therapist, 5,* 91–95.

Wolf, P. A. (1985). Risk factors for stroke (Editorial). *Stroke, 16,* 359–361.

Wyatt, H. J. (1969). Psychologic factors in arthritis. In S. Light (Ed.), *Arthritis and physical medicine* (pp. 176–190). Baltimore, MD: Waverly Press.

17

Pain Management

JEFFREY J. DOLCE AND PATRICIA C. DICKERSON

INTRODUCTION

Physical functioning and health often decrease in old age. Approximately 80% of those 65 years or older suffer from one or more chronic illnesses (Bonica, 1980; Lewis, 1984). Decline in functioning occurs in musculoskeletal, cardiovascular, pulmonary, gastrointestinal, urinary, and nervous systems. Many of these changes can be related to pain, discomfort, and functional limitations. Illnesses such as arthritic disorders, osteoporosis, neuralgias, and cancer are all common problems among the elderly that may be associated with pain (Butler & Gastel, 1980; Rowe & Besdine, 1982). Bone fractures due to falls, frequently encountered among the elderly, may also be accompanied by pain (Rubenstein & Robbins, 1984). Although pain is one of the most common complaints of the elderly (Crook, Rideout, & Browne, 1984; Haley, 1983), it is important to note that pain and discomfort are not an inevitable consequence of aging.

Some researchers even have suggested that the normal aging process may lead to a decreased sensitivity to pain. In a recent survey of 1,474 middle-aged and elderly multi-infarct patients, McDonald, Baillie, Williams, and Ballantyne (1983) found that 30% of those over age 70 did not experience pain as a major presenting symptom. On the other hand, Harkins and Chapman (1976, 1977) failed to find differences in pain thresholds between elderly and younger subjects in two studies utilizing tooth shock as a stimulus, although they did observe differences in ability to discriminate between different levels of noxious stimulation between the groups. The elderly were less able to distinguish between levels of shock than the younger subjects. The authors speculated that an age-related central nervous system processing deficit for discrimination of noxious stimuli might be the cause of this phenomenon.

Other researchers using radiant heat techniques to study responsivity to pain have found changes in energy dispersal properties in the skin of the elderly person when compared with younger skin (Procacci, Bozza, Buzzelli, & Della Corte, 1970). It appears that increased thermal dispersion of the skin may contribute to the age

JEFFREY J. DOLCE AND PATRICIA C. DICKERSON • Behavioral Medicine Unit, Division of General and Preventive Medicine, University of Alabama at Birmingham, Birmingham, Alabama 35294.

differences in thermal pain thresholds (Procacci *et al.*, 1970). Harkins, Price, and Martelli (1986) used a contact thermode probe with a rapid feedback loop to monitor temperature at the skin surface to minimize age-related thermal dispersion differences between younger, middle-aged, and elderly groups. Their results were consistent with those of previously reported studies in which elderly subjects were less likely to label suprathreshold stimulation as painful, but were more likely to rate higher shocks as painful when compared with younger subjects.

These data are thus conflicting and somewhat confusing. The confusion may be a function of differences in the criteria used for screening subjects, psycho-physiological procedures, and/or the various methods used to evaluate pain sensitivity (Harkins, Kwentus, & Prince, 1984; Harkins *et al.*, 1986). Due to the equivocal nature of these data, age-related changes in pain perception must be considered speculative at present. What is clear is that the elderly are at risk for developing pain-related problems with their accompanying disabilities and suffering. The effective management of such problems can greatly add to the quality of life for the older individual. In the following sections of this chapter we will review some of the common causes of pain in the elderly, models of pain, and assessment and treatment issues.

CAUSES OF CHRONIC PAIN IN THE ELDERLY

Headache

The muscle tension headache is the most common type of headache. In the elderly patient the most frequent causes of the muscle tension headache are cervical osteoarthritis—an arthritic condition of the cervical spine—psychological stress, and depression. These causes may interact so that pain associated with an arthritic condition may be worsened by psychological distress (Posner, 1976).

Migraine headaches are relatively rare among the elderly. Vascular headaches in this population are more frequently related to congestive heart failure, transient ischemia, increased intracranial pressure, and various metabolic disturbances. Giant cell arteritis—inflammation of the temporal artery—is the most prevalent type of vascular headache in the elderly patient and is particularly resistant to treatment with analgesic medication (Butler & Gastel, 1980; Freemoon, 1978; Posner, 1976).

Accurate diagnosis of headache in the elderly patient, particularly chronically occurring headaches with onset after age 50, is extremely important. Such headaches are not common, and they may be symptomatic of a more serious problem. A comprehensive medical examination, including a thorough history, is the most critical element in treating the elderly patient with headaches.

Degenerative Diseases

Chronic joint diseases are seen so often among the elderly that most people expect to experience some type of joint pain some time after middle age. Two of the most frequently occurring arthritic pain disorders are osteoarthritis and rheumatoid arthritis. Osteoarthritis is the more common and also the milder of the two (Brooks, Kean, Kassam, & Buchanan, 1984; Ehrlich, 1982; Wigley, 1984). Osteoarthritis is characterized by the degenerative loss of joint cartilage and hypertrophy of the bone. The exact mechanisms of degenerative joint disease are not known, but abnormal stress and injuries to subchondral bone contribute to the damage. More than 90% of patients over age 40 show radiologic evidence of osteoarthritis, particularly in the weight-bearing joints such as the knees and ankles (Wigley, 1984). It should be noted, however, that many persons with such abnormalities have no musculoskeletal or pain complaints.

Rheumatoid arthritis is a chronic systemic disease of unknown etiology that is manifested primarily by inflammatory arthritis of the peripheral joints, usually in a symmetrical distribution. The disease occurs in approximately 0.5 to 3.8% of the population, usually between the third and seventh decade (Gilliland & Mannick, 1973). Rheumatoid arthritis is the more disabling of the two types of arthritis and has a greater impact on the quality of life for the geriatric patient. Frequently, the two diseases will coexist and accompany other diseases of the musculoskeletal system. Unfortunately, the diagnosis of arthritis in any form conveys the prospect of diminished function or disability for the patient. It is important to emphasize that treatment, which balances activity with periods of rest, will increase the probability of continued mobility.

Osteoporosis, a disease characterized by a reduction in the mass of bone per unit volume to a level below that required for mechanical support, is another source of chronic pain in the elderly patient. Osteoporosis may develop as a result of a variety of diseases of diverse etiology that cause a decrease in bone mass accompanied by a rate of resorption exceeding that of bone formation. Eventually, the bone can no longer resist the mechanical forces to which it is subjected, resulting in fractures (Krane & Holick, 1983; Lane, Vigorita, & Falls, 1984). Individuals with osteoporosis frequently present with fractures of the thoracic and lumbar spine, the long bones, hip, humerus, and wrists. Women are at greater risk. Fifty percent of women over the age of 65 show evidence of sufficient bone loss to be at risk for fracture (Lukert, 1982). Although the exact etiology of osteoporosis is unknown, it appears to occur more frequently in postmenopausal Caucasian females, individuals with excessive acid intake, patients treated with heparin, and individuals with rheumatoid arthritis who have been treated with glucocorticosteriod therapy (Krane & Holick, 1983; Lukert, 1982).

Cancer

As the number of people over age 65 increases, so too does the risk of cancer. Although data have shown that 25% of the population will develop some type of neoplastic disease during their lifetime, approximately one-half of all cancers occur in the 11% of the population age 65 and older (Rimer, Jones, Wilson, Bennett, & Engstrom, 1983). Malignant disease is the most common cause of intractable pain seen in patients with terminal illness (Swerdlow, 1973; Turk & Rennert, 1981). Pain causes a significant problem in about one-third of cancer patients in treatment and in 60% to 80% of patients with terminal illness (Payne & Foley, 1984). One of the greatest problems for patients following the shock of a diagnosis of cancer is the fear of the excruciating pain and suffering associated with the disease (McGivney & Crooks, 1984). The progression of the disease accounts for 78% of pain complaints in cancer cases, while pain resulting from treatment accounts for 20% of the cases. Interestingly, one study found that patients who attributed pain to treatment reported less interference with daily activities and enjoyment than patients who attributed the pain to cancer (Daut & Cleeland, 1982).

Postherpetic Neuralgia

Postherpetic neuralgia, or the pain that sometimes persists following acute herpes zoster, is another common disorder among the elderly. The incidence of herpes zoster, as well as the prevalence of pain 1 year following the acute phase, increases with age (Demoragas & Kierland, 1957). In fact, the prevalence of post-herpetic pain increases from 4.2% among those younger than 20 years old to over 47.5% among those age 70 or older (Demoragas & Kierland, 1957). Postherpetic pain is persistent pain that has continued 2 months beyond the onset of rash and is characterized by a combination of burning or other dysesthesia, aching, and itching. Paroxysms of severe stabbing pain may also be present. Disturbances of physical, social, and psychological functioning frequently accompany the pain syndrome (Portenoy, 1986). Treatment is multimodal, including the use of phar-macological, psychological, and physical therapies (Portenoy, 1986).

MODELS OF PAIN

Pain has traditionally been conceptualized as the sensation that arises from some form of tissue damage. Clinical pain, however, has proven to be a very complex phenomenon that is not easily explained from a purely neurophysiological perspective. In recent years pain has been recognized as a complex combination of sensory, affective, cognitive, and behavioral components (Melzack & Wall, 1983; Sturgis, Dolce, & Dickerson, 1987; Weisenburg, 1977) that can be affected by beliefs, expectancies, anxiety, and depression (Dolce, 1987; Weisenburg, 1977). The sensation of pain is also regarded as an emotional-motivational event that can lead to escape and avoidance behavior (Fordyce, 1976; Weisenburg, 1977). These factors require that pain be understood as a psychological experience affected by a variety of cognitive and environmental variables, as well as the physical nociceptive re-sponse of the body to tissue damage.

In successfully managing pain problems, it is important to make conceptual distinctions between acute and chronic pain, recurrent acute pain and benign and malignant chronic pain. These distinctions, as reviewed by others (Black, 1975; Crue, 1983a, 1983b; Fordyce, 1976; Sternbach, 1974; Sturgis *et al.*, 1987), have implications for their relationship to organic disease, their likely relationship to psychological variables, and their pharmacological and psychological treatment.

Acute pain is conventionally defined as pain of recent onset (i.e., less than 6 months) that is associated with the stimulation of specialized nerve fibers (nociception). Pain of this nature generally indicates the need for medical assistance and/or a recuperation period to allow healing to occur. Acute pain is typically managed successfully by the traditional medical system through interventions aimed at treating the underlying disease and/or by blocking nociception. A disease model in which pain is seen as the result of tissue damage is typically appropriate for these acute pain problems. Behavioral and psychological variables, however, do affect the perception of acute pain and therefore should not be completely dismissed (Dolce, 1987; Turk, Meichenbaum, & Genest, 1983).

Chronic pain, on the other hand (at least in the case of *benign chronic* pain), is pain that has lasted 6 months or longer and persists despite adequate time for recovery, or in the absence of any physical findings sufficient to explain the severity of the pain problem. Pain in this sense is no longer an appropriate indicator of nociception. It ceases to function as a warning signal or serve as a guide in diagnosing underlying pathology that may be managed through the disruption of nociceptive input. Successful treatment of benign chronic pain is accomplished best by shifting to a treatment model that minimizes the role of nociception and stresses the management of pain, suffering, and disability. The distinction between acute and benign chronic pain and its implication for treatment becomes clearer when considering pain from a learning theory perspective.

In the learning theory approach, it is important to separate pain from the resulting pain behaviors (Fordyce, 1976). Pain behaviors are conceptualized as the behaviors emitted by the individual that communicate the occurrence of nociception (i.e., facial expression, gait, body posture, medication usage, etc.). When tissue damage occurs there is nociceptive input through A-delta and C-fibers of the peripheral nervous system that can produce the sensation of pain (Melzack & Wall, 1983). Nociception serves as the antecedent stimulus to the resulting pain behaviors that signal to observers the occurrence of the painful sensation. Fordyce (1976) has named pain behaviors resulting from this type of stimulus-response sequence "respondent pain behaviors." Respondent pain behaviors are thought of as behaviors that are controlled by specific and discrete antecedent nociceptive stimuli. Thus, acute clinical pain problems can be conceptualized in terms of respondent pain behaviors, i.e., the need to search for and treat the underlying physical pathology that is antecedent to the respondent pain behavior.

Benign chronic pain problems are more appropriately conceptualized in terms of "operant pain behaviors" (Fordyce, 1970, 1976). Operant behaviors differ from respondent behaviors in that they are influenced by the specific events that follow their occurrence. That is, the likelihood of an operant behavior recurring can be either increased or decreased by reward or punishment, respectively. The implication of this principle is that if respondent pain behaviors (i.e., those behaviors arising from acute pain) persist long enough in the presence of circumstances favorable to operant conditioning, then learning can occur, and pain behaviors may come under the control of environmental stimuli. The knowledge that pain behaviors can be facilitated and/or maintained by environmental factors helps clarify the situation in which complaints of pain persist despite adequate healing of the original injury. Operant pain behaviors come under the control of contingent environmental reinforcement. Treatment for operant pain behaviors, therefore, focuses on the pain behaviors themselves and emphasizes the role of environmental factors in producing and maintaining both suffering and disability (Fordyce, 1976). The goal is not curative in nature, but rather rehabilitative with an ultimate goal of reducing the patient's disability through a reduction in pain behaviors and an increase in well behaviors (Follick, Ahern, & Aberger, 1987). It is because of this learning phenomenon that chronic pain problems are increasingly conceptualized in terms of operant pain behaviors or a combination of operant and respondent pain behaviors (Fordyce, 1976; Sternbach, 1974).

Two other classes of pain problems that share aspects of operant and respondent pain behaviors are chronic malignant pain and recurrent acute pain (Crue, 1983a, 1983b). *Malignant chronic* pain is pain that is associated with an active metastatic disease process, while *recurrent acute* pain is associated with disease processes that have repeated flare-ups of acute pain related to peripheral tissue pathology (i.e., rheumatoid arthritis, postherpetic neuralgia, etc.). In each of these cases, pain is associated with tissue damage, and management must include a model of pain that adequately considers the nociceptive process. Both of these types of disorders can persist for extended periods of time and are subject to environmental contingencies. For example, Redd (1982) has noted that operant conditioning affects the level of distress experienced by cancer patients. Thus, for successful management of malignant chronic and recurrent acute pain problems it is important to consider all the factors impacting on the pain and suffering of the patient.

Loeser (1980) has presented an interactive model of pain in which he distinguishes between nociception, pain, suffering, and pain behavior. Clinical pain disorders consist of a complex combination of these four components. *Nociception* refers to the afferent impulses produced by stimulation of certain specialized nerve fibers. *Pain* is the individual's perception of the presence of, nature of, and intensity of, a noxious stimulus, and is thus defined as a subjective experience. *Suffering* is the negative affective response of anxiety, depression, or distress generated by pain and other unpleasant situations. In this model, suffering may interact with and exacerbate pain. Pain may, therefore, be more upsetting and less tolerable when patients are depressed or unhappy. *Pain behavior* is again conceptualized as the occurrence of behavior that is understood by others to communicate the presence of nociception, including complaints of pain, grimacing, limping, inactivity, taking pain medications, and disabilities.

It should be noted that the correspondence between these aspects of pain is highly variable (Melzack & Wall, 1983). Some patients report high levels of pain in the absence of observable pathology, while others with severe injuries or medical problems report little or no pain (Payne & Foley, 1984). In some cases, pain behaviors (complaints, disability) may be minimal in patients with severe disorders (e.g., cancer), but flourish in patients who appear to have recovered medically from mild injuries. Thus, the clinical team must seek to assess and manage all four of these components.

In summary, the conceptualization of pain adopted by the clinician will influence the treatment process. As previously noted, the clinician working with the elderly will encounter a number of different types of pain and must be prepared to use a model of pain that recognizes all the biopsychosocial factors that can contribute to it. It is not uncommon for elderly patients to have multiple chronic diseases, each of which can be related to pain complaints. For example, an individual may simultaneously experience acute pain secondary to a fall, recurrent acute pain secondary to arthritis, and a benign chronic pain problem. Treatment of the pain problems, therefore, should start with a complete assessment of all relevant factors including medical, environmental, and psychological variables.

ASSESSMENT AND TREATMENT

The assessment and management of pain problems in the elderly is a challenging task that can be facilitated by a multidisciplinary approach. Acute pain problems, such as a fracture related to a fall, can often be handled effectively by physicians. However, in cases of recurrent acute and chronic pain, a team consisting of knowledgeable physicians, physical therapists, psychologists, nurses, occupational or rehabilitation counselors, and social workers is often needed to manage patients successfully. It is rare for any one professional to have access to all the patient's prior evaluations, or to have the necessary knowledge to integrate the biomedical and psychosocial data on the patient. The multidisciplinary team approach allows assessment and treatment to proceed and impact on several levels.

Medical Management

Older individuals, as previously noted, are likely to present with multiple chronic illnesses (Rowe & Besdine, 1982). Unfortunately, these patients are also at risk to receive inadequate workups and little time and attention from physicians.

The primary role of medical evaluation in the assessment of pain is the determination of the extent to which organic pathology contributes to the pain problem (i.e., malignant, acute, or recurrent acute) which may be successfully treated through traditional medical intervention. Special care should be taken when evaluating cases of recurrent acute or benign and malignant chronic pain because environmental and psychological factors may confound the medical workup. The presence of behavioral and psychological factors does not rule out organic pathology. Medical assessment should include a thorough evaluation of the patient's general medical status to uncover any problems that may complicate or contradict use of a comprehensive treatment approach.

Medical management should proceed based on the degree of physical pathology uncovered during the medical workup and be designed to eliminate or modify ongoing nociception. For cases of acute, recurrent acute, and malignant chronic pain, general medical and surgical procedures are highly appropriate and necessary. Trials with antibiotics or analgesics may be useful. Other medical procedures such as nerve blocks, neuroprobe treatments, transcutaneous electrical nerve stimulation, and surgery may also be warranted.

Medications

Pharmacotherapy should be used cautiously with the elderly due to age-related changes in hepatic metabolism and renal clearance (Berlinger & Spector, 1984; Pfeiffer, 1982). Aspirin is the drug most commonly used for pain. It is frequently used in the treatment of arthritis, both for pain relief and its anti-inflammatory properties. However, aspirin is responsible for a larger number of side effects (Pfeiffer, 1982). Elderly patients frequently display exaggerated responses to narcotics (Kaiko, Wallenstein, Rogers, Brabinski, & Houda, 1982), while anti-inflammatory drugs, such as steroids, can produce gastric irritation (Harkins *et al.*, 1984).

A complete assessment of types and doses of medications taken by the elderly patient is an essential part of medical evaluation and treatment. A more complete discussion of the problems elderly have in using medications appropriately and in metabolizing medications may be found in Chapter 2 of this text.

Medication Management of Benign Chronic Pain

Addiction among patients with chronic disorders is a frequent problem. The detrimental impact of inappropriate use of medication on the chronic pain patient has been frequently observed (Black, 1975; Evans, 1981; Khatami, Woody, & O'Brien, 1979; Maruta, Swanson, & Finlayson, 1978; Sternbach, 1974; Taylor, Zlutnick, Corley, & Flora, 1980; Turner, Calsyn, Fordyce, & Ready, 1982). More specifically, the excessive use of narcotic analgesics and sedatives is associated with confusion of higher-order thought processes, impaired vocational functioning, decreased physical and social activities, and depression (Sternbach, 1974; Taylor *et al.*, 1980; Ziesat *et al.*, 1979). Chronic pain patients dependent on medications have a lower treatment success rate when compared with nondrug-abusing patients (Maruta *et al.*, 1978). In general, these complications have translated into a poorer prognosis for those pain patients who abuse medications.

The potential for medication abuse among chronic pain patients is readily apparent when one considers the positive and negative reinforcing properties of narcotic analgesics (Iversen & Iversen, 1981; Milby, 1981). Narcotic analgesics not only provide negative reinforcement by relieving pain and reducing anxiety, but also provide positive reinforcement by producing a general sensation of well-being or euphoria. In addition to these general pharmacological effects, the specific type of drug action of a medication and the schedule of administration can contribute significantly to the problem of medication abuse (Black, 1975; Fordyce, 1976; Sternbach, 1974). Potent short-acting analgesics, in contrast to slower- and longer-acting analgesics, tend to produce more euphoria and a greater feeling of detachment from the responsibilities of the world. This effect can increase the potential for drug dependence by greatly enhancing the positive reinforcing properties of using medications (Black, 1975). When medication is administered on a p.r.n. basis (when needed), rather than on a time-contingent schedule, pain behaviors become the antecedent for the reinforcing properties of medication use, thereby enhancing and maintaining pain-related problems (Berntzen & Gotestam, 1987; Fordyce, 1976; Sternbach, 1974). Such an operant conditioning paradigm develops very high rates of requests for medication (Fordyce, 1976) and is related to higher subjective pain ratings and poorer moods (Berntzen & Gotestam, 1987).

Therefore, a frequent treatment objective for patients with benign chronic pain is the gradual reduction and eventual elimination of narcotic analgesics in a manner that breaks up the conditioned pattern of medication use. The pain cocktail has become the standard technique to reduce and control these medications (Fordyce, 1976). Initially, the patient is instructed to take medications on a p.r.n., or a request-contingent basis, as they normally would for a 3- to 4-day baseline period. The types and amounts of medication are carefully recorded during the baseline phase. At the end of the baseline phase, medication administration is shifted over to the staff, and the active ingredients are placed in a cocktail or masking vehicle, which is administered orally. The cocktail is given on a time-contingent basis (rather than on a pain-contingent basis), with enough medication to equal the level taken during baseline. The active ingredients are then faded slowly over the course of treatment. The patient is informed prior to the start of this phase that medications will be gradually withdrawn, but that he or she will not be told when actual reductions are made.

During fading the patient may continue to take other medications not related to his or her pain condition (i.e., antihypertensive medications, hormones, etc.), but these medications should be monitored. It is especially important when altering medications in the elderly to monitor them closely for side effects and to fade medications very gradually (Haley & Dolce, 1986).

Medication Management of Malignant Chronic or Recurrent Acute Pain

Patients with pain due to malignant disease or a recurrent acute pain disorder have different medication requirements. With such patients, medication addiction is not the primary clinical concern. Relief of pain is the essential goal, and the use of narcotic analgesics is appropriate. The special medication strategies used in treating cancer and other terminal illnesses are described in several recent reviews (McGivney & Crooks, 1984; Payne & Foley, 1984). Putting medications on a time-contingent, rather than a p.r.n. or pain-contingent, schedule is still recommended, however, for managing pain related to both metastatic disease and recurrent acute problems (Carron, 1984; Payne & Foley, 1984). Time-contingent scheduling can provide more effective coverage of the pain problem (Carron, 1984) and reduce the probability of operantly conditioned pain problems (Berntzen & Gotestam, 1987; Fordyce, 1976).

Behavioral Management

Managing pain behaviors is an important aspect of effective treatment of clinical pain. This is particularly true for pain problems that have persisted for a significant period of time (i.e., benign and malignant chronic pain and recurrent acute pain). As time goes on, existing pain problems are increasingly likely to be affected by environmental factors. Fordyce (1976) notes that three sets of conditions can influence the frequency and maintenance of pain behaviors: (1) positive reinforcement, such as attention, sympathy and concern, compensation payments, or medications; (2) negative reinforcement, or the removal of noxious stimulation, such as anxiety-invoking situations, or the avoidance of work or other unpleasant responsibilities; and (3) extinction or punishment of "well" behavior.

Each of these factors is pertinent to the elderly patient. Older people frequently have decreased activity levels, possibly compounded by retirement and the deaths of a spouse and friends. A person may experience little stimulation to distract attention from the pain and may thereby become preoccupied with it. The elderly patient frequently has few reinforcers for healthy behavior. The increased attention from family members that often accompanies a pain problem can facilitate the acquisition of operant pain behaviors.

The avoidance of aversive events can also reinforce pain behavior. Pain patients frequently report experiencing increased pain when they are active and are, therefore, likely to reduce their activity levels. Activity avoidance is reinforced to the extent to which rest from these activities diminishes pain. Reduced activity levels may be maintained due to fear and anxiety over the consequences of being active (i.e., increased pain). The avoidance of activities reduces fear and strengthens the avoidance of activity.

It is also likely that overprotective family members may selectively punish attempts at healthy activities that they feel are too much or dangerous for their elderly relative. The identification of extinguished "well behaviors" for reactivation is an important aspect of assessment.

Cognitive impairment may also foster the acquisition of pain behaviors (Fordyce, 1978; Haley & Dolce, 1986). Cognitive impairment has been noted in chronic pain patients of all ages (McNairy, Maruta, Ivnik, Swanson, & Ilstrup, 1984). Elderly patients are particularly likely to report forgetfulness, difficulty with concentration, and/or occasional periods of confusion. Impairment may be the result of a number of reversible or irreversible causes, including medications, undetected illness, depression, sleep difficulties, stroke, and/or a dementing illness. Such impairment in conjunction with a pain problem may produce a situation where limitations due to cognitive deficits are attributed to the pain problem. Pain behaviors then serve as a convenient way of avoiding the acknowledgment of cognitive deficits and indirectly reinforce pain complaints.

A complete functional analysis of the patient's "well" and "pain" behaviors is therefore necessary. Family interactions, marital and sexual relationships, activity levels, activities of daily living, vocational activities, medication patterns, and neurological functioning all need careful exploration to determine their impact on the patient's overall level of functioning. The patient and family members should be interviewed regarding the pain problem and how the patient is behaving. Direct observation of the patient is necessary for targeting behavioral limitations. Patient self-monitoring of daily activities, pain levels, and medication utilization are also helpful. Operant pain problems can be delineated only through a careful and detailed assessment of what the patient is doing, the consequences of those actions, and the exclusion of respondent pain behaviors. Thus, information about the pain problem and the patient's level of functioning should come from multiple sources, including medical records and objective test results.

Once identified, operant pain behaviors should be extinguished, while well behaviors must be reinstated. The objective is to alter the lifestyle patterns of patients away from those of the chronically disabled. This may entail opening new leisure outlets, changes in vocation where applicable, working through retirement issues, and altering patterns of family interaction. In general, it is necessary to establish meaningful activities for each patient. In order for healthy behavior to develop and be maintained it is necessary that the targeted activities be rewarding. Finally, in addition to the treatment staff's efforts at shaping well behavior and extinguishing pain behaviors, the family should be educated to the basic conditioning factors that may occur among themselves. Specifically, they should be taught about the ways family patterns of reinforcement occur for sick behavior and how to reward well behavior.

Physical Conditioning

As previously stated, many pain patients experience increased pain with activity and reductions in pain with inactivity. The reduction of pain, which is associated with rest, can then reinforce activity avoidance and contribute to patients' disabilities. The operant conditioning aspect of inactivity is only one aspect of this problem. Extended inactivity can lead to the deconditioning of muscles needed for many normal activities, which in turn can make recovery more difficult. For example, patients with low-back pain frequently avoid even light lifting or stretching. Their back muscles may then atrophy and stiffen, leading to even greater pain when attempting to become active again. Any illness that has led to inactivity, including bed rest, following an acute injury can substantially contribute to poor physical conditioning, which may, in turn, exacerbate difficulties in returning to normal activity levels.

Exercise programs have, therefore, become a crucial aspect of many pain management programs (Doliber, 1984; Roesch & Ulrich, 1980). It appears that such programs are successful because they increase physical conditioning and provide behavior that is generally incompatible with pain behavior (Doleys, Crocker, & Patton, 1982; Fordyce, 1976). In addition, since many patients are concerned about the consequences of returning to normal activity, exercise can be useful in desensitizing the patient to the fears of being active (Dolce, Crocker, Moletteire, & Doleys, 1986b).

The use of exercise in managing the elderly patient may have additional benefits. Regular exercise improves physiological functioning in the elderly patient, and there is growing evidence that psychological and behavioral functioning may improve as well (Dishman, 1985). Regular exercise has been associated with the reduction of symptoms related to depression (Blumenthal, Williams, & Needels,

1982; Brown, Ramirez, & Taub, 1978), and anxiety (Bahrke & Morgan, 1978). When compared with a group of sedentary elderly, active elderly patients show more rapid reaction and movement times (Spirduso, 1983). Finally, both subjective (Folkins, Lynch, & Gardner, 1972) and objective (Horne, 1981) reports of sleep patterns are enhanced by exercise. These positive effects of exercise programs are, therefore, useful for dealing with many symptoms frequently encountered among chronic pain patients.

Unfortunately, exercise compliance is notoriously low in all populations (Dishman, 1982), and methods to promote and maintain increased exercise are necessary. One type of program that has been effective for increasing exercise tolerance for conditioning among chronic pain patients is the establishment of an exercise quota (Doleys et al., 1982; Fordyce, Fowler, Lehman, DeLateur, Sand, & Trieschmann, 1973). In using a quota system, goal setting is used to increase and maintain performance. Upon entry into a pain treatment program, a baseline phase of assessment is taken. During this phase, the patient is instructed to exercise, as prescribed by a physical therapist and/or physician, until weakness, fatigue, or pain causes him or her to stop. Once a stable baseline level of exercise has been established, the exercises are placed on quotas.

Quotas are first set well within the patient's achievement range at a percentage of the average of his or her baseline measures. Then they are increased gradually over the course of treatment. Initial exercise quotas are set below baseline to provide initial success for the patient and facilitate continued attempts at exercise. As an integral part of the quota system, reinforcement is provided in the form of verbal praise and rest from activities for successfully achieving set quotas. If a patient fails to meet a quota, praise is withheld. Failure to meet quotas over a period of several successive days results in a reduction of the quota level to one that has been previously attained. After the patient has successfully met this new quota several times, he or she is required to meet another quota that is slightly higher than the previous one. Exercises are tailored to the individual patient's goals and physical limitations. Because quotas are increased gradually, a therapeutically safe increase in activity level is achieved, which inhibits patients' overexertion on days when they feel good and facilitates performance on problematic days.

Quota systems have been demonstrated to increase and maintain a patient's level of performance. For example, Fordyce and his associates (1973) used a simple AB experimental design with 36 chronic pain patients to demonstrate the effective use of positive reinforcement in increasing exercise among chronic pain patients. They set quotas for several activities for each of the patients and delivered attention contingently upon the attainment of the quota for each exercise. They did not respond socially when patients failed to meet quotas. Physical activity increased significantly in these patients.

Doleys et al. (1982) used a multiple-baseline design with 26 chronic pain patients to evaluate more precisely the effects of the quota system. Verbal praise given by a physical therapist to subjects achieving their exercise quotas resulted in subjects gradually increasing and sustaining their exercise levels in a physical therapy environment. Interestingly, they found that changes were specific only to the activities placed on quotas, with no generalization to "no-quota" activities. This finding suggests that it may be necessary to apply quotas to all areas of decreased functioning.

The overall success of quota systems for increasing exercise tolerance and reducing physical limitations has been attributed to the use of reinforcement for quota achievement (Cairns & Pasino, 1977; Doleys *et al.*, 1982; Fordyce, 1976). Exercise quotas, however, also provide the patient with repeated successes at a task that they frequently fear or dread. Quota systems, therefore, may function as a desensitization process in which exposure to the feared activities deconditions the patient's concern over exercise (Dolce, Crocker, & Doleys, 1986; Fordyce, Shelton, & Dundore, 1982).

It is important to remember when working with a geriatric pain population that they differ from other pain patients. Special considerations are often required in the development of their treatment programs. Geriatric patients always require a careful medical and physical evaluation prior to establishing an exercise program. Due to an increased prevalence of chronic disabilities, identification of underlying problems that contraindicate certain types of exercise are an important component in designing an appropriate exercise program that will not aggravate existing conditions. Areas to evaluate include drug and dietary history, sensory deficits, musculoskeletal abnormalities, and cardiovascular disease (Clee, Smith, McNeil, & Wright, 1979; Fitzgerald, 1985). Peripheral neuropathy or other sensory impairment, gait disturbance, impaired equilibrium, or orthostatic hypotension indicated an increased potential for falls that can be reduced by modification of either the environment or the training program. Degenerative joint disease, also common to this group, requires assessment of joint stability with an appropriate adjustment in activity if warranted (Fitzgerald, 1985).

It is also important to review medications for possible interactions with the exercise program. Diuretics may predispose an elderly person to hypokalemia, arrhythmias, and rhabdomyolysis as well as volume depletion resulting in falls or syncope. Dosage adjustments may be required for patients on insulin or oral medication for hypoglycemia. Beta-blocking medications can also alter exercise parameters and reduce exercise tolerance in some patients. Major tranquilizers can cause orthostatic dizziness and impair thermoregulation (Rowe & Besdine, 1982).

Psychological Treatment

The general goals of psychological approaches to pain management are to reduce the experience of pain and improve the patient's overall level of functioning. Psychological treatments commonly seek to increase the patient's ability to control and manage his or her pain through teaching self-management skills. Treatment also targets the management of other related symptoms, such as anxiety and depression, that can contribute to the patient's suffering and disability. Thus, psychological approaches typically strive to alter the effective, psychophysiological, and cognitive factors that negatively impact on patients and their ability to live active and productive lives.

Affective reactions to pain contribute to the experience of pain (Keefe, 1982; Melzack & Wall, 1983; Sternbach, 1974). Depression occurs frequently among patients who have persistent pain problems (Romano & Turner, 1985), and it is especially prevalent among elderly patients with chronic illness (Gurland & Cross, 1982). When assessing for the presence or degree of depression it is important to recall that chronic pain patients often emphasize the somatic aspects of depression, such as changes in sleep and appetite, while they minimize changes in mood (Katon & Kleinman, 1982). Anxiety appears to increase the perception of pain and is common with chronic (Keefe, 1982; Sternbach, 1974) and acute pain (Martinez-Urrutia, 1975; Spielberger, Auerbach, Wadsworth, Dunn, & Taulbee, 1973). Increased muscle tension and protective posturing (Dolce & Raczynski, 1985; Kraus, 1965) may also contribute to the patient's disability. Increased muscular tension either can add to the pain of an existing disorder, such as arthritis (Acterberg-Lawlis, 1982), or may be a primary source of nociception as in myofasical pain disorders. Thus, there are a variety of affective and psychophysiological factors that should be considered in managing pain disorders.

Psychological treatments can be useful in reducing the impact of these emotional and psychophysiological reactions. Depression may be managed with a variety of approaches including increasing pleasurable activities, altering depressogenic thoughts, and providing support and the opportunity to express feelings and concerns (Beck, Rush, Shaw, & Emery, 1979). Tricyclic antidepressants may also be useful not only because they affect depressive symptomatology, but because of their analgesic effects (Butler, 1984; Pfeiffer, 1982). Sleep problems, a frequent occurrence among chronic pain patients (Wittig, Zorick, Blumer, Heilbronn, & Roth, 1982), can also improve with antidepressant treatment.

Some affective reactions are due to a patient's difficulty in adjusting to a persistent and often progressively disabling illness. Adjunctive individual, martial, and/or family therapy can be beneficial for developing more effective ways of coping with changing family, marital, and sexual roles. It is often necessary to provide information about the expected course of disease and counseling about facing disability or death. In general, intervention that enhances the patient's general ability to cope with his or her current life circumstances will help decrease distress and suffering.

Relaxation training is beneficial for managing anxiety, excessive muscular tension, and sleep problems (Haley & Dolce, 1986; Sanders, 1983). It can also help the patient control the intensity of pain (Turk et al., 1983) and strengthen the patient's belief that he or she can exert some control during periods of pain and stress (Turk & Rennert, 1981). Biofeedback training may also be helpful in reducing muscular tension and posturing (Dolce & Raczynski, 1985; Wolf, Nacht, & Kelley, 1982). While biofeedback procedures appear best suited for muscular retraining, they are not more effective than relaxation training for reducing anxiety and are more expensive to employ (Turner & Chapman, 1982). Relaxation training, therefore, appears to be the preferred treatment for managing anxiety and excessive muscular tension.

Another important area of psychological functioning includes patients' beliefs and expectancies about their illnesses and their cognitive styles for coping with pain. These cognitive variables can play an important role in how pain is experienced and managed. Patients may have limited or ineffective cognitive coping styles for managing pain and may require more effective coping techniques. Cognitive techniques, including distraction, pleasant imagery, and hypnosis, have all been found effective for enhancing patients' abilities to cope with and tolerate pain (Averill, 1973; Hilgard & Hilgard, 1975; McCaul & Malott, 1984; Rybstein-Blinchik, 1979; Thompson, 1981; Turk et al., 1983; Varni, 1981). Turk et al. (1983), however, have recently suggested that the difference between high- and low-tolerant individuals may not be related to a deficiency in the number or type of coping skills employed but rather to motivational factors and the individual's expectancies of whether he or she can effectively use the skills he or she possesses. Spanos, Radtke-Bodorik, Ferguson, and Jones (1979) have reported that individuals who display catastrophizing cognitive styles report experiencing more pain than noncatastrophizing individuals, regardless of the number or type of coping strategies employed.

These data are consistent with a growing body of research indicating that self-efficacy expectancies for coping and beliefs about disability are important cognitive variables in the management of both acute and chronic pain (Dolce, 1987). Specifically, individuals with high expectancies for coping appear more likely to apply the pain-coping skills in their repertoires and persist longer in their efforts to manage a painful stimulus. The idea that the aversiveness of an event can be decreased by having perceived control over that event is not a new one (Averill, 1973; Thompson, 1981). In support of this perspective, investigators have demonstrated that higher self-efficacy expectancies for coping are related to greater tolerance to experimental pain (Dolce, Doleys, Raczynski, Lossie, Poole, & Smith, 1986c; Klepac, Dowling, & Hauge, 1982; Neufeld & Thomas, 1977), enhanced coping with acute and recurrent acute pain (Gauthier, Cote, & Drolet, 1985; Holroyd, Penzien, Hursey, Tobin, Rogers, Holm, Marcille, Hall, & Chila, 1984; Manning & Wright, 1983), and better treatment outcome in cases of chronic benign pain (Dolce, Crocker, & Doleys, 1986a; Dolce et al., 1986b; Kores, Murphy, Rosenthal, Elias, & Rosenthal, 1985). It appears that low-efficacy beliefs serve as a cognitive barrier to patient attempts to function normally and as cues for the occurrence of overt pain behaviors.

Beliefs about being disabled can be very difficult to reverse. Roberts (1981) has noted that at discharge, patients "may be functioning at fully normal levels for age and sex, having entered treatment totally or almost totally incapacitated, and still report that they have gained no benefits from treatment even though they have collected and graphed the data which contradict this feeling" (p. 186). Despite the difficulties noted by Roberts, actual performance accomplishments are still regarded as the most effective way of raising self-efficacy expectancies (Bandura, 1982). Dolce et al. (1986b) have demonstrated that exercise quota systems can effectively raise self-efficacy expectancies for exercise among chronic pain patients. When patients have repeated successes at exercising, they receive information clearly inconsistent with beliefs about the degree of their disabilities.

The data on self-efficacy expectancies and pain indicate that patients who believe they have the ability to cope successfully with pain are significantly better at managing pain and function at higher levels. These data also suggest that psychological treatment aimed at teaching more effective coping skills should be a two-phase process. Coping skills are taught first if patients are deficient in them. Once adequate skills are acquired, success experiences are provided to raise and strengthen patients' perceptions that these skills are effective.

SUMMARY

The assessment and management of pain problems in the elderly is a complex task that is often complicated by the nature of the pain problem, iatrogenic medication problems, and psychological and environmental factors. Essential to treatment is a clear understanding of the interrelationships among the different classifications of pain and medical, psychological, and behavioral variables. Successful management is based on a comprehensive evaluation of all relevant variables. Treatment is designed to stop nociception, if present, through appropriate medical methods; eliminate operant pain behaviors; increase well behaviors; improve physical conditioning and functioning; and manage detrimental affective and psychological variables.

REFERENCES

Achterberg-Lawlis, J. (1982). The psychological dimensions of arthritis. *Journal of Consulting and Clinical Psychology, 50*, 984–992.

Averill, J. R. (1973). Personal control over aversive stimuli and its relationship to stress. *Psychological Bulletin, 80*, 286–303.

Bahrke, M. S., & Morgan, W. P. (1978). Anxiety reduction following exercise and meditation. *Cognitive Therapy and Research, 2*, 323–337.

Bandura, A. (1982). Self-efficacy mechanism in human agency. *American Psychologist, 37*, 122–147.

Beck, A. T., Rush, A. J., Shaw, B. F., & Emery, G. (1979). *Cognitive therapy of depression.* New York: Guilford Press.

Berlinger, W. G., & Spector, R. (1984). Adverse drug reactions in the elderly. *Geriatrics, 39*, 45–58.

Berntzen, D., & Gotestam, G. (1987). Effects of on-demand versus fixed-interval schedules in the treatment of chronic pain with analgesic compounds. *Journal of Consulting and Clinical Psychology, 55*, 213–217.

Black, R. G. (1975). The chronic pain syndrome. *Surgical Clinics of North America, 55*, 999–1011.

Blumenthal, J. A., Williams, R. S., & Needels, T. L. (1982). Psychological changes accompany aerobic exercise in healthy middle-aged adults. *Psychosomatic Medicine, 44*, 529–536.

Bonica, J. J. (1980). Pain research and therapy: Past and current status, and future needs. In L. Nge & J. J. Bonica (Eds.), *Pain, discomfort, and humanitarian care* (pp. 1–46). New York: Elsevier.

Brooks, P. M., Kean, W. F., Kassam, Y., & Buchanan, W. W. (1984). Problems of antiarthritic therapy in the elderly. *Journal of the American Geriatric Society, 32*, 229–234.

Brown, R., Ramirez, D. E., & Taub, J. M. (1978). The prescription for exercise for depression. *Sportsmedicine, 6*, 34–45.

Butler, R. N., & Gastel, B. (1980). Care of the aged. In L. Nge & J. J. Bonica (Eds.), *Pain, discomfort, and humanitarian care* (pp. 297–311). New York: Elsevier.

Butler, S. (1984). Present status of tricyclic antidepressants in chronic pain therapy. In C. Benedetti, C. R. Chapman, & G. Moricca (Eds.), *Advances in pain research and therapy* (pp. 173–197). New York: Raven Press.

Cairns, D., & Pasino, J. A. (1977). Comparison of verbal reinforcement and feedback in the operant treatment of disability due to chronic low back pain. *Behavior Therapy, 8,* 621–630.

Carron, H. (1984). Rational management of cancer pain. *Urban Health, 5,* 36–38.

Clee, M. D., Smith, N., McNeil, G. P., & Wright, D. S. (1979). Dysrhythmias in apparently healthy elderly subjects. *Age and Aging, 8,* 173–176.

Crook, J., Rideout, E., & Browne, G. (1984). The prevalence of pain complaints in a general population. *Pain, 18,* 199–314.

Crue, B. L. (1983a). The peripheralist and centralist views of chronic pain. *Seminars in Neurology, 3,* 331–339.

Crue, B. L. (1983b). The neurophysiology and taxonomy of pain. In S. F. Brena & S. L. Chapman (Eds.), *Management of patients with chronic pain* (pp. 21–31). New York: Spectrum.

Daut, R. L., & Cleeland, C. S. (1982). The prevalence and severity of pain in cancer. *Cancer, 50,* 1913–1918.

Demoragas, J. M., & Kierland, R. R. (1957). The outcome of patients with herpes zoster. *Archives of Dermatology, 75,* 193–196.

Dishman, R. K. (1982). Compliance/adherence in health-related exercise. *Health Psychology, 1,* 237–267.

Dishman, R. K. (1985). Medical psychology in exercise and sports. *Medical Clinics of North America, 69,* 123–143.

Dolce, J. J. (1987). Self-efficacy and disability beliefs in behavioral treatment of pain: A perspective. *Behaviour Research and Therapy, 25,* 289–299.

Doleys, D. M., Crocker, M. F., & Patton, D. (1982). Response of patients with chronic pain to exercise quotas. *Physical Therapy, 62,* 1111–1114.

Dolce, J. J., & Raczynski, J. M. (1985). Neuromuscular activity and electromyography in painful backs: Psychological and biomechanical models in assessment and treatment. *Psychological Bulletin, 97,* 502–520.

Dolce, J. J., Crocker, M. F., & Doleys, D. M. (1986a). Prediction of outcome among chronic pain patients. *Behaviour Research and Therapy, 24,* 313–319.

Dolce, J. J., Crocker, M. F., Moletteire, C., & Doleys, D. M. (1986b). Exercise quotas, anticipatory concern, and self-efficacy expectancies in chronic pain: A preliminary report. *Pain, 24,* 365–372.

Dolce, J. J., Doleys, D. M., Raczynski, J. M., Lossie, J., Poole, L., & Smith, M. (1986c). The role of efficacy expectancies in the prediction of pain tolerance. *Pain, 27,* 261–272.

Doliber, C. M. (1984). Role of the physical therapist at pain treatment centers. *Physical Therapy, 64,* 905–909.

Ehrlich, G. E. (1982). Diagnosis and management of rheumatic diseases in older patients. *Journal of the American Geriatrics Society, 30* (Suppl. 11), 545–551.

Evans, P. J. D. (1981). Narcotic addiction in patients with chronic pain. *Anaesthesia, 36,* 597–602.

Fitzgerald, P. L. (1985). Exercise for the elderly. *Medical Clinics of North America, 69,* 189–196.

Folkins, C. H., Lynch, S., & Gardner, M. M. (1972). Psychological fitness as a function of physical fitness. *Archives of Physical Medicine and Rehabilitation, 53,* 503–508.

Follick, M. J., Ahern, D. K., & Aberger, E. W. (1987). Behavioral treatment of chronic pain in applications. In J. Blumenthal & D. C. Mckee (Eds.), *Behavioral medicine and health psychology: A clinician's source book* (pp. 237–270). Sarasota, FL: Professional Resource Exchange.

Fordyce, W. E. (1970). Operant conditioning as treatment method in management of selected chronic pain problems. *Northwest Medicine, 8,* 580–581.

Fordyce, W. E. (1976). *Behavioral methods for chronic pain and illness.* St. Louis: Mosby.

Fordyce, W. E. (1978). Evaluating and managing chronic pain. *Geriatrics, 31,* 59–62.

Fordyce, W. E., Fowler, R. S., Lehman, J. F., DeLateur, B. J., Sand, P. L., & Treischmann, R. B. (1973). Operant conditioning in the treatment of chronic pain. *Archives of Physical and Rehabilitative Medicine, 54,* 399–408.

Fordyce, W. E., Shelton, J. L., & Dundore, D. E. (1982). The modification of avoidance learning pain behaviors. *Journal of Behavioral Medicine, 5,* 405–415.

Freemoon, F. R. (1978). Evaluation and treatment of headache. *Geriatrics, 33,* 82–85.

Gauthier, J. G., Cote, A., & Drolet, M. (1985). *Perceived self-efficacy as a psychological mediator of migraine headache improvement following blood volume pulse biofeedback.* Paper presented at the meeting of the Society for Behavioral Medicine, New Orleans, Louisiana.

Gilliland, B. C., & Mannick, M. (1973). Rheumatoid arthritis. In R. G. Petersdorf, R. D. Adams, E. Braunwald, K. J. Isselbacher, J. B. Martin, & J. D. Wilson (Eds.), *Harrison's principles of internal medicine* (pp. 1977–1984). New York: McGraw-Hill.

Gurland, B. J., & Cross, P. S. (1982). Epidemiology of psychopathology in old age. *Psychiatric Clinics in North America, 5,* 11–26.

Haley, W. E. (1983). Priorities for behavioral intervention with nursing home residents: Nursing staff's perspective. *International Journal of Behavioral Geriatrics, 1,* 47–51.

Haley, W. E., & Dolce, J. J. (1986). Assessment and management of chronic pain in the elderly. *Clinical Gerontologist, 5,* 435–455.

Harkins, S. W., & Chapman, C. R. (1976). Detection and decision factors in pain perception in young and elderly men. *Pain, 2,* 253–264.

Harkins, S. W., & Chapman, C. R. (1977). The perception of inducing dental pain in young and elderly women. *Journal of Gerontology, 32,* 428–435.

Harkins, S. W., Kwentus, J., & Price, D. D. (1984). Pain and the elderly. In C. Bennetti, C. R. Chapman, & G. Moricca (Eds.), *Advances in pain research and therapy,* (pp. 147–172). New York: Raven Press.

Harkins, S. W., Price, D. D., & Martelli, M. (1986). Effects of age on pain perception: Thermociception. *Journal of Gerontology, 41,* 58–63.

Hilgard, E. K., & Hilgard, J. K. (1975). *Hypnosis in the relief of pain.* Los Altos, CA: William Kaufman.

Holroyd, K. A., Penzien, D. B., Hursey, K. G., Tobin, D. L., Rogers, L., Holm, J. E., Marcille, P. J., Hall, J. R., & Chila, A. G. (1984). Change mechanism in EMG biofeedback training. *Journal of Consulting and Clinical Psychology, 52,* 1039–1053.

Horne, J. A. (1981). The effects of exercise upon sleep: A critical review. *Psychology, 12,* 241–290.

Iversen, S. D., & Iversen, L. L. (1981). *Behavioral pharmacology* (2nd ed.). New York: Oxford University Press.

Kaiko, R. F., Wallenstein, S. L., Rogers, A. G., Brabinski, P. Y., & Houda, R. W. (1982). Narcotics in the elderly. *Mental Clinics of North America, 66,* 1079–1089.

Katon, W., & Kleinman, A. (1982). Depression and somatization: A review. Part I. *American Journal of Medicine, 72,* 127–135.

Keefe, F. J. (1982). Behavioral assessment and treatment of chronic pain: Current status and future directions. *Journal of Consulting and Clinical Psychology, 50,* 896–911.

Khatami, M., Woody, G., & O'Brien, C. (1979). Chronic pain and narcotic addiction: A multitherapeutic approach. *Comprehensive Psychiatry, 20,* 55–60

Klepac, R. K., Dowling, J., & Hauge, G. (1982). Characteristics of clients seeking therapy for the reduction of dental avoidance reactions to pain. *Journal of Behavior Therapy and Experimental Psychiatry, 13,* 293–300.

Kores, R., Murphy, W. D., Rosenthal, T., Elias, D., & Rosenthal, R. (1985). *A self-efficacy scale to predict outcome in chronic pain treatment: Preliminary results.* Paper presented at the meeting of the Society for Behavioral Medicine, New Orleans, LA.

Krane, S. M., & Holick, M. F. (1983). Metabolic bone disease. In R. G. Petersdorf, R. D. Adams, E. Braunwald, K. J. Isselbacher, J. B. Martin, & J. D. Wilson (Eds.), *Harrison's principles of internal medicine* (pp. 1949–1954). New York: McGraw-Hill.

Krause, H. (1965). *Backache, stress and tension: Cause, prevention and treatment.* New York: Simon and Schuster.

Lane, J. M., Vigorita, V. J., & Falls, M. (1984). Osteoporosis: Current diagnosis and treatment. *Geriatrics, 39,* 40–47.

Lewis, C. B. (1984). Rehabilitation of the older person: A psychosocial focus. *Physical Therapy, 64,* 517–521.

Loeser, J. D. (1980). Perspectives on pain. *Proceedings of the first world conference on clinical pharmacology and therapeutics* (pp. 313–316). London: MacMillan.

Lukert, B. P. (1982). Osteoporosis—A review and update. *Archives of Physical Medicine and Rehabilitation, 63,* 480–487.

Manning, M. M., & Wright, T. L. (1983). Self-efficacy expectancies, outcome expectancies, and the persistence of pain control in childbirth. *Journal of Personality and Social Psychology, 45,* 421–431.

Martinez-Urrutia, A. (1975). Anxiety and pain in surgical patients. *Journal of Consulting and Clinical Psychology, 43,* 437–442.

Maruta, T., Swanson, D. W., & Finlayson, R. E. (1978). Drug abuse and dependency in patients with chronic pain. *Mayo Clinic Proceedings, 54,* 241–244.

McCaul, K. D., & Malott, J. M. (1984). Distraction and coping with pain. *Psychological Bulletin, 95,* 516–533.

McDonald, J. B., Baillie, J., Williams, B. O., & Ballantyne, D. (1983). Coronary care in the elderly. *Age and Aging, 12,* 17–20.

McGivney, W. T., & Crooks, G. M. (1984). The care of patients with severe chronic pain in terminal illness. *Journal of the American Medical Association, 251,* 1182–1188.

McNairy, S. L., Maruta, T., Ivnik, R. J., Swanson, D. W., & Ilstrup, D. (1984). Prescription medication dependence and neurophysiological function. *Pain, 18,* 169–177.

Melzack, R., & Wall, P. D. (1983). *The challenge of pain.* Basic Books.

Milby, J. B. (1981). *Addictive behavior and its treatment.* New York: Springer Publishing.

Neufeld, R. W. J., & Thomas P. (1977). Effects of perceived efficacy of a prophylactic controlling mechanism on self-control under painful stimulation. *Canadian Journal of Behavioral Science, 9,* 224–232.

Payne, R., & Foley, K. M. (1984). Advances in the management of cancer pain. *Cancer Treatment Reports, 68,* 173–183.

Pfeiffer, R. F. (1982). Drugs for pain in the elderly. *Geriatrics, 37,* 67–76.

Portenoy, R. K. (1986). Postherpetic neuralgia: A workable treatment plan. *Geriatrics, 41,* 34–48.

Posner, C. M. (1976). The types of headache that affect the elderly. *Geriatrics, 31,* 103–106.

Procacci, P., Bozza, G., Buzzelli, G., & Della Corte, M. (1970). The cutaneous prickling pain threshold in old age. *Gerontologia Clinica, 12,* 213–218.

Redd, W. H. (1982). Behavioral analysis and control of psychosomatic symptoms of patients receiving intensive cancer treatment. *British Journal of Clinical Psychology, 21,* 351–358.

Rimer, B., Jones, W., Wilson, C., Bennett, D., & Engstrom, P. (1983). Planning a cancer control program for older citizens. *The Gerontologist, 23,* 384–389.

Roberts, A. H. (1981). The behavioral treatment of chronic pain. In J. M. Ferguson & C. B. Taylor (Eds.), *The comprehensive handbook of behavioral medicine* (Vol. 2, pp. 172–197). New York: Spectrum Publications.

Roesch, R., & Ulrich, D. E. (1980). Physical therapy management in the treatment of chronic pain. *Physical Therapy, 60,* 53–57.

Romano, J. M., & Turner, J. A. (1985). Chronic pain and depression: Does the evidence support a relationship? *Psychological Bulletin, 97,* 18–34.

Rowe, J. W., & Besdine, R. W. (Eds.). (1982). *Health and disease in old age.* Boston: Little, Brown.

Rubenstein, L. Z., & Robbins, A. S. (1984). Falls in the elderly: A clinical perspective. *Geriatrics, 39,* 67–78.

Rybstein-Blinchik, E. (1979). Effects of different cognitive strategies on chronic pain experience. *Journal of Behavioral Medicine, 2,* 93–101.

Sanders, S. H. (1983). Component analysis of a behavioral treatment program for chronic low back pain. *Behavior Therapy, 14,* 697–705.

Spanos, N. P., Radtke-Bodorik, H. L., Ferguson, J. D., & Jones, B. (1979). The effects of hypnotic susceptibility, suggestion for analgesia, and the utilization of cognitive strategies on the reduction of pain. *Journal of Abnormal Psychology, 88,* 282–292.

Speilberger, C. D., Auerbach, S. M., Wadsworth, A. P., Dunn, T. M., & Taulbee, E. F. (1973). Emotional reactions to surgery. *Journal of Consulting and Clinical Psychology, 40,* 33–38.

Spirduso, W. (1983). Exercise and the aging brain. *Research Quarterly for Exercise and Sport, 54,* 208–218.

Sternbach, R. A. (1974). *Pain patients: Traits and treatment.* New York: Academic Press.

Sturgis, E. T., Dolce, J. J., & Dickerson, P. A. (1987). Pain management in the elderly. In L. L. Carstensen & B. A. Edelstein (Eds.), *Handbook of clinical gerontology* (pp. 190–203). New York: Pergamon Press.

Swerdlow, M. (1973). Relieving pain in the terminally-ill. *Geriatrics, 28,* 100–103.

Taylor, C. B., Zlutnick, S. I., Corley, M. J., & Flora, J. (1980). The effects of detoxification, relaxation and brief supportive therapy on chronic pain. *Pain, 8,* 319–329.

Thompson, S. C. (1981). Will it hurt less if I can control it? A complex answer to a simple question. *Psychological Bulletin, 90,* 89–101.

Turk, D. C., & Rennert, K. (1981). Pain and the terminally ill cancer patient: A cognitive-social learning perspective. In H. J. Sobel (Ed.), *Behavior therapy in terminal care: A humanistic approach* (pp. 95–124). Cambridge, MA: Ballinger.

Turk, D. C., Meichenbaum, D., & Genest, J. (1983). *Pain and behavioral medicine: A cognitive behavioral perspective*. New York: Guilford.

Turner, J. A., & Chapman, C. R. (1982). Psychological interventions for chronic pain: A critical review. I. Relaxation training and biofeedback. *Pain, 12,* 1–21.

Turner, J. A., Calsyn, D. A., Fordyce, W. E., & Ready, L. B. (1982). Drug utilization patterns in chronic pain patients. *Pain, 12,* 367–363.

Varni, J. W. (1981). Self-regulation techniques in the management of chronic arthritic pain in hemophilia. *Behavior Therapy, 12,* 185–194.

Weisenberg, M. (1977). Pain and pain control. *Psychological Bulletin, 84,* 1008–1044.

Wigley, F. M. (1984). Osteoarthritis: Practical management in older patients. *Geriatrics, 39,* 101–120.

Wittig, R. M., Zorick, F. J., Blumer, D., Heilbronn, M., & Roth, T. (1982). Disturbed sleep in patients complaining of chronic pain. *The Journal of Nervous and Mental Disease, 170,* 429–431.

Wolf, S. L., Nacht, M., & Kelly, J. L. (1982). EMG feedback training during dynamic movement for low back pain patients. *Behavior Therapy, 13,* 395–406.

Ziesat, H. A., Angle, H. V., Gentry, W. D., & Ellinwood, E. H. (1979). Drug use and misuse in operant pain patients. *Addictive Behaviors, 4,* 263–266.

18

Pet-Facilitated Therapy and the Elderly Client

Joseph E. Struckus

Introduction

Humankind has cultivated and maintained a number and variety of relationships with other animals. Animals have been used as protectors, as instruments of war, as beasts of burden, as sources of food, and as the means for recreation. All of these roles are predominantly utilitarian. The animal has been considered a "necessary machine," something to be used in promoting the material and economic well-being of the person.

The use of an animal as a pet, as a source of companionship, defies a strict utilitarian definition of purpose. An estimated 60% of American households have at least one pet, but the reasons why people keep pets and the role that pets play in human culture have only recently been investigated. Within the past decade, the study of the significance of animal–human interactions has become an accepted scientific field, and there are now a number of scholarly societies devoted to this area of research. In addition, the use of pets in certain therapeutic settings has become popular. When pets are employed as an adjunctive therapeutic device, the therapy is called "pet-facilitated."

The elderly as a clinical treatment population have been a particular focus of the research and applied work in animal–human interaction and pet-facilitated therapy. There are at least two reasons for this focus. First, the human service field has highlighted the elderly population in its effort to develop new and existing therapeutic interventions to meet the increasing need for services. Second, pets are believed to provide for some of the needs of the elderly, such as companionship, affection, unconditional positive regard, and environmental stimulation. Pets also provide incentives to exercise and interact socially and are something to care for. With the proper training of the companion animal and the proper placement procedures, there is relatively little cost to the community.

Joseph E. Struckus • Department of Psychology, Gaylord Hospital, Wallingford, Connecticut 06492.

This chapter is about the ways pets can be used to promote the mental, emotional, physical, and social well-being of the elderly. The focus is upon the developing field of pet-facilitated therapy (PFT), a discipline that uses companion animals to supplement caregiving efforts for a needy and underserviced segment of the population. The chapter will begin with a historical overview of the use of domestic animals in the therapeutic setting. The author will then review the past and current work using PFT with the elderly client, and will discuss that information in a context and language suitable for use by the behavioral researcher and clinician. This review will discriminate between programs designed for community-dwelling elderly and programs designed for institutionalized elderly. The author will also provide some recommendations and guidelines for the health care provider who is interested in using PFT as an adjunctive therapy. The chapter will conclude with an evaluation of the field's current needs and some suggestions for its future direction.

HISTORICAL DEVELOPMENT OF PET-FACILITATED THERAPY

Far from being a "new" therapy, the treatment of mental and emotional dysfunction through the use of animals can be reliably traced to the late eighteenth century. The York Retreat, founded by the Quaker merchant William Tuke, employed a treatment of "moral methods," at a time when lunatic hospitals and asylums used primarily restraint and physical punishment as forms of treatment and control. Patients were offered kindness and understanding, and were reinforced for attempts at self-control. The Retreat maintained a significant number of small animals, including rabbits and poultry, and the patients were encouraged to learn and maintain self-control by caring for the animals.

Bethel, begun as a home for epileptics in 1867 and now an extensive health facility, has used animals as part of its therapeutic milieu since its early years (Bustad, 1978). Dr. Leo Bustad, a leading figure in comparative medicine and in pet-facilitated therapy, visited the complex in 1977 and noted its similarities to the York Retreat. Small and large domesticated animals are employed in the residences and at work sites, and the facility maintains farm animals and a wild game park. Little systematic evaluation has been done on the effect of the animals on the patients, however, so despite the staff's conviction that the animals are helpful, it is impossible to draw valid conclusions about their utility.

In more recent work using animals in the individual treatment setting, Dr. Boris Levinson (1961, 1969, 1972) emerges as a prominent figure. Levinson accidentally discovered the advantages of the companion animal in psychotherapy with children, when the presence of his pet dog, Jingles, proved to be an important part of his treatment of a disturbed child. Initially withdrawn and uncommunicative, the child readily interacted with the dog, and later permitted Levinson to join in these interactions. Thus, Jingles facilitated the establishment of Levinson's therapeutic relationship with his young client. Levinson has since devoted his energies to the development and promotion of pet-facilitated therapy, and has been a leader in calling for a rigorous examination of the method of PFT and for the proper training of therapy animals.

One of the more publicized uses of pet-facilitated therapy was initiated in 1975 by David Lee, a psychiatric social worker at the Lima State Hospital in Ohio. Lima State Hospital is a maximum security forensic institution, housing about 400 patients, including sociopaths and sex offenders (Fogle, 1981). Lee introduced a variety of pet animals, including parrots, hamsters, gerbils, guinea pigs, rabbits, and even a deer into the institutional environment. He found that the pets became a medium for the direction of affectionate behaviors, and patients improved social interaction with their peers and members of the staff.

Samuel and Elizabeth Corson (1980) and their colleagues (Corson, O'Leary Corson, Gwynne, & Arnold, 1975, 1977) were among the first to examine pet-facilitated therapy systematically. The setting was a psychiatric hospital, and the subjects were patients who had failed to respond to more traditional therapies. The Corsons saw their use of pet dogs in psychotherapy "as an adjunct to facilitate the resocialization process" (1980, p. 85). Matching the temperament of their dogs to the needs of specific patients, the Corsons observed the effects of the patient's inter-actions with the dogs. Patients took on increasing responsibility for the care of the dogs, and exhibited increases in self-care behaviors and socialization on the ward. Some of the withdrawn patients had accumulated tokens from behavior modifica-tion programs but had failed to cash them in. A number of these patients found interacting with the dogs rewarding, and spent their tokens for such interaction (Corson & O'Leary Corson, 1980).

Companion animals have also been associated with medical benefits. In an epidemiological study of the relationship between social support factors and mor-tality from heart disease, Friedmann, Katcher, Thomas, & Lynch (in press) made the serendipitous discovery that heart attack victims who were pet owners had a significantly greater 1-year survival rate than did individuals who did not own pets. Additional investigation revealed that the lower mortality rate among the pet owners could not be explained as a result of increased exercise associated with dog ownership. Multivariate analysis indicated that pet ownership decreased the proba-bility of dying by about 3%, an effect comparable to a number of other healthy lifestyle characteristics.

Several investigators have observed that petting a dog can significantly reduce blood pressure (Baun, Bergstrom, Langston, & Thoma, 1984; Friedmann, Katcher, Thomas, Lynch, & Messent, 1983; Grossberg & Alf, 1985; Katcher, 1981). Katcher (1981) measured the blood pressure of 35 veterinary clinic clients after their pet dogs were removed for evaluation or treatment. The client's blood pressure was meas-ured at rest, while reading aloud from an uninteresting text, and while actively greeting the returned pet with physical contact and words. Katcher observed significant decreases in both systolic and diastolic blood pressure between the reading aloud and pet-greeting conditions. However, there were no significant differences in blood pressure between the resting and pet-greeting conditions. His results suggest that some aspect of this interchange between owner and pet has the capacity to reduce sympathetic arousal. Baun et al. (1984) confirmed and extended Katcher's findings, and highlighted the importance of a prior familiarity with the dog in the observed reduction of blood pressure. Friedmann *et al.* (1983) examined the presence of a friendly dog on the blood pressure and heart rate of 38 children, ages 9 to 16. Presence of the friendly dog was correlated with significantly lower blood pressure and heart rate. Grossberg and Alf (1985) observed reductions in blood pressure through dog petting on 48 normotensive college students, and demonstrated the value of a positive attitude toward pets in achieving this reduction.

PET-FACILITATED THERAPY WITH THE ELDERLY

While the elderly do share a number of therapeutic needs, significant differences exist between community-dwelling and institutionalized elderly to warrant very different approaches to the organization and implementation of PFT programs for those two groups. In the following sections, pet-facilitated therapy programs will be discussed in light of the particular needs of elderly living in the community and of those residing in institutional settings.

Community-Dwelling Elderly

The vast majority of the elderly reside outside of institutional settings, independently within the community. For a significant proportion of these elderly, old age brings a diminishment of family and friends, loss of earning power and responsibility, decreased mobility and opportunities for social contact, and an increasing sense of dependence upon others. Advocates of PFT believe that pets can provide an inexpensive method of allaying the negative psychological manifestations of some of these factors. They maintain that an animal companion provides solace in bereavement, attenuates the pain of social isolation and depression, offers the elderly person a renewed sense of responsibility and purpose, and actively serves a role in preventing social withdrawal and alienation. There is a considerable body of anecdotal evidence to support such claims, yet anecdotes are rarely reported unless they confirm a prior belief. Nevertheless, the few empirically based studies that have been performed offer some cautious encouragement in the use of PFT with the community-dwelling elderly.

Mugford and M'Comisky (1975) examined the therapeutic use of pet budgerigars (an Australian parakeet) among elderly pensioners aged 75–81 living alone in the community of East Yorkshire, England. This study was designed to determine whether the presence of a companion animal might improve an elderly person's self-perceptions and perceptions of social connection to his or her community. At the beginning of the study, each of the 30 participants was interviewed and completed a dependent measure that examined attitude toward self and others, as well as perceived physical and psychological health. The participant was then randomly assigned a budgerigar, a begonia (houseplant), or nothing. One half of the participants had a television, a variable considered in this experiment because of its ability to serve as a medium of interaction between the individual and larger society.

At the conclusion of the 5-month placement period, the subjects were reassessed. The results indicated that budgierigar ownership had had a positive effect upon the elderly subjects. Of the 30 participants, 12 showed marked improvement, especially in their attitudes toward other people and their own perceived psychological well-being. Begonia owners showed no statistically significant changes, positive or negative, indicating that it was not the receipt of a gift that accounted for the changes observed in budgerigar owners. Interviews with members of the pet groups indicated that not only had these individuals formed satisfying attachments to their pets, but the animals also acted as a "social lubricant," that is, a focal point for conversation with others. The experimenters hypothesized that the effect of the parakeet would be more pronounced for those participants who did not have a television. This effect was not observed. All of the budgerigars were given names by their owners, and all owners took full and responsible care of the birds. An 18-month follow-up revealed that all of the parakeet recipients still had their pets and were taking good care of them.

In evaluating the results of the Mugford and M'Comisky study, Brickel (1981) advised caution in interpretation. He noted that the methods of recruitment were not clearly defined, and thus one cannot be certain that the participants were representative of the larger elderly population. He also pointed out that only 63% of the original 30 participants were available for reassessment. While the authors themselves noted the problems of attrition, they failed to indicate how this phenomenon might have affected their results.

Robb and Stegman (1983) surveyed a randomly selected sample of elderly veterans receiving home health care through the Veteran's Administration Medical Center in Pittsburgh, Pennsylvania. A total of 56 veterans participated, including 26 pet owners and 30 nonowners. The experimenters measured morale, social interaction, mental status, psychological symptoms, ability to perform physical and instrumental activities of daily living, number of diseases, number of medications, and perceived locus of control. Three criteria were used in selecting these variables: (1) the variable had been mentioned in one or more anecdotal reports; (2) it had not been studied previously in association with companion animals; and (3) it could be measured using previously developed instruments with established validity, reliability, and prior use with elderly subjects.

No significant differences were found between the pet owner and nonowner groups with respect to the measured variables. The researchers conjectured that the strength of the pet owner bond might be an important factor and reassessed the data after dividing the sample into high-bond and low-bond subjects. Bonding status was assessed among pet owners by their response to a dichotomous question of whether they preferred people or pets, with the subjects preferring pets being assigned to the high-bond condition. Nonowners were similarly assigned using their response to the question, "Do you wish you had a pet?" One-way analysis of variance for the nine measured variables, controlling for bonding status, failed to reveal any significant differences between groups.

The authors discussed a number of conceptual and methodological issues regarding their failure to support empirically the anecdotal accounts of the effects of pet ownership. They noted their virtually all-male sample and suggested that future studies examine sex differences with regards to the effects of pet ownership. They warned against an oversimplification of the alleged relationship between association with companion animals and human health benefits. In particular, situational and personality variables that may significantly vary the effect of a PFT program on human health and well-being have yet to be identified and examined. Finally, they suggested that the health-enhancing effects of companion animals might not be measurable on a day-to-day basis, but might only impact upon human health during periods of crisis or high stress.

There was an additional difficulty with the Robb and Stegman study, not addressed by the authors. In their assessment of the bonding status of the subjects, the authors failed to consider the validity of the dichotomous questions as discriminators of high versus low bonding. If a subject prefers a pet to a person, does that make him an individual highly bonded to his pet? A more useful measure of bonding status might have been obtained with the Pet Attitude Scale (Templer, Salter, Dickey, Baldwin, & Veleber, 1981), an easily administered 18-item Likert-format scale that has some established criterion-oriented validity and face validity. A replication of the Robb and Stegman study that incorporates the suggestions presented above might provide valuable data on the psychological and physical effects of pet ownership on the elderly.

Ory and Goldberg (1983) examined the effect of pet ownership on the subjective well-being of elderly women. Structured interviews were conducted on 1,073 married white women aged 65–75. Controlling for sociodemographic, health status, and social interaction factors, the presence of a pet in the home was not a predictor of perceived happiness. However, further multivariate analyses revealed that the nature of the interaction between the subject and her pet, as well as the socioeconomic context in which the subject lived, were significant interactional factors in the evaluation of the relationship between pet ownership and perceived happiness. Specifically, a larger percentage of the women who were not attached to their pets were unhappy, when compared with those women who were attached to their pets, or even when compared with those with no pets at all. Additionally, the relationship between pet ownership and perceived happiness was dependent upon socioeconomic status (SES), with pet ownership being associated with greater happiness among those of high SES, but with less happiness among those women of lower SES.

As is typical of all correlational studies, the results of the Ory and Goldberg article suffer from an inability to distinguish cause from effect. Since an assessment of perceived happiness prior to pet ownership is not available, the conclusion that pets can produce "happier" elderly is insupportable. One could reasonably suggest that happier women are in general capable of greater responsibilities, and among those responsibilities might be the acquisition and care of a pet. The authors acknowledge that pet ownership accounted for a relatively small proportion of the variance in their measurement of perceived happiness. Physical health and the health of the subject's husband accounted for a far greater amount of the variance. Holcomb, Williams, and Richards (1985) note that the perceived attachment to a companion animal varies inversely with the opportunity for other human contact. Perhaps individuals who value greatly their marital, sibling, or friend relationships place a correspondingly smaller value on the relationships they have with their pets. A similar experiment using elderly women who have few close human relationships might have yielded dramatically different results.

The evidence derived from empirical studies in support of community-based pet-facilitated therapy with the elderly is far from overwhelming, as the results of the above representative studies suggest. Nevertheless, the development and use of these programs is burgeoning, and concerned professionals have begun the task of developing both model programs and the informational network necessary for the initiation of a public awareness program.

People and Animals Coming Together (PACT) is a model example of a thoughtfully designed and well-executed pet placement program for the elderly living at home. PACT is a community-based volunteer nonprofit organization affiliated with the Gerontology Center of The Pennsylvania State University. Its originators defined two central goals for the program: (1) to demonstrate how a group like PACT might operate to promote and support pet ownership by older people living in the community; and (2) to conduct longitudinal research to see if pet ownership has a measurable effect on the health and well-being of a sample of rural elderly people (Lago, Knight, & Connell, 1981).

PACT employs a number of criteria for assuring an appropriate match between an elderly person seeking animal companionship and the companion animal. Both the elderly person and the animal are selected and prepared for this match. Elderly clients participate in a multiple-step selection process. Clients who are either self-referred or who are referred by an intermediate individual or agency are interviewed to determine their specific needs, preferences, mental and physical limitations, and environmental restrictions. They are then matched with a volunteer sponsor who is often a friend or relative of the client, and who shares the client's interest in a type of pet. This sponsor works personally with the client from this point onward, facilitating the orientation and education of the elderly client to pet ownership and assuring the provision of follow-up attention and assistance. A counseling period follows, culminating in a mutual decision by the client and PACT about whether a pet is right for this particular person at this point in his or her life. Consideration is given to the client's desires, abilities, and resources, the availability of support and aid for the client, and the possible effect of the pet on other people in the family or household.

Potential companion animals are referred to PACT from shelters, kennels, and private donors. The animals are given thorough physical exams, are evaluated for temperament and possible behavioral problems, and are properly wormed, neutered, and immunized. PACT provides for licensing and obedience instruction, and then retains the animals for an additional period to continue behavior and temperament assessment. Such thorough preplacement screening and preparation reduces the possibility of an improper placement and a subsequent failed intervention.

Organizations like PACT provide valuable models for the development of new community-based PFT programs. As the number of these programs increases, there will be a greater need for established procedural guidelines in the implementation of a community intervention, as well as a set of evaluative criteria for determining the effectiveness of the therapeutic program.

Institutionalized Elderly

Although only 5% of the elderly in the United States live in nursing homes, this percentage represents well over 1 million individuals (Teri & Lewinsohn, 1986). Kane and Kane (1978) have pointed to the limited professional care available to the institutionalized elderly, contrasting the average umber of personnel in nursing homes (64 per 100 residents) with the number available in hospitals (243 per 100 residents). These authors have also indicated that nursing home personnel tend to be less well paid, have less professional training, and are less satisfied with their work than those in other parts of the health care system. It is important to stress that the relatively poor care provided to the elderly in nursing homes is more likely a symptom of society's disregard for the elderly than a result of a failure by nursing home staff. As Corson and O'Leary Corson (1981) suggest:

> The process of systematic exclusion of the aged from the mainstream of economic, social, and cultural life is reminiscent of the psychology of planned obsolescence based on the belief that when products get old they are to be discarded and replaced with new products designed in turn for early obsolescence. (p.146)

The Corsons have described eight characteristics of the psychosocial structure of a typical nursing home that serve to intensify personality disintegration, alienation, and an infantile type of dependence:

1. It is essentially a closed group.
2. It has a low staff–resident ratio, thus making it difficult to individualize treatment.
3. It is a highly regimented social organization, leaving very little room for the retention of a sense of individual responsibility and a feeling of dignity.
4. It is a mass-oriented social organization, leaving little room for privacy and initiative.
5. The residents tend to lose an important life-sustaining and life-enriching driving force, a sense of purpose and engagement in satisfying goal-directed activities.
6. It fails to furnish an environment conducive to the maintenance and development of positive affective states, a feeling of being needed and respected, and a feeling of being loved and an opportunity to reciprocate such feelings.
7. The residents lack socially sustaining tactile contacts.
8. Many of the residents may suffer from varying degrees of sensory deficits, particularly in vision and hearing. These losses contribute to further tactile and social isolation, thus leading to a vicious circle of social deprivation and psychological–emotional disintegration and disorientation. (p. 148)

The Corsons cite a number of other deleterious factors in the nursing home setting that contribute to a less than therapeutic experience for the elderly. Among these are the psychological and social stresses of (an often involuntary) relocation from the community to the nursing home and an isolation of the elderly from their families and long-time friendships, from their religious and cultural social groups, and from the freedom of individual living.

The rationale for instituting PFT programs in nursing home settings is twofold. First, pet animals offer the infirmed or debilitated elderly opportunities for un-critical, nonjudgmental social interaction. Even among the best intentioned and most experienced professionals, healthy people tend to send negative nonverbal signals to the sick, the infirm, the aged, and the physically and mentally retarded (Corson & O'Leary Corson, 1980). This may lead to a reciprocal pattern of social isolation, suspicion, and mistrust between the patient and the provider. Pets can form affectionate and trusting relationships with people regardless of ability, appearance, or fortune. Thus, pets can be considered especially appropriate for those individuals that suffer under the harsh prejudices of the larger society, a condition with which the elderly person must often contend. Second, pets are considered capable of providing sensory (particularly tactile) stimulation, of en-couraging caregiving responses, and of facilitating social interaction. These are conditions and behaviors often sought after in the institutional setting.

Pet-facilitated therapy programs in the nursing home setting generally fall into one of two types: either an in-residence companion animal program or a pet visitation program. In-residence programs "adopt" one or a number of animals that live in the facility and become part of the treatment community. In these programs, the elderly residents often take an active role in the day-to-day care of the animals. Pet-visitation programs generally use the services of an animal welfare, 4-H, or other animal-related volunteer program to provide visiting animals on a weekly or monthly basis. The elderly residents have the opportunity to interact with the animals, but because the animals do not live on the premises, this interaction is more limited and controlled than in the resident pet programs.

The Corsons (1980) were among the first to institute an in-residence compan-ion animal program in a nursing home setting. Benefiting from their experience with the psychiatric hospital program described previously, an adoption program was established in a private nursing facility in Millersburg, Ohio. Elderly clients who were bedridden, physically restricted, or disoriented were given a small adult dog or puppy with which to interact under the supervision of a trained staff member. Those elderly living in a dormitory-type ward were given their choice of one of a number of weaned puppies for adoption.

The results of the companion animal intervention were documented by means of a questionnaire incorporated into the nurses' notes, and through the use of a videotape recording of animal–client interactions. The authors claimed that the companion animals offered the residents a form of nonthreatening, reassuring nonverbal communication and tactile comfort. The animals additionally were said to act as effective social catalysts, encouraging increased interactions between residents and improving the overall morale of the institution. However, these claims are interpretations of results achieved, not the results themselves. The authors failed to present the data upon which the interpretations were made, and they did not offer alternative explanations for the correlational results achieved. No control was used in the evaluation of the effects of the intervention. It should be noted that the purpose of the study was the documentation of the effects of the therapeutic intervention. The authors did not intend to examine empirically the therapeutic value of companion animals. But results based on nonexperimental methodologies limit the conclusions one might make about the effectiveness of the therapeutic program.

Robert Andrysco, a student of the Corsons at Ohio State University, conducted a methodologically more rigorous study of the effects of introducing a well-trained dog-in-residence to a retirement–nursing care facility (1981). Forty-six elderly residents were randomly assigned to either the experimental or control conditions. The experimental subjects were examined prior to, during, and following introduction of the pet to the facility. Their behaviors were compared to a similar group of residents who did not participate in the PFT program. The 23 experimental and 23 control subjects were observed by both nurses and activity therapists and were rated for psychosocial functioning in the areas of activity involvement, interactions with other residents and staff, self-care, and opinions and conversations about pet animals. In addition, 10 of the experimental subjects were studied by videotape in order to observe possible changes in amount of eye contact, smiling, and tactile contact, as well as changes in verbal response time, number of words per minute, number of words in response, number of questions asked, verbalization of violence, and delusional responses.

Analysis of variance failed to detect any significant differences between the experimental and control groups on the observed psychosocial variables. Andrysco observed considerable variance within his experimental group, variance that in part accounted for the failure to find significant between-group differences. Within-subject analyses indicated that the PFT program had a beneficial effect upon a select group of the experimental subjects. Fifteen of the subjects in the experimental group significantly improved in the areas of activity involvement, verbal communication, conversations about animals, socialization with nonnursing personnel, socialization with other residents, and socialization at mealtime. Verbal and nonverbal communication improved in the 10 videotaped subjects, with significant positive changes noted in both the quantity (number of words and statements) and quality (more positive responses) of communication. Andrysco also found improved eye contact and response time during the videotaped interactions between subject and investigator when the pet was present.

There was a widely varying effect of the PFT intervention on Andrysco's group of experimental subjects. Although a majority of the elderly subjects exposed to the resident dog demonstrated significant improvement in some aspects of psychosocial functioning, 8 of the 23 subjects showed no improvement. How might this variance in performance be explained? Unfortunately, Andrysco did not have sufficient data on his subjects to attempt this evaluation. Each subject brings to the intervention a unique history of past experiences with companion animals, as well as individual perceptions of and attitudes toward the resident dog. A future study of this kind of intervention would profit from an examination of these historical, perceptual, and attitudinal antecedents.

McArthur, Brunmeier, Bergstrom, and Baun (1986) have also provided support for the belief that PFT might have some beneficial effect upon social interaction capabilities of the mentally impaired elderly. A within-subject experimental design was used to examine a sample of 28 mentally impaired elderly who met specific diagnostic and research criteria. The subjects were randomly assigned to a control or a treatment session as the first of two 10-minute videotaped conversations with the experimenter. In one session, subjects were videotaped with the researcher only, and in the other session, subjects met with the researcher and a dog. The same standard interview was used in both conditions. Components of the subject's behavior during the conversation were examined and quantified. These elemental components included looks, leans, smiles, tactile contact, temporal response time, verbalizations, topic of conversation, and negative content of verbalizations. Differences in exhibited quantifiable behaviors were examined using paired t tests.

Analysis of the examined components of the elderly subjects' behaviors revealed that when a dog was present, the subjects focused significantly less of their attention on the person present than when no dog was present. This result reviewed alone suggests that the dog served to distract the subject from person-to-person interaction. However, the authors also observed that in the presence of the dog, total attention behaviors were significantly increased, suggesting that the dog served to facilitate the subject's ability to initiate and sustain attention to the social stimulus present.

Unfortunately, it is impossible to determine whether the presence of the dog was little more than a novel stimulus. Since multiple trails of the interviewer-with-dog condition were not performed, one is not able to determine if the presence of a companion animal can *sustain* increased attention behaviors. Neither is it known whether or not the presence of an animal *per se* increases attention. A large houseplant or any prominent stimulus might produce the same effects.

In a study examining the effects of a pet visitation program on elderly nursing home clients, Robb, Boyd, and Pristash (1980) provided some evidence in support of the specific effectiveness of companion animals as social catalysts. These investigators hypothesized that the degree of animation of an object would have a direct correlation to that object's ability to initiate social interaction. They selected a wine bottle, an inanimate object that could be an interesting visual stimulus to the sample of chronically ill elderly male alcoholics; a flowering plant, alive but not capable of motion; and a caged puppy to represent full animation. The objects were introduced into the dayroom of one unit of the hospital, one at a time, each for a 90-minute period on 2 separate days. The subjects were observed for the following social behaviors: verbalizations, smiles, looks toward the object, and leans toward the stimulus.

The investigators reported that the caged puppy produced the most dramatic increase in measured social behavior. Of particular note was a change in the quality of verbalizations, with a significant reduction of monosyllabic, inappropriate, or illogical responses, and a significant increase in the frequency of relevant, conversational responding. In addition, many of the subjects who typically became verbally or physically hostile when their personal space was invaded by another resident exhibited no such hostility when interacting with other residents in the presence of the puppy.

The results of this study are compromised by some methodological confounds. The investigators used an ABCDA design in evaluating the effects of the three presented stimuli. Following baseline measurements of the dependent variables, the stimuli were introduced to the experimental setting over three successive

1-week intervals. The wine bottle was presented first, followed by the flowering plant, and concluding with the caged puppy. There was only one trial of each stimulus. There was no opportunity to vary the order of the stimuli presented, nor were there measurements taken of the dependent measures between stimulus presentations. It is impossible, therefore, to determine if the observed effect of the puppy was the result of some quality intrinsic to this particular stimulus, or was merely the result of being the last stimulus presented. Four of the five dependent measures show successive improvement over the three stimulus trials, an observation that suggests a cumulative effect of the presented stimuli.

Robb *et al.* also failed to perform a statistical analysis of their data. Using the mean number of behaviors per resident as the numerical representation of their observations, they report the changes from baseline of the dependent measures. They do not, however, report the variance implicit in each mean value, nor do they determine the significance of the reported differences between experimental conditions using an acceptable statistical device. This insufficient analysis of the data detracts from the credibility of the investigator's conclusions.

Francis, Turner, and Johnson (1985) examined the effects of a pet visitation program upon elderly living in group home settings. Thirty elderly clients participated in the experimental treatment condition, and 30 clients served in a control condition. All were chronic mentally ill people who had been discharged from psychiatric facilities. The mean age of the experimental subjects was 72; the controls averaged 76 years of age (a nonsignificant difference). The average length of time each subject had been in the group home was about 40 months.

The treatment condition consisted of weekly visitation sessions of 3 hours each, over an 8-week period, in which the participating residents were each given a puppy or a kitten. Interactions were supervised by four animal handlers who were responsible for the companion animals. The control group had weekly human visitors unaccompanied by the animals. Participants in each condition were tested prior to and following the 8-week treatment period for changes in the following eight variables: health self-concept, life satisfaction, psychological well-being, social competence and interest, personal neatness, psychosocial and mental functioning, and depression. Pretest and posttest measures were administered by different investigators in order to minimize experimenter bias. The Student's *t* test with a significance of .05 was used to evaluate differences between conditions on each variable.

There were marked differences between the two groups. The residents who had interacted with the animals significantly improved in six of the eight areas measured. They did not improve on personal neatness and health self-concept. No changes over the 8-week period were noted in the control group. Thus it appears that the visitation program was successful at facilitating some positive change among the participants in their psychological and social functioning. What remains unclear in this study is whether such changes were produced by some quality intrinsic to the companion animal interaction, or were merely the result of participation in a new and unusual activity. Robb *et al.* (1980) suggest that an animal can have a more pronounced effect upon a person because of its ability to stimulate a variety of senses simultaneously (sight, hearing, smell, and especially touch all are involved). They maintain that "the perpetual, infantile, innocent dependence of a friendly dog may inspire a natural tendency on the part of humans to offer support and protection, even when the humans appear to have withdrawn from reality" (Robb *et al.*, 1980, p. 726).

The preliminary evidence suggests that both in-residence and visitation-type pet-facilitated therapy programs can assist in making improvements among the institutionalized elderly in the areas of attention, perceived psychological well-being, capacity for appropriate interpersonal interaction, and social awareness. The data from the reviewed research suggest that well-trained companion animals share a set of characteristics that serve to promote positive change in the psycho-logical and social functioning of the elderly in nursing homes. Some of the qualities that may contribute to the animal's therapeutic value are: (1) their ability to stimu-late a number of senses simultaneously; (2) their reliable positive response to initiated contact from the client; (3) their noncritical and nonjudgmental natures; (4) their association with prior positive feelings about home; (5) their encouragement of caregiving behaviors; and (6) their need for exercise and activity, which provides an incentive for increased physical activity. These qualities might help to explain the recent proliferation of pet-facilitated therapy programs in geriatric settings.

CLINICAL RECOMMENDATIONS

Health care professionals who wish to develop PFT programs for the elderly are encouraged to follow the recommendations of Michael McCulloch, a psychiatr-ist and cofounder of the Delta Society. The Delta Society is an international profes-sional association that seeks to promote a greater understanding of animal–human interactions. It takes a great interest in pet-facilitated therapy and has been instru-mental in encouraging the development of a strong empirical base to the field. McCulloch (1986) recommends that:

1. The program developer carefully review the structure of the institution or family, the capabilities and attitudes of the caregivers and/or staff, and the specific problems to be addressed by the PFT program.
2. A careful match be made between the needs and limitations of the client and the characteristics and temperament of the companion animal.
3. Clearly established goals and outcome criteria be defined for the interven-tion, along with a set of established methods for evaluating outcome.
4. There exists an understanding of the possible risks and benefits of the intervention (the program should do no harm).
5. The staff, volunteer group, and/or family be fully informed about the program's intent, goals, and procedures.
6. The PFT program be coordinated with existing therapies, and that it should supplement, rather than replace, other forms of treatment.
7. The program coordinator continually monitor all elements of the inter-vention in order to assess potential problem areas and maintain focus upon the stated goals and directions.

8. The developer analyze the effects of the intervention and modify the program accordingly. All measured effects, and in particular failed interventions, should be documented. The conditions of failure provide an important record of the limitations of PFT, and can be used to improve subsequent interventions.

9. The developer maintain realistic expectations. PFT is adjunctive; it is not a panacea.

Potential PFT program developers would also benefit from incorporating into their programs some of the philosophical and procedural characteristics shared by the more successful existing programs. These programs thoroughly educate the elderly participants on animal care and handling prior to the match of the participant with the animal. They use carefully selected and properly trained animals. In-residence programs have the proper facilities for the housing and feeding of the animals. Pet-visitation programs use only volunteers or paid staff who are experienced in handling and caring for the animals. All of these programs have enlisted the cooperation of the nursing and general institutional staff. And finally, the successful programs have respected the rights of those individuals who do not wish to interact with the animals, recognizing that this type of therapeutic intervention is not for everyone.

CURRENT NEEDS AND FUTURE DIRECTIONS

Pet-facilitated therapy is still in its infancy, both as a treatment modality and as focus for empirical investigation. As with any young discipline, enthusiasm for its promotion and legitimation can be a double-edged sword. On the positive side, the advocates of PFT have invested a considerable amount of their time, energy, and resources into the establishment of the field. But this enthusiasm is capable of adversely affecting the legitimacy of pet-facilitated therapy. In particular, claims of PFT as a "cure-all" are completely unsubstantiated in the empirical literature and thus should not be supported by the professionals of the field. This author sees the following current concerns within the field of pet-facilitated therapy, and offers suggestions for their resolution:

1. Much of the support for PFT is derived from anecdotal accounts. There is a vital need for carefully constructed, empirically robust examinations of therapeutic interventions with companion animals.

2. There is a greater need for replication studies by sceptical or critical experimenters. Given the enthusiasm within the field, the opportunities for experimenter bias are great.

3. The relationship between PFT interventions and human health benefits has been drastically oversimplified. It is important that researchers consider the possible intervening variables that might influence the extent of the intervention. A consideration of perceptual and attitudinal variables, of the learning history of the human subject examined as it relates to pets,

and of situational factors present during the intervention is strongly warranted.

4. As the number of PFT programs continues to grow, there is a correspondingly greater need for some regulating body or agency to oversee the establishment, maintenance, and quality of new and existing programs. Organizations like the Delta Society and CENSHARE (Center to Study Human–Animal Relationships and Environments), which promote the field of pet-facilitated therapy by their support of relevant research, should take a greater role in establishing guidelines for the proper organization of PFT programs.

The elderly client has the opportunity to gain considerably from what companion animals are able to offer. The conditions that govern a successful PFT intervention are those shared by many other therapeutic interventions. No therapy can be claimed as a panacea. A careful consideration of the needs and limitations of the individual, a thorough preparation of both client and animal for the intervention, and an appropriate structure within the PFT program for evaluation and support of the intervention will increase the probability that the match between elderly client and companion animal is a therapeutically profitable one.

SOME ORGANIZATIONS INVOLVED IN PET-FACILITATED THERAPY

The American Humane Association
9725 East Hampden Avenue
Denver, Colorado 80231

CENSHARE (Center to Study Human–Animal
Relationships and Environments)
University of Minnesota
1-117 Health Science Unit A
515 Delaware Street S.E.
Minneapolis, Minnesota 55455

The Center for the Interaction of Animals and Society
University of Pennsylvania
3800 Spruce Street
Philadelphia, Pennsylvania 19104

The Delta Society
Century Building, Suite 303
321 Burnett Avenue S.
Renton, Washington 98055

The People–Pet Partnership Program
Washington State University
College of Veterinary Medicine
Pullman, Washington 99164

The Pets are Wonderful Council
500 North Michigan Avenue
Chicago, Illinois 60611

References

Andrysco, R. M. (1981, October.) *Pet facilitated therapy in a retirement nursing care community*. Presentation
     at the 1981 International Conference on the Human/Companion Animal Bond, Philadelphia, PA.
Brickel, C. M. (1981). A review of the roles of pet animals in psychotherapy with the elderly. *International
     Journal of Aging and Human Development*, 12, 119–128.
Bustad, L. K. (1980). *Animals, aging, and the aged*. Minneapolis: University of Minnesota Press.
Baun, M., Bergstrom, N., Langston, N., & Thoma, L. (1984). Physiological effects of petting dogs:
     Influences of attachment. In R. Anderson, B. Hart, & L. Hart (Eds.), *The pet connection: Its influence
     on our health and quality of life* (pp. 75–91). St. Paul, MN: Glove Publishing.
Corson, S. A., & O'Leary Corson, E. (1980). Pet animals as nonverbal communication mediators in
     psychotherapy in institutional settings. In S. A. Corson & E. O'Leary Corson (Eds.), *Ethology and
     nonverbal communication in mental health* (pp. 49–74). New York: Pergamon Press.
Corson, S. A., & O'Leary Corson, E. (1981). Companion animals as bonding catalysts in geriatric
     institutions. In B. Fogle (Ed.). *Interrelations between people and pets* (pp. 146–174). Springfield IL:
     Charles C Thomas.
Corson, S. A., O'Leary Corson, E., Gwynne, P. H., & Arnold, L. E. (1975). Pet-facilitated psychotherapy
     in a hospital setting. In J. H. Masserman (Ed.), *Current psychiatric therapies* (Vol. 15, pp. 277–286).
     New York: Grune & Stratton.
Corson, S. A., O'Leary Corson, E., Gwynne, P. H., & Arnold, L. E. (1977). Pet dogs as nonverbal
     communication links in hospital psychiatry. *Comprehensive Psychiatry*, 18, 61–72.
Fogle, B. (1981). *Interrelations between people and pets*. Springfield, IL: Charles C Thomas.
Francis, G., Turner, J. T., & Johnson S. B. (1985). Domestic animal visitation as therapy with adult home
     residents. *International Journal of Nursing Studies*, 22, 201–206.
Friedmann, E., Katcher, A. H., Lynch, J., & Thomas, S. (in press). Interpersonal aspects of blood
     pressure control: Influence of animal companions. *Journal of Nervous and Mental Diseases*.
Friedmann, E., Katcher, A. H., Thomas, S., Lynch, J., & Messent, P. (1983). Social interaction and blood
     pressure: Influence of animal companions. *Journal of Nervous and Mental Disorders*, 17, 461–465.
Grossberg, J. M., & Alf, E. F. (1985). Interaction with pet dogs: Effects on human cardiovascular
     response. *Journal of the Delta Society*, 2, 20–27.
Holcomb, R., Williams, R. C., & Richards, P. S. (1985). The elements of attachment: relationship
     maintenance and intimacy. *Journal of the Delta Society*, 2, 28–34.
Kane, R. L., & Kane, R. A. (1978). Care of the aged: Old problems in need of new solutions. *Science 200*,
     43, 913–919.
Katcher, A. H. (1981). Interactions between people and pets: Form and function. In B. Fogle (Ed.),
     Interrelations between people and pets (pp. 41–67). Springfield, IL: Charles C Thomas.
Lago, D., Knight, B., & Connell, C. (1981). PACT: A pet placement organization for the elderly living at
     home. *Aging*, 331, 19–25.
Levinson, B. (1961). The dog as "co-therapist." *American Psychologist*, 16, 357.
Levinson, B. (1969). *Pet-oriented child psychotherapy*. Springfield, IL: Charles C Thomas.
Levinson, B. (1972). *Pets and human development*. Springfield, IL: Charles C Thomas.
McArthur, M., Brunmeier, C., Bergstrom, N., & Baun, M. (1986, August). *The effect of a pet dog on the social
     interaction of mentally impaired institutionalized elderly*. Presented at the 1986 Delta Society Interna-
     tional Conference, Boston.
McCulloch, M. J. (1986). Animal-facilitated therapy: Overview and future directions. *National Forum*, 66,
     19–24.
Mugford, R. A., & M'Comisky, J. G. (1975). Some recent work on the psychotherapeutic value of caged

birds with old people. In R. S. Anderson (Ed.), *Pet animals and society* (pp. 54–65). London: Bailliere Tindall.

Ory, M. A., & Goldberg, E. L. (1983). Pet possession and well-being in elderly women. *Research on Aging, 5,* 389–409.

Robb, S. S., & Stegman, C. E. (1983). Companion animals and the elderly: A challenge for evaluators of social support. *The Gerontologist, 23,* 277–282.

Robb, S. S., Boyd, M., & Pristash, C. L. (1980). A wine bottle, plant, and puppy: Catalysts for social behavior. *Journal of Gerontological Nursing, 6,* 721–728.

Templer, D. I., Salter, C. A., Dickey, S., Baldwin, R., & Veleber, D. M. (1981). The construction of a pet attitude scale. *The Psychological Record, 31,* 343–348.

Teri, L., & Lewinsohn, P. M. (1986). *Geropsychological assessment and treatment: Selected topics.* New York: Springer Publishing.

IV

Interventions in the Health and Community Care Systems

19

Behavioral Staff Training and Management in Geriatric Long-Term Care Facilities

LOUIS D. BURGIO

INTRODUCTION

The 1980 U.S. census estimated that 1.3 million people over 65 years of age were living in long-term care settings. These people constitute a significant minority, and if current population estimates are confirmed, their ranks will swell to 3.3 million people by the year 2040 (U.S. Census Bureau, 1980). The task of providing merely basic care for a population of this size is staggering. Providing a therapeutic environment for the elderly in long-term care will require a substantial change in the focus and orientation of these settings.

Historically, as health care professionals have become more skilled in providing treatment to institutional populations (e.g., the retarded and people with psychiatric problems) the orientation of these institutions has progressed from a predominantly custodial setting to a therapeutic–rehabilitation environment. For these populations, this effort has resulted in a largely successful deinstitutionalization process with former residents often living productive lives in the community at a significantly lower financial cost.

A similar process is gradually evolving in long-term care institutions for the elderly (Barney, 1983). Many elderly are placed in nursing homes due to irreversible degenerative disease processes. For many others, however, degeneration in behavior is a result of the prevailing environmental conditions in the institution and thus, the deficits are reversible, or at least to a degree, preventable. The thesis of this chapter is that the loss of adaptive functioning in many of the institutionalized elderly is not solely a result of biological decline, but to a large extent a result of an environment that sets the occasion for and reinforces ineffective and dependent behavior (Barton, Baltes, & Orzech, 1980).

LOUIS D. BURGIO • University of Pittsburgh School of Medicine, Pittsburgh, Pennsylvania 15213.

The direct care staff is a salient factor in any institutional setting. In geriatric settings the nursing aide maintains the most contact with the patients and has the greatest responsibility for patients' basic care (Hyerstay, 1978; Reynold, 1981). Consequently, if the goal of geriatric long-term care is to progress from a primary concern for maintaining the aged patient, to restoring and optimizing patient adaptive functioning, the role of the nursing aide must undergo a profound change. To achieve this end, efficient training procedures must be developed to teach nursing aides new skills, and management systems must be designed to assure that these skills will be performed and maintained in the natural environment.

In this chapter, I will discuss the current methods of staff training and management in use within geriatric settings. This will be followed by a review of various behavioral staff training and management interventions employed in other institutional settings. Finally, I will discuss a model for applying these procedures with geriatric residents. Prior to discussing these techniques, I will review what is known about this infrequently studied but important group of care providers, and perhaps more importantly, discuss how their behavior affects the adaptive functioning of their elderly patients.

CHARACTERISTICS OF NURSING AIDES

Nursing aides constitute 45% of nursing home personnel, but they deliver up to 90% of patient care (Crawford, Waxman, & Carner, 1983; Dawes, 1981). Although very little research has examined the personal characteristics of this group, the stereotype promulgated in the popular literature is less than favorable (Dawes, 1981; see Mendelson, 1974 or Nader, 1971 for examples). Research conducted by Waxman and his colleagues (Crawford et al., 1983; Waxman, Carner, & Berkenstock, 1984) suggests that the typical aide is female, between 20 and 40 years of age, probably a member of a minority group, and of low socioeconomic status. Most aides reported having a high school diploma or less. None of the nursing aides in Waxman's research reported having any formal career training, although most had attended some form of in-service training.

Almost two-thirds of nursing aides sampled had worked in their current jobs less than 2 years, and turnover rates for these positions have been estimated to fall between 40% to 75% annually (Kraus, 1974; Stryker, 1981). Few studies have examined the reasons for this high level of staff turnover. Contrary to a commonly held assumption by many health care professionals, Crawford et al. (1983) did not find salary to be related to turnover rates. In fact, there was a slight tendency for nursing homes with high turnover to offer better monetary compensation. Finally, some data are available that suggest that nursing aides display numerous misconceptions and negative attitudes about the elderly, have trouble working with their parents, and express difficulty working with supervisors (Gillis, 1973).

These data, although preliminary, suggest that nursing aides are inadequately prepared for the responsibility of providing a therapeutic environment for elderly patients who are not aware how their behavior can affect their patients. When asked, aides themselves overwhelmingly report that they are in need of additional training (Carstensen & Fisher, 1985; Crawford *et al.*, 1973).

OBSERVATIONAL-OPERANT STUDIES OF STAFF BEHAVIOR AND STAFF–PATIENT INTERACTIONS

Research has been conducted that examined nursing aides' natural behavior patterns in the nursing home and the effect of aides' behavior on their patients. Norwich (1980) conducted a study in which the behavior of nursing staff (including nursing aides) was sampled every 5 minutes for 12 hours per day. No details were provided on the observational system, nor were the behavioral categories adequately defined. The data indicate that 64% of nursing staff's time was dedicated to patient activities, 16% was task-oriented activity, 1% was tuition (presumably, instruction giving by staff), and 18% was categorized as "other." Employing more sophisticated observational techniques, Moos, David, Lemke, and Postle (1984) categorized nursing aide behavior as only 24% patient oriented, 35% task oriented, 30% staff oriented, and 10% nonwork. Additional data suggested that aides spent roughly half of their time in areas where patients were present (e.g., the bedroom, hallway, or dining room), and the other half in areas inaccessible to patients (e.g., nurse stations or staff areas).

Baltes, Orzech, Barton, and Lago (1983) specifically designed their study to examine when, where, and how both staff and residents behave in a nursing home. These authors utilized a digital data acquisition system with a reliable, well-defined, and extensive observational code. Their findings, similar to those of Moos *et al.* (1984), indicated that 36% of staff's time was patient oriented, 24% task oriented, 27% staff oriented, and 10% walking. Location data suggest that although 67% of patient's behavior occurred in the bedroom, staff spent only 27% of their time there, preferring the hallway (41%), where the patients spent only 9% of their time.

In summary, although there are considerable discrepancies in the data presented in these studies, the more sophisticated studies (Baltes *et al.*, 1983, Moos *et al.*, 1984) suggest that aides devote roughly equal amounts of time (one-third) with patients, doing tasks, and engaging in nonwork behaviors or interacting with their colleagues. Moreover, a major portion of their day is spent in areas not frequented by their patients.

Baltes and her colleagues have also examined how aides interact with patients and how these interactions may affect patient behavior. Stimulated by an early study by Mikulic (1971), Lester and Baltes (1978) found that staff positive verbal reinforcers more often occurred contingent upon patient dependent behavior, while patient independent behaviors were more often followed by no staff response. These results were replicated when the authors examined interactions during morning care, when they used a more sophisticated observational system (Baltes, Burgess, & Stewart, 1980), and again during morning care with data analyzed with the use of sequential conditional probabilities (Barton, Baltes, & Orzech, 1980).

Finally, the authors' analysis was extended to staff–patient interaction throughout the day, and the observational code was extended beyond self-care activities with the same results (Baltes, Honn, Barton, Orzech, & Lago, 1983).

The observational-operant research conducted by Baltes and her colleagues generally supports the popular view of nursing aides as fulfilling primarily a custodial function within the nursing home, engaging in limited interaction with their patients, and interacting with them in a manner that reinforces dependent behavior.

Although there appears to be a tendency among health care professionals to blame these conditions on the disinterest and poor motivation of the nursing aides, it is undoubtedly true that the nursing aides' performance is to a large extent a function of the training provided to them by their supervisors, and the management techniques used to elicit and maintain appropriate task performance. In this regard, it may be helpful to review the current literature on nursing aide staff training and management in geriatric long-term care.

CURRENT METHODS OF STAFF TRAINING AND MANAGEMENT IN NURSING HOMES

In nongeriatric institutional settings, staff training and management has gained new emphasis, and the methods have increased in sophistication as the settings changed their focus of patient care from custodial activity to a therapeutic training model. As geriatric long-term care gradually evolves from custodial nursing care to a rehabilitation model, more attention will be given to the training and management of nursing aides. Because the role of geriatric long-term care is still evolving, an overwhelming majority of the published reports on nursing aide training has consisted of discussion articles that emphasize to the reader the importance of training nursing aides (Burke, D'Erasmo, & Burger, 1980; Buzzelli-Gibbons, 1981; Campbell & Browning, 1978; Hameister, 1977). The most frequently used method of staff training presented in this literature is didactic verbal and written instruction. Only recently have authors proposed that staff be assessed on their comprehension of the material presented during the training sessions (Almquist and Bates, 1980; Campbell and Browning, 1978; Hameister, 1978).

Some authors have recommended that the tasks presented during training be broken down into objective behavioral goals (Burke et al., 1980; Kilgore and Ralston, 1979) and that feedback and contingent supervisory praise be provided in the natural setting during the initial training period (Kilgore & Ralston, 1979; Reynold, 1981). However, in spite of an early recommendation by Hickey (1974) for the examination of "process variables," there has been an absence of systematic study of methods of staff training in geriatric long-term care.

Some authors have recognized the need for systematic and ongoing monitoring of staff performance and its effect on patient care (Hameister, 1978). Sheridan, Fairchild, and Kaas (1983) have developed a Behavioral Anchored Rating Scale (BARS) for the day-to-day evaluation of individual staff performance. The purpose of the tool is to monitor staff performance and provide the supervisor with an opportunity to praise appropriate performance and to provide guidance for those activities that need improvement. Although the rating scale is anchored by descriptions of specific behaviors, ratings are not based on direct behavioral observations, but on the supervisor's recall or impressions of staff performance.

Researchers have recognized the potential for employing nursing aides as behavior-change agents. Mishara and Kastenbaum (1974) trained nursing aides to use rewards such as wine and cigarettes to increase various appropriate behavior in chronic psychogeriatric patients. Unfor- tunately, no information is provided on the training procedure or whether procedures were used to maintain staff's behavior. Nigl and Jackson (1981) taught nursing aides to use behavior management procedures with psychogeriatric patients. Aides underwent a 4-week training course where they learned to monitor and reinforce patient behavior with tokens. Results indicated that nursing aides were successful in increasing patients' social responses. In a similar study, Sperbeck and Whitbourne (1981) used didactic presentation plus behavioral rehearsal with trainer feedback to teach behavior management procedures to nurses and nursing aides. The effects of training were assessed by changes in patient dependent responses. Three of the four targeted patients decreased dependency and maintained this change at a 6-month follow-up. Again, neither of these latter two studies described formal procedures to maintain staff therapeutic behaviors.

Barrowclough and Fleming (1986a) instructed direct care staff in the use of goal planning with elderly clients in both day-care and long-term care facilities. Staff were taught how to select target behaviors (e.g., increase client mobility, self-care skills), write clear goals and subgoals, develop client training procedures, and graph client progress. The staff-training procedures included demonstrations by the trainer, behavioral rehearsal, and real-life practice in developing treatment goals for the clients. The authors reported good skill acquisition among direct care staff; however, the absence of pretraining data renders their results open to interpretation. Based on their research, the authors have developed and published a training manual for developing goal-planning skills for geriatric direct care workers (Barrowclough & Fleming, 1986b).

Behavioral Staff Training and Management Procedures

Methods of staff training, and the subsequent management of staff behaviors, have been systematically studied, albeit in nongeriatric institutional settings. Although the application of these procedures to geriatric settings needs intensive study, due to the many similarities between the staff and settings, results from studies conducted in psychiatric settings and institutions for the developmentally disabled should be applicable to geriatric long-term care.

Numerous procedures have been used to teach new skills to caregivers. Typically, material is first presented in a classroom setting through a combination of lectures, videotape presentations, handouts, movies, modeling, role playing, reading of articles, group discussion, and homework assignments (Loeber & Weisman,

1975; Whitman, Scibak, & Reid, 1983). All of these procedures in various combinations have been used effectively, but their relative efficacy has been examined infrequently. Gardner (1972) has shown that "principles" are best taught by lectures and discussion and that "skills of intervention" are best taught by role playing. Training manuals are also used with increasing frequency in institutional staff training, but their use also requires further study. One study concluded that highly programmed written materials were not as effective as simple methods of direct instruction when training nonprofessional staff (Laws, Brown, Epstein, & Hocking, 1971).

Since most of these studies were published in the early to mid-1970s, very little staff-training research has been conducted. The reason for this is twofold. First, it was clear that a combination of didactic instruction, trainer modeling, trainer role playing, and performance feedback was sufficient to teach most skills required by caregivers. Second, it was recognized that staff-training endeavors frequently did not result in permanent changes in caregiver performance (Whitman, Scibak, & Reid, 1983). Consequently, since the mid-1970s, researchers have examined procedures for managing caregiver behavior outside of the training settings. Typically in these studies, adequate staff training is either assumed or described briefly in the methods section. Emphasis is then placed on procedures that modify and maintain staff performance on various skills outside of the training setting.

Staff management procedures can be classified as primarily antecedent or contingency management (Whitman, *et al.*, 1983). Antecedent systems focus on setting the occasion for specific staff performance. Contingency management systems set formal contingencies for correct and incorrect staff performances. Many of the more recent studies combine both strategies for changing behavior. Let us examine each method in more detail.

Antecedent Systems

Antecedent procedures are probably the most frequently used systems for changing staff behavior (Reid & Shoemaker, 1985). In its simplest form, an antecedent condition entails a supervisor instructing a staff member that a change in behavior is desired. In practice, two types of antecedent systems have been employed: instructions and modeling.

Instructions

Instructions entail an explanation by the supervisor of precisely how a task should be done. Instructions have been provided verbally (Fielding, Erickson, & Bettin, 1971) and through written presentation (Pommer & Streedbeck, 1974); both methods provide mixed results. Fielding *et al.* (1971) found that instructions that were posted on a chart on the work unit were effective in producing correct patient-escorting behavior, but verbal instruction alone was not effective in reducing staff use of physical guidance. Pommer and Streedbeck (1974) reported that written instructions regarding job duties that were posted in a work station resulted in only temporary increases in job effectiveness. Other investigators have reported minimal change (Green, Willis, Levy, & Bailey 1978), short-lived change (Montegar, Reid, Madsen, & Ewell, 1977), or no change (Quilitch, 1975).

A more detailed form of instructions, termed "increased job structure" (Whitman *et al.*, 1983), entails instructing staff how, when, where, and by whom a task should be done. An example of the procedure is the use of "Duty Cards," which indicate to each staff member what should be done in a certain location and for how long. Sneed and Bible (1979) effectively used this procedure to increase staff interaction with aggressive–disruptive retarded adults. Iwata, Bailey, Brown, Foshee, and Alpern (1976) found an increase in social stimulation activities when staff were assigned a specific activity with a certain resident. In contrast, Seys and Duker (1978) found a similar procedure unsuccessful in changing staff interactions with retarded clients.

Instructions appear to be a necessary component in any staff management program. However, instructions alone, whether verbal or written and regardless of the amount of detail supplied, do not appear to be sufficient to bring about long-term change in staff behavior.

Modeling

Modeling refers to a behavioral demonstration by a trainer of an activity to be engaged in by staff. Modeling is frequently used as one component of a staff–training or management system, but it rarely has been examined as an independent technique (e.g., Quilitch, Miller, McConnell, & Bryant, 1975). Gladstone and Spencer (1977) examined the effects of demonstrating contingent praise statements to staff to be used during toothbrushing training sessions. Data showed that staff increased their rate of verbal praise statements during toothbrushing and also generalized these skills to other personal-care tasks (e.g., face washing). Like instructions, modeling can be used effectively to teach various skills to caregivers. In most cases, for staff to maintain these skills in the natural setting, it is necessary to devise a system of consequences. In the next section, I will discuss a variety of systematically applied consequences for staff behavior.

Contingency Management Procedures

Contingency management procedures involve systematic monitoring of staff performance and the provision of consistent consequences for this performance. Various consequences have been used, from simple supervisor feedback, to money reinforcers, to multicomponent management packages that include a combination of contingent events. Each of these will be examined next.

Feedback Procedures

In its most basic form, feedback refers to information provided by supervisory personnel regarding a staff member's performance. It usually includes an evalua-tive component. Feedback has been provided in both verbal and written form, delivered publicly or privately. Verbal feedback has usually been examined in terms of supervisory praise statements used contingently upon staff performance. Montegar *et al.* (1977) used verbal approval by the ward supervisor to increase staff interaction with retarded residents. A number of studies in both retardation and psychiatric settings have used nonevaluative verbal feedback as one component of a management package (Panyan, Boozer, & Morris, 1970; Shoemaker & Reid, 1980). It has rarely been examined as an independent procedure.

One comparative study has been conducted to assess the relative efficacy of evaluative and nonevaluative verbal feedback procedures used during attendants' training of retarded residents (Brown, Willis, & Reid, 1981). Nonevaluative verbal feedback consisted of descriptive comments provided by a supervisor about a staff person's performance. Evaluative verbal feedback entailed praise statements for appropriate staff performance. Results indicated that nonevaluative verbal feedback decreased nonwork-related behaviors (e.g., watching T.V.), but verbal praise was necessary to increase appropriate behaviors such as staff interaction with residents.

Written private feedback in the form of a memo has been used. Repp and Deitz (1979) sent memos to individual staff members regarding their performance and promptness in completing administrative paperwork. Feedback was provided regarding the number of forms completed late and the number of forms completed appropriately. Improvement was indicated on both measures.

Publicly posted feedback refers to information on staff performance provided in a written manner and made visible to other staff members in the work station. A number of studies have suggested the effectiveness of this procedure (e.g., Greene *et al.*, 1978, Quilitch, 1975), although there is disagreement over the reasons for its effectiveness (e.g., peer competition, supervisor's positive or negative attention).

Quilitch (1975) used publicly posted feedback and increased job structure to increase staff involvement of residents in recreational activities. Feedback consisted of posting in the staff's office the number of residents active and the staff member responsible for patient involvement. Greene *et al.* (1978) posted the percentages of residents who were seen participating in toileting and mobility programs run by staff. Feedback was given on the number of patients involved in these activities and the staff person responsible. Increases were seen in both staff-training activity and resident-targeted behavior.

Performance feedback procedures, particularly publicly posted feedback, are probably the most potent of the staff management procedures that we have examined. However, many research questions remain. For example, what is the relative efficacy of private and public feedback? Is it necessary to publicly post feedback in the work station, or would a brief presentation in a staff meeting be sufficient? Finally, are supervisory feedback procedures practical for long-term maintenance of staff behavior?

Only a few studies to date have examined the use of a performance-based lottery (Iwata *et al.*, 1976; Patterson, Griffen, & Panyan, 1976; Shoemaker & Reid, 1980). The most systematic study was conducted by Iwata and his colleagues (1976). In this study a supervisor observed staff behavior and a sample of resident behaviors. Staff whose performance met a predetermined criterion, as indicated by the data collected by supervisors, became eligible for a lottery drawing. If a staff person's name was drawn from the lottery, the winner could rearrange his work schedule to have more days off at preferred times. Reliable improvements were found in both staff behavior and resident care. Iwata *et al.* (1976) have argued that performance-based lotteries are cost-effective systems of management because the criteria for reinforcement are appropriate performance plus the possibility of winning the lottery. Researchers need to study these procedures more fully. Specifically, they need to ask questions about long-term effectiveness and acceptability by workers' unions. Although union response to staff management procedures can be problematic, as long as workers have equal access to reinforcers, and the criteria for obtaining the reinforcers are unambiguous, unions rarely challenge these procedures.

Group Contingencies

All of the systems described above involve contingencies applied to individual staff member performance. Group contingencies refer to the requirement that the performance of a group of staff members on a unit meet a predetermined criterion for individuals in the group to receive a consequence. For example, Reid, Schuh-Wear, and Brannon (1978) required staff on each of six work shifts to reduce and maintain the total number of staff absences below a certain number in order to change their work schedule to more days off on weekends. The system resulted in reductions in the number of absences in five of the six work shifts. Although possibly confounded with a public-posting procedure, their results suggest the usefulness of a group contingency to manage institutional staff behavior. As with many of the aforementioned procedures, researchers need to examine methods of insuring the cooperation of the unions with this type of system.

Participative Management

Other researchers have studied the self-management components of participative management as they were utilized in some multifaceted programs (Korabek, Reid, & Ivancic, 1981; Seys & Duker, 1978). Burg, Reid, and Lattimore (1979) combined a staff self-monitoring and recording procedure with a supervisory monitoring system for increasing staff interaction with retarded clients. Staff recorded their own behavior by moving stickers on a small card every time he or she interacted with a resident. In addition, a supervisor monitored the same behavior at 15-minute intervals. All staff significantly increased their rate of interaction with the residents. A few studies have also examined the use of self-monitoring procedures in staff management as a component of a multifaceted program (Korabek *et al.*, 1981; Patterson *et al.*, 1976; Seys & Duker, 1978; Welch, Ludwig, Radiker, & Krapfl, 1973), and one study included self-standard setting, also within a larger system (Seys & Duker, 1978). All of these programs were successful, although the designs of the studies do not allow conclusions regarding the contribution of the self-management components.

Participative or self-management procedures place the overt control of at least part of management procedure in the hands of direct care staff. Staff participates in the development of the goal for performance, the monitoring of their own behavior,

and even, to some extent, the reinforcement process. In recent years these procedures have received increasing emphasis from researchers. Burgio, Whitman, and
Reid (1983) proposed that staff would be more receptive to these procedures and
that union resistance would be minimal. Also, since there is less supervisory
involvement from the beginning, the use of these procedures may more likely
maintain staff change in situations where the supervisor is not present. Finally, they
suggested that cross-task generalization would be more likely to occur, due to the
reduced dependence on external stimuli like the presence of the supervisor.

Burgio, Whitman, and Reid (1983) developed a procedure that included staff
participation with every component of the staff management system. The goal of
the study was to increase the rate of staff–resident interaction during unscheduled
time in a residential facility for developmentally delayed children. Staff were asked
to reach a consensus on the goal number of interactions with residents that would
be appropriate for an established period of unscheduled time. Second, wrist-held
response counters were dispensed to all staff members, who were requested to
record each occurrence of their interactions with a resident. Third, immediately
after the recording period, staff entered the number of interactions onto a graph so
that they could examine their performance in relation to the predetermined standard. Finally, immediately following the graphing of data, they completed a brief
"self-reinforcement rating form" on which they evaluated their performance. At no
time did the supervisor monitor or evaluate staff performance, but research staff
did monitor it for data collection purposes. Results indicated an increase in staff–
resident interactions comparable to that obtained in more traditional externally
controlled procedures. These results were maintained at a 6-week follow-up. A
survey of staff participating in the project suggested that they considered the
procedures to be effective and preferable to descriptions of more traditional staff
management procedures.

Research on the comparative efficacy of participative and nonparticipative
management procedures is needed. The issues of cross-skill generalization as well
as long-term maintenance of the procedures also must be examined. Finally,
researchers should explore the reasons for the significant individual differences
often found with self-management procedures. Self-management may be effective
with only certain types of staff or for changing certain behaviors, and not successful
with other behaviors.

Multicomponent Systems

Most recent staff management research focuses on developing systems that
combine many of the most effective treatment components described above. The
most comprehensive systems have been developed by Reid and his colleagues
(Ivancic, Reid, Iwata, Faw, & Page, 1981; Korabek *et al.*, 1981). Ivancic *et al.* (1981)
combined in-service training (i.e., instructions, modeling, and practice by staff)
with various prompting and feedback procedures. The prompting procedures
consisted of publicly posted instruction, intermittent verbal instruction, and modeling. Feedback consisted of verbal feedback and praise and publicly posted written feedback. The researchers found that this system effectively increased four

types of staff language interactions with profoundly retarded, multihandicapped children. Only a few minutes of supervision time each day were required to maintain the program.

Korabek *et al.* (1981) developed a similar system to improve feeding proficiency of direct care staff, but they added a self-recording component to the system. Self-recording consisted of staff marking the number of bites of food they fed to the children. As in the Ivancic study, results suggested that the procedure was both effective and time efficient.

A MODEL FOR TRAINING AND MANAGEMENT OF NURSING AIDES IN GERIATRIC LONG-TERM CARE FACILITIES

As mentioned above, there is a dearth of systematic staff-training and management research in geriatric long-term care facilities. This should come as no surprise, since the movement to reorient these institutions to the training–rehabilitation model is relatively recent. Most of the data I have reviewed in this chapter have been gleaned from projects conducted in facilities for the developmentally delayed and, to a lesser extent, psychiatric facilities. How applicable are these procedures to geriatric settings? Although modifications are necessary when transferring systems and procedures to a new setting, I believe that many of the procedures discussed can be used effectively in geriatric long-term care facilities (e.g., see the discussion of Barrowclough and Fleming, 1986a). The similarities of these institutional settings and the staff they employ make it possible to assert that claim. Institutional environments have a profound effect on patients' independent behaviors and self-esteem, regardless of whether the patient is mentally retarded, emotionally disturbed, or elderly. Across institutional environments, it is also true that workers at the level of direct care and nursing assistants have the most frequent and salient contact with patients, and thus offer the most potential for affecting patient behavior in either a beneficial or detrimental manner.

Nursing aides are usually moderately to poorly educated, poorly motivated, and often disenfranchised from their patients' treatment plan. If the training–rehabilitation model is adopted into geriatric long-term care facilities, it is crucial that state-of-the-art training procedures be employed to upgrade their skills. Moreover, in order to maintain their performance in the applied setting and increase their motivation, systematic management procedures must be adopted. In the remainder of this chapter, I will offer some suggestions for conducting staff training and management in geriatric long-term care facilities.

Initial Skill Training

A necessary, although not sufficient, condition for training staff to perform patient-related tasks is in-service training. Two questions must be addressed in this regard: which training techniques are most effective and how should the efficiency of the training techniques be assessed? The most effective training procedures include: didactic instruction, presented both verbally and in a written format; modeling of the procedure by the trainer (either with a patient or via videotape); role playing of the procedure by the trainees; and immediate performance feedback by the trainer.

Most programs that assess the outcome of their training programs do so by quizzing trainees on their knowledge of the procedure with a paper-and-pencil test. These tests assess knowledge of the procedures and are necessary, but they do not demonstrate that the trainee can perform the required skill. Consequently, the second step in the assessment phase should include a checklist assessment of skill performance in an analogue situation. The analogue situation (often the same classroom where the in-service training was conducted) allows the trainer to provide immediate corrective feedback and praise. Also, incorrect performance of the skill provides no negative consequence for the patient. The final step is the assessment of the trainee's skill performance in the natural setting. This is a crucial though often overlooked step. Performance in an analogue setting offers only limited predictive information of staff performance on the living units. These assessments should be conducted immediately following the in-service training and at regular intervals thereafter. If staff perform poorly during these assessments, they should be given remedial in-service training.

Maintenance of Previously Trained Skills with Staff Management Procedures

A number of creative management procedures have proved effective in maintaining staff performance in the natural setting. Most of these programs share three components:

1. *Antecedent instruction*. Although the programs vary in the amount of emphasis placed on antecedent procedures, all provide the staff at least a detailed description of the target behavior.
2. *Monitoring of behavior*. The targeted staff behaviors are monitored, and data are collected on the performance. Monitoring can be conducted frequently, or less frequently if the schedule of monitoring is unpredictable. Data collection is often conducted by supervisory staff.
3. *Application of consequences*. Consistent rewards should be made contingent upon appropriate staff performance. A system of contingent supervisory feedback and praise has been shown to be very effective in maintaining staff behavior change. Only minimal amounts of supervisory time are required, thus increasing the probability of long-term maintenance of the program.

A model of "behavioral supervision," which is similar to the one proposed here, has been discussed by Reid and Shoemaker (1983) for use in facilities for the developmentally disabled. Reid and his colleagues have evaluated applications of the model and have found it effective in reducing absences from work (Shoemaker

& Reid, 1980), increasing training sessions provided to patients (Ivancic *et al.*, 1981), and improving health and basic-care responsibilities of staff (Korabek *et al.*, 1981). It is important that researchers study applications of this model in geriatric long-term care programs.

Although data suggest that "behavioral supervision" is often effective in maintaining staff behavior, it may occasionally be necessary to add corrective procedures to the system. This may present difficulty since many supervisors understandably find it distasteful. Also, unions have strict regulations for the utilization of corrective procedures by management. The procedure developed by unions and management in many facilities consists of the stepwise delivery of official verbal correction of "counseling," written reprimands placed in the employee's file, suspension without pay, and finally dismissal. For employees who do not respond to positive management procedures, the addition of corrective procedures should suffice. Unfortunately, although data are not available on these procedures, anecdotal reports suggest that they are rarely applied consistently. Supervisors complain that staff often "grieve" (i.e., appeal) the application of the process. The grievance process is very time consuming, and allegedly negligent employees are often successful in their appeals. However, the frequent absence of clear behavioral goals and the lack of a coherent data collection system for staff behavior make the assessment of culpability difficult. If clear guidelines and monitoring systems were commonly available to staff, it is likely that disciplinary procedures would be unnecessary.

In summary, I have discussed the relative absence of systematic staff-training and management research in geriatric long-term care settings. I presented data that attest to the impact nursing aides have on the daily lives of institutionalized patients and the potential therapeutic role they can play. A number of training and management procedures were presented, most of which were conducted in long-term care facilities for the developmentally disabled or in psychiatric facilities. I proposed that with some modifications, many of the procedures can be applied in geriatric long-term care facilities, and I presented a model for staff training and management. In nongeriatric institutional settings, behavioral psychologists are usually responsible for the training and management activities of direct care workers. In contrast, geriatric long-term care facilities employ nursing aides who are supervised by professional nurses. Consequently, our primary goal should be to demonstrate the efficacy and practicality of these procedures to nursing supervisors and administrators. Close collaboration between behavioral psychologists and nurses is required if we are to transfer this important technology to nursing homes. Ultimately, our behavioral procedures need to be integrated into the nursing structure and orientation.

If nursing aides are not adequately performing their duties, the responsibility ultimately rests with their supervisors. Consequently, it is our responsibility, both to the staff and to the patients they influence, to provide the best training and management systems available.

ACKNOWLEDGMENTS

Thanks are due to Dr. Bernard T. Engel for his helpful comments.

References

Almquist, E., & Bates, D. (1980). Training program for nursing assistants and LPNs in nursing homes. *Journal of Gerontological Nursing, 6*(1), 622–627.

Baltes, M. M., Burgess, R. L., & Stewart, R. B. (1980). Independence and dependence in self-care behavior in nursing home residents: An operant-observational study. *International Journal of Behavioral Development, 3*, 489–500.

Baltes, M. M., Honn, S., Barton, E. M., Orzech, M., & Lago, D. (1983). On the social ecology of dependence and independence in elderly nursing home residents: A replication and extension. *Journal of Gerontology, 38*, 556–564.

Baltes, M. M., Orzech, M. J., Barton, E. M., & Lago, D. (1983). The Microecology of residents and staff: Behavioral mapping in a nursing home. *Zeitschrift fur Gerontologie, 16*, 18–26.

Barney, J. L. (1983). A new perspective on nurses' aide training. *Geriatric Nursing*, January/February, 44–48.

Barrowclough, C., & Fleming, I. (1986a). Training direct care staff in goal planning with elderly people. *Behavioural Psychotherapy, 14*, 192–209.

Barrowclough, C., & Fleming, I. (1986b). *Goal planning with elderly people.* Manchester: Manchester University Press.

Barton, E. M., Baltes, M. M., & Orzeck, M. J. (1980). Etiology of dependency in older nursing home residents during morning care: The role of staff behavior. *Journal of Personality and Social Psychology, 38*, 423–431.

Brown, K. M., Willis, B. S., & Reid, D. H. (1981). Differential effects of supervisor verbal feedback and feedback plus approval on institutional staff performance. *Journal of Organizational Behavior Management, 3*, 57–68.

Burg, M. M., Reid, D. H., & Lattimore, J. (1979). Use of a self-recording and supervision program to change institutional staff behavior. *Journal of Applied Behavior Analysis, 12*, 363–375.

Burgio, L. D., Whitman, T. L., & Reid, D. H. (1983). A participative management approach for improving direct-care staff performance in an institutional setting. *Journal of Applied Behavior Analysis, 16*, 37–53.

Burke, R. E., D'Erasmo, M. D., & Burger, S. E. (1980, September). Research brief: Training geriatric nursing assistance—A solution. *The Journal of Long-Term Care Administration*, pp. 37–41.

Buzzelli-Gibbons, K. (1981, September/October). Formal training program for nurses' aides. *Nursing Homes*, pp. 2–3.

Campbell, M. E., & Browning, E. M. (1978). Nursing assistants: An untapped resource in providing quality care to the elderly. *Journal of Gerontological Nursing, 4*, 18–19.

Carstensen, L. L., & Fisher, J. E. (1985). *Mental health needs of the elderly in nursing homes: Staff and resident perspectives.* Unpublished manuscript, Indiana University at Bloomington.

Crawford, S. A., Waxman, H. M., & Carner, E. A. (1983). Using research to plan nurses' aide training. *American Health Care Association Journal*, January, 59–61.

Dawes, P. L. (1981). The nurses aide and the team approach in the nursing home. *Journal of Geriatric Psychiatry, 14*, 265–276.

Fielding, L. T., Erickson, E., & Bettin, B. (1971). Modification of staff behavior: A brief note. *Behavior Therapy, 2*, 550–553.

Gardner, J. M. (1972). Teaching behavior modifications to non-professionals. *Journal of Applied Behavior Analysis, 5*, 517–521.

Gillis, M. (1973). Attitude of nursing home personnel toward the aged. *Nursing Research, 22*, 517–520.

Gladstone, B. W., & Spencer, C. J. (1977). The effects of modeling on the contingent praise of mental counsellors. *Journal of Applied Behavior Analysis, 10*, 75–84.

Greene, B. F., Willis, B. S., Levy, R., & Bailey, J. S. (1978). Measuring client gains from staff-implemented programs. *Journal of Applied Behavior Analysis, 11*, 395–412.

Hameister, D. R. (1977). A design of inservice education for nurses' aides in a nursing home setting. *The Journal of Continuing Education in Nursing, 8*(2), 6–12.

Hameister, D. R. (1978, Winter). Examining relationships between educational institutions and in-service training for nurses' aides. *Long-term Care and Health Services Administration*, pp. 276–286.

Hickey, T. (1974). In-service training in gerontology: Toward the design of an effective educational process. *The Gerontologist, 14*, 57–64.

Hyerstay, B. J. (1978). The political and economic implications of training nursing home aides. *Journal of Nursing Administration*, June, 3, 22–24.

Ivancic, M. T., Reid, D. H., Iwata, B. A., Faw, G. D., & Page, T. J. (1981). Evaluating a supervision program for developing and maintaining therapeutic staff–resident interactions during institutional care routines. *Journal of Applied Behavior Analysis*, 14, 95–107.

Iwata, B. A., Bailey, J. S., Brown, K. M., Foshee, T. J., & Alpern, M. (1976). A performance-based lottery to improve residential care and training by institutional staff. *Journal of Applied Behavior Analysis*, 9, 417–431.

Kilgore, M. A., & Ralston, C. M. (1979, September). Better hygiene for elderly patients. *Texas Nursing*, pp. 6–7.

Korabek, C. A., Reid, D. H., & Ivancic, M. T. (1981). Improving needed food intake of profoundly handicapped children through effective supervision of institutional staff. *Applied Research in Mental Retardation*, 2, 69–88.

Kraus, E. A. (1974). Study reveals reasons for personnel turnover rates. *Modern Nursing Home*, 11, 48–50.

Laws, D. R., Brown, R. A., Epstein, J., & Hocking, N. (1971). Reduction of inappropriate social behavior in disturbed children by an untrained para-professional therapist. *Behavior Therapy*, 2, 519–533.

Lester, P. B., & Baltes, M. M. (1978). Functional interdependence of the social environment and the behavior of the institutionalized aged. *Journal of Gerontological Nursing*, 4, 23–27.

Loeber, R., & Weisman, R. G. (1975). Contingencies of therapist and trainer performance: A review. *Psychological Bulletin*, 82, 660–688.

Mendelson, M. A. (1974). *Tender loving greed*. New York: Vintage Books.

Mikulic, M. (1971). Reinforcement of independent and dependent patient behaviors of nursing personnel: An exploratory study. *Nursing Research*, 20, 162–169.

Mishara, B. L., & Kastenbaum, R. (1974). Wine in the treatment of long-term geriatric patients in mental institutions. *Journal of the American Geriatrics Society*, 22, 88–94.

Montegar, C. A., Reid, D. H., Madsen, C. H., & Ewell, M. D. (1977). Increasing institutional staff-to-resident interactions through in-service training and supervisor approval. *Behavior Therapy*, 8, 533–540.

Moos, R. H., David, T. S., Lemke, S., & Postle, E. (1984). Coping with an intra-institutional relocation: Change in resident and staff behavior patterns. *The Gerontologist*, 24, 495–502.

Nader, R. (1971). *Old age: The last segregation*. New York: Grossman.

Nigl, A. J., & Jackson, B. (1981). A behavior management program to increase social responses in psychogeriatric patients. *Journal of the American Geriatrics Society*, 29, 92–95.

Norwich, H. S. (1980, February 14). A study of nursing care in geriatric hospitals. *Nursing Times*, pp. 292–295.

Panyan, M., Boozer, H., Morris, N. (1970). Feedback to attendants as a reinforcer for applying operant techniques. *Journal of Applied Behavior Analysis*, 3, 1–4.

Patterson, E. T., Griffin, J. C., & Panyan, M. C. (1976). Incentive maintenance of self-help skill training programs for nonprofessional personnel. *Journal of Behavior Therapy and Experimental Psychiatry*, 7, 249–253.

Pommer, D. A., & Streedbeck, D. (1974). Motivating staff performance in an operant learning program for children. *Journal of Applied Behavior Analysis*, 7, 217–221.

Quilitch, H. R. (1975). A comparison of three staff-management procedures. *Journal of Applied Behavior Analysis*, 8, 59–66.

Quilitch, H. R., Miller, S. M., McConnell, M. A., & Bryant, S. (1975). Teaching personnel to implement behavioral programs. *Educational Technology*, 27–31.

Reid, D. H., & Shoemaker, J. (1985). Behavioral supervision: Method of improving institutional staff performance. In W. P. Christian, G. T. Hannah, & T. J. Glahn (Eds.), *Programming effective human service: strategies for institutional change and client transition* (pp. 36–61). Englewood Cliffs, NJ: Prentice-Hall.

Reid, D. H., Schuh-Wear, C. L., & Brannon, M. E. (1978). Use of a group contingency to decrease staff absenteeism in a state institution. *Behavior Modification*, 2, 251–266.

Repp, A. C., & Deitz, D. E. D. (1979). Improving administrative-related staff behaviors at a state institution. *Mental Retardation*, 17, 185–192.

Reynold, S. D. (1981, June). Training the primary caregiver. *Contemporary Administrator*, p. 21.

Seys, D. M., & Duker, P. C. (1978). Improving residential care for the retarded by differential reinforcement of high rates of ward-staff behaviors. *Behavioural Analysis and Modification, 2,* 203–210.

Sheridan, J. E., Fairchild, T. J., and Kaas, M. (1983). Assessing the job performance of nursing home staff. *Nursing Research, 21*(2), 102–107.

Shoemaker, J., & Reid, D. H. (1980). Decreasing chronic absenteeism among institutional staff: Effects of a low cost attendance program. *Journal of Organizational Behavior Management, 2,* 317–328.

Sneed, T. J., & Bible, G. H. (1979). An administrative procedure for improving staff performance in an institutional setting for retarded persons. *Mental Retardation, 2,* 92–94.

Sperbeck, D. J., and Whitbourne, S. K. (1981). Dependency in the institutional setting: A behavioral training program for geriatric staff. *The Gerontologist, 21,* 268–275.

Stryker, R. (1981). *How to reduce employee turnover in nursing homes.* Springfield, IL: Charles C. Thomas.

U.S. Census Bureau (1980). *Projections of the population of the United States by age, sex, and race: 1983–2080.* Current Population Reports. Population Estimates and Projections, Series p25, #952. Bethesda, MD: Author.

Waxman, H. M., Carner, E. A., & Berkenstock, G. (1984). Job turnover and job satisfaction among nursing home aides. *The Gerontologist, 24,* 503–509.

Welch, W. V., Ludwig, C., Radiker, J. E., & Krapfl, J. E. (1973). Effects of feedback on daily completion of behavior modification projects. *Mental Retardation, 11,* 24–26.

Whitman, T. L., Scibak, J. W., & Reid, D. H. (1983). *Behavior modification with the severely and profoundly retarded: Research and application.* New York: Academic Press.

20

Behavioral Programs for Families of Dependent Elderly

Judy M. Zarit and Steven H. Zarit

Introduction: Dementia and Family Care

In the past few years, there has been increased public awareness of Alzheimer's disease and other disabling conditions of later life, including the sometimes extreme stresses that these problems create for family caregivers. The presence of involved family members often makes the difference between whether or not an elder is institutionalized, but caregiving can also take its toll, affecting the social, physical, or mental well-being of family members. All too frequently, however, the family is given little assistance or training to help reduce the burdens associated with their involvement, or to improve management of everyday tasks and problems caused by the elder's disability. In this chapter the authors summarize the problem of chronic disability in old age as it affects families, discuss assessment issues, and outline a treatment strategy to alleviate some of the stress that often accompanies active caregiving. Of particular importance in working with families of older persons are issues of identifying the client and clarifying the initial request, which are often neglected in the treatment literature. Recent research suggests that behavior management techniques used in the context of the family system can be effective in reducing the sense of burden and distress of caring for a frail older person, whether he or she lives in the community or in a nursing home or other institution. The implementation of these approaches for problems of elders and their families will be emphasized.

We are in a time of intense social change precipitated by a crisis in the economics of medical care. The crisis began with double-digit inflation in the late 1970s and culminated in current efforts to control medical costs by the use of diagnostically related groups (DRGs). The DRGs impose limits on the amount Medicare will reimburse hospitals for a particular diagnosis. During the years since

Judy M. Zarit • Child, Adult, and Family Psychological Center, State College, Pennsylvania 16801. Steven H. Zarit • Department of Individual and Family Studies, Pennsylvania State University, University Park, Pennsylvania 16803.

their imposition in 1984, their effect has been a reduction in the length of hospital stays and discharging of patients with greater medical needs. Home health agencies have proliferated, but the amount, types, and duration of services reimbursed under Medicare and Medicaid are limited, especially for more chronic, long-term problems. Most expenses likely to be incurred in long-term care for disabling and degenerative conditions are not eligible for reimbursement.

The problems of Medicare coverage are compounded by the rapid growth of the older population, especially the oldest old over age 80, who are most in need of service, and the orientation of Medicare toward acute-care services. More people than ever before are living to old age. While 4% of the population was over 65 in 1900, the current figure is 11%, and projections are for the elderly to increase to 17% early in the next century. Furthermore, the fastest growing age group in the population is people over 75, who have been termed the "oldest old" (Neugarten, 1975), in part because they tend to have higher rates of physical disabilities. While most older persons are able to live independent lives, many have chronic, disabling conditions. It is estimated that 45% of those over 64 have some limitation on activities due to a chronic illness, and 39% have major limitations (U.S. Bureau of the Census, 1982). While chronic conditions predominate in later life, Medicare coverage is basically insurance for acute-care problems. Emphasis is on reimbursement of physicians, tests, and hospitals. Psychosocial and rehabilitative approaches that might help patients and families with management of long-term disabilities are typically not reimbursed.

The types of disabilities affecting the old are quite varied. Heart disease, cancer, cerebrovascular disease, and respiratory disease are the most prevalent diseases causing impairment. Arthritis, rheumatism, and sensory impairments (vision and hearing) lead to limiting activities of over 25% of older adults (Brotman, 1982; Wilder, 1971). An additional 5–7% of those over 65 suffer from some kind of senile dementia (Mortimer, Schuman, & French, 1981). The senile dementias include Alzheimer's disease, multi-infarct dementia (a series of small strokes), and a number of less common diseases with similar symptoms (see Cummings & Benson, 1983). All of these disorders are pathological processes whose prevalence increases with advancing age, and they complicate normal age changes. It should be noted that normal age changes in physical systems, as well as in cognition and personality, do not lead to disability without a coexisting pathological process.

CARE IN A FAMILY CONTEXT

When an older person develops a chronic disability, family members often assume much of the responsibility for assistance. Rather than fading away, as some social scientists predicted at mid-century, the modified extended family has become the norm. Elders maintain their residence separate from children, but strong family ties continue, as evidenced by patterns of interaction and mutual assistance between generations (Shanas, 1979a). The number of three-generation families is a distinct minority, estimated at 8 out of every 100 households (Troll, Miller, & Atchley, 1979). Older people typically move into a child's home only when they are poor, so sick that they cannot care for themselves, or in some cases, when a spouse has died. The majority of parent–adult-child households occur when an adult child (usually a daughter) moves into the parent's home.

While the three-generation household is fairly rare, providing substantial assistance to ill or dependent parents is not. Shanas (1979b) found that the main source of help to homebound elderly is a family member. The most frequent provider is a spouse, followed in numbers by children. Other relatives, siblings in particular, play a role mainly when the older person has no children or spouse. Care may be provided to the elder's separate household, or the elder may join the household of a daughter or other relative. Except for those husbands who are caregivers, most are women. Compared to the family's role, social services contribute a small amount of home help to homebound elderly (Stone, Cafferata, & Sangl, 1987).

Frequently, caregivers have health or other limitations that make carrying out of their responsibilities difficult. Many caregivers are themselves older, including spouses and some daughters. Given increases in life expectancies, it is becoming increasingly common for daughters in their 60s to be caring for parents in their 80s. Among younger caregivers, a significant minority have obligations from family and work, which compete with their responsibilities to an elder (Stone *et al.*, 1987).

When families take on the care of a relative, they frequently find it stressful, time-consuming, and disruptive of personal and family life. Recent studies have emphasized that home care results in decreased physical or emotional well-being, diminished participation in work or social activities, increased problems in the caregiver's marital and family relationships, as well as financial costs (Adams, Caston, & Danis, 1979; Brody, 1985; Cantor, 1983; Fitting, Rabins, Lucas, & Eastham, 1986; George & Gwyther, 1986; Gilhooly, 1984; Grad & Sainsbury, 1963, 1968; Morycz, 1980, 1985; Poulshock & Deimling, 1984; Rabins, Mace, & Lucas, 1982; Sainsbury & Grad de Alarcon, 1970; Zarit, Reever, & Bach-Peterson, 1980; Zarit, Todd, & Zarit, 1986). Studies have posited that the breakdown of family supports is linked to the institutionalization of the impaired elder (Lowenthal, Berkman, & Associates, 1967; Ross & Kedward, 1977). Lowenthal *et al.* (1967) reported that institutionalization occurs in a majority of cases when there are changes in a caregiver's ability to provide assistance, rather than as the result of a worsening of the older person's physical or mental condition. They found that caregivers become physically, emotionally, or financially exhausted in their role. Family support is also critical in determining the length of stay in an institution (Bergmann, Foster, Justice & Mathews, 1979). Early intervention with families that relieves their burden before it becomes excessive has been cited as a crucial part of a program that maintains mentally and physically disabled older people at home (Macmillan, 1968).

An obvious problem for families is that of troublesome or disturbing behavior. In a study by Sanford (1975), a sample of caregivers, of whom 62% had a relative with a diagnosis of senile dementia, rated their tolerance for various behaviors. Sleep disturbance was the most difficult to tolerate. Restriction of the caregiver's social life, especially being unable to leave the home for long periods of time, was another factor that was cited often. In another study, Sainsbury and Gran de Alarcon (1970) found that families were troubled most when the patient engaged in potentially dangerous behavior, acted oddly, or was restless, troublesome at night, or uncooperative (see also Rabins *et al.*, 1982). Birkel (1987) compared caregivers of elders with cognitive impairment to those assisting physically disabled but mentally alert individuals, and found the amount of stress to be much greater among the mentally impaired group. Although adaptation to problems associated with dementia may generally be more problematic, there can be considerable variability. The authors have found, for example, that the frequency of problem behaviors was less important than how well a particular caregiver could tolerate the problem when it occurred (Zarit, 1982; Zarit *et al.*, 1986).

There is not a simple, direct relationship between problem behaviors and burden. Zarit *et al.* (1980) surveyed caregivers of senile dementia patients in the community and found that degree of impairment or frequency of problem behaviors were not as significant a predictor of burden as was the amount of social interaction with other family members. Caregivers who reported more interaction were experiencing lower feelings of burden. Further, whether the caregiver is a husband, wife, or adult child is an important factor in the amount of burden experienced. Brody (1985) and Lowenthal and Robinson (1976) have speculated that burden falls hardest on middle-aged daughters, who are caught between responsibilities to their own growing children and their aging parents. Hoenig and Hamilton (1969) found subjective burden to be greater among spouses than children, however, a finding replicated by Reever and Bach-Peterson (1979), and by Anthony-Bergstone, Zarit, and Gatz (1988).

Whether the caregiving spouse is a husband or wife may also make a difference. In a community-dwelling sample of spouses caring for a dementia patient, Zarit (1982) found that wives expressed more burden than husbands on the Burden Interview (Zarit *et al.*, 1980), and they endorsed more psychiatric symptoms on the Brief Symptom Inventory (Derogatis & Spencer, 1982). Husbands in this study used significantly more paid helpers and community services than wives, a factor that may have contributed to lower reported burden and psychological distress.

There are a number of other factors that may mediate feelings of burden. Particularly in dementias, personality change may contribute to the family's sense of burden. In Alzheimer's disease and in other dementias, personality change can occur relatively early in the disease, including exaggerations of premorbid characteristics and disinhibitions or release of behaviors. As a result, family may perceive the elder as a different person. As dementias progress, at least some families perceive the death of "personality." How often this perception occurs or its impact on caregiving has not been studied systematically. Another determinant of current stress is the quality of the relationship between caregiver and patient. The better the quality before the illness, the less burden is reported by the caregiver (Zarit, 1982). Clinical examples suggest that another critical factor is whether or not the patient continues to provide positive feedback or gratification to the caregiver. The presence of positive experiences or other recognition of the caregiver's efforts lessens feelings of strain (Zarit & Zarit, 1982).

AGISM AND INSTITUTIONALISM: HOW WE COMPOUND THE DISABILITIES OF ELDERS AND BURDENS OF FAMILIES

There is a paradoxical attitude in society's approach to disabled elderly. On the one hand, it is generally accepted that institutionalization of elders should be avoided, because the home environment can generally provide more stimulation and personal care. Concern about the costs of nursing home care both on the part of the family and government, which absorbs that cost through Medicaid if an older person's financial resources are depleted, also contributes to attitudes favoring community care. At the same time, however, much of the care older people receive has a bias toward institutionalization.

One aspect of this bias is the generally nihilistic attitude many health care providers hold toward the elderly (Kahn, 1975). All too often, no assessment or treatment is made to determine if some elements of a condition are potentially reversible. This omission is especially likely in the investigation of behavioral or social interventions that might be used as part of an overall treatment plan for remediating losses. When a child or younger adult becomes disabled, either through accident or disease, it is certain that a rehabilitation program will be planned and implemented. With older adults, rehabilitation potential is often doubted by professionals and frequently aggressive rehabilitative services are not offered (Albert & Zarit, 1977). As noted earlier, Medicare coverage only provides inconsistent coverage of specifically nonmedical services.

To cite an example of the effects of this approach, a 78-year-old man was brought by his family to a counseling center for older persons for an evaluation. The history they provided indicated he had suffered obvious symptoms of stroke during a trip abroad. After returning home in a wheelchair, the patient was evaluated by his family physician, who diagnosed a stroke, based on the presence of characteristic neurological symptoms. He prescribed medication and diet to prevent future strokes, but his advice to the wife was simply to provide protective custodial care. He did not suggest speech therapy for his aphasia or physical therapy to improve his physical mobility. Especially important, there was no discussion about the importance of exercise to maintain strength and mobility. Consequently, although the patient recovered some of his speech, he became wheelchair bound, with muscle wasting from lack of exercise.

Another dimension of this problem is that there is not always consistent help available to assist families with the stresses of caregiving. Respite services for caregivers to allow them to continue to care for the chronically ill older person are now beginning to appear in many communities. These include community adult day care, respite workers who go into the home, homemaker services, as well as rehabilitation therapists who will make home visits. As was noted above, however, only a small percentage of caregiving families utilize formal services. Costs, availability, and sometimes the quality of services available are barriers to greater utilization.

Contributing to the problems of families is the lack of integration of health care and social services. Typically, families seek help first from their family physician, who may know little or nothing about available services. If they do ask for help or express any complaints about caregiving, the advice they are likely to receive is to place the patient in a facility. Thus, while there is widespread agreement that institutionalization should be avoided or delayed if possible, the lack of integration of health and social services, limitations in the availability of current services, and the lack of a treatment–rehabilitation emphasis for chronic conditions of the elderly serves to worsen the older person's condition and place more burden on the family, until institutionalization becomes the only remaining alternative.

Once inside the institution, the older patient is even less likely to receive care that fosters rehabilitation or even maintenance of remaining abilities. It is easier for busy, overworked staff members to feed, bathe, and dress patients than it is to spend the time necessary to assist the patient in performing these functions. When these activities are taken away, people may lose both the confidence and the physical ability to perform them, leading to what Kahn (1975) termed "excess disabilities." While some will ultimately lose the ability to perform activities of daily living due to their disability, when others perform these tasks, the loss occurs more rapidly.

Families, then, are caught in a dilemma. While home care may be more desirable for personal and/or economic reasons, it can result in unacceptable costs to the caregiver's own health or well-being. Although nursing home care can relieve that strain, it places a different set of emotional and economic pressures on the family.

If the burdens associated with home care cannot be relieved, then the decision to place the elder in an institution is appropriate, and the benefits of relieving the stress on families will outweigh the drawbacks. But appropriate assistance to patients and families may reduce the need for institutional placement, or minimize the strain for families associated with home care. Even in the worst-case situation, when there is little that can be done to improve or maintain the patient's functioning, as in the case of degenerating conditions, assistance to the family may be able to relieve their burden. A program of interventions is described in the following sections.

FAMILY INTERVENTIONS

The most cost-effective alternative for caring for elderly people is to keep them in the community. It is also the preferred choice of most patients and families. When care is centered within the home, however, the critical issue becomes reducing the burden of care for family members to tolerable levels. Generally, medical aspects of care are attended to more than anything else because they are well defined, and treatment plans that are disease specific can be developed. But the issues for families are the functional, social, and psychological consequences of disease. To address these issues of patient–family interactions, one needs to look not only at the disease, but at the family system, that is, the particular context and meaning of these interactions. Unlike a medical plan, interventions for the family are more variable, because of the wide-ranging differences in family systems.

In the next sections, the authors describe an intervention plan that includes all members of the family. The interventions described below can be carried out by social workers, psychologists, family therapists, or any other professional who has contact with families that contain a dependent older person. While the program will emphasize the behavioral aspects of the intervention, it is assumed that it will be carried out in a manner consistent with sound clinical practice, in which genuineness, warmth, and empathy are present.

Defining the Problem: The Initial Phone Contact

The clinician's first task in working with chronically disabled older adults is to define the problem and determine with whom the important work of behavior change will be done. Referrals may come from a variety of sources. The initial request for services may come from the older person, from a spouse, from a family member, a neighbor, or other professional. During the initial telephone call it is important to identify who the patient is, who the primary caregiver is, and what relationship the caller has to each of them. A primary difference from most other clinical practice with adults is that the identified "patient" usually does not seek help, and may not even see himself or herself as needing help. Next, the therapist should identify the specific diagnosis, if one has been made. If there is a question about medical issues, a medical evaluation may be necessary. Families may be unsure if there has been appropriate medical evaluation or treatment of the problem, and this should be clarified first before making a behavioral intervention. This will ensure that problems that can be treated have been treated. Furthermore, if the family is still searching for a medical treatment or cure, they are not likely to comply with behavioral approaches. If the patient is cognitively impaired, it is especially important to obtain a good differential diagnosis to rule out treatable problems. If it is clear that the patient has been adequately diagnosed and treated medically, it is still a good idea to request a summary of the medical records to provide a more complete picture of the problem than the family might offer.

The next step is to determine what the presenting problem is. In carrying out this step, the therapist guides the caller toward a behavioral description of the problem. For example, if a daughter says, "My mother has gotten very forgetful lately," the therapist may inquire about what kinds of problems the mother has had in the past week that indicate forgetfulness. The therapist should continue to ask questions until he or she feels confident in understanding the specific nature of the disability.

Once the problem has been identified, the kind of help the person wants should be identified. In the example above, the daughter may be looking for something specific, like a respite-care provider to allow her some time away from the patient. In that case a referral to a respite agency would be appropriate. Or she may be asking for ways to manage her mother's memory problems more effectively, in which case she would be the identified client. She might be feeling overwhelmed about providing care for her mother. She might be worried about her caregiving father's health. She might need a referral to a specialist to determine the nature of the memory problem. She might be asking for information about the diseases that cause memory impairment. She might be looking for someone to help the whole family cope with the problem. She might be asking for therapy for the mother.

It is wise to remember that families differ in composition, needs, and goals, and that the task of the therapist is to design an intervention that will alleviate identified problems without altering the existing family structure. The therapist has to allow the family to select those goals and interventions that address what they perceive as important, without imposing values on them. As an example, the professional may make the judgment that the problems of a particular elderly patient may seem more appropriate to an institutional setting, because the professional would not endure the sacrifices involved in home care. But the family's goal of home care should take precedence, especially as there may be treatable aspects of the situation. Families do not try to maintain patients at home only out of guilt or because they are denying how stressful the situation is, as some writers have maintained. Rather, they are motivated out of a sense of how their family tries to handle dependency, and should be supported to find ways of implementing those goals that hopefully can maximize both the patient's and their own well-being.

The following case illustrates how the goals of the professional and family may not always coincide. The presenting problem was "Grandpa's anxiety." The family came to the office, including Grandpa, Grandma, their daughter, and three of her children. Grandma and Grandpa had moved in with their daughter following his heart attack. He was extremely anxious and fearful of having another heart attack, and this was of greatest concern to the daughter, who saw him withdrawing and performing fewer and fewer of the activities he had formerly enjoyed. Early in the interview the therapist noticed that Grandma was inattentive and, subsequently, that she was incontinent. This event was handled in a very matter-of-fact manner by the daughter. From questioning the daughter, it was evident that Grandma had had a dementing illness for quite some time, but that the family was very accepting of it. Since the grandfather's anxiety was identified as the problem, the intervention addressed this problem, and the family continued to manage Grandma's incontinence as they had before.

Many medical professionals believe that when a patient becomes incontinent, they must be institutionalized, presumably because families cannot handle this problem at home. However, as shown in the example above, the grandmother's incontinence was not problematic for this particular family. For another family it might be very difficult. A therapist must try to understand the family's value system as it pertains to caring for the elderly relative, rather than make assumptions about the impact of a particular problem on the family.

One particular kind of call to be aware of is the one that begins, "I need help finding a nursing home for my parent." It may be true that this person is making a straightforward request, but it is as likely that he or she has been told that the elder should be placed. Rather than take the request at face value, a complete evaluation of the situation is warranted. Sometimes minimal intervention, such as day care or respite from caregiving is all that is needed. Of course, if it turns out that institutional placement is still what the family prefers, that decision should be supported.

Once the therapist has identified the type of help being requested, he or she next determines who will be included in the intervention. This can be as inclusive or exclusive as the situation warrants. Generally, the person who calls making the request has reached a point where the problem can no longer be denied. That may not be true of the others involved in the situation. If the therapist learns that there are other interested family members, he or she may invite all of them to come to the initial assessment visit. During the visit it usually becomes evident who is motivated to continue working on the problem. The following case example will illustrate one possible direction an initial contact and assessment may take.

The initial call was made by the daughter, Jackie. She was concerned that her mother was wearing herself out caring for her husband, who had a cardiac history and some signs of cognitive impairment. She described her father as very difficult, occasionally paranoid and combative. The father had had a thorough medical examination, so an appointment was made with the mother and Jackie. During the assessment interview, Mrs. Smith was very quiet and denied having any trouble caring for her husband. Jackie continued to report incidents where her mother called her only after the situation had reached crisis proportions. It became evident that Mrs. Smith was not seeking help, but that Jackie was.

Jackie, then, became the identified client, despite the fact that her father was the "patient," and that her mother was the caregiver. The treatment focused on how Jackie could behave differently toward her mother in order to provide her mother with some respite from caregiving, and solve some of Mr. Smith's behavior problems before they became crises. While Jackie had initially wanted her mother to come to therapy to solve these problems, it was apparent that Jackie was motivated to change, while her mother was not.

Formulating the Problem

An assessment of the older person's current problems should precede the intervention. Generally, the therapist will want to assess the patient's behavioral and cognitive functioning and affective status. Behavioral competency includes the ability to carry out everyday activities. Lawton (1971) differentiates between activities involving physical self-maintenance and instrumental activities. Physical activities of daily living (ADLs) include toileting, feeding, dressing, grooming, ambulation, and bathing. Instrumental ADLs are ability to use the telephone, shopping, food preparation, housekeeping, laundry, ability to use public transportation, management of medications, and management of finances. Patients may have partial or total dependency in any of these areas. Assessment of activities of daily living identifies the areas in which the older person needs assistance.

Cognitive problems can contribute to difficulties in carrying out activities of daily living, as well as to other problems for family caregivers. Brief mental status testing can identify obvious cases of cognitive impairment consistent with dementia. Because of expectations about cognitive decline in old age, mental status should always be tested, so that cognitive problems can be ruled out in some cases. The simplest mental status questionnaire is that of Kahn, Goldfarb, Pollack, and Peck (1960) and consists of 10 empirically validated questions. Errors on two or more of the questions suggest the need for further cognitive evaluation. The Mini-Mental

State Examination (Folstein, Folstein, & McHugh, 1975) includes single items to assess, respectively, naming, drawing, following commands, and writing, as well as questions involving information and orientation. There are, however, more false positives with this procedure, especially for more poorly educated subjects (Anthony, LaResche, Niaz, Von Korff, & Folstein, 1982). More extensive testing of cognitive abilities may be appropriate, either to clarify functioning when the results of mental status testing are ambiguous, to identify strengths or weaknesses, or to serve as a baseline against which future functioning can be assessed.

Dementia is often associated with other types of behavior problems and disturbances that can be quite stressful to families. When the patient is known to have a dementia, the Memory and Behavior Problems Checklist (Zarit, Orr, & Zarit, 1985) can be used to identify specific problems and their frequencies (see Figure 1).

The patient's and family's affective status should be assessed both through direct questioning and by observation. Several instruments for rating depression have adequate reliability with older people, including the Beck Depression Inventory (Beck, Ward, Mendelson, Mock, & Erbaugh, 1961; Gallagher, Nies, & Thompson, 1982) and the CES-D (Radloff, 1977). The Geriatric Depression Scale (Brink, Yesavage, Lum, Heersema, Adey, & Rose, 1982) uses a true–false format and also omits somatic items, which may confound depression and illness in some cases.

An important part of an assessment is to conduct an applied behavioral analysis of presenting problems and difficulties of the patient and/or caregiver. For this purpose, we have developed the following activity schedule similar to that used in other cognitive and behavioral treatments, which lists the steps in an applied behavioral analysis:

1. Assessment: Identify problems and their antecedents and consequences.
2. Generate alternative solutions.
3. Select a solution.
4. Rehearse carrying out the solution.
5. Carry out the plan.
6. Evaluate outcome.

Caregivers can record specific behavior problems at the times they occur, including any antecedent events or consequences. In this way, the caregiver or designated client begins to collect baseline data from the time of the first meeting.

A careful history of current symptoms and problems should also be taken. The history contributes both to differential diagnosis and treatment planning. Differential diagnosis is much more difficult with older patients because they often present symptoms in an idiosyncratic way. For example, depression may be the presenting symptom of dementia or some other physical illness (e.g., pancreatic cancer). Conversely, memory complaints made by the patient are more often indicative of depression than dementia. An older person who is disoriented may be suffering from dementia or a delirium induced by overmedication, acute infection, or a wide variety of other illnesses. Previous history and the onset of symptoms will often clarify the diagnosis. Sometimes, however, careful neuropsychological testing is necessary to tease out the actual cognitive deficits from functional problems, and the results can be useful in developing an appropriate treatment plan. Testing, for example, can identify if certain types of cues can assist a memory-impaired individual, or if that person might benefit from having memory tasks phrased in a recognition, rather than recall, format. To cite another example, findings of language impairment might lead the clinician to investigate if problem interactions between patient and caregiver are the result of the patient's deficient use or understanding of words. Strategies for minimizing communication problems could then be developed. For a detailed discussion of differential diagnosis, see Kahn & Miller, 1978; Zarit, 1980; Zarit, Orr, & Zarit, 1985).

Along with diagnostic information, taking a history of the problem may identify changes in the patient's and/or family's life that were precipitants, or which had a worsening or ameliorating effect on the course of the problem. This information can help the clinician generate hypotheses about possible reinforcers that are no longer available or that may be used to change behavior.

The history should also include a family history, which is useful in understanding the previous level of involvement of family members with the frail older person. As when assessing any family system, questions should be asked that address the role that the identified patient played in the family, how often the family interacted prior to the onset of the problem, the impact of the problem on the extended family, and the current ability of various family members to provide assistance. It is unlikely that a family which has never been close will suddenly be able to take over total care for an ailing parent, despite a desire to "do the right thing." Spouses often attempt to take on all of the caregiving, feeling that it is unfair to ask for assistance from other family members, despite a desire on their children's part to help. These barriers to requesting help must be addressed or they will undermine the treatment plan.

Although an assessment is completed in initial sessions, the clinician continues assessing the situation over time. New problems may emerge, or the functional relation among problems may become evident. Responses of families to tasks also provides important information about their ability to change and possible obstacles in the intervention process.

At the end of the assessment, the clinician develops a plan to address those aspects of the care situation that the family finds the most stressful or burdensome and for which they want assistance. The particular interventions used will depend on both the types of problems identified and the family system, as described in the following sections.

Behavioral Treatment with Families

There are three basic components to a treatment plan for families caring for an older relative. First, information about the specific illness or problem must be shared so that all involved family members have an equal understanding of the problem. Second, problem solving is applied to current problems, and then the process of problem solving is taught. And third, a social support network for the primary caregiver is developed.

Memory and Behavior Problems Checklist (1987 revision)

Instructions to Caregiver: "I am going to read you a list of common problems. Tell me if any of these problems have occurred during the past week. If so, how often have they occurred? If not, has this problem ever occurred?" Hand the subject the card on which the frequency ratings are printed.

Reaction Ratings: For current problems (codes 2 through 5), ask: "How much does this problem bother or upset you when it happens?"

Frequency ratings

0 = never occurred
1 = occurred frequently in the past but not in the past three months
2 = has occurred recently, but not in the past week
3 = has occurred 1 or 2 times in past week
4 = has occurred 3 to 6 times in past week
5 = occurs daily or more often

Reaction ratings

0 = not at all
1 = a little
2 = moderately
3 = very much
4 = extremely

Behaviors	*Frequency*	*Reaction*
1. Asking the same question over and over again	0 1 2 3 4 5	0 1 2 3 4
2. Trouble remembering recent events (e.g., items in the newspaper, on tv)	0 1 2 3 4 5	0 1 2 3 4
3. Trouble remembering significant events from the past	0 1 2 3 4 5	0 1 2 3 4
4. Mixing up past and present (e.g., thinking a deceased parent is alive)	0 1 2 3 4 5	0 1 2 3 4
5. Losing or misplacing things	0 1 2 3 4 5	0 1 2 3 4
6. Hiding things	0 1 2 3 4 5	0 1 2 3 4
7. Unable to find way about indoors	0 1 2 3 4 5	0 1 2 3 4
8. Unable to find way about outdoors, for example on familiar streets	0 1 2 3 4 5	0 1 2 3 4
9. Wandering or getting lost	0 1 2 3 4 5	0 1 2 3 4
10. Not recognizing a familiar place	0 1 2 3 4 5	0 1 2 3 4
11. Not recognizing familiar people	0 1 2 3 4 5	0 1 2 3 4
12. Not recognizing a familiar object	0 1 2 3 4 5	0 1 2 3 4
13. Forgetting what day it is	0 1 2 3 4 5	0 1 2 3 4
14. Unable to start activities by self (besides ADL's)	0 1 2 3 4 5	0 1 2 3 4
15. Unable to keep occupied or busy by self	0 1 2 3 4 5	0 1 2 3 4
16. Follows you around	0 1 2 3 4 5	0 1 2 3 4
17. Being constantly restless or agitated	0 1 2 3 4 5	0 1 2 3 4
18. Spending long periods of time inactive	0 1 2 3 4 5	0 1 2 3 4
19. Being constantly talkative	0 1 2 3 4 5	0 1 2 3 4
20. Talking little or not at all	0 1 2 3 4 5	0 1 2 3 4
21. Being suspicious or accusative	0 1 2 3 4 5	0 1 2 3 4
22. Doing things in public that embarrass you	0 1 2 3 4 5	0 1 2 3 4

23.	Waking you up at night	0	1	2	3	4	5	0	1	2	3	4
24.	Appears sad or depressed	0	1	2	3	4	5	0	1	2	3	4
25.	Appears anxious or worried	0	1	2	3	4	5	0	1	2	3	4
25.	Appears anxious or worried	0	1	2	3	4	5	0	1	2	3	4
26.	Becomes angry	0	1	2	3	4	5	0	1	2	3	4
27.	Strikes out or tries to hit	0	1	2	3	4	5	0	1	2	3	4
28.	Destroying property	0	1	2	3	4	5	0	1	2	3	4
29.	Engaging in behavior that is potentially dangerous to others or self	0	1	2	3	4	5	0	1	2	3	4
30.	Seeing or hearing things that are not there (hallucinations or illusions)	0	1	2	3	4	5	0	1	2	3	4
31.	Any other problems (specify):	0	1	2	3	4	5	0	1	2	3	4
32.	Any other problems (specify):	0	1	2	3	4	5	0	1	2	3	4

FIGURE 1. Memory and Behavior Problems Checklist. Copyright 1987, Steven H. Zarit and Judy M. Zarit.

Information

Very often families receive inadequate explanations of what is happening to their relative. The physician may give too brief an explanation, or use jargon that the family does not understand, or the family may be too upset to retain the information given. Families often feel intimidated by the physician, which prevents them from asking questions. Providing information in a language they can understand at a time when they are not too anxious to hear it can be very helpful.

If the helping professional is unfamiliar with the particular disease the older patient has, it is a good idea to consult with the physician about the symptoms and severity of the disease. Another useful source of information about etiology and treatment is university medical centers. Standard medical reference texts can also be used to explain unfamiliar terminology (e.g., Kerson & Kerson, 1985), both to supplement the professional's knowledge and for families. It is generally true that the more information families have about an illness, the better they are able to cope with it.

In the earlier example of the gentleman who suffered a stroke and received little rehabilitative treatment, his wife understood very little about his illness. He had suffered a series of small strokes and had diminished mental status. She believed that he was purposely aggravating her by refusing to do what she asked him to do. Psychological testing made it evident that he was unable to follow more than one instruction at a time, and that he had a receptive aphasia, making it difficult for him to understand what was said to him. Once his wife learned that his impairment was part of his illness and not a deliberate attack on her, she was able to adapt her behavior to him (limiting herself to one instruction at a time), and she became much less upset with him.

In addition to explaining the symptoms and course of the illness, the treating professional must be familiar with treatment possibilities. Often the family is searching for a "cure." They would like something to be done that could make the problem go away. This attitude can be found for disorders as different as dementia and macular degeneration. In fact, the search for a cure, or even some possible improvement in function, is an appropriate response, since if anything can be done to prevent chronic disabilities, it should be. But looking for a cure can become counterproductive if the family persists long after all reasonable alternatives have been explored. Their insistence on making the patient better blinds them to the changes that could be made in their behavior or in other dimensions of management of the patient or patient's household that could improve the situation. Families may be particularly prone to quack cures.

In discussing with the family the limitations of current treatment, the professional often must tread a fine line. On the one hand, it is necessary to shift the family's focus to those aspects of the problem that they can change, yet one does not want to take away all hope. This can often be accomplished by encouraging the belief that research may uncover some new and effective treatment, while stressing the limitations of current treatments. If the family is just not ready to focus on their current situation, they can be encouraged to continue their search for a "cure." The professional might maintain a relationship with them by encouraging them to come back to report what they have found. Unfortunately, the stress on them may become too great in the meantime, as often is the case in dementias if the family does not make some adjustments early on.

Problem Solving

Once the family has learned about the illness and its effects on behavior, they will be ready to learn how they can deal with specific problems when they arise. Initially the focus is on finding solutions for the most urgent problems. The ultimate goal, however, is to teach the process of problem solving (see D'Zurilla & Goldfried, 1971; Goldfried & Davison, 1975; Zarit *et al.*, 1985). Problem solving involves a structured, behaviorally oriented approach to identifying new responses that improve coping and/or reduce the upset or distress clients feel. The use of problem solving for management of behaviors is based on the assumption that a patient's behavioral problems are, at least in part, related to the environmental or interpersonal context in which they occur. Thus, problem solving involves identifying patterns or sequences of behaviors, looking for possible antecedents or consequences, and proposing changes in the sequence that will disrupt the maladaptive pattern.

Instead of receiving advice about how to solve their problems, caregivers who learn the process of problem solving can develop more individualized approaches that take into account the specific problems their relative is having, as well as their own resources and capabilities. Each illness will present a slightly different picture, and individuals and their families will adapt in varying ways to these problems. It is difficult to identify a set of universal problems or to prescribe such pat responses as "it is good to overcome denial." What may be a problem for one person in the family may not be for another. There are few problems that are so inherently stressful that families cannot cope with them. It is thus more useful for professionals to have families identify what is most stressful and troubling to them about their current situation, and then apply a problem-solving approach.

Often family members have good problem-solving skills that they have used in the past, but they are not applying them in the present situation. For others the concept of problem solving will be new. When used successfully, the problem-solving process addresses simultaneously the practical management issues facing the caregiver, as well as the caregiver's feelings of anger and hopelessness, which may have blocked them from adopting solutions that would improve their situations. Sometimes it is necessary to urge reluctant caregivers to try it out to see if problem solving makes a difference.

Problem solving is carried out in a series of steps. The first step is having the caregiver make observations of how often and under what circumstances problems occur. This record serves as a baseline against which subsequent changes can be measured, and it also is useful for identifying possible antecedents and consequences of problem behaviors. As an example, periods of agitation in a dementia patient may follow a stretch of time in which the patient is inactive (antecedent), or it may be followed by more focused attention (consequence) than at other times of day. By keeping these records, the caregiver is, in effect, continuing the behavioral analysis which the clinician begins during the initial assessment.

Based on these observations, caregivers are then encouraged to consider possible solutions. To that end, they are urged to generate as many ideas as they can, without ruling out any possibilities prematurely because they do not seem practical. This step helps overcome the feelings of hopelessness that many caregivers have, which prevents them from exploring possible alternatives. The next step is to choose one of these strategies. If the caregiver then has trouble choosing a solution, the method of pros and cons (Beck, Rush, Shaw, & Emery, 1979) is used, in which the advantages and disadvantages of each alternative are evaluated. By demonstrating through the use of pros and cons the potential gains that could result from trying a new approach, the professional is helping the caregiver overcome feelings of helplessness and hopelessness, which often block action.

After a strategy is selected, the next step is to conduct a cognitive rehearsal (Beck *et al.*, 1979), in which the caregiver mentally rehearses the steps necessary for carrying out the plan. Potential obstacles can then be identified in advance, and the strategy refined. At that point the caregiver is ready to try out the strategy, while continuing to keep records on the occurrence of the problem. These observations will be useful for evaluating whether or not the strategy is effective.

This approach does not involve teaching families formal aspects of cognitive or behavioral interventions. While behavioral principles underlie the process, it is conducted at a common sense level, where the emphasis is on discontinuing old patterns of behavior that are maladaptive and trying something new. Typically, solutions are quite practical and down to earth, for example, the use of affection as a way of calming down an Alzheimer patient.

The following example will illustrate the problem-solving process.

Identify the problem. Mr. Brown has had significant memory problems for about 4 years. His wife is the primary caregiver, although there are two married daughters who live nearby. Mrs. Brown reports that what bothers her most are repetitive questions. (Note: This is a general complaint, and needs more specificity). She is asked to write down the questions he asks and when he asks them on an activity schedule. She is also asked to record what was happening immediately before the questions began and what happened afterward.

Mrs. Brown kept track of the questions for a week and discovered that the questions he asked most frequently were:

"What's for lunch (dinner)?"

"What time is it?"

"When are we going out?"

She further found out that he asked them most often at 11:00 a.m. and 4:00 p.m., and they occurred when he was sitting doing nothing or pacing. After asking the question, he either went back to doing nothing or got upset, depending on how she answered. She typically answered the questions each time he asked them until she lost her temper. Sometimes she reminded him that he had already asked the question, but that often increased his agitation.

Generate Solutions. The solutions discussed were:

1. Answer each question patiently when asked.
2. Remind Mr. Brown that he has already had that question answered.
3. Write answers to commonly asked questions on 3×5 cards.
4. Write meal menus and daily events on a blackboard, and refer him to it when he asks those questions.
5. Answer the question one time, then ask Mr. Brown to repeat it back the second time to see if he was paying attention.
6. Get angry.
7. Try to find an activity to occupy Mr. Brown.
8. Spend some time with Mr. Brown.

Weigh the pros and cons of each solution. Mrs. Brown was already doing either #1, #2, or #6. She understood that her husband had a memory impairment and that his problem was not inattention, so she decided not to try #5. Because the answers to his questions varied considerably, she thought #3 would not be practical. She also thought referring him to the blackboard 100 times a day (#4) would be as stressful as answering the questions. Since she had found that he was asking questions at times when he was inactive, she decided to try either #7 or #8 first.

Select an alternative and try it out. Mrs. Brown found that if she engaged Mr. Brown in conversation or found an activity for him (such as cutting coupons out of the newspaper or taking the dog for a walk), his questions decreased dramatically.

Evaluate the outcome. Mrs. Brown found that her solution took some creativity on her part, but that Mr. Brown was asking many fewer questions. She concluded that he was asking the same question over and over again because he was bored and inactive, not to irritate her. She further understood that he did not remember having asked the question before. He may have been attempting to engage her in conversation, but lacked the appropriate social skills to do so.

This example illustrates the complex interplay between problem solving and obtaining information about the problem. It is often useful to understand why a problem occurs in order to diffuse the emotional reaction to it and to select the most appropriate solution. It is also important to elicit what barriers to success the caregiver anticipates so that they do not undermine the attempt to solve the problem.

Problem solving is a process of trial and error. There are no simple solutions. Solutions come partly from observations of antecedants and consequences and partly from the ability and preferences of caregivers. A solution that works for one caregiver may not work for another caregiver coping with the same problem.

Some caregivers readily accept problem solving. They have well-developed skills that have been used to cope in the past and are simply overwhelmed in the present situation. Others, however, feel too overwhelmed to try doing anything new. They are angry at the patient, or they see it as the patient's problem. For others, making a change would mean recognizing the severity of the patient's decline, which they are reluctant to do. It is important to work carefully and slowly with caregivers so that solutions are not presented before the caregiver is ready to accept the help. A more detailed discussion of problem solving can be found in Zarit *et al.* (1985) and Pinkston and Linsk (1984).

Social Support

The need for additional sources of assistance for the primary caregiver may become apparent when using the problem-solving approach. Sometimes possible solutions involve keeping the patient more active, but the caregiver does not have the energy, time, or patience. Possible solutions, then, will involve bringing in other people to carry out those tasks or having them take the patient out. Another possibility is that the caregiver's records of stressful incidents will suggest that the accumulation of stress over the course of a day is the most significant problem, rather than any particular behavioral disturbance. That pattern suggests that the caregiver needs some rest or relief from the demands placed on him or her. When the need for help is identified, the problem-solving process can be useful for identifying and choosing additional sources of support.

Clinicians should be aware of the types of formal supportive services that are available and their limitations. Formal services, such as someone to come into the house to care for the patient, day care, or overnight respite care, can be very helpful. The amount of help actually available, however, may be limited. Services are inconsistently available, or they may be too costly for some families. Sometimes, too, agencies that serve the "frail" elderly are reluctant to take on particular problem patients, and families may need an advocate with agencies to provide assistance. Help from family and friends, when it can be arranged, tends to be more flexible and more readily accepted by the primary caregiver than help provided by an agency.

When exploring possible sources of assistance, the caregiver may express beliefs that interfere with accepting whatever help might be available. Some examples of these beliefs include: the caregiver ought to be able to do everything himself or herself; no one else can do as good a job as the caregiver; the patient will not accept anyone else. It is important to explore these beliefs with caregivers and to provide alternative perspectives on accepting help. They can, for example, consider the implications of trying to do everything, with particular attention to how that will affect their ability to continue caring for the patient in the long run. As for their concern about the patient not accepting help, the clinician can point out that gradual introduction of the new person or program to the patient is usually an effective solution to this problem.

There is a tendency for caregivers to become quite isolated, receiving fewer and fewer visits from friends and going out less often. This can be the result of the patient's behavior or physical and emotional exhaustion resulting from caregiving. Such a decrease in social contact may be the single most stressful element in caregiving because it cuts the caregiver off from stabilizing normal interactions with people. The lack of social support is believed to be one of many interacting variables involved in greater risk of emotional and physical illness. (See Handen, Chapter 5 in this text, for more details on this subject.)

Caregivers may need someone to stay with the patient so that they can have some respite. This companion can be a paid nurse's aide, a neighbor, or another family member. Caregivers may also need someone to assist with the physical management of the patient, such as bathing, feeding, and toileting. Women seem more likely to take on the whole responsibility of caregiving and are more reluctant to seek help than men. Many will "protect" other family members from knowing the extent of impairment of the patient, either because they did not want to burden others or because of embarrassment. In their efforts to protect others, these caregivers actually decrease their own effectiveness by becoming so stressed that they are no longer able to solve the problems.

Emotional support is a complex issue for someone caring for a dependent relative. Phone calls and visits from friends and family members can be helpful, but only when those who call support the work that is being done by the caregiver. Consider the case of a woman who has vowed to care for her husband at home, no matter what. If her children call her daily urging her to place him in a nursing home, those calls are not supportive, but add significantly to her distress.

Caregivers may benefit from being in a support group. Groups exist for people or families experiencing the effects of many medical illnesses, especially Alzheimer's disease, stroke, and Parkinson's disease. The groups allow the caregiver to be with others who share the same problems and who often have developed their own novel solutions to the problems they all face. The ideal group situation is one that employs the behavioral problem-solving approach outlined above. In fact, problem solving can be enhanced by the group setting when caregivers see solutions modeled by other group members.

Summary

As our population ages and the number of chronically ill elderly increases, there is a growing need for positive interventions for their caregivers. This chapter has dealt with issues of assessment and treatment aimed at a behavioral problem-solving approach for working with caregivers. The emphasis is on practical interventions designed to reduce the burdens of caregiving on families. This approach can be implemented in short-term therapy with the primary caregiver, with families, and in a group context.

References

Adams, M., Caston, M. A., & Danis, B. C. (1979). *A neglected dimension in home care of elderly disabled persons: Effect on responsible family members*. Paper presented at the meeting of the Gerontological Society, Washington, D.C.

Albert, W. C., & Zarit, S. H. (1977). Income and health care of the aging. In S. H. Zarit (Ed.), *Readings in aging and death: Contemporary perspectives* (pp. 120–127). New York: Harper & Row.

Anthony, J. C., LaResche, L., Niaz, U., Von Korff, R., & Folstein, M. F. (1982). Limits of the Mini-Mental State as a screening test for dementia and delirium among hospital patients. *Psychological Medicine, 12,* 397–407.

Anthony-Bergstone, C. R., Zarit, S. H., & Gatz, M. (1988). Symptoms of psychological distress among caregivers of dementia patients. *Psychology and Aging, 3,* 245–248.

Beck, A. T., Ward, C. H., Mendelson, M., Mock, J. E., & Erbaugh, J. (1961). An inventory for measuring depression. *Archives of General Psychiatry, 4,* 561–571.

Beck, A. T., Rush, A. J., Shaw, B. F., & Emery, G. (1979). *Cognitive therapy of depression.* New York: Guilford.

Bergmann, K., Foster, E. M., Justice, A. W., & Mathews, V. (1979). Management of the demented elderly patient in the community. *British Journal of Psychiatry, 132,* 441–449.

Birkel, R. C. (1987). Toward a social ecology of the home care household. *Psychology and Aging, 2,* 294–301.

Brink, T. L., Yesavage, J. A., Lum, O., Heersema, P. H., Adey, M., & Rose, T. L. (1982). Screening tests in geriatric depression. *Clinical Gerontologist, 1,* 37–43.

Brody, E. M. (1985). Parent care as a normative family stress. *Gerontologist, 25,* 19–29.

Brotman, H. (1982). *Every ninth American: An analysis for the chairman of the select committee on aging.* House of Representatives. Ninety-seventh Congress (Publication No. 97-332). Washington, DC: U.S. Government Printing Office.

Cantor, M. H. (1983). Strain among caregivers: A study of experience in the United States. *Gerontologist, 23,* 597–604.

Cummings, J. L., & Benson, D. F. (1983). *Dementia: A clinical approach.* Boston: Butterworth.

Derogatis, L. R., & Spencer, P. M. (1982). *The Brief Symptom Inventory (BSI): Administration and procedures manual—I.* Baltimore: Johns Hopkins University School of Medicine, Clinical Psychometric Research Unit.

D'Zurilla, T. J., & Goldfried, M. R. (1971). Problem solving and behavior modification. *Journal of Abnormal Psychology, 78,* 107–126.

Fitting, M., Rabins, P., Lucas, M. J., & Eastham, J. (1986). Caregivers for dementia patients: A comparison of husbands and wives. *Gerontologist, 26,* 248–252.

Folstein, M. F., Folstein, S. E., & McHugh, P. R. (1975). "Mini-mental state": A practical method for grading the cognitive state of patients for the clinician. *Journal of Psychiatric Research, 12,* 189–198.

Gallagher, D., Nies, G., & Thompson, L. W. (1982). Reliability of the Beck Depression Inventory with older adults. *Journal of Consulting and Clinical Psychology, 50,* 152–153.

George, L. K., & Gwyther, L. P. (1986). Caregiver well-being: A multidimensional examination of family caregivers of demented adults. *Gerontologist, 26,* 253–259.

Gilhooly, M. L. M. (1984). The impact of caregiving on caregivers: Factors associated with the psychological well-being of people supporting a dementing relative in the community. *The British Journal of Medical Psychology, 57,* 35–44.

Goldfried, M. R., & Davison, G. C. (1975). *Clinical behavior therapy.* New York: Holt, Rinehart & Winston.

Grad, J., & Sainsbury, P. (1963). Mental illness and the family. *The Lancet, 1,* 544–547.

Grad, J., & Sainsbury, P. (1968). The effects that patients have on their families in a community care and a control psychiatric service: A two year follow up. *British Journal of Psychiatry, 114,* 265–278.

Hoenig, J., & Hamilton, M. W. (1969). *The desegregation of the mentally ill.* London: Routledge & Kegan Paul.

Kahn, R. L. (1975). The mental health system and the future aged. *Gerontologist, 15* (1, Pt. 2), 24–31.

Kahn, R. L., & Miller, N. E. (1978). Assessment of altered brain function in the aged. In M. Storandt, I. C. Siegler, & M. F. Elias (Eds.), *The clinical psychology of aging* (pp. 43–70). New York: Plenum.

Kahn, R. L., Goldfarb, A. I., Pollack, M., & Peck, R. (1960). Brief objective measures for determination of mental status in the aged. *American Journal of Psychiatry, 117,* 326–328.

Kerson, T. S., & Kerson, L. A. (1985). *Understanding chronic illness.* New York: The Free Press.

Lawton, M. P. (1971). The functional assessment of elderly people. *Journal of the American Geriatrics Society, 1*(9), 465–481.

Lowenthal, M. F., & Robinson, B. (1976). Social networks and isolation. In R. H. Binstock & E. Shanas (Eds.), *Handbook of aging and the social sciences* (pp. 432–456). New York: Van Nostrand Reinhold.

Lowenthal, M. F., Berkmann, P., & Associates. (1967). *Aging and mental disorder in San Francisco.* San Francisco: Jossey-Bass.

Macmillan, D. (1968). Problems of a geriatric mental health service. *British Journal of Psychiatry, 113,* 175–181.

Mortimer, J. A., Schuman, L. M., & French, L. R. (1981). Epidemiology of dementing illness. In J. A. Mortimer & L. M. Schuman (Eds.), *The epidemiology of dementia* (pp. 3–23). New York: Oxford University Press.

Morycz, R. K. (1980). An exploration of senile dementia and family burden. *Clinical Social Work Journal, 8,* 16–27.

Morycz, R. K. (1985). Caregiving strain and the desire to institutionalize family members with Alzheimer's disease. *Research on Aging, 7,* 329–361.

Neugarten, B. L. (1975). The future and the young old. *Gerontologist, 15,* (1, Pt. 2), 4–9.

Pinkston, E. M., & Linsk, N. L. (1984). *Care of the elderly: A family approach.* New York: Pergamon Press.

Poulshock, S. W., & Deimling, G. T. (1984). Families caring for elders in residence: Issues in the measurement of burden. *Journal of Gerontology, 39,* 230–239.

Rabins, P. V., Mace, N. L., & Lucas, M. J. (1982). The impact of dementia on the family. *Journal of the American Medical Association, 248,* 333–335.

Radloff, L. S. (1977). The CES-D scale: A self report depression scale for research in the general population. *Applied Psychological Measurement, 1,* 385–401.

Reever, K. E., & Bach-Peterson, J. (1979). *The older person with senile dementia in the community and their primary caregiver.* Unpublished master's thesis, University of Southern California, Los Angeles.

Ross, H. E., & Kedward, H. B. (1977). Psychogeriatric hospital admissions from the community and institutions. *Journal of Gerontology, 32,* 420–427.

Sainsbury, P., & Grad de Alarcon, J. (1970). The psychiatrist and the geriatric patient: The effects of community care on the family of the geriatric patient. *Journal of Geriatric Psychiatry, 1,* 23–41.

Sanford, J. F. A. (1975). Tolerance of debility in elderly dependents by supporters at home: Its significance for hospital practice. *British Medical Journal, 3,* 471–473.

Shanas, E. (1979a). The family as a social support system in old age. *Gerontologist, 19,* 196–174.

Shanas, E. (1979b). Social myth as hypothesis: The case of the family relations of old people. *Gerontologist, 19,* 3–9.

Stone, R., Cafferata, G. L., & Sangl, J. (1987). Caregivers of the frail elderly: A national profile. *Gerontologist, 27,* 616–626.

Troll, L. E., Miller, S. F., & Atchley, R. C. (1979). Families in later life. Belmont, CA: Wadsworth.

U.S. Bureau of the Census (1982). *Statistical abstract of the United States, 1982–83* (103d edition). Washington, DC: U.S. Government Printing Office.

Wilder, C. S. (1971). *Chronic conditions and limitations of activity and mobility: United States, July 1965 to June 1967.* Vital and Health Statistics, Series 10, No. 61.

Zarit, J. M. (1982). *Predictors of burden and distress for caregivers of senile dementia patients.* Unpublished doctoral dissertation, University of Southern California, Los Angeles.

Zarit, S. H. (1980). *Aging and mental disorders.* New York: Free Press.

Zarit, S. H., & Zarit, J. M. (1982). Families under stress: Interventions for caregivers of senile dementia patients. *Psychotherapy: Theory, Research and Practice, 19,* 461–471.

Zarit, S. H., Reever, K. E., & Bach-Peterson, J. (1980). Relatives of the impaired elderly: Correlates of feelings of burden. *Gerontologist, 20,* 649–655.

Zarit, S. H., Orr, N. E., & Zarit, J. M. (1985). *The hidden victims of Alzheimer disease: Families under stress.* New York: New York University Press.

Zarit, S. H., Todd, P., & Zarit, J. M. (1986). Subjective burden of husbands and wives as caregivers: A longitudinal study. *Gerontologist, 26,* 561–571.

21

The Delivery of Health Care Services to Older Adults

Robert C. Intrieri and Jeffrey A. Kelly

As the elderly population of the United States increases, the demand for medical services for the aged will also increase. The medical needs of older people are varied and necessitate the services of a variety of health professionals. Previous studies (Institute of Medicine, 1978; National Institute on Aging, 1984) have pointed to the particular need for more medical personnel trained in geriatrics and gerontology. Preparing physicians and other health professionals to deal with older patients effectively and comfortably is an important social challenge.

In this chapter we will first review information on current demographic trends related to aging and health care, factors affecting mortality and longevity, and the elderly's use of health-related services and the associated economics of this use. We will next review theory and experimental findings related to physician–elderly patient interactions, findings regarding medical students' attitudes and knowledge of aging, and interventions intended to produce attitude change. Finally, we will present a behavioral model for training medical students to interact more effectively with elderly patients.

MEDICAL CARE AND THE ELDERLY: DEMOGRAPHIC TRENDS

Advances in medical science over the last 40 years have reduced mortality due to infectious disease. Susceptibility to chronic disease conditions increases with advancing age, as does the likelihood of polymedical problems. Health care needs of the older Americans are broad in scope and require the services of a variety of

Robert C. Intrieri • Pennsylvania State University, State College, Pennsylvania 16802.   Jeffrey A. Kelly • Department of Psychiatry and Human Behavior, University of Mississippi Medical Center, Jackson, Mississippi 39216.   Preparation of this chapter was supported in part by grant #53/86A from the National Fund for Medical Education and the Schering-Plough Foundation to Jeffrey A. Kelly. Robert C. Intrieri wishes to dedicate the chapter to the memory of his father, Eugene O. Intrieri.

health care professionals who are attuned to issues related to geriatric health available within these institutions (National Institute on Aging, 1984).

THE DECLINE OF MORTALITY

The expected growth in the population of older Americans is attributed to three factors. First, and most prominently, is the large number of births that occurred after World War II. This cohort of people, known as "Baby Boomers," will swell the future numbers of elderly to unprecedented levels. Second, advances in medicine have eradicated many acute and infectious diseases, thereby improving survival rates. Third, the migration rate from other countries to the United States has been steady.

The elderly population is growing older with larger numbers of people surviving to the upper-age limits. Those 85 and older make up the fastest-growing age group in the country. The increase in the "oldest-old" population is one of the major achievements of improved health care in this century. This segment of the population is expected to triple in size between 1980 and 2020. But, the expected increase in the oldest-old group raises significant public policy questions since this population is generally more frail and presents a greater need for health and social services.

Gender and Life Expectancy

The female-to-male ratio varies dramatically with age. For example, in 1985, the 30- to 34-year-old group was evenly balanced at 10.2 million each. However, the 65-plus age group had 17 million females to 11.5 million males. These statistics suggest that elderly women outnumber elderly men by 3 to 2, a rather large change from the 5 to 4 ratio that was evidenced in 1960. This gender ratio disparity increases at the upper age levels (U.S. Senate Select Committee on Aging, 1986).

Over the last 80 years, life expectancy has shown a more dramatic increase for women than for men, but this trend appears to be changing. The female–male differential in life expectancy was 7.1 years in 1985, as compared to 7.6 years in 1980 and 7.8 years in 1970.

Racial Differences in Life Expectancy

There are racial differences in life expectancy, with whites living longer than blacks. Data suggest that life expectancy at birth in 1985 was 5.8 years longer for whites than blacks. Differences at age 65 are smaller in the number of years of expected life: blacks live for an average of only 1.3 years less than whites at that age. There is a reversal of this effect in later years, with life expectancy for blacks higher than whites after age 80 (U.S. Senate Select Committee on Aging, 1986).

In summary, disparities exist for life expectancy based on gender and race.

White females have the highest life expectancy, followed by black females, and then by white males and black males. Black females have shown the largest gains in life expectancy over the last 15 years.

The Importance of Decreased Mortality

Mortality is an especially important component of population dynamics because of its implications for both individual and institutional planning. This importance is underscored in several ways. First, mortality is important to the individual because it gives some indication of the number of years a person can expect to live after a certain age. This is most salient when one starts thinking about and planning for retirement. Second, mortality is important to institutions because it provides data on the structure of the population. Accurate predictions about population structure enable policy analysts to plan future program needs, since demand for health and social services are dramatically changed after age 65. Third, understanding mortality provides insight into the human aging process and the physiological basis of chronic disease.

Models of human mortality permit the prediction of mortality and the anticipation of life expectancy. Current estimates suggest that life expectancy will not continue to advance with the current level of medical science (Fries, 1983). This "ceiling" on life expectancy has been explained in two ways. First, limitations on longevity are due to cellular aging processes. Second, life expectancy and mortality are related to increased risk from chronic degenerative diseases.

Advocates of the cellular aging model argue that reduced mortality and increased longevity will stop in the near future due to a species-specific process of senescence (Fries, 1980, 1983, 1984; Hayflick, 1975; Keyfitz, 1978; Strehler & Mildvan, 1960). As a result, efforts to increase longevity will serve to "rectangularize" the survival curve (Comfort, 1964). The curve describing survivors at any age will become nearly square and will remain so until the age when mortality due to biological senescence occurs. This perspective thus proposes that life expectancy increases because "premature death" is eliminated. When survival is truly "rectangularized," large portions of the population will live to their biologically determined end point.

In contrast, some theorists believe the major declines in mortality result from reduction in infectious disease risk due to changes in lifestyle, hygiene, nutrition, and other public health factors, and are not necessarily due to advances in medical science (McKeown, 1976; McKinlay & McKinlay, 1977; Omran, 1971). Omran's model of epidemiological transition correlates economic, demographic, and public health changes in a society. These societal changes describe a series of stages. The final stage, which the United States has reached, exhibits slow declines in mortality and slow increases in life expectancy at birth. Chronic disease is the most prominent public health hazard. Mortality models that emphasize social factors suggest that a stage has been reached in which major societal changes to improve life expectancy are unlikely. In contrast with the biological limits model, the societal risk model regards the potential reductions in mortality due to public health factors as having been fulfilled. Neither model predicts that medical science will increase life expectancy by better treatment of chronic degenerative disease. Some theorists combine both models to produce a hybrid model that suggests an even more limited potential life expectancy change.

Utilization of Human Services by the Elderly

Aging accentuates the heterogeneity of the population. Some individuals are relatively intact well into their 80s and 90s, while others suffer from the effects of age-dependent chronic diseases. An aged population has both a different structure and different health care needs than it had earlier in the life cycle. As a consequence, the type of care needed to meet these needs has changed. Treatment of acute, infectious disease has given way to treatment for chronic, long-term illnesses. Changes in demographic and mortality characteristics as well as the current trend toward chronic illnesses have mandated that the health care delivery system change. This section will highlight health care, mental health, and preventative health service utilization by the elderly.

Health Care Utilization

The elderly, as a group, are the largest consumers of health care services. Compared with younger groups, hospitalizations are twice as frequent, hospital stays are twice as long, and more medications are prescribed and used by the elderly (U.S. Senate Select Committee on Aging, 1986, 1987). About 80% of elderly community dwellers had at least one contact with a primary care physician in 1983 (Kovar, 1986). People 65 and over made about 16% of the total number of visits to physicians in 1983. Further, older adults are more likely to visit physicians than those under 65. Current statistics show that patients over 65 visit a physician six times to every five times for those under 65 (U.S. Senate Select Committee on Aging, 1986, 1987). Since Medicare has been enacted, physician contacts by those 65 and over have increased significantly, especially among the low-income elderly.

Long-Term Care

Ninety-five percent of the elderly are ambulatory or have only partial disabilities. Those with limited ability to receive ambulatory outpatient services are now eligible for skilled health care at home. Home health care is the fastest growing segment of the health care industry and is expected to have a larger impact in the future. Current estimates suggest that it is growing annually at a rate of 20–25% (U.S. Senate Select Committee on Aging, 1987). Home health care use varies with age; those aged 85 and over more frequently use Medicare-reimbursed home health services. Current government cost containment efforts, aimed at reducing the need for long-term residential care, are expected to support the continued provision of home health services.

Whether or not providing skilled health care services at home prevents entry into a long-term care facility is a question still open to empirical scrutiny. Only about 5% of the elderly require nursing home care at any single time, but about 20% will require it at one time or another. Demographers expect more people to need long-term care as the elderly population expands. Nursing home residents are typically very old, female, white, and unmarried (Manton & Soldo, 1985). The rate of nursing home use by the elderly has doubled since the inception of Medicare and Medicaid in 1966 (U.S. Senate Select Committee on Aging, 1987), and increased use is expected.

Mental Health

Recent epidemiological estimates suggest that symptoms of severe psychopathology are common in the elderly. These symptoms can influence cognitive abilities and mental functioning and may alter the course of physical illness. The prevalence of psychiatric disorders in those over 65 living in the community is estimated at between 15% to 25% (Kermis, 1986; Robbins et al., 1984; Roybal, 1984). Primary or secondary psychiatric diagnoses in nursing home residents, which are much higher, are estimated at between 40% to 75% (Kermis, 1986; U.S. Senate Select Committee on Aging, 1987).

The relationship between mental health and physical well-being among older adults is particularly worthy of attention and study. The belief that mental health affects physical health and vice versa in late life is gaining support. However, additional data are needed to specify the interaction between physical and mental health. A recent call for research underscores the importance of better studies of this relationship (National Institute of Mental Health, 1987).

Data suggest that current mental health resources are insufficient to meet the needs of the present or a growing elderly population. Results from the Epidemiological Catchment Area program indicated that when compared with younger groups, those over 65 rarely visited a mental health specialist for services (Shapiro et al., 1984). In contrast, visits to a general medical provider were higher than for other age groups. Others have found (Greene, Adelman, Charon, & Hoffman, 1986) that over 60% of primary care visits were to answer psychosocial concerns. These data suggest that it may be necessary to integrate mental health services into general medical health care systems. Providing mental health services within the context of a general medical service provision could enable older adults to develop more personal efficacy with respect to health and, ultimately, improve their well-being and quality of life.

Preventive Health Care Services

A number of chronic health conditions of the elderly may be preventable by changes in personal health habits. However, at this point little empirical research has been conducted to investigate whether habit change produces improved health status in the elderly. Health care professionals should note that changes in diet, nutritional intake, dental care, and exercise may have notable positive health effects. Appropriate attention, intervention, and education could inhibit further decreases in health status due to chronic disease.

Economics of Health Care and the Elderly

The cost of health care for the elderly was not a major issue for health policy analysis prior to the mid-1970s. Foremost at that time was concern over how to expand the system to improve the quality of care. Increased costs have raised debate about the nature of health care services that can be provided and the methods by which health care services should be delivered. National health expenditures rose from 42 billion dollars (5.9% of the Gross National Product [GNP]) to a current high of 425 billion dollars (10.7% of the GNP; U.S. Senate Select Committee on Aging, 1986). Expenditures for health care will comprise 14% of the GNP by the year 2000 if projections are accurate.

By far, the federal government is the largest payer of health care costs. National expenditures for hospital care and physicians' fees exceed costs for all other health services combined. Hospital care payments account for the largest portion (about 39%) of the health care bill. Payments to physicians rank second and comprise about 20% of health care costs.

In 1983, the Medicare system was amended to limit the amount of payments received by hospitals and physicians. Medicare's Prospective Payment System (PPS) pays hospitals a proscribed amount that is related to the average cost for a specific diagnosis. An aggregate of 471 Diagnostic Related Groups (DRGs) are used under PPS to categorize patients for reimbursement. As a result of the new system, the lowest rate of annual growth over the past 20 years was evidenced in 1985. Most policy analysts attribute the apparent slowing in health care costs to a variety of factors and not to cost containment procedures alone. Included among these factors are changing health utilization patterns, primarily a reduction in the use of in-patient services, and a low inflation rate.

Cost containment issues dominate the debate on national health care programs and will continue to do so. Cost containment efforts raise serious questions about continued public support for unlimited access to the "highest possible quality" health care. Maintaining access while preserving quality health care will set the agenda for future policy decisions for at least the next two decades. Though a substantial amount of health care costs are paid by public funds, the elderly are paying more for services out of their own pockets. The elderly paid, on average, about 15% of their total income in 1984 toward health care expenses, averaging about $1,059 per person (U.S. Senate Select Committee on Aging, 1986). The majority of these costs were not covered by Medicare, Medicaid, or private insurance. Two major protections are provided against unusually high out-of-pocket expenses: "Medigap" insurance and Medicaid. Medigap insurance is a private provider insurance plan, with premiums averaging $300–400 per person in 1984 (U.S. Senate Select Committee on Aging, 1986). Medicaid is publicly funded but is limited only to the poor whose income falls below a certain eligibility level. Medicaid provides for about 13% of all health care expenditures for the elderly. Most Medicaid payments to the elderly are used by those receiving long-term care services. Medicaid paid for about 41% of total nursing home costs in 1984.

Those 65 and older, on the average have substantially less available money than those under 65. However, the economic status of the elderly is more varied than any other age group. Some elderly have substantial resources; many others have almost none. Calculated mean income levels of the elderly are potentially misleading because a large proportion of the elderly are below or just above the poverty level. For many, social security is the main source of income.

Married couples are the most financially secure among the elderly. By comparison, elderly women who were either divorced or widowed have the lowest incomes among unmarried women (U.S. Senate Select Committee on Aging, 1986). Elderly widows or divorcees often do not have pension income or the earnings of a wage-earning spouse. These financial changes, together with decreased health status, loss of a spouse, and inflation, make the elderly economically vulnerable.

PHYSICIAN–PATIENT INTERACTIONS

Medicine has taken a decidedly technological focus over the past two decades. For example, surgical procedures to repair or replace organs have increased, and machines are being used more then ever to restore and maintain life. Today, a large percentage of the physician's time is spent keeping up to date with medical science and practice. Along with the emphasis on the high-tech aspects of medicine, American medical education has focused on the treatment of acute and infectious diseases and does not currently emphasize the primary care of chronic illness usually associated with aging processes (Glazier, 1973). Current medicine cannot always offer a dramatic breakthrough to cure these diseases; they must be endured, with treatment often intended to prevent further physical degeneration and maintain the patient's functional capacity (Rowe, 1985). As a result of these emerging treatment strategies and current demographic trends, it is no wonder that physician contacts with elderly patients are more frequent than contacts with the nonelderly.

Physicians have difficulty working with elderly patients due to their own limited knowledge, skills, experience, and attitudes about older adults (Williams, 1981). Most physicians receive little or no specific instruction about the process of aging and are not familiar with various disease clusters that are age specific. Research demonstrates that most physicians or medical students have misconceptions about aging that are similar to those of the general public. The aged are falsely thought to be ridden by physical, mental, psychological, and sexual failings (Butler, 1978). Physicians' and medical students' clinical skills are shaped by their exposure and experience in clinic settings. However, most physicians have not had and will not have training specific to the elderly, and, as a result, many of the misconceptions and biases they hold about the elderly remain unchallenged (Butler, 1978). These biases may also influence the physician's choice of a practice specialization. For example, data compiled by Kane, Solomon, Beck, Keeler, & Kane (1980) indicate that less than 5% of licensed physicians consider themselves geriatric specialists. These factors, taken singularly or in combination, make the relationship between physician and elderly patients of practical and theoretical interest.

This section will focus on selected aspects of the doctor–patient relationship that may be of crucial importance to the elderly. The discussion will center on characteristics of physicians, who are presumed to be grouped more homogeneously than either elderly patients or patient treatment settings. Three areas will be addressed: (1) factors that predict physician–patient communications, (2) the process or style of communications between doctors and patients, and (3) patient satisfaction and service utilization.

Does a Physician–Patient Relationship Exist?

Given the frequency of discussion of the relationship between patient and physician, it is important to recognize that the extent of the relationship is actually quite limited. For instance, the average frequency of physician–patient contact is about six visits per year, with a mean duration of only 13 minutes per primary-care visit (Keeler, Solomon, Beck, Mendenhall, & Kane, 1982). This means that the relationship between an average physician and patient lasts only about 1 hour and 20 minutes per year. If the same person continues to see the same physician over a 20-year period, 27 hours will be spent together. However, elderly patients are more likely to be treated by a physician who is younger than they are, and they are unlikely to see the same physician for more than a few years. Thus, the data on appointment frequency, contact duration, and the length of time with the same physician argue against labeling physician–patient interactions as true "relationships." Nevertheless, serial contacts over time form the basis for an interaction pattern that has implications for patient health, psychological well-being, and comfort. Several physician characteristics influence the interactions between physicians their elderly patients.

Physician Characteristics

Age and Gender. Age and gender are two salient and easily identified characteristics that frame the context for interactions between physicians and elderly patients. As increasing number of female medical students enter and graduate from medical school, a growing proportion of physicians are women. Because more women than men live into old age, elderly female patients will be more likely to see physicians of the same gender in the future. Concordance between physician gender and patient gender promotes rapport and facilitates self-disclosure (Levinson, McCollum & Kutner, 1984; Weisman & Teitlebaum, 1985). Furthermore, recent studies (Heins, 1979) suggest that female physicians are more egalitarian in their dealings with patients, another element crucial to establishing rapport.

Unfortunately, only a fraction of practicing physicians today are female, and few are in specialties that primarily serve the elderly. Weisman, Levine, Steinwachs, and Chase (1980) found that women are presently overrepresented in specialty areas such as pediatrics, but underrepresented in areas that more often serve the elderly, such as internal or family medicine. Specialty areas should become more evenly distributed as the number of women practicing medicine increases.

Physicians 65 and older make up at least 30% of the general practitioners. Correspondingly, 20% of their patients are 65 or older (Robert Wood Johnson Foundation, 1981). Concordance between physicians and patients in age may not be as critical as gender for several reasons. First, older physicians are not always knowledgeable of current findings related to aging processes and age-related illnesses. Second, many health problems of the elderly are closely linked to socio-political factors (i.e., pension, retirement, Social Security, and Medicare) and require a physician attuned to these issues (Robert Wood Johnson Foundation, 1981). Finally, as elderly physicians themselves grow older, they may retire or die. This, in turn, can affect the continuity of patient care. Further data are needed to evaluate empirically the implications of age and gender differences between physicians and older patients.

Social Status. Social status is determined by family background, educational achievement, and occupation. Physicians commonly enjoy upperclass status, which is usually accompanied by high income. Many elderly patients differ in socioeconomic class from their health care providers. Because social status differences are often reflected in the different styles and patterns of conversational discourse, social status discrepancies may inhibit or impede communications between some doctors and some patients (Haug & Ory, 1987). Investigators need to pay closer attention to social status variables in order to identify potential barriers between physician and patient and target them for intervention in the medical education process.

Practice Style. Practice "style," a crucial but nebulous characteristic, refers to the physician's clinical decision-making process with respect to treatment. For instance, many physicians consider the patient's ethnic and religious beliefs, treatment expectations, and payment ability before deciding on a course of treatment. In contrast, other physicians use a strict algorithmic decision-making approach based upon mathematical and scientific probabilities for treatment effectiveness. Unlike the former, the latter approach weighs social and psychological individual patient differences to a lesser degree. A technological, data-based practice style is likely to create more uncertainty for an elderly patient (Haug & Ory, 1987).

Social factors and time constraints may be linked to practice style. For instance, gaining information about how the elderly patient functions with family and friends is often crucial for accurate diagnosis and treatment planning. Physicians who see many patients for only brief periods of time may be less inclined or able to gather important psychological data about patients. They are also likely to be frustrated by the slowness of older patients. This frustration may manifest itself in annoyance or irritation that, ultimately, can undermine rapport. Keeler *et al.* (1982) found that physicians spend less time with patients 65 or older than with their younger patients. These findings are problematic because age-related physiological changes generally produce slower response times for the elderly and result in a need for more interaction time between doctors and their elderly patients.

Physiological Aspects. Butler (1978) suggests that medical education has socialized physicians to measure their success based upon cure rates. This measure of success may prove untenable with elderly patients since many have chronic illnesses that require regular revisions of diagnoses, treatment, and prognoses. Chronic illnesses force the physician to confront the uncertainties, ambiguities, and sometimes helplessness inherent in treating these conditions. Butler (1978) points out that a physician's inability to cope with the stresses of death and dying can effect the quality of patient care.

Race. Few studies have examined how race may affect physician–patient interaction. If the physician is white and the elderly patient is black, interaction and communication may be hindered due to social class differences, different cultural beliefs about health and illness, and interactional and conversational style differences. In a sample of people age 60 or older, Haug (1979) found no racial effect on challenges to physician authority. However, Santos, Hubbard, and McIntosh (1983) identified potential problems between elderly blacks and mental health therapists that are also relevant to interactions between physicians and patients. They found that black patients were talkative but withheld information more and self-disclosed less with white therapists. This suggests that racial differences between physician and patient can influence the level of communications. The paucity of minority physicians means that the minority elderly will probably receive health care from white physicians or residents.

Process of Communications

Patients and physicians often have different ideas about the purpose of their interaction. Patients are usually trying to resolve an illness, but they define it subjectively; physicians likewise are trying to resolve the patient's illness, but try to do so in an objective, scientific way. Haug and Ory (1987) point out that these interactional elements are universal for all ages. Few studies have documented interactional discrepancies between the elderly and their physicians. However, if unarticulated patient goals are not met, there may be a tendency for the patient to bring up problems that may fit the "medical model" in order to continue as a patient. Impeded by the patient's lack of specificity and clarity about problems, a physician may offer an ageist explanation that attributes disability to the aging process.

Greene *et al.* (1986) found no differences in the number of psychosocial concerns brought to physicians by young (45 years old or younger) and elderly (65 years or older) patients. They found that medical concerns and symptom descriptions predominated in both elderly and young samples. However, physician behavior differed significantly according to the ages of their patients. Physicians were less egalitarian, respectful, patient, and less engaged with elderly patients. No differences were obtained on a global rating of physician affect (e.g., emotion) during the interview.

Several factors have been identified as contributors to ineffective communications between elderly patients and physicians. Words and medical jargon used by the physician, but unfamiliar to the patient, are one source (Ley, 1977). Other aspects of verbal behavior may also inhibit skillful communications, such as age-related differences in speed of processing information. Slower processing speed may affect listening and speaking skills. Therefore, communications between a patient and a rapidly speaking physician, where pauses for questions, clarification, and/or repetition are infrequent, are likely to be ineffective (Garrity, Wilson, & Hafferty, 1984).

Another strategy that limits the effectiveness of communication is the intentional withholding of medical information from patients about their diagnosis, prognosis, or specific information about their treatment regimen. Tuckett and Williams (1984) suggest that this tactic empowers the physician and maintains the myth of medical magic. Nonverbal behaviors may create additional obstacles to good communication. This is most obvious in postures that are rigid and reflect discomfort, but may also be reflected when health care providers write notes excessively rather than talk. Posture, body, and eye movements are behavioral cues that communicate interest and empathy, and elicit patient self-disclosure (Haug & Ory, 1987). Much research is needed to clarify the role of nonverbal behaviors and their significance in the conversational interactions between physicians and elderly patients.

Setting and situational factors may also affect communication. Scheduling patients at time blocks rather than for individual appointments may put undue "ratio strain" on both the physician and the patient. Physicians with heavy patient schedules provide less clinically relevant information to the patient (Waitzkin, 1985). Office or hospital environments with high background noise may hinder effective communication with elderly patients, in general, and especially with those who have some type of hearing impairment. Physicians should evaluate such conditions thoroughly and use learning supports such as written material whenever possible. In short, physician attention and behavior to some of these issues may have an impact on communications and the resultant quality of patient care.

Interaction Outcomes of Communications

Patient Satisfaction

The patient satisfaction literature is substantial and will only be briefly reviewed here. Patient satisfaction is an important variable because it has implications for patient compliance and appointment keeping. A recent review of 21 research studies found that physician communication style was associated with satisfaction outcomes by patients (Innui & Carter, 1985). Courtesy, friendliness, and humane style were considered important variables.

Doyle and Ware (1977) found that young and old patients expressed minimal differences in satisfaction related to physician conduct. By comparison, Linn, Linn, and Stein (1982) found that a physician's personal qualities were a more important determinant of satisfaction by those 65 and over than by younger (less than 65 years old) patients. Older patients also reported greater overall satisfaction with their physicians. However, clinic-visit frequency and disease severity were the best predictors of satisfaction for both age groups. Satisfaction and compliance with suggested medical regimens were significantly related in the older group only.

A recent study examined the relationship between patient satisfaction, communication, affective care (i.e., empathy, trust, concern) and technical care (DiMatteo, Hays, & Prince, 1986). Results suggest that self-reported physician affective ability (i.e., the ability to be empathic, elicit trust, etc.) was significantly correlated with physician workload (i.e., the number of patients seen). Objective measures of physician sensitivity to verbal communications from the patient were positively related to patient appointment keeping. Nonverbal encoding skill, the ability to read and interpret patient nonverbal behavior, was significantly related to patient satisfaction with affective care and physician workload. This study provides some correlational data to support the need for programs that emphasize interpersonal skills training for health professionals. It also underscores the need for additional behavioral research that will better specify the relationships between patient–physician interactions, style, satisfaction, and age.

Attitudes

Several literature reviews document the existence of negative attitudes in society toward the elderly (Brubaker & Powers, 1976; Green, 1981; McTavish, 1971; Palmore, 1982; Tuckman & Lorge, 1953). Reviews of the attitudes of health care professionals also indicate the presence of negative attitudes and perceptions toward elderly patients (Bennett & Eckman, 1973; Coccaro & Miles, 1984; Lutsky, 1980). The professional's attitude toward a patient is thought to be integral to the type and quality of services received by the elderly because negative or stereotyped attitudes may lead to poor quality and inappropriate care (Butler, 1969, 1975; Solomon & Vickers, 1979). In addition, the attitudes of the health care provider partially determine the elderly patient's responses to clinical interventions and influence the patient's attitude toward the health care setting and self-care behavior.

Theory suggests that attitudes and perceptions mediate behavior and may be generally governed by contextual factors. According to Bem's Self Perception Theory (1972), attitudes are regarded as epiphenomena that are inferred from overt behavior and the context in which they occur. Consistent with this formulation, suboptimal patient care of the elderly has been attributed to negative or indifferent attitudes on the part of the health care provider (Coccaro & Miles, 1984). It is crucial for the practitioner to be knowledgeable of aging processes in order to form and develop a set of more favorable attitudes toward the aged patient (Coccaro & Miles, 1984).

STUDIES ASSESSING ATTITUDES TOWARD THE ELDERLY

Quality health care requires that health care providers be aware of individual differences in patients and respond differentially to them. Stereotyped attitudes or perceptions toward a specific reference group may influence clinical decision making in a deleterious manner by hindering an individual's ability to evaluate unfamiliar information efficiently and objectively. Patient stereotypes may influence decision making about a patient's care (Johnson, Kurtz, Tomlinson, & Howe, 1986).

Perceptions of the elderly by health care professionals were explored as early as 1967 by Coe, who concluded that stereotypes held by health professionals toward the elderly must be changed before elderly patients could be assured of high-quality medical treatment. Spence, Feigenbaum, Fitzgerald, and Roth (1968) demonstrated that first-year medical students held negative stereotypes about the elderly and that these attitudes did not change between the first and fourth years of medical school. Similar results were recently reported by Solomom and Vickers (1979). In a comparative study of graduate students in social work, law, and medicine, Geiger (1978) found that all students lacked both accurate knowledge of general facts about aging and career interest in working with the elderly.

Holtzman and Beck (1979) administered the Facts of Aging Quiz (FAQ; Palmore, 1977) and the Aging Semantic Differential (ASD; Rosencranz & McNevin, 1969) to health service personnel, including medical students. Significant group differences on the FAQ emerged, with better-educated groups missing fewer items. For example, medical students missed fewer items than dental students and registered nurses, who in turn missed fewer items than health care technicians. Aides and orderlies missed more items than any other group. These data support Palmore's assertion that the FAQ effectively distinguishes between levels of knowledge by occupational groups in the health field. In addition, these data lend some support to the contention that the FAQ is an indirect measure of bias.

West and Levy (1985) administered the FAQ to 170 physicians to determine their level of knowledge and misconceptions about aging and their level of age bias. Surprisingly, these data suggested that physicians' knowledge was no greater than college undergraduate students' knowledge assessed by other studies. Physicians had similar misconceptions about aging and most had antiaging biases, although these biases were not as great as those held by students. Further analyses revealed that physicians in the subspecialties who were more likely to treat the elderly knew no more about aging than pediatricians. Internal medicine specialists, aged 60 and older, were likely to know more about aging and respond less negatively toward the elderly than younger physicians in other subspecialties. These data underscore the need to provide medical professionals and professionals-in-training with basic facts about aging.

EFFECTIVENESS OF INTERVENTIONS WITH GERIATRIC MEDICAL PROGRAMS

Cicchetti, Fletcher, Lerner, and Coleman (1973) conducted one of the first evaluations of the effects of geriatric information on medical student attitudes toward the elderly using a pre–post design with first-year medical students attending an 18-week social medicine seminar. Students were assigned to either an experimental or control condition. Those in the experimental condition were given information about the elderly, and they conducted a psychosocial interview with at least one older adult client. Attitudes about aging and knowledge of psychosocial aspects of aging were assessed with a 32-item Likert-type questionnaire. Positive change was evidenced in the experimental group on only 2 of the 32 items. The investigators believed that change on these items represented knowledge acquired from the course rather than attitude change. This study was limited in several methodological respects, including the use of measures of unknown reliability and validity, little specification about the content of the intervention, and nonrigorous statistical analyses. In a similar study, Libow (1978) evaluated a summer fellowship program in geriatrics designed to develop appropriate training modules in geriatrics for preclinical medical students. The 6-week program consisted of 18 days of didactic sessions, 6 days of interviewing and interpersonal skills training, and 12 days of field experience with older adults. While the program increased student knowledge of geriatrics and aging, students' attitudes toward elderly patients remained unchanged, perhaps because study subjects were self-selected for program participation and already had favorable attitudes toward the elderly. In addition, several other methodological limitations emerged. First, the number of subjects used was limited to 11. Second, comparative data from a control group of similar students was not provided. Third, some of the instruments used to assess attitudes and knowledge of aging were developed specifically for the project and as a result may have lacked sufficient reliability and validity.

Green, Keith, and Pawlson (1983) investigated whether or not the attitudes of 148 third-year medical students and their willingness to work with elderly patients were influenced by participation in a geriatric rotation. A multidimensional questionnaire was administered pre- and postrotation to a subset of the student sample. Green *et al.* (1983) found that participation in the geriatric rotation alone did not improve student attitudes toward the elderly, nor their intention to work with elderly patients, although students who participated in the geriatric rotation rated the experience positively. The authors suggested that medical students already held both positive attitudes and a positive view toward interacting with the elderly.

An investigation by Holtzman, Beck, and Coggan (1978) showed that a program providing technical information about aging produced positive attitude change. In a pre- and posttest experimental design, medical students either took an elective course in which they were taught about the aging process and given empathy-promoting exercises or entered a clerkship that provided a technical and clinically oriented experience, emphasizing health problems in the chronically ill elderly. Modest, but statistically significant, improvement in student attitudes was evidenced for both programs, even though the interventions were brief. The authors concluded that their results provide added support for including similar programs into the medical curriculum. However, this study lacked a control group, did not randomly assign subjects to conditions, and obtained only short-term attitude data immediately after the intervention.

Several studies have explored the relationship between students' knowledge of aging and their attitudes toward older people. Holtzman, Beck, and Ettinger (1981) found a statistically significant positive relationship between attitudes and knowledge, but only for clinical-year medical students who had patient contact experiences. Perotta, Perkins, Schimpfhauser, and Calkins (1981) also found significant correlations between first-year medical student attitudes and knowledge of the aged. Interest in geriatric medicine was significantly related to knowledge, positive attitudes, or personal contact with the elderly. Wilson and Glamser (1982) developed a course that included a 3-hour didactic component and visits to a nursing home and a congregate housing facility for the well elderly. Though limited by a small sample size ($N = 61$), they obtained significant improvements in knowledge of and attitudes toward the elderly at posttesting. Broder and Block (1986) also demonstrated the effectiveness of 10 hours of didactic presentations on geriatrics for sophomore dental students, although long-term follow-up showed reductions of knowledge over time and established the need to have information about geriatrics integrated throughout medical school. Together these students suggest that the provision of educational information about the elderly increases accurate knowledge of older people and may also produce attitude change, at least in the short term.

Wilson and Hafferty (1980) developed and conducted an 8-week multicomponent geriatric education program including 8 hours of instruction in physiology, psychology, and sociopolitical aspects of aging; 4 hours of discussion between students and professionals who deliver care to the elderly; and 2 hours of student interviews with the elderly. Sixteen students participated in the program and were compared with 28 control subjects on attitude and perception measures taken immediately after the intervention and 1 year later. Seminar students' attitudes were statistically more positive than the control subjects, who showed little or no change. Following their initial study, Wilson and Hafferty (1983) readministered the measures just prior to graduation from medical school. Thirty-eight students responded, 14 seminar and 24 control subjects. the authors found that positive attitude change was maintained in the experimental group. These data support the use of an educational intervention to affect positive attitude change throughout the basic science and clinical years.

In a recent project, Donnelly, Duthrie, Kirsling, and Gambert (1987) studied the effects of geriatric training with second- and fourth-year medical students as well as physicians in their internal medicine residency. An 8-hour series of lectures on aging was used with the second-year students, while fourth-year students and physicians participated in clinical geriatric medicine rotations. All participants took pre- and posttests of their knowledge of the elderly and aging. Donnelly et al. (1987) found that fourth-year students and physicians had statistically higher scores than second-year students, suggesting that "hands on" experiences are important factors.

Two programs primarily using field experiences have been described in the literature. Birenbaum, Aronson, and Seiffer (1979) provided four medical students with extensive interview experience during a 2-month summer fellowship program. Evaluation data were positive but subjective, and the sample size was small, making interpretation difficult. Sachs, McPherson, and Donnerberg (1985) used a similar medical interviewing practice approach with a larger group ($N=231$) of medical students in a nonrandomized pre- and posttest design. Attitudes toward the elderly were assessed by 22 polar adjective pairs on a semantic differential. Results indicated a significant positive effect for the intervention and further supported the use of practica-based experiences with health older adults. The authors suggested that direct experience with the elderly is central to changing or strengthening attitudes toward older adults.

DIRECTIONS FOR PROGRAM DEVELOPMENT

As we have seen, there will be a substantially increased demand for health care services by older people in the near future. The studies reviewed here demonstrate the need to prepare health providers to care more effectively for elderly patients. Almost without exception, research conducted with medical students and health providers indicates the presence of stereotyped and often negative attitudes about aged patients, as well as substantial lack of knowledge about aging. Studies that have followed students over their educational years, or studies that have compared students early in training with those completing training, indicate that misinformation, stereotyped attitudes, and discomfort with elderly patients are maintained over time.

A number of educational intervention projects have attempted to alter student knowledge and attitudes toward the elderly. As we discussed, these projects have had mixed degrees of success. In general, it appears that by providing students with information about the elderly, about aging processes, and about chronic illnesses, it is possible to increase knowledgeability about geriatric populations. There is also reason to believe that increased knowledge about the elderly produces modest change in attitudes toward older patients (Holtzman et al., 1981; Perotta et al., 1981), probably because students' negative and pessimistic "uniformity assumptions" about the elderly are reduced with accurate information. Programs combining geriatric education with sensitization experiences and actual contact with elderly patients have produced the greatest evidence of change (Donnelly et al., 1987; Holtzman et al., 1978; Wilson & Hafferty, 1980). Unfortunately, conclusions based on research in this area must be regarded as preliminary because most evaluations of training programs have been made without random assignment of subjects to educational or training conditions, they have assessed only short-term effects using paper-and-pencil attitude or knowledge measures, and they have utilized measures lacking in validity and reliability. There has been no assessment of such critical questions as whether students who participate in gerontological education programs are more likely to take later elective courses or specialize in geriatrics, are more behaviorally skilled with elderly patients, or are evaluated with greater satisfaction by their older patients.

Many of the programs intended to improve health care trainee or student skills with the elderly have involved assessments of "special" curricula courses, workshops, or other brief interventions. The aims of these special programs have been modest: to produce short-term change in knowledge or attitude measures. These approaches may not be sufficiently comprehensive or extended to produce long-term change in students' attitudes, skills, interests, and clinical expertise with older patients. With respect to the issue of comprehensiveness, efforts to help health care professionals work more effectively with the elderly may need to be multifaceted, improving students' information and knowledge about aging and the aged; countering negative stereotypes, attitudes, and fears about aging; and teaching interpersonal skills particularly relevant to interactions with elderly patients. Examples of the latter include listening skills, attention to psychological and social concerns that may be more common in the elderly than in younger patient groups, and other social skills. While interventions to increase student knowledge of the elderly and to improve negative attitudes have been common, the training of social-behavioral skills needed to interact effectively and comfortably with elderly patients is quite rare.

This leads, in turn, to a final issue. To prepare health care professionals to work effectively with the elderly, there must be ongoing integration of geriatric education and experiences throughout a training curriculum. Thus, educational programs or special courses of the kind reviewed in this chapter must be systematically integrated with a variety of clinical experiences, consultations, clerkships, and training rotations. In such settings, students can be exposed not only to elderly patients, but to experienced professional mentors who can model the sensitivities, skills, and attitudes we wish to cultivate in students. It appears especially important to expose students to a range of elderly populations including patients who are active, in good health, and functioning independently. Too often, geriatric clinical experiences in medicine, nursing, social work, and other areas are limited to contact with patients who are terminally ill, require skilled nursing care, or are otherwise severely incapacitated. If we wish to train students to understand and appreciate the diversity of the elderly population rather than reinforce pessimism, stereotypes, and avoidances, it will be important to structure training experiences that take patient diversity into account. The challenges that await behavioral gerontologists and educators in this area are great.

ACKNOWLEDGMENTS

We gratefully acknowledge the assistance of Wauline Carter, Sue C. Jacobs, and Suzanne A. Cook for their help in preparing the manuscript.

REFERENCES

Bem, D. J. (1972) Self perception theory. In L. Berkowitz (Ed.), *Advances in experimental social psychology* (pp. 1–62). New York: Academic Press.

Bennett, R., & Eckman, J. (1973). Attitudes toward aging: A critical examination of recent literature and implications for future research. In C. Eisdorfer & M. P. Lawton (Eds.), *The psychology of adult development and aging* (pp. 575–597). Washington, DC: American Psychological Association.

Birenbaum, A., Aronson, M., & Seiffer, S. (1979). Training medical students to appreciate the special problems of the elderly. *Gerontologist, 91,* 575–579.

Broder, H., & Block, M. J. (1986). Effects of geriatric education on the knowledge of dental students. *Special Care in Dentistry, 6,* 177–179.

Brubaker, T. H., & Powers, E. A. (1976). The stereotype of "OLD": A review and alternative approach. *Journal of Gerontology, 31,* 441–447.

Butler, R. N. (1969). Age-ism: Another form of bigotry. *Gerontologist, 9,* 243–246.

Butler, R. N. (1975). *Why survive? Being old in America.* New York: Harper & Row.

Butler, R. N. (1978). The doctor and the aged patient. In W. Reichel (Ed.), *The geriatric patient* (pp. 199–206).

Cicchetti, D. V., Fletcher, C. R., Lerner, E., & Coleman, J. V. (1973). Effects of a course of the attitudes of medical students toward the elderly: A controller study. *Journal of Gerontology, 28,* 370–373.

Coccaro, E. F., & Miles, A. M. (1984). The attitudinal impact of training in Gerontology/Geriatrics in medical school. A review of the literature and perspective. *Journal of the American Geriatrics Society, 32,* 762–768.

Coe, R. M. (1967). Professional perspectives on the aged. *Gerontologist, 7,* 114–119.

Comfort, A. (1964). *Ageing.* New York: Holt, Rinehart & Winston.

DiMatteo, M. R., Hays, R. D., & Prince, L. M. (1986). Relationship of physicians' nonverbal communication skill to patient satisfaction, appointment noncompliance, and physician workload. *Health Psychology, 5,* 581–594.

Donnelly, M. B., Duthrie, E. H., Kirsling, R. A., & Gambert, S. R. (1987). The use of the combined Palmore and Dye & Sassenrath aging quizzes to assess gerontological knowledge in medical education. *Gerontology and Geriatrics Education, 6,* 11–24.

Doyle, B. J., & Ware, J. E. (1977). Physician conduct and other factors that affect consumer satisfaction with medical care. *Journal of Medical Education, 52,* 793–801.

Fries, J. F. (1980). Aging, natural death, and the compression of morbidity. *New England Journal of Medicine, 303,* 130–135.

Fries, J. F. (1983). The compression of morbidity. *Millbank Memorial Fund Quarterly/Health and Society, 61,* 397–419.

Fries, J. F. (1984). The compression of morbidity: Miscellaneous comments about a theme. *Gerontologist, 24,* 354–359.

Garrity, T. F., Wilson, J. F., & Hafferty, F. W. (1984). Improved medical care for the elderly: Intervening in medical education. *Journal of Community Psychology, 12,* 369–378.

Geiger, D. L. (1978). Note: How future professionals view the elderly: A comparative analysis of Social Work, Law, and Medical students' perceptions. *Gerontologist, 18,* 591–594.

Glazier, W. H. (1973). The task of medicine. *Scientific American, 228,* 13–17.

Green, S. K. (1981). Attitudes and perception about the elderly: Current and future perspectives. *International Journal of Aging and Human Development, 13,* 99–119.

Green, S. K., Keith, K. J., & Pawlson, L. G. 1983). Medical student attitudes toward the elderly. *Journal of the American Geriatrics Society, 31,* 305–309.

Greene, M. G., Adelman, R., Charon, R., & Hoffman, S. (1986). Ageism in the medical encounter: An exploratory study of the doctor–elderly patient relationship. *Language and Communication, 6,* 113–124.

Haug, M. R. (1979). Doctor patient relationships and the older patient. *Journal of Gerontology, 34,* 852–860.

Haug, M. R., & Ory, M. G. (1987). Issues in elderly patient–provider interactions. *Research on Aging, 9,* 3–44.

Hayflick, L. (1975). Current theories of biological aging. *Federation Proceedings of American Societies for Experimental Biology, 34,* 9–13.

Heins, M. (1979). Career and life patterns of women and men physicians. In C. Shapiro & L. M. Lowenstein (Eds.) *Becoming a physician* (pp. 217–235). Cambridge, MA: Ballinger.

Holtzman, J. M., & Beck, J. D. (1979). Palmore's facts on aging quiz: A reappraisal. *Gerontologist, 19,* 116–120.

Holtzman, J. M., Beck, J. D., & Coggan, P. G. (1978). Geriatrics program for medical students, II. Impact of two educational experiences on student attitudes. *Journal of the American Geriatrics Society, 26,* 355–359.

Holtzman, J. M., Beck, J. D., & Ettinger, R. L. (1981). Cognitive knowledge and attitudes toward the aged of dental and medical students. *Educational Gerontology: An International Quarterly, 6*, 196–207.

Innui, T. S., & Carter, W. B. (1985). Problems and prospects for health services research on provider–patient communication. *Medical Care, 23*, 521–538.

Institute of Medicine (1978). *Aging and medical education: A report of a study by a committee of the Institute of Medicine* (IOM Publication No. 78-04). Washington, D.C.: National Academy of Sciences.

Johnson, S. M., Kurtz, M. E., Tomlinson, T., & Howe, K. R. (1986). Student stereotypes of patients as barriers to clinical decision-making. *Journal of Medical Education, 61*, 727–735.

Kane, R., Solomon, D., Beck, J., Keeler, E., & Kane, R. (1980). The future need for geriatric manpower in the United States. *New England Journal of Medicine, 302*, 1327–1332.

Keeler, E. B., Solomon, D. H., Beck, J. C., Mendenhall, R. C., & Kane, R. L. (1982). Effect of patient age on duration of medical encounters with physicians. *Medical Care, 20*, 1101–1108.

Kermis, M. D. (1986). The epidemiology of mental disorder in the elderly: A response to the Senate/AARP report. *Gerontologist, 26*, 482–487.

Keyfitz, N. (1978). Improving life expectancy: An uphill road ahead. *American Journal of Public Health, 68*, 954–956.

Kovar, M. G. (1986). Expenditures for the medical care of elderly people living in the community in 1980. *Millbank Memorial Fund Quarterly/Health and Society, 64*, 100–132.

Levinson, R. M., McCollum, K. T., & Kutner, N. G. (1984). Gender homophily in preference of physicians. *Sex Roles, 10*, 315–325.

Ley, P. (1977). Psychological studies of doctor–patient communication. In S. Rachman (Ed.), *Contributions to Medical Psychology* (pp. 9–42). Oxford: Pergamon.

Libow, L. (1978). The development and administration of a geriatric program for freshman and sophomore medical students. In J. W. Brookbank (Ed.), *Improving the quality of health care for the elderly* (pp. 18–24). Gainesville: University Presses of Florida.

Linn, M. W., Linn, B. W., & Stein, S. R. (1982). Satisfaction with ambulatory care and compliance in older patients. *Medical Care, 20*, 606–614.

Lutsky, N. S. (1980). Attitudes toward old age and elderly persons. In C. Eisdorfer (Ed.), *Annual review of gerontology and geriatrics* (pp. 286–336). New York: Springer.

Manton, K. G., & Soldo, B. J. (1985). Dynamics of health changes in the oldest old: New perspectives and evidence. *Millbank Memorial Fund Quarterly/Health and Society, 63*, 206–285.

McKeown, T. (1976). *The role of modern medicine: Dream, mirage or nemesis?* London: Nuffield Provincial Hospital Trust.

McKinlay, J. B., & McKinlay, S. M. (1977). Questionable contributions of medical measures to the decline of mortality in the United States in the twentieth century. *Millbank Memorial Fund Quarterly/Health and Society, 55*, 405–428.

McTavish, D. G. (1971). Perceptions of old people: A review of research methodologies and findings. *Gerontologist, 11*, 90–101.

National Institute of Mental Health. (1987). *Research on the interaction of mental disorder and physical illness in late life* (announcement MH-87-13). Bethesda, MD: Department of Health and Human Services.

National Institute on Aging. (1984). *Report on education and training in geriatrics and gerontology* (administrative document). Bethesda, MD: Public Health Service.

Olshansky, S. J., & Ault, A. B. (1986). The fourth stage of the epidemiologic transition: The age of delayed degenerative disease. *Millbank Memorial Fund Quarterly/Health and Society, 64*, 355–391.

Omran, A. R. (1971). The epidemiologic transition: A theory of the epidemiology of population change. *Millbank Memorial Fund Quarterly/Health and Society, 49*, 509–538.

Palmore, E. (1977). Facts on aging: A short quiz. *Gerontologist, 17*, 315–320.

Palmore, E. (1982). Attitudes toward the aged: What we know and what we need to know. *Research on Aging, 4*, 333–348.

Perotta, P., Perkins, D., Schimpfhauser, F., & Calkins, E. (1981). Medical student attitudes toward geriatric medicine and patients. *Journal of Medical Education, 56*, 478–483.

Robbins, L. N., Helzer, J. E., Weissman, M. M., Orvaschel, H., Gruenberg, E., Burke, J. D., & Reigier, D. A. (1984). Lifetime prevalence of specific psychiatric disorders in three sites. *Archives of General Psychiatry, 41*, 949–958.

Robert Wood Johnson Foundation. (1981). *Medical practice in the United States—A special report*. Princeton, NJ: Author.

Rosencranz, H. A., & McNevin, T. E. (1969). A factor analysis of attitudes toward the aged. *Gerontologist, 9*, 55–59.

Rowe, J. W. (1985). Health care of the elderly. *New England Journal of Medicine, 312*, 827–835.

Roybal, E. R. (1984). Federal involvement in mental health care for the aged. *American Psychologist, 39*, 163–166.

Sachs, L. A., McPherson, C., & Donnerberg, R. (1985). Influencing medical students' attitudes toward older adults: A curriculum proposal. *Gerontology and Geriatrics Education, 4*, 91–96.

Santos, J. F., Hubbard, R. W., & McIntosh, J. L. (1983). Mental health and the minority elderly. In L. D. Breslau & M. R. Haug (Eds.), *Depression and aging: Causes, care and consequences* (pp. 51–70). New York: Springer.

Shapiro, S., Skinner, E. A., Kessler, L. G., Von Korf, M., German, P. S., Tischler, G. L., Leaf, P. J., Benham, L., Cottler, L., & Regier, D. A. (1984). Utilization of health and mental health services: Three epidemiologic catchment area sites. *Archives of General Psychiatry, 41*, 971–978.

Solomon, D. L., & Vickers, R. (1979). Attitudes of health workers toward old people. *Journal of the American Geriatrics Society, 27*, 186–191.

Spence, D. L., Feigenbaum, E. M., Fitzgerald, F., & Roth, J. (1968). Medical student attitudes toward the geriatric patient. *Journal of the American Geriatrics Society, 16*, 976–983.

Strehler, B. L., & Mildvan, A. S. (1960). General theory of mortality and aging. *Science, 132*, 14–21.

Tuckett, D. A., & Williams, A. (1984). Approaches to the measurement of explanation and information-giving in medical consultations: A review of empirical studies. *Social Science and Medicine, 18*, 571–580.

Tuckman, J., & Lorge, I. (1953). Attitudes toward old people. *Journal of Social Psychology, 37*, 249–260.

U.S. Senate Select Committee on Aging. (1986). *American in transition: An aging society* (Vols. 1–31, Serial No. 99-8). Washington, D.C.: Government Printing Office.

U.S. Senate Select Committee on Aging. (1987). *Developments in aging: 1986* (Vols. 1–3, Serial No. 100-8). Washington, D.C.: Government Printing Office.

Waitzkin, H. (1985). Information giving in medical care. *Journal of Health and Social Behavior, 26*, 81–101.

Weisman, C. S., & Teitelbaum, M. A. (1985). Physician gender and the physician–patient relationship: Recent evidence and relevant questions. *Social Science and Medicine, 20*, 1119–1127.

Weisman, C. S., Levine, D. M., Steinwachs, D. M., & Chase, G. A. (1980). Male and female physician career patterns: Specialty choices and graduate training. *Journal of Medical Education, 55*, 813–825.

West, H. L., & Levy, W. J. (1985). Knowledge of aging in the medical profession. *Gerontology and Geriatrics Education, 4*, 97–105.

Williams, T. F. (1981). The physician viewpoint. In M. R. Haug (Ed.), *Elderly patients and their doctors* (pp. 42–46). New York: Springer.

Wilson, J. F., & Hafferty, F. W. (1980). Changes in attitudes toward the elderly one year after a seminar on aging and health. *Journal of Medical Education, 55*, 993–999.

Wilson, J. F., & Hafferty, F. W. (1983). Long-term effects of a seminar on aging and health for first-year medical students. *Gerontologist, 23*, 319–324.

Wilson, R. W., & Glamser, F. D. (1982). The impact of a gerontological intervention on osteopathic medical students. *Educational Gerontology: An International Quarterly, 8*, 373–380.

22

Teaching the Use of Community Services to Elderly People and Their Families

Nathan L. Linsk, Patricia Hanrahan,
and Elsie M. Pinkston

An increasing array of home care, community-based and institutional services has accompanied the increasing numbers of elderly and disabled persons in general, as well as those with posthospitalization home care needs. The extent and availability of services are limited, however, and for those who cannot pay for their own support, eligibility requirements may limit service usage. Most home and community services for the elderly are initiated through federal programs, which often contain targeting or limiting factors. Local community programs may have limits as well. The service system frequently changes due to political and economic realities, and eligibility may change due to alterations in the recipient's needs and status. The result is a complex and confusing network that is difficult to use. In fact, elders and their families may often require considerable assistance in securing and utilizing services to which they are entitled.

An educative and enabling approach, based on principles of behavior analysis aand clinical social work, may facilitate use of community services by clients and their families. Yet procedures for linking clients with community organizations and for teaching clients and their families how to access services have been slow to develop. The process of linking elderly adults to needed services has been studied in such global terms as "assessment," "development of a care plan," "referral," and "monitoring." The more detailed study of the processes of service linkage has articulated in descriptions of case management. Austin (1983) presented a resource-dependent analysis of case management that derives relevant variables related to the nature of the local delivery system and the degree of authority and

Nathan L. Linsk • Department of Medical Social Work, College of Associated Health Professions, University of Illinois at Chicago, Chicago, Illinois 60680. Patricia Hanrahan • University of Chicago, Chicago, Illinois 60637. Elsie M. Pinkston • School of Social Service Administration, University of Chicago, Chicago, Illinois 60637.

control of the case manager. O'Connell (1988) presents a multilevel system model of case management, delineating levels of personnel and several components (status, functions, roles, focus–target, and technology).

Many have expected that an increase in community services would help prevent institutional nursing home placement. This expectation has not been realized, according to current research (Hughes, 1985; Weissert, 1985a), and may be in part due to a lack of validated assessment and referral techniques. The primary value of community-based services such as home health care and supportive home assistance may lie in improving the quality of life of impaired or disabled elders and not in deterring nursing home placement.

In this chapter we have outlined the major service programs that currently serve the elderly and disabled. We have reviewed the chief studies evaluating service provision and linkage. Next, we have presented a model of service linkage based on principles of applied behavioral analysis. This model, which was developed in the Elderly Support Project at the University of Chicago School of Social Service Administration (Pinkston & Linsk, 1984a, 1984b), is described in terms of task analysis and the development and evaluation of task strategies. Finally, we have outlined needs for future research and practice-model development.

SERVICES FOR THE ELDERLY

Informal Support: Families

The primary source of help and support for impaired elders is the family (Shanas, 1979), particularly spouses and children. In addition to direct assistance, families perform case management-like activities for their elders by identifying and securing the needed services. High levels of family support exist even for the most frail elderly (Brody, 1981; General Accounting Office of the United States, 1977). More than 80% of them receive care from informal or family sources (Soldo & Myllyluoma, 1983). An increasing amount of family care is provided by family members living in a household other than the one in which the elderly client lives (Chang & Swart, 1984; Horowitz & Dobroff, 1982).

Brody (1981) questioned three generations of family members (elderly, adult children, and adult grandchildren) about their preferences for family care of the aged. All three generations endorsed family care by nonfamily caregivers and all preferred that adult children assume responsibility for finances and act as "intimates." The children preferred formal providers more than did the older and younger generations. Brody recommended that family allowances be developed to promote family caregiving.

Caregiving is largely a female-dominated activity (Cantor, 1983; Horowitz, 1978; Osterbusch, Keigher, Miller, & Linsk, 1987; Sommers, 1985; Treas, 1977). The quality of caring varies according to whether the caregivers are adult children or healthy spouses. Each type of caregiver experiences a different kind of stress. Adult children may feel more role conflict, while spouses may respond more directly to the physical stresses of caring and seek less help to relieve the pressure (Johnson & Catalano, 1983; Rankin, 1985). Elders in need themselves turn first to family members, then to neighbors, and finally to social agencies for support (Shanas, 1979). Findings from research and practice suggest that elderly participants, significant others, and community leaders are satisfied with combined family and formal service programs (Ehrlich & Wirth, 1978; Horowitz & Shindleman, 1983; Tuzil, 1978).

Formal Community Services

The 1970s and early 1980s were marked by efforts to promote planning and coordination of services for the elderly (Estes, 1979). A national network was developed by Title III of the Older Americans Act and under the auspices of the Administration on Aging in the Human Development Services Division of the U.S. Department of Health and Human Services (HHS) (Gelfand & Olson, 1980). Under the aegis of the 10 HHS regions, each state was divided into Area Agencies on Aging (AAAs), joint ventures between the public and private sectors, with independent boards of directors and non-profit status. The AAAs, in turn, contract for and supervise specific service programs in their areas, particularly those mandated by the Older Americans Act. Although the extent of authority and responsibility of the AAAs varies, they remain a major source of teaching how agency services are organized and in linking clients to services.

Some services are especially important because they provide access either to other services or to the community beyond the narrow confines of one's home. Information and referral services provide an entry point in the complex world of service delivery systems for older adults. Case management involves a stronger emphasis on coordinating services based on an individual care plan, and on monitoring to see whether service delivery occurs. Case management sometimes provides a single entry point for access to a wide range of services, rather than having a frail elder go to a half dozen different agencies for a variety of service needs.

Both case managers and information and referral specialists can help determine whether a client is eligible for services, and give directions through the maze of service delivery systems. Eligibility criteria vary from state to state. Several states are experimenting with coordinated care programs that have the power to broaden eligibility requirements, rather than using categorical funding with programs varying in their eligibility requirements (Harrington & Newcomer, 1985).

Transportation presents a problem for many older adults due to inadequate income, insufficient access, or mobility problems (Wilson, 1984). Recent efforts to enhance access, such as reduced fare, were required under the Urban Mass Transit Act and transportation programs came into existence. These programs are sometimes limited to transporting elderly to places essential for their well-being, such as doctor appointments or grocery shopping. Transportation to visit families and for recreational purposes is frequently not available. Escort services are also available in many communities for those with impaired mobility or sensory deficits. Since transportation is a transitional service that allows people to go out of their homes, it is especially important because it provides the impaired elder with access to a wider world of reinforcers in the community.

Senior centers usually provide a variety or programs at one location. Home-delivered services may be provided under the auspices of a senior center. Other services that are sometimes offered include adult day care and rehabilitation therapy. These access services are summarized in Table 1.

There are some services that attempt to help both the health impaired and the able elderly meet a variety of needs. A number of these programs are described in Table 2.

Social Security retirement income and state, federal, or private pensions are often the major sources of income of many elderly people. Medical assistance (Medicaid) and health insurance often provide relief from financial burden, although they are insurance provisions rather than income support *per se*. Other income support sources include tax benefits, food stamps, and housing subsidies (Kutza, 1981).

The Social Security program has had a substantial impact on reducing poverty among elderly adults, although it has been less effective among elderly women, especially members of minority groups (Minkler & Stone, 1985). Older adults must retire to be eligible for Social Security payments, but Social Security Income (SSI) is available to elders with low incomes based on a means test. Private pensions depend on participation in a pension plan during past employment.

Elderly adults may also choose to supplement their incomes through continuing or modified employment past the usual retirement age. A number of older worker programs have been developed to serve those elders who are still interested in employment. An example is the Older American Community Service Employment Program, funded by the Older Americans Act. Several federally funded programs facilitate semi-employment or volunteer work with expenses reimbursed, such as Retired Senior Volunteer Program or Foster Grandparents. Job banks and placement services for older workers are often operated by senior centers and voluntary organizations.

The private sector is increasingly aware of the need to make employment available to older workers (Carnevale, 1986). Although relatively few firms have developed corporate programs for older workers, their numbers are expected to increase with the aging of the population. These programs include: part-time work options; retraining; retirement transition and job placement; and job redesign (Morrison, 1986). Support for this approach is found in gerontological research indicating that biological and intellectual functions can be preserved far longer than had originally been thought (Butler, 1986).

Another important service is the provision of legal assistance. Issues of particular interest to elders include making wills, guardianship, and consumer protection. Dealing with the complex bureaucracies involved in distributing Social Security and Medicare funds can also give rise to a need for legal services, particularly when benefits are denied (Holmes & Holmes, 1979). Senior legal programs funded by the Older American Act may be available regardless of an elderly person's financial status.

TABLE 1
Access Services for the Elderly

Service	Description	Availability
State unit on aging/area agency on aging	Responsible for planning and coordination of services for the elderly. Often provides technical assistance to community programs or award contracts to community organizations for specific services.	Locate through community resource directories, U.S. Department of Health and Human Services Administration on Aging, or National Association of State units on aging.
Information and referral	Detailed information about range of services available, including eligibility requirements, and how to apply for specific services. Generally includes names and telephone number of specific service providers.	Senior centers, hospitals, and adult day-care centers may provide this service.
Case management	Coordination of services, based on an individual care plan, usually followed by monitoring to see that the service delivery occurs and advocacy. Sometimes includes providing a single entry point for access to services.	Selected senior centers, state aging office designees, family service agencies, hospital social work departments, or other social agencies.
Transportation	Reduced fares; subsidized transportation, pickup and delivery services, specialized public transportation for elderly and disabled.	Voluntary or church organizations, Medicaid offices for recipients, specialized services for elderly through senior centers or community agencies. Priorities may be related to basic (often medical) needs.
Senior center	Central site that may provide a combination of: recreation, adult day care, medical services (screening, rehabilitation), preventative health services, information and referral, meal programs, and outreach services.	Contact community resource directories or services, state unit on aging or local Area Agency on Aging.

TABLE 2
Services for Able and Disabled Elderly

Service	Description	Availability
Income	Social Security, Supplmental Security Income (SSI), private pensions. Indirect supports include Medicaid, health insurance, food stamps, tax benefits, and housing supplements.	Social Security Office, public assistance offices, information and referral offices.
Employment	Job banks, placement and counseling services. Volunteer programs such as Retired Senior Volunteer Programs, Foster Grandparents. Private sector initiates including part-time work options, retraining, retirement transition, and placement and job readiness (Morrison, 1986).	Senior centers, information and referral programs, and unions may provide information.
Legal services and legal-aid programs	Estate planning, guardianship, consumer protection.	Subsidized services may be available to older adults with low incomes through legal services corporation, Older Americans Act, local clinics, and senior centers
Community housing	Rent supplements, maintenance and repair, construction loans.	Older Americans Act funded mainteance and repair programs. Rent supplements through Section 8 of the Housing and Community Development Act. Loans for construction through U.S. Department of Housing and Urban Development. Contact local Housing Authority, information and referral services.

Housing resources are generally inadequate and difficult to obtain for elderly individuals. Indeed, the problems of the elderly homeless are now receiving some national attention, although intervention programs have not yet begun. Housing for the elderly may entail support services to maintain existing housing. Information about local household chore services may be secured through community information and referral services. Localities may provide funding for home repair and construction, or funds may be sought through federal sources (see Table 2). Senior housing may be sought through Department of Housing and Urban Development programs, often managed through local housing bureaus. Often these services are in short supply and waiting lists are common.

Other types of housing, which may be accessed through social service programs for the elderly, include various congregate housing facilities such as apartments/hotels. These generally provide an elderly person with his or her own apartment or room in a building where meals and some recreational services are available. Many elderly live in settings, often referred to as Single Room Occupancy Hotels, where formal resources are very limited.

Elderly clients may request help locating retirement housing, which may be available as part of a multiple-use development offering a range of support for the elderly or which may exist within a retirement community.

There are many services designed to meet the needs of dependent elderly who require support. These are described in Table 3. Adult day care and protective services are particularly helpful to those who suffer from dementing illness. In-home services are helpful to those with physical and/or mental impairments. We shall consider each of these services briefly.

Adult Day Care

There are two primary models of adult day care: the health care model and the social model (Weissert, 1975). Health care models usually stress physical rehabilitation, while social models emphasize opportunities for interactions and recreation with age peers. Families and clients need to make pragmatic decisions about the utility of a program for their needs. They need to consider the ratio of staff to clients, the range of activities offered to accommodate the varying abilities of impaired elders, and whether the program serves a wide variety of needs or specializes in caring for adults with a particular type of disability, such as dementia. As a general rule of thumb, higher ratios of staff to clients are likely to mean more opportunities for positive reinforcement and individualized care. On average, the ratio of staff to adults based on daily attendance counts is one to six (Conrad, Hughes, Campione, & Singer, 1986).

Protective Services

Protective services are available for those elders who are having difficulty caring for themselves, but are not willing or able to seek help independently. Specific services may be provided depending on the nature of the client's deficits. For instance, meals may be provided to some demented elders who are living alone

TABLE 3
Services for Disabled Elderly

Service	Description	Availability
Adult day care	Supervision, recreation, and supportive intervention or training in activities of daily living. Transportation, physical therapy, or respite may be offered by some centers.	Contact hospital social worker, Area Agency on Aging, senior center. May be funded by Social Service Block Grants or Medicaid Waiver programs. May be free standing or part of nursing home, hospital, or senior center program.
Protective services	Social and legal services for individuals unable to make own decisions. May include assistance meeting basic needs or legal services.	Available through social service and legal assistance programs, with specific provisions varying from state to state.
In-Home services		
Home health service	Nursing and rehabilitation therapy provided by home nurses or home health aides.	Generally available to those who are recuperating from an acute illness, but not to those with chronic conditions. Private insurance and Medicare reimbursement. Medicaid funding may pay for more maintenance services.
Personal care	Help with self-care tasks, such as bathing, dressing, and eating.	May be based on functional assessment by nurses or social workers, often require physician orders. Contact hospital social worker or Area Agency on Aging for local information.
Homemakers	Assistance with light housework, meal preparation, supervision, or accompaniment to medical appointments.	May be based on functional assessment by nurses or social workers, often require physician orders. Contact hospital social worker of Area Agency on Aging for local information.
Companions	Supervision, socialization, which may include social outings.	Senior companion program through Administration on Aging. Local programs or private arrangements.
Home meals	Home delivered meals, generally at least once daily.	Generally available through Older Americans Act programs, but may be limited and require waiting lists.

and are no longer able to shop and make decent meals for themselves. If an elder is judged incompetent, a guardian may be appointed. Family caregivers may initiate guardianship by arranging actions with an attorney. Legal services are also available to older adults to prevent the occurrence of guardianship commitment without undue cause. Alternatively, legal advisors might help an elder choose a guardian (Holmes & Holmes, 1979).

In-Home Services

There is an increasing emphasis on the need to provide health care and other services to frail elders in their own homes, which is the preferred living situation for most. With in-home services, a community-residing elder with some disabilities may meet basic maintenance or treatment needs. Services vary by community, but may include: home health care, personal care, homemaker service, in-home companions, and home-delivered meals. Important home and community care resources (especially nutrition services, transportation and personal care) are provided through the Older Americans Act. Others are provided through Medicaid Home and Community-based Care Waivers, which allow individuals to be cared for at home rather than in nursing homes. Many states allow family members, who may otherwise require employment, to be paid as home care workers for their relatives (Linsk, Keigher, & Osterbusch, 1988).

There is some overlap among these services. For instance, assistance with eating might be offered by a personal care attendant, a homemaker, or a companion. Homemakers, as well as companions, can provide emotional support to an isolated elder. When some clients do not meet eligibility requirements for nursing assistance due to particular chronic conditions, some tasks, such as encouraging a forgetful elder to take medications, can be performed by homemakers or companions.

The programs described below are combinations of complex services designed to assist the dependent elderly individual to live in the community setting. Hospice programs provide a range of supportive services for those with terminal illnesses. A number of services have been developed under the rubrics of family-based care or family support, which include incentives for family care.

Hospice Programs

Hospice programs provide an alternative to hospital or nursing home care for older adults who are terminally ill. The hospice system consists of medical care "which emphasizes palliation and psychosocial support of terminal patients and their families" (Greer & Mor, 1986, p. 5). Some hospice programs provide supportive services to enable patients to remain at home. Some may have access to hospital beds for the last difficult days of dying. The majority of the patients who have utilized hospice services were dying of cancer. Usually family members are highly involved in assisting with care.

Family Support Programs

Family support programs, developed to sustain home care, include counseling, educational, and support group programs. Counseling may be provided by various psychosocial support agencies ranging from private practitioners with expertise in family therapy with the elderly, to family service health care providers, including hospital social workers and psychologists, and mental health agencies. Senior centers, day-care centers, or other service programs specifically for the elderly may include a family-counseling component. Family education may be provided to inform families about the processes of aging, resources available, common emotional implications, and methods of specific care. The latter may include physical care, support for emotional needs, an ways to improve daily activities and manage problem behaviors. Educational programs may be offered as part of adult education programs through local colleges, or part of community church related services, or by social agencies. Support groups for family members may be provided by the same sources, or be developed independently. These groups offer support from others in the same situation, and may also serve social action or advocacy objectives. The Alzheimer's Association has shown leadership in developing mutual help groups for families providing home care.

Incentives for Family Care

For the most part, caregiving of aged relatives is not directly compensated (Osterbusch *et al.*, 1987). Public programs to promote family care have been developed, both as specific programs and as adaptations of existing service options (Arling & McAuley, 1983; Burwell, 1986; Linsk, Osterbusch, Simon-Rusinowitz, & Keigher, 1988). Family incentives are of two types: family or caregiving allowances, whereby the client or family receive a set monthly amount to be used as they wish; and family payments, where family members are directly hired by home care agencies to provide home care. To date, family incentives are considered a last resort to arrange care for an otherwise unserved elder, and not as a way to the family in general.

SERVICE RESEARCH

Considerable research has been carried out in the last decade on a number of community-based services. Particularly relevant to our topic, linkage of families with service organizations, are a number of recent case management studies. There are also several large-scale studies that examine such specific services as day care, homemaker services, and hospice programs (Greer & Mor, 1986; Wan, Weissert, & Livieratos, 1980; Weissert, Wan, Livieratos, & Katz, 1980). In the next section we will present the research conducted with each type of service.

Research on Case Management Services

The first batch of large case management studies were funded individually by the Health Care Financing Agency (Capitman, 1986). Another study, the National Channeling Project, including a test of two models of case management in 10 sites across the country (Thornton & Dunstan, 1986). Most of the studies used random assignment of subjects to case management or to a routine services control group. The main purpose of these studies was to test the use of community services as a method of avoiding expensive institutional settings, especially hospitals and nursing homes. Most of the studies failed to achieve this cost-containment goal, and community services functioned as an add-on rather than as a substitute from institutional placement (Weissert & Cready, 1986). In the few studies that did achieve cost savings, eligibility was defined very narrowly.

Investigations also examined the impact of case management on a variety of other factors. Some case management studies have found improvements in the quality of life of elderly adults (Applebaum & Harrigan, 1986). In the Channeling Project, the number of unmet service needs was reduced, particularly among those with severe unmet needs (Thornton & Dunstan, 1986). Elderly adults also reported more satisfaction with services and more life satisfaction when using case management rather than routine services.

Although most studies have not specifically assessed the effects of case management on families, the National Channeling Project found that families reduced their worrying about obtaining sufficient help, increased their satisfaction with care arrangements, reduced personal limitations, and improved their overall life satisfaction (Christianson & Stevens, 1986a).

For the most part, case-managed community services are not associated with reduced mortality (Weissert, 1985b). In one early study, Blenkner, Bloom, and Nielson (1971) observed increased mortality among those who received special services, possibly due to the fact that the special staff were more likely to recommend institutional placement, which has a higher rate of mortality, because they felt that community services were inadequate. Secondary analysis of the study suggested that members of the experimental group had more health problems initially (Berger & Piliavin, 1976).

In the Georgia Alternative Health Service Project, investigators found a significant reduction or postponement of mortality in the group receiving case management (Skellie & Coan, 1980; Skellie, Mobley & Coan, 1982). In this study, however, the control group received substantially fewer services than the experimental group, a difference that may account for the results.

Two studies (Applebaum & Harrigan, 1986; Blenkner et al., 1971) unexpectedly found that the provision of case-managed services was associated with reduced functional ability. For example, some impaired elders gave up the struggle to bathe themselves when there was someone to do it for them. In the Applebaum and Harrigan study, contentment increased along with the decline in functional abilities. The same processes that lead to excess disabilities in institutions can occur in the community. It may, for instance, be easier for personal-care staff to feed a physically impaired elder than to clean up after self-feeding efforts.

Some approaches to service linkage, notably the Elderly Support Project, include the use of brief treatment for problems experienced by elders and/or their families (Hanrahan, Young, & Pinkston, 1985; Linsk, Green, Marlow, & Pinkston, 1980; Pinkston, & Linsk, 1984a). Steinberg and Carter (1983), on the other hand, believe that the provision of direct treatment is too time consuming for the case manager and discourage its use. Unfortunately, referral sources for the sort of brief, problem-solving approach that is appropriate for this age group are frequently unavailable (Wilson, Applebaum, & Schneider, 1986), at least in part because many service providers are biased against the elderly (Butler & Lewis, 1982; Zarit, 1980). Nevertheless, most of the large-scale case management studies relied on outsider referral for treatment of behavioral problems experienced by the elderly and their families.

Research on Day-Care and Homemaker Services

The major controlled study of adult day-care programs and homemaker services was conducted by Health Services Research (Wan et al., 1980; Weissert et al., 1980). Clients were randomly assigned to day-care services, homemaker services, combined services, or a routine services control. The day-care programs were based on a health care model that had a goal of physical rehabilitation. Homemakers provided personal care, light housekeeping, and assistance with health care, such as helping the older person get to an appointment. Positive findings favored the experimental groups on a number of measures. Day-care clients used nursing homes less frequently, had better physical functioning, and higher activity levels than controls ($p < .01$ to .05). Elders who received homemaker services had better physical functioning and were more content than controls ($p < .01$ to .05). All three experimental groups had significantly lower mortality rates than those who received routine services (20.0% versus 29.7%, $p < .01$). However, other factors besides the experimental services accounted for more of the variance in positive outcomes. These factors included diagnostic conditions and the use of other services such as hospital outpatient departments. When these variables were included in the analysis, the findings in favor of the experimental services were no longer statistically significant on most measures. At $52 per day per person, the cost of the day-care service was 71% higher than routine services. When the use of Medicare and Medicaid were included, total annual costs for the day-care group averaged $6,501 per person compared to $3,808 for controls.

Each of the experimental groups and the control group included some nursing home placement, indicating that day-care and homemaker services functioned as additions to community care instead of substitutions for nursing homes.

Research on Hospice Programs

In the National Hospice Study the conventional health care system was compared with two approaches to hospice care: home-based programs and programs with access to hospital beds (Greer & Mor, 1986). The design was quasi-experimental in that families and elders chose the setting they preferred, and outcomes among these types of settings were compared. Twenty-six sites across the country were studied. What differences occurred were not large and tended to favor hospice programs. True to their purpose, hospice patients died at home more often. The hospice programs with access to hospital beds had slight, but statistically significant, reductions in pain and symptoms. Family reports on satisfaction with care compared favorably with home care and conventional care. There were no negative effects of hospice care: survival rates and provision of palliative measures were equivalent across groups.

For the most part the findings from large-scale research on service linkage and provision are positive, although on a less ambitious level than was originally envisioned. The studies cannot demonstrate that clients avoid institutional placement due to community services of various kinds, but they do suggest that service provision does improve the client's quality of life. This most limited effect is similar to the pattern identified in a previous review of social treatment (Reid & Hanrahan, 1982). The studies are not without problems, however, particularly regarding several experimental groups that decreased their functional ability (Applebaum, 1986).

Small-Scale Studies

While most service research has consisted of large-scale studies, a few small-scale studies have been conducted. These studies have examined the inclusion of families in case management, community-based discharge planning, and caseload management. Most were quasi-experimental and used an uncontrolled single-group design. While most studies primarily examined services for elderly adults and their families, one study focused mainly on the effect of respite care on families (George, Gwyther, Fillenbaum, & Palmore, 1986). We will discuss each of these in turn.

Family as Case Managers

The Family Support Project (Frankfather, Smith, & Caro, 1981) included families with a relative at least 60 years old, functionally disabled, with an annual income under $8,000. In this project a service plan is developed during a family meeting in clients' homes. A mutual agreement specified planned agency services or cash benefits and areas of family caregiving. This contract was confirmed by letter. Families asked for help with housekeeping ($N = 36$), personal-care service (N

= 22), and counseling (N = 23). Data are given for 56 clients. family caregivers reported that as a result of the project, stress and disruption decreased across emotional, physical, social, and financial areas of functioning.

In another study (Simmons, Ivry, & Seltzer, 1985), a family service agency randomly assigned families to participation in case management planning and tasks, or to routine family services. Available progress reports confirmed that experimental group families performed more case management tasks than did those who received traditional services and received service for a briefer time, suggesting greater efficiency in the use of agency resources.

Community-Based Discharge Planning

Hubbard, Santos, and Wiora (1978) reported a study in which a case manager initiated contact with clients in the hospital, then continued to act as an ongoing liaison between the client and community services after discharge. The case manager also provided direct services, including counseling, as needed. The study was quasi-experimental, using an uncontrolled single-group design. Clients had to be at least 55 years old. Of a total of 30 cases, only two clients returned to institutions after their participation in the program. One of those two subsequently returned to the community.

Task-Centered Caseload Management

The task-centered system has been advocated as a particularly appropriate conceptual framework for case management (Epstein, 1980; Reid, 1978; Steinberg & Carter, 1983). A study by Rooney and Wanless (1985) examined the consequences of decision making in the assignment of cases to varying types of services: crisis intervention, task-centered casework, or supportive casework. Cases were assigned on the basis of need and client preference. On average, the practitioner who used a task-centered decision-making process was more efficient than others in the agency. Considerably more cases were initiated (45 versus 26) and terminated (40 versus 25).

Research on Respite

Most of the research on community care programs has focused on services to elderly adults, often with a clear effort to avoid substituting costly government services for unpaid family efforts. When older adults are moderately to severely impaired, the primary family caregiver usually spends a great deal of time providing supervision and personal care. Hanrahan, Lawler, and Pinkston (1987), for example, found that more than two-thirds of the caregivers in a study of family of adults in day care took care of their impaired relative for at least 40 hours a week, the equivalent of a full-time job.

A growing recognition of the strains on family caregivers has led to the evaluation of programs designed to relieve some of the burden. A preliminary report by George et al. (1986) describes a program in which a respite worker took over for the primary caregiver in the home for an average of 8 hours a week. Respite care was subsidized either partially or wholly for those who could not pay for the service. Subsidized care was limited, however, and families commented on the need for more time. As expected with this help, caregivers significantly increased the amount of time they spent in recreational activities, from an initial 4.6 hours a week to 11.1 hours a week. They made more statements of positive affect, a difference just short of statistical significance, and they doubled the number of their contacts with community services.   •

Results of the small-scale studies are primarily positive. Since most designs lack a comparison group, however, the findings must be considered tentative. The exception to this pattern is the research by Simmons *et al.* (1985) with families as case managers. The Elderly Support Project, presented below, is another exception. In this project, single-case designs were used to evaluate positive outcomes.

THE ELDERLY SUPPORT PROJECT

Although a number of studies have designated linkages between clients/ families and community service agencies as interventions or outcomes, few models of referral for services have been developed that specify how clients and their families access services. Both medical and mental health care practitioners generally assume that *telling* a person about a service is enough to motivate them to use it. Because there is such a large and complex array of services and uncertain outcomes in the use of services, it is important to specify methods of achieving service linkage.

In the Elderly Support Project we have developed a model about community service linkages for elderly people and their families (Pinkston & Linsk, 1984a, 1984b). There are three important elements to the program. First, community service linkages are defined as strategies for increasing the amount of reinforcement available to an older person on an ongoing basis. Access to such services as adult care, socialization, nutrition programs, or home supports may all be viewed from a behavioral perspective as ways to increase the opportunities for the individual to engage in behaviors that will be followed by positive outcomes (e.g., social contact, improved physical status, or such primary reinforcers as food or physical stimulation). Second, the process of matching need and resource is based on a twofold assessment of client need and resource capability. The process of dual assessment is critical in establishing the capability of the client to use the services and the reinforcing potential of the service outcome. The assessment is made through the joint efforts of the practitioner assisting in the linkage access, the client and his or her family supports, and the staff or the linkage agency. Third, linkages only occur when all the actors have the requisite skills and knowledge necessary to make the match. Very often, practitioners, as well as clients, must acquire appropriate skills and information. Teaching is generally provided through didactic presentation of information, often supplemented by written materials including brochures and checklists. Whenever possible the direct presentation should be interactive and allow for opportunities for rehearsal of linkage steps before they occur. The teacher, the practitioner in this case, takes responsibility for the learning of others, which means he or she will need to determine whether or not the clients learned about the service and how it will be accessed. Follow-up and evaluation are critical steps in achieving service access, and often an ongoing data base is required to ascertain outcomes.

Social workers, as well as other practitioners with frequent need to refer clients, often implement service linkage intervention in near automatic fashion, particularly if they are providing service to a large caseload in a busy setting. A medical social worker may assess need of the client through a referral from a physician and nurse and a brief interview with the patient and family (which may be by telephone). He or she may assess resource potentials by an ongoing written or unwritten data base that is supplemented from practice experience on a daily basis, and may then engage in complex teaching with service providers and clients in many short interventions interspersed in bits and pieces throughout the week. The clients may be asked to contract for service linkages and to keep a log or notes about outcomes, and to check in with the practitioner repeatedly. The social worker may frequently reassess client need or resource availability based on rapidly changing information. Steps may not always be completed because of the complex needs presented by clients. Most practitioners learn to do this using informal tools such as peer consultation, on-the-job training, or trail and error. Service linkages are not often conceptualized as sophisticated techniques, yet the success of a complex service plan may depend very much on the ways clients, families, and service agencies understand how they can work together.

The Elderly Support Project was initially developed as a home-based family and client intervention program to assist family caregivers to care effectively for elderly individuals with specific behavioral problems. We have tested the program in home-based settings, as well as in family, group, and adult day-care centers. Community service linkages have been implemented as initial or preliminary interventions or as primary interventions, but they often have been used as part of maintenance procedures to ascertain ongoing support and reinforcement subsequent to behavioral training. In the following section we have described the Elderly Support Project in five steps: assessment, contracting, training and task analysis, monitoring and evaluation, and programming for generalization.

Steps in the Elderly Support Project

Step I: Assessment

A multifocus assessment begins with the needs and abilities of the elderly adult, the needs of the family caregiver, and available resources to meet the needs. The practitioner explores the adequacy of the environment and informal support resources such as neighbors and friends. He or she spends a good deal of time in identifying behavior excesses or deficits that are associated with limited service eligibility. For example, incontinence is frequently an exclusion criterion for senior centers or adult day care; inappropriate verbal behavior excludes people from congregate meal programs and some special housing. The assessor specifies problems in behavioral terms so that a functional analysis (Kanfer & Saslow, 1969; Pinkston, Levit, Green, Linsk, & Rzepnicki, 1982; Zarit, 1980) can determine the relevant antecedents and consequences of the problem behavior or deficit that will qualify a person for or exclude a person from community resources.

Whenever possible, behavioral goals are identified in positive language, even when behavioral deficits are considered. For example, an older woman who has been very isolated and withdrawn might agree that she needs to increase her social contacts, but she may be offended if the practitioner says she needs to work on her isolation.

A number of problem categories may relate to service linkage interventions, including self-care deficits, negative verbalizations, low levels of social activities, inadequate leisure skills such as reading, television watching, and so forth.

Once problems are identified, the frequency and context of the problems must be ascertained. The first source of information is through discussion with clients and families. For instance, one family member noted that he did not like to take his severely impaired wife to activities because his arthritis made it painful for him to put on outdoor clothing. Another client reported that he and his wife only went out a few times per month because they were afraid of the neighborhood.

Often it is useful to have more direct information from observations during a home visit or from an observational report from a home care worker. Recorded observations offer a more specific and permanent source of assessment data. A log of daily notations about problem behaviors and desired alternatives can facilitate service. For example, if the client's refusal to dress himself or herself is seen as an obstacle to outside activities, the family caregiver may record daily information on any self-dressing activities. These records include what prompts or antecedents preceded the dressing (or refusal) and what followed. Even a few days of such data collection will provide sufficient information about reasons for lack of positive activities and possible alternatives. Very often such record-keeping can be continued and serve as a data base for service linkage evaluation.

Needs for service are explored within the context of problems reported by the client and family. For instance, families may find it difficult to engage in pleasant activities a man with Alzheimer's disease who spends most of his day watching television. In this case, the practitioner may choose to help the caregiver find appropriate activities and locate an adult day-care program in the area. In this way, service linkage may be important to maintain or increase a desired behavior.

It is necessary to assess the adequacy of existing service arrangements before determining that additional services are required. In one case, for example, a stroke victim was losing weight. On exploration he reported that the paid homemaker only gave him one meal all day, but he had not wanted to complain because he liked her. His daughter asked the homemaker to keep records of the food he ate, which confirmed that his food intake prior to dinner consisted of a mid-morning serving of French toast. As this example indicates, assessment of ongoing service requires the same level of specificity that is part of the emphasis of behavioral excesses and deficits.

In the Elderly Support Project, assessment usually takes place in the client's home to get an idea of the client's environment. The evaluation may reveal critical information about environmental design and problems with access to one's surroundings. For example, a client who has difficulty getting around should not be hindered by throw rugs that might slip; a client who uses a wheelchair may need ramps to facilitate access to the community; a client who has difficulty bathing might need grab bars.

A wide range of service needs have been identified by families served by the Elderly Support Project. Intensive analysis of a sample of eight cases revealed 22 service needs (Hanrahan *et al.*, 1985). All noted at least one unmet service need, such as day care, meal provision, physical therapy, community activities, and a physician referral for medication. Four families wanted more adequate housing. Two families felt that their elderly relative's prescription for antipsychotic medication was excessive, resulting in oversedation. Five were dissatisfied with the service provided. For instance, one client had a poorly fitting prosthetic device, and another had difficulty understanding the physical therapist's instructions. Other problems involved reimbursement and seeking part-time employment.

Other assessment issues that are especially important among the elderly clients include the possibility of reversible or irreversible dementia and needs for health-related services. With advanced age, mental status often changes, often due to such reversible causes as depression, illness, and malnourishment. Only a small percentage of elders experience nonreversible dementia. The practitioner should explore whether the client has had any difficulties with confusion or memory loss, and if so, a short mental status test will provide additional useful data (e.g., Folstein, Folstein, & McHugh, 1975; Kahn, Goldfarb, Pollock, & Peck, 1960). If some signs of dementia are present, then a full assessment by a geriatric physician or an interdisciplinary consultation service becomes a high priority.

Given the substantial literature that documents caregiver strain (Christianson & Stevens, 1986b), relatives providing care may also be asked to keep a log about the frequency of positive experiences in their lives (Pinkston & Linsk, 1984b; Poulshock & Deimling, 1984; Zarit, Todd & Zarit, 1986). This provides an idea about the adequacy of the caregiver's reinforcing or pleasant events. A major concern among families is the extent to which their access to reinforcement is limited by the demands of caregiving (Bowling, 1984). If caregivers have too little time to recreate, some form of respite service is needed.

As with any problem, when exploring the need for respite it is helpful to ask if it is important right now. Is there any special activity that respite would enable the caregiver to accomplish? For instance, the son of a woman with moderate dementia requested help in placing a companion so that he could take a vacation. According to him, their recent family history could be summarized as "Son hires; Mom fires." A companion was hired but fired by his mother while he was away. The practitioner reminded her that she had agreed to keep a companion while her son was away and she accepted another person. Shortly after he came back she fired the second companion. Although the agency had hoped for a longer-term placement, this case was at least a partial success in that the son met an important respite goal of his choice.

Should the relative who is providing care wish to return to work, a service package to facilitate this goal may be developed. It might be possible, for example, to combine services from a part-time paid homemaker with a personal-care attendant who is subsidized by local community care programs, or to pursue an employment option in which care provision is compensated (Linsk *et al.*, 1988).

Step II: Resource Location and Contracting

After problems and goals have been defined and measured in specific terms, an agreement is clearly stated among family members, the elderly adult and the practitioner. The participants in the agreement include those who have expressed a concern about an issue and a willingness to work with the practitioner to resolve it. Usually no more than two or three problems are identified. Service needs and goals may also be clearly stated at this time. The contract includes an agreement to participate in behavioral training to resolve problems; to use the procedures that the practitioner recommends; and to keep records on the frequency of target behaviors. When families and/or elders have identified service needs, the contract should also include an agreement to work with the practitioner to develop task strategies to secure needed services and to carry out tasks designed to accomplish service goals. The contract should clearly articulate the responsibilities of the practitioner as well. These responsibilities are to develop a treatment plan in collaboration with the family; to provide behavioral training; and to provide feedback on the efficiency of the procedures used. The practitioner assumes responsibility to locate resources and to develop a task strategy for securing resources (Linsk *et al.*, 1980; Weissman, 1975).

The use of monitored contracting has been helpful in itself in resolving service linkage problems. In the Elderly Support Project, contracting was usually paired with cueing or prompting as forms of stimulus control procedures (Pinkston & Linsk, 1984b). Contracting resulted in improvements for 80% of the behaviors targeted. More generally, the use of contracting, in addition to other procedures, correlated with successful outcomes in a review of a broad range of social interventions (Reid & Hanrahan, 1982).

Step III: Client and Family Education

The practitioner formulates an array of service options matched to the needs identified in the assessment. Clients and families are helped to generate their own resources or learn to identify and access appropriate services. The family is taught the skills needed to achieve linkage and the required steps are usually formulated into an implicit or explicit contract. The outcome of this collaboration is a set of specific tasks detailing who will perform what activity when, in order to secure a needed resource. These tasks may then be recorded on a task assignment sheet. This phase can be described in Weissman's terms as "option exploration and resource selection" (1975).

In one case, a client wished to move out of her daughter's apartment and live on her own (Green & Marlow, 1984). The practitioners helped the family decide on a division of labor. The client's granddaughter agreed to go with her to get three

Sunday newspapers to use in finding available apartments. These tasks were recorded on a task assignment sheet. The move was accomplished. A family contract arranged for social contacts with the client, her daughter, granddaughter, and a son who had not been involved previously because of conflicts between him and his sister. Social contacts increased, and in fact, the client had more contact with her family than when she lived with them.

Practitioner tasks are also clearly agreed upon in detail. The practitioner might, for instance, agree to call several adult day-care programs in order to determine which ones had openings. Joint tasks, involving the practitioner and the client or relative, may also be appropriate. For example, the practitioner might accompany the family on a visit to a day-care center as part of deciding whether or not an elderly relative should attend the program. In some cases, the client may be too impaired and the family too burdened to perform tasks. Practitioner tasks will be the main means of service linkage in these cases (Thibault, 1984).

Behavioral assessment of a client's ability to participate in tasks is an ongoing process. If a client feels fearful of taking the first step toward securing a service, the practitioner may use a joint task as a form of shaping. For instance, one depressed woman was interested in engaging in more activities in the community, but was reluctant to go out alone. The practitioner accompanied her on her initial outings, but later she was able to go alone.

Step IV: Monitoring and Evaluation

Once training and task assignments begin, the practitioner monitors completion of the tasks and changes in behavior. The task of increasing desired behavior may require an increase in reinforcement, or a decrease in the response cost. It may be necessary to reconsider the capacities of the family member who is implementing the program. A caregiver checklist has been developed for this purpose (Pinkston & Linsk, 1984b).

The evaluation of service linkage is an ongoing process that includes reviewing task progress, determining whether or not service goals have been attained, and analyzing whether securing a service has, in fact, resolved the problem. When tasks are not achieved, the practitioner should analyze the obstacles to task progress. This can be done with the family, and should be followed by an attempt to develop new tasks to resolve the problems. These procedures are similar to the methods used in the task-centered system described by Reid (1978; Reid & Epstein, 1977). Possible problems include the lack of a formal service, a change in the identified problem, and difficulties encountered by the older adult and/or family member in completing a task (Hanrahan *et al.*, 1985).

In one case, enrollment in a day-care program was frozen. Although the family and the practitioner made many efforts to contact various agencies, the situation remained unchanged. The family continued, however, to increase the clients' social contacts among friends and relatives, an effort so successful that the client no longer felt the need for day care when the program was finally available. Although the service linkage goal was not achieved, the problem that gave rise to this goal was much improved.

While many families have no difficulties in contacting service providers, for some it can be a problem. In one case, the spouse of a woman with Alzheimer's disease was having difficulty getting services for her, and keeping them once he got them. An analysis of his approach indicated that he did not communicate clearly what he expected the homemaker to do. Then he complained bitterly about her inadequate performance. The practitioner used social skills training to help the client state his expectations clearly to service providers. This procedure was helpful in securing and maintaining services for the duration of the case.

Securing a service may not resolve the problem. Records of the frequency of a problem behavior or situation should be compared to occurrence rates after a service arrangement is made. One client with mild dementia felt unable to communicate with the older people attending a day-care program. In his opinion, they were much more severely impaired than he was and it was difficult for him to talk with them. In this case, a senior center was probably a better alternative. Evaluation of each of these placements could be achieved by recording the frequency with which social contacts occur, and the client's perceived satisfaction with these interactions.

In another case, a physical therapist made an audiotape to help a client with Parkinson's disease practice exercises. The directions on the tape were hard to follow and did not include any encouraging statements. The practitioner revised the tape and found that the client increased his rate of exercise.

Step V: Generality across Time

Maintaining improvements is a key consideration when it is time to terminate a case. Service linkage may provide the necessary support to maintain progress for a client to use his or her skills in a different setting. For example, the client who has increased the frequency of his or her pleasant events at home might begin attending a day-care center to allow for more opportunities to participate in recreational activities.

Evaluation of the Elderly Support Project

The Elderly Support Project has been evaluated in two studies (Hanrahan *et al.*, 1985; Linsk *et al.*, 1980). Results about the attainment of service goals are considered tentative because of the absence of interrater reliability and the reliance on worker questionnaires and written care records as data sources. Evaluative data on changes in behavioral problems, based on behavioral observations conducted by family members, have been reported by Pinkston and Linsk (1984b).

About half of the first 17 cases referred to the project used some form of community linkage (Linsk *et al.*, 1980). In over 60% of the cases some identified services were not secured. Primary reasons for linkage failure included client failure to follow through on linkage steps or client refusal to accept the service he or she originally asked for or agreed to. In at least one case, delays in service linkage prompted the client and family to increase their reliance on friends and contacts in the community to meet their goals. In no cases did workers report linkage failure due to inability to locate needed services.

In the study by Hanrahan *et al.* (1985), goals were considered partially achieved if the problem that gave rise to a service need was alleviated, even though the service was not delivered. Goals were considered completely achieved if the service was received. The concept of service linkage was expanded to include the resolution of problems with existing services, as well as securing new services. Using this broader concept, 22 service needs were identified. About 60% of the service goals were completely attained, in the sense that the service was secured. Goals were partially attained for 18.2% of the service needs. Goals were not attained at all for 18.2%, and one case was unclear.

This latter category could be modified further. It would be helpful to distinguish between those cases in which numerous attempts were made and those in which no efforts were made. In some cases, practitioners spent 2 hours or more on the phone among various agencies in the fruitless pursuit of a resource for a client. This constitutes an accountable effort to locate a resource and should be so credited. Analysis of these cases would be enhanced by the use of systematic recording guides that would specify the nature of the obstacle to service delivery. For example, when services are delayed because the only agency that will build a ramp for a client in a wheelchair has a long waiting list, it is a failure of the service delivery system, not of the service linkage model. It would also be useful to examine the type of service goal attained in terms of the degree to which this represents a resolution of the problem that the service is meant to resolve. If a client with a history of anorexia, for instance, is no longer able to prepare meals, it is important to find out whether meals delivered to the home are eaten or thrown out. The goal of securing a service, therefore, has two dimensions: problem resolved and problem not resolved. Samples of data about the frequency with which the problem occurs would facilitate this kind of judgment.

Collecting additional information on the person responsible for performing the particular task will provide data about which types of tasks families are able to handle and which tasks require more activity from practitioners (Reid, personal communication, September, 1986). In using a task-centered and behavioral model, Thibault (1984) found that more practitioner tasks were necessary with elderly clients.

FURTHER RESEARCH

The findings from large-scale studies of service linkage and service provision suggest a variety of areas for further research. It is important to develop and evaluate training programs for home care staff and to assess the cost-effectiveness of service linkage models that provide treatment for behavioral problems.

Although case management has been the subject of considerable research, most of the models studied did not mention the treatment of behavioral problems. In the most extensive study available, the National Channeling Project, case managers were encouraged to rely on referral to other services to resolve behavioral problems, but they admitted that such referrals were inadequate (Wilson *et al.*, 1986). Mental health services have been underutilized by elderly adults (Butler & Lewis, 1982) perhaps because of a reluctance to service elderly adults (Zarit, 1980). This suggests that reliance on referral is inadequate and that the treatment of behavioral problems should be a part of the case manager's role (Zarit, 1980). There is a concern that the time involved in doing treatment would cause case management to become an overly expensive service. A cost-effectiveness study of this topic would provide policy analysts with needed information in deciding whether or not to expand the case manager's role in publicly funded programs.

Additional research into helping families resolve dysfunctional interaction patterns that interfere with the performance of case management tasks is also necessary. For those who do experience difficulty, in-session tasks may be used to assess the family's ability to analyze problems and plan ways of resolving them (Reid & Helmer, 1986). When there is a lack of agreement among relatives, such as on the amount of service needed, negotiation training or communication training may be useful in resolving this kind of obstacle.

The provision of community services is an important part of maintaining quality of life among impaired elders who choose to remain in their own homes or with their families. A wide array of services exist, although access may be limited by eligibility criteria designed to control the number of clients and related costs. Families provide competent assistance to their elders in obtaining services. The Elderly Support Project provides a model of service linkage procedures that can be used to help elders and their families resolve unmet service needs. More rigorous research of an evaluative nature is needed to confirm the usefulness of service linkages.

Although families are now recognized as critical in sustaining help for elderly people, articulating how that happens is a challenge. An educational model of services and linkage has been outlined in this chapter, including suggestions for evaluation. As clinical gerontology assumes a larger role in sustaining the old in productive societal roles, community linkage may become a respected and integral tool for practitioners, families, and elderly clients.

REFERENCES

Applebaum, R. (1986). *Two decades of research on community based long-term care: What have we learned?* Paper presented at the annual conference of the Gerontological Society of America, Chicago.

Applebaum, R., & Harrigan, M. (1986). *Channeling effects on the quality of clients' lives.* Princeton, NJ: Mathematic Policy Research.

Arling, G., & McAuley, W. (1983). The feasibility of public payments to family caregiving. *The Gerontologist, 23,* 300–306.

Austin, C. D. (1983). Case management in long-term care: Options and opportunities. *Health and Social Work, 8,* 16–30.

Berger, R., & Piliavin, I. (1976). The effect of casework: A research note. *Social Work, 21,* 205.

Blenkner, M., Bloom, M., & Nielson, M. (1971). A research and demonstration project of protective services. *Social Casework, 52,* 489–506.

Bowling, A. (1984). Caring for the elderly widowed—The burden on their supporters. *British Journal of Social Work, 14,* 489–506.

Brody, E. (1981). Women in the middle and family help to older people. *The Gerontologist, 21*, 471–479.

Burwell, B. (1986). *Shared obligations: Public policy influences on family care for the elderly* (No. 500-83-0056). Washington, DC: Health Care Financing Administration.

Butler, R. N. (1986). *Health, aging, and productivity*. Presentation at America's Aging Workforce: A Travelers' Symposium, Houston, TX.

Butler, R. N., & Lewis, M. I. (1982). *Aging and mental health: Positive psychosocial and biomedical approaches*. St. Louis: Mosby Company.

Cantor, M. (1983). Strain among caregivers: A study of experience in the United States. *Gerontologist, 25*, 597–604.

Capitman, J. A. (1986). Community-based long-term care models, target groups and impacts on service use. *Gerontologist, 26*, 389–397.

Carnevale, A. (1986). *Improving productivity in the aging workforce*. Presentation at America's Aging Workforce: A travelers' Symposium, Houston, TX.

Chang, T., & Swart, C. (1984). *Natural caregiving and frail and functionally impaired elderly in Wisconsin: A profile*. Madison, Wisconsin Department of Health and Social Services, Office of Aging.

Christianson, J. B., & Stevens, S. A. (1986a). *Channeling effects on informal care*. Princeton, NJ: Mathematic Policy Research.

Christianson, J. B., & Stevens, S. A. (1986b). *Informal care to the impaired elderly: Report of the National Long Term Care Demonstration Survey of Informal caregivers*. Princeton, NJ: Mathematic Policy Research.

Conrad, K. J., Hughes, S. L., Campione, P. F., Singer, R. H., & Goldberg, Glen, R. (1986). *Assessing the structure, population, and process of adult day care programs: Report to the American Association for Retired Persons Andrus Foundation*. Evanston, IL: Northwestern University, Center for Health Services and Policy Research.

Ehrlich, P., & Wirth, C. (1978). *Mutual help for community elderly: The Benton Model*. Paper presented at 31st annual meeting of the Gerontological Society, Dallas.

Epstein, L. (1980). *Helping people: Task centered approach*. St. Louis: C. V. Mosby.

Estes, C. L. (1979). *The aging enterprise*. San Francisco, Jossey Bass.

Folstein, M. F., Folstein, S. E., & McHugh, P. F. (1975). "Mini-mental status": A practical method for grading cognitive state of patients for the clinician. *Journal of Psychiatric Research, 12*, 189.

Frankfather, D., Smith, M. J., & Caro, F. G. (1981). *Family care of the elderly: Public initiatives and public obligations*. Lexington, MA: Lexington Books.

Gelfand, D. E., & Olson, J. K. (1980). *The aging network: Programs and services*. New York: Springer.

General Accounting Office to the United States (GAO). (1977). *Report to Congress: The well-being of older people in Cleveland, Ohio*. Washington, DC: U.S. Government Printing Office.

George, L. K., Gwyther, L., Fillenbaum, G. G., & Palmore, E. (1986). *Respite care: A strategy for easing caregiver burden?* Paper presented at the annual conference of the Gerontological Society, Chicago.

Green, G. R., & Marlow, C. (1984). Using contracts to increase independence and social contacts. In E. M. Pinkston & N. L. Linsk, *Care of the elderly: A family approach* (pp. 58–60). New York: Pergamon Press.

Greer, D. S., & Mor, V. (1986). An overview of national hospice study findings. *Journal of Chronic Diseases, 39*, 5–7.

Hanrahan, P., Lawler, E., & Pinkston, E. M. (1987). *Consequences of caregiving: Benefits and costs*. Paper presented at the meeting of the Gerontological Society of America, Washington, DC.

Hanrahan, P., Young, R. N., & Pinkston, E. M. (1985). *Case management with families of the mentally impaired elderly: A behavioral approach*. Paper presented at the annual conference of the Gerontological Society of America, New Orleans.

Harrington, C., & Newcomer, R. J. (1985). *Long term care of the elderly: Public policy issues*. Beverly Hills, CA: Sage Publications.

Holmes, M., & Holmes, D. (1979). *Handbook of human services for older persons*. New York: Human Sciences Press.

Horowitz, A. (1978). *Families who care: A study of natural support systems of the elderly*. Paper presented at 31st annual Scientific Meeting of the Gerontological Society, Dallas.

Horowitz, A., & Dobroff, R. (1982). *The role of families in providing long-term care to the frail and chronically ill elderly living in the community* (Contract No. 18-P-97541/2-02). Washington, D.C.: Health Care Financing Administration.

Horowitz, A., & Schindleman, L. W. (1983). Social and economic incentives for family caregivers. *Health Care Financing Review, 5,* 25–33.

Hubbard, R. W., Santos, J. F., & Wiora, M. (1978). A community-based model for discharge planning and aftercare for hospitalized older adults. *Journal of Gerontological Social Work, 1,* 63–68.

Hughes, S. L. (1985). Apples and oranges: A review of community-based long-term care. *Health Services Research, 20,* 461–487.

Johnson, C., & Catalano, D. (1983). A longitudinal study of family supports to impaired elderly. *The Gerontologist, 23,* 612–618.

Kahn, R. L., Goldfarb, A. I., Pollock, M., & Peck, R. (1960). Brief objective measures for the determination of mental status in the aged. *American Journal of Psychiatry, 117,* 326–328.

Kanfer, F., & Saslow, G. (1969). Behavioral diagnosis. In C. M. Franks (Ed.), *Behavioral therapy: Appraisal and status* (pp. 417–444). New York: McGraw-Hill.

Kutza, E. A. (1981). *The benefits of old age: Social welfare policy for the elderly.* Chicago: University of Chicago Press.

Linsk, N. L., Green, G. R., Marlow, C., & Pinkston, E. M. (1980). *An analysis of community linkage and behavioral strategies with families of the impaired elderly.* Paper presented at the annual conference of the Gerontological Society, San Diego.

Linsk, N. L., Keigher, S., & Osterbusch, S. E. (1988). States policies regarding paid family caregiving. *The Gerontologist, 28,* 204–212.

Linsk, N. L., Osterbusch, S. E., Simon-Rusinowitz, L., & Keigher, S. (1988). Community agency support of family caregiving. *Health and Social Work, 13,* 209–218.

Minkler, M., & Stone, R. (1985). The feminization of poverty and older women. *The Gerontologist, 25,* 351–357.

Morrison, M. H. (1986). *Corporate practices: Personnel programs and management strategies for older workers.* Presentation at America's Aging Workforce: A Travelers Symposium, Houston, Texas.

O'Connell, G. (1988). A case management: System and practice. *Social Casework, 69,* 97–106.

Osterbusch, S. E., Keigher, S., Miller, B., & Linsk, N. L. (1987). Community care policies and gender justice. *International Journal of Health Services, 17,* 217–232.

Pinkston, E. M., & Linsk, N. L. (1984a). *Care of the elderly: A family approach.* New York: Pergamon Press.

Pinkston, E. M., & Linsk, N. L. (1984b). Behavioral family intervention with the impaired elderly. *The Gerontologist, 24,* 576–583.

Pinkston, E. M., Levit, J. L., Green, G. R., Linsk, N. L., & Rzepnicki, T. L. (1982). *Effective social work practice: Advanced techniques for behavioral intervention with individuals, families and institutional staff.* San Francisco: Jossey Bass.

Poulshock, S. W., & Deimling, G. T. (1984). Families caring for elders in residence: Issues in the measurement of burden. *Journal of Gerontology, 39,* 230–239.

Rankin, E. (1985). *The family life cycle, stress and caregiver burden in home-based care of the disabled elderly.* Unpublished doctoral dissertation, University of Chicago.

Reid, W. J. (1978). *The task-centered system.* New York: Columbia University Press.

Reid, W. J., & Epstein, L. (Eds.). (1977). *Task centered practice.* New York: Columbia University Press.

Reid, W. J., & Hanrahan, P. (1982). Recent evaluations of social work: Grounds for optimism. *Social Work, 27,* 328–340.

Reid, W. J., & Helmer, A. (1986). Session tasks in family treatment. *Family Therapy, 13,* 177–185.

Rooney, R. H., & Wanless, M. (1985). A model for caseload management based on task-centered practice. In A. E. Fortune (Ed.), *Task centered practice with families and groups* (pp. 187–200). New York: Springer.

Shanas, E. (1979). The family as a support system. *The Gerontologist, 19,* 169–174.

Simmons, K., Ivry, J., & Seltzer, M. M. (1985). Agency–family collaboration. *The Gerontologist, 25,* 343–346.

Skellie, F., & Coan, R. (1980). Community-based long-term care and mortality: Preliminary findings of Georgia's alternative health services project. *The Gerontologist, 20,* 372–379.

Skellie, F., Mobley, G., & Coan, R. (1982). Cost effectiveness of community-based long-term care: Current findings of Georgia's alternative health services project. *American Journal of Public Health, 72,* 353–358.

Soldo, B., & Myllyluoma, J. (1983). Caregivers who live with dependent elderly. *The Gerontologist, 23,* 605–611.

Sommers, T. (1985). Caregiving: A women's issue. *Generations*, *9*, 9–13.

Steinberg, R. M., & Carter, G. (1983). *Case management and the elderly: A handbook for planning and administering programs*. Lexington, MA: Lexington Books.

Thibault, J. (1984). *The analysis and treatment of indirect self-destructive behaviors of elderly patients*. Unpublished doctoral dissertation, University of Chicago, School of Social Service Administration.

Thornton, C., & Dunstan, S. M. (1986). *Analysis of the benefits and costs of channeling*. Princeton, NJ: Mathematics Policy Research.

Treas, J. (1977). Family support system for the aged: Some social and demographic considerations. *The Gerontologist*, *17*, 486–491.

Tuzil, T. (1978). The agency role in helping children and their aging parents. *Social Casework*, May, 302–305.

Wan, T. H., Weissert, W. G., & Livieratos, B. B. (1980). Geriatric day care ad homemaker services: An experimental study. *Journal of Gerontology*, *35*, 256–274.

Weissert, W. G. (1975). *Aduli day care in the U.S.: A comparative study. Executive summary of final report*. Washington, DC: Transcentury Corporation.

Weissert, W. G. (1985a). Seven reasons why it is so difficult to make community-based long-term care cost-effective. *Health Services Research*, *20*, 432–433.

Weissert, W. G. (1985b). The cost effectiveness trap. *Generations*, *9*, 47–50.

Weissert, W. G., & Cready, C. M. (1986). *Comparative analysis of community care: Future research recommendations*. Paper presented at the annual meeting of the Gerontological Society of America, Chicago.

Weissert, W. G., Wan, T., Livieratos, B. B., & Katz, S. (1980). Effects and costs of day-care services for the chronically ill. *Medical Care*, *28*, 567–584.

Wiessman, A. L. (1975). Industrial social services: Linkage technology. *Social Casework*, *55*, 50–54.

Wilson, A. J. E. (1984). *Social services for older persons*. Boston: Little, Brown.

Wilson, N., Applebaum, R., & Schneider, B. (1986). *Lessons from research for case management practice in community long-term care*. Paper presented at the annual meeting of the Gerontological Society of America, Chicago.

Zarit, S. H. (1980). *Aging and mental disorders: Psychological approaches to assessment and treatment*. New York: Free Press.

Zarit, S. H., Todd, P. A., & Zarit, J. M. (1986). Subjective burden of husbands and wives as caregivers: A longitudinal study. *The Gerontologist*, *26*, 260–266.

Index

505